THE ROUGH GUIDE TO
JORDAN

ROUGH
GUIDES

Written and researched by
Matthew Teller

Contents

TEMPLE OF HERCULES, AMMAN

Introduction to
Jordan

Western travellers have been exploring the Middle East for well over a century, but Jordan is a relative newcomer to tourism, welcoming only a fraction of the numbers who visit neighbouring Egypt and Israel. Its popular image abroad encompasses not much more than camels and deserts, yet this is a country of mountains, beaches, castles and ancient churches, with an urbane people and a rich culture. It is safe, comfortable and welcoming – and by far the region's most rewarding destination.

Jordan is about 85 percent **desert**, but this one plain word covers a multitude of scenes, from the dramatic red sands and towering cliffs of the far south to the vast stony plains of volcanic basalt in the east. The northern hills, rich with olive trees, teeter over the rift of the **Jordan Valley**, which in turn runs down to the **Dead Sea**, the lowest point on earth. The centre of the country is carpeted with tranquil fields of wheat, cut through by expansive canyons and bordered by arid, craggy mountains. At Jordan's southernmost tip, beaches fringe the warm waters of the **Red Sea**, which harbours some of the most spectacular coral reefs in the world.

Jordan is part of the land bridge linking Europe, Africa and Asia, and has seen countless armies come and go. Greeks, Romans, Muslims, Christian Crusaders and more have left evidence of their conquests, and there are literally thousands of **archeological sites** from all periods in every corner of the country. In addition, Israel and Palestine, Jordan's neighbours to the west, have no monopoly on **biblical history**: it was in Jordan that Lot sought refuge from the fire and brimstone of the Lord; Moses, Aaron and John the Baptist all died in Jordan; and Jesus was almost certainly baptized here. Even the Prophet Muhammad passed through.

And yet the country is far from being stuck in the past. **Amman** is a thoroughly modern Arab capital, and poverty is the exception rather than the rule. The government, under head of state **King Abdullah II**, manages to be simultaneously

BEDOUIN MAN AND CAMELS, WADI RUM

pro-Western, pro-Arab, founded on a bedrock of Muslim authority and committed to peace with Israel. Women are better integrated into positions of power in government and business than almost anywhere else in the Middle East. Jordanians are also exceptionally highly educated: roughly four percent of the total population is enrolled at university, a proportion comparable to the UK. Traditions of **hospitality** are ingrained, and taking up some of the many invitations you'll get to tea or a meal will expose you to an outlook among local people that is often as cosmopolitan and world-aware as anything at home. Domestic extremism is very rare.

Most people take great pride in their ancestry, whether they're present or former desert-dwellers (**bedouin**) or from a settled farming tradition (**fellahin**). Across the desert areas, people still live and work on their **tribal** lands, whether together in villages or apart in individual family units. Many town-dwellers, including substantial numbers of Ammanis, also claim tribal identity. Belonging to a tribe (an honour conferred by birth) means respecting the authority of a communal leader, or sheikh, and living in a culture of shared history, values and principles that often crosses national boundaries. Notions of **honour** and mutual defence are strong. Tribes also wield a great deal of institutional power: most members of Jordan's lower house of parliament are elected for their tribal, rather than political, affiliation. The king, as **sheikh of sheikhs**, commands heartfelt loyalty among many people and respect among most of the rest.

JORDAN

MEDITERRANEAN SEA

LEBANON

SYRIA

ISRAEL

DAMASCUS
Homs
Beirut

Baghdad

Dammam

IRAQ

Turayf

(914m)

Qasr Burqu
Ruwayshid

Safawi

Azraq

SHAUMARI WILDLIFE RESERVE

Qusayr Amra

Qasr Tuba

Queen Alia International Airport

(113m)

Jebel Druze (1803m)
Bosra
Umm al-Jimal

(735m)

Dera'a
Jaber
Mafraq
Zarqa

AMMAN

Madaba

Wadi Mujib

Ma'in hot spring
MUJIB BIOSPHERE RESERVE

JAWLAN (GOLAN HEIGHTS)

Sea of Galilee
Tiberias
Nazareth
Haifa

Umm Qais
Irbid
Ramtha
Pella
Ajloun
Jerash

Salt
Fuheis

Mt Nebo
Baptism Site
Dead Sea

JORDAN VALLEY

Sheikh Hussein Bridge

King Hussein Bridge
Jericho

WEST BANK

Nablus

JERUSALEM

Hebron

N

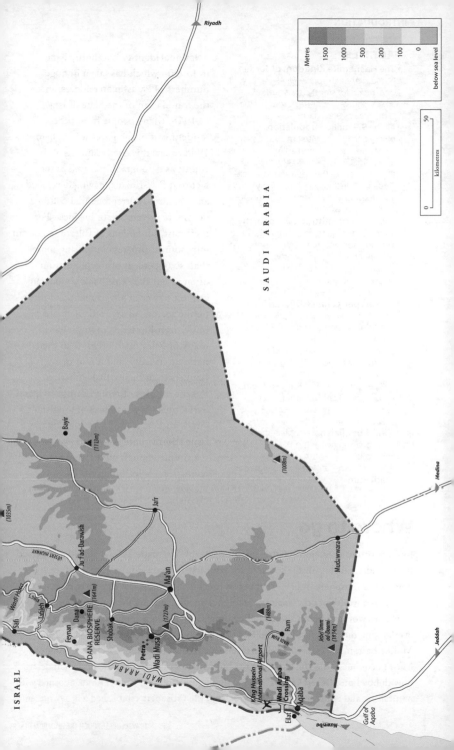

Metres
1500
1000
500
200
100
0
below sea level

kilometres
0 50

Riyadh

SAUDI ARABIA

ISRAEL

Bayir

(1713m)

(1035m)

(1008m)

DESERT HIGHWAY

Ju'f ad-Darawish

Jafr

Tafileh

Wadi Araba

Safi

Feynan

DANA BIOSPHERE
RESERVE

Dana

(1641m)

Shobak

Ma'an

Petra

Wadi Musa

(1727m)

WADI ARABA

King Hussein
International Airport

Wadi Araba
Crossing

Elat

Aqaba

Gulf of
Aqaba

Nuweiba

(1488m)

Rum

WADI RUM

Jebel Umm
ad-Daami
(1834m)

Mudawwara

Medina

Jeddah

FACT FILE

- The **Hashemite Kingdom of Jordan** (*Al Mamlakeh Al Urduniyyeh Al Hashmiyyeh*, or *Al Urdun* for short) covers around 90,000 square kilometres – roughly the same area as Portugal or Indiana.
- Of the **9.9 million population**, well over ninety percent are **Muslim Arabs**, with small minorities of Christian Arabs, as well as Muslim Circassians and Chechens. Over thirty percent of the population are non-Jordanians, including 1.3 million **Syrians**.
- **Life expectancy** is around 75 – up from 71 twenty years ago.
- Jordan is a **constitutional monarchy**, with universal suffrage over the age of 18. The king appoints the prime minister and together they appoint the cabinet. The Senate is appointed by the king, and the House of Representatives is voted in by proportional representation.
- Jordan's **per-capita GDP** is under US$6000. It has virtually no oil. Key economic sectors are phosphate and potash production, as well as tourism.
- Jordanian workers are entitled to a **minimum wage** of JD190/month (US$268).
- King Abdullah's father, **King Hussein**, and mother, **Toni Gardiner** (later Princess Muna), met on the set of *Lawrence of Arabia* in 1961.
- **King Abdullah** once appeared in a non-speaking role in the TV series *Star Trek: Voyager*.
- The 2015 film *The Martian* was filmed at **Wadi Rum**.

National identity is a thorny issue in Jordan, which has taken in huge numbers of **Palestinian** refugees since the foundation of the State of Israel in 1948. Many people from tribes resident east of the River Jordan before 1948 resent this overbalancing of the country's demography, as well as the fact that Palestinians, having developed an urbanized, entrepreneurial culture, dominate private-sector business. For their part, Jordanians of Palestinian origin – by some estimates comprising more than sixty percent of the population – often resent the "**East Bank**" Jordanians' grip on power in government and the public sector. All are Jordanian citizens, but citizenship tends to mean less to many of Palestinian origin than their national identity, and less to many East Bankers than their tribal affiliation. Recent influxes of refugees from Iraq and Syria, plus large numbers of long-stay guest workers from Egypt, muddy the issue still further. "Where are you from?" – a simple enough question in many countries – is in Jordan the cue for a life story.

Where to go

Jordan's prime attraction is **Petra**, an unforgettably dramatic 2000-year-old city carved from sandstone cliffs in the south of the country. Its extraordinary architecture and powerful atmosphere imprint themselves indelibly on most visitors' imaginations.

There is a wealth of other **historical sites**, outstanding among them the well-preserved Roman city of **Jerash**, but also including **Umm Qais**, set on a dramatic promontory overlooking the Sea of Galilee, and **Madaba**, which has the oldest known map of the Middle East, in the form of a Byzantine mosaic laid on the floor of a church. After the Muslim conquest, the Umayyad dynasty built a series of retreats in the Jordanian desert, now dubbed the "**Desert Castles**", including the bathhouse of **Qusayr Amra**, adorned with naturalistic and erotic frescoes. Centuries later, the **Crusaders** established a heavy presence

THE SEARCH FOR WATER

Jordan is one of the five **driest** countries in the world. Annual consumption per capita (calculated as renewable water resources withdrawn) is about 170 cubic metres, compared with 630 as the world average, 800 across the Middle East/North Africa region – and 1650 in North America. Almost a third of the water used in Jordan comes from non-sustainable or nonrenewable sources. Three decades of pumping from the once-abundant **Azraq oasis** (see page 195) has brought it to the point of collapse. The River Yarmouk sports a large dam shared by Jordan and Syria, and all the major valleys leading down to the Dead Sea are now dammed in an effort to stop water draining into the salty lake – which has contributed to its rapid shrinking (see page 115). Every winter the local newspapers publish reports tabulating levels of water storage in the country's reservoirs, while Jordanians anxiously wait for rain. Water rationing is in place in Amman over the summer, though a US$1.1-billion pipeline now brings fossil water to the capital from desert aquifers at Disi, and plans are afoot for desalination plants on the Red Sea.

in southern Jordan, most impressively with the huge castles at **Karak** and **Shobak**. The Arab resistance to the Crusader invasion left behind another fortress at **Ajloun** in the north.

Jordan is part of the "Holy Land": its **religious sites** include the **Baptism Site** of Jesus on the banks of the River Jordan, and **Mount Nebo**, from where Moses looked over the Promised Land. John the Baptist met his death at Herod's hilltop palace at **Mukawir** after Salome danced her seductive dance. Nearby is **Lot's Cave**, where Abraham's nephew sought refuge from the destruction of Sodom and Gomorrah.

Your most abiding memories of a visit are likely to be of Jordan's varied and beautiful **natural environment**. With its sheer cliffs and red sands, austere **Wadi Rum** – where David Lean filmed *Lawrence of Arabia* – presents the classic desert picture of Jordan. Less well-known are the gentle northern hills around the **Ajloun forests**, hosting walks through flower-strewn meadows and cool, shady woodland. In the south, tranquil **Dana** overlooks a swathe of territory from verdant highland orchards down to the sandy desert floor, offering a memorable hideaway at the **Feynan Ecolodge**. The protected **Wadi Mujib** is a giant canyon, 4km wide at the top, that narrows to a high, rocky gorge carrying a fast-flowing river down to the salty **Dead Sea**, an inland lake too buoyant for swimming but perfect for floating, your body supported by the density of the salty water. Last but not least, Jordan has some of the world's best diving and snorkelling in the coral-fringed **Red Sea** off **Aqaba**.

When to go

Jordan is a **year-round destination** – but despite its small size, you'll find wide variations in **climate**, often reliant on the topography: Amman, Petra and Wadi Rum all lie well over 800m above sea level, Dana and Ajloun are even higher (up to 1500m), whereas the Dead Sea lies 400m below sea level. The same January day could have you throwing snowballs in Ajloun or topping up your tan on the Red Sea beaches.

The best time to visit is **spring** (March–May), when temperatures are toasty but not scorching, wild flowers are out everywhere (even the desert is carpeted), and the hills and valleys running down the centre of the country are lush and gorgeously colourful.

AVERAGE TEMPERATURES AND RAINFALL

	Jan	Feb	Mar	Apr	May	Jun	Jul	Aug	Sept	Oct	Nov	Dec
AMMAN (800M)												
Min/max (°C)	3/12	4/13	6/16	9/23	14/28	16/31	18/32	18/32	17/31	14/27	10/21	6/15
Min/max (°F)	37/54	39/55	43/61	48/73	57/82	61/88	64/90	64/90	63/88	57/81	50/70	43/59
Rainfall (mm)	69	54	41	15	5	0	0	0	0	5	33	46
AQABA (SEA LEVEL)												
Min/max (°C)	10/21	11/23	14/26	17/31	18/36	24/38	26/39	26/40	25/37	21/33	16/28	12/23
Min/max (°F)	50/70	52/73	57/79	63/88	64/97	75/100	79/102	79/104	77/99	70/91	61/82	54/73
Rainfall (mm)	8	5	4	0	0	0	0	0	0	0	1	6
DEAD SEA (400M BELOW SEA LEVEL)												
Min/max (°C)	11/20	13/22	16/25	20/29	24/34	27/37	28/39	29/40	27/37	24/32	18/27	13/22
Min/max (°F)	52/68	55/72	61/77	68/84	75/93	81/99	82/102	84/104	81/99	75/90	64/81	55/72
Rainfall (mm)	10	9	7	2	0	0	0	0	0	1	5	8
PETRA (1100M)												
Min/max (°C)	2/12	4/14	6/17	10/23	14/29	17/33	18/34	19/34	17/32	14/27	8/20	4/15
Min/max (°F)	36/54	39/57	43/63	50/73	57/84	63/91	64/93	66/93	63/90	57/80	46/68	39/59
Rainfall (mm)	36	31	30	11	4	0	0	0	0	2	13	33

The worst of the rain is over by March, though it doesn't entirely peter out in Amman and the hills until late April. Humidity is pleasant everywhere, and low, clear sunlight draws a spectacular kaleidoscope of colour and texture from the desert rocks. There's only one drawback – a desert wind, loaded with dust and grit, which blows regularly each spring or early summer out of the Arabian interior. It's known across the Middle East as the *khamseen* ("fifty"), after the fifty days it traditionally persists (although in Jordan it rarely lasts longer than a few days), and can darken the sky and raise the temperature by 10°C, coating everyone and everything in a layer of sand.

In **summer** (roughly June–Sept), Amman can sizzle – up to 40°C in the city centre – though it's a dry heat, rarely uncomfortable, and the hills catch some cooler breezes. Temperatures at the Dead Sea and Aqaba, though, have been known to top 45°C, with Aqaba in particular suffering from an intolerable hot wind that makes you feel like you're basting in a fan-assisted oven. High, hazy light flattens the brown landscape and bleaches any beauty out of the desert. Copy the locals, and treat the hours between noon and 3pm as a time to snooze in the cool indoors.

Typical **autumn** weather (mid-Sept to mid-Nov) mostly passes Jordan by, with only a few weeks marking the shift out of high summer – if you catch it, this can be a lovely time to visit. The first rains fall in early or mid-October, making the parched countryside bloom again and temperatures drop to more manageable levels.

In **winter** (roughly Dec–Feb), Amman can be desperately chilly, with biting winds sweeping through the valleys, rain showers and even snowfall, although the sun is still never far away. With short days and freezing nights, Petra winters can be taxing; exceptional lows of -8°C have been recorded. Rum is more temperate, but Aqaba makes a fine retreat, with sunshine and warmth even in the depths of January (average Red Sea and Dead Sea water temperatures vary little either side of a balmy 24°C all year).

Author picks

After "Is it safe?", the question people always ask author Matthew Teller is "What's your favourite place?" That tends to change with every visit, but after 25 years – and dozens of trips – he's built up a few personal favourites.

Desert hideaways Wadi Rum (see page 320) offers classic Jordanian desertscapes. A quirky choice would be Azraq (see page 192), to go on safari and visit a holy tree – but for all-round quality of experience, Feynan (see page 340) trumps all.

Urban flavours A stroll on Rainbow Street (see page 80) or around Jabal Al Lweibdeh (see page 83) can open up Amman. Salt has a great little souk (see page 172), while Madaba exemplifies Jordan's easy-going, warm-hearted urban charm (see page 208).

Rural retreats Jordan's countryside is much overlooked. Ajloun (see page 146) is a highland beauty, and Umm Qais (see page 158) never fails to inspire – though unforgettable Dana (see page 238) wins out every time.

Evocative ruins Jordan is packed with them. Petra's Treasury (see page 264) takes the biscuit, while Roman Jerash (see page 133) always fascinates. Get off the beaten track to sample Shobak castle (see page 246), Qasr al-Abd (see page 175) and haunting Qasr Kharana (see page 187).

Hidden campsites Although the nature reserves offer nights under canvas, you could also strike out alone. Try the rural camping at Rasoun (see page 150) or Shobak (see page 245) – then hold onto your hat for the amazing clifftop site at Nawatef (see page 245).

Best views How to choose? Mount Nebo (see page 220) is a jaw-dropper, Wild Jordan Center (see page 82) has a stunning urban panorama, and Dana (see page 238) astounds, but the view from Umm Qais (see page 158) will replay itself in perpetuity every time you close your eyes.

If you do only one thing in Jordan… Go stargazing at Feynan (see page 340). Or walk through the Siq at dawn (see page 263). Or meet the locals in Al Ayoun (see page 152). Make that three things.

> Our author recommendations don't end here. We've flagged up our favourite places – a perfectly sited hotel, an atmospheric café, a special restaurant – throughout the Guide, highlighted with the ★ symbol.

STREET MARKET, SALT

RURAL CAMPING

20
things not to miss

It's not possible to see everything that Jordan has to offer in one trip – and we don't suggest you try. What follows, in no particular order, is a selective taste of the country's highlights: striking natural landscapes, absorbing ruins and memorable experiences. All highlights are colour-coded by chapter and have a page reference to take you straight into the Guide, where you can find out more.

1

1 WADI RUM
See page 320
Experience the atmosphere of the open desert in the stunning company of sheer mountains, red dunes and vast, silent panoramas.

2 JORDANIAN CUISINE
See page 36
Sample some of the Middle East's finest restaurants in Amman – or scoff Jordan's national dish, *mansaf*, at a bedouin gathering in the desert.

3 AJLOUN
See page 146
Set amid the northern hills is a magnificent Crusader-period castle, within easy reach of a tranquil nature reserve.

4 BAPTISM SITE
See page 122
A pilgrimage spot alongside the River Jordan at the place where Jesus was baptized, commemorated by dozens of ancient churches and hermitages.

5 RED SEA DIVING AND SNORKELLING
See page 310
You don't have to be a diver to come nose to nose with a turtle: coral reefs and multicoloured fish await just beneath the surface of this warmest and clearest of seas.

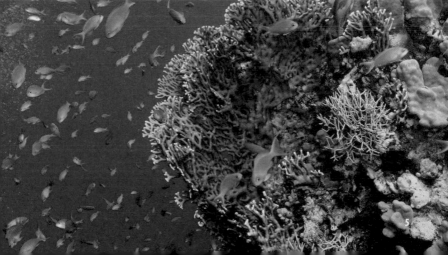

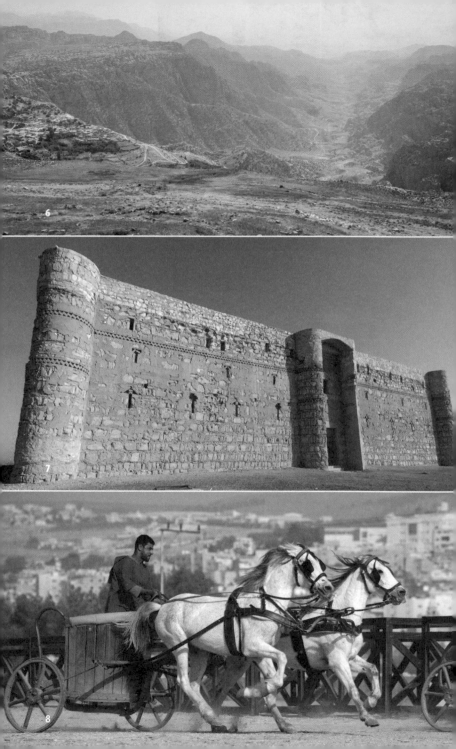

6 DANA

See page 238

Jordan's flagship nature reserve, covering a sweep of territory from highland cliffs to the sandy desert floor. Whether you come for the hiking, the natural environment or the silence, you won't want to leave.

7 THE "DESERT CASTLES"

See page 184

Venture east of Amman to explore a string of early-Islamic forts, palaces, hunting lodges and caravanserais, dotted across the stony desert plains.

8 JERASH

See page 133

A spectacularly well-preserved Roman city, complete with colonnaded streets, grand temples, intimate marketplaces and mosaic-floored churches.

9 HIKING

See page 49

There are plenty of opportunities to get off the beaten track in Jordan's back country for a day or a week, whether alone or with an adventure tour company.

10 FEYNAN ECOLODGE

See page 342

Hole up at this beautifully designed ecofriendly desert hotel, far from the nearest road, for rugged walking, fascinating cultural encounters and epic star-gazing.

11 TAKING TEA
See page 39
The hospitality of Jordanians is legendary: whether you're passing through a city or crossing the desert, you're bound to be invited in for tea.

12 ANCIENT AMMAN
See page 69
Roman columns and the ruins of an Islamic-era palace tower over Amman, gazing down on a huge Roman theatre in the heart of the city.

13 PETRA
See page 250
Magnificent ancient city hidden away in the craggy mountains of the south – one of the world's must-see attractions.

14 MODERN AMMAN
See page 80
Take time out from ruin-hunting to explore the capital's buzzing cafés, galleries and restaurants – a side of the city few visitors experience.

15 THE DEAD SEA
See page 112
Enjoy spectacular sunsets at the lowest point on earth, floating effortlessly on this inland lake supported only by the density of the salty water.

13

14

15

16

17

18

BETHLEHEM
NABLUS
HERODIUM
JERUSALEM MT-OF-OLIVES
RAMALLAH
HEBRON
QUMRAN
DEAD SEA
JERICHO
LAKE TIBERIAS

LAKE TIBERIAS 106 Km 351 NNW
NABLUS 86 Km 318 NW
JERICHO 27 Km 289 WNW
RAMALLAH 52 Km 284 WNW
JERUSALEM mt-of-OLIVES 46 Km 269 W

QUMRAN 25 Km 262 W
BETHLEHEM 50 Km 260 W
HERODIUM 47 Km 254 WsW
HEBRON 65 Km 224 SW

19

20

Tailor-made trips

Distances are small in Jordan, and the landscapes are hugely varied. A couple of hours' travel could see you losing or gaining hundreds of metres in altitude and moving in quick succession from village to city and forest to desert. The trips below give a flavour of what the country has to offer and what we can plan and book for you at www.roughguides.com/trips.

A WEEKEND IN AMMAN

Two days to sample the capital, from history to art to fine dining.

DAY ONE

❶ Downtown breakfast Spurn the delights of your hotel buffet and go for a traditional Jordanian breakfast of hot beans, flatbread and scalding sweet tea at *Hashem*. See page 101

❷ Jordan Museum Lose yourself in the country's best museum, amid fascinating displays on history, art and culture. See page 75

❸ Citadel Hill The ruins of this early-Islamic hilltop palace make for a fine contrast with the buzzing modern city. See page 78

❹Dinner Head to Rainbow Street and take your pick: fine dining, salads and wraps, hot dogs and pizza – or falafel and tea. See page 98

DAY TWO

❶ Art galleries Devote a morning to exploring Jabal Al Lweibdeh's art, from the National Gallery to funkier contemporary spaces. See page 80

❷ Cave of the Seven Sleepers Venture out to this pilgrimage spot in the far-flung outskirts for a fresh take on the city. See page 86

❸ Royal Automobile Museum This fine collection of vintage vehicles, amassed by the late King Hussein, is a fascinating way to learn more about Jordan's modern history. See page 85

❹ Dinner Time for some posh Arabic nosh. Sample the top-quality cuisine of *Fakhr el-Din* or *Tannoureen* – or head out of town to comfortable, informal *Zuwwadeh*. See page 101

JORDAN'S GREAT OUTDOORS

See the best of Jordan's dazzlingly varied landscapes in a week of travel between deserts, forests, mountains and seas.

❶ Ajloun Forest Head north of Amman into the forested highlands for long walks in quiet countryside, home-cooked food and community crafts projects. See page 148

❷ Umm Qais Jordan's northernmost point offers panoramic views out over the Sea of Galilee and Golan Heights, set among rolling green hills and plunging valley gorges. See page 158

You can book these trips with Rough Guides, or we can help you create your own. Whether you're after adventure or a family-friendly holiday, we have a trip for you, with all the activities you enjoy doing and the sights you want to see. All our trips are devised by local experts who get the most out of the destination. Visit **www.roughguides.com/trips** to chat with one of our travel agents.

❸ **Dead Sea** Float your cares away at the world's largest open-air spa, situated 400m below sea level at the lowest point on Earth. See page 112

❹ **Dana** Don't miss this tranquil highland village of stone cottages and yawning vistas out over rocky domes and soaring cliffs. Walk, camp, daydream – you won't want to leave. See page 238

❺ **Wadi Rum** Legendary desertscapes – red dunes, granite cliffs, hidden springs and ancient inscriptions. Take it all in with a night or two under the stars at a bedouin camp. See page 320

❻ **Azraq** Drive out across empty desert to reach Jordan's only oasis, offering birdwatching and desert tours. See page 192

CULTURE AND HISTORY

Cover the cream of Jordan's ancient sites, from Roman cities to the majestic Petra.

❶ **Amman** Start your explorations in the capital, replete with biblical history, Roman architecture and fascinating Islamic ruins. See page 62

❷ **Umm Qais** Visit the stupendously located Roman city of Gadara, high above the Sea of Galilee, where Jesus performed the Miracle of the Gadarene Swine. See page 158

❸ **Umm al-Jimal** Far out in the black volcanic desert north of Amman sit the evocative ruins of this frontier Roman town, with fine architectural detail surviving. See page 182

❹ **"Desert Castles"** Take a day to explore this fascinating string of early-Islamic forts, bathhouses and caravanserais east of Amman on a convenient, easy-to-navigate loop of roads. See page 184

❺ **Madaba** Start out in this genial Christian town, packed with Byzantine mosaic art, then head to nearby Mount Nebo, where Moses gazed over the Promised Land, and Mukawir, where John the Baptist lost his head. See page 208

❻ **Shobak** Further south, this was the Crusader headquarters in Jordan – a virtually impregnable hilltop fortress. See page 245

❼ **Petra** Last but not least, visit the legendary "rose-red city" of the Nabateans, lost for centuries, but still full of the power to amaze. See page 250

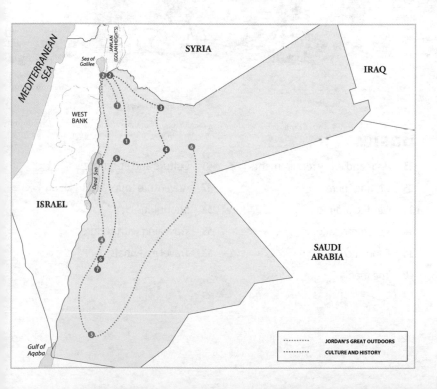

TAKING A BREAK AT WADI RUM

Basics

Visas and entry requirements

All visitors to Jordan must hold a passport valid for at least six months beyond the proposed date of entry to the country.
On arrival at all airports, as well as at most land and sea borders – apart from the King Hussein/Allenby Bridge and the Eilat–Aqaba border – most nationalities are routinely issued with a **single-entry visa**. If you arrive at Aqaba, it's free; if you arrive anywhere else, it costs JD40 (payable in cash, Jordanian dinars only).

The visa fee is **waived** if you hold the **Jordan Pass** (see page 55) or if your trip has been booked through a licensed Jordanian tour operator and you'll be spending at least two nights in Jordan.

Multiple-entry visas are available in advance only, from Jordanian embassies and consulates, for JD120 or the local equivalent.

Citizens of around fifty developing countries – listed at ⓦ visitjordan.com – cannot obtain a visa on arrival and must instead apply at the nearest Jordanian embassy at least three months prior to travel.

Both single- and multiple-entry visas are valid for a stay of **thirty days**. If you're planning to stay longer than that, you must register at any police station in the last couple of days before the thirty-day period is up – a simple, free, five-minute procedure which grants a three-month extension. For any queries, ask your hotel (or an Arabic-speaking friend) to call the Borders and Residence Department (☎ 06 550 5360, ⓦ psd.gov.jo), part of the Public Security Directorate, on your behalf.

If you plan to enter Jordan for the first time via the King **Hussein/Allenby Bridge**, or via the crossing from **Eilat to Aqaba**, you must already hold a visa – they are not issued at these crossing points. If you left Jordan via the King Hussein/Allenby Bridge and are returning via the same bridge, you don't need to buy another visa as long as your current one is still within its thirty-day validity period.

Always carry your passport on you: you'll need it to check into hotels and to ease your way through any checkpoints.

Visas at Aqaba

If you enter Jordan at **Aqaba** – which stands at the centre of the Aqaba Special Economic Zone (ASEZ) – you are granted a **free thirty-day visa** on arrival at Aqaba's airport, seaport or the land crossing from Saudi Arabia (Durra). You are then at liberty to travel around Jordan as you like. **Extending an ASEZ visa** can be done only at the offices of ASEZA (Aqaba Special Economic Zone Authority) in Aqaba itself.

If you intend to cross by land from **Eilat** (Israel) to Aqaba you must already hold a Jordanian visa in advance.

If you arrive in Jordan elsewhere – other than the King Hussein/Allenby Bridge – and you let the passport officials know that you intend to go directly to Aqaba, you are in theory entitled to get a free ASEZ visa rather than paying for a standard visa. In these cases, though, you must register at the ASEZA offices in Aqaba within 48 hours of your arrival in Jordan: if you miss this deadline, you become liable for the cost of the visa plus a fine.

Getting there

Jordan is served by daily nonstop flights from London and easy one-stop connections from around the UK, as well as nonstop routings from major European, North American and Southeast Asian hubs.
Queen Alia International Airport in **Amman** (AMM; ⓦ qaiairport.com) handles almost all incoming flights to Jordan. A few flights arrive at King Hussein International Airport in **Aqaba** (AQJ; ⓦ aac.jo), which is also linked to Amman by daily short-hop shuttles on the national carrier Royal Jordanian.

EMBASSIES AND CONSULATES
Full lists are at ⓦ visitjordan.com.

JORDANIAN EMBASSIES ABROAD
Australia ☎ 02 6295 9951, ⓦ jordanembassy.org.au.
Canada ☎ 613 238 8090, ⓦ embassyofjordan.ca.
Ireland ☎ 086 242 3083, ⓦ jordanconsul.ie.
South Africa ☎ 012 346 8615, ⓔ pretoria@fm.gov.jo.
UK ☎ 020 7937 3685, ⓦ jordanembassy.org.uk.
USA ☎ 202 966 2664, ⓦ jordanembassyus.org.

EMBASSIES AND CONSULATES IN AMMAN
Australian ☎ 06 580 7000, ⓦ jordan.embassy.gov.au.
Canadian ☎ 06 590 1500, ⓦ jordan.gc.ca.
Irish ☎ 06 553 3616, ⓦ dfa.ie.
South African ☎ 06 592 1194, ⓦ www.dirco.gov.za.
UK ☎ 06 590 9200, ⓦ ukinjordan.fco.gov.uk.
US ☎ 06 590 6000, ⓦ jo.usembassy.gov.

> ## ROUTE CHANGES
> **Flight routes** in and out of the Middle East are notoriously prone to short-notice changes. By the time you come to research your trip, you may find a greater choice of airlines and routes than we've described here – or, perhaps, the opposite. Check online or contact the Jordan Tourism Board (see page 59) for the latest info.

When to travel

The **best times to visit Jordan**, weather-wise, are spring (March–May) and autumn (Sept & Oct), although this is also when airfares and package deals are at their most expensive. In summer, you face the disadvantages of heat – though it's rarely extreme – and the peak season for tourism from the Gulf countries. Ramadan, the holy month of fasting, falls in April and May each year until 2023, when it nudges into late March too. Winter, when fares are lower, can be chilly for sightseeing.

Airfares also peak in the periods surrounding major **Islamic holidays** such as Eid al-Fitr and Eid al-Adha (see page 58), when thousands – or, in the case of the hajj pilgrimage to Mecca, millions – of people are on the move. For weeks before the hajj (which takes place in July until 2023), whole planes get block-booked for pilgrims on many routes into the Middle East – not just flights into Saudi Arabia, but also connections via Jordan and neighbouring countries. For two weeks after the pilgrimage, few planes out of the region have spare capacity. It pays to check when Islamic holidays are due to fall; book well ahead if you want to fly at or near those times.

One thing to watch when planning an itinerary is your scheduled **arrival time**: many flights from London, for instance, are afternoon departures, landing in Amman in the late evening – which means your head may not actually hit the pillow until midnight or later. In addition, many return flights to London take off from Amman at breakfast time, necessitating a predawn wake-up call.

Flights from the UK and Ireland

There are nonstop flights daily **from London** Heathrow to Amman (5hr) with Royal Jordanian (W rj.com) and British Airways (W ba.com). You might find return fares for under £400, but it's rare: £450–500 is more common. EasyJet (W easyjet.com) flies once a week from Gatwick to Aqaba (5hr), from around £250–300 return.

If you're starting from **elsewhere in the UK or Ireland** you could opt for a BA shuttle flight into Heathrow to pick up a connection, or explore options on Lufthansa (W lufthansa.com) via Frankfurt, Austrian (W austrian. com) via Vienna or Air France (W airfrance.com) via Paris. Turkish Airlines (W thy.com) operates flights from Heathrow, Gatwick, Birmingham, Manchester and Dublin to Istanbul, where you can pick up an onward connection to either Amman or Aqaba.

Flights from the US and Canada

From **North America**, Royal Jordanian flies nonstop to Amman from New York, Chicago, Detroit and Montreal. RJ's code-sharing deals offer good connections from a range of other cities. Delta (W delta.com) flies from many US cities to Paris, and from there onward to Amman, code-sharing with Air France. United (W united.com) offers good connections with European airlines such as Lufthansa and Austrian, while British Airways (W ba.com), Air Canada (W aircanada. com) and others also fly (or code-share) from major cities with a change of plane. Turkish Airlines (W thy.com) has nonstop flights from Chicago, New York, Washington and Los Angeles into Istanbul, for a shuttle onward to Amman or Aqaba. EgyptAir (W egyptair.com) does the same from New York via Cairo.

Expect round-trip **fares** of around US$900–1300 from the east and Midwest, US$1500–2000 from the west, and Can$1000–1700 out of Canada. Flight time is eleven hours from the east coast or fifteen hours from the west coast, not including stops on the ground.

Flights from Australia, New Zealand and South Africa

There are no direct flights to Jordan **from Australasia** – though, thanks to code-sharing, it's relatively easy to put together a one-stop routing: Qantas or Thai to Bangkok, for instance, then direct to Amman with Royal Jordanian. Alternatives include Emirates via Dubai or Etihad via Abu Dhabi. From **South Africa**, you're looking at one-stop routings on Emirates, Etihad, Qatar, EgyptAir or Turkish.

Return **fares** from Australia are likely to be in the range Aus$2000–2700. From New Zealand, reckon on NZ$3000–3500, and from South Africa around R6000–9000.

Organized tours

Many **organized tours** follow a fairly set pattern – a week or so in Jordan, comprising stays in Amman, Petra, Aqaba and/or the Dead Sea, with sightseeing on the way and excursions to sites like Jerash and Wadi Rum. The advantage of these packages is that they get you a good-value flight-plus-accommodation deal; by booking a tour in advance you can end up staying in posh hotels for bargain prices. The disadvantage, of course, becomes clear if you fancy an extra day or two on your own to explore Petra once you get there.

Where fixing up an organized tour really comes into its own is if you have a particular kind of holiday in mind. If you want to know all about Jordan's archeological sites or learn how to scuba dive, or if you have your heart set on seeing a Sinai rosefinch (Jordan's national bird), **specialist tour operators** can sell you ready-made packages or tailor-make a tour to suit your requirements. Adventure companies can often throw in activities such as camel trekking, desert camping or snorkelling, and many operators specialize in pilgrimage tours to sites of biblical interest. You can also arrange tours directly with specialist tour companies in Jordan (see below).

Though Jordan remains safe, the sometimes uncertain political and security situation across the wider Middle East can mean you may find more – or, sadly, fewer – possibilities than we cover here when you come to research your holiday.

TOUR OPERATORS IN THE UK

CULTURAL/HISTORICAL TOURS

Abercrombie & Kent ☎ 01242 547760, W abercrombiekent. co.uk. Upmarket tailor-made trips.

Ancient World Tours ☎ 0333 335 9494, W ancient.co.uk. Archeological and historical itineraries.

Andante Travels ☎ 01722 713800, W andantetravels.co.uk. Small-scale, personalized, expert-led archeological/historical tours.

Audley Travel ☎ 01993 838415, W audleytravel.com. High-quality tailor-made trips both on and off the beaten track.

Corinthian Travel ☎ 020 3583 6089, W corinthiantravel.co.uk. Upscale cultural journeys.

Cox & Kings ☎ 020 3553 7925, W coxandkings.co.uk. Highly respected and long-established company offering gilt-edged cultural and historical tours.

Intrepid ☎ 0808 274 5111, W intrepidtravel.com. Breezy itineraries for independent-minded travellers.

Jordan Tours ☎ 01446 774018, W jordantours.co.uk. Small tailor-made firm with the personal touch.

Kirker Holidays ☎ 020 7593 1899, W kirkerholidays.com. Luxury tailor-mades.

Kuoni ☎ 0800 092 4444, W kuoni.co.uk. Large holiday operator with a choice of introductory trips.

Martin Randall Travel ☎ 020 8742 3355, W martinrandall.com. Small-group cultural tours, led by experts on art and archeology.

On The Go Tours ☎ 020 7371 1113, W onthegotours.com. Lively group tours, as well as tailor-made trips and unusual insider angles on exploring Petra.

Original Travel ☎ 020 7978 7333, W originaltravel.co.uk. Upmarket short breaks and family holidays to Jordan.

Scott Dunn ☎ 020 3553 1706, W scottdunn.com. Luxury tailor-made tours, staying in some out-of-the-way corners.

Steppes Travel ☎ 01258 787512, W steppestravel.com. Expertly prepared tailor-made trips.

Titan ☎ 0800 988 5823, W titantravel.co.uk. Classic escorted tours of major historical sites.

Voyages Jules Verne ☎ 020 3811 6201, W vjv.com. Major Jordan operator with years of experience, offering a range of well-thought-out holiday options.

ADVENTURE TOURS

Exodus ☎ 020 3733 2877, W exodus.co.uk. Small-group adventure tour operators, featuring walking, trekking, scrambling and cycling for individuals and families.

Explore ☎ 01252 883619, W explore.co.uk. A wide range of small group tours, treks and expeditions.

Families Worldwide ☎ 01962 302062, W familiesworldwide. co.uk. Specialists in adventure holidays for families.

G Adventures ☎ 0344 272 2060, W gadventures.co.uk. Pacy small-group tours for a youthful clientele.

Imaginative Traveller ☎ 01728 862230, W imaginative-traveller.com. Well-respected adventure operator with a good range of tours.

In The Saddle ☎ 01299 272997, W inthesaddle.com. High-quality tours on horseback.

KE Adventure ☎ 01768 773966, W keadventure.com. Great range of treks and adventure tours from a Jordan specialist.

Naturetrek ☎ 01962 733051, W naturetrek.co.uk. Small-group birdwatching and botanical tours of Jordan with expert guidance.

Nomadic Thoughts ☎ 020 7604 4408, W nomadicthoughts.com. Tailor-made trips to Jordan.

A BETTER KIND OF TRAVEL

At Rough Guides we are passionately committed to travel. We believe it helps us understand the world we live in and the people we share it with – and of course tourism is vital to many developing economies. But the scale of modern tourism has also damaged some places irreparably, and climate change is accelerated by most forms of transport, especially flying. We encourage our authors to consider the carbon footprint of the journeys they make in the course of researching our guides.

NOMADS ☎ 01457 873231, ⓦ www.nomadstravel.co.uk. Small operation run by Tony Howard and Di Taylor, the British climbing duo who opened up Rum to international tourism in the 1980s. They provide detailed, knowledgeable advice on all aspects of independent exploration of Jordan's wilder corners.

Peregrine Adventures ☎ 020 7206 0079, ⓦ peregrineadventures. com. Range of tours in and around Jordan and its neighbours.

Planet Dive ☎ 01273 921001, ⓦ planetdiveholidays.com. Good range of dive options at Aqaba, plus side-trips to Rum and Petra.

Ramblers ☎ 01707 818268, ⓦ ramblersholidays.co.uk. Great walking holidays.

Ride World Wide ☎ 01837 825440, ⓦ rideworldwide.co.uk. High-quality horseriding holidays.

Unicorn Trails ☎ 01767 777187, ⓦ unicorntrails.com. Horseriding holidays.

Walks Worldwide ☎ 01962 302085, ⓦ walksworldwide.com. Leading walking and outdoors operator to Jordan, with a broad range of tours, including family trips.

Wild Frontiers ☎ 020 8741 7390, ⓦ wildfrontiers.co.uk. Adventure trips, including on horseback in Wadi Rum.

World Expeditions ☎ 0800 074 4135, ⓦ worldexpeditions.com. A good range of trekking and adventure expeditions.

PILGRIMAGE TOURS

Guiding Star ⓦ guidingstarltd.com. A leading pilgrimage operator with offices in Jerusalem and Amman, founded in 1961. Combining Christian sites with adventure excursions and cultural exploration, they are exceptionally well connected, and can design a unique itinerary on request.

Maranatha Tours ☎ 01255 871423, ⓦ maranatha.co.uk. Specialist in biblical pilgrimage tours.

McCabe Pilgrimages ☎ 020 8675 6828, ⓦ mccabe-travel.co.uk. Pilgrim tours to Jordan.

Worldwide Christian Travel ☎ 0845 458 8308, ⓦ christian-travel.com. Biblical and pilgrimage tours.

TOUR OPERATORS IN NORTH AMERICA

Abercrombie & Kent ☎ 1 800 554 7016, ⓦ abercrombiekent. com. Fully escorted luxury tours to Jordan and its neighbours.

Bestway Tours ☎ 1 800 663 0844, ⓦ bestway.com. Cultural specialists, with a great range of tour options.

Caravan-Serai Tours ☎ 1 206 545 7300, ⓦ caravan-serai.com. Leading specialists to the Middle East, with a range of excellent, culturally aware tours to Jordan and all across the region. Owned and run by the award-winning Jordanian-born businesswoman Rita Zawaideh.

Cox and Kings ☎ 1 323 452 4433, ⓦ coxandkingsusa.com. Long-established top-of-the-range tour operator, with several Jordan offerings.

Far Horizons ☎ 1 415 482 8400, ⓦ farhorizons.com. Expert-led archeological and historical tours of Jordan.

HLO Tours ☎ 1 800 736 4456, ⓦ hlotours.com. Specialists in tailor-made trips, with many years of experience in the Middle East.

IsramWorld ☎ 1 800 223 7460, ⓦ isram.com. Long-established tour operator with a diverse selection of Middle Eastern offerings.

Maranatha Tours ☎ 1 602 788 8864, ⓦ maranathatours.com. Specialist in biblical pilgrimage tours.

Martin Randall Travel ☎ 1 800 988 6168, ⓦ martinrandall. com. British company running small-group cultural tours, led by expert lecturers.

On The Go Tours US ☎ 1 866 606 2960, Canada ☎ 1 866 890 7038, ⓦ onthegotours.com. Leading worldwide operator to Jordan, with a variety of cultural and adventure itineraries.

Spiekermann Travel ☎ 1 800 645 3233, ⓦ mideasttrvl.com. Experts on Middle Eastern travel, with hosted tours around Jordan.

Wilderness Travel ☎ 1 800 368 2794, ⓦ wildernesstravel.com. Cultural exploration around Jordan and beyond.

Ya'lla Tours ☎ 1 800 644 1595, ⓦ yallatours.com. Middle East specialist, with a wide range of trips and packages covering Jordan.

TOUR OPERATORS IN AUSTRALIA & NZ

Abercrombie & Kent Australia ☎ 03 9536 1800, New Zealand ☎ 0800 441 638, ⓦ abercrombiekent.com.au. Classy operator with a strong reputation – upmarket luxury tours.

Adventure World Australia ☎ 1300 295 049, ⓦ adventureworld. com.au; New Zealand ☎ 0800 238 368, ⓦ adventureworld.co.nz. Agents for a wide array of international adventure companies – well worth a browse.

Martin Randall Travel Australia ☎ 1300 559 595, New Zealand ☎ 0800 877 622; ⓦ martinrandall.com. British company running small-group cultural tours, led by expert lecturers.

On The Go Tours Australia ☎ 1300 855 684, New Zealand ☎ 0800 447 769; ⓦ onthegotours.com. Leading operator to Jordan, with unique cultural and adventure itineraries.

Peregrine Adventures Australia ☎ 1300 854 445, ⓦ peregrineadventures.com. Broad range of Jordan tours that reach some lesser-known highlights.

World Expeditions Australia ☎ 1300 720 000, New Zealand ☎ 0800 350 354; ⓦ worldexpeditions.com.au. Australian-owned adventure company, with a broad programme of trekking and adventure expeditions.

Overland routes

Before the war in Syria, many **independent travellers** visited Jordan overland, either popping across from one of the neighbours or as part of a longer odyssey between Istanbul and Cairo. Travel through Syria is no longer possible, though border-crossings at other points are straightforward. Most nationalities can get a Jordanian visa (see page 25) on arrival – except at the King Hussein/Allenby Bridge between Jerusalem and Amman, and the Wadi Araba/Yitzhak Rabin crossing between Eilat and Aqaba, where Jordanian tourist visas are not issued.

From Damascus

At the time of writing the war in **Syria** was continuing, and the country was closed to tourists. There's

ISRAEL AND WEST BANK LAND BORDERS

For details of current fees, regulations and transport for **crossing into Jordan** via the King Hussein/Allenby Bridge, the Sheikh Hussein/Jordan River Bridge and the Rabin/Wadi Araba border go to the **Israel Airports Authority** site ⓦ iaa.gov.il.

no knowing when that situation will change. When it does, transport to Amman from the capital, **Damascus**, barely 100km north of the Jordanian frontier, will likely be easiest by *serveece* (shared taxi). Ask around for the latest information.

From Jerusalem

No public transport runs directly between **Jerusalem** and Amman: the only way to go is with a combination of bus, taxi and serveece. All traffic is funnelled towards the single border-crossing open to the public, located a short way north of Jericho in the West Bank. It is known as the **Allenby Bridge** (*Jissr Allenby* in Arabic; *Gesher Allenby* in Hebrew) or the **King Hussein Bridge** (*Jissr al-Malek Hussein*).

Bridge **opening hours** are limited (Sun–Thurs 8am–midnight, Fri & Sat 8am–3pm; ☎ 02 548 2600), and you should arrive well before closing to avoid being stranded (at the latest: Sun–Thurs 8.30pm, Fri & Sat 11.30am). The Israeli and Jordanian terminals are around 5km apart, separated by no-man's-land either side of the bridge itself. Walking across, or taking a private car, is forbidden: you must take public transport. This crossing point is also notoriously subject to the ebb and flow of Middle Eastern politics, and can close at short notice.

Although you must have a **visa** to enter Jordan, they are not issued at this bridge – which, thanks to a complex piece of official doublethink, is not viewed by Jordan as an international border. If you try to cross without already holding a Jordanian visa, you'll be turned back by Israeli security.

Israeli buses from West Jerusalem don't go to the bridge; they only drop off at a parking area beside Highway 90, by a security barrier. Instead, use the *serveeces* (shared taxis) which depart frequently from East Jerusalem for NIS42 per person plus NIS5 per bag – the main operator is Taxi Nejmeh (☎ 02 627 7466), a short walk east of Damascus Gate on the main street, in a courtyard beside the *Golden Walls* hotel. Set out early in the morning, or book your ride in advance: serveeces stop running by about noon (10am on Fri & Sat), after which your only certain option of reaching the bridge is a private taxi for NIS250 or more. Buses also run to the bridge from Jericho.

At the Israeli bridge terminal (foreigners' hall), your bags are taken away for X-ray while you pay the Israeli **departure tax**, currently NIS176 (around US$45), plus

a NIS5 fee. You can pay the tax in advance online, at ⓦ borderpay.metropolinet.co.il. If you intend to use your passport for overland travel beyond Jordan, be sure to tell the Israeli officials not to stamp your passport (see page 30).

Then you reclaim your bags and must wait up to an hour for a **bus** which makes the short trip across the bridge to the Jordanian arrivals terminal – the fare is JD7 plus JD1.50 per bag, payable in cash dinars only. During the trip the bus driver will collect all passports; on arrival, you go into the foreigners' arrivals hall to reclaim your passport, which won't have been stamped by the Jordanian officials. Here you'll find a snack bar, a bank and an ATM. **Taxi** drivers gather outside, charging around JD30–35 to Amman, or *serveeces* do the one-hour journey to Tabarboor station in Amman for JD6–7 per person.

With luck, the journey from Jerusalem to Amman can take as little as two hours; without it (or with security/immigration delays) you could be hanging around most of the day. If you need speed, you can pay roughly US$250 for **VIP service** city-to-city from agencies such as ⓦ amman2jerusalem.com – but this excludes the bridge shuttle bus. A slightly cheaper, but still very quick, option is to take a taxi to the bridge, then at the Israeli departures terminal go to the marked VIP office run by Laufer Aviation (ⓦ lauferghi.com): for around US$110 they can whisk you through all the formalities and zip you direct in a private minibus to Jordanian arrivals, from where you can jump in a taxi to Amman.

From Tel Aviv and Nazareth

From **Tel Aviv**, the easiest way to get to Jordan using public transport is to take a bus or train to Jerusalem, then a tram or taxi to the Damascus Gate of Jerusalem's Old City, from where you can take a *serveece* to the border (see above).

A more expensive and long-winded way – which avoids travel through the West Bank – uses the northern crossing point over the River Jordan, a bridge about 6km east of the Israeli town of Beit She'an (*Beisan* in Arabic), known to the Israelis as the **Jordan River crossing** (Sun–Thurs 6.30am–9pm, Fri & Sat 8am–7pm; ☎ 04 609 3410), and to the Jordanians as the **Sheikh Hussein Bridge** or simply the Northern Crossing. Don't confuse the Sheikh Hussein Bridge, in the north, with the King Hussein Bridge, near the Dead Sea.

THE ISRAELI STAMPS PROBLEM

If you intend to visit Israel, the West Bank or Gaza as part of a longer journey in the region, you need to bear in mind that it is the official policy of almost all Middle Eastern and North African countries (exceptions include Egypt, Jordan and Morocco) to refuse entry to people who have **evidence of a visit to Israel** in their passports.

Israel no longer **physically stamps** passports of tourists – issuing a printed slip of paper on arrival instead – but "evidence" can include Jordanian entry or exit stamps from the border-posts at the Sheikh Hussein/Jordan River Bridge, the King Hussein/Allenby Bridge and the Wadi Araba/Yitzhak Rabin crossing (Aqaba–Eilat), as well as Egyptian stamps from the border-posts at Taba (near Eilat) and Rafah in northern Sinai. Visas issued in Israel for travel to any country and flight itineraries that specify Tel Aviv (or TLV) may also bar you, as may anything in Hebrew discovered in your belongings.

We've had some reports of travellers holding such evidence getting into certain countries (Tunisia, Oman and the UAE, among others) without any difficulty, but this can't be relied upon. Lebanese officials are the least flexible in this regard.

The best advice is to construct your **itinerary** so that you visit Israel last, after Lebanon and the rest. Alternatively, you can apply in your home country, well in advance, for a **second passport**: many countries issue these to people travelling around the Middle East as a matter of routine, but it's then up to you to ensure that your tally of entry and exit stamps in each passport adds up, and that you don't hand the wrong passport over to the wrong border official.

If you hold only one passport, there is no foolproof method of avoiding a giveaway stamp. If you're feeling lucky, and you've entered Jordan by air, sea or across the land borders from Iraq or Saudi Arabia, then you could try using *only* the King Hussein (Allenby) Bridge to cross from Jordan to the West Bank and back (while making sure that your Jordanian visa does not expire in the meantime). At this bridge Israeli and Jordanian immigration officials will usually stamp you both in and out on a **piece of paper**, thus avoiding any permanent evidence of having been "on the other side" (as many travellers refer to Israel, to avoid detection by eavesdropping officials). However, the success of this depends on not running into an official who decides to stamp your passport regardless.

It's a well-known ploy of travellers who have unwittingly acquired evidence of a visit to Israel to **lose their passports** deliberately in Egypt or Jordan and apply for new ones from their embassies. However, an unused passport issued in Cairo or Amman is as much evidence to some consular officials of a visit to Israel as a border stamp. Even if the loss of your old passport was genuine, you may still find yourself refused entry to certain countries on this suspicion alone.

To get to the Sheikh Hussein Bridge, take a bus from Tel Aviv to **Beit She'an** (2hr 30min; NIS38–45; more frequent connections via Afula), then a taxi to the border (around NIS50). You pay an Israeli departure tax, currently NIS101 (or about US$25), plus around NIS6 for a bus across the bridge. On the Jordanian side, you must get your visa (JD40; free with Jordan Pass, also free if you've booked your trip through a Jordanian tour company and will stay at least two nights in Jordan). There is no onward public transport – the only option is a taxi to Irbid (around JD25) or Amman (around JD50).

Alternatively, a bus runs from **Nazareth** direct to Irbid and Amman, using the same crossing point. Departures (usually Sun, Tues, Thurs & Sat 8.30am; NIS80) are from outside 97 Paulus VI Street. Contact the bus operator Nazarene Tours for more information (☏ 04 647 0797, ⊕ nazarene-tours.com).

Flying from Tel Aviv to Amman (around 30min) costs around US$310 one-way on Royal Jordanian (☏ 074 750 6666, ⊕ rj.com) – but offers the lure of spectacular scenery over desert hills and the Dead Sea.

From Eilat

Another crossing point from Israel is in the south, between the neighbouring Red Sea resort cities of **Eilat** (Israel) and Aqaba (Jordan), known to the Israelis as the **Yitzhak Rabin Crossing** or Arava Crossing (Sun–Thurs 6.30am–8pm, Fri & Sat 8am–8pm; ☏ 08 630 0555), and to the Jordanians as the **Wadi Araba** or Southern Crossing. From Eilat bus station, it's reached most easily by taking a taxi (around NIS50) or by simply walking 2km to the border. Note that Jordanian tourist visas are not issued here: you must already have a Jordanian visa to cross here. There's an Israeli departure tax, currently NIS101 (or about US$25). Once you're through the formalities, a taxi into central Aqaba (5km) costs around JD15.

From Cairo and the Sinai

From **Cairo**, just jump on a **plane**: the overland journey is long – almost 24 hours – uncomfortable, difficult and passes through territory in the Sinai peninsula which, at the time of writing, was deemed dangerous by most Western governments. Royal Jordanian and EgyptAir **fly** from Cairo to Amman (1hr 30min; around US$180–220), and you can also find flights from Alexandria and Sharm el-Sheikh.

At the time of writing, the British Foreign Office (**W** fco.gov.uk) **advised against all but essential travel** to many of the places we mention below, including Dahab, Nuweiba and Taba. **Check the security situation carefully before you travel**.

Jordanian JETT and Egyptian SuperJet **buses** depart once or twice weekly from the Almaza terminal in Heliopolis (**☎** 02 2290 9013). The fare on either is around US$100 including the Nuweiba–Aqaba ferry, payable in dollars only. The East Delta bus company (**☎** 02 2405 3482) runs cheaper daily services from the Turgoman/Cairo Gateway terminal.

Ferry service from Egypt to Aqaba in Jordan is chaotic. From **Nuweiba** there is a **fast ferry** (catamaran; 1hr) – though this was suspended at the time of writing – and a **slow ferry** (daily 1pm; US$90; 3hr). The timetable is notoriously unreliable and can change from month to month. **Expect lengthy delays**. There may be a tax of about EGP50. Arrive at the port, 8km south of Nuweiba, at least two hours early to buy tickets (with US dollars only). On boarding, you'll have to hand over your passport, which will be returned to you at Aqaba passport control, where visas are free (see page 25). A *serveece* into central Aqaba (9km) is about JD2 per person, a taxi about JD8. Check for details of extra departures in peak season (during summer, at the end of Ramadan, and around the hajj and Eid al-Adha).

A smaller tourist ferry operates from **Taba**, 70km north of Nuweiba, to Aqaba, but it is intended for hotel guests in Egypt who want to visit Jordan for a day or two: you can't buy a one-way ticket, and if you try to board with bags or suitcases, you may be stopped from travelling. A return ticket, valid up to eight days, costs US$106.

For details of either route, contact AB Maritime (Cairo **☎** 02 2260 4949, Nuweiba **☎** 069 352 0365; **W** abmaritime.com.jo).

A cheaper and often easier alternative is to go **overland** through the Israeli resort of Eilat (see opposite). **Taba**, on the Egyptian–Israeli border, is well served by transport from Nuweiba, Dahab and Cairo. The crossing is open 24 hours daily, but it can be difficult to find transport inside Israel during the Jewish *shabbat*, so avoid turning up here between 2pm Friday and 7pm Saturday. There may be a small Egyptian departure tax (around EGP50), and most nationalities are routinely issued with a free Israeli visa on arrival. Once in Israel, a combination of city buses and walking will get you through **Eilat** to the Jordanian border (*hagvul ha-yardeni* in Hebrew), but it's easier to take a taxi (around NIS80–100). Crossing from Eilat into Jordan is straightforward (see opposite). Total journey time is about two or three hours – though the passport stamps you pick up will disqualify you from subsequently entering Lebanon and many other Middle Eastern countries (see opposite).

Getting around

Jordan's public transport is a hotchpotch. Bus routes cover what's necessary for the locals, and there is little or no provision for independent travellers. With some highly visitable places inaccessible by public transport, the best way to see the whole of Jordan is to rent a car for at least part of your stay.

By bus and serveece

The most common way of getting between cities is by **bus**, most of which are fifteen- or eighteen-seater minibuses. Some larger buses and air-conditioned coaches also serve as public transport. Throughout this book, we use "bus" as a catch-all term, though in most cases minibuses are the only transport option available.

Timetables are rarely in operation: buses tend to depart only when they're full. This means that, on less-travelled routes especially, you should factor in sometimes quite considerable waiting time for the bus to fill up. Once you get going journeys are rarely arduous: roads are decent, and the longest ride you're likely to need – from Amman to Aqaba – is four hours or less. All buses and minibuses have their point of origin and destination painted in Arabic script just above either brake light on the rear of the vehicle.

Locals know the system by word-of-mouth, but no official information about bus travel exists: in most situations, you simply have to turn up at the point of departure (which may not be advertised as such – we offer guidance in relevant parts of the Guide where possible) and ask around. You're unlikely to **wait** long for a bus on popular inter-city routes – Amman to Madaba, say, or Jerash to Irbid – but longer trips, or more isolated destinations, may be served by only one or two buses, or by a handful of departures clustered together at a certain time of day. Miss them, and you'll have to come back tomorrow. Guides and hotel staff may be able to help, but given the lack of information even they often can't advise effectively on public transport. If you are travelling around quieter regions by bus, keep your itinerary loose.

Bus fares are low. As a guide, a thirty-minute hop between towns costs around JD1. Slightly longer journeys, such as Amman to Jerash, or Karak to Tafileh, are in the order of JD1.50–2. Rip-offs are rare: if you ask the fare, you'll invariably be told the truth. Expect higher fares on routes serving major tourist sites: Petra to Aqaba is around JD5–7. There is no price competition between minibus operators.

A few companies operate large, **air-conditioned buses** in competition with the minibuses on some long-distance runs. The main one is Jordan Express Tourist Transport, or **JETT** (Ⓦjett.com.jo), with daily timetabled services from Amman to Aqaba, Petra and other destinations; **Hijazi** operates Amman–Irbid, mainly for Yarmouk University students; and there are a few others. These offer the advantages of comfort and speed over the minibuses, and most allow you to book in advance (in person only, at the company's offices).

On most inter-city routes, **shared taxis** or service taxis (universally known as *serveeces*) tout for business alongside the buses. A *serveece* (pronounced "ser-VEES") is a white car, seating four to seven passengers, which offers, at a slightly higher price, the single advantage of speed over the same journey by bus – though being squashed into the back seat on a long journey can counter in discomfort what might be gained in time. *Serveeces* also operate the system of departing when full, but because there are fewer seats they leave more frequently. If you're carrying bulky or heavy luggage, you may find that *serveece*- and some minibus- drivers will charge you a small supplement per bag.

For getting around within cities, most places have their own systems of short-hop buses and *serveeces*.

Bus and *serveece* **etiquette** says that a foreigner should ideally not be sitting next to a Jordanian of the opposite sex. You may find that the locals shuffle themselves around to make sure that men are sitting next to men and women next to women.

Hitchhiking

Hitching a ride on well-travelled routes such as Amman to Petra will likely take you hours (or days), since drivers won't have a clue why you can't just get the bus like everyone else. However, in areas where buses may be sporadic or nonexistent – the eastern desert, the southern portions of the King's Highway, the link road from the Desert Highway into Wadi Rum, or just from one village to the next on quiet country roads – local drivers stick to a well-established countryside protocol about picking people up if they have space. The way to show you're hitching is to hold out your arm and loosely flap your index finger.

The first rule – apart from foreign women never hitching alone – is that you should always be prepared to pay something, even if your money is refused when offered. Trying to freebie your way around the country will inspire contempt rather than camaraderie. Travellers who decide to hitch should do so always in pairs. The risk of unpleasantness is minuscule but nonetheless does exist; women should never sit next to local men, and if you're alone, spontaneous offers of hospitality should be accepted only with caution. Water and a hat are vital accoutrements: dehydration is probably the greatest threat.

For a great account of hitchhiking across Jordan, search for "Is Jordan safe?" at Ⓦ engagingcultures.com.

By car

Compared with Egypt or Lebanon, **driving in Jordan** is a breeze; compared with the West, it's a challenge. Apart from driving on the right and always obeying a police officer, rules of the road tend to have individual interpretations. Most roads aren't marked out in lanes, so overtaking on both sides is normal – always accompanied by a blast or two on the horn – as is pulling out into fast-moving traffic without looking. There is no universally accepted pattern of right of way. It's wise to follow the locals and sound your horn before many types of manoeuvre; out in the sticks, look out for children playing on the hard shoulder and give a warning honk from a long way back. Traffic lights are always respected – cameras record red-light runners – as are most one-ways. Right of way on roundabouts goes to whoever's moving fastest.

Road surfaces are generally good, although there are lots of **unmarked speed bumps** and **rumble strips** in unexpected places (including main highways), as well as killer **potholes**. Look out for drifting sand in the desert: if you're going too fast when you hit a patch of sand, you can be spun off the road before you know it. Speed limits – posted fairly regularly – are generally 100km/h or 110km/h on open stretches of highway and 90km/h on main roads, dropping to 80km/h, 60km/h or 40km/h in built-up areas. Mobile police **radar traps** are very common – if you're caught speeding, expect traffic police (who may or may not speak English) to demand to see your driving licence and car registration documents before issuing you with a spot fine of JD20 or more, all recorded and receipted.

On major roads, **directional signs** are plentiful and informative; most have English as well as Arabic. Large brown signs around the country direct tourists to major sites, superseding older blue signs. On unsigned back roads, the only fail-safe method of finding the right direction is to keep asking the locals.

Night driving is considerably more scary. Lighting is often poor, so speed bumps, uneven road surfaces, children or animals (or objects) in the road and potholes all become invisible. Slow-moving trucks and farm vehicles often chug along in the dark without lights or reflectors. It's common – if inexplicable – practise on dark country roads to flip to main beam when you see somebody coming, dazzling them blind. Many people flash their headlights to say "get out of the way", but some do it to say "OK, go ahead", others merely to say hello: you must make up your own mind at the time which it is.

Although a normal driving licence from home is sufficient, an **International Driving Permit** can be useful, since it has an Arabic translation; these are available very inexpensively from motoring organizations in your home country.

Car rental

For the freedom and flexibility it brings, a **rental car** is a worthwhile investment, best arranged before you arrive. The rental market is huge, but most local firms cater more to Jordanians' friends and family than to westerners – although you can get some great deals on the fly, many of these tiny outfits are no more than a guy with a phone renting out old cars on the cheap with no insurance, no papers and no service.

Amman has more than a hundred **car rental firms**, all of which can match or undercut the international agencies' rates – but few of which maintain equivalent levels of quality and service. The best-value and most conscientious outfit is **Reliable**, located in Abdoun, not far from 5th Circle (☎06 592 9676, ⌨rentareliablecar.com). They charge about JD25–30 a day for a new or one-year-old car (manual or automatic) with air conditioning, comfortable for four people, including unlimited mileage and full insurance. Prices drop for longer rental periods. They'll bring the car to you, and you can drop it off for free, at the airport or anywhere in Amman, 24 hours a day – and their customer service is excellent. Collision damage waiver (CDW) costs a few dinars more, but is worth it. Options such as theft protection (TP) are unnecessary.

Cheaper deals are available elsewhere (as low as JD15–20/day) – but this will buy you an older vehicle, dodgier paperwork and less reliable backup when you're out on the road.

The global names have broader coverage – and higher prices. Hertz (☎06 581 2525, ⌨hertz.jo), Avis (☎06 569 9420, ⌨avis.com.jo) and Europcar (☎06 550 4031, ⌨europcar.jo) have multiple offices in Amman and Aqaba, plus also the Dead Sea, the King Hussein Bridge, the Eilat–Aqaba border and other points around the country. A listing of other firms is at ⌨visitjordan.com.

For all but the most dedicated adventurers, a normal car is fine for getting around Jordan. **Four-wheel-drive vehicles** cost from about JD50 a day. These are essential for getting to out-of-the-way archeological sites and touring the desert, but you need familiarity with 4x4 driving – and a local guide with you – before you head off-road. It's a good idea to keep several litres of drinking water in the car, in case you get stranded in some remote spot.

If you're involved in an accident, to claim costs back from the insurance company you'll need a full written report from the police, and from the first doctor on the scene who treated any injuries.

Fuel

All **fuel** sold in Jordan is unleaded – standard **90 octane** (*tisaeen*) or pricier **95 octane** (*khamsa wa-ti-saeen*). Diesel (*deezel*) is rarely available. Almost all petrol stations have attendants to do the pumping for you: either hand over, say, JD10 or JD20 before he starts, or just ask for "full". Most stations accept cash only.

Accidents

Despite the Jordanian driving style, **accidents** are infrequent, and rarely amount to more than a prang. However, under Jordanian law, any accident involving a car and a pedestrian is automatically deemed to be the fault of the driver: if you hit anybody, cause any sort of injury, or even if someone falls out of a window onto your stationary vehicle, **you will be held responsible** by the police and (often worse) by the victim's family. Complex negotiations involving large sums of money may ensue. If you hit an **animal** – goats, sheep, donkeys and camels roam more or less freely beside roads – you will have to pay the owner compensation. With a goat costing, say, JD100, and a camel ten times as much, you'd do well to keep your eyes peeled.

If you're in any sort of accident while behind the wheel of a rental car, call the rental company first: if they're trustworthy they will then call the police on your behalf and send someone out (for free) to pick you up. Otherwise, call the police yourself on ☎911.

By taxi and car-with-driver

Taxis are generally yellow with green panels in Arabic on both front doors, and they'll go anywhere if the price is right. Inexpensive and quite often essential within Amman, their good value declines the further afield you want to go: renting a taxi to cover the transport-thin eastern desert, for instance, will cost you almost twice as much as if you drove there yourself in a rental car (but, obviously, with less of the stress).

As far as **fares** go, taxis are metered within Amman. Elsewhere you'll probably have to negotiate with the driver before setting off. Ballpark figures for particular routes are given in the guide, but where you're inventing your own itinerary, you'd do well to ask the advice of a disinterested party (such as a hotel receptionist) beforehand. Then check rates and services with **Jordan Taxi** (W jordan-taxi.com), which offers a private hire service nationwide.

Smartphone-based ride-sharing taxi services **Uber** (W uber.com) and **Careem** (W careem.com) operate in Amman, undercutting traditional taxi prices.

Most rent-a-car agencies can provide a **driver** for the day for about JD30 on top of the price of the rental; on a longer trip, JD50 a day should cover his food and accommodation costs. However, if you want your driver to also be a (qualified) guide, explaining sites along the way, you need to book with a local tour company – and pay accordingly.

Jordanian women wouldn't get in the front seat next to a male driver. Wherever possible, foreign women should follow suit and sit in the back. Very few women drive yellow taxis, though many do now drive for Careem and Uber.

By train

No scheduled passenger **trains** operate in Jordan. The historic, narrow-gauge Hejaz Railway (W jhr. gov.jo), running from Damascus to Amman and south into the desert (see page 88), has been taken out of service and now only hosts occasional specials, usually chartered by foreign tour operators and steam enthusiasts, though there are also some weekly excursions for local families. A proposal to launch tourist shuttles on the freight line between Aqaba and Wadi Rum – used for trains carrying phosphates to port from desert mines – has so far come to nothing.

By plane

Royal Jordanian (T 06 510 0000, W rj.com) operates the only **domestic flights**, two or three times daily between Amman (Queen Alia) and Aqaba. Flight time is little over thirty minutes. At around JD50 one-way, it isn't prohibitively expensive, and means you can travel from city centre to city centre in around an hour and a half (including check-in and ground transfers), compared with more than four hours overland. In addition, the airborne views over the desert, the Dead Sea and the Petra mountains are exceptional; sit on the right-hand side heading south.

By bike

Cycling around Jordan is a very pleasant way to travel, although few locals cycle (mostly in the flat Jordan Valley) and you're likely to be regarded as mad if you try. Apart from the heat and steep hills, the chief dangers are oblivious drivers and – occasionally – groups of stone-throwing children in remote villages. Although it may seem counterintuitive, you should try to dress conservatively if you're planning a solo ride in the hinterlands: rural villagers may look askance at lurid skin-tight Lycra.

Bike Rush (W facebook.com/bikerush) is one of Jordan's few **bike rental** firms. Also check the Cycling Jordan group and Amman Cycling Club on Facebook for details of spare-parts outlets, weekend bike trips and to make contact with like-minded locals. The adventure tour operators Terhaal (W terhaal.com) and Experience Jordan (W experiencejordan.com) run mountain-bike excursions and tours around Madaba, the Dead Sea, Petra and Rum.

Accommodation

Accommodation in Jordan runs the gamut from the cheapest fleapit dives all the way up to international-standard luxury five-star hotels. Amman, Petra and Aqaba have a wide choice covering all price brackets, and Jordan's Dead Sea hotels are some of the best spa resort complexes in the world.

The **Jordan Hotel Association** (W johotels.org) grades their member hotels and campsites from one to five stars. **Room rates** can vary dramatically, according to demand and the time of year. The **high season** (March–Nov) peaks in April and October, when it can be difficult to find a room at any budget in Petra and Aqaba. Hotels in Aqaba can stay busy all winter long (Nov–Feb), when the luxury hotels on the Dead Sea are also often full – block-booked by groups or conference delegates, or packed with wealthy Ammanis on weekend breaks.

Most hotels above two-star include sixteen percent **government sales tax** and ten percent **service charge** in their rates, but many websites quote headline prices before tax – be sure to check total prices before committing. If demand is low, a little gentle bargaining can often bring discounts.

Standards vary widely within each price bracket and sometimes within each hotel. Things to look out for are air conditioning (or, at the most basic places, at least a ceiling fan – not a table fan) in summer and some form of heating in winter; both are essential almost everywhere. South- or west-facing rooms that receive direct sunshine are liable to become ovens on summer afternoons and stay uncomfortably hot

> ## HOTEL PRICES – A ROUGH GUIDE
>
> Each hotel review in this book includes the rate charged at the time of writing for the **least expensive standard double room** in high season. This, however, can be misleading, especially in Jordan: room prices can rise and fall from week to week (sometimes day to day), depending on demand. Renovations might push prices up. Competition might push prices down. Information gathered this year will be out of date next year. Online booking sites might offer discounts – and so on. Nothing infuriates honest hoteliers more than people insisting on paying the price quoted in a guidebook. You should use the figures we quote as a rough guide, not as gospel truth.

during the night; you'd do well in Aqaba, for instance, to reject a sea view in favour of a cooler, north-facing balcony. Even cheaper hotels should offer 24-hour hot water.

For those on a **backpacker** budget, there's a network of traveller-style hotels in all the major towns, and you'll easily get onto the grapevine for bargain excursions. In the **mid-range**, you can take advantage of some excellent-value small hotels – many family-run – dotted on and off the beaten track, as well as comfortable lodges and cabins within several of Jordan's nature reserves. At the **top end**, Jordan's finest hotels compete with the best in the world.

With the rise of Airbnb (🌐airbnb.com), **bed and breakfasts** – or **B&Bs** – have taken off in Jordan. You'll find dozens of choices, from rooms to apartments to guesthouses and more, for all tastes and budgets.

Budget hotels

Jordan's **cheapest hotels** – to be found in all town centres – are essentially dosshouses, catering to labourers, long-distance truckers and other hard-up folk. Universally filthy, they're best avoided by even the most frugal travellers: washing facilities are likely to be spartan or nonexistent, and there might be only one squat toilet to share.

Slightly up from these are **budget hotels** aimed at least partly at western tourists, offering a choice of shared or private rooms, housing two, three or four beds, perhaps with some **en-suite** rooms as well. It's perfectly acceptable to check things out before agreeing to pay: see if the sheets are clean (it's common practice in these places to leave the sheets a couple of weeks between changes; insist on clean bedding before taking the room), the bed is stable, the flyscreens on the windows are intact, the ceiling fan works, the water in the bathroom is hot (or at least lukewarm), the toilets don't smell too much, and so on. It's a good rule to keep your **passport** with you at all times: with the risk of pickpocketing at virtually zero, the hotel "safe" (often just an unlocked drawer) is rarely safer than your own pocket.

Women travelling alone or together on a rock-bottom budget will have to play things by ear. In general – although not always – budget hotels that are geared towards western backpackers will be safe and welcoming for women, whereas those that are mainly geared up for locals should be avoided. Paying slightly more to stay in hotels with better security and privacy is wise.

If **breakfast** is provided at all, it will generally comprise tea, pockets of flatbread, butter or marg, jam, processed cheese and perhaps a hard-boiled egg. Some places might include it in the room rate; others may charge a dinar or two extra.

Mid-range hotels

Mid-range hotels are generally decent, family-run establishments that take a pride in offering good service. Other than at Petra, they're just as likely to be targeting visiting Arab families as foreign tourists and thus can't afford to get a reputation for slovenliness. Lobbies are often done up in grandiose style, featuring gilt, fake marble and lots of glitter: don't be too dazzled, though, since a fancy lobby can sometimes prelude distinctly drab or gloomy rooms.

If you're after colonial character, you'll be disappointed: being a bedouin backwater, Jordan missed out on the grand age of hotel-building – and Amman's venerable *Philadelphia Hotel*, built soon after the 1921 foundation of the emirate, was rather short-sightedly bulldozed in the 1980s. Instead, look for character in the modest but comfortable rural lodges and cabins within several of Jordan's nature reserves, notably Dana, Ajloun and Azraq.

Luxury hotels

The **luxury** end of the market can offer remarkable value for money. An over-concentration of top-end hotels means that, with prudent advance booking (which can bring you bed and breakfast for less than the room-only walk-up rate), you could bring the cost of a five-star splurge down to a half or even a

out. **Unadventurous travellers can
easily find themselves stuck in a rut of
low-quality falafel and kebabs, departing
the country never having tasted the best
of what's on offer.**

third of what you might pay in Europe for equivalent facilities. There are very few independently owned luxury hotels left in Jordan: almost all belong to one or other of the big global hotel groups – InterCon-tinental (which includes Crowne Plaza and Holiday Inn), Mövenpick, Marriott, Kempinski and the like. All five-star hotels can cater for nonsmoking guests on request, generally with nonsmoking floors.

Camping

Jordan has limited facilities for **camping**. Just a handful of independently run sites exist, often in beautiful locations but with a minimum of amenities. Some hotels, notably at Petra, allow you to camp in their grounds. Several of the RSCN's nature reserves have excellent campsites, including Dana and Ajloun, but you have to pay for the tents that are provided: pitching your own tent is prohibited.

At Wadi Rum, all the local desert guides (and most of the outside companies that take tourists to Rum) have campsites for their own customers, comprising traditional bedouin black goat-hair tents pitched in some beauty spot, often with a decent toilet block, kitchen and even makeshift showers: all bedding and amenities are supplied. It's always preferable, of course, to sleep under the stars. If you want to visit (and camp) independently, note that a tent is not normally necessary outside the winter months, but Rum can be chilly at night year-round, and tents do keep away scorpions – as well as the winter and spring rains.

Elsewhere you should be judicious: the authorities disapprove of rough camping on the grounds of safety – though if you camp far away from habitation and tourist hot spots, no one will bother you. Always avoid lighting fires: wood is a very scarce commodity in Jordan. Ideally, use a multi-fuel stove or camping gas. Camping prices given in this Guide are for two people and one pitch, unless otherwise specified.

Food and drink

**Bedouin tradition values home cooking
over eating out. As a consequence, most
of Jordan's restaurants are simple places
serving straightforward fare. Excellent
restaurants do exist, but must be sought**

How to eat

Unless you stick to a diet of familiar "international" cuisine and take every meal in upmarket hotels or restaurants, you're likely to be **eating with your fingers** at least some of the time – especially if you sample local styles of cooking, whether at low-budget hummus parlours or gourmet Lebanese restaurants. In budget diners, the only cutlery on the table will be a spoon, used to eat rice and soupy stews. More upmarket restaurants will provide cutlery, but even here, flaps or pockets of flatbread (similar to the pitta bread seen in the West) count as knife, fork and spoon – torn into pieces for scooping up dips, mopping up sauces, tearing meat off the bone and constructing personal one-bite sandwiches.

Since the left hand is traditionally used for toilet purposes, Jordanians instinctively always eat **only with the right hand**. In restaurant situations no one will be mortally offended if you use your left hand for a tricky shovelling or tearing manoeuvre, but using your left hand while eating from a communal platter in someone's house would be considered unhygienic.

When to eat

Most people have **breakfast** relatively early, before 8am. **Lunch** is eaten between 1 and 3pm, and many people take a break around 6pm for coffee and sweet pastries. The main meal of the day is eaten late, rarely before 8pm; in Amman and Aqaba, restaurants may not start to fill up until 9.30 or 10pm. However, in keeping with the bedouin tradition of relying on home cooking, you'll find that even quite large towns in the bedouin heartland of southern Jordan, such as Madaba or Karak, have a bare handful of small, plain restaurants that do a roaring trade in early-evening takeaways and close up by 9pm.

Breakfast

The traditional Jordanian **breakfast** is a bowl of hot *fuul* (boiled broad/fava beans mashed with lemon juice, olive oil and chopped chillis), served with a long-handled ladle from a distinctive bulbous cooking jar and mopped up with fresh-baked *khubez* (flatbread) – guaranteed to keep you going for hours. Hummus, a cold dip of boiled chickpeas blended with lemon juice, garlic, sesame and olive oil, is lighter. Both *fuul* and hummus can be ordered to take away (*barra*) in plastic pots. Bakeries that have an open oven (*firin*) offer a selection of savoury pastries, including *khubez bayd* (a kind of small egg pizza) and bite-sized pastry triangles (*ftayer*) filled with cheese (*jibneh*), spinach (*sabanekh*), potato (*batata*) or meat (*lahmeh*). Larger bakeries also have chunky breadsticks, sesame-seed bread rings (*kaak*), thick slabs of crunchy toast (*garshella*) and rough brown bread (*khubez baladi*). Along with some olives (*zaytoon*) and runny yoghurt (*laban*) or creamy yoghurt (*labneh*), it's easy to put together a picnic breakfast.

Prices are nominal. A bowl of *fuul* or hummus costs around JD0.75; small baked nibbles half that. Bread is sold by weight, with a kilo of large *khubez* (about five pieces) or small *khubez* (about eleven pieces) roughly JD0.50.

Hotel breakfasts vary wildly. At budget establishments, expect pretty poor fare (thin bread, margarine, processed cheese, marmalade and so on). Larger hotels, though, pride themselves on offering absurdly lavish breakfast buffets, encompassing hummus and other dips, dozens of choices of fresh fruit, fresh-baked bread of all kinds, pancakes with syrup, an omelette-chef on hand and a variety of cooked options from hash browns, baked beans and fried mushrooms to "beef bacon" (a substitute for real bacon, which is forbidden under Islam). Some offer Japanese specialities such as miso soup and sushi.

Street snacks

The staple **street snack** in the Middle East is **falafel**, small balls of a spiced chickpea paste deep-fried and served stuffed into *khubez* along with some salad, a blob of *tahini* (sesame-seed paste) and optional hot sauce (*harr*). Up and down the country you'll also find **shawarma** stands, with a huge vertical spit outside to tempt in customers. *Shawarma* meat is almost always lamb (only occasionally chicken), slabs of it compressed into a distinctive inverted cone shape and topped with chunks of fat and tomatoes to percolate juices down through the meat as it cooks – similar to a Turkish-style doner kebab. When you order a *shawarma*, the cook will fill a flatbread pocket with thin shavings of the meat and a little salad and hot sauce.

Depending on size, a falafel sandwich costs about JD0.50, a *shawarma* sandwich about JD1.

Restaurant meals

The cheapest **budget diners** will generally only have one or two main dishes on view – *fuul*, stew with rice, roast chicken and the like – but you can almost always get hummus and salad to fill out the meal.

In better-quality Arabic **restaurants**, the usual way to eat is to order a variety of small starters (meze), followed by either a selection of main courses to be shared by everyone, or a single, large dish for sharing. Good Arabic restaurants might have thirty different choices of meze, from simple bowls of **hummus** or **labneh** up to more elaborate mini-mains of fried **chicken liver** (*kibdet djaj*) or **wings** (*jawaneh*). Universal favourites are **tabbouleh** (parsley salad), **fattoush** (salad garnished with squares of crunchy fried bread), **warag aynab** (vine leaves stuffed with rice, minced vegetables and often meat as well) and spiced **olives**. **Kibbeh** – the national dish of Syria and Lebanon and widely available at better Jordanian restaurants – is a mixture of cracked wheat, grated onion and minced lamb pounded to a paste; it's usually shaped into ovals and deep-fried, though occasionally you can find it raw (*kibbeh nayeh*), a highly prized delicacy. Portions are small enough that two people could share five or six meze as a sizeable starter or, depending on your appetite, a complete meal. Bread and a few pickles are always free.

Meze are the best dishes for **vegetarians** to concentrate on, with enough grains, pulses and vegetables to make substantial and interesting meat-free meals that cost considerably less than standard meaty dishes. Filling dishes such as **mujeddrah** (lentils with rice and onions) and **mahshi** (cooked vegetables stuffed with rice) also fit the bill.

Main courses are almost entirely meat-based. Any inexpensive diner can do **half a chicken** (*nuss farooj*)

FUMING

Jordan has a desperate **tobacco** problem: according to World Health Organization figures, around sixty percent of men and ten percent of women are smokers – the highest rates in the Arab world. Although **smoking** in enclosed public places has been outlawed by the Jordanian parliament, enforcement is patchy at best. As you move around the country you're very likely to encounter smoke-filled hotel lobbies, cafés and restaurants. Sometimes an establishment will allocate a no-smoking zone (generally in the farthest corner and hardly ever with an actual physical barrier) but often it's just a free-for-all. Very few eating places call themselves **smoke-free** – mostly espresso-style cafés and fast-food joints in West Amman. Find out more about the domestic campaign to have the law enforced at ⓦ smokefreejo.com and on social media.

with rice and salad. Lamb **kebabs** are also ubiquitous; the chicken version is called **shish tawook**. Lots of places also offer meaty stews with rice at lunchtime; the most common is with beans (*fasooliyeh*), although others feature potatoes or a spinach-like green called *mulukhayyeh*.

Jordan's national speciality is the traditional bedouin feast-dish **mansaf** – chunks of boiled lamb or mutton served on a bed of gloopy rice, with pine nuts sprinkled on top and a tart, creamy sauce of *jameed* (pungent goat's-milk yoghurt) on the side to pour over. You'll also find some delicious Palestinian dishes, including **musakhan** (chicken steamed with onions and sumac, a sour-flavoured red berry) and **magloobeh** (essentially chicken with rice). A few places, mainly in Amman and the north, do a high-quality Syrian **fatteh** (meat or chicken cooked in an earthenware pot together with bread, rice, pine nuts, yoghurt, herbs and hummus, with myriad variations).

Good **fish** (*samak*) is rare in Jordan. **Pork** is forbidden under Islam and only appears at expensive Asian restaurants.

Costs

Simple meals of chicken, stew or kebabs won't cost more than about JD5 for a stomach-filling, if not a gourmet, experience. Plenty of Arabic and foreign restaurants dish up varied, high-quality meals for JD10–12. It's possible to dine sumptuously on meze at even the most expensive Arabic restaurants in the country for less than JD20 a head, although meaty main courses and wine at these places can rapidly torpedo a bill into the JD40s a head without too much effort.

Sweets

A western-bred, guilt-ridden "naughty-but-nice" attitude to **confectionery** can only stand in the face of the unabashedly sugar-happy, no-holds-barred Levantine sweet tooth: most Arabic sweets (**halawiyyat**) are packed with enough sugar, syrup, butter and honey to give a nutritionist the screaming horrors.

The traditional Jordanian way to round off a meal is with fresh fruit. Restaurants may offer a small choice of desserts, including some of the items described below, but inexpensive places frequently have nothing sweet. However, all large towns have plenty of patisseries making *halawiyyat* fresh: it's common to take a quarter- or half-kilo away in a box to munch at a nearby coffee house.

There are three broad categories of *halawiyyat*: large round trays of hot, fresh-made desserts, often grain-based, which are sliced into squares and drenched in hot syrup; piles of preprepared, bite-sized honey-dripping pastries and cakes; and stacks of dry sesame-seed or date-filled biscuits. The best of the hot sweets made in trays is **knaffy** (or *kunafeh* or *kanafa*), a heavenly Palestinian speciality of buttery shredded filo pastry layered over melted goat's cheese. **Baglawa** (the local way to say *baklava*) – layered flaky pastry filled with pistachios or other nuts – comes in any number of different varieties. Juice stands often lay out tempting trays of **hareeseh**, a syrupy semolina-almond cake, sliced into individual portions. Of the biscuits, you'd have to go a long way to beat **maamoul**, buttery, crumbly rose-scented things with a date or nut filling. Everything is sold by weight, and you can pick and choose a mixture: a quarter-kilo (*wagiyyeh*) – rarely more than JD2 – is plenty for two.

Large restaurants and some patisseries also have milk-based sweets, often flavoured deliciously with rosewater. King of these is **muhallabiyyeh**, a semi-set almond cream pudding served in individual bowls, but the Egyptian speciality **Umm Ali** – not dissimilar to bread pudding, served hot, sprinkled with nuts and cinnamon – runs a close second.

Curiously elastic, supersweet **ice cream** (*boozeh*) is a summer standard. During Ramadan, bakeries and patisseries make fresh *gatayyif* – traditional **pancakes** – often on hotplates set up on the street. Locals buy stacks of them for stuffing at home with nuts and syrup.

Fresh fruit and picnic food

Street markets groan with **fresh fruit**, including apples from Shobak and oranges, mandarins and bananas from Gaza and the Jordan Valley. Local bananas (or the common Somali ones) are smaller, blacker and sweeter than the bland, oversized clones imported from Latin America. In the late spring, Fuheis produces boxes of luscious peaches; local grapes come from the Balqa and Palestine. Exquisite **dates**, chiefly Iraqi, Saudi and Omani – though there are now a few Jordanian producers – are available packed year-round and also fresh in late autumn, when you'll also see stalls selling small, yellow-orange fruits often still on the branch; these are *balah*, sweet, crunchy unripe dates that seldom make it to the West. Look out for **pomegranates** around the same time, while spring and summer are the season for local melon and watermelon.

For picnic supplements, most towns have a good range of stalls or mobile vendors selling **dried fruit** and roasted **nuts and seeds**. Raisins, sultanas, dried figs and dried apricots can all be found cheaply everywhere. The most popular kind of seeds are *bizr* (dry-roasted melon, watermelon or sunflower seeds), the cracking of which in order to get at the minuscule kernel is an acquired skill. Local almonds (*looz*) are delectable. Pistachios and roasted chickpeas are locally produced; peanuts, hazelnuts and cashews are imported. It's often possible to buy individual hard-boiled eggs from neighbourhood groceries, and varieties of the local salty white cheese (*jibneh*) are available everywhere.

Tea, coffee and other drinks

The main focus of every Jordanian village, town and city neighbourhood is a **coffee house**, where friends and neighbours meet, gossip does the rounds and a quiet moment can be had away from the family. The musicians, poets and storytellers of previous generations have been replaced everywhere by TV music or sport, although a genial, sociable ambience survives. Unlike the contemporary espresso bars which predominate in West Amman and elsewhere, traditional coffee houses – which also serve tea and other drinks – are male domains and bastions of social tradition; foreign women will always be served without hesitation, but might feel watched.

The national drink, lubricating every occasion, is **tea** (*shy*), a strong, dark brew served scalding-hot and milkless in small glasses. The traditional method of tea-making is to boil up loose leaves in a pot together with several spoons of sugar to allow maximum flavour infusion. In deference to foreign taste buds, you may find the sugar being left to your discretion, but the tannins in steeped tea are so lip-curlingly bitter that you'll probably prefer the Jordanian way.

Coffee (*gahweh*), another national institution, has two broad varieties. **Turkish coffee** is what you'll come across most often. Made by boiling up cardamom-flavoured grounds in a distinctive long-handled pot, then letting it cool, then reboiling it several times (traditionally seven, though in practice two suffices), it's served in small cups along with a glass of water as chaser. Sugar is added beforehand, so you should request your coffee unsweetened (*saada*), medium-sweet (*wasat*) or syrupy (*helweh*). Let the grounds settle before sipping, and leave the last muddy mouthful in the cup.

Arabic coffee, also known as **bedouin coffee**, is an entirely different, almost greenish liquid, unsweetened and pleasantly bitter, traditionally made in a long-spouted

---

EATING DURING RAMADAN

Throughout the month of **Ramadan** (see page 58), Muslims are forbidden by both religious and civil law from **smoking** and from **eating or drinking** anything – including water and, in the strictest interpretations, even their own saliva – during the hours of daylight. Throughout Ramadan, almost all cafés and restaurants nationwide (apart from those in big hotels) stay closed until sunset. Thereafter, most do a roaring trade into the early hours. Markets, groceries and supermarkets are open during the day for purchases, with slightly truncated hours.

All shops close for an hour or two around dusk to allow staff to break the fast with family or friends – and this is a great time to join in. For restaurants of all kinds, including those in hotels, make the sunset "breakfast" meal **iftar** a real occasion, with special decorations, themed folkloric events or music and general merriment. Even the cheapest diners will rig up party lights and lay out tables and chairs on the street to accommodate crowds of people, all sitting down together to share the experience of breaking the day's fast. Many people have two or three light dinners as the evening goes on, moving from one group of friends or relatives to the next.

Officially, eating in public during fasting hours is a **criminal offence**, punishable by up to a month in prison and/or a JD25 fine. For **foreigners**, nothing too serious will happen if you inadvertently light up a cigarette in public during the day, but the locals will not thank you for walking down the street munching a sandwich: if you do, expect lots of shouting and perhaps some unpleasantness. All four- and five-star hotels serve both food and soft drinks to foreigners during daylight, although they will only do so in places out of view of the street. If you're travelling on a tight budget and are buying picnic food for both breakfast and lunch, you'll need to exercise a good deal of tact during the day in eating either behind closed doors or well out of sight in the countryside.

It is illegal for supermarkets and the majority of restaurants (that is, all those below a certain star rating) to sell **alcohol** for the entire month. At the time of writing, it was possible for non-Jordanians to buy and consume alcohol during Ramadan in five-star hotels and a handful of independent restaurants (mostly in Amman), but you may find the rules have changed when you visit.

brass pot set in hot embers. Public coffee houses don't have it, and you'll only be served it – often, rather prosaically, from a thermos flask – in a social situation by bedouin themselves, for example if you're meeting with a police officer or government official, or if you're invited to a family tent in the desert (see page 44).

Coffee houses also serve **soft drinks** and a wide range of seasonal herbal teas, including mint, fennel, fenugreek, thyme, sage and camomile. In colder seasons at coffee houses and street stands, you'll come across the winter-warmer **sahleb**, a thick milky drink made from a ground-up orchid tuber (or, nowadays, just cornflour) and served very hot sprinkled with nuts, cinnamon and coconut.

A coffee house is also the place to try a tobacco-filled **water pipe**, known by different names around the Arab world but most familiarly in Jordan as a "**hubbly-bubbly**", **shisha** or **argileh**. Some upscale restaurants offer them as a postprandial digestive. It is utterly unlike smoking a cigarette: the tobacco is nearly always flavoured sweetly with apple or honey, and this, coupled with the smoke cooling as it bubbles through the water chamber before you inhale, makes the whole experience pleasant and soothing – though, in health terms, one lungful of shisha smoke is equivalent to an entire cigarette. Smoking shisha for an hour, you inhale the same amount of smoke as from about 100 cigarettes.

Water

Although Jordanians drink **water** freely from the tap, you might prefer not to: it is chlorinated strongly enough not to do you any harm (it just tastes bad), but the pipes it runs through add a quantity of rust and filth you could do without. All hotels above three stars have water filtration systems in place, which help cut out the unpleasantness, as do water bottles with purifying filters. Bottles of **mineral water**, both local and imported, are available inexpensively in all corners of the country. A standard 1.5-litre size costs roughly JD0.40 if you buy it individually, less if you buy a six-pack from a supermarket or grocery. Expect to pay more in out-of-the-way places – JD2 or so inside Petra. Check that the seal is unbroken before you buy. Inexpensive diners always have jugs of **tap water** (*my aadi*) on the table, but in restaurants waiters will quite often bring an overpriced bottle of mineral water to your table with the menu – which you're quite entitled to reject. Recycling facilities for plastics are few and far between; bringing your own water bottle with a filter is much more environmentally friendly.

Fresh juice and squash

Most Jordanian towns have at least one stand-up **juice bar**; these are great places for supplementing a meagre breakfast or replenishing your vitamin C. Any fruit in view can be juiced or puréed. Sugar (*sukkr*) and ice (*talj*) are automatically added to almost everything; however, considering ice blocks are often wheeled in filthy trolleys along the roadside and broken up with a screwdriver, you might like to give it a miss – if so, request your juice *bidoon talj*. "Without sugar" is *bidoon sukkr*. Most freshly squeezed juices, and mixed juice cocktails, cost around JD0.50 for a "small" glass (actually quite big), double that for a pint. Mango, strawberry and other exotic fruit cost a little more.

More popular, and thus easier to find, are cheaper ready-made fruit squashes. Dark-brown **tamarhindi** (tamarind, tartly refreshing) and **kharroob** (carob, sweet-but-sour), or watery **limoon** (lemon squash) are the best bets; other, less common, choices include **soos** (made from liquorice root, also dark brown and horribly bitter) and **looz** (sickly sweet white almond milk). All are around JD0.30 a glass.

Alcohol

Drinking **alcohol** is forbidden under Islam. That said, Jordan is not Saudi Arabia, and alcohol is legal and widely available – but you have to look for it: the market streets and ordinary eateries of most towns show no evidence of the stuff at all.

Apart from in big hotels, the only restaurants to offer alcohol are upmarket independently owned establishments and tourist resthouses at some archeological sites. Most big supermarkets and some smaller convenience stores sell alcohol. Amman has a lot of **bars**, not all of them inside hotels. Places such as Aqaba and Petra that serve tourists (or Madaba, with a prominent Christian population) also have some bars. Elsewhere, expect to find little or no alcohol at all.

Drinking alcohol in public, or showing signs of **drunkenness** in public – which includes on the street, in cafés or coffee houses, in most hotel lobbies, on the beach or even in the seemingly empty desert or countryside – is utterly taboo and will cause great offence to local people.

The biggest local **beer** is Amstel, brewed under licence and very palatable. It's available in cans and bottles, and also on draught in some bars: a large glass costs around JD7. You'd do better with **Carakale** (Ⓦcarakale.com), Jordan's first craft microbrewery, based in Fuheis – choose from a variety of ales, stout and porter, sold in bottles at supermarkets, beer shops and some bars and restaurants in Amman and Madaba.

There's a good range of Jordanian **wine**, with the best now able to compete on the world stage. Leading the way are the **Saint George** wines of Zumot (Ⓦzumot-wines.com) – notably the fruity Cabernet and Merlot, which have won numerous global wine awards, and fresh, very drinkable Chardonnay/Sauvignon Blanc. Haddad, trading as Eagle (@eagledis.com), are best known for their bright **Mount Nebo** whites, alongside the **Jordan River** range which includes a Cabernet Sauvignon, a rich, plummy Shiraz and a light, spicy Chardonnay. These – along with widely available Palestinian "Holy Land" wines – are around JD8–12 a bottle, much less than imported wines. The top local spirit is anise-flavoured **araq** (similar to Turkish *raki*), drunk during a meal over ice, diluted with water. A bottle of premium *araq* – whether from Zumot, Eagle or more prestigious Lebanese distilleries – will set you back JD15 or so.

The media

With the widespread use of English in public life, you'll have good access to news while in Jordan. Despite a worsening trend for censorship in recent years, major news sites and satellite channels remain accessible, international newspapers and magazines are on sale and there's some independent local media in English.

In Arabic

Among the region's conservative and often state-owned **Arabic press**, Jordan's newspapers, all of which are independently owned, have a reputation for relatively well-informed debate, although strict press laws – and the slow process of media liberalization – cause much controversy. The two biggest dailies, *ad-Dustour* ("Constitution") and *al-Ra'i* ("Opinion"), are both centrist regurgitators of government opinion; *al-Ghad* ("Tomorrow") has a fresher outlook. There's a host of other dailies and weeklies, ranging from the sober to the sensational. Local news websites abound.

In English

English-language newspapers are widely available from the kiosks in all big hotels and also from some bookshops, as well as online. Look out for excellent regional papers such as Abu Dhabi's *The National* (@thenational.ae), Beirut's *Daily Star* (@dailystar.com.lb) and Cairo's *Al-Ahram Weekly* (@weekly.ahram.org.eg). The *International New York Times* and most British dailies and Sundays generally arrive one or two days late (JD2 and upwards).

For **local news** in English, the *Jordan Times* (@jordantimes.com) is published daily except

Saturdays, featuring national news focused closely on the royals, plus agency reports and pro-government comment. The website @7iber.com (pronounced *hibber* – it means "ink") runs a more enticing mix of stories in Arabic and English. Artmejournal (@artmejo.com) has features and interviews from Jordan's art scene, with exhibition listings. *My Kali* (@mykalimag.com) is an online LGBTQ magazine.

There's a lively market for Jordanian print **magazines**, with a range of English-language monthlies including glossy *Living Well* (@livingwell.jo). Plenty of international magazines are available, from *Cosmopolitan* to *The Economist*.

TV and radio

Jordan **TV** (@jrtv.gov.jo) isn't up to much. Almost all hotels have satellite TV, featuring CNN, BBC World News, Al Jazeera English, plus a few movies and sitcoms in English, alongside dozens of Arab, European and Asian channels.

As well as stations devoted to Quranic recitation, local news, phone-ins, contemporary pop and old-time crooners, Amman has several English-language FM music **radio** stations playing western hits, including Play 99.5, Beat 102.5 and Bliss 104.3.

Culture and etiquette

Your experience of Jordanian people is likely to be that they are, almost without exception, decent, honest, respectful and courteous. It seems only right that you should return some of that respect by showing a grasp of some basic aspects of Jordanian, Arab and Muslim culture.

If it's possible to generalize, the three things that most annoy local people about foreign tourists in Jordan are **immodest dress**, **public displays of affection** and **lack of social respect**. In this section we try to explain why, and how to avoid causing upset.

As you travel through the country you will doubtless see dozens of tourists breaking these taboos (and others), sometimes unwittingly, sometimes deliberately. Nothing bad happens to them. Jordan is a relatively liberal society and there are no Saudi-style religious police marching around to throw offenders in jail. Jordanians would never be so rude as to tell visitors to their country that they are being crass and insensitive; instead, they'll smile and say, "Welcome to Jordan!" – but still, the damage has been done. You might prefer to be different.

FROM A WOMAN'S PERSPECTIVE – SOME SAMPLE EXPERIENCES

"It's easy for women to travel alone in Jordan. You'll be pleasantly surprised, as I was, by people's reactions – the best preparation is just to head out with self-confidence, curiosity and a sense of humour. People are extremely willing to help, and almost everyone invited me for tea – a boy selling tablecloths, taxi drivers, even the guardian in the museum.

Travelling for a time with a male friend felt a little unreal. Suddenly, people stopped talking to me and paid attention only to him. This was probably due more to respect for me than condescension, but I couldn't help feeling a little upset – though it put me in a great position to just observe events.

It is vital to be able to take things lightly. For instance, I was followed by a bunch of teenage boys for at least an hour through the whole of Salt. They had a great time, running around and making jokes. My mistake was to try and get away. I should have stayed and talked to them, lived up to my role and – best of all – taken a picture. They'd have loved that."

Anna Hohler, journalist

"One day in Karak, I was doing some exercises in my hotel room. The door was locked, the shades were down. I happened to glance up. Above the closet there was a small set of windows (hadn't noticed them before), with a man's face, quickly disappearing.

The following morning, when I saw Mr Peeper in the lobby, he stared right at me without an ounce of shame. Being spied on is no surprise in any culture, but his lack of shame was a cultural lesson for me – not about relations between men and women in Jordan (because I think Jordanian women command a great deal of respect), but rather because I was assumed not to question his rights over my body.

You can regulate the respect you receive according to the way you dress. Complying with the standards of the place you're visiting relieves you from harassment. It also signals your intention to understand. The assumptions about western women are so image-based that changing your image will change your reception. It's as simple as that."

Karinne Keithley, dancer

"Living and working in Jordan was rewarding and very comfortable. Modifying my dress and behaviour to match social norms helped immensely. Just wearing loose clothes and long-sleeved shirts made me feel more confident and relaxed, especially in more traditional areas, and allowed local people to take me seriously. Being friendly with men I didn't know inevitably got me in trouble, since they interpreted it as flirting: I tried never to smile at men on the street and to keep my interactions with waiters and shopkeepers on a reserved and businesslike footing. This doesn't mean I didn't get stared at – I did. But I came to accept that in some places, as a foreigner, I was an exotic sight to be seen, as much as Jordanian people are exotic to visitors.

The flipside of avoiding men's stares was that I could smile and look freely at women. Since most women adopt a serious, frozen expression on the street it was a great surprise, smiling tentatively at a woman passer-by or exchanging a few words of greeting, to see her face light up with a broad smile in response. I had an immediate, spontaneous connection which surpassed words and cultural differences."

Michelle Woodward, photographer

Incidentally, you may also see Jordanians acting and dressing less conservatively than we recommend here. That is, of course, their prerogative – to shape, influence or challenge their own culture from within, in whatever ways they choose. Tourists do not share the same rights over Jordanian culture – the onus is on visitors to fit in.

Dress codes

Outward appearance is the one facet of interaction between locals and western tourists most open to misunderstandings on both sides. A lot of tourists, male and female, consistently flout simple dress codes, unaware of just how much it widens the cultural divide and demeans them in the eyes of local people. Clothes that are unremarkable at home can come across in Jordan as being embarrassing, disrespectful or offensive.

Jordanians and Palestinians place a much greater emphasis on personal grooming and style of dress than people tend to in the West: for most, consciously "dressing down" in torn or scruffy clothes is unthinkable. In addition, for reasons of modesty, many people expose as little skin as possible, with long sleeves and high necklines for both sexes.

Male dress codes

Visiting tourists who wear shorts on the street give roughly the same impression that they would wandering around Bournemouth or Baltimore in their underpants. **Long trousers** are essential in the city, the country and the desert, whatever the weather – clean and respectable light cotton, denim or canvas ones in plain colours (not flimsy, brightly patterned beach-style trousers). If you must wear shorts, go for the loose-fitting knee-length variety rather than brief, shape-hugging athlete's shorts. Any top that doesn't cover your shoulders and upper arms counts as underwear. Wearing a T-shirt is acceptable, but a **buttoned shirt** tucked into trousers broadcasts a sounder message about the kind of value you place on cultural sensitivity. Jordanian men never, in any situation, walk around in public topless.

Female dress codes

To interact as a western woman in Jordanian society with some degree of mutual respect, you'll probably have to go to even greater lengths than men to adjust your normal style of dress, although it is possible to do so without compromising your freedom and individuality too much. **Loose-fitting, opaque clothes** that cover your legs, arms and chest are a major help in allowing you to relate normally with local men. On women, shorts appear flagrantly provocative and sexual, as do Lycra leggings. T-shirts are also generally best avoided. The nape of the neck is considered particularly erotic and so is best covered, either by a high collar or a thin cotton scarf.

Hair is another area where conservatism helps deter unwanted attention. Jordanian women who don't wear a headscarf rarely let long hair hang below their shoulders; you might like to follow suit and clip long hair up. To some people, women with wet hair are advertising sexual availability, so you may prefer to dry your hair before going out. If your hair is blonde, you must unfortunately resign yourself to a bit more inquisitive attention – at least when walking in more conservative areas.

Social interactions

Social interaction in Jordan is replete with all kinds of seemingly impenetrable verbal and behavioural rituals, most of which can remain unaddressed by foreigners with impunity. A few things are worth knowing, however.

The energy which Jordanians put into social relationships can bring shame to westerners used to keeping a distance. Total strangers greet each other like chums and chat happily about nothing special, passers-by ask each other's advice or exchange opinions without a second thought, and old friends embark on volleys of salutations and cheek-kisses, joyful arm-squeezing or back-slapping, and earnest enquiries after health, family, business and news. Foreigners more used to avoiding strangers and doing business in shops quickly and impersonally can come across as cold, uninterested and even snooty. Smiling, learning one or two of the standard **forms of greeting** (see page 392), acknowledging those who

(see page 392)

WORDS OF WELCOME

Ahlan wa sahlan is the phrase you'll hear most often in Jordan. It's most commonly rendered as "welcome", but translates directly as "family and ease", and so might come out better in English along the lines of "Relax and make yourself at home [in my house/shop/city/country]". With hospitality a fundamental part of Arab culture, there's no warmer or more open-hearted phrase in the language. Everybody uses it, in all situations of meeting and greeting, often repeated like a mantra in long strings.

As a visitor, you needn't ever say *ahlan wa sahlan* yourself, but you'll have to field torrents of them from the locals. The proper response – even if you're walking past without stopping – is *ahlan beek* (*beeki* if you're talking to a woman). Alternatively, you can acknowledge the welcome with a smile and *shukran* ("thank you") or an informal *ahlayn!* ("double *ahlan* back to you!").

The catch-all word used to invite someone – whether welcoming an old friend into your home or inviting a stranger to share your lunch (surprisingly common) – is **itfuddal**, often said together with *ahlan wa sahlan*. Translations of *itfuddal* (*itfuddalee* to a woman, *itfuddaloo* to more than one person) can vary, depending on circumstance, from "Come in" to "Go ahead" to "Can I help you?" to "Here you are", and many more. A respectful response, whether or not you want to take up the offer, is to smile and say *shukran* ("thank you").

We list many more Arabic terms at the end of this Guide (see page 391).

GESTURES AND BODY LANGUAGE

There's a whole range of **gestures** used in Arab culture which will either be new to you or which carry different meanings from the same gesture in your home country. Rather than nodding, **yes** is indicated by inclining your head forwards and closing your eyes. **No** is raising your eyebrows and tilting your head up and back, often accompanied by a little "tsk" noise (which *doesn't* indicate impatience or displeasure). Shaking your head from side to side means **I don't understand**. A very useful gesture, which can be used a hundred times a day in all kinds of situations, is **putting your right hand over your heart**: this indicates genuineness or sincerity, and can soften a "no thanks" to a street-seller or a "sorry" to a beggar, or reinforce a "thank you very much" to someone who's helped you. Many people in the south of Jordan will instinctively touch their right hand to their heart after shaking hands.

One hand held out with the palm upturned and all five fingertips pressed together means **wait**. A side-to-side wrist-pivot of one hand at chest level, palm up with the fingers curled, means **what do you want?** If someone holds their flat palm out to you and draws a line across it with the index finger of the other hand, they're asking you for whatever **document** seems relevant at the time – usually a passport. You can make the same gesture to ask for the bill (check) in a restaurant.

Pointing at someone or something directly with your index finger, as you might do at home, in Jordan casts the evil eye; instead you should gesture imprecisely with two fingers, or just flap your whole hand in the direction you mean. **Beckoning** with your palm up has cutesy and overtly sexual connotations; instead you should beckon with your palm facing the ground and all four fingers together making broom-sweeping motions towards yourself.

In all Arab cultures, knowingly showing the **soles of your feet or shoes** to someone is a direct insult. Foreigners have some leeway to err, but you should be aware of it when crossing your legs while sitting: crossing ankle-on-knee means your sole is showing to the person sitting next to you. Copying the Jordanian style of sitting on a chair – always keeping both feet on the floor – is safest. Sitting on the floor requires some foot-tucking to ensure no one is in your line of fire. Putting your feet up on chairs or tables is not done.

Another major no-no is **picking your teeth** with your fingers; you'd break fewer social taboos if you were to snort, spit into a plastic bag, jiggle a finger in your ear and pick your nose in public. Most diners and restaurants offer toothpicks, which should be used surreptitiously behind your palm.

are welcoming you and taking the time to exchange pleasantries will bring you closer to people more quickly than anything else.

People **shake hands** in Jordan much more than in the West, and even the merest contact with a stranger is normally punctuated by at least one or two handshakes to indicate fraternity.

Personal space

Personal space is treated rather differently in Arab cultures from in the West: for all intents and purposes, it doesn't exist. Queuing is a foreign notion, and in many situations hanging back deferentially is an invitation for other people to move in front. Jordanians also relate to the natural environment rather differently from westerners. Sitting alone or with a friend in the most perfectly tranquil spot, you may find someone coming up to you blocking the sunset and eager for a chat. It can be difficult, if not impossible, to convey your desire to be alone.

Invitations

It's almost inevitable that during your time in Jordan you'll be **invited** to drink tea with someone, either in their shop or their home. It's quite likely too that at some point you'll be invited for a full meal at someone's house. Jordanians take **hospitality** very much to heart, and are honestly interested in talking to you and making you feel comfortable. However, offers tend to flow so thick and fast that it would be difficult to agree to everyone, yet people are often so eager it can also be difficult – and potentially rude – to refuse outright.

First and foremost, whether you're interested or not, is to take the time to chat civilly; nothing is more offensive than walking on without a word or making an impatient gesture, even if they're the twentieth person that day to stop you. If you're invited and you don't want to accept, a broad smile with your head lowered, your right hand over your heart and "*shukran shukran*" ("thank you, thank you") is a clear, but socially acceptable, no. You may have to do this several times

– it's all part of the social ritual of polite insistence. Adding "*marra okhra, insha'allah*" ("another time, if God wills it") softens the "no" still further, indicating that you won't forget their kind offer.

Below, we've gone into detail about what to expect if you've been **personally invited** to a private gathering. However, if you're attending a "bedouin dinner" as part of a tour-group itinerary, the event is commercial: you're paying for the experience, so the same social norms and values don't apply. In this situation, your bedouin hosts will be tourism professionals, probably with good English anyway.

Before the meal

If you're **invited to eat** with someone at home and you choose to accept, the first thing to consider is how to repay your host's hospitality. Attempting to offer money would be deeply offensive – what is appropriate is to bring some token of your appreciation. A kilo or two of sweet pastries handed to your host as you arrive will be immediately ferreted away out of sight and never referred to again; the gesture, however, will have been appreciated. Otherwise, presenting gifts directly will generally cause embarrassment, since complex social etiquette demands that such a gift be refused several times before acceptance. Instead, you can acknowledge your appreciation by giving gifts to the small children: pens, small toys, notebooks, football stickers, even picture postcards of your home country will endear you to your hosts much more than might appear from the monetary value of such things.

It's worth pointing out that you should be much more sparing and – above all – generalized in praising your host's home and decor than is common in the West, since if you show noticeable interest in a particular piece, big or small, your host may feel obliged to give it to you. Minefields of complex verbal jockeyings to maintain dignity and family honour then open up if you refuse to accept the item in question. Many local people keep their reception rooms relatively bare for this reason.

If you're a **vegetarian**, you would be quite within social etiquette to make your dietary preferences clear before you accept an invitation. Especially in touristy areas, vegetarianism is accepted as a western foible and there'll be no embarrassment on either side. Elsewhere, it can help to clarify what seems an extraordinary and unfamiliar practice by claiming it to be a religious or medical obligation. All best efforts notwithstanding, though, veggies should prepare themselves to have to sit down in front of a steaming dish of fatty meat stew and tuck in heartily, while still looking like they're enjoying it.

During and after the meal

This section outlines some of the things which may happen once you **sit down to eat** with a family. It may all seem too daunting for words to try and remember everything here. The bottom line is, you don't: you'd have to act truly outrageously to offend anyone deeply. Your host would never be so inhospitable as to make a big deal about some social blunder anyway.

Once you arrive for a meal, you may be handed a thimbleful of bitter **Arabic coffee** as a welcoming gesture; down it rapidly, since everyone present must drink before sociabilities can continue. Hand the cup back while **jiggling your wrist**: this indicates you don't want any more (if you just hand it straight back, you'll get a refill). The meal – often a *mansaf* (see page 38) – may well be served **on the floor** if you're in a tent, generally with the head of the household, his adult sons and any male friends squatting on one knee or sitting cross-legged around a large communal platter; western women count as males for social purposes and will be included in the circle. As **guest of honour**, you may be invited to sit beside the head of the household. Even if wives and daughters are present, they almost certainly won't eat with you, and you may find that they all stay out of sight in another part of the tent or house for the duration of your visit. If they do, it would be grossly impertinent to enquire after them.

Once the food appears (generally served by the women), and the host has wished you "*sahtayn!*" ("[May you eat] with two appetites!"), you should confine yourself to eating – strictly with your **right hand only** – from that part of the platter directly in front of you. Reaching across is not done. Your host may toss over into your sector choice bits of meat – probably just ordinary bits, but perhaps the tongue, brains or, as an outside possibility, the eyes – which, if they land in front of you, it would be inexplicable to refuse. It's possible that everyone present will share a single glass of water, so if the only glass visible is put in front of you, it's not a cue for you to down it.

While eating, locals will be careful not to lick their fingers, instead rolling their rice and meat into a little ball one-handed and popping it in from a short distance; however, it takes ages to learn how to do this without throwing food all over yourself, and you'll have enough social leeway to subtly cram in a fistful as best you can. It's no embarrassment – in fact, it's almost obligatory – to make a horrible greasy mess of your hands and face. People do not linger over eating, and rarely pause to chat: you may find that everyone chomps away more or less in silence.

Pause (or slow down) **before you're full**, partly because as soon as you stop you'll be tossed more food, and partly because no one will continue eating

THE MEANING OF COFFEE

In **tribal bedouin culture**, where the mark of a man is how he treats his guests, and where what is unsaid has as much (or more) resonance than what is said, **coffee** plays a hugely significant symbolic role.

In some areas, merely starting to make coffee is a signal to families in neighbouring tents that something is afoot: by pounding freshly roasted beans in a *mihbash* – a form of pestle and mortar, sometimes wood, sometimes metal – using a distinctive rattling or jangling sound, a man (it's always a man) can send out a wordless invitation from his tent for all within earshot to gather round. He brews the coffee with cardamom in a *dalleh*, a long-spouted pot set in the embers, and then serves it to everyone present in tiny thimble-sized cups, always beginning with the guest of honour and proceeding clockwise around the circle. The first cup is known as **l'thayf** ("for the guest"), to indicate hospitality. The second is **l'kayf** ("for the mood"), to indicate a relaxed atmosphere. The third is **l'sayf** ("for the sword") to show that any animosity has evaporated. Then, and only then, can the social interaction or discussion begin.

However, if the guest of honour places their first cup in front of them without drinking, this is a signal that they have a request to make of the host – or that there is some underlying problem between them. Only when the request has been met, or the problem solved, will the guest drink. For a guest to leave without drinking even the first cup is a serious snub – such a dispute may require independent arbitration.

A guest could, if they wish, spark a feud by commenting *gahwahtak saydeh* ("your coffee is hunted" – that is, tainted or bad). If, in the opinion of those present, the beans are indeed off, there is no problem. If, however, the coffee is good, the guest is then deemed to be deliberately insulting the host. The consequences could be serious.

Coffee, too, can serve as a symbol of revenge. A man could gather his neighbours and declare one cup of coffee to be a "**blood cup**", meaning whoever drinks it accepts the task of cleansing family honour by taking revenge on a named enemy. But then if the person who drinks fails to exact revenge, they themselves face dishonour and exile. Coffee, in this instance, is life or death.

There are many more such traditions – and they aren't limited to tent-dwelling bedouin. Even in modern homes, where the beans might be pre-roasted and the coffee machine-made, the **rituals and meanings** remain unchanged. Coffee is more than just a drink: it's an integral part of Jordanian culture.

after you – the guest of honour – have fully stopped (so if you sit back too soon you'll be cutting the meal short). Never finish all the food in front of you, since not only does this tag you as greedy, it's also an insult to your host, who is obliged to keep your plate well stocked. Bear in mind, too, that dinner for the women and children consists of whatever the men (and you) leave behind.

When you've finished, your right hand over your heart and the words **al-hamdulillah** ("thank God") make clear your satisfaction.

Everyone will get up and walk away to wash hands and face with soap, before adjourning to lounge on cushions, perhaps around the fire. **Coffee** will be served in tiny handleless cups; take three before returning the cup with a jiggle of your wrist. Then there'll be endless glasses of sweet, black **tea**, along with bonhomie, conversation and possibly an *argileh*. It's your host's unspoken duty to keep the tea flowing whatever happens, so after you've had enough – or if you don't want any at all – stem the tide by saying *"da'iman"* ("may it always be thus") and then simply ignore your full glass.

Answering questions

People will be genuinely (and innocently) interested in you as visitors, and their **questions** may flow thick and fast. Aside from "What's your name?" and "Where are you from?", you're likely to be asked about how many children you've got, what their names are, why you don't have more, and so on. If you have none, *lissa* ("later") or *masha'allah* ("according to God's will") are two respectful, comprehensible ways to say so. Other useful phrases are given in the Glossary (see page 398). Having a few **photos** or digital images to show of children, parents, brothers, sisters, nephews and nieces can break the ice, should any ice need breaking. However, note that men in Jordan never enquire after another man's wife – not even her name; the conversation should stay strictly on work and children.

If you're travelling as an **unmarried couple**, saying "We're just good friends" means little and merely highlights the cultural divide. Being able to show a wedding/engagement ring (a cheap fake will do), even if you have no nuptials planned, makes things instantly clear and understandable. The Language section at the end of this Guide explains how to say "We're getting married next year" in Arabic, along with other handy phrases (see page 391). For a **woman travelling alone**, a ring – indicating an absent husband – is a powerful signifier of respectability.

Although you can talk about most **political issues** freely, locals will not want to embarrass you, or potentially raise hackles, by embarking on political conversation in anything but the broadest terms. You can, though, feel free to ask questions of your own; once you do, you'll find most people aren't backward about speaking their mind on issues surrounding Israel, Arab affairs, domestic reform or the wider world. Let them make the running: if they wish, for instance, to criticize the king or royal family – which can be a criminal offence – be sure not to follow suit. The same goes for **religion**: people are generally free to practise their religion unhindered, but since it is illegal to proselytize or encourage anyone to convert to any religion other than Islam, it is prudent to avoid initiating debate on religious issues.

Photography

Here's a quote from a Jordanian involved in rural tourism development: "People underestimate how much of an invasion of privacy **taking pictures of women** is." He was talking about bedouin women in the desert – but the rule applies pretty much across the board, in towns and cities nationwide too. **Always ask permission** before you photograph women in any context, even in the street – and, if you're in or near a family house or tent, ask permission of the men too. Some people don't mind, others do. Any refusal will be given graciously and smilingly, but perhaps a little diffidently – ask twice if necessary to be sure you don't mistake a no for a yes.

Elsewhere, the obvious caveats apply around military installations and international borders, but otherwise there are few issues.

Couples: displaying affection

Couples travelling together need to be aware of Jordanian social norms. Put simply, **public displays of affection** between men and women are not acceptable. Even if you're married, walking arm-around-waist or arm-over-shoulder, touching each other's face or body or kissing each other are likely to be viewed as deeply distasteful – as if you were bringing the intimacy of the bedroom into the public sphere. It is possible occasionally to see husbands and wives walking hand-in-hand, but it's rare.

LGBTQ travellers

Homosexual conduct in private between consenting adults is **legal** in Jordan, but social disapproval of an overtly gay lifestyle is strong: dalliances between young, unmarried men are sometimes understood as "letting off steam", but they are accepted – if at all – only as a precursor to the standard social model of marriage and plenty of children. Although women form strong bonds of friendship with each other to the exclusion of men, public perception of lesbianism is almost nonexistent. Amman has a small underground scene that is mostly invisible to outsiders. *My Kali* (W mykalimag.com) is an online LGBTQ magazine that frequently pushes boundaries.

A by-product of the social divisions between men and women, though, is that visiting LGBTQ couples can feel much freer about limited **public displays of affection** than straight couples: cheek-kissing, eye-gazing and hand-holding between same-sex friends in public is normal and completely socially acceptable.

Sexual harassment

Sexual harassment of women travellers in Jordan is rare. Most harassment never goes beyond the **verbal** – perhaps including hissing or making kissy noises – and unless you're sufficiently well versed in Arabic swearwords to respond in kind (worth it for the startled looks and the apologies), there's unfortunately not much that can be done about it.

A tiny fraction of incidents involve **physical touching**. If you take the fight to your harasser, by pointing at him directly, shouting angrily and slapping away his hand, you're likely to shame him to his roots in front of his neighbours. Accusing him of bringing himself and his country into public disrepute – *aayib!* is Arabic for "shame!" – is about the most effective dissuasive action you could take. Onlookers are likely to be embarrassed and apologetic for you having suffered harassment. Unmarried or unrelated men and women do not touch each other in public (apart from possibly to shake hands in a formal setting), and any man who touches you, even on the elbow to guide you, has overstepped the mark and knows it.

More serious incidents – blocking your path or refusing to leave you alone – are even less likely, and violence is extremely rare. In Jordan, strangers are much more likely to help a foreigner in distress than might be the case at home, and in an emergency you shouldn't hesitate to appeal directly for help to shopkeepers or passers-by, or to bang on the nearest front door.

CAMEL RIDES

Many visitors from the West come to Jordan never having laid eyes on a **camel**, yet almost all arrive with received wisdom about the creatures. Myths about the simplicity of desert life, the nobility of the bedouin and the Lawrence-of-Arabia-style romance of desert culture all seem to be inextricably bound up in western minds with the camel. In truth, the bedouin long since gave up using camels either as a means of transport or as beasts of burden: Japanese pick-ups are faster, sturdier, longer-lived and less bad-tempered than your average dromedary. However, some tribes still keep a few camels, mostly for nostalgic reasons and the milk, though some breed and sell them. The bedouin that live in or close to touristed areas such as Petra and Rum have small herds of them to rent out for walks and desert excursions. There are no wild camels left in Jordan: any you see, in however remote a location, belong to someone.

If you're in any doubt about whether to take the plunge and have a **camel ride**, then rest assured that it's a wonderful experience. There's nothing to compare with the gentle, hypnotic swaying and soft shuffle of riding camelback in the open desert. Wadi Rum is the best place in Jordan to try it out, with short and long routes branching out from Rum and Disi all over the southern desert. Take as long as you like, but anything less than a couple of hours' riding isn't really worth it.

As a beginner's tip, the key to **not falling off** a camel is to hang onto the pommel between your legs – the animal gets up from sitting with a bronco-style triple jerk that flings you backwards, then forwards, then back again. If you're not holding on as soon as your bottom hits the saddle you're liable to end up in the dust. Once up and moving, you have a choice of riding your mount like a stirrupless horse, or copying the locals and cocking one leg around the pommel.

Adventure tours and trekking

Taking an organized tour once you arrive in Jordan can turn out to be the most rewarding way to get to some of the more isolated attractions in the hinterland – and to get closer to the people, too.

There are hundreds of Jordanian tour operators dealing with incoming tourism, but most are fairly set in their ways, offering virtually identical seven-day tours around a circuit of sights from Amman to Jerash, Madaba, Karak, Petra, Wadi Rum, Aqaba and the Dead Sea. Only a handful can take you **off the beaten track** – and fewer still can take you out of the tourist bubble for one-on-one encounters with local people. Some of the best are listed below, along with a handful of **voluntourism** and **responsible tourism** operators. We list recommended desert guides at Wadi Rum in our account of the destination (see page 330).

ADVENTURE OPERATORS AND SPECIALIST INDEPENDENT GUIDES IN JORDAN

A Piece of Jordan ☎ 079 990 2916, ⓦ apieceofjordan.com. This small but well-connected community tourism operation is run by the wonderful Stephanie Altwassi, who has roots in both Petra (Jordan) and Birmingham (UK). As well as supporting crafts projects and offering "eco experiences" with local families – picking olives, baking bread, and so on – Steph can fix up trips around Jordan that get you under the skin of the country in a way few others are able to.

Ammarin ☎ 079 975 5551, ⓦ ammarinbedouincamp.com. The Ammarin tribe run this wonderful camp at Little Petra; they also offer hiking and adventure guiding in and around the outer fringes of the Petra region.

Bait Ali ☎ 079 925 7222, ⓦ facebook.com/baitaliwadirum. Ambitious desert camp on the outskirts of Wadi Rum. Their connections with the Swalhiyeen tribe, who occupy the lands north of Rum, give access to terrain that other guides in the area do not cover. As well as camels, jeeps and hiking, they offer adventure sports such as quad biking and horseback safaris.

Baraka Destinations ☎ 077 666 7660, ⓦ barakadestinations. com. Unique small company led by award-winning tourism entrepreneur Muna Haddad that works at grassroots level around Jordan to develop sustainable, community-led initiatives. Haddad, who helped bring the Jordan Trail into existence, has focused on Umm Qais and Pella, developing superb rural lodging and memorable visitor experiences.

Discovery Circle Tours ☎ 06 464 1959, ⓦ discoverycircletours. com. Long-standing general inbound operator with a refreshingly innovative approach, often trumping the competition on range, flexibility, price and service. Equally at home in the cultural sector as with adventure/experiential ecotourism, able to cater at short notice to families and individuals.

Dynamix in Jordan ☎ 079 519 9689, ⓦ dynamixinjordan.com. Adventure specialists, with reliable knowledge of canyons, treks, climbs and trails all across the back country.

Engaging Cultures ⓦ engagingcultures.com. Very unusual Jordan-based operation, offering the kind of insight and cultural immersion on touring itineraries that is otherwise extremely hard to find. Detailed knowledge of the whole country and great contacts among local communities mean they can get you under the skin of the place more quickly than just about anyone else, on a variety of broad general-interest trips and excursions. A fine choice.

Experience Jordan ☎ 077 041 7711, ⓦ experiencejordan.com. Local adventure firm with vast knowledge of the outdoors and a wealth of experience in everything from rural hikes in the Ajloun forest to canyoning above the Dead Sea or desert trekking in the wilds of Rum. Nationwide expertise means they can put together any sort of trip, at any budget – and their decades-long links with Palestinian tourism open up doors across the river too. Specialists for the long-distance Jordan Trail trek.

Feynan/EcoHotels ☎ 06 464 5580, ⓦ feynan.com. Managed by the engaging (and award-winning) Nabil Tarazi, the *Feynan Ecolodge* in the southern deserts of Wadi Araba works with a number of trained guides from the local tribes in the area, offering an unparalleled calibre of backcountry expertise and cultural insight for hikes and wilderness adventures both short and long.

In2Jordan ☎ 06 585 9699, ⓦ in2jordan.com. This innovative UK/European/Jordanian enterprise specializes in yoga/relaxation weekends and horseriding retreats in the mountains around Petra. They are also well connected to arrange hosted dinners with local families and day- or long-distance walks around the country, as well as tailor-made itineraries into the nature reserves.

Jordan Beauty ☎ 078 880 2045, ⓦ jordanbeauty.com. Specialists in hiking and trekking, specifically in the Petra area, with excellent local knowledge. Also able to construct innovative, keenly priced tours around the country.

Jordan Inspiration ☎ 077 213 2067, ⓦ jitours.com. Small, flexible company based in Wadi Musa, with a wide range of tour options in Petra and around the country.

Jordan Tracks ☎ 079 648 2801, ⓦ jordantracks.com. Specialized team based in Wadi Rum, focusing on desert services but also able to put together modest trips around Jordan.

La Beduina ☎ 06 554 1631, ⓦ labeduinatours.com. These specialists in fully supported adventure trips and treks in and around Petra also offer nationwide itineraries including diving, mountainbiking and horseriding.

Mahmoud Twaissi ☎ 077 725 4650, ⓦ mahmoudtwaissi. wordpress.com. Born and bred in Petra, Mahmoud is in the top rank of Jordan's national tour guides, highly experienced and with a particular focus on hiking and nature tourism.

Murad Arslan ☎ 077 654 1381, ⓦ facebook.com/ muradarslan.111. One of Jordan's top licensed adventure guides, Murad has years of experience leading groups and individuals through Jordan's backcountry, including for several of the companies listed in this section.

Petra Moon ☎ 079 617 0666, ⓦ petramoon.com. One of Jordan's leading adventure tour operators. Very well connected, they can set you up with good local guides for hikes, low-impact jeep trips into the remote countryside around Petra or long-distance horse or camel rides, with full backup support all the way.

Raami Tours ☎ 03 215 4551, ⓦ raamitours.com. A bedouin-owned and -operated tour company based in Umm Sayhoun outside Petra, offering specialist knowledge and unrivalled access to far-flung corners of the southern deserts. Raami himself

has travelled the world – and knows how to deliver tip-top experiences.

Terhaal ☎ 06 581 3061, ⓦ terhaal.com. Outstanding eco-aware adventure tour company that has been instrumental in opening up new hiking and mountain biking routes off the King's Highway around Madaba. Specialists in canyoning in the Dead Sea gorges, with many unique routes and combinations, as well as the long-distance Jordan Trail. Also with scuba and other options, including Petra hikes and scrambling in Rum – alongside a full programme of regular group trips that are open to all.

Tropical Desert ☎ 077 778 8900, ⓦ tropicaldesert.me. Run by the tireless Hakim Tamimi, these experts in outdoor adventure specialize in trekking, canyoning and rock climbing in all sorts of out-of-the-way places. Check ⓦ facebook.com/TropicalDesert for details of regular weekend excursions.

Wild Jordan (RSCN) ☎ 06 461 6523 or ☎ 079 700 0086, ⓦ wildjordan.com & ⓦ rscn.org.jo. Wild Jordan is the ecotourism arm of Jordan's pioneering Royal Society for the Conservation of Nature (RSCN), which creates and protects all of Jordan's nature reserves as part of a national programme emphasizing nature conservation (including wildlife reintroductions) and environmental issues. It has exclusive responsibility for developing sustainable tourism in the reserves: no other operator runs trekking and camping inside the Dana reserve, canyoning and gorge walking within Wadi Mujib, forest walks in the woodland reserves at Ajloun, safari drives at Shaumari, or birdwatching at the Azraq Wetlands (all of which are protected areas). Their environmental credentials are impeccable, and they work closely with local people, developing socioeconomic projects to support communities living in and near the reserves. The ecofriendly lodges and cabins they design to accommodate visitors are staffed by locals. Prices are higher than elsewhere – but your money could barely go to a better cause. Their headquarters are in Amman (see page 82).

Zikra Initiative ⓦ facebook.com/zikrainitiative. Award-winning voluntourism outfit which seeks to draw both Ammanis and foreign visitors into the world of Jordanian village life, showcasing craft and culinary traditions in the deprived communities of Ghor Al Mazraa, at the southern end of the Dead Sea, and other locations through paid "Exchange Tourism" programmes.

Trekking

It's easy for anyone of moderate ability to embark on **half- or full-day country walks** from most towns – as the local Facebook group "Walking Jordan" attests. What you can't expect is any kind of trail support: no signposts, no refreshment facilities and often no trail markers; there are also virtually no maps useful for walkers available. In recompense, you'll generally be walking alone in pristine countryside. For greater insight, and a full range of detailed route descriptions, your best bet is to get hold of one of the few books on the subject – *Jordan: Walks, Treks, Caves, Climbs and Canyons* by Di Taylor and Tony Howard (see page 390).

AERIAL ADVENTURES

The **Royal Aero Sports Club** of Jordan (☎ 079 730 0299, ✆ rascj.com), based at Aqaba airport, runs **sightseeing flights** over the Wadi Rum desert in ultralight aircraft (JD75/30min). They also offer a serene one-hour journey at dawn by **hot-air balloon** over the deserts of Wadi Rum (JD130/person, minimum three people). All these must be booked in advance.

The same outfit doubles up as **Skydive Jordan** (☎ 079 870 6622, ✆ facebook.com/SkydiveJordanOfficial), offering tandem jumps from high above the Dead Sea, from JD195.

The **Royal Jordanian Gliding Club** (☎ 079 001 9999, ✆ facebook.com/RoJoGC), based at Marka airport in Amman, can take you up for a uniquely silent view of the capital (from around JD40). They also fly ultralights.

Trekking is in its infancy in Jordan, other than in the unique mountains and deserts of Wadi Rum, where it plays an important role in the local economy. As at Petra, trekking services at Rum are offered by local people who still proudly consider themselves bedouin. Plenty of the best routes in and around Rum – as well as ancient caravan trails around Petra – are known only to the locals.

Elsewhere, only a few companies and individual guides understand the theory and practice of trekking. Through its "**Wild Jordan**" office, the Royal Society for the Conservation of Nature offers carefully controlled access to the country's nature reserves – environmentally fragile, protected landscapes that are largely off-limits to visitors: the RSCN allows trekking only on designated trails with qualified RSCN nature guides. On no account should you enter the reserves without permission, or stray off-trail.

Outside these places, in the rugged mountains near Aqaba or the green hills of the far north, for example, there are no marked trails and very few guides. Indeed, it is highly unlikely that while walking you'll come across anyone other than locals, some of whom may be happy to guide you – and all of whom will welcome you with the full warmth of Jordanian hospitality. Offers of tea and refreshment are likely to flow thick and fast as you pass through rural villages.

You'll find guidance on camping in our Accommodation section (see page 36).

The Jordan Trail

The **Jordan Trail** (✆ jordantrail.org) is a 600km walking route that goes from the country's northernmost limits at Umm Qais to the southern coast beside Aqaba. The website is excellent, with detailed advice, tips for transport and accommodation, contacts for local guides (if needed) and precise, stage-by-stage maps for each of the trail's 36 day-stages. Established by Jordanian volunteers over several years – many of the guides and companies named in our listings were involved – it's been designed to take in the best of Jordan's topographical diversity. Wherever you start, it's straightforward to consult the online maps, find a local trailhead, and get out into epic countryside on foot for anything from a day to a month. The website has full information, maps, GPS points and detailed walking notes. We pinpoint accessible stages throughout this Guide.

Terrain

Jordan's **terrain** is spectacularly varied. Anyone expecting a desert country will be astonished by the Alpine-style meadows of north Jordan, which are carpeted in flowers in springtime, when warm breezes carry the aromas of herbs and pine. The hills of **Ajloun** in April are simply captivating – a gentle terrain, with no real hazards other than the lack of water. The RSCN's forest reserves at Ajloun and Dibeen offer access into the area, as does the locally developed Al Ayoun Trail (see page 152).

The **Dead Sea hills**, also dubbed the "Mountains of Moab", offer a more savage prospect, gashed by wild **canyons** which flash-flood after rains. They require respectful treatment. Their northern reaches fall within the boundaries of the RSCN's **Wadi Mujib reserve**, where you can tackle the spectacular descent of the Mujib gorge, though independent adventure guides also offer access to similar exploration of neighbouring canyons outside the reserve such as Wadi Zarqa Ma'in or Wadi Mukheiris.

The southern part of the Moab hills around **Karak**, with excellent trekking and canyoning, is also outside the Mujib reserve. Hiking here, alongside water in the midst of harsh desert terrain, is always a pleasure. This part of the country is still very much off the beaten track, but you may be able to find a company or a specialist guide organizing trips to the beautiful and varied canyon of **Wadi ibn Hammad**.

Further south is the RSCN reserve at **Dana**, its ancient village perched like an eyrie above the wild Wadi Dana. This is, understandably, the pride of the RSCN, who organize some excellent treks past oases and ancient copper mines down to the **Feynan Ecolodge** in the Wadi Araba desert, as well as other routes in far-flung parts of these hills, including around their remote **Rummana Campsite**.

The fabulous ancient city of **Petra** is concealed beyond the next range of hills to the south. While you could spend days hiking around this remarkable site, most walkers will feel the urge to explore further. Navigating paths through this craggy range of mountains is, however, extremely complex, and waterholes are few: until you gain confidence in the area, you should take a local guide. Independent guides offer a superb **four-night wilderness trek** from Feynan all the way to Petra, and local companies in Wadi Musa can set up excellent week-long camel- or horseriding treks from Petra to Rum.

At **Wadi Rum**, don't let the multitudes of tour buses deter you. Out in the desert, away from the very few, well-travelled safari routes taken by day-trippers, all is solitude. The **rock climbing** in Rum is world-famous, but for the walker there is also much to offer, both dramatic **canyon scrambles** and delightful **desert valleys**. Again, be sure of your abilities if you go without a guide: bedouin camps are rare and only those intimate with Rum will find water. Far better is to get to know the local bedouin and hire a guide: a real desert experience is just as much about the people as the place. The rigorous ascent of the mighty **Jabal Rum** by a bedouin hunting route – well known to qualified guides – or the relatively easy scramble to the summit of **Jabal Umm ad-Daami**, Jordan's highest mountain, is a world-class experience open to any fit and confident person.

Clothing, equipment and preparation

You should take a minimalist approach to **clothing** and **equipment**. Heavy boots aren't necessary; good, supportive trainers or very lightweight boots are adequate. Quality **socks** are important and should be washed or changed frequently to keep the sand out and minimize blisters. Clothing, too, should be lightweight and cotton or similar: **long trousers** and **long-sleeved tops** will limit dehydration and are essential on grounds of modesty when passing through villages or visiting bedouin camps. A sunhat, proper protective sunglasses and high-factor sunblock are also essential, as are a light windproof top and fleece. Basic trip preparation also includes carrying a mobile phone (bear in mind that coverage can be patchy, particularly on mountains and in canyons), a watch, a medical kit and a compass, and knowing how to use them all. You should carry a minimum of **three litres of water per day** for an easy walk, perhaps six or eight litres per day for tough treks. On **toilet** procedures, if you're caught short in the wilds, make sure that you squat far away from trails and water supplies, and bury the result deeply. Toilet paper is both unsightly and unhygienic (goats will eat anything!); the best way to clean yourself is with water, but if you must use paper, either burn it or store it in a plastic bag and dispose of it correctly when you get back to a town.

Part of your preparation for trekking in Jordan must involve familiarizing yourself with the dangers of **flash floods**, most pertinently if you intend walking in narrow valleys and canyons, even in the desert: deluges are life-threatening.

There are no official search and rescue organizations. However straightforward your hike may seem, you must always tell someone responsible (such as a reliable friend or the tourist police) where you are going. You must then follow or stick close to your stated route, and check in when you return or reach your destination.

Hiring trekking/adventure guides

Fees for trekking guides can vary. In Rum, you should reckon on roughly JD40–60 per person for a high-quality full-day jeep tour with a knowledgeable English-speaking guide in a vehicle seating four to six people (per-person prices drop the more of you there

---

PIGEON-FANCYING

At sunset in towns and villages all across Jordan, you'll often see small, tight flocks of pigeons wheeling overhead. **Pigeon-fancying** is surprisingly popular, and has taken on something of a shady image, since the point of it is not to race the birds, but rather to kidnap prize specimens from other people's flocks. In every neighbourhood, as the sun goes down, people emerge onto the flat rooftops and open up their ramshackle pigeon coops, sometimes twirling a lure on a length of rope to keep the flock dipping and swooping, sometimes holding a female bird up so that the males will circle around. Neighbours will often deliberately exercise their flocks at the same time, to try and persuade each other's birds to defect; similarly, some well-trained flocks can be enticed to fly off to another part of town to bring back new individuals. Newspapers report that enthusiasts gain three or four new birds a week, yet lose roughly the same number. Many fanciers keep their identities secret, since – for obvious reasons – they're popularly seen as being not entirely trustworthy.

are), including dinner, overnight desert camping with everything provided, and breakfast. (Cheaper deals are widely available – but you get what you pay for.) Guiding on scrambles and climbs that require ropes for safety costs considerably more, in the order of JD150–200 a day, and rightly so: it's a responsible job. To be guided on a private one-day adventure trek – for instance through a gorge such as Wadi bin Hammad near Karak, Wadi Ghweir near Dana or one of the canyons above the Dead Sea – expect to pay in the order of JD100–120, less if it's on easier terrain (and less if you join a scheduled group trip, such as through one of the operators we've listed in this section). The RSCN sets its own rates within each of the reserves, publicized on its website. Whatever you're planning, it's always best to book ahead.

If you've enjoyed your trip, **tipping your guide** is entirely appropriate. Ten percent would be fine, but you may want to give more – or perhaps a gift of a useful item of clothing or equipment. RSCN guides working in the reserves are not allowed to accept tips.

Shopping

Unlike Syria, Palestine and Egypt, the trading history of Jordan mostly revolves around goods passing through rather than being produced; no city within the boundaries of modern Jordan has ever come close to matching the craftsmanship on display in the souks and workshops of Cairo, Jerusalem, Damascus and – formerly – Aleppo.

Traditionally, people in Jordan have simply made whatever they needed for themselves – carpets, jugs, jewellery – without their skills being noticed or valued by outside buyers. Today, although a handful of outlets around the country sell local (and some imported) **crafts**, Jordan has no Cairo-style craft bazaars. You may come across items of aesthetic value here and there, but your chances of picking up bargain antiques are very small, and any that you might come across almost certainly originate from outside Jordan. For the record, Jordanian law forbids the purchase of any item dating from before 1700.

There are only three rules of **bargaining**: first, never start the process unless you want to buy; second, never, even in jest, let a price pass your lips that you're not prepared to pay; and third, never lose your temper. However, the lack of a tradition of bazaar-style haggling results in a reluctance among Jordanian merchants even to embark on the process. In most everyday situations, you'll rapidly be brought up short against an unbudgeable last price – which, unlike in Cairo or Jerusalem, really is the last price, take it or leave it.

Embroidery and weaving

The field where Transjordanian people have the strongest tradition is in **hand-embroidered textiles**, although up to a few decades ago such fabrics tended to stay within the confines of the town producing them and generally never came onto the open market. Embroidered jackets, dresses and cushion covers are now available everywhere, in both traditional and modern styles, but relatively few are high-quality, handmade items.

Sheep's wool and **goat's hair** have been used since time immemorial to weave tents, carpets, rugs, cushions, even food-storage containers, for family use; the two fibres woven together form a waterproof barrier. Rarer **camel hair** went to make rugs. Up until the 1920s, **natural dyes** were always used: indigo (planted in the Jordan Valley), pomegranate, onion peel and mulberries were all common, as was the sumac berry (red), kermes insect dye (crimson), cochineal (pink), and even yellowish soil. Salt, vinegar or soda were added in order to make the colours fast.

Since the 1980s, local and international development projects – Save The Children among them – have been involved in nurturing traditional bedouin **weaving**. By doing so, and by establishing retail outlets in Amman and elsewhere for the sale of woven items, they have managed to rejuvenate a dying craft, and simultaneously create extra sources of income for the weavers, who are almost without exception rural women. The quality of carpets, rugs and home furnishings produced under these various projects is first-rate, although prices are high as a result.

The older, more traditional colours – deep reds, navy blues, greens, oranges and blacks – as well as the traditional styles of stripes and diamonds, are being augmented these days by brighter, chemically dyed colours and more modern patterns, to appeal to a new, western-inspired clientele, but there is usually a good range of traditional and modern pieces on offer. In Madaba, Jerash and Irbid you may see carpet shops featuring **upright treadle looms**; these are operated only by men, and almost exclusively in the cities, to produce mainly derivative items for sale. These have their own appeal, but the majority of traditionally designed woven pieces are made by women, who use only a **flat ground loom**, which they set up either in front of their home tent in springtime or at village workshops.

A more affordable woven craft is **weaving with straw**, a skill of northern Jordanian women, to produce large multicoloured trays, mats, storage containers or wall-hangings. Baskets made of local bamboo, woven by men in Himmeh (aka Mukhaybeh) on the River Yarmouk, often find their way to Amman for sale in crafts centres.

Jewellery

Many Jordanians have inherited their parents' and grandparents' preference – stemming partly from previous generations' nomadic existence, and partly from a rural mistrust of urban institutions – for investing their money in **jewellery** rather than banks. Until recently, bedouin brides wore their personal wealth in silver jewellery, and retained the right throughout their married lives to do with it what they wanted, husbands' wishes notwithstanding. Owning jewellery was – and still is – something of a safety net for women against the possibility of abandonment, divorce or widowhood.

Traditionally, the bedouin much preferred **silver** to gold; indeed, it's just about impossible to find genuine old **gold** in Jordan. The Gold Souk – a collection of tiny modern jewellery shops huddled together in Downtown Amman – has excellent prices, but almost everything is of generic modern design.

If you're after more distinctive jewellery, you should be aware that, although there are a few Jordanian designers producing new, handmade items, practically all the new jewellery you'll see in craft shops has been imported from Turkey, India or Italy. Chunky bedouin jewellery that looks old generally turns out to have been made no earlier than about 1920, and much old "silver" is in fact a mix of eighty percent silver and twenty percent copper. Practically all the "old" necklaces you might see will have been strung recently on nylon thread using stones and silver beads from long-dispersed older originals.

However, none of this detracts from the fact that beautiful and unique items are available; especially striking are necklaces that combine silver beads with beads of coloured glass, amber or semiprecious stones. Different stones have different significance: blue stones protect the wearer from the evil eye, white stones stimulate lactation during breast-feeding, and so on. You might also find rare Circassian **enamelwork**, dramatically adding to a silver bracelet or necklace's charm. However, note that all precious stones in Jordan are imported, mostly from Turkey.

Metalwork, wood and glass

In Amman, **copper** and **brass** items, such as distinctive long-spouted *dalleh* coffeepots, candlesticks, embossed or inlaid platters and the like, are generally mass-produced Indian and Pakistani pieces. You might find original Yemeni or Iraqi curved silver daggers on sale, in among the reproductions.

Wood is a scarce resource in Jordan, and although you may discover some Jordanian-carved pieces (simple cooking implements, mostly, of local oak and pistachio) practically all the elegant wooden furniture you'll come across – wardrobes, chairs, beautiful inlaid chests and the like – originates in Syria. You might spot some original hand-carved wooden implements used in the bedouin coffee-making process, such as a *mihbash*, or grinder, and a *mabradeh*, an ornamented tray for cooling the coffee beans after roasting. Prices in Amman for **olive-wood** or **mother-of-pearl** pieces from Bethlehem or the famous **blown glass** of Hebron (formerly made in Na'ur, just outside Amman) can be half what you might pay in Jerusalem.

Travelling with children

Children are universally loved in Jordan, and travelling with your family is likely to provoke spontaneous acts of kindness and hospitality from the locals.

Children are central to Jordanian society – many couples have four or five, and double figures isn't uncommon. Middle-class extended families tend to take pleasure in indulging children, allowing them to stay up late and play endlessly, but as a counterpoint, children from low-income families can be seen out on the streets at all hours selling cigarettes. The streets are quite safe and even very young children walk to school unaccompanied.

Only the cheapest hotels will bar children; most will positively welcome them (with deals on extra beds or adjoining rooms), as will all restaurants, although discounts may have to be negotiated. There are a few precautions to bear in mind. Foremost is the **heat**: children's sensitive skin should be protected from the sun as much as possible, both in terms of clothing (brimmed hats and long sleeves are essential) and gallons of sunblock. Heatstroke and dehydration can work much faster on children than on adults. Sunglasses with full UV protection are vital to protect sensitive eyes. Children are also more vulnerable than adults to **stomach upsets**: you should definitely carry rehydration salts in case of diarrhoea. Other things to watch out for include the crazy **traffic** (especially for British children, who'll be used to cars driving on the other side of the road), **stray animals** that may be disease carriers, and **jellyfish** and poisonous corals off Aqaba's beaches.

Children will love **riding camels** in Wadi Rum, and even Petra's threadbare **donkeys** may hold an appeal. Most of the archeological sites will probably be too rarefied to be of more than passing interest (aside, possibly, from exploring towers and underground passages at Karak, Shobak or Ajloun **castles**); spotting vultures, ibex and blue lizards at Dana or Mujib may be a better bet, and the **glass-bottomed boats** at Aqaba are perennial favourites. Children born and brought up in urban environments will probably never have experienced anything like the vastness and silence of the **open desert**, and you may find they're transfixed by the emptiness of Wadi Rum or the eastern Badia.

Travel essentials

Addresses

Following strenuous efforts by cartographers and government officials, Jordan now uses **street addresses** in some areas – but it's only in the big cities that streets sport nameplates and buildings are numbered. Problems arise in spelling – there's no universally accepted method of transliterating Arabic into English, so online mapping systems may not use the same spelling as the street sign in front of you – and also in usage: many people still ignore the system, navigating instead in relation to prominent landmarks or by asking passers-by. Mail is delivered only to PO boxes at post offices.

Costs

Though sometimes surprisingly expensive, Jordan is generally pretty **good value**. It's possible to see the sights, eat adequately, sleep in basic comfort and get around on public transport for roughly £70/US$90 a day for two. If you like things more comfortable – staying in good mid-range hotels, eating well, perhaps renting a car to see some out-of-the-way places – reckon on nearer £120/US$150 a day for two. To travel independently while hiring drivers and guides, staying in five-star hotels and generally living the high life, a realistic minimum is £250/US$320 a day for two. All these figures – which are rounded and approximate – exclude the cost of getting into **Petra**, which at £100/US$130 for a two-day ticket for two people, could bust your budget, though the **Jordan Pass** (see opposite) can help offset some costs.

Jordan has a government **sales tax**, which applies at different rates, depending on the goods/services involved, up to about sixteen percent: bear in mind that, in many situations, the price you see (or are told) doesn't include this tax, which is only added on when you come to pay. In Aqaba, sales tax is lower than the rest of Jordan. In addition, hotels and restaurants above a certain quality threshold automatically add a ten percent **service charge** to all bills. They are legally obliged to state these charges somewhere, although it can be as surreptitious as a tiny line on the bottom of a menu.

Crime and personal safety

The sense of **honour** and **hospitality to guests** embedded deep within Arab culture, coupled with a respect for others, means that you're extremely unlikely to become a victim of **crime** while in Jordan. Along with the ordinary police, Jordan maintains a force of English-speaking **tourist police**, identifiable by their armbands with English lettering. Posted at all tourist sites nationwide, they can deal with requests, complaints or problems of harassment. Any representation by a foreigner, whether to the tourist police or the ordinary local police, will generally have you ushered into the presence of senior officers, sat down and plied with coffee, with your complaint taken with the utmost seriousness. The nationwide police emergency number is ☎911. Dial ☎199 for an ambulance. Otherwise you're only likely to tangle with the police if they catch you speeding.

Terrorism and **civil disorder** in Jordan are extremely rare. At the time of writing, the British Foreign and Commonwealth Office (FCO) had no warning against travel anywhere in Jordan, other than to within 3km of the border with Syria, because of the small risk of stray firing from across the frontier. There is no reason for tourists to venture anywhere near the border, anyway. Across the country, all big hotels have barriers keeping vehicles clear of the entrance, and **airport-style security** for everyone entering the building (including compulsory baggage X-ray and body search). Armed police patrol all major tourist sites. Regardless of the impression you might get from the nightly news – and as long as you stay clear of the **border zones with Syria and Iraq** – you'd be in no more danger travelling round Jordan than you might be in your home country.

Note that it is illegal to **insult the king** or the royal family, possess **drugs** or pornography, preach Christianity in public or encourage people to convert to any **religion** other than Islam.

Customs and duty-free

You're permitted to buy two hundred cigarettes, one litre of spirits and two litres of wine **duty-free** on arrival in Jordan. All borders and airports have duty-free shops which open for long hours, but if you forget to buy your allowance of alcohol, cigarettes, perfume or electronic goods when you arrive, you

THE JORDAN PASS

The **Jordan Pass** (W jordanpass.jo) is designed to save time and money as you move around the country. It is a virtual pass, displayed on your phone as a scannable QR code. You buy the pass online, and it then grants free entry to many museums and attractions in Jordan, including **Petra** – though you have to decide in advance whether you want one, two or three days in Petra before choosing which Jordan Pass to **buy** (JD70/JD75/JD80 respectively).

If you get the pass before you reach Jordan, showing it on arrival at the airport or land/sea borders will **waive your visa fee**, saving JD40.

These two savings alone – the visa fee and Petra admission – add up to more than the cost of the pass. Throw in other sites for which the pass grants free entry – Jerash, Wadi Rum, Amman's Citadel and Roman Theatre, and many others – and the pass becomes a bargain for those keen to tour Jordan's historical sites.

However, not everything is included. At the time of writing several major attractions – including the Jordan Museum in Amman, Mount Nebo, the Baptism Site, the Church of the Map in Madaba and the popular Petra By Night walk, as well as the nature reserves at Dana, Ajloun, Wadi Mujib and elsewhere – were not included on the pass. Buying a so-called "universal" pass and then still having to shell out for major attractions is a bit galling.

That said, many people – especially first-time visitors – save money using the pass. It's worth looking into.

---

can go to the Duty-Free Shop on Tunis Street near 5th Circle in Amman (T 06 520 6666, W jdfshops. com) within fourteen days, where the whole range is available. Bring your passport.

The area around Aqaba is a **Special Economic Zone**, with lower taxes and its own customs rules: on all roads into the city, you'll have to pass through a customs station. On departing the zone, you may be subject to checks: personal items, plus up to two hundred cigarettes and one litre of alcohol that you bought in the zone, are exempt from duty.

Electricity

The **supply** in Jordan is 220V AC, 50Hz – the same as in Europe. Most new buildings and big hotels have British-style square three-pin sockets. Older buildings tend to have two-pin sockets for European-style thick-pronged, round plugs.

Health

No **immunizations** or vaccinations are required to enter Jordan. However, before you travel, it's a good idea to make sure you're up to date with immunizations against hepatitis A, polio, tetanus (lockjaw), tuberculosis and typhoid fever. You should consult a doctor at least two months in advance of your departure date, as there are some immunizations that can't be given at the same time, and several take a while to become effective.

TRAVEL CLINICS

Australia & NZ TMVC T 1300 658844, W traveldoctor.com.au.

Canada CSIH T 613 241 5785, W csih.org.
Ireland TMB T 01 271 5200, W tmb.ie.
UK MASTA T 0330 100 4200, W masta.org.
US CDC T 1 800 232 4636, W cdc.gov/travel.

Dehydration

Top of the list of Jordan's maladies, well ahead of the worst creepy-crawlies, is **dehydration**, which can work insidiously over days to weaken you to the point of exhaustion without your ever showing any signs of illness. If you're sweating profusely during activity (such as hiking), even experienced walkers can go from alert and vigorous to dizzy and apathetic in as little as half an hour, due to heat exhaustion and loss of body fluids. It is essential to carry *lots* of water with you on these walks: one bottle is not enough

An adult in a temperate climate should normally drink two litres of water a day; from day one in the Middle East, you should be drinking three litres – and, if you're exerting yourself in hot conditions, more than double that. It's a matter of pride among the desert bedouin not to drink water in front of foreigners, but if you copy them you're likely to make yourself ill. Drinking to quench your thirst just isn't enough in a hot climate: you must drink well beyond that if you're to head off lethargy and splitting headaches. Alcohol and caffeine exacerbate the effects of dehydration.

Heat exhaustion and sunstroke

The Jordanian sun can be scorchingly intense, and – obvious though it sounds – you should do all you can to **avoid sun exposure**, especially if you're travelling in high summer (May–Sept). Head protection is essential. Lightweight, a hundred percent cotton clothes – such as long-sleeved shirts, and long trousers or ankle-length skirts – will allow air to circulate close to your skin to keep you cool and limit both sunburn and dehydration. If you feel very hot, dizzy and faint but aren't sweating, you may have **sunstroke**: get out of direct sun and into air conditioning and/or cold water as soon as possible. Call a doctor if symptoms worsen.

Travellers' diarrhoea

If you arrive in Jordan directly from the West (or Israel), give your **stomach** a chance to acclimatize: avoid street food for a few days and spend a little extra to eat in posher, but cleaner, restaurants. Every eating place, from the diviest diner upwards, will have a sink with soap for washing your hands. Nonetheless, few travellers seem to avoid **diarrhoea** altogether. Instant recourse to **drugs** such as Imodium or Lomotil that plug you up (they actually paralyze your gut) is not advisable; you should only use them if you have to travel. The best thing to do is to wait, eat small amounts of dry food such as toast or crackers, if you feel able, and let it run its course, while constantly replacing the fluids and salts that you're flushing away. Maintaining fluid intake (even if it all rushes out again) is vitally important. **Oral rehydration solutions** such as Dioralyte or Electrosol are widely available worldwide, sold in sachets for dissolving in a glassful of clean water. They're marketed as being for babies, but will make you feel better and stronger than any other treatment. If you can't get the sachets, make up your own solution with one heaped teaspoon of salt and twelve level teaspoons of sugar added to a standard-sized (1.5-litre) bottle of mineral water. You need to keep downing the stuff, whether or not the diarrhoea is continuing – at least a litre of the solution per day interspersed with three litres of fresh water. Bouts of diarrhoea rarely last longer than 24–48 hours.

If it goes on for longer than four days, seek medical advice. Nasty but easily treatable diseases such as giardiasis and amoebiasis must be tested for by a stool examination. If there is blood in your diarrhoea, you may have dysentery and must see a doctor.

Bites and stings

Malaria is not present in Jordan, though mosquitoes and sandflies are. Snakes are frightened of humans; if you walk slowly and noisily, any snakes present will slither away. To avoid tangling with scorpions and spiders never walk barefoot, and if you're camping always shake out your shoes and clothes before wearing them.

Treatment in Jordan

Every town has a **pharmacy** (*saydaliyyeh*), generally staffed by fluent English-speaking professionals trained to western standards. Unless you're obviously a hospital case, this is where you should head first, since a pharmacist charges nothing for a "consultation", and can either prescribe a remedy on the spot or refer you to a local doctor. If you're given a medicine, find out explicitly from the pharmacist what the dosage is, since printed English information on the box might be sketchy.

If you need a **doctor** (*doktoor*), ask your embassy to recommend one or check first with a pharmacist. All doctors are trained in English, many in hospitals in the UK or US. If you're in real trouble, aim for the emergency room of a **hospital** (*moostashfa*) – and call the emergency helpline of your embassy (see page 25) to ask for advice. Consultation fees and medical costs are much lower than back home, but you should still get signed receipts for everything in order to claim money back from your insurance company when you return.

Insurance

It's essential to take out a good **travel insurance** policy to cover against theft, loss of property and illness or injury. Before paying for a new policy, however, it's worth checking whether you are already covered: home insurance may cover your possessions when overseas, many private medical schemes include cover when abroad and premium bank accounts or credit cards often have travel insurance included. After exhausting these possibilities, contact a specialist travel insurance firm.

Mail

Airmail **letters and postcards** can take a week or two to Western Europe, up to a month to North America or Australasia. Asking someone to write the destination country in Arabic can help avoid things going astray. It's safest to ignore the street postboxes and instead send your mail from larger post offices, all of which have a box for airmail (*barid jowwy*). Stamps (*tawabe'a*) cost pennies, but parcels are expensive (JD10–15 for 1kg). International courier firms are well represented in Amman and Aqaba.

Maps

For all general purposes, the **maps** in this Guide should be adequate. Many international map publishers cover Jordan, but few offer close detail and most omit newer roads and mark villages or archeological sites inaccurately. The *Reise Know-How* 1:400,000 map is probably the best available outside Jordan. Others, including city maps and plans for Petra and other sites, are available at hotel bookstalls in Jordan, many produced by the Royal Jordanian Geographic Centre (⊗ rjgc.gov.jo).

The coverage of Jordan on **Google Maps** is disappointing, with less detail than you might expect.

For a spectacular annotated satellite overview of Jordan's **archeological sites**, go to the excellent ⊗ megajordan.org.

Money

The Jordanian unit of currency is the **dinar**, abbreviated to **JD** (or JOD). Most people refer to the dinar as a "*jaydee*" or a "*lira*". One dinar is divided into **1000 fils** or **100 piastres** (*qirsh*). Locals always think in piastres; they only refer to fils when talking to foreigners. A hotel, restaurant or shop bill will show either "14.65" or "14.650", both of which mean 14 dinars and 65 piastres (that is, 650 fils). In this Guide, we stick to two decimal places only.

Banknotes are JD50, JD20, JD10, JD5 and JD1, all with Arabic on one side and English on the other. For coins, there's a gold, seven-sided **half-dinar coin** inset with a circular silver bit in the middle; a smaller **quarter-dinar coin**, also gold and seven-sided but without the silver inset; and silver coins of **ten piastres** and **five piastres**. All coins state their value on them somewhere in tiny English lettering.

In verbal exchanges, you'll find that people quite often leave the denomination off the end of prices. If they say something costs "*ashreen*" (twenty), it's up to you to decide whether they mean 20 fils (a throwaway amount), 20 piastres (ie 200 fils; the price of a street snack or a short bus ride), or 20 JDs (the cost of a room in a small hotel). Nicknames also pop up: 10 piastres is a *barizeh* and 5 piastres is a *shilin*.

Changing and carrying money

Few banks in the West keep Jordanian dinars on hand, but you should be able to order them with a few days' notice. It's a good idea to bring JD80 or so with you in cash, to cover visa and transport costs on arrival.

Most hotels and shops above the cheapest level accept **credit and debit cards**, but Jordan is a **cash** society: just about everywhere the preferred method of payment is local banknotes. You can't pay in dollars, euros or other currencies.

Security-wise, Jordan is safer than anywhere in the West: you can carry wads of cash around in your pocket without concern. You're more likely to be invited for tea than mugged.

For **changing money**, every town has a welter of banks, with identical exchange rates, and there are also plenty of independent change offices. **Cash machines** (ATMs) are widespread, always with an English option. You can generally withdraw a maximum of around JD250 a day, depending on your card provider, but watch for hidden fees and commission charges: it's worth checking your terms and conditions before you leave home – and switching to a card tailored for holiday use if you can. There's no **black market** in currency exchange.

Opening hours and public holidays

Jordan's working week runs from **Sunday to Thursday**. Public sector office hours are 8am–3pm; private sector businesses tend to follow a split pattern, perhaps 8.30am–1pm and 3.30–6.30pm. The weekend is officially **Friday**, though banks, government departments and many businesses also close on **Saturdays**.

Although Muslims pray together in the mosque on a Friday, the concept of a "sabbath" or "day of rest" does not translate: downtown **shops and markets** are generally open seven days a week, roughly 9am–9pm. More upmarket shops tend to open 9/9.30am–6/7pm, perhaps closing for two or three hours at lunchtime. Almost everywhere shuts for a couple of hours around

Friday midday prayers. All **transport services** operate seven days a week, though there are fewer services on Fridays (none at all on some routes).

During **Ramadan**, the Muslim holy month of fasting, everything changes. Shops and offices open from 9am to 2 or 3pm (closed Fri), while street markets operate every day until about an hour before sunset. Banks and government departments may only be open for two or three hours in the morning. Some shops might reopen for a couple of hours after dark.

Fixed public holidays

Jordan's secular **national holidays** tend to be low-key affairs; banks, businesses and government offices are closed, but shops might open as normal. Even though Jordan's Christians are mostly Orthodox and follow the Julian calendar, which varies from the Gregorian calendar used in the West by a couple of weeks, everyone has agreed to celebrate Christmas Day together as a national holiday on December 25 (Muslim shops and businesses don't close).

PUBLIC HOLIDAYS

Jan 1 New Year's Day
May 1 Labour Day
May 25 Independence Day
Dec 25 Christmas Day

Islamic holidays and Ramadan

Islamic **religious holidays**, based on the Hijra calendar, are marked by widespread public observance. All shops and offices are closed and non-essential services are liable to be suspended. The following dates are approximate, since each holiday is announced only when the new moon has been seen clearly by an authorized cleric from Jordan's Ministry of Islamic Affairs. Quoted dates could vary by a couple of days. The start of the holy month of Ramadan is also included here; Ramadan is not a holiday, but since it comprises thirty days of restricted business hours, its first day is a useful date to know.

ISLAMIC HOLIDAYS

Eid al-Isra wal-Miraj Night Journey to Heaven. March 22, 2020; March 11, 2021; March 1, 2022; Feb 18, 2023.
1st day of Ramadan April 24, 2020; April 13, 2021; April 2, 2022; March 22, 2023.
Eid al-Fitr Three days. Begins May 24, 2020; May 13, 2021; May 3, 2022; April 22, 2023.
Eid al-Adha Four days. Begins July 31, 2020; July 20, 2021; July 10, 2022; June 28, 2023.
1st of Muharram Islamic New Year. Aug 20, 2020; Aug 9, 2021; July 30, 2022; July 19, 2023.
Mawlid an-Nabawi Prophet Muhammad's birthday. Nov 10, 2019; Oct 29, 2020; Oct 19, 2021; Oct 8, 2022, Sept 27, 2023.

Phones

Landline numbers are nine digits long – seven digits prefixed by a two-digit area code: **02** covers northern Jordan, **03** southern Jordan, **05** the Jordan Valley and central and eastern districts, and **06** the Amman area.

Mobile phone numbers are ten digits long – seven digits prefixed by a three-digit code (currently 077, 078 or 079).

Most Jordanians have given up on landlines and instead rely on mobile phones – many people have two, on different networks. To follow suit you can walk into

---

USEFUL NUMBERS

EMERGENCIES
Police ☎911
Ambulance ☎199
Traffic accidents ☎190

PHONING HOME
To the UK ☎0044
To the Republic of Ireland ☎00353
To the US or Canada ☎001
To Australia ☎0061
To New Zealand ☎0064
To South Africa ☎0027

CALLING JORDAN FROM ABROAD
First dial your **international access code** (00 from the UK, Ireland and New Zealand; 011 from the US and Canada; 0011 from Australia), followed by **962 for Jordan**, then the Jordanian number **excluding the initial zero**.

any phone or electronics shop (there are dozens in every town), buy a local SIM card, plug it into your unlocked handset and be up and running with a Jordanian number in minutes, for around JD10. Topping up with scratchcards (buyable everywhere) is straightforward. Calling and texting off a local number is very inexpensive – much cheaper than roaming from your home network. Basic handsets can be purchased for perhaps JD20–30.

Smoking

Smoking is banned in public places, including airports, museums and on public transport. However, enforcement is minimal and in effect it's impossible to escape cigarette smoke anywhere in the country (see page 37).

Time

Jordan is usually two hours ahead of London, seven hours ahead of New York and eight hours behind Sydney. Daylight Saving Time operates from the last Friday in March to the last Friday in October.

Tipping

In a good restaurant, even when a service charge is included, it's customary to round the bill up slightly as well. Low-budget local diners don't expect **tips** and will never press you for anything. In most everyday situations a half-dinar tip (ie JD0.50) is a perfectly satisfactory indication of your appreciation for a service, such as a hotel porter loading your bags onto a bus or taxi. Taxi drivers deserve ten percent of the meter charge; if a driver has spent half a day shuttling you from place to place, JD5–10 is in order. An appropriate tip for a bellboy in a four- or five-star hotel who brings your bags up to your room is JD1. Guidance on tipping specialist guides is given in "Adventure tours and trekking" (see page 48).

Tourist information

The **Jordan Tourism Board**, or **JTB** (Ⓦ visitjordan. com), part affiliated to the Ministry of Tourism and part private, publicizes the country's tourist assets abroad under the **Visit Jordan** brand. It is very active on Twitter, Facebook and other social media. In most countries, the account for handling promotion of Jordan is awarded to a local PR company, so contact details can, and do, change.

VISITJORDAN.COM

In Australia ☏ 02 9449 3088.
In Canada ☏ 514 750 9715.
In Jordan ☏ 06 567 8444.
In the UK ☏ 020 7326 9880.
In the US ☏ 1 877 733 5673 or ☏ 703 243 7404.

USEFUL WEBSITES

Ⓦ **visitjordan.com** Jordan's official tourism portal.
Ⓦ **kingabdullah.jo** Detailed features on history, the royal family, politics and tourism.
Ⓦ **jordantimes.com** Leading English-language newspaper.
Ⓦ **wildjordan.com** Excellent information on Jordan's nature reserves.
Ⓦ **www.nomadstravel.co.uk** For climbing and trekking enthusiasts.
Ⓦ **maani.us/jordan** Superb "Field Guide to Jordan": download their app or buy the book.
Ⓦ **jmd.gov.jo** Weather forecasts and climate data (Arabic only).

Travellers with disabilities

Jordan makes few provisions for its own citizens who have **limited mobility**, and this is reflected in the negligible facilities for tourists. The best option is to plump for an organized tour; sightseeing is liable to be complicated enough – leaving the practical details to the professionals will take a weight off your mind. Throughout the country, pavements are either narrow and broken or missing altogether, kerbs are high, stairs are ubiquitous and wheelchair access to hotels, restaurants and public buildings is pretty much nonexistent. Hotel staff and tourism officials, although universally helpful, are generally poorly informed about the needs and capabilities of tourists with limited mobility. Travelling with an able-bodied helper and being able to pay for things like a rental car (or a car-with-driver) and good hotels will make things easier.

All Jordan's ancient sites are accessible only by crossing rough and stony ground. Scrambling around at Jerash or Karak is hard enough for those with full mobility; for those without, a visit represents a major effort of energy and organization. Petra has better access: with advance planning, you could arrange to rent a horse-drawn cart to take you from the ticket gate into the ancient city, from where – with written permission obtained ahead of time from the tourist police – you could be picked up in a car and driven back to your hotel.

Amman

SHOPPING IN DOWNTOWN AMMAN

1 Amman

Consistently overlooked and underrated by travellers to the Middle East, the Jordanian capital Amman stands in marked contrast to its raucous neighbours, with none of the grand history of Damascus, not a whiff of Jerusalem's tension and just a tiny fraction of Cairo's monuments. It's an approachable city with unexpected charm, bathed in a new spirit of dynamism: investment is pouring in, new buildings are going up, neighbourhoods are being rejuvenated and the city is humming with cafés, galleries and commerce. If you're dreaming of medieval mosques, gloomy spice bazaars and fading romance, go elsewhere; if you want a handle on how a young, buzzy Arab capital is making its way in the world, Amman is for you.

Amman is a thoroughly twentieth-century invention: it was only a small town when Emir Abdullah chose it to be his **new capital** in 1921. The sense of Amman being a village-made-good is highlighted when you spend some time on the busy Downtown streets. Here the weight of history – a constant presence in the heart of many Middle Eastern cities – is absent. Amman, instead, is distinguished by a quick-witted self-reliance. This energy stems in large part from displacement: most Ammanis identify themselves as originating from somewhere else. Circassians, Iraqis and above all Palestinians have arrived in the city in large numbers, voluntarily or forcibly exiled from their homelands – and joined, in the last few years, by post-conflict Syrians and Sudanese. The distinctive cultures they have brought are still jostling for living space with the culture of the indigenous bedouin. Indeed, scratching beneath Amman's amiable surface reveals a whole cluster of personalities jockeying for supremacy: western-educated entrepreneurs make their fortunes cheek-by-jowl with poverty-stricken refugees, Christians live next door to Muslims, conservative Islamists and radical secularists tut at each other's doings, Jordanians of Palestinian origin assert their identity in the face of nationalistic tendencies among "East Bank" Jordanians, and so on. What it is to be Ammani is a dispute that shows no signs of resolution.

For the time-pressed ruin-hunter, then, there's little more than an afternoon's sightseeing to be done; however, if you're on a long, slow journey of familiarity you could easily spend several days exploring the slopes of Amman's towering hills, getting under the city's skin while seeing nothing in particular. The capital's impressive **Roman Theatre** and eighth-century **Umayyad Palace** are the only significant monumental attractions, augmented by the **Jordan Museum**, but of equal, if not greater, interest is contemporary Amman's burgeoning arts scene. The arts centre of **Darat Al Funun**, the **National Gallery** and regular music events can add a surprising perspective to your experience of the city's life. The city also makes a good base for day-trips (see page 89).

Brief history

The first known settlement near Amman, a Neolithic farming town near the **Ain Ghazal** spring in the hills to the northeast of the modern city, dates from over nine thousand years ago. This was one of the largest such towns discovered in the region, three times bigger than contemporary Jericho. Artisans from among its two thousand inhabitants produced strikingly beautiful human busts and figurines in limestone and plaster, some of the earliest statuettes ever discovered – now on display in the Jordan Museum.

Highlights

❶ **Roman Theatre** Hugely impressive 2000-year-old ancient arena at the heart of the capital. See page 69

❷ **The Downtown souks** Immerse yourself in the noise and bustle of Downtown Amman's market streets. See page 73

❸ **Jordan Museum** The most comprehensive overview of Jordan's archeological heritage, packed with fascinating history and thought-provoking exhibits. See page 75

❹ **Jabal Al Qal'a (Citadel Hill)** Lofty summit overlooking the city centre, offering amazing views and well-preserved Roman, Byzantine and Islamic ruins. See page 78

❺ **Rainbow Street** Explore the quirky shops and cafés of this attractive old hillside neighbourhood. See page 80

❻ **Contemporary art** Get a new angle on Amman at the city's thriving art galleries. See page 80

❼ **Arabic cuisine** Gorge on street snacks – or dine in style at sophisticated, elegant restaurants citywide, serving some of the region's best Arabic cuisine. See page 101

❽ **Shopping** Whether browsing in dusty bazaars or glitzy malls, shopping puts you at the heart of what makes Amman tick. See page 105

HIGHLIGHTS ARE MARKED ON THE MAP ON PAGE 64

1

AMMAN

■ ACCOMMODATION
Crowne Plaza ... 1

● SHOPPING
Chamber Gyld ... 2
Readers ... 1

① (200m) & ② (700m) ▲

Jordan University, Sweileh, Jerash & the North ▲

Mecca Mall (1km), City Mall (2km), Royal Automobile Museum (3km) & King Hussein Park

⑤ (7km),

GHAZI ARABIYYAT

SPORTS CITY CIRCLE

GARDENS STREET

WADI SAQRA STREET

Safeway

MEDINA STREET

OMAR BIN ABDULAZEEZ

SEE 'SHMEISANI, JABAL HUSSEIN AND ABDALI' MAP

MECCA STREET

HARAMAIN SQUARE

McDonald's

AL-SHAREEF ABDULHAMEED SHARAF

ABDULHAMEED BADEES

❼
SHMEISANI

AL-RIYADH

BAGHDAD

MECCA STREET

SHAT AL-ARAB

UMM
UTHAYNA
❼

WADI SAQRA CIRCLE

AL-AMEER SHAKER BIN ZEID

ILYA ABU MADHI

ABDULLAH GHOSHEH

MEDINA STREET

AL-MALEK FAISAL BIN ABDULAZEEZ

SA'D BIN ABI WAQQAS

Orfali
Gallery
❻

DULAH

SHMEISANI CIRCLE

Jordan Gate
Towers
1

MOUSA BIN NUSAYR

QURTUBAH

ABDULLAH BIN OMAR

WADI SAQRA

QUEEN NOOR

Foresight32
Gallery

5TH
CIRCLE

7TH
CIRCLE

ZAHRAN

6TH
CIRCLE

TUNIS

ZAHRAN

4TH
CIRCLE

FANZI AL

Wadi Seer

JETT
Buses

❼
WAKALAT STREET

SWEIFIYYEH

MAWLOUD MUKHLES

M. ALI JINNAH

AL-MUTANABBI

Safeway

Sweifiyyeh
Mosaic
❽

SAEED AL-MUFTI

JAMEEL AL-TUTANJI

FAWZI QAWUQJI

FAWZI AL

PRINCESS BASMA STREET

❶
Cozmo

AIRPORT ROAD

❷

SA'D ZAGHLOUL

ASMA

AL-QAHERAH

ABDOUN

AL-NEEL

ABDOUN
CIRCLE

SEE 'JABAL AMMAN,
JABAL AL-LWEIBDEH
& ABDOUN' MAP

AIRPORT ROAD

MUSTFA KAMEL

❾

N

8th Circle ◀

▼ Queen Alia Airport (35km), Dead Sea, Madaba & the South

▼ Queen Alia Airport & Dead Sea

HIGHLIGHTS

1. Roman Theatre
2. The Downtown souks
3. Jordan Museum
4. Jabal Al Qal'a (Citadel Hill)
5. Rainbow Street
6. Contemporary art
7. Arabic cuisine
8. Shopping

EATING

B@C in Abdoun	8
Bakdash (Medina St)	2
Bakdash (Wakalat St)	7
Blue Fig	9
Pizza Reef	1
Pizza Rimini	3
Reem Al Bawadi	4
Tannoureen	6
Zuwwadeh	5

Tabarbour Bus Station

SPORTS CITY

QUEEN ALIA STREET

ABU SUFYAN

IBN ARABI

ISAM AL-AJLOUNI

AL-ISTIQLAL

NABLUS

INTERIOR CIRCLE

JABAL HUSSEIN

Housing Bank Centre

BI'R AL-SABA'

KHALED

FIRAS CIRCLE

KING HUSSEIN STREET

JETT Buses

AL-JALEEL

AL-RAMAH

BIN AL-WALEED

YAFA

AL-ISTIQLAL

JABAL AL-QUSOOR

ABDALI PROJECT (UNDER DEVELOPMENT)

STREET

AL-SHAREEF AL-HUSSEIN BIN ALI

MUKHABARRAT STREET

King Abdullah Mosque

Jordan National Gallery of Fine Arts

JABAL AL-LWEIBDEH

KING HUSSEIN

ROYAL PALACES

MULQI

AHMED BIN HANBAL

WADI SAQRA

6

SHARI'A COLLEGE

LWEIBDEH CIRCLE

Darat Al Funun

STREET

National Archeological Museum

JABAL

Grand Hyatt

3RD CIRCLE

7

InterContinental

PRINCE MUHAMMAD STREET

4

HASHMI STREET

Raghadan Bus Station

Mahatta, Marka & Zarqa

AL-KULLIYAH

2ND CIRCLE

8

A M M A N

AL-ISLAMIYAH

1ST CIRCLE

SHA BAN

JABAL AL-QAL'A

1

MITHQAL AL-FAYEZ

ZAYD BIN HARETHAH

RAINBOW

5

STREET

DOWNTOWN

Roman Theatre

IBN KHALDOUN

AL-BUHTARI

Muhajireen Police Station

City Hall

ALI BIN ABI TALEB

AL-MUHAJEREEN

3

8

MANGO STREET

KING TALAL STREET

SAQF SAYL

Husseini Mosque

2

JABAL AL-JOFEH

AL-YA

SEE 'DOWNTOWN' MAP

JABAL AL-AKHTHAR

RAS AL-AIN

Abu Darwish Mosque

JABAL AL-ASHRAFIYYEH

USAMAH BIN ZAYD

AL-DUSTOUR

AL-QUDS

JABAL AL-NATHIF

TAREQ BIN ZIYAD

PRINCE HASSAN STREET

AL-YARMOUK

AL-MUTHANNA BIN HARETHAH

BIN HARETHAH

0   1

kilometre

Royal Tank Museum (4km)

Wihdat & Azraq Highway

1

AMMAN ORIENTATION

Amman is a **city of hills**, and any map of the place can only give half the story. Although distances may look small on paper, the reality is that traffic and people are funnelled along streets often laid on valley beds or clinging to the side of steep hills: to reach any destinations above Downtown you'll generally have to zoom (or zigzag) up sharp gradients.

DOWNTOWN AND JABAL AL QAL'A

The area known in English as **Downtown**, in Arabic as *il-balad* (literally "the city"), is the historical core of Amman; Roman Philadelphia lies beneath its streets, and as late as the 1940s this small area comprised virtually the whole of the city. Downtown forms a slender T-shape nestling in the valleys between six hills. At the joint of the T, and the heart of the city, is the imposing **Husseini Mosque**, which faces along **King Faisal Street**, the commercial centre of Downtown and home to most of its budget hotels. The other main thoroughfare of Downtown – Hashmi Street and King Talal Street, together forming the cross-piece of the T – runs in front of the mosque, passing to the west most of Amman's street markets, and to the east the huge **Roman Theatre**. Towering over Downtown are several hills, including **Jabal Al Qal'a** ("Citadel Hill"), site of a partly restored **Umayyad Palace**.

JABAL AMMAN

Amman's wealth is concentrated in upmarket **West Amman**; other districts to the north, south and east are poorer and more populous. The various neighbourhoods of **Jabal Amman** form the heart of the city's rich western quarter. Running along the crest of the ridge is **Zahran Street**, the main east–west traffic artery, punctuated by numbered intersections known as **circles** (not all of them are roundabouts, and most feature overpasses and/or multilevel, crisscrossing tunnels that keep the traffic moving). Closest to Downtown, **1st Circle** marks a characterful district with some elegant old stone buildings, focused on the cafés and galleries of cobblestoned Rainbow Street. The area around **2nd Circle** has back streets comprising close-knit neighbourhoods with rows of shops and diners. Offices, upmarket residential districts and big hotels cluster around busy **3rd Circle**. The slopes around **4th** and **5th Circles** are where the Prime Ministry and many embassies are located (as well as more big hotels). Overlooked by the Jordan Gate twin towers, **6th Circle** lies near the cafés and boutiques of Sweifiyyeh and Umm Uthayna. The start of the Airport Road/ Desert Highway (heading south) is marked by **7th Circle**, which features supermarkets, petrol stations and drive-through fast-food outlets. Busy **8th Circle** hosts hard-working neighbourhoods at the western limits of the city proper.

JABAL AL LWEIBDEH, ABDALI AND SHMEISANI

The next hill north of Jabal Amman is **Jabal Al Lweibdeh**, a historic residential neighbourhood that's home to the **National Gallery** and several other art galleries. Lweibdeh abuts the unromantic commercial area of **Abdali**, now transformed into a new business district centred on a cluster of skyscrapers. Above Abdali lies **Shmeisani**, a lively financial district sprinkled with restaurants and pavement cafés. Beyond here, the northwestern suburbs dribble on for miles out to **Jordan University**.

SWEIFIYYEH, ABDOUN AND BEYOND

South of Shmeisani, **Sweifiyyeh**, the city's most upmarket shopping district, lies below 6th Circle, alongside the lavish mansions of **Abdoun**, residence of most of Jordan's millionaires and reachable from 4th and 5th Circles.

Within spitting distance of Abdoun's villas, the **Wadi Abdoun** valley marks a division between rich West Amman and poor East Amman – of which **Muhajireen** and **Ras Al Ain** are closest to Downtown, the latter hosting the Jordan Museum.

Amman during the Old Testament

Around 1800 BC, during the Bronze Age, the hill now known as **Jabal Al Qal'a**, which overlooks the central valley of Amman, was fortified for the first time. According to Genesis, the area was inhabited by giants before the thirteenth-century-BC arrival of the **Ammonites**, named as descendants (along with the Moabites) of the drunken seduction of Lot by his own two daughters. By 1200 BC, the citadel on Jabal Al Qal'a had been renamed **Rabbath Ammon** (Great City of the Ammonites) and was capital of an amply defended area which extended from the Zarqa to the Mujib rivers.

Rabbath – or Rabbah – is mentioned many times in the Old Testament; the earliest reference, in Deuteronomy, reports that, following a victory in battle, the city had seized as booty the great iron bed of King Og, last of the giants. Later, the book of Samuel relates that, around 1000 BC, the Israelite **King David** sent messengers to Rabbah with condolences for the death of the Ammonite king. Unfortunately, the Ammonites suspected the messengers were spies: they shaved off half their beards, shredded their garments and sent them home in ignominy. In response to such a profound insult, David sent his entire army against Rabbah, although he himself stayed behind in Jerusalem to develop his ongoing friendship with **Bathsheba**, who soon became pregnant. On David's orders, her husband **Uriah** was placed in the front line of battle against Rabbah and killed. David then travelled to Rabbah to aid the conquest, threw the surviving Ammonites into slavery and returned home to marry the handily widowed Bathsheba. Their first child died, but their second, Solomon, lived to become king of Israel.

The feud between neighbours simmered for centuries, with Israel and Judea coveting the wealth gathered from lucrative trade routes by Ammon and its southern neighbours, Moab and Edom. In the absence of military or economic might, Israel resorted to the power of prophecy. "The days are coming," warned **Jeremiah** in the sixth century BC, "that a trumpet blast of war will be heard against Rabbah of Ammon." The city was to become "a desolate heap" with fire "destroying the palaces". In a spitting rage at the Ammonites' celebration of the Babylonian conquest of Jerusalem in 587 BC, **Ezekiel** went one better, prophesying that Rabbah was to be occupied by bedouin and to become "a stable for camels".

From Alexander the Great to modern times

After Alexander the Great conquered the region in 332 BC, his successor Ptolemy II Philadelphus rebuilt Rabbah and named it **Philadelphia**, the "city of brotherly love". Turmoil reigned following the Seleucid takeover in 218 BC until the Romans restored order by creating the province of Syria in 63 BC. Philadelphia was at its zenith as the southernmost of the great **Decapolis** cities (see page 135), and benefited greatly from improved trade and communications along the **Via Nova Traiana**, completed in 114 AD by Emperor Trajan to link Bosra, the provincial capital, with the Red Sea. The **Romans** completely replanned Philadelphia and constructed grand public buildings, among them two theatres, a nymphaeum, a temple to Hercules and a huge forum, all of which survive.

In Byzantine times, Philadelphia was the seat of a bishopric and was still a regional centre when the Arabs conquered it in 635; the city's name reverted to Amman under the Damascus-based **Umayyad** dynasty. Amman became a regional capital and, around 720, its Umayyad governor expanded the Roman buildings surviving on Jabal Al Qal'a into an elaborate palatial complex, which promptly collapsed in the great earthquake of 749. Following the **Abbasid** takeover shortly afterwards, power shifted east to Baghdad and Amman's influence began to wane, although it continued to serve as a stop for pilgrims on the way south to Mecca.

Over the next centuries, travellers mention an increasingly desolate town; by the time **Circassian** refugees (see page 68) were settled here by the Ottomans in the 1870s, Amman's hills served only as pastureland for the local bedouin – Ezekiel's furious prophecy come true. The Circassians, however, revived the city's fortunes, and when the **Emirate of Transjordan** was established in 1921, Emir Abdullah chose Amman to be its capital.

Twentieth-century Amman

Up to 1948, Amman comprised only a village of closely huddled houses in the valleys below Jabal Al Qal'a, with a handful of buildings on the lower slopes of the surrounding hills. But in that year **Palestinians**, escaping or ejected from the newly

1

THE CIRCASSIANS

The first people to settle in Amman in modern times were Muslim refugees from Christian persecution in Russia. The **Circassians** (or Cherkess), who began arriving in the 1870s, trace their origins back to mountain villages above the eastern Black Sea, in the region of the **Caucasus** around present-day Georgia and Chechnya.

In the 1860s, Russian military offensives in the Caucasus forced 1.5 million people out of their homes into exile in Ottoman Turkish territory. Some headed west towards the fertile lands of the Balkans (establishing Muslim communities in and around Bosnia), while others drifted south into the Ottoman province of Syria. Stories began to filter back to those left behind of life in a Muslim land, and many Circassian and Chechen villages went en masse into voluntary exile. European governments lent their weight to the Ottoman policy of dumping the refugees on ships bound for distant Syria.

Meanwhile, **Amman** had been uninhabited for virtually a thousand years. In 1877, Selah Merrill, a visiting American archeologist, "spent part of one night in the great theatre ... The sense of desolation was oppressive. Kings, princes, wealth and beauty once came here to be entertained, where now I see only piles of stones, owls and bats, wretched *fellahin* (peasants) and donkeys, goats and filth." The first Circassian refugees arrived the following year, setting up home in the galleries of the theatre; others founded new villages in the fertile valley of Wadi Seer to the west and among the deserted ruins of Jerash to the north. The presence of settlers caused some conflict with local tribes, but the Circassians held their own in skirmishes with the bedouin, and soon a mutual respect and a formal pact of friendship emerged between them. After 1900, Circassian labour was central to the building of the Hejaz railway line, and Circassian farmers became famed for their industry. One of their great innovations was the reintroduction of the **wheel**: with no roads to speak of, wheeled transport hadn't been used in Transjordan for centuries.

When, in the 1920s, **Emir Abdullah** established a new state and chose Amman to be its capital, he bound the Circassian community into his new administration: loyal and well-educated families were the mainstay of both the officer corps and the civil service. Over the years, overt expressions of Circassian culture faded: Arabic became the lingua franca, the use of national dress died out and, with the rise in land prices following the influx of Palestinian refugees in 1948, many Circassians sold their inherited farmlands around Amman for the building of new suburbs. However, their internal identity remained strong, and Circassians today form an integrated minority of around 100,000. See ⓦ circassianidentity.blogspot.com for more.

established State of Israel, doubled the city's population in just two weeks. Makeshift camps to house the refugees were set up on the outskirts, and, following another huge influx of Palestinian refugees from the West Bank, occupied by Israel in 1967, creeping development began to merge the camps with the city's sprawling new suburbs.

A fundamental shift in Amman's fortunes came with the outbreak of the **Lebanese civil war** in 1975. Beirut had been the financial, cultural and intellectual capital of the Middle East, but when hostilities broke out, many financial institutions relocated their regional headquarters to the security of Amman. Most subsequently departed to the less parochial Gulf, but they nonetheless brought with them money, and with the money came Western influence: today there are parts of West Amman indistinguishable from upmarket neighbourhoods of American or European cities, with broad leafy avenues lined with mansions, and fast multilane freeways swishing past strip malls and glass office buildings. A third influx of Palestinians – this time expelled from Kuwait following the 1991 **Gulf War** – again bulged the city at its seams, squeezing ever more urban sprawl along the roads out to the northwest and southwest.

Into the 21st century

When King Hussein signed a **peace treaty** with Israel in 1994, ending a state of war that had persisted since 1948, many Ammanis hoped for the opening of a new chapter in the city's life; Amman's intimate links with Palestinian markets and its generally

1

Western-oriented business culture led many to believe wealth and commerce – not to mention Western aid – would start to flow. Building development burgeoned across the city, but for several years many of the new hotels and office buildings were white elephants, with Amman seeing little economic comeback from political rapprochement with Israel.

Since the early years of this century, that situation has changed. Substantial quantities of **US aid** are starting to have an effect. Jordan's political and economic institutions are strengthening. With the government's increasing **liberalization** of the economy, confidence in Amman as a city on the up is growing. Private sector investment has rocketed, much of it coming from Arab countries. Refugees have continued to arrive – notably **Iraqis**, following the 2003 Gulf War, and **Syrians**, following the 2011 uprising and subsequent war – adding to the social mix but putting extra strain on the city's infrastructure. Horrendous **traffic**, resulting from the failure to implement a coherent transport strategy, is damaging both business performance and quality of life.

Yet with its carefully nurtured international image as the moderate and hospitable face of the modern Arab world – an image that rings true for visitors – Amman today can be said to enjoy a greater influence in the region and the world than at any time since the Romans.

Downtown

Although you shouldn't leave Amman without having spent at least some time in **Downtown**, the cramped valleys between towering hills shelter comparatively few obvious sights. Downtown's appeal is in its street life – the spiritual and physical heart of the city. This is the district that most strongly resembles the stereotype of a Middle Eastern city – loud with traffic and voices, Arabic music blaring from shopfronts and people selling clothes, coffee, cigarettes or trinkets on the street. The handful of Roman ruins that survive here have been irreverently incorporated into the everyday bustle of the city: the banked seating of the huge **Roman Theatre** is frequently dotted with small groups of locals seeking refuge from the traffic noise.

The Roman Theatre

Hashmi St • Sun–Thurs & Sat 8am–5pm, Fri 9am–4pm • Joint ticket with Odeon JD2; free with JP

The **Roman Theatre**, dominating the heart of Downtown, was the centrepiece of Roman Philadelphia, and also the initial focus for Amman's modern settlement late in the nineteenth century. As you approach from Hashmi Street, a long Corinthian colonnade and some original Roman paving are the only physical remains of Philadelphia's **forum**, the marketplace which filled the now-landscaped gap between the theatre and the street.

Cut into a depression in the hillside, the Roman Theatre itself is impressively huge, and the view, as well as the ability to eavesdrop on conversations between ant-like people on the stage below, definitely repays the steep climb to the top.

The structure was built between 169 and 177 AD, during the reign of Emperor Marcus Aurelius, for an audience of almost six thousand, and is still occasionally filled today for concerts. Above the seating is a small, empty **shrine** with niches; the dedication isn't known, although part of a statue of Athena was discovered during clearance work.

FREE WITH JORDAN PASS

Throughout this Guide, "free with JP" means that the attraction grants free admission to holders of the **Jordan Pass** (see page 55).

1

AMMAN: DOWNTOWN

Abdali

Jordan National Gallery of Fine Arts

PARIS CIRCLE
(SQUARE DE
PARIS)

JABAL
AL-LWEIBDEH

Luzmila
Hospital

Beit
Sitti ❷

Darat
Al Funun

Makan
Art Space

Dar al-Anda

3rd Circle & Wadi Saqra

OMAR AL-KHAYYAM STREET

PRINCE MUHAMMAD STREET ❷
✉
❻

❺

1st Circle

KING HUSSEIN STREET

CINEMA AL HUSSEIN STREET

❹

❺
❹

❶

Umayyad
Palace

Jordan
Archeological
Museum

Ticket Office

MATHAE STREET

Temple of
Hercules

Arab
Bank

KING FAISAL STREET
❽
❼

Duke's Diwan

❶ Gold
Souk

SHABSOUGH STREET

Cairo
Amman
Bank

HASHMI STREET

HASHMI STREET ←

Nymphaeum

Wild
Jordan
❿ ❸

Nabad
Gallery

❷

OTHMAN BIN AFFAN

BASMAN STREET

QUBERTAY STREET

JABAL
AMMAN

NOFA
Creative Space

Jordan River
Designs

❽ ❶
Al Safadi
Mosque

❶❷

FAWZI MALOUF

❼
❶
❻

❺

❾

RAINBOW STREET

Mango
House

Royal Film
Commission

❿
⓯

MANGO STREET

Al-Pasha
Turkish
Bath

Jacaranda
Gallery

❶❶

MANGO STREET

KHIRFAN STREET

Fruit & Vegetable
Market

❹

Husseini
Mosque

Souk
Sukkr

KING TALAL STREET

SAQF AS SAYL (QURAYSH STREET)

Tree

N

JABAL
AL-ASHRAFIYYEH

KING TALAL STREET

Mehajireen, Ras al-Ain & Jordan Museum

Church of
The Saviour

SAQF AS SAYL

ITALY STREET

PRINCE HASSAN ST

AHNAF BIN QAIS STREET

Wihdat

●SHOPPING

Al Afghani	4
Balian	6
Bawabet al-Sharq	9
Books@Café	10
Gold Souk	1
Jordan River Designs	7
Mlabbas	8
Ola's Garden	11
Soap House	5
Urdon Shop	2
Wild Jordan Nature Shop	3

●EATING

Auberge	7
Beit Sitti	2
Books@Café	15
Cantaloupe	11
Darat Al Funun	1
Duinde (Salam Kanaan Gallery)	12
Eco-Tourism Café (Al Arasheed Courts)	8
Habibah (main)	5
Habibah (takeaway)	9
Hashem	4
Jafra	6
Montage	14
Al Quds (Jerusalem)	3
Sufra	13
Wild Jordan	10

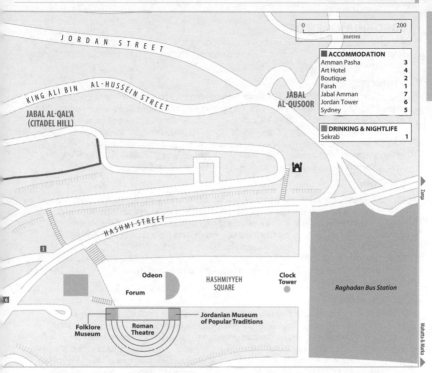

Standing on the stage or in the orchestra – the semicircle in front of the stage – you can get a sense of the ingenuity of the theatre's design: the south-facing stage is flooded with sun throughout the day, while virtually every spectator remains undazzled and in cool shadow. To discover the incredible acoustics, stand in the middle of the orchestra and declaim at the seating, and your normal speaking voice will suddenly gain a penetrating echo; step off that spot and there's no echo. Furthermore, two people crouching down at opposite ends of the orchestra can mutter into the semicircular stone wall below the first row of seats and easily hear each other.

The Folklore Museum and Jordanian Museum of Popular Traditions

Within the Roman Theatre, to the sides of the stage, are two small museums, housed in vaults beneath the auditorium. On the right as you walk in, the **Folklore Museum** displays mannequins engaged in traditional crafts and a reconstruction of an old-fashioned living room. The more worthwhile **Jordanian Museum of Popular Traditions**, opposite, enlivens the theme of traditional clothing, jewellery and customs by rooting it firmly in the present-day life of ordinary people. The vaulted rooms are full of examples of national dress, with detailed notes and occasional photographs to set them in context. Other exhibits include pieces of antique bedouin jewellery and a fascinating range of stones used in healing, as well as mosaics downstairs gathered from Madaba and Jerash (and viewable up close).

The Odeon

Hashmi St • Sun–Thurs & Sat 8am–4pm, Fri 9am–3pm • Joint ticket with Roman Theatre JD2; free with JP

1

JORDANIAN IDENTITY

Although Jordan has a homogeneous population, society is characterized by overlapping **layers of identity**. You'll often come across expressions of religious and social sensibility that sound refreshingly unfamiliar to Western ears.

ETHNICITY

Almost Jordan's entire population is **Arab**. This is a hard term to define, linked to language more than ethnicity, but also marks a pan-national identity, largely because nation-states are relatively new: many people in Jordan feel a much stronger cultural affinity with Arabs from nearby countries than, say, Britons might feel with Belgians. The bedouin add a deeper layer of meaning by often regarding themselves to be the only true, original Arabs. Jordan has tiny ethnic minorities of **Circassians** and **Chechens** (who are Muslim), **Armenians** (Christian) and **Kurds** (Muslim) – all of whom are closely bound into Jordanian society – as well as **Dom** gypsies (also Muslim).

RELIGION

Roughly 92 percent of Jordanians are **Sunni Muslim**, and the observance of Islam is a central part of daily life for most people across the country. The **call to prayer** (see page 382) sounds five times a day in every city, town and village. Jordan's largest religious minority, totalling around six percent, are **Christians**, most of whom are Greek Orthodox, but also including Melkite Catholics, Roman Catholics, Syrian Orthodox, Armenian Orthodox, Coptic Orthodox, Maronites and some Protestants (Lutherans, Baptists, Episcopalians and others). There are also small communities of **Shia Muslims**, **Druze** and **Bahai**. Expats aside, there are no **Jews** in Jordan.

NATIONALITY

There persists a perceived difference between people whose origins lie in families long resident on the east bank of the River Jordan and people whose families originate on the west bank of the river. All are **Jordanian** citizens, yet Jordanians of **Palestinian** origin are estimated to number between half and three-quarters of Jordan's population. Roughly seven percent of people in Jordan are expats, including guest workers – many of them **Egyptian**, **Sri Lankan** and **Filipino** – alongside sizeable populations of **Iraqi** and **Syrian** refugees.

TRIBE

A **tribe** is an extended grouping of families who cultivate a distinctive tradition of history and folklore (mainly oral) and assert ownership of a particular territory. Not all tribes are desert-dwelling – there are many whose background is rural, and others who have become urbanized. Tribal territories, which predate nation-states, often extend across international borders. Some tribes are made up of clans and branches which have taken on tribe-like status; others have banded together in larger, often pan-national, tribal confederations.

For a lot of Jordanians, **tribal identity** is at least as strong as religious or national identity. Many people make a distinction between two broad social tribal traditions. The **bedouin** (see page 385) originate in families who are current or former desert-dwellers: they may once have been nomadic, but are almost all now settled. Some still live in tents in or near the desert, following traditional lifestyles, but many do not: a police officer in Amman or a marketing executive in Aqaba might be as bedouin as a camel-guide in Wadi Rum. By contrast, the **fellahin** originate from a settled, rural, farming tradition, often in the north and west of Jordan. They frequently have strong historic links – often of family or tribe – to rural communities across the borders in Syria and Palestine.

THE NEXT GENERATION

More than a third of Jordanians are **under 15**. This is one of the **best-educated** countries in the developing world: almost everyone you meet will be able to hold some sort of conversation in English (and possibly French, Spanish and German too). Students from all income groups and social backgrounds mix freely at the universities, where the traditional emphasis on engineering and the sciences – Jordan is a world leader in medical fields including ophthalmology and cardiology – is giving way to new technology. Amman has a thriving **start-up** scene. The heritage-style image of Jordan as a nation of simple tent-dwellers, scratching a living from the desert sands, bears little relation to reality.

Facing onto the forum area outside the Roman Theatre is the **Odeon**. This renovated freestanding theatre, seating about five hundred, dates from slightly earlier than its bigger neighbour and was probably the venue for either parliamentary-style council meetings or small-scale drama. In antiquity, the whole building would probably have been roofed.

Amman's grand old **Philadelphia Hotel**, the country's first (and, for many decades, only) hotel, was built in 1925 beside the Odeon on the banks of the Sayl Amman, which was then a stream flowing through the city centre. Sadly, the hotel was demolished in 1988 to make way for Downtown redevelopment – which, at that stage, didn't end up taking off.

Several nineteenth-century travellers reported seeing the remains of a large **propylaeum**, or ornamental gateway, on the edge of the forum; this still stood in 1911 but has since disappeared. If you stop in front of the theatre and look back towards the street, high on the summit of Jabal Al Qal'a opposite you'll spot the columns of the Temple of Hercules (see page 78). Originally, the propylaeum stood at what was the foot of a tremendous monumental staircase leading down from the temple, linking the religious and social quarters of the city.

Husseini Mosque

Hashmi St • Daily except Fri at caretaker's discretion • Free; ask at the right-hand gate to be let in; dress suitably decently

From the Roman Theatre and Odeon, lively **Hashmi Street** storms west past *shawarma* stands, juice bars, patisseries and cafés towards the commercial hub of Downtown and the focal, pink-and-white-striped **Husseini Mosque**. Like almost everything else in Amman, this is a relatively recent construction, although a mosque has stood here since 640 (and, before that, a Byzantine cathedral). However, any remnant of the original building was erased when Emir Abdullah ordered the site cleared for construction of the current mosque in 1932. Though modestly sized, it remains one of Amman's most important places of worship, and is often also the focus for political demonstrations (especially after Friday noon prayers).

Souk Sukkar

The area around the Husseini Mosque remains the heart of Amman's souks. To the east lies a warren of alleys known as **Souk Sukkar**, where stalls sell everything from dates and spices to soap and mops. Souk Sukkar translates as "Sugar Market" – though some say the area was actually named after 1950s entrepreneur Samir Sukkar, who built the first shops.

King Talal Street

To the west of Husseini Mosque, the main street funnelling traffic out of Downtown is **King Talal Street**, lined with stores selling ordinary household goods, fabric and bric-a-brac. A little way down on the left, hidden behind a row of shopfronts, is the city's main fruit and vegetable market.

Opposite the mosque, the building on the corner where King Talal Street begins formerly held Amman's best-loved coffee house, the grand old **Arab League Café** – a stalwart here for over fifty years, with its fine balcony overlooking the bustle below. In 2002, after a wrangle between the building's owners (one wanted to keep it as it was; the other wanted to rebuild), the café was gutted – to the horror of seemingly everyone in the city bar the owners themselves. The site has now been redeveloped.

1

STREET NAMES

Street names in Amman are a recent innovation. For decades, the city survived without them: people simply named roads after local landmarks. Every street has now been given a name, which appears in Arabic and English on prominent signs. Yet the system is taking time to bed in, and some anomalies remain. Probably the most confusing thing for visitors is that the sequence of major traffic intersections along Zahran Street on Jabal Amman – known to everyone as 1st Circle, 2nd Circle, and so on – are signposted instead with the names of royals and politicians. Our list below decodes them, and a few others.

Sharia is "street" and always precedes the name. Both *duwaar* (circle) and *maydan* (square) are used to mean "traffic intersection". Many streets are named after royals: *al-malek* is "King" and *al-malka* or *al-malekah* is "Queen". Similarly, *al-amir* or *al-ameer* is "Prince" and *al-ameera* "Princess" – so "Prince Muhammad Street" translates as *Sharia al-Amir Muhammad*.

Bear in mind, too, that no rules govern the **transliteration** of street names and place names into English: you might see "Shmeisani", "Al Shumaysani" and "Ash Shimisany" all referring to the same place. Similarly "Sweifiyyeh"/"Swayfiya", "Abdoun/Abdun" and so on.

Official name	Common name
DOWNTOWN	
Quraysh Street	Saqf As Sayl
JABAL AMMAN	
King Abdullah I Square	1st Circle (*duwaar al-awwal*)
Wasfi at-Tall Square	2nd Circle (*duwaar al-thaani*)
King Talal Square	3rd Circle (*duwaar al-thaalith*)
Prince Ghazi bin Muhammad Square	4th Circle (*duwaar al-raabe*)
Prince Faisal bin al-Hussein Square	5th Circle (*duwaar al-khaamis*)
Prince Rashid bin el-Hassan Square	6th Circle (*duwaar al-saadis*)
Prince Talal bin Muhammad Square	7th Circle (*duwaar al-saabe*)
King Abdullah II Square	8th Circle (*duwaar al-thaamin*)
SHMEISANI AND BEYOND	
Jamal Abdul-Nasser Intersection	Interior Circle (*duwaar al-dakhliyyeh*)
Square de Paris	Lweibdeh Circle
Arar Street & Sharif Nasser bin Jameel Street	Wadi Saqra
Wasfi At Tall Street	Gardens Street
Yubil Circle (jct Gardens/Medina St)	Waha Circle (*duwaar al-waha*)
Queen Rania Al Abdullah Street	University Street
King Abdullah II Street	Medical City Street

Saqf As Sayl

The main street parallel to King Talal Street follows the course of the Roman *decumanus maximus*, which was formed by paving over the free-flowing stream beneath. The street – officially Quraysh Street – is still popularly known as **Saqf As Sayl** (Roof of the Stream), but these days the *sayl* is dry, having been tapped upstream. This is Amman's liveliest quarter, with cobblers, CD stalls and hawkers of soap and toothbrushes competing for space under the pavement colonnades with a secondhand clothes market.

The Nymphaeum

Saqf As Sayl, behind the Husseini Mosque • The site is fenced and is usually off-limits, though the guardian may not object to you exploring

Excavation and restoration work on the Roman **Nymphaeum** has been going on for years, seemingly without end. It's very similar in design to the huge nymphaeum at Jerash, which has been dated to 191 AD; at that time, Philadelphia too was at its zenith. However, apart from the immensity of the building (and its newer reconstruction), there's not much to see. Nymphaea – public fountains dedicated

1

to water nymphs – were sited near rivers running through major cities throughout the Greco-Roman world. This one, facing onto an open plaza at the junction of the two principal city streets, the east–west *decumanus* and the north–south *cardo*, was originally two storeys high and must have been quite a sight. Colonnades of Corinthian columns would have drawn even more attention towards the concave building, which was lavishly faced in marble, with statues of gods, emperors or city notables filling the niches all around.

Jordan Museum

Ras Al Ain • Mon, Wed, Thurs, Sat & Sun 9am–5pm, Fri 3–6pm; hours vary in winter • JD5 • ☎ 06 462 9317, ⓦ jordanmuseum.jo

Southwest of the Husseini Mosque, King Talal Street and Saqf As Sayl meet at a large traffic intersection. To the south rises the hill of Ashrafiyyeh, while dead ahead (west), in the valley of the Sayl Amman, is an area known as **Ras Al Ain** ("Source of the Spring"). Here, just past an open colonnaded plaza known as Sahat Al Nakheel ("**Palm Square**") featuring a public fountain at its centre, stands the **Jordan Museum**, a sleek building housing the world-class national archeological collection.

From the atrium, adorned with a Byzantine mosaic and a striking Nabatean relief, probably of the goddess Atargatis, turn left. The chronological tour begins with one of the highlights – the **oldest human statues in the world**, roughly 9,500 years old, discovered at Ain Ghazal near Amman and superbly displayed, eerie and spotlit. Displays track the development of **flint** tools – becoming finer as large-brained *homo sapiens* evolved – to reach the mysterious Tulaylat al-Ghassul mural, the earliest-known painting of human figures in costume, engaged in some kind of ritual procession four thousand years ago.

After a room devoted to **bedouin** culture, the **Bronze Age** displays are crowned by an exquisite wooden box from Pella, inlaid in ivory (from a species of Middle Eastern elephant now extinct) with a depiction of two Middle Eastern lions (also now extinct) beneath the sun-disc of the Egyptian god Horus. Beside a copy of the **Mesha Stele** (see page 231) stands the squat, imposing figure in stone of an **Ammonite king** from the eighth century BC. Displays on communication follow, including charts showing the development of **alphabets**, and a Hellenistic room discussing the arrival of **coinage** after Alexander the Great's invasion.

The **Nabatean** hall, with exquisite sculpture and delicate eggshell-ware pottery, features a haunting bust of the Syrian rain god Hadad. **Roman** displays include a

RENOVATING DOWNTOWN

Since 2007, the government and municipality have been engaged in extensive **rebuilding and renovation** work throughout the Downtown area. The first district to see a transformation was **Ras Al Ain**, at the western end of Talal Street, with the construction of three buildings: City Hall, the Al Hussein Cultural Centre and the Jordan Museum, all designed in an airy, contemporary style by leading Jordanian architect Jafar Touqan. The intention was to bring affluent West Ammanis into a Downtown neighbourhood they might otherwise never visit: the regeneration of what was formerly a traffic island of dusty waste ground in a low-income district is one of Amman's recent success stories.

Then the presentation of the archeological remains atop **Jabal Al Qal'a** was revamped, and focused on a new visitor centre – though people living within low-income communities on the lower slopes of the same hill were left out of the scheme, raising hackles citywide. In 2014 the "**Hashemite Plaza**", around the Roman Theatre and Odeon, was redesigned and rebuilt, with new seating areas, better access and a bit of greenery.

Public finances are under pressure, and larger-scale redevelopment has been put on hold for now, but you may find more reconstruction under way – including, perhaps, new hotels, shops and transport facilities – when you visit.

1

WALKING IN AMMAN

Walking in Amman is a mixed bag. It's absolutely the only way to get around Downtown, but once you venture further out, the distances between sights lengthen and the uptown hills feel like mountain peaks.

You can walk from one end of **Downtown** to the other in about twenty or thirty minutes, staying on the flat the whole way. **Jabal Al Lweibdeh** and the lower reaches of **Jabal Amman** (below 3rd Circle) are residential and can be explored on foot, but elsewhere, if you try to walk, you'll generally find yourself slogging along beside streams of traffic in neighbourhoods designed for driving.

However, one of the most delightful discoveries of old Amman – largely ignored by visitors and locals alike – are the **flights of steps** which trace direct paths up and down the steep Downtown hills, dating from the days in the 1930s and 1940s when hillside residences were otherwise inaccessible. Countless flights – many weed-ridden and crumbling – crisscross the area below 1st Circle on Jabal Amman, the nose of Jabal Al Lweibdeh, the flanks of Jabal Al Qal'a and the hills above the Roman Theatre, passing now and then through private backyards, beneath washing lines or past deserted, once-grand villas. If you're decently dressed and sensitive to the fact that you're tramping through people's gardens – as well as to the possibility that the steps you happen to have chosen might not go anywhere – you're basically free to explore.

---

winsome statue of Apollo and a beautiful marble panel from a Byzantine chancel screen, discovered in Petra. There's also a room devoted to the **Dead Sea Scrolls**, as well as galleries focusing on Jordan in the Islamic period through to modern times.

King Faisal Street

The Husseini Mosque, at the fulcrum of Downtown, faces up **King Faisal Street** (also known as Faisal Square), modern Amman's oldest thoroughfare, occupying the valley between Jabal Amman to the south and Jabal Al Qal'a to the north. Although it follows exactly the course of the Roman *cardo*, any trace of the ancient past has been built over: the oldest buildings, with elegant arched windows and decorated stone balconies, date only from the 1920s. Nonetheless, this street and the numerous souk alleyways which branch off its south side, filled with textile merchants, shoe shops, bakeries and cafés, hold the spirit of old Amman. Indulging in a tea and an *argileh* on the balcony of one of the local coffee houses hiding in or hanging over nearby alleyways is a great way to absorb the Downtown atmosphere.

At its northern end, Faisal Street forks. To the right, King Hussein Street climbs to Abdali. To the left, amid a welter of always busy shops selling cut-price pirated CDs and DVDs, Prince Muhammad Street accesses Jabal Amman and Jabal Al Lweibdeh; just past the fork, signs pick out **Hashem**, perhaps Amman's most famous restaurant, turning out plates of hummus 24 hours a day (see page 101).

Duke's Diwan

12 King Faisal St • Open at owner's discretion, at most daily except Fri 8am–sunset • Free

One of the most charming houses on King Faisal Street, known as the **Duke's Diwan**, dates from 1924. The building formerly served as the main post office, an annexe of the Ministry of Finance and, from the 1950s, as the *Haifa Hotel* (whose sign still lies in one of the rooms). It has been renovated as a labour of love by a prominent Jordanian businessman, Mamdouh Bisharat, who owns land in the village of Mukhaybeh (see page 162). King Hussein dubbed him the "Duke of Mukhaybeh" – hence "Duke's Diwan" (a *diwan* is a place for meetings and gatherings). The entrance gives onto a long flight of steps. At the top is an atmospheric suite of seven rooms around a central hallway, decorated with old photos of Amman, paintings and cabinets of bric-a-brac.

ROMAN THEATRE

1

Students, artists and Ammani old-timers often gather here to read and chat. Roam around as you like; you'll inevitably be invited to drink tea on the balcony. The *diwan* also hosts occasional informal concerts and artistic events.

Gold Souk

Flanking the Duke's Diwan are the wonderful pastry shop **Habiba**, renowned for its delicious *kunafeh* (see page 98), and the **Gold Souk**, tiny jewellery shops clustered together in a little network of alleys. Buying gold can be a protracted affair (see page 107) but it's a pleasure to browse, stroll and chat. Nearby is Shabsough Street, named after the Shabsough tribe of Circassians who first settled here, from which stairs rise up to Jabal Al Qal'a.

Jabal Al Qal'a (Citadel Hill)

Ruins: Sun–Thurs & Sat 8am–7pm, Fri 9am–6pm; winter till 5pm; last entry 1hr before closing • JD3; free with JP

Jabal Al Qal'a (**Citadel Hill**) has been a focus for human settlement since the Paleolithic Age, more than eighteen thousand years ago. Unfortunately, when the Romans moved in to occupy the area, they cleared away whatever they found, including the remains of the Ammonite city of Rabbath Ammon, and chucked it over the side of the hill: Bronze Age, Iron Age and Hellenistic pottery shards have been found mixed up with Roman remains on the slopes below. Of the remains surviving today, the most impressive is the huge **Umayyad Palace** complex on the upper terrace of the Citadel, dating from the first half of the eighth century. On the middle terrace below and to the south lies the Roman **Temple of Hercules**, its massive columns dramatically silhouetted against the sky. East of the temple, Roman fortifications protect the grassy lower terrace, which has no visible antiquities.

ARRIVAL AND DEPARTURE   JABAL AL QAL'A (CITADEL HILL)

By taxi The easiest way to reach the summit is by taxi (JD1 from Downtown).

By car If you're driving, head east out of Downtown towards Zarqa, come off, pass under the highway, rejoin it heading west, then exit right. At the traffic lights bear left steeply up the hill, along King Ali bin Al Hussein St. Near the top a hairpin left turn brings you to the car park.

On foot The ascent on foot (20min from Downtown) is extremely steep. About 150m along Shabsough St as you head east, and just past the second turning on the left, a side street has a wide flight of steps leading left up the hillside. Turn right at the top, and head up any way you can from here: there are crumbling steps most of the way, often leading through private backyards, though note you'll still have to circle around to enter the site at the ticket office.

Temple of Hercules

The **Temple of Hercules**, its towering columns visible from Downtown, dates, like the Roman Theatre, from the 2nd century AD. The temple stands on a platform at the head of the monumental staircase which formerly led up from the lower city: the blocks on the cliff edge mark the position of the staircase, and afford a tremendous panoramic view over the city centre that is particularly striking at **sunset**, when – in addition to the visual dramatics – the dozens of mosques in the city all around start broadcasting the call to prayer almost simultaneously.

The temple's columns, which were re-erected in 1993, formed part of a colonnaded entrance to the **cella**, or inner sanctum. Within the *cella* a patch of bare rock is exposed, which, it's thought, may have been the sacred rock that formed the centrepiece of the ninth-century-BC Ammonite Temple of Milcom on this spot. The Roman dedication to Hercules is not entirely certain but, given the quantity of coins bearing his likeness found in the city below, pretty likely. Look out for the giant **marble hand** displayed nearby, part of an immense statue also thought to be of Hercules.

Jordan Archeological Museum

Opposite the Temple of Hercules stands a modest building, built in 1951, which at the time of writing was still called the **Jordan Archeological Museum**, displaying some interesting pieces including Ain Ghazal statues. However, now that it's been superseded by the main Jordan Museum, the future of this little museum – now very old-fashioned – remains unclear. There has been talk of reworking it as a new museum devoted to the history of Amman.

Umayyad Palace

Climbing the signposted path from the Temple of Hercules, you pass a small ruined **Byzantine church** on the right, dating from the fifth or sixth century, which reused many of the columns from the nearby temple. The church formed part of a Byzantine town which probably covered much of the hill.

The remains of a large Umayyad mosque on the left indicate the beginning of the huge **Umayyad Palace** complex, which stretches over the northern part of the hill. Part of the palace was built over pre-existing Roman structures, and an entire colonnaded Roman street was incorporated into it. Built around 730, when Amman was a provincial capital, the complex probably combined the residential quarters of the governor of Amman with administrative offices. It was still in use during the Islamic Abbasid (750–969) and Fatimid (969–1179) periods, although much of the brand-new palace was never rebuilt following a devastating earthquake in 749.

The entrance hall

Beyond the mosque you come to the impressive domed **entrance hall**, reached by crossing the first of four plazas. Built over an earlier Byzantine building (which is why it's in the shape of a cross), the hall is decorated with stucco colonnettes and Persian-style geometric patterns, set off by foliage rosettes and a hound's-tooth zigzag. Much renovation has been carried out here in recent years, not all of it subtly – the new stucco around the interior walls deliberately clashes with the original work, and in 1998 a new dome was constructed above the building, though archeological controversy persists about whether there ever was a dome here in antiquity. To one side of the building are the remains of a small **bathhouse**, beside a large round cistern and what may have been an olive-pressing works.

The colonnaded street

Beyond the entrance hall is the second large plaza, from which the **colonnaded street** leads ahead. This was the heart of the administrative quarter, surrounded by nine separate office or residential buildings (of which only four have been excavated), each in the typical Umayyad style of a self-contained *bayt* – small rooms looking onto a central courtyard. The *bayts* were constructed within the pre-existing Roman enclosure, possibly a temple, whose exterior walls are still visible in places.

The residential quarters

At the far end of the colonnaded street, a decorated doorway takes you through the Roman wall into the third plaza and the private **residential quarters** of the ruler of Amman. Rooms open from three sides, but the plaza is dominated by a huge *iwan* – an audience room open on one side – which leads through to a domed, cruciform **throne room**, or *diwan*. According to Umayyad protocol, the ruler stayed hidden behind a curtain during audiences; the tiny passageway between the *iwan* and the *diwan* could have served this purpose. To either side lie the residential *bayts* for the ruling household. At the back of the *diwan*, a doorway leads through to the fourth and final plaza – a private affair, looking north over the massive Roman retaining wall to the hills opposite.

1 West Amman

Outside of Downtown and Citadel Hill, you're most likely to visit sprawling, relatively wealthy **West Amman**, home to practically all of the city's upmarket hotels, as well as restaurants and nightlife. Key areas to explore include **Jabal Al Lweibdeh**, an attractive residential neighbourhood that is home to the **National Gallery**, and the lower reaches of **Jabal Amman**, particularly around **1st Circle**, where the cafés and quirky shops of **Rainbow Street** make for some of the city's most pleasant strolling.

Jabal Amman: around 1st Circle

West Amman is too large to attempt aimless exploratory rambling, though if you have a spare afternoon to fill, you might like to take a wander through the leafy streets **around 1st Circle** on **Jabal Amman**. When Amman was a small town occupying the Downtown valley floors, this gentle neighbourhood was the preserve of the elite, including royalty, families wealthy through business or commerce, politicians and ambassadors, British commanders of the army, and so on. The quiet streets either side of **Rainbow Street** are still lined with many fine old villas dating from the 1920s and 1930s.

We've outlined a route beginning at 1st Circle, but you could instead pick up a detailed (free) *Jabal Amman Walking Trail* leaflet at Wild Jordan (see page 82).

Rainbow Street

Perhaps Amman's most famous thoroughfare, **Rainbow Street** has become known for two things: cafés and traffic. Of the former there are dozens, both on and just off the street: this has become one of the city's prime spots for socializing. All tastes are catered for – there are traditional coffee houses, zingy contemporary espresso bars, cosy hideaways for organic-tea-lovers and swanky DJ venues, alongside antiques shops, craft studios, edgy fast-food hangouts, top-quality restaurants…it's quite a whirl. All attractions, though, are crammed onto what is effectively a narrow, semi-residential one-way street: traffic on weekend evenings in particular can be disastrous. It can take half an hour to drive a few hundred metres.

On foot, though – cafés, shops and restaurants notwithstanding – Rainbow Street is a window into another Amman. As you head east from 1st Circle, the street (named after the renovated Rainbow Cinema on the right) bustles with activity on the stroll to the walled-off **British Council**. Beyond here, the road dips sharply; partway along on the left is the **Al Safadi mosque**, with a fine old minaret. On a minor street to the right, an anonymous-looking townhouse, in a dark shade of plaster and sporting curved Art Deco-style balcony railings, was where King Talal lived for a time before his accession, and where both the late King Hussein and his brother Prince Hassan were born.

NOFA Creative Space

Othman bin Affan St • Daily except Fri 10.30am–6pm • ☎ 077 740 1222, ⓦ facebook.com/nofacreativespace

There's a cluster of elegant little 1920s stone villas around the junction of Rainbow Street and Othman bin Affan Street. One houses the splendid Jordanian restaurant Sufra; turn left here, and the second villa on the right has been beautifully restored and reopened as the **NOFA Creative Space**, a venue for talks, readings, music recitals, screenings and exhibitions. It's worth popping in to sample the atmosphere, and to linger in their gorgeous garden.

Nabad Gallery

46 Othman bin Affan St • Daily except Fri 10am–1.30pm & 4–7pm • ☎ 06 465 5084, ⓦ nabadartgallery.com

As Othman bin Affan Street descends and curves around the edge of the hill you'll spot the beautiful **Nabad Gallery**, housed in a particularly fine old villa with a secluded rear terrace. This has rapidly earned a reputation as one of the city's leading art galleries,

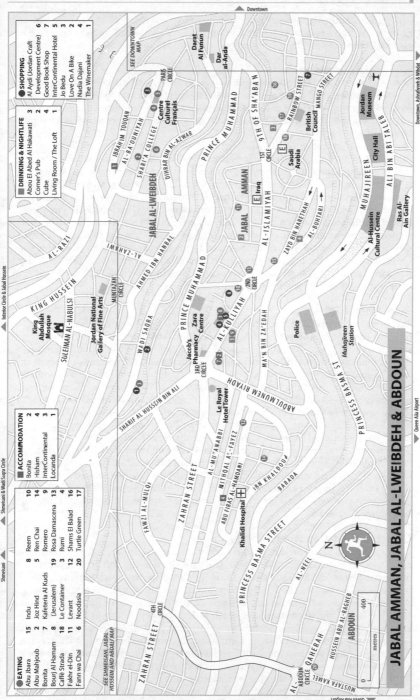

JABAL AMMAN, JABAL AL-LWEIBDEH & ABDOUN

● EATING			
Abu ibara	15	Indu	8
Abu Mahjoub	2	Joz Hind	5
Bonita	3	Kafeteria Al Kuds	7
Bourj Al Hamam	8	(Jerusalem)	
Caffe Strada	18	Le Container	4
Fakhr el-Din	11	Levant	12
Fann wa Chai	6	Noodasia	
		Reem	10
		Ren Chai	14
		Romero	9
		Rosa Damascena	13
		Rumi	16
		Shams El Balad	17
		Turtle Green	20

■ ACCOMMODATION	
Bonita	2
Hisham	3
InterContinental	4
Locanda	1

■ DRINKING & NIGHTLIFE	
Abou El Abed Al Hakawati	3
Corner's Pub	2
Cube	4
Living Room / The Loft	1

● SHOPPING	
Al Aydi (Jordan Craft	6
Development Centre)	
Good Book Shop	7
InterContinental Hotel	5
Jo Bedu	3
Love On A Bike	2
Nadia Dajani	4
The Winemaker	1

Downtown

SEE DOWNTOWN MAP

Downtown, Ashrafiyyeh & Wihdat

Queen Alia Airport

SEE SHMEISANI, JABAL HUSSEIN AND ABDALI MAP

Interior Circle & Jabal Hussein

Shmeisani & Wadi Saqa Circle

Shmeisani

Queen Alia Airport

1

with a consistently high-quality range of temporary shows. Check the website and Facebook to find out what's on – or just drop by on the off-chance. Next door is the swanky **Urdon Shop**, selling upmarket crafts all made in Jordan.

Wild Jordan Center

36 Othman bin Affan St ☎ 06 463 3542, ⓦ wildjordancenter.com • **Ecotourism unit** ☎ 06 461 6523, ⓦ wildjordan.com & ⓦ rscn. org.jo • **Farmers' market** Fri 11am–6pm, ⓦ souqalshams.com • Reachable from 1st Circle by taking the fourth turning on the left (signposted) and following the street round, or by walking down the stairs at the end of the "Souk Jara" lane, Fawzi Malouf St, or by walking left (slightly uphill) from the T-junction at the bottom end of Rainbow St, ignoring the set of steep stairs heading down the hill into Downtown.

The striking **Wild Jordan Center**, designed by architect Ammar Khammash for the Royal Society for the Conservation of Nature (RSCN), is the headquarters of the RSCN's **ecotourism unit**, which manages visits to Jordan's nature reserves. As well as information about how to visit the reserves, you'll find a **nature shop** selling all kinds of pieces designed in traditional style by Jordanian craftworkers. An organic **farmers' market**, Souq Al Shams, is held on site every Friday, and there are often free **exhibitions** of photographs or art inspired by Jordan's natural environment. The cool, shaded balcony of the excellent **café** here (see page 104) offers one of Amman's most spectacular **views**, looking over the valleys of Downtown and across to Jabal Al Qal'a. Opposite, between the hills, rises a gigantic flagpole with an enormous Jordanian flag fluttering lazily. The pole stands a shade under 127m high, and the flag itself is 30m by 60m – impressive, but no longer a world record.

Fawzi Malouf Street

Two of the most attractive villas in the area, both well signposted, are beside each other on **Fawzi Malouf Street** – also known as "**Souk Jara Street**" after the summer street market here (see page 105) – about 250m east of the British Council. On the Rainbow Street corner stands an elegant symmetrical villa set back from the street and faced in local stone, with a stepped portico and tall, slender windows; it is now used as showrooms for the crafts of **Jordan River Designs** and **Bani Hamida**. Alongside it is a one-storey villa – once home to Major Alec Kirkbride, the first British Ambassador to Jordan – with a beautiful portico of pointed arches, wrought-iron window-bars, and a lovely garden centred on a star-shaped fountain. Both these houses were built in the late 1920s by Salim Al Odat, an architect originally from Karak.

Just round the corner with Asfour Street is a pair of houses built for Egyptian businessman and adviser to Emir Abdullah, Ismail Bilbaysi, a smaller one dating from the 1930s with a semicircular balcony featuring a lavishly painted ceiling visible from the street, and beside it a much larger villa designed in the 1940s in a consciously medieval Mamluke style, with bands of alternating pink and white stone and pointed arches.

Omar bin al-Khattab Street (Mango Street)

Continuing east past more cafés and crafts outlets down Rainbow Street, you come to the distinctively modernistic **Mango House** on the right, at the corner with **Omar bin al-Khattab Street** (aka **Mango Street**). In smooth, reddish stone with curving, pillared balconies, it was built in the late 1940s by Kamal and Ali Mango, members of one of Amman's most prominent business dynasties. On the other side of Rainbow Street is a long, low house, the whole facade of which is sheltered beneath an elegant Circassian-style porticoed balcony; its most famous resident was Said Al Mufti, a Circassian who was prime minister in the 1950s and also mayor of Amman. Following Mango Street to the right brings you past more cafés and another fine villa, now home to the **Royal Film Commission**, before – on the right – the widely known **Books@Café**, an attractive bookshop and café-bar shoehorned into another historic old house. A few doors further is the print gallery **Jacaranda**, past which the road climbs to a mini-roundabout; to the right is the **Al Pasha hammam** (see page 96), while straight on leads in the direction of 2nd Circle, past numerous shops.

Khirfan Street
At the bottom (east) end of Rainbow Street, turning right at the T-junction leads into **Khirfan Street**, an old residential quarter on the slope of Jabal Amman's hill which offers great views out over Downtown towards mountainous Jabal Al Ashrafiyyeh opposite. Several of the buildings along the narrow street are traditional three-storey villas in the Syrian style, with high balconied walls concealing central courtyards. A few minutes' walk along, at no.60, is the wonderful **Ola's Garden** handmade jewellery emporium (see page 106).

Jabal Al Lweibdeh
Amman has a dynamic **contemporary arts** scene, and some of the best galleries are within walking distance of each other in the charming neighbourhood of **Jabal Al Lweibdeh** (also spelled **Weibdeh**, **Webdeh**, **Lwiebda**, **Luwaybida** and so on, with or without **Al** or **El**), just north of Jabal Amman and overlooking the hubbub of Downtown. The area has a relatively high proportion of Christian (and foreign expat) residents, and you'll find a tangibly different atmosphere from other parts of the city: streets are quieter and you might hear the unfamiliar sound of church bells. Its shaded lanes and attractive stone architecture have also drawn in artists, writers, quirky cafés, independent shops and a progressive-minded start-up scene. For better or worse, Lweibdeh is becoming hip.

Paris Circle (Square de Paris)
Aim first for **Paris Circle**, also signed as **Square de Paris**, a little roundabout on top of Jabal Al Lweibdeh's hill that has been prettified (and renamed) by the French Embassy. It serves as a gateway to the area, flanked by small independent shops, while cafés, fashion stores, design outlets and neighbourhood groceries hide among the often-grand, stone-built villas on its side streets. The wonderful Beit Sitti cookery school (see page 102) is also nearby.

Darat Al Funun
13 Nadim Al Mallah St • Daily except Fri 10am–7pm • Free • ☎ 06 464 3251, ⓦ daratalfunun.org • A short walk down (east) from Paris Circle past the Luzmila Hospital; from Downtown, head for Omar Al Khayyam St, which leads steeply up behind the Downtown post office – turn right at the first hairpin and you'll soon see a high stone wall with gates to left and right into the complex

An idyllic refuge from Amman's bustle and a centre for contemporary Arab art, **Darat Al Funun** ("little house of the arts") comprises a set of three 1920s villas in a beautiful, shaded hillside garden, within which lie the remains of the small sixth-century Byzantine **Church of St George**. The "Blue House" at the top of the steeply terraced complex houses changing exhibitions, and its wooden porch – a common feature of Circassian architecture, added to the building as an acknowledgment of the Circassian presence in the city – serves as a tiny **café**, Amman's most beautiful and peaceful. On the same level is the former home of Emir Abdullah's court poet, now a private studio for visiting artists. Below is the main building, the former official residence of Lieutenant-Colonel Frederick Peake, or "Peake Pasha", British Commander of the Arab Legion in the 1920s and 1930s. It sports a wonderful semicircular portico and has been superbly renovated by Jordanian architect Ammar Khammash to house well-lit **galleries**, studios and an excellent **art library**. Legend has it that, on his stay in late 1921 as a guest of Peake, T.E. Lawrence wrote much of *Seven Pillars of Wisdom* in this building.

Exhibitions at Darat Al Funun vary from grand overviews of contemporary Arab art to small shows from local artists, with everything publicized on the gallery website.

1

ART IN AMMAN

Aside from the National Gallery and the galleries mentioned in this section (Darat Al Funun and Dar Al Anda), there are many ways to access Amman's burgeoning **art scene**: below are just a few.

Nabad (see page 80) stands just off Rainbow Street, showcasing changing exhibitions in an atmospheric, traditional villa setting. Nearby is **Jacaranda Images** (see page 82), devoted to prints and photography, and the quirky Wadi Finan gallery (Ⓦ wfinangallery.com). Umm Uthayna hosts the **Orfali Gallery** (Ⓦ orfali.net), which also holds concerts and other events, and the **Foresight32 Gallery** (Ⓦ foresightartgallery.com), another exhibition venue and cultural centre. Ask around: there are several more.

As well as bank buildings and hotels, **cafés** such as *Blue Fig* (see page 103), *Duinde* (see page 100) and others host shows by local artists, as does the Al Hussein Cultural Centre and Ras Al Ain Gallery in Ras Al Ain. It's also worth looking online at the work of **Ammar Khammash** (Ⓦ khammash.com), an artist, designer and architect who has worked on several high-profile projects in the capital and nationwide.

For more ideas, take a look at Ⓦ universes.art/en/art-destinations/jordan. The "artist's hub" Ⓦ artmejo.com includes an exhibition calendar, interviews and gallery listings; its founder, culture journalist Hind Joucka, leads her own personalized art tours around Amman (search on Airbnb to book). Current shows are also publicized in the *Jordan Times* and at Ⓦ 7iber.com.

There are also plenty of **lectures and performances**, often staged atmospherically in the ruined church, and all events are free to the public. Even if you aren't interested in the art, dropping in is worthwhile to gain a sense of a flourishing side of Jordanian culture that's barely touched upon by most visitors.

Dar Al Anda

3 Dhirar Bin Al Azwar St • Sun–Thurs 10am–4pm • Free • ☎ 06 462 9599, Ⓦ daralanda.com

Across from the Al Saadi mosque, decorated walls announce **Dar Al Anda**, a **gallery** and **cultural centre** staging concerts, workshops and arts events. The original 1939 building has been beautifully restored, and – along with newer structures around the courtyard – now houses a library for children, a studio, a guest apartment for resident artists, and more. Opening hours can vary, but it's worth popping by to see what's happening.

Jordan National Gallery of Fine Arts

Muntazah Circle • Mon, Wed, Thurs, Sat & Sun 9am–7pm (winter till 5pm) • JD3 • ☎ 06 463 0128, Ⓦ nationalgallery.org

Ten minutes' walk west from Paris Circle on the flat along quiet, shady Shari'a College Street, past the Terra Sancta religious academy, will bring you to Muntazah Circle, an oval expanse of green lined with elegant townhouses. One of these, on the right, is the **Jordan National Gallery of Fine Arts**, also reached on a short, signposted walk from Abdali. This is the country's premier establishment showcase for contemporary art, with artists from Jordan and the wider Arab and Islamic worlds, all represented in a changing programme of shows drawing on the permanent collection of the two thousand works. Exhibitions are split between the main building and an annexe in a townhouse opposite; take time to stroll in the pleasant garden between the two.

King Abdullah I Mosque

Suleiman an-Nabulsi St, Abdali • Open for visitors daily except Fri 8–11am & 1–2pm; women visitors must wear a headscarf and *abaya* (black cloak), supplied at the prominently signed visitor entrance • JD2

Its giant blue mosaic dome a common feature in images of Amman, the **King Abdullah I Mosque** was built in the 1980s by the late King Hussein in commemoration of his grandfather, the first ruler of modern Jordan. Though now superseded in size and grandeur as a congregational mosque, it remains both a key visual landmark and one of the only large mosques in the country that admits non-Muslims. You first pass through a small **Islamic museum**, mostly comprising old photos, before entering the serene, carpeted **prayer hall**, capable of holding thousands of (male) worshippers – the smaller women's section is off to one side.

Tiraz Centre

19 Riyadh Al-Mufleh St, behind 4th Circle • Sat, Sun & Tues–Thurs 10am–4pm, by appointment only: always call ahead • JD2 • ☎ 06 592 7531, ⓦ tirazcentre.org

Housed in an elegant townhouse between 4th and 5th Circles, the **Tiraz Centre** showcases a unique collection of traditionally embroidered Arab dresses. Collector **Widad Kawar** has assembled more than two thousand historic items, from wedding gowns to religious robes. Variations in styles, colours and patterns represent different tribal and regional traditions, now largely lost to modernity. The gallery displays textiles and jewellery from across Jordan and Palestine, including the extraordinary three-metre-long dresses of Salt, worn with swags of cloth ostentatiously folded over and over around the body.

King Hussein Park

Off King Abdullah II St • Daylight hours • Taxi roughly JD3–4 from city centre

Amman's favourite green space is **King Hussein Park**, a large tract of hilly land on the western outskirts of the city. Many people come out here – especially on a Friday – to stroll, picnic or play games. There's a monument to King Hussein at the highest point of the park, and you'll also spot the minarets of the **King Hussein bin Talal Mosque**, inaugurated in 2006.

Royal Automobile Museum

King Hussein Park • Mon & Wed–Sun 10am–7pm • JD3; audioguide JD2 extra • ☎ 06 541 1392, ⓦ royalautomuseum.jo

Following King Hussein's death in 1999, King Abdullah II established the **Royal Automobile Museum** in his father's memory. This fine building, designed by star Jordanian architect Jafar Touqan, blends in with its natural surroundings by being partly sunk into the earth and clad in untreated stone. The airy, spacious exhibition areas are filled with vehicles with a royal connection, ranging from a 1916 Cadillac through some elegant Rolls-Royces (and even a 1952 Triumph Thunderbird motorbike) to a Porsche 911 turbo. Images, dioramas and noticeboards give background information to the various vehicles so beloved of King Hussein and his predecessors. It's a unique, fascinating way into twentieth-century Jordanian history, superbly presented. Petrol-heads will be enthralled.

THE ABDALI PROJECT

The shiny new developments rising above the Abdali district (pronounced AB-d'lee) form Amman's highest-profile megaproject. Occupying a wedge of land that was formerly home to the headquarters of the national intelligence agency, the $5-billion **Abdali Project** (ⓦ abdali.jo), backed by a public-private consortium that includes big Lebanese and Kuwaiti investment, comprises a mix of residential, commercial, retail and hotel space – all of it very upscale. At its heart is **The Boulevard**, a 370m-long pedestrianized street of shops and cafés. It's a nice enough place to stroll, with fountains and elevated walkways, but can feel a bit sterile – not unlike the corporate developments that dominate parts of Beirut and Dubai.

Atmosphere aside, Abdali is creating **jobs** – desperately needed in this hard-pressed city – and also sending a powerful signal to the world about Jordan's stability and economic resilience. Building work will continue into the 2020s.

1

Children's Museum
King Hussein Park • Sun, Mon, Wed, Thurs & Sat 9am–6pm, Fri 10am–7pm • JD3 • ☎ 06 541 1479, ⓦ cmj.jo
Alongside the Royal Automobile Museum is the wonderful **Children's Museum**, another superbly designed building – by Jordanian architects Faris & Faris – that is packed with toys, games, hands-on exhibits, art equipment and all kinds of fun for kids, from toddlers to teens.

East Amman

West Amman is the most accessible part of the city outside Downtown, and you're unlikely to have much reason to visit the city's other, chiefly low-income neighbourhoods, often collectively dubbed **East Amman**, even though they spread to the north, east and south. The deepening gap of culture and affluence between the two "halves" of the city leads local wags to claim that you need a passport these days to cross from West to East Amman; that's an exaggeration, but if you venture out to the handful of landmarks in the east – the **Hejaz Railway Museum**, for instance, or the **Cave of the Seven Sleepers** pilgrimage site – you'll certainly feel as if you've left the ritzy shops and hotels of West Amman far behind.

Hejaz Railway Museum
King Abdullah I St in Mahatta, about 2km east of Downtown • Sun–Thurs 8am–2pm • JD1 • ☎ 06 489 5413, ⓦ jhr.gov.jo • Taxi roughly JD1–2 from Downtown
The Mahatta district, at the foot of the hill that climbs towards Marka, is home to the **Hejaz Railway Museum**, occupying one of the century-old red-roofed stone buildings of Amman's old railway station on the Hejaz line, which originally ran between Damascus and Medina (see page 88). The museum itself is a modest affair, comprising models, railway memorabilia, maps, bits of old equipment and so on. Just as exciting is the chance to roam the yards and train sheds – still home to many fine old locomotives – and chat with the engineers or explore the restored Pullman carriages. You can normally turn up unannounced, though it's always best to phone ahead.

Abu Darwish Mosque
Jabal Al Ashrafiyyeh, around 1km south of Downtown • Access for worshippers only • Taxi JD1–2 from Downtown
Perched over Downtown to the south is **Jabal Al Ashrafiyyeh**, the highest and steepest hill in the city, topped by the **Abu Darwish Mosque**, built in 1961 by a Circassian immigrant and visible from points all around the city. On the inside it's unremarkable, but outside, it's an Alice-in-Wonderland palace, striped in vibrant black and white, complete with a row of black-and-white chess pawns atop its walls and multicoloured fairy lights after dark. Other than admiring the exterior, the only reason to come up here is for the panoramic **view**, yet there are no clear sightlines from street level; you'll have to – subtly – get onto the roof of one of the apartment buildings just down from the mosque. Any effort will be amply rewarded, though, especially early in the morning or after sunset: from this high up, the entire city is laid out like a relief map at your feet.

Cave of the Seven Sleepers
Ahl Al Kahf St in Abu Alanda, 7km south of Downtown • Daily 8am–5pm • Free • By car, head 4km south from Downtown, through the low-income neighbourhood of Wihdat, to reach Middle East Circle (*duwaar ash-sharq al-awsat*), then continue south 2.5km to a signposted turn to Abu Alanda, which brings you up the hill to a little roundabout – turn right onto Ahl Al Kahf St and the cave is just over a kilometre farther on; alternatively, taxi from Downtown JD10 return, including waiting time

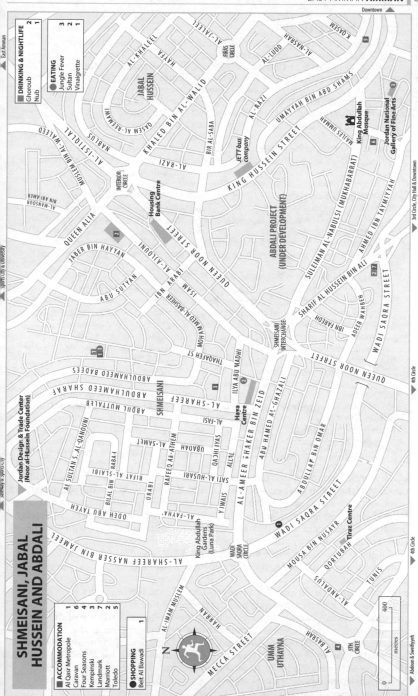

SHMEISANI, JABAL HUSSEIN AND ABDALI

ACCOMMODATION
Al Qasr Metropole	1
Caravan	6
Four Seasons	4
Kempinski	3
Landmark	7
Marriott	2
Toledo	5

SHOPPING
Beit Al Bawadi	1

DRINKING & NIGHTLIFE
Ghoroub	2
Nub	1

EATING
Jungle Fever	3
Sultan	2
Vinaigrette	1

1

THE HEJAZ RAILWAY

The plan to build a **railway** to facilitate the **Muslim pilgrimage**, long touted in the Ottoman capital, Istanbul, was finally approved by the sultan in the 1890s. At that time, a camel caravan travelling the 1300km from **Damascus** to the holy cities of **Medina** and **Mecca**, in the Hejaz region of western Arabia, took the best part of two months – a difficult journey through harsh country that left the pilgrims vulnerable to exhaustion, disease and bandits. The train, it was proposed, would cut this to a mere three days. The route chosen for the line (and the adjacent **Desert Highway** that came later) followed almost exactly the pilgrimage route in use since the sixteenth century. By 1908, with goodwill funds pouring in from all over the Islamic world, modern, comfortable carriages, a luxury Pullman car and even a rolling mosque (with 2m minaret) were running three times a week along the full length of the line from Damascus to Medina, bringing new wealth and sophistication to villages such as Amman and Ma'an along the route.

During World War I, Faisal and Abdullah, the sons of Sherif Hussein of Mecca, and the British colonel T.E. Lawrence ("of Arabia"), organized the **Arab Revolt** in the Hejaz. They moved north up the rail line, harassing the Turkish supply lines, blowing up trains and eventually taking Damascus. After the war and the collapse of the Ottoman Empire, there was only enough money to rebuild the line as far as Ma'an, well short of the holy cities. With its raison d'être negated, the railway lay semi-dormant for decades, and the only passenger services – between Damascus and Amman – came and went, subject to fluctuations in diplomatic relations.

In 1992, a British advertising company hit on the idea of filming an ad for extra-strong mints on the old Hejaz steam locomotives, paying the railway handsomely for the privilege. More enquiries came in, following which profits from passenger service paled into insignificance beside the requests for **special charters** from diplomats and train buffs wanting nostalgic rides into the desert, and from film crews and tour operators capitalizing on the legend of Lawrence. Five-star package tours to Jordan have been known to include an afternoon ride on a steam-drawn Pullman, with the added "surprise" of a mid-desert Lawrence-style raid on the train by mounted bedouin warriors.

These charters all head south from Amman into the desert. Service on the line northwards to Damascus – used far more for freight than passengers – has now been halted, with part of the route subsumed into the planned **Amman–Zarqa light railway**. Jordan's transport ministry is also starting to put plans in place for a **new national rail network** that may, it is hoped, link up with a Saudi line being built northwards from Riyadh. The Hejaz railway itself has finally reached the end of the line – but the dream that inspired it is back on track.

In the southeastern outskirts, tucked away in the run-down suburb of Abu Alanda, the **Cave of the Seven Sleepers** – known in Arabic as *Ahl Al Kahf* – is a pilgrimage site associated with a story recorded in the Quran about seven young Christian men who escaped Roman religious persecution by hiding in a cave. God put them to sleep for hundreds of years, and when they awoke, their attempts to buy food with ancient coins aroused incredulity. The youths were taken to the governor – by that time a Christian – who realized that a miracle had occurred, and ordered celebrations. Their work of enlightenment done, the men returned to the cave, where God put them to sleep for good.

The atmospheric cave, one of many Byzantine **rock-cut tombs** nearby, is set into the hillside next to a modern mosque, built to service the tide of people who come to pay their respects. In antiquity, a small church was built literally on top of the cave: the *mihrab* of its later conversion into a mosque is directly overhead. The decorated entrance, shaded by an ancient olive tree, is topped by five medallions, one of which is a cross. Inside are alcoves with four sarcophagi, one of which has a much-worn hole through which you can peek at an eerie jumble of bones. The walls show remains of painted decoration, with a curious eight-pointed star recurring many times – a Byzantine Christian symbol.

1

Royal Tank Museum

King Abdullah II Park, Muqabalein, 5km south of Downtown • Thurs & Fri 10am–5pm • JD5 • ☎ 06 438 1881, ⓦ rtm.jo • Taxi roughly JD2 from Downtown

Of the few military museums around Amman, most of which are devoted to memorializing past wars, the **Royal Tank Museum** is perhaps the most engaging. It displays more than a hundred tanks and other armoured vehicles deployed over the last century of conflict in a spacious, contemporary gallery building.

ARRIVAL AND DEPARTURE   AMMAN

Amman is Jordan's transit hub, but the many points of **arrival** and **departure** are far-flung, and unless you opt for the simplicity of a **taxi** they nearly always involve a rather complicated journey across the city to reach (or to get away from). However, one thing you can always count on is a generally helpful attitude from bystanders. The worst that might happen to you on your first day in Amman would be an overabundance of offers of help or a slightly inflated taxi fare. There are plenty of options for **car rental** (see page 33).

BY PLANE

QUEEN ALIA INTERNATIONAL AIRPORT

Amman's main Queen Alia International Airport (code AMM, abbreviated locally to QAIA; ☎ 06 401 0250, ⓦ qaiairport. com) is located on the edge of the desert, 35km south of Amman and about 18km east of Madaba. It's signposted off Jordan's main north–south highway, known in the south as the Desert Highway and around Amman as the Airport Road. Off the plane, signs direct you to the desks where you buy a visa (JD40), routinely issued to most nationalities

on arrival (see page 25) – or show your Jordan Pass (see page 55) for a free visa. There are bank counters and ATMs before the visa desks, though it's prudent to save time it's prudent to bring cash with you.

Domestic flights Royal Jordanian (☎ 06 510 0000, ⓦ rj. com) flies to Aqaba (2–3 daily; 30min; around JD50).

Taxis Airport taxis – which have fixed, non-negotiable fares (posted prominently in Arrivals) charge JD20–22 into Amman (depending on the district) or Madaba, JD35 to the Dead Sea and JD78 to Petra. Prices include baggage. Driving time to central Amman is 30–45min. On the return journey, a taxi from anywhere in Amman should cost around JD18–20.

Buses from the airport Sariyah Airport Express buses (info ☎ 06 489 1073) head to Tabarboor station (daily every 30min 6.30am–5pm, then hourly 6pm–midnight; 45min; JD3.25 including baggage), dropping off at 7th, 6th, 5th and 4th Circles and in Shmeisani.

Buses to the airport Sariyah Airport Express buses (info ☎ 06 489 1073) leave from Tabarboor station (daily every 30min 6.30am–5pm, then hourly 6pm–midnight; 45min;

DAY-TRIPS FROM AMMAN

Distances in Jordan are small. It's easy to base yourself in Amman and make a series of day-trips out to nearby attractions. The main draw is floating your day away at the **Dead Sea** (see page 112); you could combine this with a visit to the nearby **Baptism Site** of Jesus (see page 122). Alternatively the amiable old town of **Madaba** (see page 208) is within easy reach – and, with your own transport, you could construct a gentle, circular day-trip from Amman to Madaba, then the Mount Nebo mosaics, then the Dead Sea (with or without the Baptism Site), and back to Amman. If you start early, and maintain a reasonable pace, this circuit is also possible by bus.

A pleasant day-trip into the hilly countryside **west of Amman** could take in the Hellenistic palace of **Qasr al-Abd** (see page 175) and the adjacent caves and crafts workshops of **Iraq Al Amir** (see page 174), the beautiful old Ottoman capital of **Salt** (see page 170) and a stroll in the lanes of old **Fuheis** (see page 173).

North of Amman, the Roman ruins at **Jerash** (see page 133) make for a great half-day excursion, set in some lovely rolling countryside. Combine Jerash with a visit to **Ajloun Castle** (see page 147) – or make a day of it with a walk on Ajloun's **Al Ayoun Trail** (see page 152).

East of Amman, a circuit of roads takes in the fascinating "**Desert Castles**" (see page 184) – this is easy to do by taxi or private car, but impossible on public transport.

A COUNTRY WALK ON THE JORDAN TRAIL

The national **Jordan Trail** (see page 50) winds north–south across the country, passing just west of Amman. The closest section to the capital is stage 3.1, a full-day countryside walk between villages from Fuheis to Iraq al-Amir, accessible by public transport at both ends. For more, see ⓦ jordantrail.org.

1

BUS DEPARTURES

We list the frequency of service on certain **bus routes** – but, as covered in Basics (see page 31), the vast majority of buses **do not run to a timetable** and simply depart whenever they are full. No official information exists, and hotel owners may not be able to advise either; in most situations, you have to turn up and take pot luck. You're unlikely to wait long on popular intercity routes out of Amman – to Salt, Madaba, Zarqa or Jerash, for instance – but further-flung destinations may only be served by one or two buses, or by a handful of departures clustered together at a certain time of day (often early in the morning, say 7–9am).

JD3.25 including baggage), picking up from marked stops at the Housing Bank Centre beside Interior Circle in Shmeisani, then 4th, 5th, 6th and 7th Circles. Ask your hotel to confirm the schedule. If you're flying with Royal Jordanian, you can avoid queuing at the airport by using RJ's City Terminal at 7th Circle (daily 8am–8.30pm; ☎ 06 510 0000). Here, you can check your bags in and receive a boarding card anytime between 24hr and 8hr in advance of your departure. You can then go back into the city or, if your flight is imminent, take RJ's private bus direct to the airport (every 30min; JD4, plus JD2/bag; 40min) where you're led through a fast-track gate direct to passport control.

MARKA AIRPORT

A few flights – mainly regional and domestic charters on variable schedules – come into Amman Civil Airport (code ADJ) in Marka, 5km east of Downtown. It shares its runway with a large military air base alongside. A taxi into the centre costs JD2–3.

BY BUS OR SERVEECE

Amman has numerous terminals scattered all over the city for local and international transport by bus or *serveece* (shared taxi) – we cover the main ones below. Which you use depends partly on where you're coming from (or going to), and partly on what form of transport you're using. Things can change at short notice: it always pays to check details of your journey in advance with a hotel receptionist or some other disinterested party. Note that some intercity buses do not run on Fridays.

TERMINALS

Abdali *Serveeces* and some buses to and from some Middle Eastern cities such as Medina and Riyadh – and, formerly, Damascus – operate out of transport offices on King Hussein St in the Abdali district (pronounced *AB-d'lee*). Most tourist hotels lie within a JD1–2 taxi ride.

JETT office Buses run by JETT (☎ 06 566 4146, ⊛ jett.com. jo) – and their partner firms – to and from Aqaba, Petra, Damascus, Cairo and other cities use the JETT office at 224 King Hussein St, about 1km uphill from Abdali (and several more kilometres uphill from Downtown).

Muhajireen A small patch of asphalt beside Princess Basma St, at the bottom of the hill from 3rd Circle – roughly

2km southwest of Downtown – is the terminus for minibus destinations west of Amman, including the Dead Sea, Wadi Seer, Shuneh Al Janubiyyeh and some to/from Madaba. A taxi to/from most central hotels is JD1–3.

Raghadan & Mahatta The Raghadan station – in the heart of Downtown beside the Roman Theatre – hosts only *serveeces* serving neighbourhoods within Amman: buses to and from nearby destinations such as Zarqa, Salt and Madaba operate from Mahatta station, 2km east of Raghadan off King Abdullah I St, pending an overhaul of transport services in the area. Onward taxi fares are about JD1–3.

Tabarboor (North station) Known as North station (*mujemma ash-shamal*), located 5km north of Abdali where Al-Urdon/Jordan St meets Al-Shaheed St, this is the terminus for buses and *serveeces* serving towns north of Amman – including Jerash, Ajloun, Irbid and Salt – as well as some to/from Madaba. Sariyah Airport Express buses serving Queen Alia airport, and *serveeces* to/from the King Hussein/Allenby Bridge (for Jerusalem) are also based here. Reckon on a taxi fare of about JD3 to reach the city centre hotels, or much less than that in a *serveece* bound for Raghadan or Wihdat.

Wihdat (South station) Known as South station (*mujemma al-janoob*), located 5km south of Downtown near Middle East Circle, off Mosaab bin Omayr St, this is the terminus for buses and *serveeces* to and from the south of Jordan – chiefly Aqaba, Petra, Ma'an, Karak and some from Madaba – as well as a handful of international buses. It lies a JD3–4 taxi ride from any hotels, or you could take a local *serveece* bound for Raghadan or Tabarboor and get off en route.

TO JERASH AND THE NORTH

Tabarboor is the main departure point for buses and *serveeces* to destinations in the north of Jordan. For the quickest journey to Irbid, take one of the large, a/c coaches from Tabarboor station run by Hijazi (JD2), or others run by JETT (JD2) from their Abdali office. For Umm Qais and the far north, change in Irbid. For Pella and the northern Jordan Valley, take a bus from Tabarboor to Dayr Alla and change there.

Destinations Ajloun (1hr 30min); Dayr Alla (1hr); Irbid (every 15–30min; minibus 1hr 15min, large bus 2hr); Jerash (1hr).

TO AZRAQ AND THE EAST

The only direct public transport between Amman and destinations east are minibuses from Tabarboor to Mafraq, where you should change for Umm Al Jimal and the far desert; and minibuses from Tabarboor or Mahatta to Zarqa, where you should change for Hallabat and Azraq. There is no public transport along the Amman–Azraq highway apart from a minibus from Mahatta to Muwaqqar, making it impossible to reach Qasr Kharrana and Qusayr Amra without your own transport; many travellers resort to hiring a taxi or joining a "tour" run by a hotel (see page 185).

Destinations Mafraq (1hr); Muwaqqar (45min); Zarqa (35min).

TO SALT AND THE WEST

Transport to towns west of Amman include minibuses from Tabarboor or Mahatta to Salt; from Tabarboor to Fuheis; and from Muhajireen to Wadi Seer. The day-trips by bus formerly run by JETT (☎06 566 4146, ⊛ jett.com.jo) from its Abdali office to the Ma'in hot springs weren't operating at the time of writing.

Destinations Fuheis (35min); Salt (35min); Wadi Seer (30min).

TO THE DEAD SEA

Early-morning minibuses from Muhajireen station might run direct to the "Amman Beach" resort on the Dead Sea, but only if there's demand – likely on a Friday. Others stop short at the crossroads town of Shuneh Al Janubiyyeh, about 15km north of the Dead Sea. From Shuneh, occasional minibuses head to the village of Sweimeh, 3km northeast of the Dead Sea hotels; the driver might be willing to take you on to Amman Beach for a little extra, but it's not guaranteed. The day-trips by bus formerly run by JETT (☎06 566 4146, ⊛ jett.com.jo) from its Abdali office to the Dead Sea weren't operating at the time of writing.

Destinations Amman Beach (7–9am depending on demand; 1hr); Shuneh Al Janubiyyeh (1hr).

TO MADABA AND THE SOUTH

Minibuses to Madaba run from four stations on slightly different routes: Tabarboor (your best bet), Mahatta, Muhajireen and Wihdat. There is no direct public transport to destinations south of Madaba along the picturesque King's Highway: all minibuses and *serveeces* from Amman use the Desert Highway. However, the *Mariam Hotel* runs its own transport from Madaba to Petra along the King's Highway (see page 219). Aside from Madaba, all other destinations in the south are served from Wihdat station. A bedouin pick-up for up to four people to Feynan, organized through the *Feynan Ecolodge* (see page 342), costs JD81.

Destinations Graygra for Feynan (4hr); Karak (2hr); Ma'an (2hr 30min); Madaba (30min); Qadisiyyeh for Dana (3hr); Shobak (2hr 45min); Tafileh (2hr 30min).

TO PETRA

By minibus & serveece Minibuses to Wadi Musa/Petra (3hr) leave from Wihdat station. Departures are more common in the morning (from 6.30am onwards) than the

---

PETRA SCAMS

It's worth being aware of the **scams** used by some taxi-, *serveece*- and bus-drivers plying the heavily travelled tourist route from Amman to Petra. No public buses, minibuses or *serveeces* from Amman to Petra follow the scenic **King's Highway**, and any drivers who claim they do are trying to gouge you for an inflated fare. For comparison purposes, the true cost of hiring a private taxi to drive you from Amman along the King's Highway to Petra is around JD70–80.

Some of the budget hotels in Amman take advantage of this to offer cut-price "**tours**" to Petra along the King's Highway, stopping off at various places on the way. You'll get what you pay for on these: often a driver who speaks little English, a cramped, all-day drive and whistle-stop photo breaks. They can, nonetheless, be an economical way to glimpse the countryside. Beware of drivers on the day claiming, for instance, that the section of the King's Highway through the Wadi Mujib canyon is closed so they have to go on the Desert Highway instead: this is invariably just a ploy to get out of a long drive. The most reliable of these King's Highway jaunts to Petra is run by the excellent *Mariam Hotel* in Madaba (see page 219).

Many Amman *serveece*- and taxi-drivers have deals running with certain hotels in Wadi Musa: they bring tourists directly to the hotel, and the hotel pays them **commission** for each one, passing that cost on to you in the form of a higher room rate. You may find that your taxi driver offers to **phone ahead** to a hotel on your behalf while driving: if you're able to understand Arabic, you'll hear that, rather than asking if they have a room available, he's instead asking how much commission the hotel would pay him if he brought you to the door. If the hotel refuses to cough up, he'll turn to you and claim it's full before offering to try another. The best way to avoid all this is to insist that you get dropped off in the middle of Wadi Musa town so you can find a hotel independently. In any case, not all hotels in Wadi Musa are recommendable: if a place hasn't made it into our listings, there's a reason.

1

afternoon. *Serveece*-drivers tend to quote prices higher than normal to start with; some hopefuls to Petra start as high as JD10, although the real price is JD5–8 (or JD5–7 on the bus). If you can't find transport, take a bus or *serveece* to Ma'an, where you might catch a connecting bus (if not, a Ma'an–Petra taxi is JD10–12).

By JETT bus A daily coach to Petra run by JETT leaves from its Abdali office at 224 King Hussein St (☎06 566 4146, ⊚jett.com.jo), departing at 6.30am (JD11 one-way). Should you choose to make a day-trip of it, the same coach leaves Petra about 4.30–5pm, arriving back in Amman around 7.30–8pm; in between, you get about six hours in Petra – enough to see a few highlights.

TO AQABA

By minibus & serveece From Wihdat station, minibuses (5hr; about JD7–8) and *serveeces* (4hr; about JD8–9) depart regularly for Aqaba, the drivers touting for business by barking "*Aqabaqabaqaba!*" over their revving engines.

By JETT bus Large a/c JETT coaches (☎06 566 4141, ⊚jett.com.jo) depart to Aqaba (4hr 30min; JD9) roughly 6–8 times daily from each of four Amman locations (first bus 7–8am, last 6–7pm) – Tabarboor station, 224 King Hussein St in Abdali, Wihdat station and 7th Circle. There are also more comfortable "VIP" departures from Abdali and 7th Circle (1–3 daily; JD11–19), and one overnight departure from Abdali (daily midnight; JD9). Call ahead to confirm schedules and book a seat.

By plane Royal Jordanian (☎06 510 0000, ⊚rj.com) has 2–3 flights a day to Aqaba from Amman's Queen Alia airport (30min; around JD50).

TO DAMASCUS

At the time of writing the war in Syria was continuing, and the borders were closed to tourists. There's no knowing when that situation will change. When it does, transport between Amman and the Syrian capital Damascus, barely 100km north of the Jordanian frontier, will likely be easiest by *serveece* – or perhaps by JETT bus. Ask around for the latest information.

TO JERUSALEM AND THE WEST BANK

As the crow flies, Amman and Jerusalem are only about 50km apart, but the Jordan Valley and a heavily fortified frontier bridge lie in the way. No buses or *serveeces* run directly between the two cities. The only way to go is with a combination of buses and taxis/*serveeces*. With luck the journey from Amman to Jerusalem can take as little as 2hr; without it (or with security/immigration delays) you could be hanging around most of the day. If you need speed, you can pay extra for VIP service.

King Hussein Bridge All forms of transport require you to change midway at a bridge known as the King Hussein Bridge (*Jissr Al Malek Hussein*) or Allenby Bridge (*Gesher*

Allenby in Hebrew, *Jissr Allenby* in Arabic), located 4km west of Shuneh Al Janubiyyeh in the Jordan Valley. It's open limited hours (Sun–Thurs 8am–midnight, Fri & Sat 8am–3pm). The Jordanian and Israeli terminals are around 5km apart, separated by no-man's land either side of the bridge itself. Walking across, or taking a private car, is forbidden without high-level permission: you must take public transport. This crossing point is notoriously subject to the ebb and flow of Middle Eastern politics, and can close at short notice.

By serveece or taxi From Tabarboor station in Amman, *serveeces* run direct to the bridge (1hr; about JD5). Opposite the terminal gates is a line of car rental companies; if you've driven down from Amman, you can park your car down marked alleyways between the offices for a negotiable JD1/day, payable at the end. A taxi from Amman costs about JD25. Within the terminal, departure formalities involve filling out a short form (which is stamped instead of your passport), paying the departure tax (JD10) and then loading your bags onto a shuttle bus (JD7/person plus JD1.50/bag) which – once it's full – heads off to cover no-man's land across the bridge, dropping you at the Israeli arrivals terminal.

By bus An alternative option from Amman is to take the 6.30am daily JETT bus from their Abdali office (☎06 566 4146, ⊚jett.com.jo); book one day ahead, or turn up no later than 6am to guarantee a seat. The JD11 fare (which doesn't include JD10 departure tax) takes you across to the Israeli terminal. Beware of the bus driver taking the passports of all the passengers to give en masse to the Israeli immigration officials. It's normal practice now for the Israelis not to stamp passports, but if you need yours to stay clear of stamps, it's worth asking to present your own passport.

At Israeli arrivals At the arrivals terminal you disembark, queue to load your bags onto belts for X-raying, queue for a passport check, queue to go through a metal detector, then queue for the formal Israeli immigration procedure, where you may be questioned at length about your travel plans; if you pass scrutiny, you will be given a (free) Israeli visa. It's normal practice now for officials not to stamp passports, but if you need yours to stay unsullied, it's worth asking. Once you're through, there is a bank counter to change money, but no ATM. Turn right to find the pick-up point for a *serveece* to Jerusalem, run by Taxi Nejmeh: the 1hr ride, which drops you by the Damascus Gate of the Old City, costs 42 Israeli shekels (NIS) plus NIS5/bag; you can pay in dinars (about JD10) or US dollars (about $14). They'll charge a hefty NIS300 (roughly US$75–80) or so for a private taxi into Jerusalem. There is also a bus to Jericho for NIS15 plus NIS3/bag.

VIP service If you need speed, you can pay roughly US$250 for VIP service city-to-city from agencies such as ⊚amman2jerusalem.com – but this excludes the bridge shuttle bus. An alternative is to take an ordinary taxi from Amman to the VIP terminal at the bridge. Pay around JD75 and they will whisk you immediately through all the passport and security formalities, zip you across the bridge in a private minivan and escort you officially to the front of every queue in the Israeli arrivals hall, then out to the taxi stand.

TO NAZARETH

By bus Israeli company Nazarene Tours (☎+972 4 647 0797, ⌨ nazarene-tours.com) runs buses between Amman and Nazareth – the largest Palestinian city inside Israel – a few times a week (usually Sun, Tues, Thurs & Sat, but it can vary; around JD17). Pick-up is 2pm from outside *Wardat Al Bustan Hotel*, 327 Queen Rania/University St beside Majdi Mall. Be there 30min early, to be safe. Buses go first to Irbid to pick up more passengers, then cross via the Sheikh Hussein Bridge, where you pay a departure tax of JD10.

TO TEL AVIV

By plane The short flight from Amman's Queen Alia airport to Tel Aviv on Royal Jordanian (☎06 510 0000, ⌨ rj.com) costs around JD270 one-way but offers the lure of spectacular views over the Dead Sea (1–2 daily; 30min).

TO CAIRO

By bus Buses do run from Amman to Cairo, though it's an uncomfortable journey of at least 20hr; you'd do better to break your journey in Aqaba and/or the Sinai along the way. To reach Cairo, you need a full Egyptian tourist visa (JD15), issued at airports, seaports and most land borders (not Taba), sometimes in US dollars only (around $21). JETT (☎06 569 6151, ⌨ jett.com.jo) and its Egyptian partner SuperJet run buses to the Almaza terminal at Heliopolis in Cairo (Sun, Tues & Thurs 11am; JD33); the fare excludes the Aqaba–Nuweiba ferry. It's advisable to book up to a week ahead. Other Abdali-based bus companies compete, all of them cheaper and even less comfortable.

By plane Royal Jordanian (☎06 510 0000, ⌨ rj.com) and EgyptAir (☎06 463 6011, ⌨ egyptair.com) fly several times daily to Cairo (1hr 30min; around JD160 one-way).

AROUND THE MIDDLE EAST

JETT and other transport companies around Abdali run regular buses and *serveeces* direct to other cities including Jeddah, Madina, Riyadh, Dammam, Kuwait, Baghdad and points further afield – as well as, formerly, Beirut, Damascus and Aleppo. Middle Eastern airlines fly from Amman to their hub cities – all the usual legacy carriers, as well as a handful of cheaper, perkier Gulf-based low-cost airlines, including Air Arabia (☎06 460 2222, ⌨ airarabia.com), Fly Dubai (☎06 500 4445, ⌨ flydubai.com) and Jazeera (☎06 562 6141, ⌨ jazeeraairways.com).

GETTING AROUND

Due to its geography and the unplanned nature of its expansion, Amman doesn't have an integrated **transport system**: buses and *serveeces* compete on set routes around the city (you'll never have to wait long beside a main road to flag one or other of them down), but none runs to a timetable. Few people pay heed to roadside bus stops: most buses and all *serveeces* will stop anywhere. The excellent **Amman Unofficial City Transport Map** – the first ever made, conceived by a volunteer group of local enthusiasts – details all bus and *serveece* routes. Download it at ⌨ maannasel.net/map or as a smartphone app for Android or iOS.

AMMAN–JERUSALEM: THE BUREAUCRACY

The **bureaucracy** surrounding the journey from Amman to Jerusalem is very confusing. The **Jordanians** view the West Bank as being intimately linked with Jordan: if you have a single-entry Jordanian visa and cross the King Hussein/Allenby Bridge to spend time in the West Bank or Israel, then return *the same way* to Jordan, the Jordanians don't see you as ever having left the country and you don't need to buy a new Jordanian visa, as long as your current one is still within its validity – indeed, Jordan does not issue visas at this bridge anyway. Bear in mind that the cost saving is negated by the unusually high departure tax imposed by Israel. If you return to Jordan having used any other route out or in, you must buy a new Jordanian visa.

However, once you cross the King Hussein Bridge from Jordan into the West Bank, the **Israeli** authorities view you as arriving in Israel proper, and routinely issue free tourist visas on arrival, which are usually valid throughout Israeli- and **Palestinian**-administered West Bank territory and Israel itself (though officials will sometimes impose restrictions). The Palestinians currently do not control their own borders or issue their own visas. As a foreigner, you'll be waved through any checkpoints on the "Green Line" between the West Bank and Israel proper, a border you'll find marked on Jordanian and Palestinian maps but not Israeli ones.

1

HEAVY TRAFFIC

Traffic in Amman – especially West Amman – can be horrendous at the best of times. Add to that an influx during the summer of tens of thousands of visitors from Saudi Arabia and the Gulf, almost all of whom drive their own cars, and the problem reaches crisis levels. All this isn't helped by the local driving style: lane discipline is nonexistent, cars are frequently parked (or double-parked) to block the flow of traffic, roundabouts are a free-for-all, poor traffic-light phasing often leads to gridlock, and so on. Many pinch points experience all-day congestion, and you should allow up to an hour to cross the city during the day. Thursday afternoons (the start of the weekend getaway) and Friday afternoons/evenings are notoriously bad.

BY SERVEECE

Serveeces (shared taxis) are essential for getting quickly and easily up the hills surrounding Downtown, and for crossing between districts. They operate like small buses, with between four and six passengers cramming in and everyone paying a flat fare. You can get in or out wherever you like on the set route. All Amman's city *serveeces* are white cars, with black, stencilled panels in Arabic on both front doors stating the district they're going to. The cars tend to form long nose to tail lines at the bottom of the Downtown hills; the first passengers in the queue pile into the last car in line, which pulls out and grinds its way past the others up the hill and away. All the rest then roll backwards one place and the same thing happens again.

Routes and stops No official information exists; aside from the Unofficial City Transport Map mentioned above, the best way to find out which *serveece* goes where is to ask passers-by or local shopkeepers. If you want to pick up a *serveece* partway along its route, a bunch of people queuing on the kerbside is a sure sign of a stop. When you want to get out, saying "*allah yaatik al-afyeh*" ("God give you strength") will have the driver veering over to the kerb for you. Fares are pennies – under JD1/person. *Serveeces* run frequently during the day (around 7am–7pm); at night they tend to operate as private taxis.

BY TAXI

Roughly a quarter of all cars in Amman are yellow taxis; the metered fares are cheap and you can be whisked to places that might take hours to get to by any other means. Unless you're starting from a remote neighbourhood or are planning a journey in the middle of the night, you'll rarely have to wait long to be able to hail one. Smartphone-based ride-share firms Uber (uber.com) and Careem (careem.com) operate in Amman.

Navigation Although most drivers know their way around pretty well, no Ammani relates to street names. Unless you're going somewhere obvious, like Wihdat station or the Roman Theatre, first give the name of the neighbourhood you're heading for, then, as you get closer, tell the driver which building you want, or maybe a nearby landmark: if he's not familiar with it, he'll quite likely just drive around asking passers-by for directions.

Costs In a yellow taxi, you should insist on the meter being switched on before you start moving, though practically all drivers will do it anyway as a matter of course. The meters always work; if a driver claims it's broken and tries to negotiate a fixed fare with you, simply say "*ma'alesh*" ("forget it") and wait for another taxi to come along. A 10min ride should cost less than JD2, with a crosstown journey perhaps JD4 or JD5. Don't misplace the decimal point: we've had reports of first-time visitors seeing "1600" on the meter, and handing over JD16 instead of JD1.60. Not every driver will point out the mistake. Uber and Careem can undercut metered taxi rates slightly.

Luxury taxis A fleet of silver-coloured luxury taxis branded Al Moumayaz (06 579 9999), with trained drivers and a central radio dispatch system, charge slightly higher fares. They also operate electric/hybrid vehicles and (unusually) employ some women drivers.

BY BUS

City buses These compete with *serveeces* on popular routes around the city – but, with little information available, they are unlikely to be of much use to short-stay visitors. A citywide Bus Rapid Transit scheme (ammanbrt.jo) – where large buses run on car-free lanes down the centre of main highways – has been under construction for several years, and may be operating when you visit.

BY TRAIN

Light railway A planned light railway between Amman and Zarqa is currently on hold.

BY BIKE

Bike Rush (Sun–Thurs noon–9pm; 079 945 4586, facebook.com/bikerush), on Shaashaa St below 1st Circle, rents bikes from JD10/day – though you'd have to be brave to tackle Amman's steep hills (and unpredictable traffic). They also run weekend off-road excursions out of the city.

INFORMATION

Leaflets There's a small office within the *JARA Cafe* at 36 Rainbow St (Sun–Thurs 9am–4pm; ☎ 06 463 4770), run by the Jabal Amman Residents' Association to showcase the Rainbow St area, with old photos relating the history of Amman and leaflets outlining self-guided walks. Interesting, but despite the big sign outside, it's not a tourist information centre.

Online Aside from ⓦ visitjordan.com, the best approach is to plug into the local knowledge at ⓦ beamman.com, which is packed with listings, ideas, reviews, travel tips and features. The independent media site ⓦ 7iber.com (pronounced *hibber*) also has cultural listings and events calendars.

Maps Bookshops in five-star hotels stock reasonable maps – invariably better than the tourist-board handouts. The local media initiative Plurality (ⓦ facebook.com/pluralityME) publishes the excellent "Culinary & Cultural" foldout map, which pinpoints dozens of cafés, restaurants, shops, markets and galleries around the city. Find it at local shops on Rainbow St and in Lweibdeh and Abdoun (including JoBedu, Mlabbas and Books@Cafe).

Nature reserves For details about Jordan's nature reserves and to book guided walks, overnight stays or meal-stops at any of them, drop into the Wild Jordan centre (see page 82).

ACCOMMODATION

Amman has accommodation to suit all budgets. Hoteliers citywide are tuned into the needs and expectations of Western tourists, but outside the luxury end of the market, you'll find that their margins are tight: standards are sometimes make do, although the welcome extended to guests is invariably warm.

Where to stay Staying outside Downtown may mean you're further from Amman's headline antiquities, but the cafés and street life outside your hotel in, say, Shmeisani are just as much an Amman "attraction" as the Roman ruins far away in Downtown. Bear in mind that Madaba is closer to Amman airport (18km) than Amman itself (35km) – and it has a decent range of hotels: if you rate a small-town base over a big-city one, Madaba is an attractive proposition.

Rates and booking All the room rates quoted here are very open to negotiation: prices in Jordan fluctuate according to season and daily demand, and the figures here should be taken as guidelines rather than gospel.

Airbnb The site ⓦ airbnb.com has taken off in Amman: it lists dorm beds to guesthouse rooms to entire furnished apartments, at prices that compete keenly with hotels of equivalent standards.

DOWNTOWN

Downtown Amman is crammed with inexpensive hotels, but most of them aren't up to snuff – tape holding the windows together, unchanged beds, ancient bathrooms. Hostel-booking websites don't help, falsely publicizing many shabby or sinister establishments as backpacker-friendly. Despite this, Downtown holds some good-value inexpensive hotels. Key attributes aside from cleanliness are a/c in summer (or at least a ceiling fan: a table fan won't do) and heating in winter. Rooms on higher floors tend to be less prone to dust and traffic noise. Hotels reviewed in this Guide are safe for all.

Amman Pasha 4 Shabsough St ☎ 06 461 8262, ⓦ ammanpashahotel.com; map p.70. Popular, keenly priced tourist hotel in a great location on a busy Downtown corner opposite the Roman Theatre. Rooms are spotless and well kitted out, service is warm and there's a friendly buzz about the place. Loads of optional extras include tours, cooking classes, a hammam and more – plus a rooftop café for those views. JD34

★ **Art Hotel** 32 King Faisal St ☎ 06 463 8900, ⓦ art hoteljordan.com; map p.70. Classy mid-range hotel – the best in the Downtown area – comprising forty rooms,

---

AMMAN'S ANNUAL FESTIVALS

As well as side events during the **Jerash Festival** (see page 136), the capital hosts its own **Amman Summer Festival** from mid-July to mid-August in the King Hussein Park, featuring DJs, dance troupes, music shows and a kids' zone with puppetry, face painting and more. **Amman Stairs**, part of the Summer Festival, comprises informal evenings of music and art staged on some of the staircases that climb the hills of Amman's older neighbourhoods, including Jabal Al Lweibdeh and Jabal Al Qal'a. **Citadel Nights** features music, stalls and traditional food on Jabal Al Qal'a each night during Ramadan (9pm–2am).

The **Amman International Theatre Festival** in March stages experimental drama from around the world in Arabic and English; the **Al-Balad Theatre** (ⓦ al-balad.org) hosts the **Baladk Street Art Festival** in May (ⓦ facebook.com/baladkproject), a summer music festival every other July and a storytelling festival in September; while throughout the year there's a sequence of short **film festivals** (ⓦ film.jo), featuring screenings of Jordanian, Spanish, French, Filipino, Arab and other arthouse movies alongside music and cultural events.

1

AMMAN'S HAMMAMS

Hammams (Turkish baths) are common in Cairo, Damascus and many other Middle Eastern and North African cities, elegant and civilized places to steam the city dust out of your pores. Amman is an exception: its short recent history means that it doesn't share the centuries-old urban traditions of its neighbours. Other than in five-star hotels, there are only a very few hammams in the city, most prominently these two.

Al Pasha Turkish Bath Mahmoud Taha St, opposite Ahlia girls' school ☎ 06 463 3002. Beautifully designed in traditional style, this hammam offers two hours of soaking, scrubbing, lathering and olive-oil massaging with professional male or female therapists for JD25. There are separate times for male and female access, though you can book ahead as a mixed group or a couple; call for details. Decor is looking a bit tired these days, but it's still a pleasant city centre retreat. Fifth turn on the right coming from 1st Circle along Rainbow St. Daily 10am–midnight.

Alf Layla Wa Layla Turkish Bath 191 Medina St (Madina Al Munawwara St) ☎ 06 552 8868. Out in West Amman, in a retail zone of shops and restaurants off Gardens St, this fresh, superclean hammam offers the full range of soak, steam, scrub and massage treatments, starting from around JD30. Standards are high, and the place is split between areas for men and women. Daily 10am–midnight.

spread over three floors of a historic building (with a lift) on the main drag, surrounded by cafés, restaurants, shops and activity. This accomplished hideaway offers pristine, high-quality, en-suite three-star rooms that maintain a sense of style, with air-conditioning and double glazing. Some have balconies and artistic murals covering the walls. JD45

Boutique 32 Prince Muhammad St, opposite Jafra restaurant ☎ 079 797 0611, ⓦ the-boutique-hotel-amman.com; map p.70. Not swanky enough to qualify as a boutique hotel, but still a decent cheap option in the Downtown bustle, this hotel occupies the upper floors of a 1930s building, where tiled floors, knick-knacks and art on the walls create a pleasant ambience. The six rooms are small but en suite and with a/c, and there are cheaper beds in a six-person dorm room and in a tent on the roof. Also offers cut-price tours nationwide. Dorms JD8, doubles JD32

Farah Cinema Al Hussein St ☎ 06 465 1443, ⓦ farah hotel.info; map p.70. Dynamic, ambitiously run budget hotel, up an alley behind an old cinema, with a lift, decent decor and a pleasant front garden. Out of 24 rooms, five are en suite, with a/c, heating and hot water; for the remainder, every three rooms share two bathrooms. Four- and six-bed dorms available. Staff are friendly and attuned to backpacker needs: expect cut-price transport around Jordan, deals on airport runs, and so on. Dorms JD10, shared-bath JD26, en-suite JD36

Jordan Tower 48 Hashmi St ☎ 06 461 4161, ⓦ jordan toweramman.com; map p.70. Well-run travellers' hotel in the middle of Downtown, steps from the Roman Theatre. Cheerful, well-kept rooms – some with small en-suite bathrooms – are spread across four floors: this is a decent, secure, clean, simple place that knows its clientele. A roof terrace and options for airport pick-ups, luggage storage and budget tours around the country add to the appeal. Shared-bath JD28, en-suite JD37

Sydney 9 Shaaban St ☎ 077 823 4715, ⓦ sydneyhotel amman.com; map p.70. Reliable hostel-style place, just up the slope from Downtown towards 1st Circle, a short (but steep) walk from Rainbow St. There's a range of rooms on offer, from dorms to triples, doubles and twins, with/ without en-suite bathroom. A few wrinkles in facilities, such as mediocre bathrooms, are eased by large communal areas and cheerful staff, who offer budget tours and airport transfers. Dorms JD7, shared-bath JD26, en-suite JD36

JABAL AMMAN

The largest and most diverse area of West Amman, Jabal Amman runs the range from small, simple hotels up to the largest and grandest establishments in the city. Once you get beyond 3rd Circle, though, there's not much within walking distance, and taxis become essential for moving around.

★ **Bonita** 1 Qiss bin Saedah St, near 3rd Circle ☎ 06 461 5061, ⓦ bonitaamman.com; map p.81. More like a cheerful guesthouse than a hotel, Bonita has six rooms (five doubles and a single), located above a good Spanish restaurant and tapas bar – within walking distance of more cafés, shops and nightlife – and is often booked up weeks ahead. Staff are friendly and approachable; the rooms, though modest in size, have been recently refurbished with laminate flooring and an almost domestic warmth of character, with en-suite bathrooms and a/c. A great choice. JD52

Crowne Plaza 6th Circle ☎ 06 551 0001, ⓦ crowneplaza. com; map p.64. Not a pretty building, and now dwarfed by the giant Jordan Gate twin towers directly behind, but nonetheless an excellent five-star hotel. Rooms are comfortable and service is outstanding. This is a great choice for a first night in the city if you're driving in from the airport – turn off the Airport Highway at 7th Circle, just nearby. The hotel is within walking distance of the shops and restaurants of both Sweifiyyeh and Umm Uthaina. JD150

Four Seasons 5th Circle ☎ 06 550 5555, ⊕ fourseasons. com; map p.87. Perhaps the grandest hotel in the country – a palatial, fifteen-storey landmark. Rooms are the largest in Amman – exceptionally well appointed, with every detail taken care of. The public areas are stunningly opulent, and there's a large spa and a clutch of top restaurants and bars. JD210

Hisham Abu Firas Al Hamdani St, between 3rd & 4th Circles ☎ 06 464 7540, ⊕ hishamhotel.com.jo; map p.81. Small, long-established hotel in the embassy quarter with an excellent reputation, a fine bar-restaurant and courteous staff. Expect modern interiors, tiled floors, chic textiles, designer bathrooms, big mirrors and lots of dark wood. Service can be a little hit-and-miss but very large corner rooms – such as #401 (king) or #403 (twin) – stand out. Only 25 rooms. Book ahead. JD105

InterContinental Between 2nd & 3rd Circles ☎ 06 464 1361, ⊕ intercontinental.com; map p.81. One of the city's landmarks; some taxi drivers still call it by its old name of *Funduq Al Urdun* (Jordan Hotel), harking back to the days in the 1960s when it was the only luxury hotel in the country. Now at world-class standard, it has modern, spacious, well-appointed rooms and is packed with all kinds of diversions, from a crafts gallery to live music. Star features include the cafés in the lobby and on the rear terrace, one of the city's best bookshops and an excellent Indian restaurant. JD180

Jabal Amman Rainbow St ☎ 06 463 7733, ⊕ jabal ammanhotel.com; map p.70. Rather classy apartment-hotel in a great location at the lower end of Rainbow St, with shops, cafés, restaurants, nightlife and the Downtown atmosphere all within easy walking distance. The attractive apartments – six studios, four one-beds and five two-beds – are spacious and stylishly contemporary, all with a breakfast bar and kitchen facilities as well as modern bathrooms. Upper-floor ones have rooftop views. JD91

★ **Landmark** Sharif Al Hussein bin Ali St, off 3rd Circle ☎ 06 560 7100, ⊕ landmarkamman.com; map p.87. Notable for being Amman's only independent Jordanian-owned, Jordanian-operated five-star hotel, the *Landmark* stands out for its real sense of pride. Staff aren't just going through the motions: they're engaged, working to make things the best possible. Overlook the unlovely exterior (a 1970s tower) – interior public areas feature cool but quirky character and the rooms (260 in total) are unusually large, some with contemporary styling, others traditional. The hotel also supports an array of social projects in Jordan on empowerment, equality and human rights: this is a fine place to spend your money. JD100

JABAL AL LWEIBDEH AND ABDALI

The few accommodation options in Jabal Al Lweibdeh – mostly small, family-run hotels – benefit from the area's peaceful, residential ambience, with a whiff of historical character in its old stone houses and courtyard gardens. Restaurants and galleries are within walking distance. Abdali, alongside, is now dominated by a purpose-built business district of offices, upscale apartment complexes and swanky hotels, though a popular, more affordable survivor clings on nearby.

Caravan Police College Rd, near King Abdullah Mosque ☎ 06 566 1195, ⊜ caravanhotel@outlook.com; map p.87. A welcoming old hotel with a solid reputation to uphold, reaching back to 1967. The 29 rooms are clean and decent, all with fan and some with balcony – and the location, behind the National Gallery and very near the former Abdali bus station, is handy. JD37

Locanda 52 Al-Baouniyah St, Lweibdeh ☎ 06 460 2020, ⊕ locandahotel.com; map p.81. Friendly, artistically-minded little boutique-style hotel in a renovated 1950s buildings in this quiet, cheerful neighbourhood. Each of the fourteen rooms is named after a famous Arab musician, with decor to match – expect high standards in design and service, and a relaxed vibe throughout. JD70

Toledo King Hussein St, Abdali ☎ 06 465 7777, ⊕ toledo hotel.jo; map p.87. Rather good tourist hotel in a convenient location, backing onto the main King Hussein St artery but also built into the side of the mountainous hill of Jabal Hussein. From street level on the Abdali side, take the lift to the seventh floor for the Moorish-style lobby and main street entrance (accessed from Jabal Hussein's Al Razi St). This was Amman's first hotel to be awarded the Green Key, a global rating system based on environmental policy. The rooms are classy – spacious, recently renovated, well equipped and pleasant to spend time in. Try to nudge the quoted room rate down a bit. JD76

SHMEISANI

Effectively West Amman's financial district, business-minded Shmeisani has a breezy, modern feel and is packed with shops, cafés and restaurants – chiefly catering to the office crowd. You're also on higher ground out here, which can temper the summer heat by a few, crucial degrees. Traffic can be a problem, though, with main roads into the area often nose to tail during the day.

★ **Al Qasr Metropole** Arroub St ☎ 06 566 6140, ⊕ alqasrmetropole.com; map p.87. Quality upper-mid-range hotel on a quiet residential street behind Shmeisani. Cosy rooms are very light and bright, with smartly contemporary facilities – go for those on the upper floors, which have balconies and panoramic city views. The buzzing lobby atmosphere is ideal for businesspeople bored with five-star isolation. Also has an excellent bar and super-stylish restaurants. JD120

Kempinski Abdul Hamid Shoman St ☎ 06 520 0200, ⊕ kempinski.com; map p.87. Shiny five-star haven, perfectly placed in the heart of Shmeisani's commercial district, with shops, cafés and restaurants on the doorstep. The styling is fresh and ultramodern throughout – no stuffy

1

opulence, wood panelling or swirly carpets here. Instead, think cool, spacious rooms, chic public areas and sharp, genial service. JD190

Marriott Issam Al Ajlouni St ☎06 560 7607, ⓦamman marriott.com; map p.87. A popular and long-standing city landmark, looming high above Shmeisani. Weighing value against quality, this is one of the best options in the luxury bracket for its unfussy comfort and intelligent service. Facilities include a health club with two swimming pools and an always lively American sports bar-cum-restaurant. A great choice if you prefer five-star character to mere opulence. Regular deals and promotions. JD180

AIRPORT

Amman Airport Hotel Queen Alia International Airport ☎06 445 1000, ⓦammanairporthotel.com. Reasonable four-star hotel, 1km from the airport terminal (by free shuttle bus), with 304 rooms. The breakfast isn't up to much, and service can be vague, but if you're arriving late or flying out early – or if you want to save the bother of tangling with urban traffic – sleeping here, 35km south of the capital, has some merit. JD125

EATING

Amman has some fine options for **eating out**. For more opinions on dining in the capital, look at the reviews and comments at ⓦbeamman.com and ⓦtasteofjordan. me. Also worth getting hold of is the "Culinary & Cultural" city map produced by local media initiative Plurality (ⓦfacebook.com/pluralityME), available at bookshops and independent stores in Rainbow, Lweibdeh and Abdoun.

Restaurants and street food There are numerous first-rate Arabic restaurants, but also places offering affordable and surprisingly good Indian, Chinese, European and other international cuisine. All the better restaurants, and virtually all the non-Arabic places, are located in uptown districts. On a tighter budget, you'll find dozens of inexpensive local restaurants, many in Downtown. There's also plenty of opportunity for cheap and tasty snacking: falafel sandwiches and bowls of *fuul* or hummus are unbeatable, and street shawarma stands are everywhere.

Cafés, patisseries and juice bars Ammanis have an incorrigible sweet tooth, which they are constantly placating with visits to the city's many patisseries, for honey-dripping pastries and cakes, or its coffee houses and cafés, for syrupy-sweet tea and coffee (and soft drinks by the crateful). Traditional coffee houses are holding their ground against the advance of western-style pavement cafés and espresso bars in Abdoun, Shmeisani and other uptown neighbourhoods (including within all the big shopping malls), where people watching is easier and women can feel more comfortable. If you fancy refreshment on the hoof, stop in at one of the juice bars dotted around the city.

Valet parking Many upmarket restaurants and cafés provide valet parking for customers. A reasonable tip, presuming that you're not left standing around waiting, is JD1.

CAFÉS

TRADITIONAL COFFEE HOUSES & STREET FOOD

Auberge Alley off Prince Muhammad St (unmarked entrance), Downtown; map p.70. One floor below the *Cliff Hotel*, this small café is uncompromisingly male and rather dour with it. However, the coffee is good and the tiny balcony is a great place to watch the street life. Also on offer are simple, low-priced Arabic meals (around JD10). Daily around 9am–midnight.

Eco-Tourism Café (Al Rasheed Courts) King Faisal St, opposite the Arab Bank, Downtown; map p.70. With a bizarrely misleading name for a perfectly ordinary locals' coffee house, this place is relaxed and foreigner-friendly, attracting a younger, hipper crowd than most. The balcony – Downtown's best – is a pleasant place to hang out and chat with local 20-somethings, many of whom migrate here from uptown West Amman for an after dark *argileh* (roughly JD2–4) in the kind of traditional surroundings Abdoun cannot muster. Daily around 9am–midnight.

★ **Habibah** King Hussein St, near the corner with King Faisal St, Downtown; map p.70. The best patisserie in the city, if not the country, piled high with every conceivable kind of sweetmeat, pastry and biscuit, all very affordable. Their shop sign is in Arabic only, but it's unmissably big, with a symmetrical blue-on-white logo; there's a café upstairs for eat-ins. Smaller pop-in branches are dotted around the city, including very nearby – just off King Faisal St beside the Arab Bank, where fresh, hot *kunafeh* (a Palestinian dessert) is served continuously, for a few JDs per plate, depending on size. Daily 8am–late.

★ **Kafeteria Al Kuds (Jerusalem)** Rainbow St, Jabal Amman; map p.81. Not to be confused with the Downtown *Al Quds* restaurant, this tiny hole-in-the-wall joint, near the British Council, serves what many claim to be the best falafel in Amman. Catch them when the falafel is fresh-fried and crispy hot, and you'll never look back (from under JD1). Daily around noon–9pm or later.

★ **Reem** 2nd Circle; map p.81. A hole-in-the-wall pavement stand, famous for serving Amman's most flavourful and succulent *shawarma*, bar none, for under JD1. At lunchtime, early evening and around midnight, this little place is single-handedly responsible for slowing the traffic around 2nd Circle – cars, limos and taxis triple-park as drivers head over from around the city to collect family-sized orders. Daily 11am–late.

KING ABDULLAH MOSQUE

1

Sultan An-Nahda St, Shmeisani; map p.87. Huge, popular pavement-side café in the middle of Shmeisani (one of several on this main drag), with a big terrace to watch the people and traffic stream by. Hole up with a tea, coffee or soft drink (JD1–2) – but after a while, especially if it's busy, the waiters may ask you to order again or move. Daily 10am–late.

CONTEMPORARY CAFÉS

B@C in Abdoun 10 Omar bin Ikrimah St, off Fawzi Qawuqji St, Abdoun ☎06 592 3036, ⍟facebook.com/bacinabdoun; map p.64. An addition to the *Books@Cafe* family, with a similarly upmarket style – a combination of bookshop and friendly espresso bar-cum-café, selling gourmet coffee and healthy meals (think omelettes, salads, soups and the like, for JD4–11 or so). No alcohol. Daily 9am–11.30pm.

★ **Bakdash (or Bekdash)** 256 Medina St (Madina Al Munawwara St) ☎079 555 7371, ⍟bit.ly/Bakdash; map p.64. The legendary *Bakdash* ice cream parlour opened in Damascus's Hamidiye souk in 1895, and is reportedly still doing business there, amid the war. In 2013, this branch opened, alongside many other hugely popular Syrian eating establishments on Medina St. It's worth making the trip out here for a cup (JD2) of what is universally acclaimed as the Middle East's best ice cream – pounded by hand with mastic, which gives it a unique elasticity, scented with rosewater and rolled in pistachio nuts. There's another branch on Wakalat St in Sweifiyyeh, and on King Ghazi St in Downtown. The rival *Bekdash* outlet in Sweifiyyeh's Galleria Mall is an impostor. Sat–Thurs 10am–1am, Fri 2pm–2am.

★ **Books@Café** 12 Omar bin al-Khattab St (Mango St), off Rainbow St, Jabal Amman ☎06 465 0457, ⍟booksatcafe.com; map p.70. When it opened in 1997 this was Jordan's first-ever internet café – combining a bookshop with a café-bar and the novelty of online access. The fact that, all these years later, it's still at the cutting edge of the city's social scene is testament to how perfectly it – and its owner, the irrepressible Madian Al Jazerah – hit the spot back then (and clung on tight). The decor is wild, flowery and ultra-retro, the ambience always light and the coffee top-notch. Hang out during the day with a smoothie and a salad, or tuck into burgers, *calzone*, wraps and lighter bites (around JD6–14) – then prepare for a night of cocktails and mellow beats. Wonderful terrace views. Daily 9am–1am.

Caffè Strada 15 Mohammed Rashid Ridha St, off Rainbow St, Jabal Amman ☎06 461 0017, ⍟cstrada.com; map p.81. Of Rainbow St's many smart, designer-style tea-bar-cum-espresso cafés, this one is the tops – coffee to die for (and baristas who know how to handle it), a wide choice of teas, appealing decor of brick and pine, good food, decent prices (from JD2)… It's all there. And it's smoke-free, too. Daily 7am–11pm.

Darat Al Funun 13 Nadim Al Mallah St, Jabal Al Lweibdeh ☎06 464 4131; map p.70. This gallery complex and arts centre has what must be the quietest, most attractive little open-air café in Amman, hidden among shady gardens, with a beautiful open-air terrace. There aren't many places in the city centre where the loudest noise is birdsong. From JD2. Daily except Fri 10am–6pm.

Duinde (Salam Kanaan Gallery) 67 Rainbow St, Jabal Amman ☎06 465 9459, ⍟salamkanaan.com; map p.70. Beautiful, atmospheric little corner café in this strollable neighbourhood, with an eclectic array of shabby-chic furniture, works by local artist Salam Kanaan and found objects creating a seductively laidback ambience. Snacks and light bites start at a couple of JDs. Daily noon–midnight.

★ **Fann wa Chai** 25 Kulliat Al Sharea St, Jabal Al Lweibdeh ☎079 808 2004, ⍟fannwachai.com; map p.81. Cool and cosy café in a quiet part of town, with a relaxed ambience and a pleasant outdoor terrace. There's art on the walls (the name means 'art and tea'), books to dip into and plants dotted about, and as well as serving sandwiches and salads (JD2–6) along with teas and coffees, they also hold talks and music events. It's a justifiably popular spot. Daily 9am–midnight.

Jungle Fever At National Gallery of Fine Art, Jabal Al Lweibdeh ☎079 570 0220, ⍟facebook.com/jfcoffee andteahouse; map p.87. Cheerful, colourful café on the top floor of the gallery, with a terrace overlooking the little park and sculpture garden in one direction and the mosque and church in the other – hole up for juices, smoothies, coffee (JD2–4) or choose from a long list of teas, served hot or cold (JD3–4). Sat–Thurs 9.30am–11pm, Fri noon–11pm.

Montage Royal Film Commission, 5 Omar bin al-Khattab (Mango St), Jabal Amman ☎06 461 3296, ⍟facebook.com/montagejo; map p.70. Pleasant contemporary styled café, good for espresso and light snacks (cheese toastie JD1.75) that spreads over the side terrace of the old villa housing the Royal Film Commission – perfect for relaxing with a book from the on-site film library, while taking in views over the Downtown rooftops. Often stages music or cultural events; watch out for the summer season of open-air screenings. Daily 9am–11pm.

★ **Rumi** 14 Shari'a College St, Jabal Al Lweibdeh ☎06 464 4131, ⍟facebook.com/rumicafejo; map p.81. Friendly little corner café in this charming area, perfect for espresso, lattes, an intriguing variety of teas, cakes and light bites, with soy milk options and atmospheric oriental-style decor. A peaceful hideaway to hole up for an hour or two. From about JD2. Daily 7am–11.30pm.

★ **Shams El Balad** 69 Muath bin Jabal St, Jabal Amman ☎06 465 1150, ⍟facebook.com/shamselbaladcafe; map p.81. Lovely, sunny contemporary-styled café in an old house on the hilly lanes below Rainbow St, done up with simple wooden furniture and typewriters hanging on the walls. Local produce is on offer, such as breads, cheeses and oils, accompanied by good coffee, all of which can be enjoyed on a shaded open-air terrace. Indoors is smoke-free. Light bites from around JD3–5. Daily 9am–11pm.

★ **Turtle Green** 46 Rainbow St, Jabal Amman ☎ 079 554 0601, ⓦ facebook.com/turtlegreentbar; map p.81. Wonderfully relaxed and unpretentious little neighbourhood nook, serving organic teas, good coffee and light snacks (around JD2–8) to a laptop-gazing, phone-tapping clientele. Makes for a perfect pit stop halfway along Rainbow St. Sun–Thurs & Sat 8am–11pm, Fri 10am–11pm.

ARABIC

★ **Abu Jbara** 46 Al Buhturi St, behind 2nd Circle; map p.81. This little local chain is legendary in Amman for its hummus in particular. This cheery branch, on a lively little street of local restaurants, bakeries, clothes shops and pharmacies, has been known to cause its own traffic jams, as Ammanis rush to get bags of takeaway hummus, *fuul* and falafel. Copy them – or eat in; either way, a meal is a few dinars. Branches around the city, including a hugely popular 24hr outlet on Medina St (Madina Al Munawwara St). Daily 6am–midnight.

Abu Mahjoub Shari'a College St, Jabal Al Lweibdeh; map p.81. Much-loved little restaurant in this charming, old-fashioned neighbourhood. Founded in 1961 – and still run by the same family – it offers what aficionados claim is some of the best hummus and falafel in the city. You'd be hard pressed to spend more than a couple of dinars. Sat–Thurs 7.30am–7pm, Fri 11am–7pm.

Bourj Al Hamam InterContinental Hotel, between 2nd & 3rd Circles ☎ 06 464 1361; map p.81. Exquisite Lebanese cuisine in an elegant hotel restaurant, serving all the classic meze dishes with style and pinpoint authenticity. Generally packed nightly: this is a classy dining spot for businesspeople and the city's elite. Expect at least JD25 a head. Daily noon–midnight.

★ **Fakhr el-Din** 40 Taha Hussein St, behind Iraqi Embassy, between 1st & 2nd Circles ☎ 06 465 2399, ⓦ fakhreldin.com; map p.81. One of Jordan's best restaurants, catering to the royal and diplomatic upper crust and housed in a tastefully renovated 1920s villa. The food – formal Lebanese cuisine with a Syrian twist – is as impeccable as the service, yet judicious choices can keep the bill around JD20 a head – not, however, if you indulge in the highly acclaimed, but expensive, raw meat platter. Unusually for an Arabic restaurant, dessert is worth leaving space for: both the *osmaliyyeh* (crispy shredded pastry over fresh cream, doused in syrup) and *muhallabiyyeh* (rose-scented almond cream pudding) are exquisite. Reservations essential, especially in summer for outdoor dining amid lemon trees. Daily 1–4.30pm & 7–11.30pm.

Haret Jdoudna Madaba. Superb Arabic restaurant, worth the 30km trip to Madaba (see page 220).

★ **Hashem** Off Prince Muhammad St, Downtown; map p.70. A fast-paced diner and an Amman institution, founded by restaurateur Hashem Al Turk in the 1920s. There are just two dishes to choose from – *fuul* or hummus. Ask for *fuul* and you'll get the standard Jordanian version, but there are plenty of tasty, fresh variations; *fuul masri* is Egyptian-style, without the chilli but with a dollop of *tahini*, while *qudsiyyeh* is Jerusalem-style – *fuul* with a blob of hummus in it. Flatbread, chopped onion and a sprig of mint are free (the restaurant gets through a staggering 50kg of onions a day). The stand opposite sells bags of cheap falafel balls as a side dish, and tea waiters periodically stride around shouting *shy, shebab?* (tea anyone?) – grab a glass off the tray. You can eat well for JD2–3. Almost all the waiters are Egyptian, earning a shade above the minimum wage; tips are optional. Daily 24hr.

★ **Jafra** Prince Muhammad St, Downtown ☎ 06 462 2551; map p.70. Wonderful upper-floor café-restaurant and hangout, a step from the Downtown bustle but with an enticing, easygoing atmosphere all its own. The main room is huge, invariably dim and misty from *argileh* smoke, the tiled floor packed with wooden tables, low stools and old sofas. Plaintive Arabic classics croon through the hubbub. Find a nook in among the vintage bric-a-brac and old photos on the wall to sample sweet tea, thick coffee or straightforward meze and light bites:

SECONDHAND SMOKE

It's very difficult to avoid **secondhand smoke** wherever you go in Amman: cigarette smoke and more fragrant postprandial *argileh* smoke are both very common, with acrid cigar smoke an occasional hazard in the five-star hotel restaurants. To avoid it, try eating earlier than is usual – lunch at 12.30pm, say, or dinner at 7.30pm – and thereby leaving before the place fills up. Nonetheless, you may still find people around you lighting up before, during and after the meal, oblivious to diners at neighbouring tables. When reserving, mention clearly that you'd like to be seated in a no-smoking area (which, if it exists, is almost always hidden away in the back somewhere) – but, depending on the restaurant's facilities and how busy it is, you should still be prepared to have to put up with fumes: smoke-free areas are simply not in high demand.

1

COOKING CLASSES AT BEIT SITTI

One of the most innovative developments in Amman's dining scene in recent years is **Beit Sitti**, a project set up by Maria Haddad and her sisters Dina and Tania in which visitors **cook their own meal** under supervision. In a spotless modern kitchen installed in a charming historic townhouse, you get to spend a couple of hours handling ingredients, learning techniques and hearing stories of culinary endeavour from chefs – generally wives and mothers with a lifetime of cooking behind them – as you prepare a three-course Arabic meal. Then, of course, you scoff your handiwork together, often on the shaded front terrace, with a gorgeous view over the Downtown rooftops. Wine is also available. It's a wonderful, insightful experience – cultural as much as culinary – that has rapidly become a hit among locals as well as visitors.

Reservations – which are essential, at least one day ahead – are very flexible: they can accommodate bookings for breakfast, lunch or dinner, at times to suit you. If you're booking as an individual or couple, they will try to slot you in with the next available group – or you can pay extra for a private session of your own.

Beit Sitti 16 Mohammad Ali Al Sadi St, Jabal Al Lweibdeh ☎077 755 7744, ⊛beitsitti.com; map p.70. Groups (minimum five people) pay from about JD30/person including apron and equipment; smaller groups pay slightly more. Roughly 2hr 30min–3hr. Booking essential.

even a gut-busting meal won't cost more than JD10 a head. Daily 9am–2am.

Levant Behind Le Royal hotel, off 3rd Circle ☎06 462 8948, ⊛levant-jo.com; map p.81. *Levant* is a favourite for its Armenian twist on the standard meze menus: try the *sujuk* (spicy sausages), Lebanese-Armenian *freekeh* (roasted green wheat) with salty cheese, and more – but remember to leave space for the dense, creamy desserts. Prices are high (JD20 a head and beyond) but the quality matches up. Daily 1pm–midnight.

Al Quds (Jerusalem) King Hussein St, Downtown; map p.70. The best restaurant in Downtown (which isn't saying much), serving a range of rather overcooked Arabic specialities, including the celebrated bedouin speciality *mansaf* (lamb with rice). Prices are reasonable – a full meal needn't set you back more than JD5 or so – but the menu is in Arabic only and the grumpy waiters won't stop to chat. Daily 7am–11pm.

Reem Al Bawadi Just off Duwaar Al Waha (junction of Medina St & Gardens St), Tla'a Al Ali ☎06 551 5419; map p.64. Delightfully over-the-top affair, complete with tent, fake castle, fountains, palm trees and neon lights. The menu is in Arabic only, but the waiters are happy to translate – they're used to foreigners. Few restaurants offer such untrammelled good service – formal but not stiff, warm yet discreet. Come as much for the old-school atmosphere, and to take a leisurely three or four hours over lunch or dinner in a comfortable, unhurried setting. From JD15/head. Families welcome. No alcohol. Daily 11am–midnight.

Rosa Damascena 2nd Circle ☎06 461 0010; map p.81. Wonderful Syrian restaurant in a convenient, easy-to-find location. Stylish, contemporary decor (wood furniture, tiled floors) is offset by a charming informality –

and superb food, including lamb stews and perfect kubbeh, as well as delectable ghazl al banat, a lacy dessert of spun sugar. Prices are moderate, around JD15–20 a head. Daily 8am–midnight.

★ **Sufra** 28 Rainbow St, Jabal Amman ☎06 461 1468, ⊛facebook.com/sufrarestaurant; map p.70. Wonderful restaurant on Amman's most happening street, in an old house – once home to an Armenian family – that's been updated in tasteful shabby-chic style, with colourful patterned tile floors and chandeliers. As well as the usual Lebanese meze, expect to see a host of Jordanian, Palestinian and bedouin specialities, from the feast dish *mansaf* to *magloobeh* (meat and aubergine with rice), *sayadiyyeh* (fish with onions and almonds) and *musakhan* (spiced chicken with pine nuts), plus plenty of other more obscure options. It's not cheap – expect to pay JD20 or more – but quality of food, service and ambience is tip-top. Don't miss it. Sun–Thurs 1–11.30pm, Fri & Sat 9.30am–11.30pm.

★ **Tannoureen** Shatt Al Arab St, Umm Uthayna ☎06 551 5987, ⊛tannoureen.co; map p.64. This is probably the best Arabic restaurant in Jordan – award-winning Lebanese cuisine of the highest quality in a grand, elegant setting. Hardened restaurant critics declare the meze here to be "out of this world" – the only difficulty is choosing from the long list of options, both hot and cold. Try to leave space for a main course: the *shish tawook* is exquisite, and the kebabs and mixed grill perfectly tender and flavour-rich. Desserts are spectacular, but not many diners make it that far. The courteous service is unusually warm and understated, as is the decor, which includes many paintings of old Jordanian and Palestinian villages. All in all, quite an experience. From JD25 a head. Booking essential. Daily 1–5pm & 7pm–midnight.

★ **Zuwwadeh** Hijaz St, Dabouq, just beyond the Baccalaureate School, 3.5km west of King Hussein Park ☎ 079 560 2858, ⓦ facebook.com/zuwwadeh; map p.64. This excellent and reasonably priced Lebanese restaurant – for twenty years a fixture in the lanes of Fuheis village, now in the suburb of Dabouq – remains a favourite informal out-of-town dining spot; at weekends in particular the place is crowded with families and groups of friends. The kebabs and *fatteh* (JD6–9) are superb, but you could choose from their inventive list of meze (JD2–6) and still dine lavishly for JD15 or so. There's nightly live music from an accomplished *oud* player. One speciality of the house is an alcoholic *argileh* (JD8) – instead of water in the bubble chamber, the management substitute *araq*. Book ahead, at weekends especially. Daily 10am–1am.

ASIAN

Indu InterContinental Hotel, between 2nd & 3rd Circles ☎ 06 464 1361, ⓦ facebook.com/induamman; map p.81. Expensive but spectacularly good Indian food, served in a subtle, sophisticated dining area away from the bustle of the hotel's lobby cafés and restaurants. Tandoori is a speciality, and there are plenty of options for vegetarians. Look out for the changing menus of regional Indian dishes. From JD20 a head. Daily 1–4pm & 7–11.30pm.

Noodasia Abdoun Circle ☎ 06 593 6999, ⓦ facebook.com/noodasiajo; map p.81. Lively Asian restaurant in the heart of Abdoun. Decor is chic and contemporary (think dark wood and polished chrome), and the food delicious: the spring rolls are perhaps the best in Amman, pad thai or Szechuan beef are popular staples and the sushi is outstanding. Presentation is immaculate, service efficient. Lunch specials start from JD8, with regular buffet nights at a bargain JD16–22. Daily noon–3.30pm & 7–11.30pm.

★ **Ren Chai** Off 4th Circle ☎ 06 462 5777, ⓦ renchai.com; map p.81. Amman's leading Chinese restaurant, offering a swanky, super-cool fine-dining experience, whether on the open terrace or in the sleek designer interior. Dim sum, soups and sizzling mains are all authentically prepared, while delicacies including abalone and lobster fill out a long, varied menu. From JD25 a head. Daily 12.30–11.30pm.

EUROPEAN AND NORTH AMERICAN

Blue Fig Prince Hashem St, Abdoun ☎ 06 592 8800, ⓦ bluefig.com; map p.64. Designed by one of Jordan's top architects, this casual café/bar and restaurant draws in a sleek, chic crowd. The ambience is cool and sophisticated, with world music and fusion beats booming out. The walls display works by local artists, and there are regular live music sessions. Booking essential on Thurs nights and Fri (especially for breakfast/brunch, from around JD10). Branches around town. Daily 8.30am–1am.

Bonita 1 Qiss bin Saedah St, near 3rd Circle ☎ 06 461 5061, ⓦ bonitaamman.com; map p.81. The best Spanish restaurant in town, known for its paella (one of which is vegetarian) at around JD20 for two, and also serving "international" cuisine: go for pasta or steak (JD7–15). Alongside is a tapas bar with Mexican beer, dozens of cheap nibbles and some live bands. Daily: restaurant 12.30pm–midnight; bar 6pm–midnight.

Cantaloupe Rainbow St, Jabal Amman ☎ 077 773 3333, ⓦ cantaloupe.jo; map p.70. This self-styled "gastropub" doubles as one of Amman's chic-est lounge-restaurants. Cool, dark, jazzy and stylish – think black leather sofas and minimalist lines – it resides at the top of a building on Rainbow St's lower end: panoramic views from the wraparound windows (and outside terrace in summer) encompass most of the Downtown area – breathtaking at night. Starters of tempura, wings, skins and bresaola (JD7–12) are followed by salads, pasta, Norwegian salmon, chargrilled king prawns (JD7–18) and steaks (JD30). Despite the pretension, service is friendly and down-to-earth: this is a quality spot. Daily 5pm–1am.

★ **Joz Hind** 8 Shari'a College St, Jabal Al Lweibdeh ☎ 077 933 4783, ⓦ bit.ly/jozhind; map p.81. Much-loved neighbourhood restaurant steps from Paris Circle in relaxed, independent-spirited Jabal Al Lweibdeh. The name is a play on words: *joz hind* is coconut in Arabic, but it also means "Hind's husband" – Hind will probably say hi when you arrive, and her cheery Italian husband Luca does the cooking. The filling and healthy food is all freshly prepared with local organic produce, listed on a board (and Facebook) each morning – soups and salads to start (JD4), then usually a choice of three mains (JD6–8): pasta, meat or something veggie – and served on funky glazed crockery, with drinks in jam jars or tin mugs. Seating is limited: be prepared to share space. Sat, Sun, Tues & Thurs noon–4pm, Mon & Wed noon–8.30pm.

Le Container 129 Arar St (Wadi Saqra) ☎ 079 679 6000, ⓦ facebook.com/lecontaineramman; map p.81. Launched in late 2018 as Amman's first osteria, or traditional rustic Italian restaurant, this place shares space with the Winemaker outlet for local Saint George wines alongside. Details are sketchy at the time of writing, but expect high-quality imported deli items – hams, salami, foie gras, and the like – alongside a gastronome's selection of salads, steaks, pasta, seafood and burgers (JD7–20), washed down with St George vintages from next door's stock. Sporadic hours: call to check.

★ **Pizza Reef & Pizza Rimini** Reef: 244 Medina St, Tla'a Al Ali ☎ 06 568 7087; Rimini: 35 Azab St ☎ 06 568 6324; map p.64. The chefs at *Pizza Reef* make some of the best pizza in the city – thin-crust, wood-fired fresh to order and inexpensive (around JD7 for two people). They can make up anything you fancy, with or without meat

1

or cheese – their unique *labneh*-and-rocket offering with extra rosemary is delectable. Nearby sister outlet *Pizza Rimini* (coming up Gardens St, turn right before Duwaar Al Waha and continue 100m) does all the same stuff as well as takeaways. Reef: Mon–Sat noon–1am; Rimini: daily except Tues noon–1am.

Romero 3 Mohammed Hussein Haykal St, off 3rd Circle, opposite InterContinental Hotel ☎06 464 4227, ⊕romerogroup.jo; map p.81. Splendid Italian restaurant – an Amman institution that has been around since 1979, updated with style and elegance. The pastas, risottos and meaty mains are spot on, and there's a long wine list. Service is uniquely calm and friendly, and the food outstanding. Expect a bill north of JD25 a head. Daily 1–11.30pm.

Vinaigrette Al Qasr Metropole Hotel, Shmeisani ☎06 566 6140, ⊕facebook.com/vinaigrettejo; map p.87. Bar-cum-restaurant perched on the top (seventh) floor atop one of the highest hills in Amman – the view from the floor-to-ceiling windows all round is fantastic. Contemporary styled, with decor in bamboo and untreated wood, a relaxed vibe and accompanying jazzy beats. The food covers familiar Mediterranean-cum-international ground with a fishy edge, from calamari salad and smoked salmon blinis to mussels and sushi (via frog's legs and veal). A meal will cost JD20, maybe more if you push the boat out. Book for a window table. Daily noon–midnight.

★ **Wild Jordan** 36 Othman bin Affan St, off Rainbow St, Jabal Amman ☎06 463 3542, ⊕wildjordancenter. com; map p.70. Landmark organic café/restaurant within the Royal Society for the Conservation of Nature's (RSCN) Wild Jordan Center, with a stunning view over Downtown from the balcony. Prices are high, but that's because the food is mostly organic, with many ingredients grown locally on the RSCN nature reserves around Jordan. Examples include spinach and mushroom salad with hazelnut and lime dressing, smoked salmon on wild rocket, lean steak sandwich and wholewheat spaghetti with light pesto (all around JD11). The smoothies are sensational – and don't miss the thirst-quenching frozen lemonade with fresh mint. Smoke-free throughout. Daily 9am–11pm.

DRINKING AND NIGHTLIFE

Amman has a wide range of **bars**, from swish upmarket hotel pubs to dingy dives in back alleys. All those in Downtown Amman – of which the *Jordan Bar*, behind the *Cliff Hotel*, is typical – are fairly seedy hangouts devoted to sedentary drinking, with no attraction other than the alcohol. Uptown neighbourhoods in West Amman offer a classier ambience along with ear-blasting sound systems and small dance floors (Thurs is the big night out), and during the summer months many of the big hotels host swanky open-air rooftop lounge bars. Many of the places we describe as "cafés" – such as *Blue Fig* and *Books@Café* – double up as bars; treat these reviews below as additions to them.

Abou El Abed Al Hakawati Just off Rainbow St, Jabal Amman ☎06 463 4567, ⊕facebook.com/elhakawaty; map p.81. This Beirut-style café-restaurant (closed for renovation at the time of writing, but due to reopen by the time you read this) fills a fine old house dating from 1927. Come to eat – the Lebanese menu is great (from JD10) – but this also counts as a relaxed, easygoing bar venue on the upper level, where a broad column-free space has been opened up for expansive night-time views while big screens play sport or music videos and beers go down. Daily 10am–1am.

★ **Corner's Pub** 12 Ibrahim Al Muwaylehi St, Jabal Amman ☎077 775 5166, ⊕facebook.com/thecorners pub; map p.81. Popular little nightspot on a corner behind 2nd Circle, often packed with a youngish crowd enjoying drinks and live bands. Cheerful, unpretentious and very local. Daily noon–1am.

Cube Shepherd Hotel, Zaid bin Haritha St, behind 2nd Circle ☎079 985 5955, ⊕facebook.com/cubeamman; map p.81. Popular, long-running bar and club, with a lively crowd dancing to local and international DJs and a legendary Wednesday 80s night. Door policy can be strict. Tues–Fri 9pm–3am.

★ **Ghoroub** Landmark Hotel, Shmeisani ☎079 833 1313, ⊕facebook.com/ghoroubsunsetlounge; map p.87. This funky, upscale Moroccan-styled lounge resides on the thirteenth floor of this five-star hotel, offering spectacular views across the city – a deeply atmospheric place to hole up for cocktails (JD9–10), also with a decent bar menu (JD4–13). Daily 6pm–1am.

Living Room/The Loft 3 Mohammed Hussein Haykal St, off 3rd Circle, opposite InterContinental Hotel ☎06 465 5998, ⊕romerogroup.jo; map p.81. Cosy haven above the classy *Romero* restaurant: climb the stairs to enter a classy, wood-panelled bar, lounge and dining area, where you can relax with a beer or tuck into familiar favourites such as steak, ribs, salads and sushi. Happy hour offers (1–7pm) include sushi platters (JD10–12) and beers from JD3.50. Upstairs again is *The Loft*, a jazzy open-air rooftop bar. Daily 1pm–1am.

Nub Al Qasr Metropole Hotel, Shmeisani ☎06 566 6140, ⊕facebook.com/thenubjo; map p.87. Cosy basement pub-restaurant. Eat if you like (the menu covers salads and gourmet burgers; JD4–12) or savour a beer (including local Carakale for JD6) and a range of whiskies from around the world (JD5–9 for a glass). Daily noon–1am.

Sekrab Off Rainbow St beside Jabal Amman hotel ☎079 173 5722, ⊕facebook.com/sekrabjo; map p.70. Colourful bar filled with upcycled junk – also with

"SOUK JARA" STREET MARKET

In the summer months, don't miss **Souk Jara** (mid-May to mid-Sept every Fri 10am–10pm; ⓦ facebook.com/soukjara), a popular, easygoing flea market of antiques, crafts, T-shirts and other streetwear, art and food, established by JARA (the Jabal Amman Residents' Association). It's held on Fawzi Malouf Street, off the lower end of Rainbow Street, and often includes impromptu concerts, film screenings and other activities.

a very cool rooftop terrace, open in summer – that focuses on cocktails (from JD4), runs regular happy hours and stages music and DJ events (usually around JD10 admission, including a drink). Also serves bar food (burgers, pasta, nachos etc: JD7–11). Daily 5pm–1am.

SHOPPING

A great way to experience Jordanian culture is by going **shopping** – and can bring you closer than almost any other activity to understanding what makes Amman tick. An excellent way to spend your first morning in the city would be to set yourself a modest shopping goal: a domed alarm clock that sounds the call to prayer, for instance, or a set of decorative Islamic prayer beads. Head out with a few dinars and roam the Downtown shopping streets till you have what you want: the item may be worth little, but the process of finding it and buying it will be a memorable experience.

WHERE TO SHOP

Downtown King Talal St, in Downtown, is lined with shops selling household goods where you could browse for interesting everyday items; good buys include a Turkish coffee service (a tiny pot for boiling the grounds plus six handleless cups on a tray) or an *argileh*, often steel but occasionally brass (check the joints carefully for leaks). There are many outlets near the Husseini Mosque where you could pick up a simple but attractive cotton-polyester *jellabiyyeh* (full-length robe) for less than JD10, or a *keffiyeh* (chequered or plain headcloth) for around JD2.50. And some food items, such as a box of succulent dates or a kilo of fresh-roasted coffee ground with cardamom, can make great souvenirs.

West Amman Other fascinating areas for window shopping (and people watching) include Sweifiyyeh (the grid of streets to the southwest of 6th Circle) – packed with all kinds of shops from designer boutiques and jewellery shops to groceries and cafés (and the chic Al Baraka Mall): one innovation here is pedestrianized Wakalat St, with upmarket fashion and pavement cafés. Abdali's Boulevard is in similar style. Rainbow St and the lanes off Paris Circle in Jabal Al Lweibdeh hold small, independent shops for crafts, quirky street fashions and more.

SHOPPING MALLS

Amman's shopping malls can be great to explore – less glitzy than Dubai's, not as bland as those in Europe, and often buzzing with people browsing or hanging out. Two of the biggest are Mecca Mall and City Mall, though there are many more. Spread over multiple floors, these behemoths – with abundant parking – take in literally hundreds of shops, dozens of cafés and restaurants, cinemas and other entertainment, kids' zones and more. Don't spurn malls as some kind of foreign import: many ordinary Ammanis shop here, and they represent, in their own way, as much an authentic expression of modern Jordanian culture as the Downtown bazaars.

CRAFT AND DESIGN

Compared to Cairo, Jerusalem, Damascus and Aleppo, which all have – or, sadly, had – centuries-old souks and long traditions of craftsmanship, Amman is a modern lightweight, with no memorable bazaars to explore. Where the city scores is in its range of bedouin crafts from Jordan and Palestine at prices a fraction of Jerusalem's, and some amazingly inexpensive gold (see page 107). There's only a handful of genuine craft shops in Amman, several located around 2nd Circle, and they tend to be associated with projects to revive or nurture the skills of local artisans; prices are legitimately high and you're purchasing quality goods. Souvenir shops which are simply retail outlets for local or imported merchandise are more numerous, with prices that don't necessarily relate to quality.

Al Afghani Talal St, Downtown ☎ 079 558 8144, ⓦ facebook.com/alafghanim; map p.70. Amman's oldest and most famous souvenir business, *Al Afghani* was founded in Hejaz in 1862 and Palestine in 1870, and moved to Jordan after 1948. Still in the same family, they now have a number of branches around town. The Downtown shop opposite the Husseini Mosque is a wonderful little Aladdin's cave, crammed to the ceiling with everything from Bohemian glass to ornate Cairene Ramadan lamps. Serious browsing is better undertaken at the bigger, friendlier branches at Jabal Al Lweibdeh (just off Paris Sq), Gardens St or Mecca Mall. Sun–Thurs & Sat 10am–10pm, Fri 2–10pm.

★ **Al Aydi (Jordan Craft Development Centre)** 1 Talat Harb St, 2nd Circle ☎ 06 464 4555, ⓦ jordancraftcenter.

com; map p.81. Best place to buy locally produced handmade crafts, located on a signed backstreet behind the *InterContinental Hotel*. Staff work as advisers and design consultants to about a hundred local craftspeople – mostly rural women – who share in the shop's profits. There's a huge variety of pieces, from olive-wood carving to mother-of-pearl, hand-blown glassware, textiles (including lovely hand- and machine-embroidered jackets and dresses), jewellery, ceramics, baskets and more, both old and new. It also stocks a huge collection of carpets – Jordanian, Iraqi and Kurdish – ranging from antique pieces to newly mades. Daily except Fri 9am–6pm.

★ **Balian** 8 Rainbow St, Jabal Amman ☎ 06 462 3399, ⓦ armenianceramics.com; map p.70. Master ceramicist Neshan Balian arrived in Jerusalem in 1917 from Turkey. His family followed, and in 1922 they opened a workshop to produce beautiful, distinctive hand-painted Armenian tiles. Generations on, Balian remains one of the best-known businesses in Jerusalem, now with an outlet in Beirut and a shop and workshop in Amman. This wonderful little place, at the downhill end of Rainbow St, serves as an outlet for Balian's distinctive style, with pieces from individual tiles to complete room decorations. Daily except Fri 9am–6pm.

Bawabet al-Sharq 25 Rainbow St, Jabal Amman ☎ 06 463 7424, ⓦ facebook.com/bawabetalsharq; map p.70. Store for handmade textiles and embroidery commissioned by shop owner Randa Qubti from local women's cooperatives around the country. Sun–Thurs 10am–7pm, Fri 1–7pm.

Beit Al Bawadi 238 Arar St (Wadi Saqra) ☎ 06 560 4920, ⓦ beitalbawadi.com; map p.87. Swanky showroom-style outlet for high-quality ceramics in contemporary Islamic designs from the nonprofit JOHUD (Jordanian Hashemite Fund for Human Development). Daily except Fri 8am–6pm.

Chamber Gyld 19 Nahr Dyala St, Abdoun ☎ 077 770 3330, ⓦ chambergyld.com; map p.64. This seriously upmarket concept store stocks anything from handmade jewellery and fashion accessories to home furnishings – all unique pieces made by local designers. A major reason to visit is because this is one of the few stockists of T-shirts, tote bags and crafts by The Orenda Tribe (ⓦ theorendatribe.com), a Jordanian initiative working with refugee children and marginalized communities on "Art For Hope" educational projects. Buy their stuff – they do good work (T-shirts from JD20). Daily except Fri 10am–8pm.

Gold Souk King Faisal St, Downtown; map p.70. This network of alleys off the north side of the main street in Downtown Amman has dozens of tiny shops, selling modern gold jewellery (see page 78) at highly competitive prices. Daily except Fri 10am–11pm.

★ **Jo Bedu** 10 Baouniyyeh St, Jabal Al Lweibdeh ☎ 06 461 8144, ⓦ jobedu.com; map p.81. Quirky, hugely successful independent business selling T-shirts and street fashion items printed with witty designs and logos sourced from Jordanian artists and designers – anything from "Mind the camel" road signs to hip-hop imagery and ironic Arabic wordplays tapping into urban pop culture, in thousands of designs and every size from babywear to XXXL. Stylish, unique and more joyously Ammani than all the gewgaws in all the souvenir shops put together. Also at 5 Hisham Hijjawi St in Abdoun. Sun–Thurs & Sat 10am–10pm, Fri noon–10pm.

Jordan River Designs Rainbow St, 1st Circle ☎ 06 461 3081, ⓦ jordanriver.jo; map p.70. A project originally set up by Save The Children, selling simple, bright and pricey handmade home furnishings from a lovely old 1920s-era villa at the lower end of Rainbow St. In the same courtyard is an outlet for superb carpets woven by women of the Bani Hamida tribe, where you can pick up a small wall hanging for JD30 and reasonably sized rugs from around JD70. Sat–Thurs 9am–7pm, Fri 10am–7pm.

Love On A Bike 23 Dhi Qar St, off Wadi Saqra ☎ 079 643 3311, ⓦ loveonabike.com; map p.81. Quirky and much-loved little studio and shop selling all kinds of colourful bits and bobs – from textiles to artworks – designed by artist Rima Malallah. Call ahead before making a visit. Variable hours, usually: daily except Fri noon–6pm.

★ **Mlabbas** 28 Rainbow St, Jabal Amman ☎ 06 464 6473, ⓦ mlabbas.com; map p.70. Best of Rainbow St's crop of independent design shops, with clothing and accessories from mugs to smartphone cases designed in witty style by local artists and illustrators, alongside books and art. Also has a kiosk outlet in Taj Mall, Abdoun. Daily 9.30am–11pm.

★ **Nadia Dajani** InterContinental Hotel forecourt, between 2nd & 3rd Circles ☎ 06 461 2272, ⓦ nadia dajani.com; map p.81. Showroom and main outlet store for this Jordanian designer's superb jewellery. Her work – produced at a workshop employing women from low-income areas of Amman – stands out for its focus on Jordanian themes, with styles evoking Roman jewellery from Jerash, Nabatean designs from Petra, folkloric charms and amulets, natural themes from Dana, and more. Everything is unique, gorgeously designed and handcrafted to the highest standards. Sun–Thurs & Sat 10am–9pm, Fri noon–7pm.

★ **Ola's Garden** 60 Khirfan St, 1st Circle ☎ 079 539 0136, ⓦ facebook.com/ola.garden; map p.70. A short walk along the street at the lower end of Rainbow St, this tiny shop sells paintings, mosaics, jewellery, home furnishings and clothes created by designer Ola Mubaslat. Her designs feature natural and organic forms; browsing is a pleasure and Ola deserves a much higher profile than she has. Daily except Tues 11am–6.30pm.

BUYING GOLD

Prices for gold jewellery in Amman are some of the lowest in the world. Not only is there a constant, massive demand in Jordan for gold, used in marriage dowries, but workmanship on gold jewellery is charged by weight here – which turns out to be very economical by world standards. The upshot is that it's well nigh impossible to find the same quality of work or purity of gold outside Jordan for less than three or four times the Amman price. In the Downtown Gold Souk, you can be paying a measly few dinars per gram for finished pieces in **21-carat gold** (which is very popular, partly because its orangey-yellow hue looks good against darker skin, and partly because its purity and investment value make it most desirable for dowries).

When buying, you have to know, at least sketchily, what you're looking at and what you want, and you have to be prepared to devote some hours to making a purchase. Browsing from shop to shop to get a sense of the market can be a pleasure: Jordan is mercifully free of the kind of tedious hard-sell haggling for which the Middle East is notorious. Be aware that there are no hallmarks; instead, look for a stamp indicating **gold purity** in parts per thousand: "875" indicates 21-carat, while "750" is 18-carat. When you buy, you will be given two receipts: one for the per-gram market value of the item, another for the cost of the workmanship. The honour system among gold merchants – both in the Downtown Gold Souk and elsewhere – is very strong, and means that it is very unlikely you'll be misled. Styles of jewellery vary – although everyone will happily make you up a necklace of a gold tag shaped with your name in Arabic – and, with prices as low as they are, commissioning a custom-made piece to your own design doesn't command the kind of absurd prices that the same thing in the West might do.

Silver is sold in the same way as gold, although it is much less popular and you may have to search for it; prices, though, can be absurdly low. All **jewels** or precious stones on sale in Jordan are imported.

Soap House 8 Rainbow St, Jabal Amman ☎06 463 3953, ⓦfacebook.com/trinitaejo; map p.70. Fragrant outlet up an alleyway at the less-explored lower end of Rainbow St selling a range of handmade olive-oil soaps, luxury moisturizing creams and Jordanian Dead Sea skincare products. Everything is of the highest quality, a touch pricey for everyday use, but good for gifts to remember. Daily except Fri 10am–6pm.

Urdon Shop 44 Othman bin Affan St, off Rainbow St, Jabal Amman ☎06 463 1921, ⓦurdonshop.jo; map p.70. Upmarket outlet for a wide range of heritage products sourced by the King Abdullah II Fund for Development (KAFD), including pottery, jewellery, textiles, Dead Sea cosmetics and more – everything 100 percent Jordanian. Also has a small café-restaurant on the roof, with great views. Daily 9am–11pm.

Wild Jordan Nature Shop 36 Othman bin Affan St, off Rainbow St, Jabal Amman ☎06 463 3718, ⓦwildjordancenter.com; map p.70. This "nature shop" sells designs in traditional style by Jordanian artisans, who are often rural women. These range from unusual contemporary jewellery to painted ostrich eggs and hand-woven bags, items in goat leather, handmade olive oil soap and more. Also on sale are organic herbs, dried fruits and spices. All profits are ploughed back into conservation work. Daily 10am–10pm.

The Winemaker 129 Arar St, Wadi Saqra ☎06 461 4125, ⓦfacebook.com/thewinemakeramman; map p.81. Jordan's poshest off-licence (liquor store). Zumot, under the St George brand, make some of the finest wines to come out of the Middle East, winning global awards for quality – and this elegant shop, their headquarters, is the best place to pick up a few bottles to take home. Prices start around JD10, and climb into the hundreds. Book in advance for a proper tasting session. Daily except Fri 9am–8pm.

BOOKS

Books@Café 12 Omar bin al-Khattab St (Mango St), off Rainbow St, Jabal Amman ☎06 465 0457, ⓦbooksatcafe.com; map p.70. This lovely café, like its B@C sister outlet in Abdoun, sells an eclectic range of books, especially strong on art and design but encompassing much more. Daily 9am–1am.

Good Book Shop 11 Haleem Abu Rahmeh St, off Rainbow St, Jabal Amman ☎06 461 3939, ⓦthegood bookshop.com; map p.81. Wonderful locally run shop, with armchairs, sofas, plenty to browse and great coffee. Also stages weekly book club discussions, open to all (Sat 4pm). Daily 10am–10pm.

InterContinental Hotel Between 2nd & 3rd Circles ☎06 464 1361, ⓦintercontinental.com; map p.81. Aside from newspapers, magazines and novels, the hotel's surprisingly good lobby bookshop focuses on Jordan and the Middle East – everything from travel guides and photo

1

books to politics and Islam. Daily 8am–9pm.
Readers Cozmo Mall, off 7th Circle ☎06 582 8488, ⓦ facebook.com/readersbookshop; map p.64. Airy, spacious outlet for books of all kinds in English and Arabic, with coffee on hand. Also with a branch in Taj Mall, Abdoun. Daily 10am–10pm.

DIRECTORY

Children's activities As well as the Children's Museum (see page 86), aim for the Haya Cultural Centre (☎06 566 5195, ⓦ hcc.jo) in Shmeisani – it stages plays, puppet theatre, music and activities for children, and has a small playground and café; call ahead for details. Mecca Mall, on Mecca St, has child-friendly karting and skating, as do most of the other city malls. Teenagers will love paintballing in the forests north of Amman (see ⓦ mountainbreeze.jo). There's also the Amman Waves water park, off the airport road (ⓦ ammanwaves.com) and the modest Luna Park carnival zone at King Abdullah Gardens in Shmeisani. For more ideas, go to ⓦ beamman.com.

Embassies and consulates See page 25.

Hospital The Khalidi Hospital (☎06 464 4281, ⓦ khmc.jo), near 4th Circle, is one of Jordan's best and has a 24hr emergency room.

Pharmacies Jacob's Pharmacy on 3rd Circle (daily 8.30am–midnight; ☎06 464 4945). Also pharmacies near the Khalidi Hospital.

Police The courteous English-speaking Tourist Police are on duty 24hr at the airport (☎079 019 1140), the Jabal Al Qal'a ruins (☎079 019 1272), the Roman Theatre (☎079 019 1269), Rainbow St (☎079 019 1261) and elsewhere; they take any queries or complaints seriously. Their administration (☎06 530 1465 or ☎079 019 1265, ⓦ psd.gov.jo) comes under the Public Security Directorate, which is part of the Ministry of Interior. The main Downtown

USEFUL ARABIC PLACE NAMES

Amman	عمّان	Jordan	الأردن

WITHIN AMMAN

1st Circle	الدوار الاول	JETT station	مجمع جيت
2nd Circle	الدوار الثاني	Jordan University	الجامعة الاردنية
3rd Circle	الدوار الثالث	Kan Zaman	كان زمان
4th Circle	الدوار الرابع	Mahatta station	مجمع المحطة
5th Circle	الدوار الخامس	Marka	ماركا
6th Circle	الدوار السادس	Middle East Circle	دوار الشرق الاوسط
7th Circle	الدوار السابع	Muhajireen station	مجمع المهاجرين
8th Circle	الدوار الثامن	Ras Al Ain	راس العين
Abdali	العبدلي	Sahab	سحاب
Abdoun	عبدون	Shmeisani	الشميساني
Ahl Al Kahf	اهل الكهف	Sport City	المدينة الرياضية
Downtown	وسط البلد	Sweifiyyeh	الصويفية
Hejaz train station	محطة الحجاز	Tabarboor	طبربور
Interior Circle	الدوار الداخلية	Tabarboor station	مجمع الشمال
Jabal Amman	جبل عمّان	Tla'a Al Ali	تلاع العلي
Jabal Al Ashrafiyyeh	جبل الاشرفية	Trust office	مكتب شركة الثقة
Jabal Hussein	جبل الحسين	Umm Uthayna	ام اذينة
Jabal Al Lweibdeh	جبل اللويبدة	Wihdat	الوحدات
Jabal Al Qal'a	جبل القلعة	Wihdat station	مجمع الجنوب

NEAR AMMAN

For destinations further afield in Jordan, see the end of each relevant chapter.

Baptism Site	المغطس	Queen Alia International Airport	مطار الملكة علياء الدولي
Dead Sea	البحر الميّت		
King Hussein Bridge	جسر الملك حسين	Sweileh	صويلح
		Zarqa	الزرقاء

OUTSIDE JORDAN

Beirut	بيروت	Jericho	اريحا
Cairo	القاهرة	Jerusalem	القدس
Damascus	دمشق	Nazareth	الناصرة
Dera'a	درعا	Tel Aviv	تل ابيب

police station is halfway along King Faisal St, opposite the Arab Bank; there's also a police station opposite the *InterContinental Hotel*.

Post office The main Downtown post office (daily 7am–7pm, Fri till 1pm; shorter hours in winter) is on Prince Muhammad St, but most big hotels offer more convenient postal services at a small premium. For sending valuables, you're better off using couriers such as Aramex (☎ 06 535 8855, ⓦ aramex.com), DHL (☎ 06 580 0800, ⓦ dhl.com.jo) or FedEx (☎ 06 551 1460, ⓦ fedex.com/jo).

The Dead Sea and Baptism Site

KEMPINSKI ISHTAR HOTEL

The Dead Sea and Baptism Site

2

A few kilometres west of Amman's city limits, the rugged highlands of central and northern Jordan drop away dramatically into the Dead Sea Rift. This giant valley marks a geological dividing line as well as a political one, with the Arabian plate to the east shifting a few centimetres a year northwards, and the African plate to the west moving slowly southwards. Between the two is the River Jordan, defining Jordan's western border as it flows into the large, salty inland lake of the Dead Sea, famed as the lowest point on Earth. Taking a dip here and relaxing on the beaches is an unmissable experience, not least because of the world-class luxury resort hotels ranged along the shore.

This whole area is within easy reach of the capital, and also stands within an hour or so's drive of Amman's Queen Alia International Airport: for many visitors the **Dead Sea** serves as a perfect first- or last-night stop in Jordan. There are also some fine day-trip possibilities, including up to Madaba (see page 208), Mount Nebo (see page 220) and the Ma'in hot springs (see page 225), or north to Salt (see page 170) and south to Karak (see page 230).

Aside from beaches, the area's main historical draw is the **Baptism Site** of Jesus, located on the east bank of the River Jordan about 8km north of the Dead Sea shore. The combination of archeology, the extraordinary natural environment and the momentous associations of the place makes this one of the Middle East's most important religious destinations. Continuing the biblical theme, in the barren hills overlooking the southeastern part of the Dead Sea is **Lot's Sanctuary**, built over the cave where Abraham's nephew sought refuge from the destruction of Sodom and Gomorrah.

The Dead Sea

Forming what has been called the world's biggest open-air spa, the amazing **DEAD SEA** (*al-Bahr al-Mayit* in Arabic) is a major highlight of a visit to the Middle East. Swimming in it is a memorable experience, quite unlike anything else on the planet.

The lake occupies the Great Rift Valley, a geological cleft which can be traced from Turkey all the way into East Africa. Its shoreline – at 400m below sea level – marks **the lowest point on Earth**, and, as such, is stiflingly hot for much of the year.

The Dead Sea got its name in antiquity due to its uniquely salty water, which kills off virtually all marine life: seawater is about three or four percent salt, but Dead Sea water is over thirty percent. It is fed mainly by the River Jordan, flowing south from Galilee, but due to the geological upheavals it has no outflow; instead, water evaporates off the surface at the rate of millions of litres a day, leading to continuous precipitation of salt onto the beach and a thick atmospheric haze overhead which dampens sound down to almost nothing – there's little to hear but lapping water anyway. The haze also filters out harmful UVB sunrays, handily allowing tanning but not burning (though you should still wear sun cream to protect against UVA).

Many people come for **therapeutic tourism**: Dead Sea water (and mud) have medically proven benefits, and have been known to put severe skin diseases and joint problems into long-term remission. Beneficial calcium, magnesium, bromine, sulphur and bitumen are found in extremely high concentrations, and, in addition, the air is unusually highly oxygenated. Dead Sea skin care products are a popular

Highlights

❶ **The Dead Sea** Float your day away at the lowest point on Earth. See page 112

❷ **Amman Beach** The top (non-hotel) choice for a straightforward day by the Dead Sea – a public beach with pools and recreation facilities. See page 116

❸ **Dead Sea Panorama** Viewpoint complex perched on the slopes, offering sensational views – not least at sunset. See page 117

❹ **Dead Sea Museum** Excellent displays on the ecology, geology and history of the Dead Sea. See page 117

❺ **Mujib Biosphere Reserve** Walking trails wind through spectacular canyons in this protected nature reserve on the Dead Sea shore. See page 118

❻ **Lot's Sanctuary** Well-preserved Byzantine church complex on the hills above the Dead Sea, with a fine archeological museum alongside. See page 120

❼ **Baptism Site** Pilgrimage site of world renown on the banks of the River Jordan – come to reaffirm your faith or to take in the remarkable history and dramatic natural environment. See page 122

HIGHLIGHTS ARE MARKED ON THE MAP ON PAGE 114

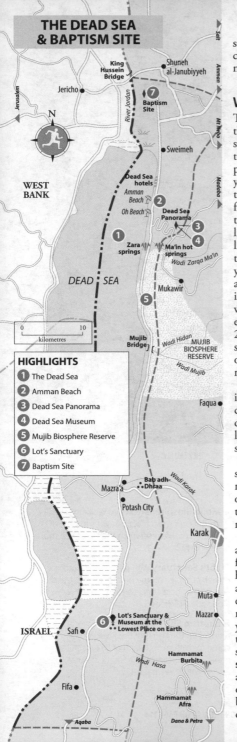

THE DEAD SEA & BAPTISM SITE

West Bank

Jerusalem

Jericho

King Hussein Bridge

Shuneh al-Janubiyyeh

Baptism Site **7**

River Jordan

N

Sweimeh

Dead Sea hotels

Amman Beach

Oh Beach **2**

Dead Sea Panorama **3**

4

1

Zara springs

Ma'in hot springs

Wadi Zarqa Ma'in

DEAD SEA

Mukawir

5

0   10
kilometres

Mujib Bridge

Wadi Hidan   MUJIB BIOSPHERE RESERVE

Wadi Mujib

Faqua

HIGHLIGHTS

1 The Dead Sea
2 Amman Beach
3 Dead Sea Panorama
4 Dead Sea Museum
5 Mujib Biosphere Reserve
6 Lot's Sanctuary
7 Baptism Site

Bab adh-Dhraa

Mazra'a

Wadi Karak

Potash City

Karak

Muta

Mazar

6 Lot's Sanctuary & Museum at the Lowest Place on Earth

ISRAEL   Safi

Hammamat Burbita

Wadi Hasa

Fifa

Hammamat Afra

Aqaba   Dana & Petra

---

souvenir. All the big hotels have medical centres, which are often booked solid for months ahead.

What to expect

The main reason to visit the Dead Sea is that the lake's high salinity makes the water so **buoyant** that it's literally impossible to sink; Olympic swimmers and hopeless paddlers alike become bobbing corks. As you walk in (bring **flip-flops**: beaches tend to be gravelly), you'll feel your feet being forced up from under you – you couldn't touch the bottom if you tried, and if you lie back you'll find the water supports you like a cradle. You ride too high in the water to swim: should you attempt a few strokes you'll probably just splash ineffectually – and may also get water in your eyes, which is a very unpleasant experience. The salty water will also make you very aware of every cut and blemish: avoid shaving for 24 hours before a dip. Nonetheless, the sensation of floating unaided and silent on a flat, hot sea surrounded by hazy mountains is worth the discomfort.

Other diversions include covering yourself in the hot, sulphurous black **mud** that collects in pools on the beach; letting it dry in the sun before washing it off will leave you with tingling muscles and baby-soft skin.

Scorching heat (well over 40°C in summer) and exceptionally low humidity make **dehydration** a danger: while you're out in the open you should be drinking twice or three times as much water as normal to compensate.

The Dead Sea is a popular spot for a weekend outing: roads, hotels and facilities can get crowded on Fridays and holidays. Bikinis and regular swimwear are fine at the private (paid) beaches, but elsewhere a T-shirt and long shorts are a minimum. One thing to bear in mind, if you're planning a dip but want to avoid the big hotels, is that you should make sure you have access to a **freshwater shower**: Dead Sea brine is thick and oily, and leaves an uncomfortable layer of salt on your skin that you'll want to wash off before dressing. Lastly, expect **flies** – lots of them.

THE DYING DEAD SEA

The future of the Dead Sea is in doubt. In the 1950s, the lake's surface area was about a thousand square kilometres; today, it's about six hundred and still falling. The **water level** has already dropped by a startling 35m, and is continuing to fall by a metre a year. The problem is that greater and greater inroads have been made into the lake's freshwater sources: today, far more water evaporates from the lake than flows into it. There are several **dams** across the River Jordan (as well as across its tributary, the Yarmouk), and – as part of its national water conservation programme – Jordan has dammed all the major rivers in its territory that formerly flowed directly into the Dead Sea, including the Zarqa Ma'in, the Mujib and the Hasa. In addition, both Israel and Jordan have developed major mineral and potash industries at the southern end of the lake which depend on large-scale evaporation for production.

Since the 1970s, **Lynch's Strait**, a channel of water that formerly connected the northern and southern parts of the lake, has dried out, turning the Lisan peninsula into a land bridge. Dangerous **sinkholes** are opening up in the soft ground on both shores. If things continue as they are, some estimates say the Dead Sea will dry up completely in fifty years.

In 2013, the World Bank gave the financial go-ahead to the **Red Sea–Dead Sea conduit**, a plan formulated by the Israeli and Jordanian governments with the Palestinian Authority to pipe seawater 250km from the Red Sea at Aqaba to replenish the Dead Sea. The 400m drop in altitude would mean that large quantities of hydroelectric power could be generated, and there would also be shared desalination plants creating up to 850 million cubic metres a year of potable water by reverse osmosis, thus substantially easing the region's critical shortage of water. The brine residue left after desalination would then be pumped into the Dead Sea to restore its natural water level. The project stalled over financing disputes and diplomatic flare-ups, though in 2018 Jordan announced that it was determined to press ahead regardless. Construction is due to begin in 2021.

However, not everyone is happy. **EcoPeace** (ecopeaceme.org), a coalition of Israeli, Palestinian and Jordanian environmental groups, has voiced several concerns – not least that the Dead Sea needs immediate action, and implementing the Red–Dead plan would take several years and billions of dollars. In addition, as it currently stands, the Red–Dead scheme allows the **unplanned exploitation** of the Dead Sea's resources to continue, with no bar on the numbers of hotels being built, and no imperative for **sustainable development**. There have, as yet, also been no detailed environmental studies on how the addition of huge quantities of seawater might affect the Dead Sea's delicate ecological balance – or on the possible impact of a pipeline breach in the open desert. Time will tell whether the Red–Dead conduit is the answer.

The Dead Sea beaches

Emerging from the hills after the steep descent from the capital, the Amman–Dead Sea highway passes a busy little intersection before meeting a T-junction: the highway bends left towards the **Dead Sea hotels**, while a minor road cuts right to the Baptism Site (see page 122). The old road to Jerusalem formerly led straight on at this junction, but the King Abdullah Bridge which carried it over the river was bombed in the 1967 war, then rebuilt but never reopened; it has now been superseded by the King Hussein Bridge (see page 170), 8km upstream.

Although you'll pass one or two hotels near the T-junction – as well as turn-offs to Sweimeh village nearby – the Dead Sea's main **hotel zone** lies about 8km south, past the mammoth King Hussein Bin Talal Convention Centre (hiltonkinghusseincentre.com). The hotel zone comprises a cluster of four- and five-star properties complete with pools, spas, showers, bathtubs, flushing toilets and a fairly extensive acreage of irrigated and hand-watered gardens, planted in what is naturally barren, salty soil. Almost all the fresh water for this hotel strip is piped from Wadi Mujib, which remains severely depleted. In such a desperately water-poor country, it's a moot point whether luxury development in this particularly arid spot is entirely a good thing.

This area at the lake's northeastern corner includes almost the only developed **beaches** on the Jordanian shore, the remainder of which is mostly lined with jagged, salt-

> ## DEAD SEA FROM THE AIR
> The **Royal Aero Sports Club of Jordan** (☎ 079 730 0299, ⓦ rascj.com) has a base by the Dead Sea, and operates sightseeing flights over the Dead Sea, Baptism Site and/or Mount Nebo by **ultralight** – a two-seater plane, where you sit behind the pilot (JD50/20min; JD75/30min; JD90/45min) – or **gyrocopter** (JD60/20min). Book well in advance.

encrusted rocks. **Hotels** usually allow beach access to non-guests – expect a **fee** over JD25 per person for a day visit, including towels, showers and access to hotel pools – but they may turn you away if they're particularly busy; phone ahead wherever possible. Otherwise there are two options for beach access: Amman Beach and Oh Beach Resort.

Amman Beach
2km south of the hotel zone • Daily 9am–8pm • JD25 • ☎ 05 356 0804 • Some early-morning buses may run direct here from Amman (see page 91)

Don't be fooled by **AMMAN BEACH**'s name: the city is about an hour away (and over 1200m up in the hills). This is the most easily accessible low-budget option for Dead Sea beach-bumming – not least because the car park serves as the terminus for public buses from Amman and elsewhere. It's a reasonably well-run resort with trees and plenty of shade, though facilities are a bit tired. It can get very crowded on Fridays and Saturdays.

The beach is OK, if a bit gravelly, with freshwater showers, little play areas for children and café/restaurants offering simple buffet food (around JD13–17). The main beach area is a basic affair, with no pool and slightly scruffy facilities; women here might attract less attention covered up with a T-shirt and long shorts. The other area – entry is to the right of the main entrance – has a swimming pool and better facilities: women can feel comfortable wearing a bikini, there are lots of loungers (free), you can hire towels and the lockers are usable.

Oh Beach Resort
4km south of the hotel zone • Daily 9am–midnight or later • JD20–50 (prices approximate; higher Thurs eve, Fri & Sat) • ☎ 05 349 2000, ⓦ www.ohresort.net • No public transport

About 2km south of Amman Beach, **OH BEACH RESORT** tries to be a super-swanky day retreat, with sandy beaches and contemporary urban styling – infinity pools, cushioned lounges, pool bars, luxury spa and so on. The location is good, but service and quality standards in food and facilities can be poor. Visit during the day midweek and you could have the place to yourself.

South of Oh Beach, the road continues along the Dead Sea shoreline towards Aqaba, roughly 275km away. We cover the route later in this chapter (see page 118).

ARRIVAL AND DEPARTURE | THE DEAD SEA BEACHES

The Dead Sea is easy to reach on a fast, signposted dual-lane road that branches off the Amman–Airport highway. With your own transport, it's easy to construct a circular day-trip route from either Amman or Madaba to take in the Baptism Site, the Dead Sea and Mount Nebo.

Buses to the Dead Sea Minibuses from Amman (1hr 30min) leave from Muhajireen station. Early-morning buses (7–9am) run direct to Amman Beach, but only if there's demand – guaranteed on a Friday. Others may stop short at the crossroads town of Shuneh al-Janubiyyeh (1hr; see page 170), about 15km north in the Jordan Valley. You can also reach Shuneh by bus from Salt (30min), Dayr Alla (40min) and Madaba via Mount Nebo (1hr). From Shuneh,

occasional minibuses head to the village of Sweimeh (20min), 3km northeast of the hotel zone; the driver might be willing to take you on to Amman Beach for a little extra, but it's not guaranteed.

Buses from the Dead Sea The last minibus back to Amman departs from Amman Beach at around 5pm, the last from Shuneh around 6pm (both an hour or two earlier in winter). These times are very approximate: check departure details with staff at Amman Beach (or bus drivers) as soon as you arrive.

Day-trip by taxi A taxi seating three or four passengers from Amman and back, including 2–3hr waiting time at the Dead Sea, should be about JD50. For a one-way ride, reckon on about JD20–30, but you may have to bargain – and bear in mind that it can be hard to find transport once you're at the Dead Sea: you'd do better to charter a cab both ways. Many budget hotels in Amman can also arrange transport for a day at the beach.

To Feynan A ride from any of the Dead Sea hotels to Feynan, organized through the *Feynan Ecolodge* (see page 342), costs JD70.

ACCOMMODATION

There are no towns within easy reach of the Dead Sea, so if you stay overnight, pretty much your only dining and entertainment options lie within your hotel or a neighbouring one (if such a thing exists). More hotels and leisure complexes are planned on the Dead Sea in the years ahead; building works may be ongoing when you visit.

Crowne Plaza 1.5km south of Dead Sea hotel zone ☏ 05 349 4000, ⓦ crowneplaza.com. Huge 420-room resort complex with a white-sand beach, a variety of pools, several restaurants and big, luxuriously appointed guest rooms. If searching online, don't mix it up with the *Crowne Plaza Dead Sea* in Israel. **JD120**

Dead Sea Spa Hotel Dead Sea hotel zone ☏ 05 356 1000, ⓦ dssh.jo. Decent four-star hotel that offers a more down-to-earth experience than its ritzy neighbours, away from the corporate ambience. It's especially good if you're looking to avoid splurging at the big-name hotels alongside, either on a day-trip or on a weekend break. The guest rooms are large and comfortable, and the on-site medical centre was the pioneer for therapeutic tourism in Jordan. **JD95**

★ **Hilton** Dead Sea hotel zone ☏ 05 349 3000, ⓦ hilton.com. The newest addition to this hotel strip, with spacious contemporary designed rooms arrayed across a complex of buildings set among exotic gardens, as well as several pools, an expanse of private beach, and a spa (not yet open at the time of writing). **JD140**

Holiday Inn 4km north of Dead Sea hotel zone ☏ 05 349 5555, ⓦ holidayinn.com. Away from the others, at the northern end of the hotel strip, this pleasant, upmarket resort hotel features a sequence of palm-shaded swimming pools and neat, spacious rooms done up in contemporary design. A good option for families, with a decent sandy beach (if not very large), a shaded kids' pool and switched-on service. **JD110**

Kempinski Ishtar Dead Sea hotel zone ☏ 05 356 8888, ⓦ kempinski-deadsea.com. A leading luxury hotel. Set amid the gardens, lagoons and numerous palm-shaded pools are separate enclaves, including private villas and beach complexes, featuring designer interiors done up in a mock Babylonian style (Ishtar was the Babylonian goddess of love). The public areas are cool and airy, and the spa area is vast, including twenty treatment rooms alongside pools and steam rooms galore. **JD140**

Marriott (Jordan Valley Marriott) Dead Sea hotel zone ☏ 05 356 0400, ⓦ marriott.com/qmdjv. Excellent holiday hotel, built in a large U-shape around three swimming pools, including an infinity pool facing west across the Dead Sea. Its public areas are airy and well designed, while the guest rooms are exceptional. Eight cafés, bars and restaurants occupy several levels within the main reception building and seafront locations across the site, and there's beach volleyball, a tennis court, on-site spa and, of course, a beach. **JD130**

★ **Mövenpick** Dead Sea hotel zone ☏ 05 356 1111, ⓦ movenpick.com. The lobby of this tasteful resort hotel is supremely elegant – cooled by a flowing artificial stream and waterfall – while the bar features a stunning wooden ceiling, hand-carved in Damascene style. Guest rooms are housed in two-storey buildings of local stone and plaster, designed to imitate and blend in with the lumpy Dead Sea landscape of low, rounded marl hills, and arranged around quiet courtyards with fountains and flower gardens. Further down the complex are a variety of restaurants – Italian, Asian, fine dining – plus a large open-air pool and steps leading down to the beach, as well as the ultra-chic Zara Spa. **JD120**

Dead Sea Panorama

16km southeast of the hotel zone • Daily 9am–5pm (Nov–Feb till 4pm) • JD2 • ☏ 05 349 1133 • No public transport

On the main road 5km south of Amman Beach, a marked turn-off climbs into the mountains: follow it up 9km of steep switchbacks to reach the **DEAD SEA PANORAMA** complex. This sensitively designed building perches on a cliff edge with spectacular views over the Dead Sea: footpaths lead away from the parking area to viewpoints, and there's a short walking trail that covers a circular route around the site.

Within the main building, the excellent **Dead Sea Museum** covers four themes in fascinating detail: the **geological origins** of the Dead Sea; the **ecology** of the region; the area's **archeology and history**; and issues surrounding future **conservation**. The museum is spacious, modern and air-conditioned, and the exhibits and accompanying videos make for an absorbing visit. Next door is an RSCN **nature shop**, selling handmade crafts and jewellery. There's also a fine **restaurant** here.

From a T-junction above the Panorama, a turn-off heads down 2km to the Ma'in hot springs spa resort (see page 225). The main road leads up to the plateau, passing through Ma'in village and ending after about 30km at Madaba (see page 208).

EATING   DEAD SEA PANORAMA

Dead Sea Panorama 16km southeast of Dead Sea hotel zone ☎05 349 1133. A pleasant, upmarket restaurant on the hillsides above the Dead Sea. Sample high-quality Arabic food in the a/c interior or out on the terrace. Reckon on around JD20 a head for a fine selection of hot and cold meze, salads, kebabs and grills. Alcohol is served. It's a popular spot for weekend dining: book ahead. Daily noon–midnight (Nov–Feb till 10pm).

South along the Dead Sea road

South of the Dead Sea's main hotel and beach zone, the shoreside road continues all the way to Aqaba, roughly 275km away. This is a reasonably fast, mostly empty **driving route**, offering spectacular scenery that shifts from the deep blue of the Dead Sea to the sandy deserts of the Wadi Araba (see page 339) – though don't get carried away: mobile police speed traps are common.

GETTING AROUND   THE DEAD SEA ROAD

The way to move around here is by **car** or **taxi** (organized from hotels in Amman, Madaba or at the Dead Sea itself). Local **buses** that follow this road are few and far between – some express buses between Amman and Aqaba go this way, but they don't stop – and the attractions don't really merit attempting an excursion by public transport. Adventure tour operators (see page 48) often come this way, dropping off or picking up clients at the mouth of one or other of the canyons either side of Wadi Mujib (see pages 221 and 235).

Zara springs

12km south of Amman Beach • Open access • Free

The series of thermal springs at **Zara** lies downstream from the hot waterfalls of Hammamat Ma'in (see page 225). This is a very popular Friday outing spot, with cars lined up along the highway and people alternating between dipping in the Dead Sea and washing the salt off in the warm spring water. Men can splash around freely, but even in the secluded valleys women would do best to venture in fully clothed. Note that the pools and beach aren't all that clean. A few hundred metres south of Zara are the remains of King Herod's baths and Dead Sea port at **Callirhoë**, although there's little left to see other than a handful of column drums and the remnants of a harbour wall.

Mujib Biosphere Reserve

27km south of Amman Beach • Visitor centre daily 8am–4pm • Day-access to Dead Sea beach JD10/person • ☎ 079 720 3888 or contact the RSCN Wild Jordan centre in Amman on ☎ 06 461 6523, ⓦ wildjordan.com (see page 82)

Beside cliffs on the Dead Sea shore road, the **Mujib Bridge** forms a graceful 140m span across the outflow of the River Mujib. On the lake side of the bridge you can splash around in the refreshing river water. The Mujib Valley system, which extends eastwards high into the mountains, is the centrepiece of the **Mujib Biosphere Reserve**, run by Wild Jordan, the ecotourism arm of the Royal Society for the Conservation of Nature (RSCN). Below the bridge, on the cliff side of the road, is the strikingly designed **visitor centre**. Staff here have maps, brochures and light refreshments, and can advise on walking routes, though you should always **book in advance** for hikes directly or through the RSCN's Wild Jordan centre in Amman (see page 82). There's also access to a modest **beach** on the Dead Sea, by the chalets.

This is the main entrance to the reserve, and the best way to access the **canyoning routes** and **water trails** that characterize Mujib. The upper highland entrance, at Faqua village off the King's Highway (see page 230) is unattended and further from the canyoning action.

WILD JORDAN RESERVE PRICES

Prices at Jordan's **RSCN-run nature reserves** are high. The RSCN make no apologies for this, saying that the reason they exist is to protect Jordan's natural environment, and that they have built lodges and developed tourism – under their **Wild Jordan** brand – as a tool for generating funds to help conservation and support rural communities. You may or may not agree with their pricing policy, but this kind of responsible tourism is virtually unknown in the Middle East, and the RSCN are pioneers. For now, until tourism schemes emerge that are truly community-owned, paying extra to visit the RSCN reserves is a good way to ensure that your money goes to benefit rural people and habitats.

2

Wadi Mujib trails

Siq Trail April–Oct; 2hr 30min; JD21/person self-guided • **Ibex Trail** Year-round; 4hr; JD21/person including compulsory guide • **Canyon Trail** April–Oct; 4hr; JD31/person including compulsory guide • **Malaqi Trail** April–Oct; 6hr; JD44/person including brunch & compulsory guide • All routes closed during Ramadan

The easy but dramatic **Siq Trail** heads into the Mujib Gorge, leading you between towering sandstone cliffs to the base of a waterfall before returning; you may be wading or even swimming some sections. A tougher alternative is the dry **Ibex Trail**, which heads from the Mujib Bridge south to a steep access route up into the mountains, traversing a number of valleys on the way to a ranger station: you may spot ibex roaming wild here. You should be a confident swimmer to tackle the **Canyon Trail**, which includes negotiating the Mujib river. Longer routes include the wet **Malaqi Trail**, a classic canyoning route, graded difficult, which initially follows the Ibex Trail before descending into the Mujib Gorge and heading upstream to the confluence with the Wadi Hidan, then returning – via a 20m waterfall abseil – to the Mujib Bridge.

More options are outlined on Wild Jordan's website. For detailed trail reports, see Tony Howard's fine book on Jordan walks (see page 390).

ACCOMMODATION   MUJIB BIOSPHERE RESERVE

Mujib Biosphere Reserve chalets West of the Mujib Bridge, on the Dead Sea shore ☏ 079 720 3888 or book via the RSCN's Wild Jordan centre in Amman (see page 82) on ☏ 06 461 6523, ⊛ wildjordan.com. On the Mujib river delta near the bridge stands a cluster of fifteen modest chalets, compact and simple but still comfortable. Each is en suite and has a/c, plus comes with its own shaded terrace looking north over a quiet beach which is pleasant for a float (and has showers). The chalets are open year-round, but even the staff admit that the a/c isn't enough to ease the blistering temperatures of high summer (June–Aug). Alongside is a pleasant restaurant block offering meals (JD6–21) and lunchboxes (JD6) – though only with advance booking at least a day ahead. Check in first at the Mujib Bridge visitor centre, from where staff will drive you over to the chalets in their 4x4. **JD76**

Mazra'a

24km south of Mujib Bridge

South of Mujib, the Dead Sea road continues south, hugging the salt-spattered shore below rocky cliffs until it comes to **MAZRA'A**, a small town on what was the **Lisan Peninsula** – now a belt of dry land across the lake. Exploring the peninsula isn't encouraged by the Arab Potash Company, whose massive factory complex stands nearby, but it's still possible to turn off at the company's sign, drive out a little way and then venture into the soft white sand on foot. You might stumble upon one of the old **Byzantine monasteries** that lie ruined here, unexcavated, in an eerie landscape forever sultry and thick with haze.

Ghor Mazra'a (*ghor*, meaning "depression", refers to the agricultural lands around the village) and neighbouring **Ghor Haditha** are the location for an experiment in "exchange tourism" run by the Zikra Initiative (see page 120).

Bab adh-Dhraa

About 1km south of Mazra'a is a turn-off leading up into the hills to Karak; take this road for about 1km and the *tell* appears on the left

2

> ## THE ZIKRA INITIATIVE
>
> Mazra'a and its village neighbours are home to some of the poorest people in Jordan, isolated until relatively recently and often subject to discrimination for their dark skin colour. In 2007, Amman entrepreneur Rabee Zureikat began working with the community to find ways to alleviate their poverty. Instead of the usual forms of charity and giving, flowing in one direction from city to countryside – and often demeaning both parties in the process – he hit upon the idea of **exchange tourism**. Both sides can give, and both receive: urbanites provide money and resources, while villagers show creative skills handling natural materials, cooking using traditional techniques and recounting life experiences. It's a resourceful attempt to bridge a gap of memory, to show both parties that knowledge and outlooks carried from previous generations can still benefit "modern" life.
>
> On that basis Zureikat founded the **Zikra Initiative** (*zikra* means "memory"), establishing active projects of exchange between Amman and Mazra'a: Ammanis (and tourists) pay a relatively modest sum (around JD30–35) for a day in Mazra'a being invited into people's homes, learning how to weave, bake bread, cook local food – and listening to stories from this otherwise marginalized community (with everything translated for non-Arabic speakers). There may also be the chance to hike in the surrounding hills, or help out picking tomatoes on village farms. It's a fabulous idea, executed with dignity and charm – and the project, as well as Zureikat himself, has won numerous global awards. Contact Zikra Initiative on Facebook well in advance to find out what's possible.
>
> As an alternative, contact the local **Al Numeira Environmental Association** (🌐alnumeirae.wordpress.com) about their modest programmes for community tourism by bicycle in the Mazra'a area, promoting recycling and sustainable lifestyles.

The Bronze Age *tell* (archeological mound) of **Bab adh-Dhraa** is a sparse site, offering a thick city wall and a handful of foundations – but the attraction is in relating the place to a name. Bab adh-Dhraa is the site of a large town which flourished around 2600 BC – some graves in the huge **necropolis** across the road date from as early as the fourth millennium – and is the leading candidate for biblical **Sodom**, location of so much depravity that God felt compelled to raze the city and kill its inhabitants (see opposite). Standing on the *tell* today, amid barren rocks on the hazy shores of a salt lake, you can only wonder what on earth the poor Sodomites must have been up to in these rooms to deserve such a fate.

Lot's Sanctuary and Museum
Signed east off the Dead Sea road at Ghor Safi, 22km south of the Karak turning

Near Safi village lies **Lot's Sanctuary**, a rich archeological site that has thrown up evidence of Early and Middle Bronze Age habitation, as well as Nabatean pottery, Byzantine mosaics and the earliest example of carved wood yet discovered intact in Jordan: a door that dates from the seventh-century Umayyad period. The location – not to mention the notion of standing in Lot's sandalprints – is dramatic enough to warrant a visit.

Museum at the Lowest Place on Earth
About 1km east of the Dead Sea road • Daily 8am–4pm • JD2, free with JP • ☎ 03 230 2845; crafts 🌐 facebook.com/saficraftsjordan

On the way to the archeological site, the **Museum at the Lowest Place on Earth** is set in a grand, semicircular building designed to showcase the historical heritage of the southern Dead Sea area. Highlights within the modern, well-lit galleries include finds from the Lot's Sanctuary site, including a complete **mosaic** pavement. There are also some extremely rare Greco-Roman **textiles** discovered at Khirbet Qayzun on the Dead Sea shore – felt hats and women's wool-fringed head veils – as well as early Christian **tombstones** from Zoara (Safi's biblical name). One display section explains the area's importance as a **sugar-processing centre** during the Mamluke period (twelfth to fifteenth centuries), when dozens of mills processed sugar cane in industrial quantities for export to Europe: Zoara, then known as Zughar, may have given its name to the product.

The museum also has a small shop and café run by the local **women's cooperative**, selling their handmade crafts.

The sanctuary, cave and ruins

From the museum, a track continues steeply up the hill to a parking area; the guardian will accompany you up to the sanctuary site

Entering the **sanctuary** site involves a tiring climb of almost three hundred steps. The first area you come to is a **court**, part of which has slipped down the hill, but which originally supported the floor of the **church** above. The main **apse** has seating for the bishop and is slightly raised. Five **mosaics** – one dated April 606, another May 691 – have been renovated, and may be uncovered for viewing once a site shelter is in place. The **narthex** was originally entered from the right, via a doorway from the court below; this ingenious piece of design enabled visiting Jewish and Muslim pilgrims to avoid stepping inside the church and instead head straight for the holy **cave** – where Lot is said to have sought refuge from the destruction of Sodom and Gomorrah – the entrance to which is to the left of the apse. A beautifully carved **lintel** over the cave entrance, marked with crosses, presages an interior mosaic which mimics the round stones embedded in the roof. All around the church was spread a **monastery**: the remains of six or seven cells are dotted around the parched hillside. The views over the Dead Sea and the nearby town of Safi are stunning.

Safi and beyond

SAFI, at the southern tip of the Dead Sea, is the phosphate capital of Jordan, although – under the name Zoar – it also has a history as one of the five biblical "cities of the plain", along with Sodom and Gomorrah. The southernmost portion of the Dead Sea has been corralled into huge evaporation pans for Jordan's phosphate and chemical industries and, with its neighbour, the lush farming village of **FIFA** a bit further south, Safi shares a natural hothouse that is one of the most intensively farmed areas of Jordan, with bananas, tomatoes and other fruits as staple irrigated crops.

SODOM AND GOMORRAH

The tale in Genesis of how God punished the depravity of the inhabitants of **Sodom and Gomorrah**, and how **Lot** and his wife escaped, is one of the best-known biblical stories. After arriving in Canaan (Palestine), Lot and his uncle Abraham began to bicker over grazing grounds. They separated, and Lot pitched his tents at the southeastern corner of the Dead Sea near Sodom, one of the five "cities of the plain" (the others were Gomorrah, Zoar, Admah and Zeboyim). "But," as Genesis warns, "the men of Sodom were wicked and sinners before the Lord exceedingly." One evening, Lot was visited by two angels, come to warn him of the city's impending divine destruction. Lot, his wife and two daughters fled and "the Lord rained upon Sodom and Gomorrah brimstone and fire." Every one of the five cities was destroyed, and every person killed. As they were fleeing, Lot's wife disobeyed a divine order not to look back at the destruction, and was turned into a pillar of salt.

Seemingly the last people left alive in the world, Lot and his daughters sought refuge in a cave in the mountains. Calculating that, with all potential mates vaporized, they were likely to die childless, the daughters hatched a plan to get their father so drunk he wouldn't be able to tell who they were, whereupon they would seduce him and thus preserve the family. Everything worked to plan and both daughters gave birth to sons; the elder named her child **Moab**, and the younger Ben-Ammi, or "father of **Ammon**".

The last of these bizarre biblical episodes has been commemorated for centuries, and possibly millennia, at a cave-and-church complex in the hills above Safi. Ruins within Safi itself, as well as at four other scanty Early Bronze Age sites nearby (Bab adh-Dhraa, Numayra, Fifa and Khanazir), show evidence of destruction by fire. At Numayra, archeologists also found the skeletons of three men whose bones were crushed by falling masonry. These five could possibly be the "cities of the plain". The only fly in the ointment is that they were razed around 2350 BC, several hundred years before the generally accepted era of Abraham and Lot, although archeologists are still debating the precise timescales involved.

Just beyond Fifa, a scenic turn-off climbs to Tafileh (see page 237), while continuing south brings you into the long **Wadi Araba**, with drifting sand and wandering camels all the way south to Aqaba. We cover this route in Chapter 7 (see page 339).

Bethany: the Baptism Site

Daily 8.30am–6pm (Nov–March till 4pm); last entry 1hr before closing • JD12 • ☎ 05 359 0360, ⓦ baptismsite.com

One of the most important recent discoveries in Middle Eastern archeology has been the identification of a site on the east bank of the River Jordan, near the Dead Sea, as **Bethany-beyond-the-Jordan**, the place where John the Baptist lived, and where he most likely **baptized Jesus Christ**. Archeologists have uncovered a wealth of sites – 21 at the last count – along **Wadi Kharrar**, a small side-valley of reeds and flowing water that runs for 2km from its source down to the **River Jordan**. These discoveries – eleven Byzantine churches, five baptismal pools from the Roman and Byzantine periods, caves of monks and hermits, and lodges for pilgrims – plus a wealth of medieval accounts of pilgrims

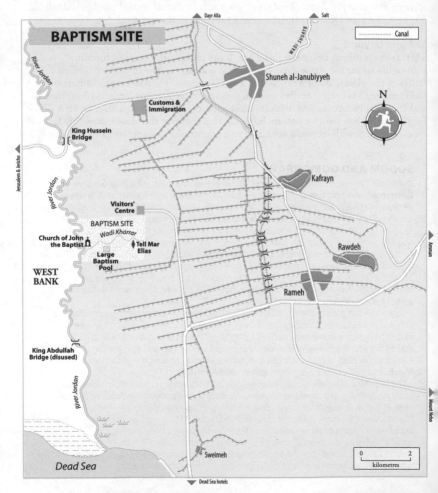

and travellers to the area, rapidly convinced both Jordanian and international opinion as to the veracity of the site.

This is almost the lowest point on earth, over 350m below sea level; the air is thick, hot and heavy. On the banks of the Wadi Kharrar, you're in the midst of the biblical **Plains of Moab**; views across the baked ground, punctuated by the occasional wizened tree, enable you to pick out individual buildings and cars in the Palestinian city of Jericho, across what is now an international border. Underfoot is a soft, chalky marl that seems to deaden sound; only when you get close to Wadi Kharrar itself can you hear the chirping of birds and the soughing of the dense beds of reeds and tamarisk that line the watercourse. Flanking the River Jordan itself is a jungle-like thicket, tropically hot and humid – more akin to Southeast than Southwest Asia.

Visiting outside winter (Nov–Feb) means that you'll have to cope with scorching temperatures, often topping 45°C in summer. The best advice is to arrive at 8am and explore in the relative cool of the morning. There can also be lots of flies. Nonetheless, for its historical resonance, natural austerity and religious power, this is an extraordinary place.

Biblical accounts of the Baptism Site

This stretch of desolate plain flanking the River Jordan has been a focus for spirituality since Old Testament times: Judaism, Christianity and Islam all recall momentous events which took place in this relatively small part of the southern Jordan Valley. The first mention is in Genesis, when **Lot** separated from Abraham and "chose the plain of Jordan" to pitch his tents, after which **Jacob** wrestled with God a little way north at Penuel. A sizeable proportion of the Book of Numbers is set at the Israelites' camp, "pitched in the plains of Moab by Jordan opposite Jericho", following which **Moses** delivers a long address in Deuteronomy before going up "from the plains of Moab unto the mountain of Nebo", where he died. **Joshua** led the tribes across the river, which miraculously halted its flow, an event mirrored centuries later in 2 Kings, when the prophets **Elijah** and **Elisha** again stopped the flow of the river, as a chariot and horses of fire took Elijah up to heaven – according to ancient tradition, from the rounded hillock alongside Wadi Kharrar now known as Tell Mar Elyas (Elijah's Hill).

It was because of the associations with the prophet Elijah that, a thousand years later, John, an ascetic holy man with a prophetic vision, took up residence near the same hillock, using the numerous small springs of sweet water to symbolically cleanse people of sin, locals soon flocked to this **John the Baptist**. Most biblical mentions describe the baptisms taking place "in Jordan", which probably referred loosely to this general area. The River Jordan, which often flooded to a width of 1km or more, would have been deep and rapid (in Aramaic, *yardeen* – from which "Jordan" is derived – means "fast-flowing water"), offering no easy access from the often-steep bank. By contrast, the dozens of tiny side-springs, some of which rise within pools barely 100m from the river, are protected and more manageable as immersion points.

The Gospel of St John mentions "**Bethany-beyond-the-Jordan**, where John was baptizing"; the spot – unconnected with Bethany near Jerusalem – was also known as Bethabara or Beit-Abara, "the House of the Crossing Point". A later account says that **Jesus** "returned again across the Jordan to the place where John had first started baptizing". There is no explicit mention of when or where John baptized Jesus, but the accumulated weight of tradition and historical evidence places it in or near Wadi Kharrar, with plentiful supplies of spring water, alongside the Roman road between Jericho and Nebo (thereby within easy reach of potential converts), but far enough out of reach to mean that John could criticize King Herod with impunity.

Pilgrim accounts of the Baptism Site

As early as 333 AD, the anonymous **Pilgrim of Bordeaux** identified the site of Bethany-beyond-the-Jordan as lying five Roman miles (just under 7.5km) north of the Dead

2

A PROLIFERATION OF CHURCHES

In recent years many **new churches** have been built at the Baptism Site, as the world's Christian denominations clamour to be represented at this hugely important spot. The planning process is strict, and all the new buildings are modest and unintrusive – many rather beautiful. Coptic, Armenian, Ethiopian, Syrian Orthodox, Roman Catholic, Greek Orthodox, Anglican, Lutheran and Baptist churches are all present, along with other institutions and prayer centres, as well as monasteries and/or pilgrim hostels belonging to the Greek Orthodox, Latin and Russian Orthodox churches.

If you wish to visit in order to affirm your Christian faith, you can request to be taken for a **private baptism** and religious ceremony at any of several baptism pools and centres around the site. Someone from your own party can officiate or you can ask for a local priest to conduct the ceremony. Check ⓦ baptismsite.com well in advance to fix things up – or, if it's last minute, call ☎ 077 784 2300 at least 48 hours ahead to see what can be arranged.

Sea, corresponding almost exactly to the point where the Wadi Kharrar enters the river: "here is a place by the river, a little hill on the far bank, where Elijah was caught up into heaven". From then on, many ancient texts mention several churches in the same area dedicated to John the Baptist and Elijah. The sixth-century pilgrim **Theodosius** described the riverside "Church of St John, which the emperor Anastasius built [in about 500 AD]; this church is very lofty, being built above chambers on account of the flooding of the Jordan" – a description which corresponds almost exactly with one of the churches uncovered recently. The place was important enough to merit inclusion on the **Madaba mosaic map** (see page 213).

The accounts continued through the Middle Ages, with Bethany-beyond-the-Jordan taking its place in a **pilgrimage route** linking Jerusalem, Jericho, Hesban and Mount Nebo. From the twelfth to the eighteenth century, Bethany was home to **Greek Orthodox monks**, who were reported still to be present as late as the beginning of the twentieth century (the whole site is still in the custody of the Greek Orthodox Church), but most ruins lay undiscovered while knowledge of the whereabouts of Bethany-beyond-the-Jordan faded from collective memory.

Archeological investigations at Tell Mar Elias and along Wadi Kharrar had to be abandoned at the outbreak of **war** in 1948, and for many years the site lay in a militarized border zone. It was only after the 1994 **peace treaty** between Jordan and Israel that the area could be swept for landmines and again opened for study. The momentous discoveries that rapidly followed convinced the Jordanian authorities, and then the broad mass of specialist opinion worldwide, that the long-lost "Bethany-beyond-the-Jordan" had been rediscovered.

Along Wadi Kharrar

The site comprises six square kilometres focused around the small **Wadi Kharrar**, which runs westwards for 2km on a meandering course from beside the rounded hillock of **Tell Mar Elyas** down to join the River Jordan amid fourteen small springs around the **Church of John the Baptist**. Midway along is a set of ancient **baptism pools**.

Tell Mar Elyas (Elijah's Hill)

At the head of little Wadi Kharrar stands the low **Tell Mar Elyas** (**Elijah's Hill**). A few metres south of the *tell*, a number of remains have been uncovered. The most prominent sight is a large freestanding **arch**, raised in 1999 from 63 stones (to commemorate the death at 63 of King Hussein) over the foundations of a rectangular church dating from the fourth or fifth century. Since 2000, when the then pope celebrated Mass beneath this arch and, in a gesture of reconciliation, faced west to bless Jerusalem then east to bless Mount Nebo, the site has been known as the **Church of John Paul II**.

A few metres away are the foundations of a larger rectangular building, with some fragments of a mosaic floor remaining, which has been dubbed a **prayer hall**. Around here is a complicated web of water channels, pool-beds, a pear-shaped well (once circular, but distorted by earth movements) and a large **cistern**, still with its plastered interior. The cistern was formerly covered by a barrel vault of sandstone, quarried 20km away at Sweimeh, and topped with a mosaic floor – remnants of which have been preserved. With the level of settlement in antiquity, and the numbers of baptisms performed here, a great deal of water was needed: pipes and aqueducts channelled water to the site from several kilometres away, but still the 100-cubic-metre cistern wasn't enough, and a second, smaller cistern was built nearby.

The small *tell* features a trinity of trinities – three churches, three caves and three baptism pools – encircled by a wooden catwalk. Proceeding clockwise, on the west side of the *tell* is a cave which forms the apse of a small **Byzantine church**, with little niches to the east and south and tiny fragments of its mosaic floor. An open chapel on the northwest side leads round to the large, late-Byzantine **northern church**, now sheltered from the elements, which incorporates a strange black stone into its apse to commemorate the fire which accompanied Elijah's rise to heaven. Its detailed mosaic floor includes an intriguing cross motif in diamonds and an inscription in Greek that dates it to "the time of Rhotorius" (early sixth century). Up a couple of steps on the northeastern side of the *tell* are two **pools** from the Roman period, one cut later with the addition of a 14m-deep well. Further round is a large rectangular pool, plastered, and with a line of four steps leading into it – for group baptisms, it's been suggested.

The Pilgrims' Station, Baptism Pool and caves

Paths lead down from the *tell* area to the footpath along the south side of Wadi Kharrar, which features several sites attesting to the faith of Byzantine pilgrims and ascetics. Around 500m west of the *tell* are the remains of a *lavra*, a complex of hermits' cells, while further west is a large **Baptism Pool**, designed to hold three hundred people, built roughly on its lower courses but with well-dressed sandstone ashlars further up. Channels fed water from the **Spring of John the Baptist** to the pool; a fifth- or sixth-century building excavated on a small promontory directly above the pool, with views over the whole valley, may well have been a hostel for visiting pilgrims (it has now been dubbed the **Pilgrims' Station**).

Immediately to the west, the *ghor*, or broad valley floor, gives way to the *zor*, the narrow, deep-set floodplain flanking the River Jordan itself. Cut into the loose marl of these cliffs, and now accessible by modern steps, are two **caves**, each featuring prayer niches; one of the caves has three interior apses. The seventh-century writer John Moschus records the pilgrimage to Sinai of a monk John, from Jerusalem; while recovering from a fever in the *lavra* of Safsafas, John the Baptist appeared to him and said, "This little cave is greater than Mount Sinai: our Lord Jesus Christ himself visited me here."

Church of John the Baptist

The Old Testament prophet Jeremiah spoke of the "**jungle of the Jordan**", and the contrast in the natural environment between Tell Mar Elyas and the churches on the banks of the Jordan itself couldn't be stronger. This narrow strip flanking the river is quite unlike anywhere else in the country: paths from the wild and knobbly lunar landscape of the desert-like *zor* plunge into a wall of woody tamarisk bushes so thick that, had a way not been cut, it would be impossible to force your way through. Inside the thicket of reeds and tamarisk, the air is steamy and tropical, full of the chirruping of birds and the hum of insects, and marked by a constant babble of water from the fourteen springs that flow all around (indeed, the name "Kharrar" is thought to be onomatopoeic).

2

From the shuttle bus drop-off point, a five- or ten-minute walk through the "jungle" – past a number of springs and rest areas – brings you to a clearing marked by a modern pool and the sheltered remains of the sixth- or seventh-century **Church of John the Baptist**, situated alongside two more churches, which were built more or less on top of one another; the floor of the lower one, tiled in triangular, square and octagonal flags of marble, has been exposed, and there are also marble Corinthian capitals from long-fallen columns lying nearby. Beneath a shelter is the altar and mosaic floor of the main **Church of the Trinity**, a basilica formerly raised up above the level of the river on an arched vault to protect it from flooding – exactly as medieval pilgrims recorded. Pillars from this vault still lie where they fell in antiquity, on the north side of the church building. Byzantine stairs, three of them black marble or bitumen, interspersed with white marble from Asia Minor, lead from the apse – and a marble fragment commemoratively marked "IOY. BATT." (a Latin abbreviation of "John the Baptist") that was found in the church is on display in the Visitors' Centre. Other chapels, churches and pilgrimage sites, from various dates, dot this area.

The River Jordan
About 200m west of the Church of John the Baptist, via a laid path through the tamarisks, stands the modern Greek Orthodox **Church of St John**, alongside other modern churches. Opposite, shaded steps lead down to a wooden platform on the **River Jordan** itself – not the grand, Amazon-like spectacle of imagination, but rather a low, muddy stream, these days barely a metre deep and less than 10m wide at this point. In plain view across the water, in the Israeli-occupied West Bank, is a rival complex known as Qasr al-Yahud – a white stone terrace, complete with chapel. (Alternative Israeli baptism sites further north are unashamedly commercial affairs.)

Linger here awhile, if you can: despite its modest appearance these days, the Jordan is one of the world's great rivers, with huge religious and historical significance. There are very few other places along its course where you can get this close to the water – and none has such drama. The walk back to the shuttle bus leads you on a different route via two more river lookouts, perched high above the banks.

ARRIVAL AND DEPARTURE

By car The Baptism Site is signposted from the T-junction at the end of the highway from Amman (about 45min). The highway bends left (south) to the Dead Sea hotels, while a minor road turns right (north) to the Baptism Site. Note that if you're approaching from the Dead Sea hotels, you have to follow the highway round to the right and then make a U-turn in order to access the Baptism Site road. From the junction, it's 5km to a gateway across the road, where you pay the admission fee and receive a free brochure (with a map). A little ahead is the parking area in front of the palm-shaded Visitors' Centre.

By bus No public transport runs within 5km of the site.

By taxi A taxi from Amman is about JD25 – but hotels in Amman, Madaba and at the Dead Sea can organize return taxi transport, often as part of a day-tour of nearby sites and attractions; prices vary, depending what else is on the itinerary.

INFORMATION

Visitors' Centre The Visitors' Centre has toilets, souvenir shops and refreshment kiosks, and is where the official site guides wait. If you're visiting independently in a car (or privately hired taxi), an official site guide (free with the JD12 entry ticket) can accompany you, in your own vehicle, for a tour around the site – private vehicles without a guide are banned. Otherwise, you must wait at the Visitors' Centre for a free shuttle bus (every 15–20min), which makes a round trip to the separate areas of the site. Allow a minimum of 1hr – though an in-depth tour of the whole site could take up to 3hr. **Exploring the site** Other than in winter, it's very hot here: bring a hat and water, and expect lots of flies. The standard shuttle bus tour starts off at Tell Mar Elyas (Elijah's Hill) before dropping off at the Baptism Pool, from where you proceed on foot to the Church of John the Baptist and down to the river. The bus returns you to the Visitor Centre.

Fresh drinking water is provided at several points (but you should carry your own), and there are toilets available. You can also – with advance notice – elect to tackle the hot and tiring walk from the Visitors' Centre to Tell Mar Elyas and onwards on a marked trail along the south bank of the Wadi Kharrar to John's Church and the River Jordan. It's about 4km in total, but allow 3hr one-way. Note that the pools and springs are mostly or completely dry from May until late Oct.

Jerash and the north

UMM QAIS

Jerash and the north

The rolling hills of northern Jordan hold some of the loveliest countryside in the whole Middle East, with acres of olive and fig trees, patches of ancient pine forest and fields of wheat interspersed with fertile, cultivated valleys that point the way west down to the deep Jordan Valley. This is the most densely populated part of the country, and every hill and wadi has its village. Many of the local people are from ancient Syrian or Transjordanian families, but plenty of towns also have a significant population of Palestinians, who continue to farm the East Bank of the Jordan much as they did the West Bank and Galilee before having to flee in the wars of 1948 and 1967. This area has also borne the brunt of Jordan's refugee crisis from Syria's war: the towns of Ramtha and Irbid lie just over the border from Dera'a, the seat of the Syrian revolution in 2011, and have absorbed countless families escaping the fighting.

In biblical times, this was the greater part of the area known as the **Decapolis** (see page 135), and extensive ruins of important Roman cities survive, most notably those of **Jerash**, north of Amman, and **Umm Qais**, in the far northwest. West of Jerash, the ruins of an Arab-built Crusader-period castle dominate the hills above Ajloun, which is also the location for the lovely **Ajloun Forest Reserve**, set amid isolated woods of evergreen oak, now also the venue for fascinating rural walks and local village projects.

To the west is the swelteringly subtropical **Jordan Valley**, more than 200m below sea level, carrying the trickling River Jordan south to the Dead Sea. Ongoing excavations here at the Decapolis city of **Pella** have revealed continuous habitation for at least five thousand years before the Romans arrived. Above the southern Jordan Valley, the rolling hills of the **Balqa** region that rise towards Amman hide low-key towns and villages, such as the graceful old Ottoman capital **Salt** and its neighbour **Fuheis**.

Weaving around and between all these is the long-distance **Jordan Trail** (see page 160), which can be easily broken down into day-stages, covering some of the most scenic walking terrain in the country.

EXPLORING NORTHERN JORDAN

On even the tightest itinerary, **Jerash** deserves at least half a day, preferably more – and if you can, you should clear a night to stay (and walk) in and around the wonderful **Ajloun Forest**, though it's hard to reach without a car.

However, most tourists never venture further north than Jerash – such a pity, since this can be a rewarding area to visit, very different from Jordan's deserts. Even if you're relying on public transport, it's easy to construct a **one-night tour**: start with a bus from Amman's Tabarboor station to **Ajloun**, for a morning exploring the castle, the town and the olive groves. Then move on to the Roman ruins at **Jerash** before taking a late-afternoon bus to **Irbid**. Next day, return direct to Amman or extend the trip with a bus to **Umm Qais**.

Renting a car (see page 33) gets you easy access to the beautiful **Ajloun Forest Reserve** or rural walks such as the **Al Ayoun Trail**, as well as worthwhile sites off the beaten track. If you're starting from the Dead Sea, for instance, you could drive through the Jordan Valley to Pella, continue to Umm Qais for lunch, and head via Irbid to Ajloun for dinner and overnight in the Ajloun Forest Reserve, with a half-day walk the next morning and an easy drive on to Salt, Jerash or Amman.

ROMAN GENERAL IN HIS CHARIOT, JERASH

Highlights

❶ Jerash Explore the Roman streets, then watch the choreographed spectacle of gladiatorial combat and chariot racing in the restored hippodrome. See page 133

❷ Ajloun Castle A half-ruined Saracen castle, lording it over the rolling countryside. See page 147

❸ Ajloun Forest Reserve Ajloun's lush hills offer great walks, rural hideaways and cultural encounters, notably on the Al Ayoun Trail. See page 148

❹ Umm Qais Roman ruins perched on a cliff edge with magnificent Galilee views. See page 158

❺ The Yarmouk Gorge road A great scenic drive, with spectacular views of the Golan Heights. See page 162

❻ Sharhabil bin Hassneh EcoPark A peaceful hideaway in the Jordan Valley for rural walks and bike rides. See page 164

❼ Pella See the ruins, then stay for some countryside hospitality. See page 165

❽ Salt Elegant Ottoman-era hilltown of honey-stone villas and winding lanes. See page 170

❾ Qasr al-Abd A white palace, two millennia old, set amid beautiful countryside west of Amman. See page 175

HIGHLIGHTS ARE MARKED ON THE MAP ON PAGE 132

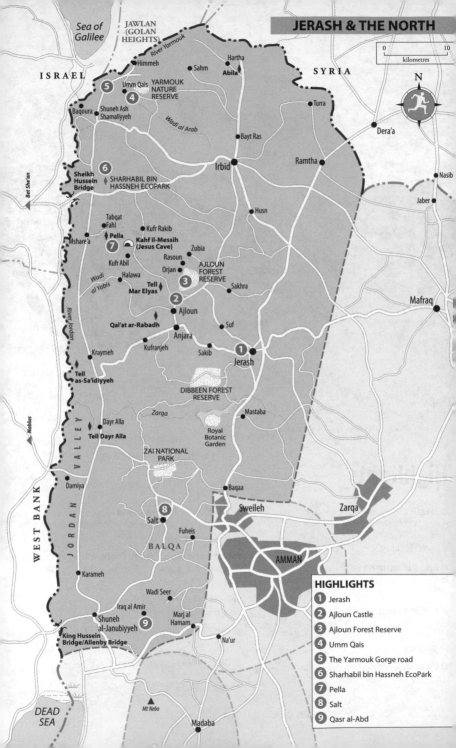

JERASH & THE NORTH

Sea of Galilee

JAWLAN (GOLAN HEIGHTS)

River Yarmouk

ISRAEL

SYRIA

Himmeh

Hartha

Sahm

Abila

Turra

Dera'a

⑤ Umm Qais
④ YARMOUK NATURE RESERVE

Baqoura

Shuneh Ash Shamaliyyeh

Wadi al Arab

Bayt Ras

Ramtha

Nasib

Jaber

Sheikh Hussein Bridge

⑥ SHARHABIL BIN HASSNEH ECOPARK

Bet She'an

Irbid

Husn

Tabqat Fahl

Kufr Rakib

Mshare'a

⑦ Pella

Kahf il-Messih (Jesus Cave)

Zubia

Mafraq

Kufr Abil

Rasoun

Orjan

③ AJLOUN FOREST RESERVE

Sakhra

Halawa

Wadi al Yabis

② Tell Mar Elyas

Ajloun

Suf

① Jerash

Qal'at ar-Rabadh

Anjara

Sakib

River Jordan

Kraymeh

Kufranjeh

Tell as-Sa'idiyyeh

DIBBEEN FOREST RESERVE

Mastaba

Zarqa

Nablus

Dayr Alla

Tell Dayr Alla

Royal Botanic Garden

ZAI NATIONAL PARK

Damiya

Baqaa

Sweileh

Zarqa

⑧ Salt

Fuheis

BALQA

AMMAN

JORDAN VALLEY

WEST BANK

Karameh

Wadi Seer

Iraq al Amir

⑨ Marj al Hamam

Shuneh al-Janubiyyeh

Na'ur

King Hussein Bridge/Allenby Bridge

Mt Nebo

DEAD SEA

Madaba

0   10
kilometres

N

HIGHLIGHTS

1 Jerash
2 Ajloun Castle
3 Ajloun Forest Reserve
4 Umm Qais
5 The Yarmouk Gorge road
6 Sharhabil bin Hassneh EcoPark
7 Pella
8 Salt
9 Qasr al-Abd

Jerash

Ruins: daily 8am–6pm (Nov–March till 4pm) • JD10, free with JP

One of the best-preserved Roman cities in the eastern Mediterranean, set in the bowl of a well-watered valley about 50km north of Amman, **JERASH** is the principal focus of a trip into northern Jordan. With its monumental and sophisticated public buildings tempered by charmingly human touches, the ancient city is likely to inspire even if you are on the jaded final leg of a ruin-hopping tour of the region.

Jerash is a huge site which easily merits a full day; if you have only a couple of hours, you could rapidly absorb the **Oval Plaza** – with its temple and theatre – the **Cardo**, the **Sacred Way** leading up to the **Temple of Artemis** and the **North Theatre**, but you wouldn't really be doing the place justice. Make sure you time your visit to coincide with one of the shows of Roman-style **chariot racing** staged in the **hippodrome**: they are quite a spectacle.

Approaching Jerash

Most visitors **approach Jerash** from Amman. Aim first for the big intersection at Sweileh on Amman's northwestern outskirts – reachable from Shmeisani on Queen Rania/ University Street or from 8th Circle on King Abdullah II/Medical City Street. From there, the main highway into northern Jordan, signed for Jerash, plunges steeply down the slope into beautiful countryside, with hills on the horizon sometimes snowcapped as late as April. Then comes **Baqaa**, the biggest of Jordan's UN-run Palestinian refugee camps – today a city of 100,000-plus. After crossing a bridge over the **River Zarqa**, you'll spot a well-signed turning marked for South Jerash. This road follows the west bank of the **Wadi Jerash**, lush with eucalyptus and olive trees, for 6km into Jerash itself, a bustling regional capital of around 45,000 people that sprawls over slopes beside the ruins. Information on accessing the site comes at the end of our account (see page 145).

Modern Jerash suffers economically from its proximity to Amman, Zarqa and Irbid, and is desperately **under-resourced**: it's essentially a farmers' town, reliant on income from olive processing and tourism. There's a handful of good restaurants, but nowhere to stay (bar one small hotel) and nothing to do. Almost everyone visits on a day-trip from somewhere else – and virtually no one investigates beyond the ruins.

Brief history

Known by give or take the same name for more than two thousand years, Jerash has a long and colourful **history** taking in emperors, invading armies and – like much of Jordan – modern reinvention after centuries of abandonment.

Ancient times

Set in the fertile hills of **Gilead**, which is mentioned frequently in the Old Testament as being a populated and cultivated region, the Jerash area has attracted settlement since prehistory: Paleolithic and Neolithic implements have been uncovered nearby, and archeological investigation around the South Gate of the city has revealed evidence of settlement going back to the Middle Bronze Age (around 1600 BC).

Gerasa (the ancient name for Jerash) was founded around 170 BC, the relatively small settlement of that time focused around the Temple of Zeus and the low hill opposite. Very little evidence of this **Hellenistic** period survives today.

The Roman era

By the time of Gerasa's foundation, the idea of the **Decapolis** had emerged (see page 135). Gerasa and its Decapolis neighbours were "liberated" by the Romans under Pompey in 63 BC and granted autonomy under the higher authority of the **Province of Syria**. The century which followed saw unprecedented growth and stability, and it was during the first century AD that the basic town plan as it survives today was laid down:

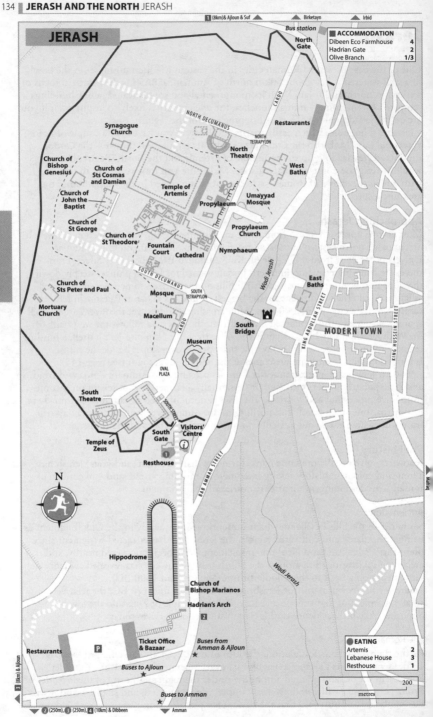

JERASH

1 (8km) & Ajloun & Suf   Birketayn   Irbid

Bus station

North Gate

ACCOMMODATION
Dibeen Eco Farmhouse   4
Hadrian Gate   2
Olive Branch   1/3

NORTH DECUMANUS

Restaurants

CARDO

NORTH TETRAPYLON

Synagogue Church

North Theatre

West Baths

Church of Bishop Genesius

Church of Sts Cosmas and Damian

Temple of Artemis

Propylaeum

Umayyad Mosque

Church of John the Baptist

Church of St George

Propylaeum Church

Church of St Theodore

Fountain Court

Cathedral

Nymphaeum

SOUTH DECUMANUS

Church of Sts Peter and Paul

Mosque

SOUTH TETRAPYLON

Wadi Jerash

East Baths

Mortuary Church

Macellum

CARDO

MODERN TOWN

KING ABDULLAH STREET

KING HUSSEIN STREET

Museum

South Bridge

OVAL PLAZA

South Theatre

SOUTH STREET

Temple of Zeus

South Gate

Visitors' Centre ⓘ

Resthouse 1

BAB AMMAN STREET

Mafraq

N

Hippodrome

Wadi Jerash

Church of Bishop Marianos

Hadrian's Arch 2

Restaurants

P

Ticket Office & Bazaar

Buses from Amman & Ajloun

EATING   2
Artemis
Lebanese House   3
Resthouse   1

Buses to Ajloun

0   200
metres

3 (8km) & Ajloun

2 (250m), 3 (250m), 4 (10km) & Dibbeen   Amman

Buses to Amman

THE DECAPOLIS

From the time of Alexander the Great, a group of around ten important cities of the Middle East began to be associated together. Bastions of urban **Greek** culture in the midst of a **Semitic** rural population, these cities were founded or refounded during or following Alexander's consolidation of power in the Levant in the late fourth century BC. **Decapolis** means "Ten Cities" in Greek, but Classical authors disagreed on both the number and identity of the ten: one list, from the first century AD, comprises, in modern-day Jordan, Philadelphia (Amman), Gadara (Umm Qais), Gerasa (Jerash) and Pella; in modern Syria, Damascus, Raphana, Hippos, Dion and Canatha; and in Israel, Scythopolis (Bet She'an). Although it's tempting to imagine the Decapolis cities working together in a formal league of cooperation, no records survive of such a pact, and it seems instead that the term was used simply to refer to the geographical area of northern Transjordan and southern Syria: the gospels of Matthew and Mark, for example, mention the Decapolis only as a region. All that can be said for sure is that the Decapolis cities shared a common history and culture.

After the **Roman** armies arrived in 63 BC, the area enjoyed a sizeable degree of both affluence and autonomy. The population within the cities – by this stage predominantly of Middle Eastern origin – spoke much more Greek than Latin (the latter was only used on formal occasions and in official documents), and were almost certainly also fluent in **Aramaic**, the language spoken in the countryside. Even in its heyday, Gerasa, for instance, remained at core a Semitic society, its ancient local traditions overlaid with Greco-Roman ideas.

By the second century, the Decapolis appears to have expanded; a list from this period names eighteen cities, including, in Jordan, Abila (Qwaylbeh), Arbela (Irbid) and Capitolias (Bayt Ras, near Irbid). However, historical confusion subsequently reigns supreme, with some authors indicating the Decapolis to be a part of Syria, others seeming to show that Syria was a part of the Decapolis, and still more including cities that seem to have played no part in the common history and culture of the original ten. It was **Emperor Trajan** who effectively broke the cultural bonds in the Decapolis and sowed the seeds of this confusion. His Province of Arabia, created in 106 AD, included only some of the cities: Pella and Scythopolis, for instance, remained within the Province of Syria. Bosra became the new provincial capital, and although Decapolis centres such as Gerasa and Philadelphia subsequently experienced a golden age in culture and sophistication, Trajan's reorganization ensured that their horizons now encompassed more than merely their own region: they were bonded firmly into the greater Roman order. By the time of the division of empire into east and west under **Diocletian** at the end of the third century, the notion of a special, parochial link between the cities of the Decapolis was dead.

a colonnaded north–south axis cut by two colonnaded side streets, along with a temple to Zeus (built over the pre existing temple) fronted by an oval plaza, expansion of the temple to Artemis and construction of the **South Theatre**.

In 106, when **Emperor Trajan** reorganized Roman authority in the region around his new Province of Arabia, Gerasa lost its autonomy and was governed from the provincial capital, Bosra. Gerasa gained a link by a branch road to Trajan's new highway running between Bosra and the Red Sea, while other main roads linked the city with Philadelphia and Pella. Suddenly, Gerasa found itself not only close to the provincial capital but also astride the highly lucrative trade routes guarded by the Nabateans. In 129–130, Gerasa briefly became the centre of the Roman Empire, as Trajan's successor, **Hadrian**, wintered in the city; in his honour, the Gerasenes built a new monumental arch outside the southern walls and embarked on major expansion works, including widening of the main street and renovation of temples and public buildings. Hadrian's visit ushered in a golden age for the city, and Gerasa's population may have touched 25,000 during the late second and early third centuries.

Civil disorder in Rome in the 190s heralded the end of the boom. Taxation increased to help cover greater military expenditure – which fuelled further resentment, as well as crippling inflation – and the Persian **Sassanians** began to whittle away at the eastern flanks of the empire. Trade was seriously affected, and in Gerasa the lavish programme of public works was cut back.

THE JERASH FESTIVAL

Jordan's major summer festival of music and the arts was founded in 1980 as the **Jerash Festival**, staged over two to three weeks during July and early August amid the city's ancient ruins. Audiences of thousands pack Jerash's open-air Roman theatres (as well as venues in Amman) to see big-name Arab performers and star-studded evenings of jazz, pop and opera, running alongside craft fairs and art exhibitions. You can usually buy tickets for roughly JD10–20, sometimes even on the day, and extra public buses are laid on each evening to get people to and from Amman. Check ⓦ jerashfestival.jo or ⓦ visitjordan.com for more information, or keep an eye on the *Jordan Times* for daily listings.

A sea change took place when, in 324, **Christianity** became the official religion of the eastern empire. Gerasa embraced the new religion shortly afterwards, and during the fifth and sixth centuries dozens of churches went up, though pre-existing buildings were ransacked for stones and columns, giving a botched, make-do feel to many of Gerasa's churches. By the late seventh century, the city was literally crumbling from shoddy workmanship and lack of maintenance. **Persian** forces were able easily to occupy the once-grand metropolis for a dozen years or so from 614.

After the Romans

After the Muslim victory over the Byzantines in 636, it was long theorized that Gerasa – subsequently arabized to **Jerash** – had slipped into anonymous decline: a small, jerry-built **Umayyad** mosque and a handful of kilns were the only evidence from the Islamic period in the city. However, a recent dig uncovered a large congregational **mosque** from the Umayyad period in the heart of the city centre, with what has been suggested is a governor's house attached. Work is ongoing, but Jerash may have been stronger and more populous in the early Muslim period than was previously thought. Nonetheless, a cataclysmic earthquake in 749 seems to have brought the city to its knees, and for a thousand years Jerash lay deserted.

At the beginning of the nineteenth century, **European** explorers – including, on a four-hour visit, Burckhardt (see page 255) – were taken around the ruins by local bedouin, and news of the "discovery" of the ancient city of Gerasa spread rapidly. Archeological investigation at Jerash has been continuous and wide-ranging ever since, although large areas remain untouched beneath the grass.

In modern times, a new lease of life for the ancient city came from an unexpected quarter. In 1879, in the same process of migration and resettlement that brought **Circassian** settlers to the deserted ruins of Amman, the Ottoman authorities directed refugee Circassians to settle in the ruins of Jerash. They occupied what is believed to have been the Roman residential quarters on the east bank of the river, and the bustling town which has since grown up there, now capital of its own governorate, still has a substantial population of Circassians.

Hadrian's Arch

The first monument you see as you approach Jerash from the south – and as you climb the steps from the ticket office – is the huge **Hadrian's Arch**, poised over a traffic junction. The 11m-high triple-arched gateway, which originally stood at almost 22m and which has been restored and partially reconstructed, was built to honour the visit of the Emperor Hadrian to Jerash in 129–130 AD. The huge arches, which probably had wooden doors, are flanked by engaged columns unusually decorated with capitals at the bottom rather than the top. Over 400m from the city walls, the positioning and structure of the arch point to a grandiose scheme for southward expansion of Gerasa. The municipal authorities seem to have been envisioning the arch as an enormous city gate, since its side walls were left untrimmed to enable tight bonding with new perimeter walls. The plan remained unrealized, however, and when it became clear, maybe a century or so later, that the city wasn't going to expand, two small side-pavilions, with niches mirroring the arch's side entrances, were added.

The Hippodrome
On the west side of Hadrian's Arch, an array of small arches belongs to the reconstructed south wall of the **Hippodrome**, which has undergone extensive renovation work. This was the scene of ancient Gerasa's sporting festivals and chariot races; 1500 years on, it is again (see below). At 244m long, and seating up to fifteen thousand spectators, it is impressively large for Jerash, but is nonetheless the smallest hippodrome so far discovered in the Roman Empire: the Circus Maximus in Rome could accommodate over 157,000 people. Jerash's arena has garnered international attention, though, for the preservation of remnants of its original starting gates as well as some areas of original seating.

Walking north towards the Visitors' Centre takes you past a series of shops built into the Hippodrome on the left, and the small, ruinous Byzantine **Church of Bishop Marianos** on the right, erected in 570 among Roman and Byzantine tombs on what was then the main Gerasa–Philadelphia road.

The South Gate
North of the Hippodrome is a restaurant (see page 146), guides office and **Visitors' Centre**, which has been recently renovated, with a good interpretation hall and mini-museum (free). Past this, you'll come to the reconstructed **South Gate**, the principal

---

CHARIOT RACING AT JERASH
Jerash is the backdrop for a revival of the Roman sport of **chariot racing**, with choreographed contests and displays of Roman military prowess staged in the restored Hippodrome. **RACE** ("Roman Army and Chariots Experience") organizes the reconstructions, which have been based on extensive research by academics and enthusiasts – including such luminaries as the technical adviser for the Oscar-winning film *Gladiator* and an Italian actor who drove chariots in the 1950s epic *Ben-Hur*. After surveying Roman hippodromes around the world, experts settled on Jerash as being the most suitable, for its modest size, good state of preservation and well-visited setting.

Shows take place on Saturday, Sunday, Monday, Wednesday and Thursday at 11am and 2pm, and Friday at 10am; shows are occasionally cancelled in bad weather, and times may be altered in winter and during Ramadan – check in advance online (45min; tickets on the door JD12, no need to book ahead; w jerashchariots.com).

From the earliest days of Classical Greece, around 650 BC, right through to the fall of Constantinople in 1453, chariot races followed a broadly similar format – four chariots competing around seven anticlockwise laps of the arena. The Jerash re-enactments follow the same guidelines. *Ben-Hur* summons up images of gleaming, armour-plated war-chariots racing improbably quickly behind four horses, but in reality the Romans (unlike the Britons and the Celts) used chariots only for racing, not in battle, so they built less visually impressive, but much faster, 50kg wickerwork chariots, drawn by two horses. The new Jerash chariots fall somewhere between Hollywood romanticism and the flimsy, but historically accurate, truth.

The shows are low-key affairs, but include live commentary in English. Expect legionaries in authentic Roman battledress, gladiators armed with swords and tridents and, of course, charioteers, everything meticulously choreographed. All the costumes and equipment have been manufactured in Jordan, and everyone involved in the show is from Jerash – most are ex-army or police. RACE keeps around seventy locals in salaried employment as actors, technical crew and stable-hands: for this reason, if no other, the project deserves your support.

entry point into the ancient city – officials here check you have a ticket and send you back to the ticket office to buy one if you don't (see page 145). It seems from the wheel ruts on the thresholds that the west door was reserved for wheeled traffic, and the central and east doors were used principally by pedestrians. Near the gate is a section of the 3m-thick wall which originally ran for over 3.5km around the city, a fourth-century strengthening of the original, thinner first-century wall.

The Oval Plaza

Beyond the South Gate, the split-level **South Street** runs between what is believed to be a Hellenistic settlement on the right, and the restored vaults supporting the lower terrace of the **Temple of Zeus** complex to the left. It gives onto what is one of the most impressive pieces of Roman urban design in the world, the **Oval Plaza**. The plaza comprises a large central paved area enclosed by two curving colonnades, both irregular bent ellipses and of different lengths, forming an elegant, smooth entry into the city proper while deftly linking the east–west axis of the Temple of Zeus with the north–south axis of the main street, the Cardo. Approaching from the south, the shorter western arm of the colonnade draws your eye (and your feet) towards the opening of the Cardo, which may originally have been marked by a prominent triple arch. Beautiful stone paving swirls around the plaza, following the curve of the Ionic colonnades. Two slightly wider intercolumnar spaces on the west show where small side streets led in from residential districts. The podium in the centre of the plaza may have supported a statue; in the seventh century, a water tank was built around it, and pipes are still visible set into the paving.

The South Theatre

From the plaza, a track climbs west up to the **South Theatre**, the most magnificent of all Jerash's monuments and the largest of the city's three theatres. Now extensively restored, it was built in the 90s AD to seat over three thousand, the cost of construction partly offset by contributions from wealthy Gerasenes. Inscriptions record such generosity, and lower seats on the shadier western side of the auditorium are numbered (notable citizens could presumably reserve these prime spots). You enter the theatre at the orchestra, and there are plenty of acoustic games to play: talking while standing at the midpoint of the orchestra gives an effect as good as a PA system, and if two people at opposite ends stick their heads into the round indentations below the seats they can hear each other's mutterings quite clearly. The stage has been restored in stone – it was probably wood originally – and the *scaenae frons*, or backdrop, would have had another storey on top of the beautifully carved detail that exists today.

The Temple of Zeus

Adjacent to the theatre on the same hill, the **Temple of Zeus** in its heyday must have towered over the city, and, like its sister temple of Artemis in the city centre, was intended to be visible from all parts of Jerash. Originally surrounded by gigantic Corinthian columns 15m high (the three that are standing now were re-erected in 1982 in the wrong place), the temple was built in 162–163 AD on the foundations of a first-century predecessor, which itself replaced a temple from the second century BC.

The inner sanctum is plain and simply decorated, and the massive front wall is 4.5m thick, to accommodate stairs up to the roof. In front of the temple, huge dismembered columns have lain untouched since the day of some cataclysmic **earthquake** in antiquity; the slope they lie on, now covered with earth and overgrown, probably conceals a monumental staircase. From above, the layout of the *temenos*, or sacred terrace, below the temple is clear, with remains of an altar to the left; the far side of the *temenos* is supported on the restored vaults visible from South Street. What is also clear from here is the vast extent of ancient Gerasa: as well as the entire sweep of the ancient ruins, much of modern Jerash is visible. Behind a minaret in a distant space between buildings in the town, you can spot a surviving remnant of the eastern city wall.

The Cardo (Colonnaded Street)

The colonnaded **Cardo**, the main boulevard of ancient Jerash, leads north from the Oval Plaza into the city centre. Some 800m long, the street was originally laid out with Ionic columns, but at some point during the remodelling of the city in the second century, it was widened as far as the Temple of Artemis and the columns updated to the grander Corinthian order. Along the Cardo, the columns supported a continuous architrave, and a wide covered pavement on both sides gave access to shops behind. Because of the gentle gradient, each column stands a few centimetres higher, and is slightly shorter, than the last; where the column height would have been too small to maintain strict architectural proportion, the architrave was halted, bracketed into the side of the next column and begun again at a higher level. The diagonal street paving is marked by deep grooves worn by centuries of metal-wheeled traffic, while round drain covers give access to an underground sewerage system.

Macellum

The four tallest columns in this section mark the entrance on the left to the **macellum**, the ancient food market, an octagonal courtyard built around a central fountain and surrounded by small shops. Originally there were massive tables in four corners of the courtyard; strikingly carved supports survive in the farthest corner.

Museum
Included in site ticket

Opposite the *macellum*, steps lead up to the small site **museum**, the garden of which is dotted with carved sarcophagi and chunks of statuary. Inside are exhibits tracing the settlement of Jerash from Neolithic times, including a good explanation of ancient coinage.

The South Tetrapylon

The Cardo meets the first of Jerash's two major cross streets, the **South Decumanus**, at an intersection known as the **South Tetrapylon**. At the centre of this circular plaza are four freestanding podia, each of which was decorated with shell niches and held four columns topped by a square entablature. A statue probably stood between the four columns of each podium. This impressive structure was designed to turn a simple street junction into a grand meeting point flanked with shops, while not impeding traffic circulation from street to street.

To the east, the South Decumanus crossed the river into what were probably Gerasa's residential neighbourhoods at the **South Bridge**. The bridge has been restored, but a modern fence bars access.

On the southwest corner of the junction, excavations have revealed a large congregational **mosque** from the eighth-century Umayyad period, set crooked to the street so that its three *mihrabs* faced south towards Mecca.

What has been suggested is a **governor's house** stands alongside to the southwest, indicating that this spot may have been the city's nexus of power at the time. Investigation is continuing, but this building is already providing a fascinating link between the pagan Gerasa of the ancient world and modern, Muslim Jerash.

The Nymphaeum

Beyond the South Tetrapylon, the Cardo was expanded to its widest extent, and Byzantine raising of the pavement included the addition of small niches down at ankle level, either for small statues or, possibly, streetlights. The wheel-ruts from chariot traffic are particularly pronounced in this section. Eight tall columns on the left mark the entrance to the Cathedral (see page 143), while beyond, fronted by four even taller columns, is Gerasa's lavish **Nymphaeum**. Completed in 191 AD, and dedicated to dancing, singing water nymphs, the Nymphaeum was a grandiose **public fountain**: imagine the sight and sound of water splashing in abundance from such a finely carved monument. Even today, dry, the carving which survives on the two-storey semicircular recess is impressive. Originally, the lower storey was faced in green marble, while painted plaster covered the upper storey; traces of the green-and-orange design survive in the topmost niche on the left. Concealing the holes in the lower niches, statues were probably designed to appear to be pouring water into the basin below, from which lion's-head fountains spat water into shallow basins at pavement level. One of Jerash's most endearing small details is the basin carved as four fish (or dolphins) kissing, their eyes serving as drainage holes. The huge red granite laver in front is a Byzantine embellishment.

3

The Temple of Artemis complex

Beyond the Nymphaeum, thirteen ordinary-sized columns are followed by four gigantic ones marking the entrance to the **Temple of Artemis**. The most important edifice in the ancient city, this temple was approached via a long east–west **Sacred Way** which originated somewhere in the residential eastern quarters and cut across the Cardo at the point marked by the four huge columns. The best way to discern the route is to pick a path to the east through the jumble of rubble opposite the four columns and stand on top of the apse of what is called the **Propylaeum Church**, ingeniously created from elements of the Roman street. In the sixth century, when the cult of Artemis had passed into historical memory, the Christian inhabitants of Gerasa sealed off the old Sacred Way with the apse and used the colonnades of the street as the divisions within the church between nave and aisles. Between here and the Cardo, a **plaza** – decorated with beautiful spiral-twisted columns topped with a delicately carved architrave that now lies in chunks nearby – became the atrium of the new church. Behind, down below the Propylaeum Church, a Roman bridge carrying the Sacred Way once spanned the river. One of the few monuments of Gerasa to survive in modern Jerash is the huge **East Baths** building, which you can see on the other side of the river: ongoing excavations here have produced a series of spectacular discoveries, including life-size statues of Aphrodite and Zeus in 2017, and in 2018, statues of six of the nine Greek Muses – the first to be found in the Middle East.

The Propylaeum

On the west side of the Cardo, a portico leads you to the **Propylaeum**, a massive, ornately decorated gateway dedicated in 150 AD, which gives onto a monumental staircase of seven flights of seven steps. At the top – but still well below the temple proper – is a terrace with the foundations of a small **altar**; from here, another monumental staircase, originally over 120m wide, takes you up to the level of the **sacred courtyard**, or *temenos*, with a dramatic view of the temple.

3

The temple

The Temple of Artemis is set far back in a vast **courtyard** some 161m deep and 121m wide, which was originally lined on all four sides with a colonnade and is now cluttered with the ruins of Byzantine and Umayyad pottery kilns and workshops. The temple has clung onto its huge **portico**, whose clustered limestone columns have turned peachy bronze over the centuries. Inserting a long stick or a key between the drums of any of them (the fourth on the left is a favourite) demonstrates how these mammoth pillars were designed to sway gently, in order to absorb the effects of earth tremors and high winds – and have been doing so for almost two millennia without toppling.

The inner sanctum

The temple's *cella*, or **inner sanctum**, is today exposed, but would originally have been surrounded by a peristyle of six columns across each short side, eleven on each longer side; the capitals of those that stand are still in place, but some elements of the entablature have never been found, pointing to the possibility that the temple was never completed. The inner walls of the *cella* would have been richly decorated with slabs of marble supported on hooks fitting into the holes all round the walls, which were pilfered during the Byzantine period to adorn churches. At the back is the single focus of all this wealth of extraordinary architecture along the Sacred Way: the **niche**, now empty, which once housed an image of Artemis, daughter of Zeus and goddess of the forests, who cared for women and brought fertility to all creatures.

The North Theatre

From the Temple of Artemis courtyard, a track leads north to the rear of the restored **North Theatre**. Much smaller than its southern twin, this was originally constructed in the 160s AD to be a small performance space or council chamber; many of the seats in the lower rows are marked with Greek names, referring to tribes which voted in the city council. On the two ends of the semicircular orchestra wall, lovely little **stone reliefs** show women and boys dancing and playing different musical instruments. Upper rows of seats were constructed early in the third century to give a total capacity of around 1600, but by the fifth century the building seems to have fallen out of use as a theatre. Much reconstruction and renovation work has been done here, not least in the **orchestra**, with its beautiful marble flooring. The restored theatre saw its first public performance in more than 1500 years when, in 1997, the Palestinian poet Mahmoud Darwish gave a reading to a packed house.

In front of the theatre is a reconstructed **plaza**, with huge Corinthian columns on one side of the street faced by an equally huge colonnade on the other; the latter is flanked by unusual double columns ingeniously knitted into the walls of the theatre itself.

The North Tetrapylon

Beside the North Theatre's plaza, the **North Decumanus** meets the Cardo at a rebuilt junction-point known as the **North Tetrapylon**. Simpler than the South Tetrapylon, this dates from the late second-century remodelling of Gerasa and comprises arches on all four sides leading into a small, domed central space. On the eastern side of the street rise the huge arches of the **West Baths**, which includes a room fronted by two columns that has somehow clung onto its elegantly constructed domed brick roof. A fraction south, you'll find the ruins of a small **Umayyad mosque**, with a reused Roman shell niche serving as a makeshift *mihrab*.

The North Gate

Beyond the North Tetrapylon, the northernmost section of the Cardo, is the quietest part of Jerash. Ignored during the city's second-century face-lift, this part of the street retains its original, plain Ionic colonnade, and is the same width as when initially laid out in the first century AD. The peaceful walk ends after some 200m at the **North Gate**, dating from 115 AD, from which a road once led on to Pella. The gate is a cleverly designed wedge shape, in order to present a square facade both to the Cardo and to the Pella road.

Retrace your steps partway down the Cardo to explore the Cathedral and surrounding ruined churches.

The Cathedral

Fifteen Byzantine **churches** have so far been uncovered in Jerash, and wending a path through the largely unexcavated southwestern quarter of the ruins to visit nine of them, starting with the Cathedral and ending up near the South Theatre, brings you out of the main crush of the central sights.

The elaborate **Cathedral Gateway**, marked by eight large columns on the Cardo just south of the Nymphaeum, originally formed the entrance to a now-vanished second-century **temple**, thought to have been dedicated to Dionysus. During the fourth century, the old temple was converted into the large church that survives today, at the head of a monumental **staircase**. The walls flanking the stairs originally supported high enclosed and roofed colonnades on both sides, but earthquakes toppled the lot. The old pagan temple probably faced west – as does the Temple of Artemis – but the new church had to face east: the Byzantine architects seem to have been unconcerned about aesthetic harmony and calmly plonked the apse of the new church plumb across the head of the staircase. A small shell niche **Shrine to Mary** was placed on the blank exterior wall of the apse. It was originally dedicated to "Michael, Holy Mary and Gabriel" and it's still possible to read the Greek for Gabriel in red paint on the right of the band beneath the shell.

Left or right from the shrine, the narthex brings you round into the **Cathedral** itself, a shadow of its former self. Little is known about this building: no sign of a dedication has been found and historians aren't sure if it even was Gerasa's cathedral. Colonnades, of which only bits and pieces remain scattered about, divided the nave and the aisles, and the high side walls were decorated with elaborate glass mosaics. Pale pink limestone flagstones survive in the aisles. To the south is a small **chapel**.

Fountain Court and around

Immediately west of the cathedral, a portico beautifully paved in red and white octagons and diamonds leads into the atrium, known as the **Fountain Court** after the square fountain in its centre fed by water brought from the reservoir at Birketayn (see page 144). Roman historians, including Pliny, hinted that Gerasa held festivals to Dionysus (the god of wine) at which water miraculously turned into wine. After the Dionysian temple here had been converted into a church, it duly became the venue for festivals celebrating Jesus's performance of the same feat at Cana. During these festivals, so the historian Epiphanius records, the square fountain in this court miraculously began to flow with wine.

To the side of the paved portico is a small room known as the **Glass Court**, named for the huge quantity of glass fragments discovered there. The weeds and rubble carpeting its floor conceal beautiful mosaics, reburied for protection. Left (west) of the Glass Court, a staircase leads up to the tiny **Sarapion Passage**, its octagonal flags running beneath precarious lintels out to the **Stepped Street**. Turning left up the street brings you past the maze of tiny rooms forming the Byzantine **Baths of Placcus**, which date from an unusually late 455 AD, evidence that luxurious Roman bathing habits died hard. Dominating the baths to the left are twin colonnades of the **Church of St Theodore**, dating from 496. Nothing remains of the main superstructure of the building, the marble paving of the nave and aisles or the glass mosaics which covered both the interior walls and the semidome over the apse; all that does remain is the huge apse itself, nosing out dramatically above the Fountain Court below.

The western churches

A path from St Theodore's leads west over scrubby hillocks, reaching after 150m a group of three interconnected **churches** built between 529 and 533. Out here, you're away from the main cluster of ruins – it's a fine area to walk and ponder the extent of Roman Jerash, and just how much lies unexcavated beneath the grass.

Church of Saints Cosmas and Damian

On the right as you approach from St Theodore's, the **Church of Saints Cosmas and Damian** houses the best of Jerash's viewable mosaics, although the only way to see them is to lean over the high wall around the church; the church doors are locked. Cosmas and Damian were twin brothers born in Arabia in the late third century, who studied in Syria and became famous for providing medical services for free. Their church is floored with a large mosaic open to the elements, which shows birds and animals in a geometric grid of diamonds and squares. Just below the chancel screen, the dedicatory inscription is flanked by portraits of the donors of the church; to the left is Theodore swinging a censer in his official robes as a kind of church trustee, and to the right his wife Georgia, her hands upraised.

From the Church of Saints Cosmas and Damian, it's possible to work your way back to the Visitors' Centre through the adjacent circular **Church of John the Baptist** and **Church of St George**, both with fragments of floor mosaics surviving.

Synagogue Church and south to Mortuary Church

Heading north from Cosmas and Damian takes you to the ruined **Synagogue Church**, way up on high ground and invisible from below. A Jewish synagogue originally stood here, oriented westwards towards Jerusalem, with a floor mosaic depicting the Flood and various Jewish ritual objects. On its conversion into a church in 530 or 531, during a period of Jewish persecution under Emperor Justinian, a new geometric mosaic was laid over the original, and the orientation of the building reversed, with an apse laid in what was formerly the synagogue's vestibule.

South of Synagogue Church lie the ruins of the **Church of Bishop Genesius**, built in 611 just three years before the Persian invasion and featuring a prominent benched apse. On a hill 300m south, tucked inside the southwestern city walls not too far from the South Theatre, the **Church of Saints Peter and Paul** and, close by, the **Mortuary Church** are slowly being reclaimed by Mother Nature.

Birketayn

2km north of Jerash North Gate

Amid the bustle of modern Jerash town centre, two small roads branch off the main route north to Irbid, passing in front of Gerasa's North Gate. The road on the left climbs towards

ANCIENT ORGIES

The **Maiumas festivals** were nautical celebrations of ancient origin which involved, among other things, the ritual submersion of naked women. By the time of Gerasa's heyday, the festivals seem to have become thinly veiled excuses for open-air **orgies**, and were duly **banned** by the city's early Christian rulers. In 396 AD the rule was relaxed, provided that the festival followed "chaste customs"; however, the pleasures of the flesh seem to have proved irresistible, since three years later the ban was reimposed. Some 130 years passed before the festival was again resurrected and incorporated by the Gerasenes into their Christian faith as a kind of **harvest celebration**, purged of eroticism.

Suf, but an easy walk along the other, leading directly away from the gate, brings you to **Birketayn** (Arabic for "two pools"). Set in a shaded valley in a crook of the road, this is a Roman double reservoir – restored in the 1960s – which fed water into Gerasa. Birketayn was the venue for the notorious **Maiumas festivals** (see opposite).

> ### FREE WITH JORDAN PASS
> Throughout this Guide, "free with JP" means that the attraction grants free admission to holders of the **Jordan Pass** (see page 55).

Overlooking the reservoir stands the thousand-seat **Festival Theatre** and, beyond, a path leads through the trees to the ruined **Tomb of Germanus**, standing amid sown fields, some columns upright and others – along with the empty sarcophagus – entwined in thistles down the slope.

ARRIVAL AND DEPARTURE   JERASH

By car Jerash is about 50km north of Amman and about 40km south of Irbid. After the drive from the capital (see page 133) you'll reach a set of traffic lights in central Jerash overlooked by the giant Hadrian's Arch; a left turn leads to Ajloun, but if you go straight ahead for 50m you'll see a side-turning to the left just in front of the arch which heads down to a free parking area and a fake tourist bazaar, within which is the site ticket office.

By bus and serveece Public buses and *serveeces* arrive

at Jerash's bus station, sited just beyond the northern limit of the ruins – though buses to and from Amman and Ajloun will also pick up and drop off at the road junction by Hadrian's Arch, at the southern end of the ruins. Note that public transport out of Jerash ends by about 5.30pm; after that time, you'll have to either hitch or negotiate a taxi fare (around JD30–40 to Amman).

Destinations Ajloun (30min); Amman Tabarboor (1hr); Irbid (35min).

INFORMATION

Tickets Tickets cost JD10 (free with JP) from the ticket office (daily 8am–6pm, Nov–March till 4pm) located within the tourist bazaar below Hadrian's Arch. If you try to enter the ruins elsewhere, you'll be sent back here.

Visitors' Centre From the ticket office, steps lead up to Hadrian's Arch, from where it's a 400m walk beside the Hippodrome to reach the Visitors' Centre, which houses an excellent interpretive exhibition on the history and architecture of Jerash. Alongside the Visitors' Centre is the

Resthouse restaurant (see page 146), an office coordinating local guides and the mighty South Gate, the main entrance to the ancient city.

Guides Hiring a guide to lead you around the ruins can bring a visit to life: these fluent professionals are generally very knowledgeable. They wait at the office beside the Visitors' Centre, opposite the *Resthouse* door; just ask, and you'll be passed along to the next in line. Expect to pay around JD20 for a tour lasting roughly 1hr 15min.

ACCOMMODATION

IN TOWN
Hadrian Gate On the main road beside Hadrian's Arch ☎ 077 779 3907; map p.134 The only hotel in Jerash. Run by the cheerful and accommodating Walid, it has five immaculate doubles and triples, most en suite: go for the private en-suite room 105 on the roof, with a panoramic terrace. It's overpriced but friendly and pleasant – and in a perfect location. **JD50**

OUT OF TOWN
Dibeen Eco Farmhouse About 10km southwest ☎ 079 535 5555, ⓦ facebook.com/dibeenfarmhouse; map p.134 This family-run organic farm offers an unexpected slice of rural living. Set in rolling pine-forested countryside outside Jerash, it has six tidy guest rooms, one en suite, and offers the kind of welcome hotels can't touch. Hike in the woods, help out picking fruit or olives, chopping wood or

feeding the chickens – or just relax, listen to stories from Zeid and the family and gorge on farm-to-fork food. **JD45**
Olive Branch In the hills 8km northwest ☎ 02 634 0555, ⓦ olivebranch.com.jo; map p.134. This soulless hotel is in a peaceful location offering a panoramic view over forested hills. The rooms are all en suite, some with a balcony, but interiors are very tired and the food is poor. You can camp in their grounds – which include a shaded swimming pool – for JD15 (less with your own tent). Follow road signs to Suf until, 7.5km from Jerash, you see a sign pointing left to Ajloun; from the sign, a minor road winds 1.5km through olive groves to the hotel. Buses from Jerash to Suf can drop you at the sign. An alternative route to the hotel comes off the Jerash–Ajloun road: take an Ajloun minibus, ask to be dropped at the hotel's sign, and walk 2km along the turn-off road. A taxi from Jerash is about JD6–8. **JD50**

3

THE ROYAL BOTANIC GARDEN

The idea to establish a **Royal Botanic Garden** (RBG) for Jordan took shape in 2005. The site chosen is the hilly area of **Tell Ar Rumman**, to the west of the Amman–Jerash road and about 25km north of the capital, overlooking the lake formed by the King Talal Dam. At 180 hectares, with more than 300m of elevation difference between mountain summits and the lakeshore, the garden is able to grow most of the country's native plant species, in five **Jordanian habitats** re-created within the site: deciduous oak forest, pine forest, juniper forest, Jordan Valley and freshwater wadi. Habitat-based **conservation** is a key theme – as is **social inclusion**: the people (and their flocks) living in the area are an integral part of the conservation model, with environmental education and research into sustainable land use playing a key role.

So far the RBG has established a native plant nursery, a seed bank, a national herbarium and other projects, alongside fostering research into medicinal plants and rangeland rehabilitation. Eventually, it is intended to be a demonstration site open to the public, showcasing "sustainable living and environmentally compatible solutions that can be easily replicated by the average Jordanian", with themed **gardens**, nature trails, **birdwatching**, a **butterfly house**, **boat trips** on the lake, a wholefood **café-restaurant** and ecolodge **accommodation**. Call or check online (☎ 06 541 3402, 🖰 royalbotanicgarden.org) for up-to-date information.

EATING

For **eating**, few visitors bother to explore beyond lunchtime buffets at the *Resthouse* in the site itself (see below), but there's a scattering of countrified restaurants around town – or you could head into modern Jerash, to take your pick of the local *shawarma* and falafel stands.

Artemis 250m south of the Ajloun road ☎077 978 8828, 🖰facebook.com/artemisrest; map p.134. This countryside tourist restaurant has a reputation for quality and decent service, offering a range of meze (JD3–7) and standard Arabic grills (JD6–9) in an upmarket hilltop setting. It's an easy 10min walk from the ruins, or a 3min taxi ride. Hours vary.

★ **Lebanese House** 100m east of Artemis restaurant, 250m south of the Ajloun road ☎02 635 1301, 🖰lebanese-house.com; map p.134. Widely known as

Umm Khalil ("Khalil's Mother"), a familiar name given to the *patronne* of years gone by – Antoinette Rami, a refugee from the Lebanese civil war who fled to Jordan – this classy Lebanese restaurant has been a Jerash fixture since 1977. The quantity of Jordanian families dining here and the impeccable standard of the food speak volumes. The staff, though formal, are well used to foreigners – expect a genial and accommodating welcome, and a bill of around JD15 a head. It's an easy 10min walk, or a 3min taxi ride. Hours vary.

Resthouse Beside the Visitors' Centre ☎02 635 1437; map p.134. This run-of-the-mill tourist restaurant makes it into our reviews solely for its convenient location (and its a/c): the lunchtime buffets are adequate but overpriced, at around JD16. An adjacent café section sells cold bottled beer. Hours vary.

Ajloun

Northern Jordan's verdant hills are cut through by countless lush valleys. Even in the height of summer, when the hills are baked brown and dry, you'd miss a good deal of the kingdom's beauty if you neglected the chance for a trip into the countryside. Thick forests of pine, oak and pistachio covered these slopes until the early 1900s, when large areas were cleared to provide timber for the Hejaz Railway (see page 88), both for track-building and fuel. Enough survived, though, in the **AJLOUN** region around the highland market town of the same name, to give plenty of walking and picnicking possibilities in what are some of the most southerly natural pine forests in the world. Use the town – or, better, the rural tourism projects around the **Ajloun Forest Reserve** nearby – as a base to get way off the beaten track for a day or three, walking silent hillside tracks and exploring the magnificent Crusader-period castle perched among the olive groves. In 2019 plans were approved to build Jordan's first **cable car** in Ajloun; details were scarce at the time of writing, but the project may be under way when you visit.

Ajloun town

Ajloun town itself (pronounced "adge-loon"), 25km west of Jerash via a beautiful road that lopes over the hills among stands of pine and olive trees, has been a centre of population for a thousand years or more. Marking the centre of the town, 150m along the market street from the bus station, is a **mosque**, probably from the early fourteenth century; the square minaret base, simple prayer hall and carved Quranic inscriptions set into the walls are original.

Ajloun Castle

Daily 8am–6pm (Nov–March till 4pm) • Joint ticket with Tell Mar Elyas JD3, free with JP • Shuttle buses run from Ajloun bus station (frequent Fri & Sat, less so on other days; 10min), and a taxi costs JD8–9 return; it's a stiff 3km walk from the town centre – head up the steep road keeping the minaret on your left

The history of the town is bound up in the story of **Ajloun Castle** – in Arabic, the *Qal'at ar-Rabadh* – which towers over it from the west. The hill on which the castle sits, Jabal Auf, is a perfect location, offering bird's-eye views over the surrounding countryside and over three major wadis leading to the Jordan Valley. It's said to have formerly been the site of an isolated **Christian monastery**, home to a monk named Ajloun. By 1184, in the midst of the Crusades, the monastery had fallen into ruin, and an Arab general and close relative of Salah ad-Din, **Azz ad-Din Usama**, took the opportunity to build a **fortress** on the ruins, partly to limit expansion of the Crusader kingdoms (Belvoir castle stands just across the River Jordan to the west and the Frankish stronghold of Karak is ominously close), partly to protect the iron mines of the nearby hills and partly to show a strong hand to the squabbling clans of the local Bani Auf tribe. Legend has it that, to demonstrate his authority, Usama invited the sheikhs of the Bani Auf to a banquet in the newly completed castle, entertained and fed them, then threw them all into the dungeons. The new castle also took its place in the chain of beacons which could transmit news by pigeon post from the Euphrates frontier to Cairo headquarters in twelve hours. From surviving records, it seems that Ajloun held out successfully against the Franks.

Expanded in 1214–15 by Azz ad-Din Aybak (who also worked on Qasr Azraq), Ajloun's castle was rebuilt by the Mamluke sultan **Baybars** after being ransacked by invading **Mongols** in 1260. Ottoman troops were garrisoned here during the seventeenth and eighteenth centuries, but when the explorer Burckhardt came through in 1812, he found the castle occupied only by forty members of a single family. Earthquakes in 1837 and 1927 caused a great deal of damage, and consolidation work on the surviving structures is ongoing.

Visiting the castle

These days, the castle is entered from a modern parking area below the walls. A **moat bridge** cuts through the east wall. A long, sloping passage leads up to an older, arched entrance, decorated with carvings of birds, and just ahead stands the original entrance to Usama's fortress. Although the warren of chambers and galleries beyond is perfect for scrambled exploration, with all the rebuilding over the centuries it's very difficult to form a coherent picture of the castle's architectural development; there's even – in this Muslim-built, wholly Muslim-occupied castle – one block carved with a cross, presumably part of the monk Ajloun's monastery. However, a climb to the top of any of the **towers** gives breathtaking views over the rolling landscape, and these more than make up for any historical confusion.

Off to the side of the castle road are acres of olive groves, carpeted in spring with wild flowers – perfect **walking** territory.

ARRIVAL AND DEPARTURE   AJLOUN TOWN

By bus The bus station is in the town centre.
Destinations Amman Tabarboor (1hr 30min); Irbid (45min); Jerash (30min); Kraymeh (30min).

By car Ajloun is 25km west of Jerash and 30km south of Irbid. If you're driving from Jerash, don't miss (after 18.5km) the right turn signposted to Ajloun in the middle of Anjara town (see page 154). After exploring Ajloun, if you're seeking a route down to the Jordan Valley, there are two options. You could go back to Anjara and take the main road via Kufranjeh – or opt for a more scenic back route down between the hills. Halfway up the road towards Ajloun Castle, turn off at the *Jabal Castle* hotel, fork left after 4km and then right 4km further. The rustic village of Halawa appears after another 7km, in the middle of which there's a steeply sloping fork; the road to the left (which runs past the post office) will eventually deliver you after 10km of lovely countryside around Wadi al-Yabis (also known as Wadi Rayyan) to the Jordan Valley highway – or if heading direct to Pella, follow the signs from Halawa.

ACCOMMODATION AND EATING

Ajloun has two **hotels**, both located on the quiet castle road. Despite being decades past their best, they remain popular with holidaying Jordanian and Saudi families, and may need booking ahead in summer. On balance, you'd do better to stay at the Ajloun Forest Reserve (see below) or take advantage of homestays and rural B&Bs in nearby villages (see page 152). Picnicking on the castle slopes is a good alternative to sampling the basic **restaurants** in town – or make a detour towards the castle for one of the area's loveliest community-run cafés.

Ajloun Hotel The castle road ☎ 02 642 0524. The higher of the two hotels on the castle road, this place is smaller and shabbier than the nearby *Qal'at Al Jabal* (see below), with marginally lower prices and barely adequate rooms. __JD33__

Qal'at Al Jabal (Jabal Castle) The castle road ☎ 02 642 0202. With a nice garden in front, this old place limps on, year after year. A cavernous, gloomy lobby preludes old-fashioned rooms, some of which boast spectacular castle views: room 201, for instance, is spacious and en suite, and has a fine balcony. __JD36__

★ **Summaga Café** Opposite the castle ☎ 079 702 3723, ⓦ facebook.com/summagacafe. A friendly community-run café at the top of the castle road, with airy views across to the fortress and enveloping countryside. Run by a women's-led cooperative of 25 organic farms, it offers all sorts of local goodies, from honey to olive oil, on a menu that includes varieties of breakfast omelettes (JD6), lunches or dinners of salads and roast meats or veg (around JD11) and a range of fresh juices, coffees and herb teas (JD2–3). Lovely. Daily 9am–10pm.

Ajloun Forest Reserve

Around 85km north of Amman • JD8; fee waived if you book a walk or stay overnight • Book all activities at least a day in advance, on ☎ 079 906 2210 or via the RSCN Wild Jordan centre in Amman ☎ 06 461 6523, ⓦ wildjordan.com (see page 82)

One of Jordan's most beautiful hideaways is the Royal Society for the Conservation of Nature's **AJLOUN FOREST RESERVE**, spread over remote hillsides about 9km north of Ajloun. This is lovely countryside, situated around 1200m above sea level – the coolness compared to Jerash is noticeable, and when it's sweltering a short drive away in the Jordan Valley it can be balmy and fresh up here.

The reserve comprises 13 square kilometres of rolling Mediterranean woodland – mainly evergreen oak, with some pistachio, carob and wild strawberry trees along with olive groves. The **fauna** covers some very European names: wild boar, foxes and badgers are all common (alongside striped hyena, Asiatic jackals and wildcats), as are **birds** such as tits, finches and jays. **Roe deer** – previously extinct in the wild – have been successfully reintroduced to the reserve by the RSCN. Staying a night or two, or just booking for a meal and a walk, is strongly recommended.

Tourism investment has been pouring into rural Ajloun in recent years – not least via the US government's USAID programme – and there are now competing interests at play in and around the forest reserve. As well as the walks and visits outlined in this section, run by the RSCN's **Wild Jordan** ecotourism unit (see page 82), the local Al Ayoun community has developed its own trails (see page 152).

Walks in the Ajloun Forest Reserve

Roe Deer Trail 2km; 1hr; self-guided free, guided JD11 • **Rasoun Trail** 7km; 3hr; JD17/person • **Orjan Village Trail** 12km; 6hr; JD25/person including lunch • **Prophet's Trail** 8.5km; 4hr; JD23/person including lunch • **Ajloun Castle Trail** 18km; 9hr; JD32/person including lunch and donkey transport • **Rockrose Trail** 8km; 4hr; JD17/person • Return transport by minibus is included for all except the circular trails

From the reserve visitor centre, several **walking trails** head out into the trees. The **Roe Deer Trail** is a short circuit heading up through the forest to a nearby hilltop and back – especially beautiful in springtime when wild flowers carpet the ground.

WALKS AROUND AJLOUN

Ajloun is **hill-walking** country. In this chapter we outline walks within the **Ajloun Forest Reserve** (see oppsite) and on the community-run **Al Ayoun Trail** (see page 152) – but there are other options too. **National walking routes** pass this way, or you could head off-piste: outside the rainy (and occasionally snowy) winter months, the gentle terrain of north Jordan lets you make your own explorations – preferably in the springtime, when the flowers are at their best.

ON THE JORDAN TRAIL

Stage 2.1 of the national **Jordan Trail** (15.4km; moderate; 5hr; see page 50) begins at **Ajloun Castle**. Dropping down to the south, it offers hilly views as it passes west of Anjara town, climbing past an **abandoned village** – with its spring still flowing – to follow a cliff above Wadi Mahmoud into the village of **Khirbet as-Souq**, where there's a simple homestay. The Jordan Trail website (ⓦjordantrail.org) has full information, maps, GPS points and detailed walking notes.

A TWO-DAY TREK TO PELLA

A fine **two-day trek** leads 36km from the fortress of Ajloun down to the ruins of Pella (see page 165). Bring water, since places to replenish supplies are widely spaced. From the castle walls at Ajloun you can see the line of the route: west along the ridge, then down right into the thickly forested valley and up west to a saddle between rounded hills, on the far side of which is concealed the **Wadi al-Yabis** (also known as Wadi Rayyan). The walk down this long and varied valley is particularly beautiful, first passing through **natural forests** to reach a knoll on its right side, with **Ottoman ruins**; this makes for an idyllic **campsite**, with a view to the setting sun behind the Palestinian hills. The second day covers about 20km, with a pleasant morning walk down through **olive groves**. The path crosses and recrosses the stream, until a larger stream enters from the right after a couple of hours. Cross the confluence and take a track north through well-tended **orchards** where birds dart between pomegranate blossoms in spring. The trail rises steeply to the hilltop village of **Kufr Abil**, from where various options down 6km of country lanes take you almost to the Jordan Valley, emerging above the village of **Tabaqat Fahl** at the ruins of Pella.

Don't rely on our brief outline: this and other walks in the area are described in detail in *Jordan: Walks, Treks, Climbs & Caves in Al Ayoun Jordan* by Di Taylor and Tony Howard (see page 390).

Longer trails must be done with an RSCN **guide**, in a group (min four, max twenty). The **Soap House Trail** leads through the woods and up to the stunning Eagle Viewpoint at 1100m before continuing down into Rasoun village. The **Orjan Village Trail** extends the Rasoun Trail to reach springs, copses and olive groves around Orjan village. The **Prophet's Trail** heads off in the other direction, south past caves and across hillside meadows before climbing to Tell Mar Elyas (see page 153); an extension, graded as "difficult", continues on an all-day route to Ajloun Castle, dubbed the **Ajloun Castle Trail**. Another route is the **Rockrose Trail**, a scenic countryside walk of moderate difficulty, crossing wooded valleys and ridges on a beautiful looping path.

Wild Jordan Ajloun (Royal Academy for Nature Conservation)

Hours vary • Free • ⓦ wildjordan.com

Just before you drive into the reserve, you pass on the right a long, low, cantilevered building of stone. This beautiful landmark, designed by Jordanian architect Ammar Khammash, was originally intended to be an academy for training nature guides. At the time of writing, it was being prepared for reopening as **Wild Jordan Ajloun**, a rural twin for Amman's original Wild Jordan centre (see page 82). Approached via a bridge arching over a disused quarry, the building seems to float above the treetops beyond. Exactly what will be on offer inside isn't clear, but from the sleek lobby, with its deliberately rough finish, you will turn right for a **café-restaurant**, with shaded

> ### WILD JORDAN RESERVE PRICES
>
> **Prices** at Jordan's **RSCN-run nature reserves** are high. The RSCN make no apologies for this, saying that the reason they exist is to protect Jordan's natural environment, and that they have built lodges and developed tourism – under their **Wild Jordan** brand – as a tool for generating funds to help conservation and support rural communities. You may or may not agree with their pricing policy, but this kind of responsible tourism is virtually unknown in the Middle East, and the RSCN are pioneers. For now, until tourism schemes emerge that are truly community-owned, paying extra to visit the RSCN reserves is a good way to ensure that your money goes to benefit rural people and habitats.

tables out back, or turn left to enter a sinuous, skylight-illuminated corridor. This leads to a **nature shop**, selling RSCN crafts, as well as to outlets employing local women producing floral-infused olive oil **soap** and all-natural **biscuits** and energy bars for national distribution. You can view the workshops and chat with the women; there's no pressure to buy, but if you do, profits stay in the villages. Deeper into the building are conference rooms, a library and lecture hall.

ARRIVAL AND DEPARTURE   AJLOUN FOREST RESERVE

By car From Ajloun town centre, with the castle road to your left, drive straight on (north) up the hill on the road towards Irbid. After 4.7km, turn left towards Ishtafeina (or Eshtafena) village. (If you're coming the other way, this junction lies 24.6km south of the Yarmouk University campus in Irbid city centre.) From here the reserve is clearly signposted down 4km of twisting country lanes, on a hill above Umm Al Yanabeea village. Whatever you're planning to do, check in first at the Visitor Centre reception office, beside the parking area.

By taxi A taxi from Ajloun to the Visitor Centre is about JD8–10. There's no public transport.

ACCOMMODATION

The cabin **accommodation** within the Ajloun Forest Reserve is situated amid olive groves just behind the Visitor Centre buildings. The silence up here is wonderful.

★ **Ajloun Cabins** By the Visitor Centre ☎ 079 906 2210, ⓦ wildjordan.com. Comfortable, with even a whisper of style, these attractive, Scandinavian-style cabins – in three grades: economy, standard and deluxe – have cement floors, raised wooden verandas and comfy beds and sofas, all with en-suite bathrooms and heaters. Breakfast is included, as are views of the forest. Booking essential. **JD94**

Visitor Centre ☎ 079 906 2210. Breakfast and other meals are usually taken at the Visitor Centre's (shaded) rooftop tables, in front of sumptuous views extending out to Palestine and as far as the snowcapped Jabal ash-Sheikh peak on the Syria/Lebanon border. Even if you're not staying, you can book ahead for lunch or dinner here (JD12–18/person) – hearty fare, using local ingredients, organic whenever possible. Walkers' lunchboxes are also available (JD6).

Orjan and Rasoun

As part of their remit for supporting socioeconomic development in the communities hosting nature reserves, the RSCN and Ministry of Tourism launched development projects in **ORJAN** and **RASOUN**, two adjacent villages on the northern edge of the Ajloun Forest Reserve. The aim of the programme is to provide local people with new sources of income, thereby reducing their dependence on natural resources, promoting environmental conservation and giving a boost to the rural economy. At the time of writing, though, the RSCN had made the decision to centralize the projects – soap-making and biscuit-baking – in their "Wild Jordan Ajloun" building, a short distance from the villages at the entrance to the Ajloun Forest Reserve. Check online for the latest information.

Rasoun Heritage Museum

Rasoun village • Daily except Fri 9am–3pm • Free, by appointment only, either via the Ajloun Forest Reserve or direct on ☎ 077 220 8001, ⓦ facebook.com/rasoun.museum

A local homeowner in Rasoun village, Mohammad Suleiman – better known as Abu Issam – has opened up the small **Rasoun Heritage Museum** in his home. The items in his collection speak to a rustic past: tools for farming and cooking, artefacts such as coffeepots, coins and ephemera including early postage stamps. Equally enticing is the chance to spend some time in a family setting, sipping tea and hearing stories of rural Jordanian life.

ARRIVAL AND DEPARTURE ORJAN AND RASOUN

By car To reach Orjan and Rasoun, follow directions to the Ajloun Forest Reserve; just before a left turn climbs to Umm Al Yanabeea village, the road around the edge of the reserve is signposted ahead for both villages, which lie just a few kilometres further.

On foot From the Ajloun Forest Reserve visitor centre, take the (guided) 7km Rasoun Trail (see page 148) to reach Rasoun.

ACCOMMODATION AND EATING

Orjan and Rasoun, like Ajloun, are popular rural getaways for Jordanian and Saudi/Gulf travellers, who come for the greenery and mild climate more than the cultural exchange; a few families in the villages oblige with independent B&B **accommodation**. You could also stay in the RSCN reserve (see page 150), or even the hotels by Ajloun Castle (see page 147), and arrange transport over. However, the options below are much more pleasant, with a warmer welcome and more interesting atmosphere. With notice, the local Al Ayoun Trail guides (see below) can fix you up with a home-cooked **lunch** or **dinner** in someone's house (roughly JD8–11/person), even if you're not staying – well worth sorting out in advance.

★ **Eisa Dweekat Family Homestay** Orjan ☎ 079 682 9111, ⓦ facebook.com/eisa5dweekat. A lovely homestay just past Rasoun on the edge of Orjan village, with one of the area's leading guides – Eisa is knowledgeable, well-connected and super-hospitable. He has added five en-suite double/triple rooms to his home, turning this into a peaceful rural mini-hotel, with comfortable beds, excellent bathroom facilities and superb home cooking (lunch or dinner JD15pp). Eisa is justifiably in demand: this is a popular spot. Book ahead. Per person: **JD25**

Mohammad Dweikat Orjan ☎ 077 229 3291. Simple village homestay comprising one large shared room in the house of Mohammad Dweikat (brother of Eisa), with four single beds – basic, but welcoming, comfortable and superclean, with private shower. Food is all local, and memorably good. Per person: **JD20**

Rasuon Camp Across the valley from Rasoun ☎ 079 793 0071, ⓦ facebook.com/rasuoncamp. This basic countryside camp (spelled "Rasuon" on Facebook) is run by local character "Sheikh" Zuher Al Shar'e. It has a range of options, from single-person tents up to larger tents sleeping four or six and basic cabins. There are simple washing facilities, and meals provided (around JD10). To get here, ask any local guide for directions. Camping per person: **JD15** Cabin for two people: **JD46**

★ **Wadi Tawaheen Rest House** Near Orjan ☎ 077 684 6239. This wonderful little countryside café lies hidden away in the Wadi Orjan, easily walkable (or driveable) in a few minutes from Orjan village, its shaded tables perched just above the bubbling, rushing river. It's a simple spot, serving delicious food – bread from a traditional *taboon* oven, local *za'atar* and jams (breakfast JD3–5, lunch or dinner around JD10) – and to one side is a little two-bedroom lodge sleeping up to four. Lodge **JD30**

Al Ayoun Trail

Three villages in Ajloun's **AL AYOUN** municipality (*ayoun* means springs) which borders the reserve – Rasoun, Orjan and Baoun – have clubbed together to develop a new walking path. Jordan's first-ever community-run cooperative tourism enterprise, the **Al Ayoun Trail** runs for 12km between all three villages, crossing some beautiful and otherwise unvisited countryside. The rationale is for the community to direct attention towards their (stunning) natural setting, to boost local income directly through guiding fees and trail support – and, perhaps, to spark further development in tourism and infrastructure from outside parties. It's all about social engagement and developing the guest/host relationship which lies deeply embedded in Arab culture: **this is not a nature trail**, and though much of it passes through open country, you are also routed quite deliberately into the villages – in part walking on asphalt roads. The idea is to book ahead with a **guide**, to learn about the area, engage with individuals in each village (someone will prepare lunch in their home, someone else may invite you for tea, others may want to show you a particular site), to see and be seen, to stop and be stopped. It's a slow, people-focused ramble.

The trail

The Al Ayoun Trail begins in **Rasoun** village, a short drive from the Ajloun Forest Reserve visitor centre. Past Rasoun village centre, the trail forks to the right down into the Wadi Orjan, lush with figs, pomegranates, carob and cherries, then enters **Orjan** village. The path climbs, offering views into Wadi al-Yabis/Wadi Rayyan, before dropping into Wadi Abu Kharoub, lined with carob trees, and up again past olive groves and a cemetery into **Baoun** village. After zigzagging through the village and beyond, the trail picks up a shepherd track which crosses the hills and climbs to a mosque at **Listib**, ending at the hilltop site of **Tell Mar Elyas**.

Along the way there are small Roman sites, Bronze Age dolmen fields and Byzantine hermitages. There's even the modest Aisha al-Baouniya Cultural Forum, established in Baoun to honour the sixteenth-century mystic and poet Aisha al-Baouniya, one of Islam's most renowned female Sufi theologians.

Trail extensions

Trails have also been opened up either side of Al Ayoun, linking to Zubia, Ajloun Castle and Pella, some of them part of the national **Jordan Trail** (@jordantrail.org; see page 50). We outline a couple of extension walks earlier in this chapter (see page 149).

3

ESSENTIALS	**AL AYOUN TRAIL**

Local guides You can walk the Al Ayoun Trail independently – but, frankly, that's not really the point: the idea is to walk with a guide. If you don't fancy walking all of the path – or any of it – you can still book ahead to be met, hosted and guided on foot for as much as you want and driven for the rest. The best point of contact, and one of the area's best walking guides, is Eisa Dweekat (☎079 682 9111, @facebook.com/eisa5dweekat). Alternative contacts include Mohammed Swalmeh (☎077 221 9604, @mohdswalmeh@live.com) and Mahmoud Hawawreh (☎077 213 6376, @mahmoud_hawawreh@yahoo.com). Expect to pay around JD75–90/day for a guide.

Accommodation and eating With notice, the local guides can fix you up with homestay accommodation, with or without a home-cooked lunch or dinner in someone's house. They can also arrange meals at the homestays for non-guests (roughly JD10–15/person) – well worth arranging in advance.

Tour operators Jordanian firms offering excursions to the trail include @experiencejordan.com.

Walking guidebooks The best resource is *Jordan: Walks, Treks, Climbs & Caves in Al Ayoun Jordan* by Di Taylor and Tony Howard (available on Amazon). Profits from the book support the local communities. It covers trails either side of Al Ayoun, including to Pella and Ajloun, as well as routes and ideas of all sorts for seeing more (and understanding more) of northern Jordan. It's invaluable (see page 390).

Abraham Path The Al Ayoun Trail has long been supported by the Abraham Path Initiative (@abrahampath.org), an international project fostering the development of a long-distance walking route from Turkey to Palestine. Look online for background and practical info.

Tell Mar Elyas

Daily 8am–6pm (Nov–March till 4pm) • Joint ticket with Ajloun Castle JD3, free with JP

A holy site sacred to Muslims and Christians lies tucked away in the hills west of Ajloun. **Tell Mar Elyas** (or Elias) is generally accepted as the birthplace of the prophet Elijah, named in the Bible as "Elijah the Tishbite" (Tishbe has long been associated with Listib, a region lying 8km west of Ajloun) and who is also proclaimed in the Quran as a "messenger".

The modest archeological remains, on a windswept hilltop, are of a huge, cruciform **church**, roughly 33m by 32m. Only the foundations and a course or two of stones are left. One of the exposed floor **mosaics**, in white letters on a red background, has been dated to 622 AD – a time of upheaval in Jordan, with the Byzantine forces in full retreat in the face of the Islamic armies sweeping northwards. There has been, as yet, no satisfactory reason put forward as to why the authorities were building churches amid such political instability. Beside the apse is a **sacristy**, floored with a plain mosaic, and there are some beautiful mosaic designs surviving against the north wall, including multicoloured chevrons and an elaborate drinking vessel with grapes. At the western end of the church is a section on a slightly lower level, possibly a narthex, which incorporates a deep **well** beside an ancient oak.

Many of the trees in the area are bedecked with strips of cloth, tied by pilgrims – both Christian and Muslim – as a mark of respect for the prophet. A good time to visit is on Elijah's commemoration day of **July 21**, when there are special celebrations – but arriving at this lonesome spot on any afternoon, especially on foot, to be met by a fiery sunset behind the hills of Palestine, is quite an experience.

ARRIVAL AND DEPARTURE   TELL MAR ELYAS

By car The memorable drive from Ajloun leads along a quiet country lane clinging to the contours of the forested slopes. From Ajloun centre, head up the hill towards the castle, then turn off at the *Qal'at al-Jabal* hotel. At a crossroads after 1km, go steeply down to the left. After 4km, a junction is marked with a sign to Mar Elyas (and another to the village of Wahadneh, where there's a modern church dedicated to Elijah); head right at the sign for just under 2km, go left for 1km, then take an unsigned dirt track left uphill for 400m to the parking area at the foot of the *tell*.

On foot Tell Mar Elyas is on many walking routes in the area, including the Al Ayoun Trail (see page 152) and Prophet's Trail (see page 148).

Anjara
3km south of Ajloun • Buses from Ajloun (5min) and Jerash (25min)

The small market town of **ANJARA** sits south of Ajloun, on the main road up from the Jordan Valley towards Jerash. Local legend has it that Jesus, Mary and the disciples once stopped overnight at a cave near the town, where Jesus gave a sermon. There's nothing in the Bible about this, but it is known that Jesus crossed the Jordan many times, and Anjara then (as now) straddled a junction of roads.

Sayyidat al-Jabal
From Anjara's central junction, the square steeple of the church, with its distinctive red roof, is clearly visible just below the main road • If the gates aren't open, ask around locally – Father Nimat lives nearby and will be happy to unlock the shrine for you

The exact location of the cave where Jesus supposedly stayed near Anjara is unknown. In the 1920s, an Italian Catholic priest, Father Foresto, decided a plot of land in the town would have to do for a **commemorative church**, and arranged for a 150-year-old life-size wooden statue of the Madonna to be brought over from Italy. The church went up in the 1950s, and then in 1971 Father Nimat – who is still the chief cleric in Anjara – built a shrine for the statue in the churchyard, known as **Sayyidat al-Jabal** (or Our Lady of the Mountain), and had its walls decorated with (rather kitsch) murals. Following the seal of approval from the Vatican that this is indeed a sanctified Catholic site, Christian **pilgrims** now flock to Anjara to visit the diminutive shrine in its rubbly artificial grotto.

Dibeen Forest Reserve
Hikers free; JD2/car • rscn.org.jo

A large area of cool, fragrant, pine-forested hillside 10km southwest of Jerash, the **Dibeen Forest Reserve** – like its neighbour near Ajloun – is a beautiful, remote getaway. In 2004 the forest (about 8 square kilometres) was declared a protected area under the RSCN, who have begun a scheme to promote environmental conservation and launch sustainable development with local people. International developers have also got their eyes on this forest: after many disputes, a super-luxury **hotel** was reported to be going ahead in 2016, managed by Aman Resorts under the name *Amanbadu*, but there's no sign of it and no news about progress.

Nonetheless, Dibeen remains a fine option for woodland **walks** or **picnics** with a view amid the stands of Aleppo pine and evergreen oak, although there are no facilities. It is a very popular spot for family outings and barbecues, so expect weekends to be busy; it's not unknown for there to be four hundred cars parked in and around the forest on summer Fridays and Saturdays. The nearby *Dibeen Eco Farmhouse* (see page 145) is a great overnight option.

ARRIVAL AND DEPARTURE	DIBEEN FOREST RESERVE
By car Head from Jerash towards Ajloun, then after 100m turn left and follow signs; this road continues through the Ghazza Palestinian refugee camp and down into the lush Wadi Haddada past the reforestation projects at Jamla	before reaching Dibeen. **By bus** No public transport runs nearby. **By taxi** A taxi from Jerash is about JD7.

Irbid

Although **IRBID** has been inhabited since the early Bronze Age and has also been identified as the Decapolis city of Arbela, almost nothing survives from its ancient past. This busy university city of around 750,000 people was crowded before the Syrian war erupted on its doorstep; since 2013 it has struggled to absorb huge numbers of people seeking refuge from the fighting. Located around 75km north of Amman, Irbid remains friendly enough, with rambling souks filling the downtown alleyways, but there's little to merit a diversion. It is most often visited as a staging post for journeys into the far north of Jordan; if time is short, give it a miss.

Dar as-Saraya antiquities museum

Tell Irbid • Sun–Thurs & Sat 8am–4pm, Fri 10am–4pm • JD2, free with JP

Rising above the bustle of the downtown markets is Irbid's *tell*, its steep streets now lined with offices. Behind the municipality building, the old Ottoman **Dar as-Saraya** (Governor's House), built in the mid-nineteenth century, has been restored to serve as a rather good **antiquities museum**. Rooms around the courtyard exhibit fine pottery from Pella and other Jordan Valley sites, as well as Greco-Roman statues from Umm Qais and a splendid mosaics collection. Staff here can provide information about Irbid and the local area, and will also direct you down the street to Beit Arar.

Beit Arar

Tell Irbid • Daily except Fri 8am–3pm • Free

Beit Arar, an atmospheric Ottoman courtyard house, was once home to the nationalist poet Mustafa Wahbi al-Tal (1897–1949), who wrote under the pseudonym "Arar". It's a pleasant place to relax and browse through the displays on the poet's life.

Museum of Jordanian Heritage

Yarmouk University • Sun–Wed 10am–4.30pm • Free • From the main university gate, continue straight ahead until the second roundabout, and the museum is the second building to the right, part of the Institute of Archeology and Anthropology

About 2km south of Irbid city centre is the campus of Jordan's highly regarded **Yarmouk University**, around which a funky quarter of studenty restaurants and music stores has evolved, centred on Arshaydat Street, known to all as University Street. Yarmouk's modest **Museum of Jordanian Heritage** is worth a visit; all periods of Jordan's history are explained clearly on informative panels, and illustrated with interesting artefacts, from 9000-year-old statues to antique farm tools. Upstairs, displays focus on traditional crafts.

ARRIVAL AND DEPARTURE	IRBID

BY CAR
Irbid is perhaps Jordan's least car-friendly city. Signage is poor, traffic is horrendous and parking is a nightmare. Factor in plenty of time to cross the city – and expect to get lost, bored and frustrated behind the wheel.

BY BUS
Irbid has numerous bus stations, of which three serve destinations other than local villages. Minibuses link all the bus stations with the downtown area, but they are marked in Arabic only – ask around for help. A taxi fare across the

city from any of them shouldn't come to more than JD2.

New Amman station The New Amman station (*mujemma amman al-jdeed*) is about 500m east of the Sports City junction. Buses and large Hijazi coaches serve Amman's Tabarboor station, while JETT runs frequent coaches to/ from their Amman Abdali offices and less frequently to/ from Amman 7th Circle.

Destinations Ajloun (45min); Amman (at least every 30min; 1hr 15min); Aqaba (6hr); Jerash (35min); Mafraq (45min).

Valleys station The Valleys station (*mujemma al-aghwar*) is located off Palestine St about 2km west of downtown.

Destinations Mshare'a (for Pella; 45min); Sheikh Hussein Bridge (1hr).

North station The North station (*mujemma ash-shomali*) is about 1.5km north of downtown on Fadl al-Dalgamouni St.

Destination Umm Qais (45min).

INTERNATIONALLY

To Damascus At the time of writing the war in Syria was continuing, and the country was closed to tourists. There's no knowing when that situation will change. When it does, ask around at Irbid's New Amman bus station for information on transport to Damascus or the nearest Syrian city, Dera'a. Routes run via the Jordanian border town of Ramtha, 20km east of Irbid.

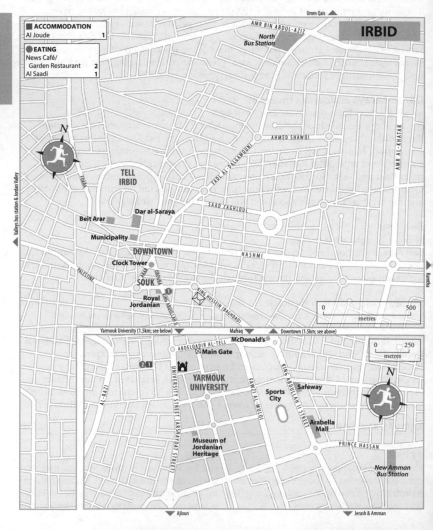

To Nazareth Buses to Nazareth – the largest Palestinian city in Israel – run a few times a week (usually Tues, Thurs, Sat & Sun, but variable). All buses originate in Amman, so are subject to traffic conditions, but pick-up in Irbid is around 3–3.15pm. The fare is around JD18, and buses cross via the Sheikh Hussein Bridge (see page 164), 30km west of Irbid, where you pay a departure tax of JD10. Contact the bus operator Nazarene Tours (☎+972 4 647 0797, ⊛nazarene-tours.com) for detailed information and bookings. A more laborious method is to take a bus or *serveece* for about JD4 from Irbid's Valleys station to the Sheikh Hussein Bridge terminal (taxi roughly JD25), from where a shuttle covers no-man's-land between the two customs posts. On the other side, a taxi to the Israeli town of Bet She'an, a few kilometres west, costs about 50 shekels (US$13).

ACCOMMODATION

For a city of this size, Irbid's **accommodation** is poor. There's a little cluster of cheap hotels near the downtown souks, but none is recommendable. A few business hotels are signposted around the edges of the centre, but there's only really one tourist hotel worth mentioning.

Al Joude Manama St, off University St ☎02 727 5515; map p.156. Irbid's best hotel (which isn't saying much) offers spacious en-suite rooms – some carpeted, others with laminate flooring – that are shabby and old, but adequate. Staff are friendly, and the cheerful *News Café* downstairs provides a room-service menu. Free parking is another bonus, as is the location, within walking distance of the university quarter. **JD42**

EATING

Irbid's **downtown souks** are packed with eating options, but they mostly cover street-food basics: falafel and *shawarma*, plus patisseries for Arabic sweet treats such as *kunafeh*. **University Street** is more enticing; here virtually every establishment is an eating house of some kind, and the turnover is massively high: what's here this year might be gone the next. The best advice is to copy the locals and browse your way along the street, or just aim for your favourite brand of **fast food**: burgers, pizzas, fried chicken and doughnuts all feature strongly. For picnic ingredients, the large 24hr Safeway **supermarket** isn't far away.

News Café/Garden Restaurant Al-Joude hotel, off University St ☎02 727 5515; map p.156. Buzzing basement joint, popular with students and other trendy types, that has decent salads (from JD3) and pizza (from JD4), plus pastas, sandwiches and the like, washed down with decent coffee or cold beer. It's a popular spot to smoke an *argileh* (from JD3.50). The hotel's outdoor *Garden Restaurant* serves similar stuff. Daily 10am–midnight or later.

Al Saadi King Hussein St (Baghdad St) ☎02 724 2454; map p.156. This is one of the better choices in the downtown area – a fairly basic place offering standard Arabic meze and grilled meats for around JD8–10 a head. Sun–Thurs & Sat 9am–10pm, Fri 2–10pm.

The far north

The land hard up against the Syrian border in the **far north** of Jordan is hilly farming country, especially beautiful in springtime when a riot of colour covers the fields between groves of olives and figs. The ancient trees around the picturesque village of **Umm Qais**, perched on the very edge of the Transjordanian plateau, are famed for producing some of the choicest olives in the region, although the village is best known for the atmospheric ruins of **Gadara** – where Jesus performed one of his most famous miracles – and for spectacular views out over the Sea of Galilee. Below coils the dramatic gorge of the **River Yarmouk**, which flows west to meet the River Jordan just south of the Sea of Galilee, and which now marks the border between Jordan and the Israeli-occupied Golan Heights (*Jawlan* in Arabic). Travel along the gorge is restricted. Nestled among palm trees and banana plantations below the heights is **Himmeh**, graced with a laidback air that belies the Israeli watchtowers within shouting distance. Further east, tucked away in the peaceful Wadi Qwaylbeh north of Irbid, lie the part-excavated ruins of **Abila**, another of the Decapolis cities, featuring a hillside rock-cut cemetery decorated with Byzantine frescoes.

Umm Qais

Off the beaten track 30km northwest of Irbid, tucked into the angle of borders formed by Jordan, Israel and the Golan, the windswept village of **UMM QAIS** is well worth the effort of a long journey, whether you visit on a day-trip from Irbid or stay overnight to relish the still twilight and fresh, chilly mornings. The main attraction is exploring the remote, widespread ruins of the Decapolis city of **Gadara**, on the edge of modern Umm Qais, some of which are jumbled together with the striking houses of black basalt and white limestone of an abandoned Ottoman village. It's a popular choice for Friday outings, when its parking area can be filled with family cars and youth-club buses, and the ruins swamped by teenagers more interested in having a raucous good time than absorbing the atmosphere. Umm Qais is unmissable, but do pick your moment to visit.

Since the foundation of the State of Israel in 1948, Palestinians who were expelled from or fled their homes have come to Umm Qais specifically to savour the spectacular **views** over their former homeland – the waterfront city of Tabariyyeh (Arabic name for Tiberias), the choppy lake itself, and the villages and lush countryside of the Galilee. The tradition is continued today by many Palestinian Jordanians.

Brief history

After the death of Alexander the Great in 323 BC, Gadara was founded by the **Ptolemies** as a frontier station on their border with the Seleucids to the north (*gader* is a Semitic word meaning "boundary"). In 218 BC, the Seleucids took the city, but came under siege a century later from the Jewish Hasmoneans; when the Roman general **Pompey** imposed order throughout Syria in 63 BC, he personally oversaw the rebuilding of Gadara as a favour to one of his favourite freedmen, a Gadarene.

The Roman era

The city won a degree of autonomy under the Romans, and became a prominent city of the Decapolis (see page 135). **Roman rule** – particularly following Trajan's annexation of the Nabatean kingdom in 106 AD – brought stability and prosperity. As at Jerash, Gadara saw large-scale **public building works** during a second-century golden age, including construction of the great baths at Himmeh. Literary sources

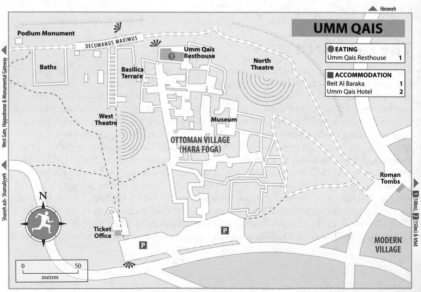

UMM QAIS

Podium Monument

DECUMANUS MAXIMUS

Baths

Basilica Terrace

Umm Qais Resthouse

North Theatre

West Theatre

Museum

OTTOMAN VILLAGE
(HARA FOGA)

Roman Tombs

N

Ticket Office

MODERN VILLAGE

West Gate, Hippodrome & Monumental Gateway

Shuneh ash-Shamaliyyeh

Himmeh

● EATING
Umm Qais Resthouse — 1

■ ACCOMMODATION
Beit Al Baraka — 1
Umm Qais Hotel — 2

0   50
metres

MIRACLE OF THE GADARENE SWINE

Gadara's main claim to fame centres on a story recounted in the New Testament about **Jesus** crossing the Sea of Galilee. The following version is in Matthew 8:28–32:
And when he came to the other side, to the country of the Gadarenes, two demoniacs met him, coming out of the tombs, so fierce that no one could pass that way. They cried out, "What have you to do with us, O Son of God? Have you come here to torment us before the time?" Now a herd of many swine was feeding at some distance from them. And the demons begged him, "If you cast us out, send us away into the herd of swine." And he said to them "Go." So they came out and went into the swine; and the whole herd rushed down the steep bank into the sea, and perished in the waters.

describe Gadara at this time as a city of great cultural vitality, a centre for philosophy, poetry and the performing arts, where pleasure-seeking Romans came from all over the empire. As early as the third century BC, a native of the city, **Menippos**, had risen to become renowned in Greece as a **Cynic** philosopher and satirist. By the second century AD, the city's Cynic streak was flourishing in the hands of **Oenomaos**, a nihilist and critic, although perhaps the city's best-known sons are **Philodemus**, a mid-first-century-BC Epicurean philosopher, and **Meleager**, a highly regarded love poet. **Theodoros of Gadara** was a famous rhetorician of the first century BC, who taught the Emperor Tiberius. Later, two Gadarenes of the third century AD stand out: **Apsines** taught rhetoric in Athens; and the scientist **Philo** refined Archimedes' calculations of mathematical pi.

3

After the Romans

By 325 AD Gadara was the seat of a **bishopric**, but its proximity to the decisive battles at Pella and Yarmouk, when Muslim armies defeated the Christian Byzantines, led to the establishment of Muslim rule over the city decades before the foundation of the Umayyad caliphate in Damascus in 661. However, a series of **earthquakes** not long afterwards destroyed much of Gadara's infrastructure, and the town went into rapid decline.

At some point in the Middle Ages, Gadara's name changed to **Umm Qais**, possibly derived from the Arabic *mkes* (frontier station) or *maqass* (junction). Little is known about it until 1806, when the German traveller Ulrich Seetzen identified the ruins as those of Gadara.

Modern times

During the 1890s, a small village grew up on the Roman ruins, the inhabitants reusing the precut stones to build their homes around courtyards. A modern village soon developed nearby, but people continued to occupy the Ottoman cottages – known as the **Hara Foga**, or "upper village" – right through until 1986, when the 1500 inhabitants accepted token payments from the Ministry of Tourism to leave their homes, in order to enable archeologists to investigate.

However, not a single square of land was cleared. In the 1990s the government changed its tune, announcing a project to convert the Hara Foga into a **tourist village**, for private-sector profit. A few houses were renovated – among them the buildings now housing the *Umm Qais Resthouse* and the museum – but work then stalled, to the satisfaction of many of the displaced locals, who saw the plan as a betrayal.

Other schemes have come and gone, but for much of the year the abandoned Ottoman village and its once-grand Roman neighbour stand quiet, tour groups sweeping in and out, weeds growing higher and dust-devils infiltrating the long narrow streets.

Locals still mourn the displacement as marking the end of their generations of self-sufficiency, evoking memories of life in the Hara Foga through poetry, plays and film. New projects are helping visitors access some of these stories through walks and homestays; ask around for the latest.

ACTIVITIES AROUND UMM QAIS

At the very northern tip of Jordan, **Umm Qais** serves as the trailhead for several **walking routes** into the hilly countryside nearby, not least the long-distance Jordan Trail.

THE JORDAN TRAIL

The 23.8km first stage of the national **Jordan Trail** (Ⓦ jordantrail.org; see page 50) is a long hike, recommended in spring before the summer heat kicks in. Starting from Umm Qais, the route drops to the dam in mighty Wadi Al Arab, skirting the lake before climbing to farmland, dodging between villages on a loop that ends in Wadi Ziglab at the **Sharhabil bin Hassneh Ecopark**, where there is accommodation (see page 165). The Jordan Trail website has full information, maps, GPS points and detailed walking notes.

GUIDED WALKS AND CULTURAL HERITAGE

Baraka Destinations (Ⓣ 077 666 7660, Ⓦ barakadestinations.com), a local tourism firm, has been working with villagers to develop **guided walks** through the **Hara Foga** – Umm Qais's abandoned Ottoman village – for visitors to hear stories of times past and experience contemporary hospitality. They also offer the chance to join a local **beekeeping** expert for a trip to his hives (and buy the honey), a **cooking** class with a local family, **basket-weaving**, **olive-picking**, **cycle-riding** and more. Check their website for details and bookings.

YARMOUK FOREST RESERVE

The **Yarmouk Forest Reserve** was established in 2010 as part of a larger project run by the Royal Society for the Conservation of Nature (RSCN) to manage ecosystems in the Jordan Rift Valley. Spread over a small area (20 square kilometres) of the hills beside Umm Qais, the reserve overlooks the River Yarmouk, which marks the border between Jordan and Syria. It protects a swathe of **deciduous oak forest** (85 percent of Jordan's surviving cover), along with two species of rare orchid, mammals including otters, hyenas, wolves and the threatened **mountain gazelle**, reptiles, fish and birds. The first hiking trails opened to the public in 2018. Check Ⓦ rscn.org.jo or talk to Baraka Destinations for the latest.

The ruins

Daily 8am–6pm (Nov–March till 4pm) • JD5, free with JP • Guided tour (2hrs; JD21; advance booking essential at Ⓦ barakadestinations.com)

At the western edge of the modern village of Umm Qais, as you approach the ancient site you'll pass two **Roman tombs** in a hollow to your left; the basalt doorways are beautiful, and it's tempting to link them to the miracle story recounted in the New Testament, but that appears to be supposition.

From the ticket office, up some steps above the car park, a Roman street leads you into the abandoned Ottoman village, where you can wander freely in and out of the weed-ridden courtyards and dusty alleys. The street leads to the evocative **West Theatre**, built entirely of basalt; its three thousand spectators – including VIPs in freestanding high-backed power chairs – had a fine view west over the city (now a grassy hill dotted with olive trees).

The Basilica Terrace

North of the West Theatre is Gadara's most dramatic space, the **Basilica Terrace**, cut into the bedrock on one side and supported by vaulted shops below on the other. Its main feature, closest to the theatre, is a square Byzantine **church** dating from the fifth or sixth century. A small narthex opens into an outer circular passageway, still paved with coloured geometric tiles, which encloses a central octagon demarcated by basalt columns which probably supported a dome. Within the octagon, a small depression and apse housed the altar, behind which stands a thin, pink marble column carved with a cross. On the north side of the terrace, the white limestone paving and columns of the **atrium** stand in stark contrast to the black columns of the church.

The atrium gives onto Gadara's main, paved street, the **Decumanus Maximus**, the clear line of which can be traced east and west – but the main draw is the simply spectacular **view**, a breathtaking, wind-exposed 180° sweep taking in the Jordan Valley, the Sea of Galilee (with the city of Tiberias in plain view), the Yarmouk Gorge and, most impressive of all, the Golan Heights rearing up in front, pointing the way north towards snowcapped Jabal ash-Sheikh on the Lebanese border. Linger here.

The North Theatre and museum

Museum: daily 8am–5.30pm (Nov–March till 3.30pm) • Entrance included in main ticket

Above and to the east of the Decumanus Maximus rise the restored arches of the on-site restaurant (see page 162). Following the street around the edge of the hill brings you to the grassy bowl of the **North Theatre**, its stones plundered to build the Ottoman cottages. At the highest point of the hill is the site **museum**, occupying the former residence of the Ottoman governor. It's an elegant building on two storeys, with a portico and a lovely, peaceful internal courtyard. Highlights of the collection include a headless marble statue of Tyche found in the West Theatre, mosaics and carved sarcophagi.

The western quarters

What we've described here comprises only a small part of Roman Gadara: the city originally extended for a kilometre west from the Basilica Terrace. It remains largely unexcavated beneath the fields.

Walk 100m west of the Basilica Terrace to find a ruined **podium monument** of unknown usage. Opposite stands a ruined **baths** complex. Some 250m further on is a colonnaded section of the street, and away to the left are the remains of more baths and a small forum. After another 100m you'll spot a circular structure, the foundations of the tower of a gate across the street, within which steps lead down into a locked underground mausoleum. Gadara's **West Gate**, with an exposed section of basalt street, is 200m further on. Alongside the modern tarmac road (which formerly ran to Tiberias) are the remains of a **hippodrome**, culminating, 300m further on, in a partly reconstructed **monumental gateway** to the city, designed to impress visitors approaching from the Jordan Valley below. Looking back from here gives an idea of the enormous size of Gadara in its heyday, and the impossible task of excavating it all.

ARRIVAL AND DEPARTURE   UMM QAIS

By bus Buses to and from Irbid's North station stop on Umm Qais's main street (45min).

By car The route to Umm Qais from Irbid is signed through Irbid city centre, though the jagged route can be hard to follow. Once you're free of the northern outskirts, about 7km north of Irbid, traffic lights mark a point where the Umm Qais road branches left. From here it's another 20km of mostly countryside driving to reach Umm Qais itself. After your visit, you could take the main road back to Irbid

or follow it the other way, down towards Himmeh and into the Yarmouk Gorge. Alternatively, turn right out of the site car park and follow a secondary road – badly broken up in its initial stages – as it drops down off the cliff edge in a series of spectacular hairpin bends into the scenic Wadi Al Arab, passing a giant dam and lake before reaching Shuneh ash-Shamaliyyeh (North Shuneh) on the floor of the Jordan Valley, roughly 11km from Umm Qais. It's a splendid drive.

ACCOMMODATION

★**Beit Al Baraka** Just off the main street; book via Baraka Destinations ☎077 666 7660, ⓦbaraka destinations.com; map p.158. This wonderful B&B makes a comfortable overnight visit – or a longer stay – in Umm Qais viable. Located in the village, it embodies ideals of sustainable tourism, with locally made furniture and textiles creating a relaxing, arty vibe in the sleek lounge area and three twin bedrooms. All the food is locally made – breakfasts are huge, varied and delicious – and

Baraka Destinations, who manage the place, offer a host of activities in and around Umm Qais, from cooking with a local family to honey-collecting, olive-picking, bike rides, guided walks and more. Prices are high to support the village economy: this quiet nook offers access to rural life that would otherwise be unavailable to visitors. Grab the opportunity with both hands. **JD140**

Umm Qais Hotel Main street ☎02 750 0080; map p.158. A basic dive, on the village's main drag. Standard rooms with shared bathrooms are on the reception level, while marginally better en-suite rooms are up above; comfort

and cleanliness vary, though all are pretty bad. There's also a five-room apartment, sleeping six (JD50). **JD25**

EATING

There are good *fuul*-and-falafel **diners** either side of the hotel (the *fuul* up here, prepared with sumac and other spices, makes an interesting change from Amman-style), but otherwise – unless you book ahead with Baraka Destinations for "Galsoum's Kitchen", a sensational farm-to-table dinner in the home of a local family (JD15pp) – there's only really one choice in town.

★ **Umm Qais Resthouse** In the ruins ☎ 02 750 0555, ⓦ facebook.com/ummqaisresthouse; map p.158. You

shouldn't leave Umm Qais without sitting awhile on the terrace of this restaurant within the ancient city itself, occupying a sensitively renovated Ottoman building overlooking the ruins. This gives the single best view in the country, a spectacular panorama out over the Sea of Galilee and Golan Heights. A meal here of Arabic meze and grills costs around JD15–20 and, since the place is under the same management as Amman's *Romero* restaurant, one of the capital's best, the food is very good. Daily 10am–10pm or later.

Himmeh (Mukhaybeh)

4km from Umm Qais • Follow signs for Jordan Himmeh – head north down the steep hill out of Umm Qais to a crossroads, from where the village is 4km straight on; buses from Umm Qais (15min)

In Roman times, Gadara's lavish baths complex, built around the seven hot springs at **HIMMEH**, was grand enough to bear comparison with the fabulous imperial baths at Baiae, near Naples. Modern Himmeh – also known as **Mukhaybeh** – is a shadow of its former self, and has been divided by modern boundary-drawing: most Roman remains are now in what the locals call "Syrian Himmeh", on the north bank of the Yarmouk in territory currently occupied by Israel (inaccessible from the Jordanian side), and there is little or no historical interest in the village of "**Jordan Himmeh**".

Hemmed in by the towering Golan Heights – with its easily visible Israeli jeep patrols – and lying some 200m below sea level, the village is crowded with palm trees and banana plants that thrive in the sweltering, subtropical conditions.

ACCOMMODATION   HIMMEH (MUKHAYBEH)

Mamdouh Bisharat's home Himmeh ☎ 079 616 6000. Mamdouh Bisharat, a leading Jordanian philanthropist and patron of the arts who runs a cultural salon in Amman (see page 76) – and who is widely known as the "Duke of Mukhaybeh" after a nickname bestowed on him by King Hussein – has a farm in Himmeh employing many local

people, and takes an active interest in the village's fortunes. He has very kindly offered Rough Guides readers the chance to stay – by prior arrangement only – at his private villa in the village, which has its own spring and Roman pool. Call for details.

The Yarmouk Gorge road

Himmeh is as far east along the River Yarmouk as you're allowed to venture, but with your own transport you can head west alongside a portion of the deep and dramatic **Yarmouk Gorge** (all buses go back up the hill to Umm Qais). The **views** on this tense frontier road are spectacular (even better looking east than they are looking west), gazing down into the Yarmouk, across to the Sea of Galilee and up to the Golan Heights. The **wrecked bridge**, still hanging over the gorge, was bombed in 1946 by Jewish paramilitaries to disrupt British Army transport routes in and out of Palestine. Drive slowly and remember you are under constant surveillance here from both the Jordanian army and the Israeli army; although you might be able to snatch a photo or two of the beautiful scenery, or of the bridge, you may find the soldiers objecting. There are **checkpoints** every few hundred metres, for which you should always stop and show your passport. After 6km of this you come to a junction where the only option is to turn left, and this road delivers you after another 7.5km to the town of **Shuneh ash-Shamaliyyeh** (North Shuneh), at the head of the Jordan Valley, a pleasant enough little market town. It's a short drive south towards **Pella** (see page 165).

Baqoura

From the Shuneh junction, head north for 3.4km to a checkpoint, where they might let you through to drive another 1.2km to the end of the road at an army base, where you must park your car; if you explain that you're interested in seeing Baqoura, an officer may find some transport and accompany you: they won't let you explore here alone

Northwest of Shuneh lies **Baqoura**. This tiny sliver, less than a kilometre square, was occupied by Israel in 1967 and returned to Jordan under the 1994 peace treaty. It is a **military zone**: visiting isn't easy, but it's popular as a local beauty spot and retains an intriguing cross-border identity. From the army base, a road heads down for about 1km and crosses the Yarmouk on a rickety bridge alongside a half-ruined **hydroelectric station** – the first in the Middle East, built in 1927 by Russian engineer Pinchas Rutenberg and damaged by Iraqi shelling in 1948.

Up above is a hilltop parking area known as the **"Island of Peace"**, with a breathtaking **view**: from here you can see the confluence of the Yarmouk and the Jordan just below, with the cultivated fields of the Israeli kibbutz Ashdot Yaakov all around, the route of the old railway line from Haifa to Damascus visible and cars passing on the Israeli highway opposite. This beautiful area was formerly where Israeli and Jordanian day-trippers mixed freely, until 1997 when a Jordanian soldier, Ahmed Daqamseh, murdered seven Israeli schoolgirls here. Daqamseh was released from prison in 2017. His name remains notorious.

3

Abila

12km north of Irbid • Buses run infrequently from Irbid (25min)

Lying in the lush Wadi Qwaylbeh north of Irbid, the lonely ruins of the Decapolis city of **Abila** have only just begun to be excavated from the grassy fields. Opposite a columned seventh-century church, prominent on a hilltop, one slope of the valley shelters Abila's Roman-Byzantine **cemetery**, comprising dozens of **tomb caves**, some beautifully painted – persistent exploration is required. The caves that hold frescoes are gated and locked, but it's likely that the guardian (a local shepherd) will arrive to lead you around. Some **frescoes** are in remarkably good condition, offering delightful portraits of men and women, and a spectacular scene of dolphins covering a ceiling. The experience of stumbling across portraits of long-dead Abilenes gazing back into your torchlight from the rock-cut coffins that once held their bones is one to remember.

Working your way north (right) along the cave-dotted slope brings you, after about 2km, to a modern building which overlooks the Roman **bridge** across the stream, leading into the ancient city centre past the remains of a large Byzantine church. You can make out the bowl of a **theatre** next to a section of basalt-paved Byzantine **street**. Follow the track curling up to the hilltop **church**, with its alternating basalt and limestone columns. Olive groves conceal the Hartha road from the church; once on the road, you could hitch a ride back to Irbid, or wait for the (infrequent) buses.

ARRIVAL AND DEPARTURE   ABILA

By car From Irbid, follow signs towards Umm Qais (heading north) until you reach a junction after 7km, where the Umm Qais road branches off left. Continue straight on here until you reach a quiet fork at a mosque close to Wadi Qwaylbeh (11km north of Irbid). You should head right at the fork – you can get out here and walk, or continue to drive for 900m, then before parking up and walking left across the fields. This will bring you to a dry-stone wall teetering over the steep flank of the wadi, beyond which lie the tomb caves.
By bus Take a bus from Irbid's North station towards Hartha and alight at the fork in the road 11km north of Irbid and a kilometre or so from the ruins.

The Jordan Valley

The deep cleft of the **Jordan Valley** carries the River Jordan south from the Sea of Galilee (some 200m below sea level) to the Dead Sea (400m below). It's a distance of only 104km as the crow flies, although the meandering river twists and writhes for more than three times that length. Set down in a deep gorge flanked by a desolate floodplain (the *zor*), the river is never visible from the main road, which runs through the *ghor*, or cultivable valley floor, well to the east. Flanked by 900m-high mountains on both sides and enjoying a swelteringly subtropical climate of low rainfall, high humidity and scorching temperatures, the valley, with its fertile alluvial soil, is perfect for **agriculture** on a large scale: this vast open-air greenhouse can produce crops up to two months ahead of elsewhere in the Middle East and can even stretch to three growing seasons annually. As early as five thousand years ago, foodstuffs from the valley were being exported to nearby states, and irrigation systems and urban development progressed hand-in-hand soon after. Agriculture has remained at the heart of the valley economy, from the wheat, barley, olives, grapes and beans of the Bronze Age to an extensive sugar-cane industry under the Mamlukes. Since the late nineteenth century, rapid development – and, in particular, the building of the **King Abdullah Canal** in the 1960s to irrigate the eastern *ghor* – has led to a burgeoning agricultural industry that supplies most of Jordan's tomatoes, cucumbers, bananas, melons and citrus fruits, as well as producing a surplus for export.

In contrast to the prosaic vistas of concrete piping, plastic greenhouses and farm machinery that characterize the area today, well over two hundred **archeological** sites have been catalogued in the valley, although – with the notable exception of the Roman-Byzantine remains at **Pella** – almost all of them are Neolithic or Bronze Age settlements on the summits of *tell*s, with little to see other than stone foundations. South of Pella, a few kilometres from the river's outflow into the Dead Sea, lies the **Baptism Site** of Jesus (see page 122).

GETTING AROUND   **THE JORDAN VALLEY**

By bus Transport in the Jordan Valley mostly comprises buses shuttling north and south along the main road between the hub towns of Shuneh ash-Shamaliyyeh (North Shuneh), Kraymeh, Dayr Alla and Shuneh al-Janubiyyeh (South Shuneh), stopping at all points in between. If you don't decide to stay overnight in the valley, you could take a half- or a full-day trip through it by bus, starting from Irbid and heading south to Amman, or vice versa.

By car Bearing in mind the excessive heat – summer temperatures regularly top 45°C – and the lack of tourist facilities, the best way to see the valley is in your own vehicle.

Sheikh Hussein Bridge

Sun–Thurs 6.30am–9pm, Fri & Sat 8am–8pm • Bus about JD4 to/from Irbid's Valleys station (1hr); taxi about JD25 to/from Irbid (45min), about JD50 to/from Amman (2–3hr)

Well signposted off the valley highway about 9km south of Shuneh ash-Shamaliyyeh is the **Sheikh Hussein Bridge** (or **Jordan River Crossing**), which heads into Israel. First you come to the turning for the trucks terminal; 4km south is the turning for cars and buses, which share a terminal.

Buses from Nazareth to Irbid and Amman cross using this bridge, and you can also cross here independently, using local buses from Irbid (see page 155).

The village of Mshare'a, access point for Pella (see opposite), lies 5km south of the bridge turn-off for cars and buses.

Sharhabil bin Hassneh EcoPark

9km north of Pella • Daily 8am–sunset • JD1 • ☎ 079 800 0470, ⓦ jordanecopark.com

Not all the attractions in the Jordan Valley are archeological or agricultural. Tucked away in the hills about 9km south of Shuneh ash-Shamaliyyeh, the **SHARHABIL BIN**

ACTIVITIES IN SHARHABIL BIN HASSNEH ECOPARK

WALKS

Short **circular walks** of between thirty minutes and an hour and a half lead around the protected area, such as the 6.3km route around the perimeter of the lake. Guides are available for JD2–5 per person. Longer **trails** head out to explore further afield. The EcoPark is also on the national **Jordan Trail** (W jordantrail.org; see page 50): stage 1 is a walk here from Umm Qais; stage 2 leads from the EcoPark past Pella to Beit Idis village.

CYCLING

Mountain bikes are available to rent from the Visitor Centre (JD10/day).

ADVENTURE HIKE

Contact Amman tour operator Tropical Desert (W tropicaldesert.me) for details of their full-day wet/dry **adventure hike** around the lake using inflatable boats.

ZIPLINE

A 530m-long **zipline** – the longest in Jordan – whizzes passengers through the trees at up to 60km/h (JD20).

3

HASSNEH ECOPARK offers a rare opportunity to explore the rolling valley landscape through walks and bike rides. Centred on the lake formed by the Ziglab Dam, the EcoPark was created by **EcoPeace**, a consortium of Jordanian, Palestinian and Israeli environmental campaigners. From 2005 they rejuvenated a damaged and heavily polluted stretch of terrain, which is now maintained mostly by volunteers, in conjunction with bedouin living on the land and villagers from local communities. Informational signboards around the park explain the work being done and identify **flora** such as acacia and tamarisk, as well as birds, snakes, frogs and more.

From the main gate, paths and driving routes lead to the Visitor Centre, set amid shady picnic areas, from where you can explore at will. Rising behind the Visitor Centre, the **Ziglab Dam** holds back a long, narrow lake of fresh water: it's a magnificent sight, beneath raptors circling in the silent heat.

ARRIVAL AND DEPARTURE   SHARHABIL BIN HASSNEH ECOPARK

By car Directly opposite the truck turn-off for the Sheikh Hussein Bridge crossing point, a minor road heads east, climbing for 1km to the main gate of the EcoPark, where you pay admission. From here it's a short drive to the car park, and a stroll to the Visitor Centre.

By bus Buses running north and south along the main road can drop you at the turn-off, from where you must walk 1km to reach the EcoPark.

ACCOMMODATION AND EATING

Cabins By the Visitor Centre ☎ 079 800 0470, W jordan ecopark.com. The EcoPark has seventeen simple cabins under the pines and olive trees, designed chiefly for groups, though individuals are welcome. The cabins, sleeping two, three or four people, are plain, wooden and unadorned – though they do have a/c, a necessity down here. Toilets and showers are separate. The EcoPark lives up to its name, using solar power, composting and water recycling. You can pitch a tent and lunch and/or dinner are available (JD5–7). Book everything well in advance. Rates include breakfast. Camping **JD7**, cabins **JD35**

Pella

For archeologists, **PELLA**, comprising a large *tell* overlooking a well-watered valley protected by hills, is thrilling, and possibly the most significant site in all of Jordan; evidence has been found of human activity in the area for nearly a million years, with extensive remains from almost all periods from the Paleolithic through to the Mamluke. The *tell* itself has been occupied for the last six thousand years almost without interruption. However, though it's worth the journey, Pella can appear rather underwhelming to non-archeologists, with little more than three ruined Byzantine churches to divert attention from the lovely hill-walking all around. Nonetheless, it's a beautiful spot, and makes a pleasant stop on a journey along the Jordan Valley.

Brief history

The reasons for Pella's long history have much to do with its location on the junction of major **trade routes**: north–south between Arabia and Syria, and east–west between the Transjordanian interior and the Mediterranean coast. With its positioning almost exactly at sea level – the Jordan Valley yawns below – Pella has a comfortably warm climate and is watered both by springs in Wadi Jirm and by a reasonable annual rainfall. In addition, it was surrounded in antiquity by thick oak forests, since felled, which at more than one point provided the backbone of the city's economy.

Ancient times

Stone Age hunters roamed the area's forests and savannas until about a million years ago, bagging native game such as elephants, deer and lions. By five thousand years ago, a **Neolithic** farming village was established, and remains have been uncovered of a larger, terraced settlement southeast of the *tell*. Around four thousand years ago, during the **Bronze Age**, there was a thriving city at Pella: discoveries dating from at least four main periods of occupation around the sixteenth and fifteenth centuries BC include luxury items imported from Egypt, Syria and Cyprus such as bronze pins, stylized sculpture, gold thread, alabaster bottles, cuneiform clay tablets and inlaid ivory boxes. In the thirteenth century BC, Pella was the principal supplier to Pharaonic Egypt of wood for chariot spokes. **Iron Age** cities flourished up to the seventh century BC, but during the Persian period (539–332 BC) it seems that the area was abandoned.

The **Hellenistic** period is the first for which the name of Pella can be found in historical records, and was a time of considerable affluence for the city. In 218 BC, the Seleucid king Antiochus captured Pella on a sweep through Palestine and Transjordan, and soon the site spread over the *tell*, the slopes of Tell Husn opposite, the so-called "Civic Complex" area on the valley floor and the peak of Jabal Sartaba.

The Romans and after

In 83 BC, the Jewish **Hasmonean** leader Alexander Jannaeus crossed into Transjordan from Palestine and sacked pagan Pella and its neighbours Gadara, Gerasa and others. The arrival twenty years later of Pompey and the **Roman** army imposed order in Pella as elsewhere in the Decapolis region, and the city settled down to a period of stability, minting its own coins and embarking on a programme of building. However, one legacy of the city's location above a perpetually flowing spring is that, due to a rise in alluvium levels, it's been impossible to excavate in the valley-bed. Consequently, virtually nothing of the Roman period apart from a small theatre survives, although coins found here depict a nymphaeum, various temples, what is probably a forum, baths and lavish public buildings dotted throughout the city.

A massacre of twenty thousand Jews in a single hour at Caesarea in Palestine in 66 AD fuelled a widespread Jewish revolt against Roman rule, and amid the turmoil the nascent **Christian community** of Jerusalem fled en masse to the relative safety of Pella – though they returned by the time of the rebuilding of Jerusalem, around 130 AD.

Pella reached its zenith during the **Byzantine** fifth and sixth centuries, with churches, houses and shops covering the slopes of the *tell* and Tell Husn, and pottery from North Africa and Asia Minor indicating significant international trade. However, by the seventh century, the city was again in decline; in 635, Muslim forces defeated the Byzantine army near Pella, and the city reverted to its pre-Hellenistic Semitic name of **Fahl**. The devastating **earthquake** of 749 destroyed most of Pella's standing structures, and the city lay abandoned for several centuries, with small groups of farmers coming and going throughout the Abbasid and Mamluke periods.

The ruins

Daily 8am–6pm (Nov–March till 4pm) • JD2, free with JP

Although there may not be any buildings of substance left in Pella, it's certainly in a beautiful location. Spring water cascades out of the ground on the floor of the **Wadi Jirm**; and the imposing bulk of the sheer **Tell Husn** to one side, the long, low *tell* on the other and **Jabal Abu al-Khas** between them (on which stands the modern, triple-arched *Resthouse*) enclose the little valley with high slopes of green, leaving only the vista westwards over the Jordan Valley.

West Church

Before you reach the main site, you'll see the remains of the **West Church** behind barbed wire on the edge of the modern village. The church was built in the late fifth or early sixth centuries, in Pella's prime, and is one of the largest Byzantine churches uncovered in the entire Middle East.

Civic Complex Church

The **main valley** is dominated by the standing columns of the **Civic Complex Church** on the edge of the bubbling spring. All the re-erected columns belong to the church's atrium; to the east, in front of a finely paved portico, are two exquisite columns of green swirling marble, one of which cracked in two as it fell in antiquity. The church itself, its columns collapsed like a house of cards, has three apses, and was originally decorated with glass windows, glass mosaic half-domes, stone mosaics on the walls and floor, and chancel screens of marble. The **monumental staircase** in front was added in the seventh century, when the valley floor was some 2 to 3m below its current level.

Theatre

To one side of the church is the bowl of a small Roman **theatre**, built in the first century AD to seat about four hundred; many of its stones were plundered to build the church staircase. Across the whole area of the modern springs, there may once have stretched a **forum**, with the stream channelled below through subterranean vaulting, some of which is still visible.

East Church

The steep path between the Civic Complex ruins and the *Resthouse* coils up the hillside past the columns of the small, atmospheric **East Church**, built in the fifth century overlooking the lower city and originally accessed by a monumental staircase from below. The atrium has a small central pool.

The tell

The **tell** itself – on the left as you face the *Resthouse* – is likely to excite only archeologists. Although several different excavations have revealed dozens of levels of occupation over millennia, all there is to see for the lay person are the crisscrossing foundations of coarser and finer walls at different levels and a couple of re-erected columns. Of most accessible interest is a small **Mamluke mosque** close to the modern dig-house, with a plaque commemorating the decisive Battle of Fahl of 635. Excavations alongside it have unearthed the massive stone blocks of a **Canaanite temple** dating to 1480 BC, the largest yet discovered from that period. You'd have to be very keen to scale the precipitous **Tell Husn** opposite, in order to poke around the sixth-century Byzantine fortress on its summit.

Pella Museum

No fixed hours; check online or ask at the *Resthouse* • ⓦ pellamuseum.org

Behind the *Resthouse*, Jordanian architect Ammar Khammash has built the private **Pella Museum**. It explores Jordan's history before archeology, showcasing fossils and exploring geological formations. Admission is strictly by appointment only.

WALKS AROUND PELLA

Longer exploration of the area around Pella can take the form of a combination of **ruin-hunting** and **adventure hiking**. Research your options by consulting the book *Jordan: Walks, Treks, Climbs and Caves in Al Ayoun Jordan* by Di Taylor and Tony Howard (see page 390), which includes detail on walking routes from Pella into the highlands around Ajloun.

ON THE JORDAN TRAIL

Pella lies midway along Stage 1.2 of the national **Jordan Trail** (ⓦ jordantrail.org; see page 50). The full stage is a long walk (23.7km) beginning at the Sharhabil bin Hassneh EcoPark, but if you choose to start at Pella you could tackle a less taxing 11km, climbing Wadi Jirm to upland meadows to reach the "**Jesus Cave**" in Beit Eidiss village, where there is a simple homestay. It's also possible – and easier – to do this stretch in the reverse direction, ending at Pella. From Beit Eidiss, the next stage, 1.3 (16.2km; 4–6hr; difficult), climbs into the oak woodlands around Zubia, ending at **Rasoun** (see page 150). The Jordan Trail website has full information, maps, GPS points and detailed walking notes.

TO JABAL SARTABA

If you head past the East Church in Pella's ruins to curve up behind the *Resthouse*, you'll find rough trails leading across the hills for an hour or more out to the peak of **Jabal Sartaba**. Here stand the remains of a Hellenistic fortress, rather less dramatic than the remoteness of the location and the stunning views across the hills and valleys west into Palestine and east towards Ajloun.

ARRIVAL AND DEPARTURE
PELLA

The ruins of Pella are situated beside the modern village of **Tabaqat Fahl**, about 2km up a steep hill from the town of **Mshare'a** on the valley-floor highway, 18km south of Shuneh ash-Shamaliyyeh.

By bus One or two buses a day run direct to Tabaqat Fahl village from Irbid's Valleys station (1hr 15min), but there are more frequent departures from Irbid to Mshare'a (1hr), from where it's not difficult to hitch or even walk up the steep hill.

ACCOMMODATION AND EATING

★ **Beit Al Fannan** Pella, behind the Resthouse; book via Baraka Destinations ☎ 077 666 7660, ⓦ baraka destinations.com. This small, beautiful home ('House of the Artist' in Arabic), standing alone on the hillside with sublime views over the Pella ruins, was built by Jordanian artist Ammar Khammash. After seeing the benefits that sustainable tourism outfit Baraka Destinations had brought to Umm Qais (see page 160), Khammash offered the house to them for conversion into a holiday rental. It's a magical place to spend a night, or a week. You walk 200m along a hillside track to reach what is a quirky, rustic cottage, comfortable with sofas and balconies and art on the walls, but also appealingly rough around the edges. Sounds swirl around – a distant call to prayer, nearby cicadas – the bedroom is bedecked in candles, and everywhere there are books, design pieces and art works to investigate, as well as art materials for keen dabblers. Meals are served at your table by the caretaker family who live along the track. It's a serene hideaway for two. **JD120**

Pella Countryside Hotel Tabaqat Fahl ☎ 02 656 0899, ⓦ pellacountrysidehotel.com. As you enter the modern village, you'll see prominent signs pointing left to this little place, run by the super-friendly Deeb Hussein – whose family have been in the area since 1885. It's a lovely spot, a modern building on a backstreet among peaceful olive groves. The twelve modest en-suite rooms (with a/c) are simple but very clean, with an excellent dinner and breakfast included. **JD45**

Pella Resthouse Pella, overlooking the ruins ☎ 077 718 8880, ⓦ facebook.com/pellaresthouse. This triple-arched restaurant is a haven, designed by Ammar Khammash, with a spectacular terrace perched high above the ruins. The food is good – grilled meat, chicken, fish and the like – and they serve cool refreshments. Lunch is around JD10–12/person. Daily 10am–sunset.

Kahf il-Messih (Jesus Cave)

Numerous little-explored routes lead out from Pella, including northwards into the hills by car or on foot to **Kahf il-Messih** (the "**Jesus Cave**"), marked by a spreading oak tree, with its arched entrance facing north. Local legend – thoroughly unsubstantiated – has it that Jesus stayed in the cave for some days before going to meet John for his baptism. It has Roman-style *loculi*, or alcoves for bodies, cut side by side into the bedrock. The **oak** tree is also the object of some veneration by the locals. Beside it is a flat rectangular area for treading grapes, complete with rock-cut channels and pools for collecting the juice.

The rolling hills all around are laced with caves and dotted with the odd archeological ruin (a small mosaic-floored church has been unearthed on one of the hills opposite). The village of **Kufr Abil**, a stop on the long walk between Ajloun and Pella (see page 165), is only a few kilometres south of here.

ARRIVAL AND DEPARTURE

By car Drive up from the Jordan Valley to Pella, but instead of taking the side-turn up to the *Pella Resthouse*, just keep going straight: the road is rocky and bad, but taken slowly is passable in an ordinary car. Some 200m beyond the *Resthouse* junction is a fork; head uphill for 2.4km, turn right, then continue on, ignoring the small roads that join from the side. After 7.3km, in the middle of the village of Kufr Rakib, take the right fork. As you leave the village, beneath the twin arches, take the right fork again, then a small road on the right after 1km, and left after another

KAHF IL-MESSIH (JESUS CAVE)

1.3km into the locality of Beit Eidiss village. The Jesus Cave is 300m further on. Along the way you could take a short diversion: at the fork 200m past the *Pella Resthouse* head straight on, and after 1.6km you'll arrive at a photogenic rock arch, through which flows the warm Wadi Hemmeh. Circle around to view it from the other side, where you'll also spot a small building which once housed the hot spring itself, now reduced to a stagnant pool.
On foot You can walk from Pella (11km), as part of the national Jordan Trail (see page 50).

Kraymeh and around

Buses run from Ajloun (30min) and the valley villages to the north and south

On the floor of the main Jordan Valley, 20km south of Mshare'a, lies the town of **KRAYMEH**. Just beyond the town, opposite an isolated mosque with a stone minaret, a road branches west towards the huge mound of **Tell as-Sa'idiyyeh**, some 2km away, home to a large city in the Late Bronze Age, during the thirteenth and twelfth centuries BC. Halfway along the right-hand slope of the *tell*, a reconstructed Iron Age **stone staircase** leads up from a spring-fed pool to the summit; excavation trenches display remnants of an Egyptian-style public building (Sa'idiyyeh may have been a northern outpost of the Egyptian empire) and city wall. The *tell* gives stunning views along the length of the valley, though the River Jordan itself, only a few hundred metres away, is still invisible in its gorge.

Dayr Alla

Buses run to Dayr Alla from Amman Tabarboor (1hr), Salt (40min) and the valley villages to the north and south; the *tell* is a short walk 1km north from the town centre

About 9km south of Kraymeh is the market town of **DAYR ALLA** (the name translates as "High Monastery" and has nothing to do with Allah or Islam). Rising beside the road about 1km north of the town is the large **Tell Dayr Alla**. Some historians link the site with biblical Penuel, where Jacob wrestled with God; others associate it with Succoth, site of an ironworks that produced pieces used in the Temple of Solomon in Jerusalem. One excavation uncovered an inscription in red and black ink on plaster, dated around 800 BC, relating tales of prophecy by **Balaam**, a seer mentioned in the Bible (Numbers 22–24). The *tell* itself, punctured by deep excavation trenches exposing anonymous walls and rooms, is barely worth the effort of the climb.

Dayr Alla Museum

Daily except Fri 8am–1pm & 2–5pm • Free

Heading down the street that hugs the south flank of the *tell* brings you to an office; as well as providing information and impromptu refreshment, staff can unlock the small **Dayr Alla Museum**, which houses a collection of interesting bits and bobs from sites throughout the valley as well as an explanation of the Balaam text.

South of Dayr Alla

South of Dayr Alla points of interest are few and far between. About 10km south you may spot an old road sign pointing west to the Palestinian city of **Nablus**, harking back to the days before 1967 when territory on both sides of the river was Jordanian (the turn-off leads to a bridge now reserved for agricultural traffic). Some 6km further lies the humdrum town of **Karameh**, site of a major dam.

Shuneh Al Janubiyyeh (South Shuneh)

Buses from Amman Muhajireen (1hr), Salt (30min), Dayr Alla (40min), the Dead Sea (30min) and Madaba via Mt Nebo (1hr); taxis to/from King Hussein Bridge cost about JD5 (5min)

Set among the farming villages of the valley floor a few kilometres south of Karameh, the market town of **SHUNEH AL JANUBIYYEH** (South Shuneh) is the main settlement in these parts. The traffic lights in the centre of Shuneh mark a major crossroads: one road heads west to the King Hussein Bridge, another climbs east into the Wadi Shuayb towards Salt, north is the Jordan Valley, and a few kilometres south you'll reach the highway up to Amman, the turn for the Baptism Site, and the Dead Sea.

King Hussein Bridge/Allenby Bridge

4km west of Shuneh Al Janubiyyeh – take the side road heading west from the central traffic lights

The **King Hussein Bridge**, also known as the **Allenby Bridge**, is the main crossing point from Jordan into the Palestinian West Bank. It's also the quickest route for moving between Amman and Jerusalem; we give details in Basics on **arriving** (see page 29) and in Chapter 1 on **departing** (see page 92) via this bridge.

The Balqa hills

The gentle hills which roll westward from Amman down to the Jordan Valley through the historic **Balqa** region – of which the graceful old town of **Salt** is capital – are laced with lush valleys and dotted with quiet, pleasant towns such as **Wadi Seer** and **Fuheis**. Near Wadi Seer is one of the few examples of Hellenistic architecture surviving in Jordan – the impressive white palace of **Qasr al-Abd**, set in open countryside near an ancient cave system known as **Iraq al-Amir**. All these places are easily accessible by bus from Amman, and could together form an unusual half- or full-day trip by car.

Salt

For many centuries, **SALT** was the only settlement of any size in Transjordan. A regional capital under the Ottomans, the town – whose name derives from the ancient Greek *saltos*, meaning "thick forest" – came into its own in the late nineteenth century, when merchants from Nablus arrived to expand their trading base east of the river. Into what was then a peasant village of shacks boxed between precipitous hills, the merchants brought sophisticated architects and masons to work with the honey-coloured local limestone; buildings were put up in the ornate Nabulsi style to serve both as grand residences and as merchandise centres. With open trade to and from Palestine, Salt's boom continued into the 1920s; the new Emirate of Transjordan was formally proclaimed in 1921 in the town's main square, but by then the railway from Damascus had reached nearby Amman, and Emir Abdullah chose the better-connected town to be his capital. As quickly as Salt had flourished, it went into decline: superseded by Amman, it was cut off by war in 1948 from its traditional trade outlet to the Mediterranean at Haifa, then again in 1967 from its Palestinian twin, Nablus.

As a consequence, Salt has seen none of the headlong modernization that has afflicted the capital: much of its **Ottoman architecture** has survived, as has a small town's atmosphere, perfect for aimless exploration.

Standing under one of the huge eucalyptus trees that line the lower end of Maydan Street, you are surrounded by three towering hills: to your right are the bare rocky slopes of **as-Salalem**, to the left rises the tree-adorned peak of **al-Jada'a**, and straight ahead is **al-Qal'a**, named for the Mamluke fortress on its summit which was demolished in 1840 and finally swept away recently for a white-domed mosque.

Historic Old Salt Museum (Abu Jaber House)

Al-Ain Square • Daily 8am–4pm; winter till 3pm • JD1, free with JP

Stroll up Dayr Street and through the commerce-heavy, crowded central streets to the graceful arched facade of the **Abu Jaber House**, one of the city's most beautiful buildings, built over twenty years from 1886 using local sandstone, Belgian stained glass, Italian marble and hand-painted Jerusalem tiles. Now restored, it houses the **Historic Old Salt Museum**, with good displays on local history and trade, as well as fine views from the top-floor frescoed salon over the rooftops, and a lovely café. Pick up a town map from the front desk showing a **heritage trail** around the city centre, linking more than a dozen architectural points of interest in a looping walk.

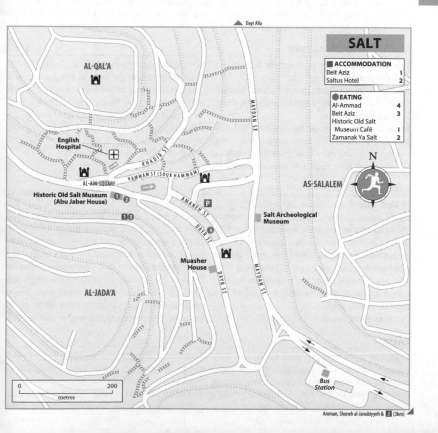

Jabal Al Qal'a

Facing the Abu Jaber House, on the other side of Al-Ain Square, tiny Khadir Street has several flights of steps leading steeply up **Jabal Al Qal'a**. Partway up you'll see the colonnaded honey-stone **English Hospital**, its gates still bearing an "EH" monogram; the building is now the Middle East's first vocational training centre for people with disabilities. The view from Jabal Al Qal'a's **summit**, bathed in sunshine, out over the town to the rolling Balqa hills beyond, is worth the hard climb.

Souk Hammam

From Al-Ain square, dive into narrow Hammam Street (the eponymous hammam was razed in the 1930s for lack of customers). This lane, known as **Souk Hammam**, is lined with buildings which date from Salt's golden age, including a wonderful old mosque. The street hosts Jordan's oldest – and, some say, best – souk, an ordinary little market of food and household goods that nonetheless is full of atmosphere, wreathed in the aroma of spices and lifted by the gorgeous honeystone Ottoman architecture.

Salt Archeological Museum

Maydan St · Sun–Thurs & Sat 8am–5pm, Fri 9am–4pm; winter closes earlier · JD2, free with JP

At the east end of Souk Hammam, turn right to reach the arched and pillared facade (on the left) of the **Salt Archeological Museum**, housing a fascinating modern collection that includes a working model of a Mamluke sugar mill and an impression of a Neolithic dolmen landscape. The Ottoman-era building is equally interesting, known as **Beit Touqan**, once the stately residence of the Touqan family (King Hussein's third wife, Queen Alia, was a Touqan).

ARRIVAL AND DEPARTURE   SALT

By bus The bus station is in the town centre, 200m south of the Archeological Museum.

Destinations Amman Mahatta (40min); Amman Tabarboor (35min); Dayr Alla (40min); Shuneh Al Janubiyyeh (30min); Sweileh flyover (15min).

By car Signage into Salt can be confusing – and, once you arrive, the narrow hilly streets in the historic centre, one-way system and heavy traffic makes for gridlock. On the way out, if you're heading for the Jordan Valley it's

worth knowing that the road from Salt down to Shuneh Al Janubiyyeh follows the beautiful and dramatic Wadi Shuayb, a flowing stream lush with undergrowth all year and carpeted with wild flowers in spring; this is a much more impressive route down to the valley floor than the highway from Amman. North of Salt, on the Dayr Alla road, the Zai National Park is perfect picnic territory – thick forest with rough trails and plenty of wild nooks.

ACCOMMODATION

★**Beit Aziz** Prince Hassan St ☎079 953 5900, ⓦfacebook.com/beitaziz; map p.171. A charming B&B in an attractive old family home dating from 1905, located a short walk above the main square with a balcony overlooking the downtown streets. The original building, with vaulted ceilings, pointed arches and walls of stone, holds two bedrooms, while a modern extension has three more. Traditional crafts dot the public areas and service is warm and friendly. <u>JD40</u>

★**Saltus Hotel** Naqab Al Dabbour ☎079 542 1790,

ⓦfacebook.com/saltushotel; map p.171. This fine three-star hotel is run by the big Zara hotel corporation, in partnership with a local vocational training institute. The 23 rooms are comfortable and stylishly furnished; modern mosaics and local art lift the tone. The food is excellent and staff bend over backwards to help – most are students from the hospitality training college next door, doing six months here before deployment to one of Jordan's luxury hotels. Reserve well in advance. It lies in a residential hilltop location east of the centre: ask for directions or a pick-up when you book. <u>JD40</u>

EATING

Al-Ammad Amaneh St, nine doors up from the Cairo Amman Bank; map p.171. King among the town centre's restaurants, this unprepossessing place has been churning out quality shish kebabs to the Salti cognoscenti for a century or more (from JD5). There's no sign in English or

Arabic; spot it by the small plaque beside the door which outlines its history (in English). Daily roughly 10am–10pm.

Beit Aziz Prince Hassan St ☎079 953 5900, ⓦfacebook.com/beitaziz; map p.171. The rooftop restaurant of this

---

WALKS AROUND SALT AND FUHEIS

Salt, Fuheis and Iraq Al-Amir are all way-stations on the national **Jordan Trail** (ⓦjordantrail.org; see page 50). This is pleasant walking country – hilly, green and quiet – and these three points benefit from public transport at both ends, accessible to/from Amman. The Jordan Trail website has full information, maps, GPS points and detailed walking notes for these and all routes.

FROM SALT TO IRAQ AL-AMIR

This is a tough, full-day walk (22.2km; difficult), leading from the city centre of Salt down into the valley and out through the suburbs onto steep, green hillsides, dropping down past small farm holdings and rural settlements. After skirting the outskirts of Fuheis, the long, winding route continues southwards over the hills on country lanes between farm plots – and past a spring – to end in the village of Iraq al-Amir, by the gates of the Qasr al-Abd palace.

FROM FUHEIS TO IRAQ AL-AMIR

An alternative full-day trail starts from Fuheis (15.2km; easy). The route officially begins at the Carakale brewery, 2km west of Fuheis Al-Balad, though you could start in the village if you prefer. From the brewery the trail drops down into the valley, then joins the trail from Salt, heading south to end in Iraq Al-Amir village.

3

---

small hotel, with superb views over the city, is a great place to take the weight off with a hot drink, or linger for the traditional cooking (meze roughly JD2–4, mains around JD5–6). Daily 9am–10pm.

Historic Old Salt Museum Café Abu Jaber House, Al Ain Square; map p.171. Lovely upper-floor café-restaurant within the museum, with views over the square below and a range of decent lunchtime meals (JD6–8), snacks (JD2–4) and – best of all – desserts and pastries (JD2–4). Daily 10am–3pm.

Zamanak Ya Salt On a lane beside the Abu Jaber House

ⓞ077 614 0166; map p.171. This 120-year-old building – once split between four families, two Muslim, two Christian – is now home to the first café in Salt to be run by a woman, Nadia Abu Al Samn. In a traditional setting, enhanced by displays of antique coffeepots, embroidered dresses and other artefacts, she serves snacks (around JD5) and full meals (around JD8–10) of authentic local food, often accompanied by live music. Even if you're not hungry, take a few minutes to sit with a fragrant coffee and soak up the atmosphere. Daily 8am–3pm & 5–10pm.

Fuheis

Set among rolling hills near Salt – and just 15km northwest of Amman – **FUHEIS** (pronounced "fhayce") is a prosperous small town, 95 percent Christian, with a scattering of nineteenth-century churches. Its easy-going atmosphere – and, in summer, Jordan's best peaches – make it a pleasant stop-off.

The upper half of town, known as **al-Allali** (with a large calligraphic sculpture in the central Shakr roundabout), is newer and less attractive; carry on down the steep hill to the older part, known as **al-Balad**. Between the two lies Jordan's biggest cement factory, which employs more than seventy percent of the town but which has, for years, inflicted clouds of cement dust and soaring rates of asthma on local people. It remains both a blessing and a curse.

Al-Balad, centred on a roundabout with a statue of St George killing the dragon, comprises a district of quiet lanes and 100-year-old stone cottages alongside the deep Wadi Rahwa. It makes for an interesting short wander, and the lanes come into their own in the golden light of late afternoon.

During August, Fuheis hosts a small-town **carnival**. You may also find music and cultural events staged in the week or two before **Christmas**.

ARRIVAL AND DEPARTURE   **FUHEIS**

By car On the road north from Amman past Jordan University, just beyond the centre of Sweileh (a crossroads town on the northwestern fringes of Amman), take the

clearly marked turn-off towards Salt, then follow Fuheis signs onto a minor road that winds through pine forest, passing the Royal Stables at Hummar before entering Fuheis at the Shakr roundabout.

By bus Buses run from Al Balad to/from Amman's Tabarboor station, but if you're coming from Wadi Seer, Salt or Jerash, you'll need to go via Sweileh; dozens of buses stop at or near the large roundabout beneath Sweileh's trademark flyover,

from where you can pick up the Amman–Fuheis buses (ask locals where to stand). The last bus back to Amman leaves around 9pm in summer, 7pm in winter.

Destination Amman Tabarboor (35min).

By taxi A taxi to/from Amman is around JD12–15.

Wadi Seer

Buses from Amman's Muhajireen and Mahatta stations drop off at the bus station (30min), above a roundabout in the town centre

The town of **WADI SEER** ("Valley of Orchards") – small and peaceful, filled with trees and birdsong – has the atmosphere of the countryside, even though it's barely 12km from central Amman, within spitting distance of 8th Circle on the western outskirts. Add to the **natural beauty** a couple of small-scale **archeological gems** and the area around the town, including its eponymous valley, merits an exploratory picnic. That said, if you choose a Friday for your outing, you'll discover that most of Amman has had the same idea.

Originally settled by Circassian immigrants in the 1880s, Wadi Seer boasts many nineteenth- and early twentieth-century **Ottoman stone buildings** in the streets around the centre, including a red-roofed mosque of yellowish limestone with one of the most beautifully carved **minarets** in the country.

Wadi Seer is the staging post for a journey out to the striking Hellenistic palace of **Qasr al-Abd**, next to the village of **Iraq al-Amir**. This is a lovely part of the country in which to dawdle, and the walk along the road from Wadi Seer to Iraq al-Amir slopes gently downhill all the way, hugging the side of a fertile valley and passing through several villages. The **scenery** is soft on the eye, the valley thick with fig, olive, cypress and pomegranate trees and watered by a perpetually flowing stream; springtime sees a riot of poppies and wild iris. However, banish thoughts of riverside footpaths and unspoiled nature: the walk is all on the asphalt road and this is Jordanian country life in the raw – litter, half-built houses, curious children and all.

Ad-Dayr

4km west of Wadi Seer

About 4km west of Wadi Seer, the road reaches the valley floor and passes a **Roman aqueduct**; the spartan *al-Yannabeea* **café** (daily 7am–midnight) occupies a perfect spot on the grassy bank here – good if you fancy a cold drink, though the food isn't up to much. Just before the café, a detour for the energetic leads steeply up to the left; after about 500m, a fork to the left gives access to rough paths up the hillside. A short scramble will bring you to two eerie **caves** known as **ad-Dayr** (meaning "the monastery"). They look rather like a medieval pigeon-fanciers' den: the interiors are lined with small triangular niches, and stone grilles are still in place over the cave windows.

Iraq al-Amir

10km west of Wadi Seer

Beyond the *al-Yannabeea* café, 4km west of Wadi Seer, the road continues straight – apart from one left fork marked in English – for another 6km or so to the village of **IRAQ AL-AMIR** (meaning "Caves of the Prince"). Just before you get here, you'll spot the smoke-blackened caves high up to the right of the road. Once you reach them there's nothing to see but the view across the fields and a single ancient Hebrew inscription beside one of the cave entrances, referring to the family who built the white palace visible down in the valley.

Women's cooperative

Daily except Fri 8am–3pm • ☏ 077 593 1563, ⓦ iraqalameer.com

In old stone cottage in Iraq al-Amir village, a **women's cooperative** produces a variety of top-quality crafts, including handmade paper (the only such centre in Jordan), textiles,

USEFUL ARABIC PLACE NAMES

Baoun	باعون	Mshare'a	المشارع
Dibeen	دبين	Orjan	عرجان
Halawa	حلاوة	Ramtha	الرمثا
Hartha	حرثا	Rasun	راسون
Irbid	اربد	Shuneh Al Janubiyyeh	الشونة الجنوبية
– New Amman station	مجمع عمّان الجديد	Shuneh ash-Shamaliyyeh	الشونة الشمالية
– North station	المجمع الشمالي	Suf town	بلدة سوف
– Trust office	مكتب شركة الثقة	Sweileh	صويلح
– Valleys station	مجمع الاغوار	Tabaqat Fahl	طبقة فحل
Jordan Valley	غور الاردن	Wadi Qwaylbeh	وادي قويلبة
Karameh	الكرامة	Wadi al-Yabis	وادي اليابس
Kraymeh	الكريمة	Yarmouk Reserve	محمية اليرموك
Kufr Abil	كفر ابيل	Yarmouk University	جامعة اليرموك
Kufr Rakib	كفر راكب		

foods such as *zaatar* and olives, ceramics and more, all of which you can buy. They also have a small **restaurant** on site: book ahead to eat here.

Qasr al-Abd

Daily 8am–6pm (Nov–March till 4pm); when you arrive, the guardian will probably materialize to unlock the gates • JD1, free with JP • 1hr drive from Amman; Iraq al-Amir is quiet, so plan return transport in advance – the bus from Wadi Seer takes 20min so if you're relying on a bus back (even if you're choosing to walk down), ask the bus driver when the last one leaves; a taxi is about JD8–10 including waiting time

After passing through Iraq al-Amir village, the road ends about 1km further on at the gates of the **Qasr al-Abd**, a strikingly beautiful pre-Roman country **villa** set on a platform above the fields. The villa was begun in the years around 200 BC by Hyrcanus, a member of the powerful Tobiad family, as the centrepiece of a lavish, cultivated estate; its name, meaning "Palace of the Servant", derives from a fifth-century-BC member of the clan, who is mentioned in the Old Testament as being a governor, or "servant", of Ammon. Hyrcanus died in 175 BC and the palace was never completed; indeed, for some reason the huge limestone building blocks – some up to 25 tonnes in weight – were originally laid precariously on their 0.5m edges, and dutifully collapsed at the first earthquake, in 365 AD. Since then, the building has been only sporadically occupied, possibly during the Byzantine period by Christian monks. It was only in the 1980s that the palace could be partially reconstructed by industrial cranes; before then, the fallen masonry was too heavy to be reassembled.

Inside, only a few courses of the internal walls still stand, although picture windows still ring the building and stairs lead up to a now-collapsed second storey. The main attractions, though, are outside. Around the walls are elegant **carvings of wild animals**, though it's unlikely such beasts roamed the area even in antiquity. At ground level on both sides of the building are dolomite **leopards** doubling as fountains, and around the top of the walls are eagles and lions. The best of all, high up on a back corner, is a **lioness** – complete with mane for some reason – suckling her cubs.

Museum

Open on request – ask the guardian • Included in entry ticket, but tips welcome (JD2–3)

Off to one side is a small modern building housing a **museum**, housing photos of the site and some informative notes, including translations of a text by the first-century Roman historian Josephus describing the villa and its animal carvings in uncannily accurate detail. If the electricity is on, the guardian will play the excellent historical slide show for you; even if it's off, he still deserves a tip.

The eastern desert

QASR KHARANA

The eastern desert

For hundreds of kilometres east of Amman, the stony plains of the eastern desert extend unbroken to the Iraqi border – and beyond, clear to Baghdad. This is the harshest and least populated part of Jordan, with a bare handful of roads linking small, dusty towns and frontier villages. The two exceptions are Zarqa, an industrial city and transport hub, and Mafraq, the amiable but little-visited capital of the northeast, nudging the Syrian border. However, the main reason to come this way is to follow a circuit of desert roads that runs past a string of early-Islamic inns and hunting lodges, collectively dubbed the "Desert Castles".

For its mosaics and its remote atmosphere, **Qasr Hallabat** makes a fine opener to the "**Desert Castles**" loop, matched by elegant **Qasr Kharana** and the uniquely frescoed **Qusayr Amra**. At the circuit's farthest point, 100km east of Amman, lie the castle and twin villages of **Azraq**, Lawrence of Arabia's desert headquarters, set in a once-majestic oasis in the heart of the **northern Badia**, which stretches out to the Syrian and Iraqi borders. Close by in southern Syria, and often visible, is the **extinct volcano** of Jabal Druze (or Jabal Al Arab), rising to 1800m and surrounded for hundreds of kilometres by blisteringly hot plains of basaltic lava known as the **Hawran**. Near Mafraq, irrigated fields temper the monotony, but further east – and south as far as Azraq – the desert is shadowy and grimly blackish, stark bedrock overlaid by dark boulders and glassy basalt chips too hot to touch. Out here stand the silhouetted ruins of **Umm al-Jimal**, enormously romantic in the cool evening, while a host of minor attractions include the holy tree of **Biqyawiyya** and the striking **Qasr Burqu**, a ruined black castle on the shores of a mirage-like lake, which lies remote in the far desert, not far from the Iraqi border.

Desert travel is sometimes approached as a chore, but you'll have much more satisfaction if you abandon the urgency of getting from A to B and treat the desert as a destination in its own right. Adventurous explorers out here will be rewarded with extraordinary hospitality, diverse environments and some stunning natural drama.

GETTING AROUND
                                               THE EASTERN DESERT

By bus Public transport in the desert is predictably thin. From Amman, take a bus to either Zarqa – from where buses head to Azraq (via Hallabat) – or Mafraq, for buses to Umm al-Jimal and the desert towns further east.

By car The best way to see the sights is by car – either in a rented vehicle or a taxi chartered via your hotel.

On a tour Wild Jordan arranges off-road and wildlife tours (see page 181).

Border areas with Syria At the time of writing the war in Syria was continuing. The British government was advising against all but essential travel to within 3km of the Syrian border. Check the latest at ⓦ fco.gov.uk.

Northeast of Amman

If you're relying on public transport, the only feasible access to the eastern desert is via the industrial cities of **Zarqa** or **Mafraq**, both located **northeast of Amman** along the main Syria-bound highway. Neither is even remotely geared up for tourism, though: if you're driving, bypass them both and aim for the big skies further east.

Zarqa

Some 20km northeast of Downtown Amman, and connected to the capital by a ribbon of low-income suburbs, industrial **ZARQA** is Jordan's second-largest city. There's little reason to spend time here except to catch an onward bus – to nearby **Khirbet as-Samra**,

QUSAYR AMRA

Highlights

❶ Umm al-Jimal This ruined city, out in the "black desert" near the Syrian border, offers romance, isolation and fascinating history. See page 182

❷ The "Desert Castles" loop Take one or two days from Amman to follow a circuit around the eastern desert, visiting ancient sites and modern villages. See page 184

❸ Qasr Hallabat Magnificently restored palace-fort, with fine mosaics and bags of atmosphere – it's a richly satisfying place to visit. See page 186

❹ Qasr Kharana Atmospheric "desert castle" with magnificent views; cool, dark and musty. See page 187

❺ Qusayr Amra Bawdy eighth-century frescoes adorn this diminutive desert bathhouse. See page 188

❻ Azraq Palm-fringed oasis town, with a unique wetland nature reserve and splendid ecolodge. See page 192

❼ Burqu Wander on the shores of a mirage-like lake guarded by a ruined black castle, out in the deep desert. See page 202

HIGHLIGHTS ARE MARKED ON THE MAP ON PAGE 180

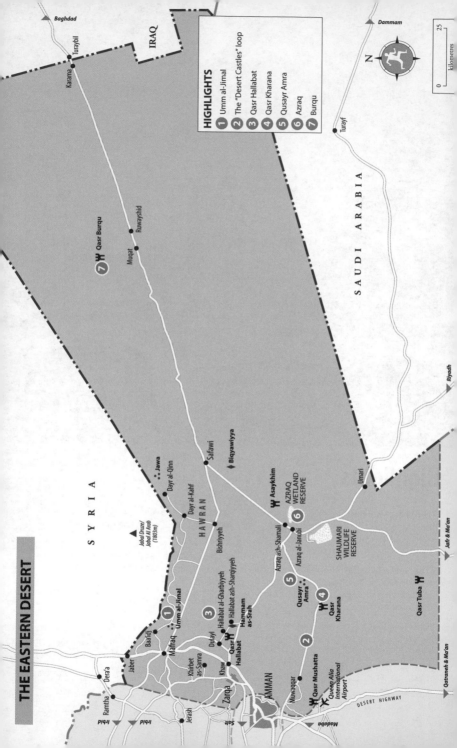

THE EASTERN DESERT

HIGHLIGHTS

1. Umm al-Jimal
2. The "Desert Castles" loop
3. Qasr Hallabat
4. Qasr Kharana
5. Qusayr Amra
6. Azraq
7. Burqu

N

0 ——————— 25
kilometres

Baghdad

IRAQ

Turaybil

Karama

Dammam

Turayf

SAUDI ARABIA

Riyadh

Ruwayshid

Muqat

Qasr Burqu ⑦

Safawi

Biqyawiyya

SYRIA

Jawa

Dayr al-Qinn

Dayr al-Kahf

Jabal Druze/
Jabal Al Arab
(1803m)

HAWRAN

Bishriyyeh

Asaykhim

AZRAQ
WETLAND
RESERVE

Umari

Jafr & Ma'an

Azraq ash-Shamali

Azraq al-Janubi ⑥

SHAUMARI
WILDLIFE
RESERVE

Umm al-Jimal ①

Ba'aij

Mafraq

Dulayl

Hallabat al-Gharbiyyeh

Hallabat ash-Sharqiyyeh

Hammam
as-Srah

Qusayr
Amra ⑤

Qasr
Kharana ④

Qasr Tuba

Jaber

Dera'a

Khirbet
as-Samra

Khaw

Qasr ③
Hallabat

Zarqa

AMMAN

Muwaqqar

Qasr Mushatta ②

Queen Alia
International
Airport

DESERT HIGHWAY

Qatraneh & Ma'an

Madaba

Salt

Jerash

Ramtha

Irbid

Irbid

Qasr ③
Hallabat

EXPLORING EASTERN JORDAN

Of all Jordan's regions, the east is the least-visited. Few tourists bother to come out here – but even if you're relying on public transport, it's easy to construct a **one-night tour**: start with a bus from Amman to Zarqa, head east to Qasr Hallabat, then continue to Azraq. Next morning return to Zarqa and switch buses for Mafraq and then Umm al-Jimal, before continuing from Mafraq to Jerash or back to Amman.

Renting a car (see page 33) buys you the freedom to roam at your own pace, opening up sites such as Kharana and Amra that have no public transport access. Many of Amman's budget hotels offer competitively priced one-day trips by taxi to Kharana, Amra and Azraq (see page 185).

To add a twist of adventure, talk to the Wild Jordan team at the RSCN/Royal Society for the Conservation of Nature (w wildjordan.com; see page 49) about fixing up a half- or full-day excursion from Azraq – maybe an off-road tour of sites such as **Asaykhim** and **Biqyawiyya** nearby, or **birdwatching at dawn** in the wetlands nature reserve, or even a desert wildlife **safari** drive at Shaumari. They can also arrange guided trips to far-flung desert locations, including **Burqu**.

Bear in mind that, as long as the **war in Syria** continues, it's advisable to stay clear of the border, certainly no closer than 3km. If you're travelling in the border region north of the Mafraq–Safawi–Ruwayshid–Karama road, it's best to do so with a trusted guide, ideally from a reputable local firm.

with its Roman-Byzantine ruins; to **Hallabat**, at the start of the "Desert Castles" loop; or direct to **Azraq**.

ARRIVAL AND DEPARTURE
ZARQA

By bus Zarqa has two bus stations, 1km apart. The New Station serves Amman as well as Madaba and elsewhere. A shuttle bus runs from here to the Old Station, or you could walk left on the main road for 500m and then aim for a main roundabout by the old Hejaz Railway tracks, overlooked by a red-roofed church steeple.

New Station destinations Amman Mahatta (25min); Amman Tabarboor (35min); Madaba (1hr).
Old Station destinations Azraq (1hr 20min); Hallabat (40min); Jerash (45min); Khirbet as-Samra (30min); Mafraq (30min).

Khirbet as-Samra

Ruins: open access

If time is spare, you might take a couple of hours to visit isolated **KHIRBET AS-SAMRA**, about 20km northeast of Zarqa. Decked in wild flowers in spring and baked brown in summer, these hills were once crossed by caravans travelling the Roman Via Nova Traiana between Syria and the Red Sea; the town – then named **Hattita** – flourished for five hundred years or more. A Roman cohort was garrisoned here during the fourth century, and archeologists have uncovered eight **Byzantine churches**, all with mosaic floors.

Unfortunately, Hattita is better in the telling than the seeing: all the mosaics have either been removed or covered over for safekeeping and it's hard to make sense of the site. The sense of countrified **isolation** is as good a reason as any to visit. (Khirbet as-Samra is best known in Jordan for its huge wastewater treatment plant, but fortunately this isn't in sight or smell of the old village.)

Walking around the **ruins** will bring you to a large reservoir, near which is the **Church of St John**, a tiny place identifiable by its white limestone (instead of the otherwise ubiquitous black basalt) and paved floor, complete with apse. Further on are the foundations of the west wall of the original **Roman fort**, traceable around to the exposed East Gate, with the threshold and bases of flanking twin towers visible. The site guardian will help guide you around and show you photos from the French team who excavate here (w afsr.org); he deserves a tip.

By car From the main roundabout in Zarqa by the old Hejaz Railway tracks, head straight for 4km, then turn left towards Hashmiyya, then right after another 13km. You'll see the ruins at Khirbet as-Samra after 6km.

By bus Buses run from Zarqa (30min).

Mafraq

Roughly 70km north of Amman – and just 12km south of the Syrian border – lies the ramshackle town of **MAFRAQ**. Squeezed between it and the Jordan Valley to the west is the whole of the northern Jordanian agricultural and industrial heartland, but to the east yawns the open desert, and Mafraq's mood is of a tussle with the elements scarcely won. Dust fills the long streets, buildings are squat and ranged close together and many people wear the billowing robes of desert dwellers. Students from the big Al al-Bayt University add a bit of zip, but you're unlikely to have a reason to visit.

The main change in recent years has been the massive influx of families fleeing the **war in Syria**. Hard-hit Mafraq's population has more than doubled, to 200,000, while 11km east in windblown desert the giant **Zaatari refugee camp** at one stage housed over 150,000 people. At the time of writing Zaatari's population had settled just under 80,000, making it Jordan's fourth-largest "city" – a place of trauma, hardship and despair. It's run by the UN, guarded by the Jordanian army and is not open for visits.

By bus Mafraq's two bus stations lie 1.5km apart. Buses from Amman and Zarqa come into the Bedouin station, which otherwise serves mostly desert destinations. Local *serveeces* shuttle to the Fellahin station, for buses to Irbid (which lies 45km northwest on a fast road) and Jerash.

Bedouin station destinations Amman Mahatta (1hr); Amman Tabarboor (1hr); Dayr al-Kahf (45min); Ruwayshid (2hr); Safawi (1hr); Umm al-Jimal (30min); Zarqa (30min). Fellahin station destinations Irbid (45min); Jerash (40min).

Umm al-Jimal

Daily 8am–6pm (Nov–Feb till 4pm) • JD2, free with JP • ⓦ ummeljimal.org

In 1913, the American archeologist H.C. Butler wrote: "Far out in the desert there is a deserted city all of basalt, [rising] black and forbidding from the grey of the plain." The romance and sense of discovery accompanying a visit to **UMM AL-JIMAL** (literally "Mother of Camels") remain, even though the plain is now irrigated, and a modern village with good roads has grown up around the ruins. The site, about 75km northeast of Amman, has been well excavated and is rewarding to explore – you could spend a couple of hours here, though the sun can be fierce: bring water, and plan to visit before 11am or after 3pm. There's been a lot of conservation work done here recently; you may find access and on-site information have improved when you visit.

Umm al-Jimal's appeal lies in its **ordinariness**. Although it is roughly contemporary with the grand city of Jerash, only a day's ride westward, Umm al-Jimal has no temples or impressive monumental buildings. There's not even any evidence of the town's original Roman name, which remains unknown. The archeologist who excavated the ruins, Bert de Vries, perceptively explained Umm al-Jimal as "a symbol of the real life of Rome's subjects".

Brief history

Umm al-Jimal was occupied from roughly the first to the eighth centuries. Following Queen Zenobia of Palmyra's rebellion against Rome around 270 AD, the village was rebuilt as a military station on the fortified frontier of the Roman Empire. It prospered as an agricultural and commercial centre; a sixth-century conversion to Christianity resulted in fifteen churches going up. The town continued to prosper after the Muslim conquest, though an eighth-century onslaught of earthquake, plague and war led to the town's abandonment, until it was resettled in the early twentieth century by Syrian Druze families and local bedouin.

The ruins

Start a one- or two-hour walking tour at the **barracks**, which date from the fifth century. In the eastern wall, the basalt slab door, which still moves on its hinges, gives onto a courtyard. The late Byzantine **corner tower** is inscribed with crosses and the names of the four archangels: Gabriel, Raphael, Michael and Uriel.

The houses

Picking a path between **houses 102 and 116**, and left around **House 104**, will deliver you to the **double church**, two adjacent basilicas tucked into the houses around them, fronted by a small ablutions basin. Nearby **House XVI**'s lockable double doors would have fitted together snugly, and inside is a good example of a corbelled ceiling, the strong basalt beams supporting a much greater load than limestone could. Back behind

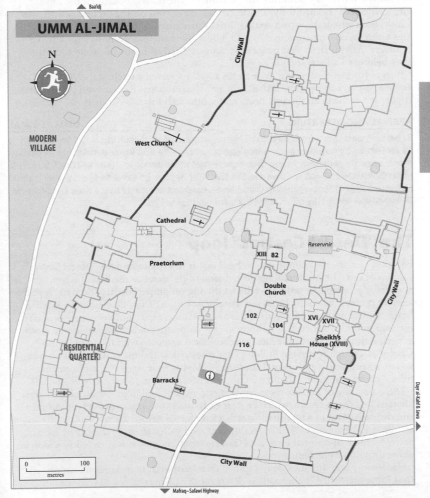

4

you, the sheikh's house (**House XVIII**) is outside on the left. Its large internal courtyard has a cantilevered staircase on the left and two in front forming a V-shape; stables were ranged at ground level, with bedrooms above. If you leave the courtyard through the gate here, you'll spot a beautiful double-arched window three storeys up. Archeologists have cleared and restored much of this house: it's now in great shape, with interpretive signage (tying in with the virtual tour at ⊚ummeljimal.org) and serves as a focal point for a visit.

From here, wandering north through the loose, clinking basalt leads to a huge **reservoir** – now fenced off – that was originally Roman. Just west of the reservoir, a scramble through **House 82** brings you into **House XIII**, with mangers and an interlocking stone ventilation screen – partially obscured by a recently built arch – dividing space for livestock within the house.

West Church and the cathedral

It's a 150m walk across to the four graceful and strikingly silhouetted arches of the **West Church**. The structure that remains is the division between the nave and a side-aisle; beautiful Byzantine crosses are carved on the arches. A little way south, the **cathedral** sports a reused lintel stone mentioning Valens, Valentinian and Gratian, co-emperors in 371 AD. Close by is the **praetorium**, with a triple doorway. As you stroll you may come across a herd of beautiful **white camels** – they belong to a local sheikh.

Fans of Roman roads could drive to see a well-preserved stretch of the **Via Nova Traiana**, which survives near **BAA'IDJ** village. The cambered Roman road points north (right) across the fields towards Bosra and south (left) towards Amman.

ARRIVAL AND DEPARTURE — UMM AL-JIMAL

By bus Buses run to Umm al-Jimal from Mafraq (30min).
By car From the big interchange on the eastern edge of Mafraq, where the north/south Amman–Syria highway crosses the east/west Irbid–Mafraq–Safawi road, drive east (signposted Iraq) for 11.5km to a turn-off for Umm al-Jimal. The turn-off leads directly to the ruins in around 4.5km, and continues ahead to reach Dayr al-Kahf (see page 202). To get to the Via Nova Traiana at Baa'idj, take the perimeter road around Umm al-Jimal to the West Church and fork left. After 7km, turn left turn at the T-junction, right at a small roundabout and straight on at a bigger roundabout, then continue for 600m.

The "Desert Castles" loop

For most visitors, the main reason to head east is to explore Jordan's "**Desert Castles**", a group of early-Islamic buildings dotted around the desert – the best of which are now easily accessible by ordinary vehicles driving on proper roads. Most date from the **seventh century**, when the **Umayyad** dynasty was ruling from Damascus: bedouin at heart, the Umayyad caliphs seem to have needed an escape from the pressures of city life, and so built a network of hunting lodges, caravanserais and farmhouses to serve as rural retreats. Nineteenth-century archeologists came up with the term "Desert Castles", although few of the buildings are true castles, and many were built on what was then semi-fertile agricultural land. Archeologists have suggested replacement titles – desert complexes, country estates, farmsteads – but none exactly fits the bill.

These are some of Jordan's most atmospheric ancient buildings – most notably **Qasr Kharana** and **Qusayr Amra**, which lie near each other on a fast road between Amman and the oasis town of **Azraq** (itself worth a stop for its nature reserve, ecofriendly lodge and links to Lawrence of Arabia). A different road to Azraq, from the city of Zarqa, passes by the well-restored fortress of **Qasr Hallabat**, making it easy to follow a loop in either direction from Amman.

Harder-to-reach sites include the ruined **Qasr Mushatta**, near Amman's airport, and **Qasr Tuba**, marooned in the roadless desert south of Kharana.

THE "DESERT CASTLES" LOOP: A SUMMARY

Clockwise from Amman: Hallabat–Azraq–Amra–Kharana.
Anticlockwise from Amman: Kharana–Amra–Azraq–Hallabat.
Off the main loop: Mushatta.
4x4 and desert guide essential: Tuba, Burqu.

GETTING AROUND

Transport options around the **"Desert Castles" loop** – which starts and finishes in Amman, with the two villages of Azraq as its furthest point – are limited. Buses reach some destinations, but many travellers prefer the convenience of a one-day tour by taxi. If there's at least two of you travelling together, you could potentially save money – and gain in convenience – by **renting a car** (see page 33) and driving yourself.

BY BUS

Two of the best sites (Kharana and Amra) have no buses running nearby. You could cobble together a looping route by taking a bus from Amman to Zarqa, then switching to reach Hallabat, then moving on to Azraq. From there, though, the only viable option is a bus back to Zarqa – or hitching along the Amman road to reach Amra, then Kharana, then into Amman itself. Be prepared to pay for each ride.

BY TAXI

"Tours" are run by several of Amman's budget hotels. For around JD20/person (usually with a minimum of three people to make the trip viable), you get door-to-door transport to Kharana, Amra, Azraq and back, with a decent amount of waiting time at each; sometimes Hallabat is included (if it isn't, try and get it added), but lunch is not. This is the cheapest and easiest way to see the loop in a day: you're unlikely to get a better price if you negotiate directly with a taxi driver in Amman, who may not know the route anyway. Book at least one day ahead. Upmarket hotels, of course, can do the same thing for a higher price.

BY CAR (ANTICLOCKWISE LOOP)

Amman to Azraq via Kharana and Amra To copy most "Desert Castles" tours from Amman, follow the loop anticlockwise by joining the Azraq road in the southern outskirts of the capital. Drive south out of Downtown Amman along Prince Hassan St (aka Madaba St) through Wihdat and past the major intersection Middle East Circle (*duwaar ash-sharq al-awsat*). In the industrial district of Sahab, about 5km south of Middle East Circle, you'll come to the flyover that carries the road from Azraq. Head left (east) on this road – also signposted for Iraq and Saudi Arabia – beyond the factories and into the desert. About 17km on you'll reach hilltop Muwaggar village, where there's a large Umayyad reservoir dating from the early 720s AD and still in

THE "DESERT CASTLES" LOOP

use. Beyond Muwaggar, it's a straight run for 38km east to Qasr Kharana, then another 15km to Qusayr Amra. Roughly 17km beyond Amra is a junction where the road from Zarqa merges; Azraq lies 8km ahead.

Azraq back to Amman via Hallabat From Azraq al-Janubi, head west 8km to the junction of the Amman road, then continue towards Zarqa (also signposted Syria) for 44km until you reach the Hallabat turn-off to the right. After Qasr Hallabat, instead of retracing your steps, continue on through Hallabat al-Gharbiyyeh village 4km west to Dulayl, to pick up highway signs pointing left to Zarqa and Amman.

BY CAR (CLOCKWISE LOOP)

Amman to Azraq via Hallabat From Amman, the clockwise route is to follow Hashmi St east from Downtown Amman until you reach a main roundabout in Zarqa city centre overlooked by a red-roofed church steeple. From here, follow signs to Iraq – they will take you straight for 4km (to where Hashmiyya is signed left; don't turn left). Continue straight for another 7km to a large, isolated interchange at Khaw, then straight again for 4km to a junction where Azraq is signed to the right. Take this turn – this is the main road to Azraq, which lies 65km ahead. After 13km you'll see a sign for Hallabat pointing left. It leads you for 2km through Hallabat ash-Sharqiyyeh village to a T-junction. Turn left and you'll see Hammam as-Srah after 300m, and then, 3km further in Hallabat al-Gharbiyyeh village, Qasr Hallabat signposted on the left. Once you've finished, retrace your steps to rejoin the Zarqa–Azraq road. From the Hallabat turn-off, it's 52km east to Azraq.

Azraq back to Amman via Amra and Kharana From Azraq al-Janubi, head west 8km to a major junction and follow signs to Amman. Qusayr Amra is 17km further, Qasr Kharana is 15km beyond Amra, and then it's 55km more (past Muwaggar village) to reach a junction in Amman's southern suburbs; head right to join traffic streaming into Downtown.

REMOTE SITES

Although Qasr Burqu (see page 202) and Qasr Tuba (see page 192) can be grouped archeologically with the sites on the loop, they are so far off any beaten tracks that it's only possible to reach them with a local guide and a 4x4 vehicle, best booked through a tour operator with expert knowledge (see page 48) – or via staff at Azraq Lodge.

4

Qasr Hallabat

Daily 8am–6pm (Nov–Feb till 4pm) • Joint ticket for all "Desert Castles" JD3, free with JP

QASR HALLABAT, perfectly situated on a small hill 30km east of Zarqa, is one of the most elaborate of the "Desert Castles". A Roman fort was built on this site in the second century to guard the desert frontier, and parts of it still survive, but the key period of the building's history was the sixth century, in the generally overlooked gap between the end of Roman control and the Muslim conquests. At that time, the **Ghassanids** – a group of Christian tribes who had migrated out of Yemen in preceding centuries – had risen to play a prominent role, introducing a specifically Arab identity and Arab system of governance to the region well before Islam. It seems they rebuilt Hallabat as a **country palace**, with mosaic floors, chapel and monastery. When the Muslim **Umayyads** took over, in the late seventh century, Hallabat simply seems to have been refurbished, with mosaics altered slightly, the monastery converted into storerooms and a mosque added to one side in white limestone, contrasting with the black basalt used by the Ghassanids.

A Spanish archeological team has done extensive work here in recent years, clearing rubble, bringing order to the site and renovating key structures. Hallabat is now perhaps the most satisfying of all the "Desert Castles" to explore, full of atmosphere – and still largely unvisited.

The ruins

From the Visitor Centre – where a small **museum** may or may not be open – walk 200m up a stony path to the hilltop site. You come first to the beautifully rebuilt Umayyad **mosque**, many of its doorway arches sporting distinctive scalloping.

Beside the mosque, a modern door beneath a wobbly **entrance arch** – one shake and it'd be rubble – leads into the main building's spacious, L-shaped **courtyard**, stone-flagged and flanked in black and white. To left and right, tall basalt walls lead into rooms filled with blocks inscribed in Greek, laid higgledy-piggledy; they originally formed an edict of Emperor Anastasius I (491–518), but the earthquake of 551 tumbled the lot. The Ghassanids, who no longer felt beholden to imperial decrees, reused the stones at random. In several places you can see remnants of the plaster they slapped over the top, etched in a herringbone pattern.

A scramble to the **corner towers** – the highest points of the ruins – can help with orientation; from here, as well as panoramic views over the undulating desert hills, you can spot older blocks from the tiny original Roman fort which occupied one corner of the site. Opposite, a water channel runs under the stairs, carrying rainwater from the roof to cisterns under the courtyard and outside the walls. Filling the centre of the building is a large square room complete with a dazzling carpet mosaic in a diamond design; the adjacent portico also features mosaics of birds and fish.

Hammam as-Srah

Included in main ticket

Beside the road roughly 3km east of Qasr Hallabat, in the adjacent village of Hallabat ash-Sharqiyyeh, lies a small Umayyad bathhouse, **HAMMAM AS-SRAH**. Similar to, though smaller than, Qusayr Amra, its *caldarium* (hot room) is nearest the road, followed by the *tepidarium* (warm room) with the hypocaust system of underfloor heating and terracotta flues in the walls. The *apodyterium* (changing room) is furthest away, next to the original entrance, where there's some decorative cross-hatching on the walls. Recent conservation work here has restored much of the building's beauty, and an elegant, wooden dome has been erected overhead.

> **FREE WITH JORDAN PASS**
>
> Throughout this Guide, "free with JP" means that the attraction grants free admission to holders of the **Jordan Pass** (see page 55).

| ARRIVAL AND DEPARTURE | QASR HALLABAT |

By bus Buses running between Zarqa and Azraq drop off on the main street of the village of Hallabat al-Gharbiyyeh, a few hundred metres from Qasr Hallabat (which is signposted).

By car Qasr Hallabat is 50km from Amman via the clockwise loop (see page 185), and 60km from Azraq via the anticlockwise loop (see page 185).

Qasr Mushatta

Daily 8am–6pm (Nov–Feb till 4pm) • Joint ticket for all "Desert Castles" JD3, free with JP

The largest of the "Desert Castles", **QASR MUSHATTA** (Arabic for "Winter Palace") lies 25km southeast of Amman, just beyond the north runway of Queen Alia Airport – the ruins are often visible on takeoff and landing.

Qasr Mushatta probably dates from the 740s and is moderately well preserved, although it was never finished. The **site** is enclosed by a square wall 144m along each side, with collapsed towers all round and portions of intricate Classical-style carving surviving. Similar pieces at one time covered all of the exterior, but as a sop to Kaiser Wilhelm of Germany before World War I, the Ottoman sultan Abdul Hamid II had most of them stripped off and presented to the Pergamon Museum in Berlin, where they are still on display. The whole site is littered with unfinished work, capitals and column drums; along with the carving, everything hints at a splendour of design that was never fully realized.

As you walk in, remnants of a **mosque** lie to the right, its *mihrab* set into the external wall. The palace buildings themselves are massive, built of unusual burnt brick above a stone base. The triple-arched entrance hall has a colonnade of beautiful swirling greenish marble columns, very striking against the reddish brick. Ahead is the huge triple-apsed **reception hall**. All around are interconnected rooms, some still with their high, barrel-vaulted ceilings in place; if you decide to explore, tread heavily to warn any resident **snakes** of your presence. Behind the impressive arched *iwans*, at the back of the hall on both sides, ancient toilets stick out of the wall, complete with run-off drain.

4

| ARRIVAL AND DEPARTURE | QASR MUSHATTA |

By car Head south out of Amman on the airport highway. Exactly 6.5km past the Madaba exit look for a small white mosque on the northbound (left-hand) side of the highway, followed 200m later (also on the northbound side) by a minor turn-off. This is the road you want. Continue south until you can make a U-turn, then return northbound and turn right down the turn-off (which lies 4km north of the exit for the airport). Drive straight along the turn-off road, following Air Cargo signs past industrial estates and across the old Hejaz Railway tracks. After 7.5km, just before a checkpoint, you'll see the ruined palace on the left.

Qasr Kharana

Daily 8am–6pm (Nov–Feb till 4pm) • Joint ticket for all "Desert Castles" JD3, free with JP

Of all the sites in the eastern desert, **QASR KHARANA** – also spelled **Kharrana**, **Kharaneh**, **Harraneh**, **Harrana**, and so on – was probably the one which gave rise to the misnomer "Desert Castles". Marvellously cool and perfectly still inside, Kharana is one of Jordan's most atmospheric and beautiful ancient buildings. It's worth coming here to soak up the peace and quiet for an hour or two.

Standing foursquare beside the road, and visible for miles around, Kharana looks like a fortress built for defensive purposes, with round corner towers, arrow slits in the wall and a single, defendable entrance. However, on closer examination, you'll find that the towers are solid (and thus unmannable) and that only 3m-tall giants with extra-long arms could fire anything out of the arrow slits. Rather, it seems most likely that Kharana – positioned at the meeting point of many desert tracks – was a kind of rural **conference centre**, used by the Umayyad caliphs as a comfortable and accessible place to meet with local bedouin leaders, or even as a site where the bedouin themselves could meet on neutral ground to iron out tribal differences. It was probably built in the late seventh century; a few lines of graffiti in an upper room were written on November 24, 710.

The ground floor

Circle left around the building to reach the sunken Visitor Centre at the back of the site. From here, you approach the main entrance facade head-on. Look up to see a distinctive band of diagonal bricks up near the top of the walls, a decorative device still in use on garden walls all over Jordan today.

As you enter, to left and right are long, dark rooms probably used as stables. The **courtyard** is surprisingly small, and it's here you realize how deceptive the solid exterior is: the whole building is only 35m square, but its doughty towers and soaring entrance make it seem much bigger. An arched **portico** originally ran round the courtyard, providing shade below and a corridor above – when it was in place, virtually no direct sunlight could penetrate into the interior. All the rooms round the courtyard, including those upstairs, are divided into self-contained units, each called a **bayt**, comprising a large central room with smaller rooms opening off it. This is typically Umayyad, and the same system was used in the palace at Amman, as well as at Mushatta and Tuba. Weaving in and out, you can explore your way around the deliciously musty and cool ground floor to get a sense of how the maze-like *bayt* system works. Each *bayt* most likely held a single delegation – the central, well-lit room used for meetings or socializing, the flanking, darker rooms for sleeping or storage. Kharana had space for a total of eight delegations and their horses.

The upper floor

Of the two **staircases**, the left-hand one as you come in delivers you to the more interesting upper western rooms; at the top of the stairs, it's easy to see the springs of the portico arches below. The room immediately to your left upstairs is lined with stone **rosettes**. Next door, a more ornate room holds a few lines of eighth-century **graffiti**, in black painted Kufic script in the far left-hand corner above a doorway. All around are graceful blind arcades and friezes of rosettes, with the semidomed **ceiling** supported on squinches.

Work your way through the **northern bayts**, which are open to the sky, round to the large **east room**, with a simple houndstooth design. From the southeast corner there's a nice view along the whole width of the *qasr* through alternately lit and dark areas. The **southern room**, with a row of little arched windows over the courtyard, has the only large window, looking out above the entrance: this may have been a watchpost. One of the small, dark rooms on the south wall has a unique **cross-vaulted ceiling**, with decorated squares and diamonds not found elsewhere. Take the stairs up again to the **roof** to watch the dustdevils spinning across the flat, stony plain.

ARRIVAL AND DEPARTURE   QASR KHARANA

By car Kharana lies 15km southwest of Qusayr Amra. It's roughly 60km southeast of Amman via the anticlockwise loop (see page 185), and 40km southwest of Azraq via the clockwise loop (see page 185).

Qusayr Amra

Daily 8am–6pm (Nov–Feb till 4pm) • Joint ticket for all "Desert Castles" JD3, free with JP

If you're not ready for it, you might miss the squat **QUSAYR AMRA**, beside the Amman–Azraq road 15km east of Kharana. *Qusayr* is the diminutive of *qasr*, meaning "little castle" (the building is also often called "Qasr Amra"). A small **bathhouse**, Amra was built to capitalize on the waters of the Wadi Butm, named after the *butm* (wild pistachio) trees which still form a ribbon of fertility winding through the desert, now arbitrarily cleft by the highway. A short walk in the wadi bed beyond Amra can transport you within minutes into total silence among the trees.

Amra was where the **Umayyad** caliphs came to let their hair down, far from prying eyes in Damascus. Probably built between 711 and 715 by Caliph **Walid I**, it is unmissable for the **frescoes** covering its interior walls. Joyously human, vivid and detailed, they stand in stark contrast to the windswept emptiness of the desert, and feature an earthly paradise of luscious fruits and vines, naked women, cupids, musicians, hunters and the kings of conquered lands. The first Islamic edict ordering the destruction of images came from one of Walid's successors, when Amra's frescoes were just five years old, but for some reason they were overlooked and have managed to survive 1300 years of fire and graffiti.

The Visitor Centre includes an **interpretation room**, with good information about the building and its history. As you approach, what you see first is the **water supply system** – a cistern, well and *saqiya*, or turning circle (an ox or a donkey went round and round this circle to draw up water).

The central aisle and arches

The main door opens southwards into the main hall, which is divided into **three aisles**; facing you at the back is a small suite of rooms probably reserved for the caliph. At first sight, the frescoes are disappointingly sparse, scratched with graffiti and – after the brightness of the desert sun – almost invisible. But if you wait a few minutes to let your eyes adjust, the frescoes become much easier to see, and much more rewarding to linger over.

On the sides of the **arches** facing you, setting the tone of the place, are a topless woman holding up a fish [**e** on our map] and a nude female dancer welcoming visitors [**f**]. Above the entrance is a woman on a bed [**a**], with figures by her side, a pensive

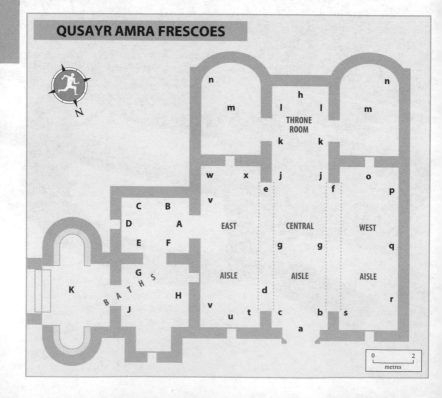

QUSAYR AMRA FRESCOES

woman reclining with a winged angel [**b**] and a female flautist, a male lute-player and a dancer [**c**], with another nude woman [**d**]. The **central aisle** that you're standing in mostly has real or fantasized scenes from **court life**: aside from women, there are horsemen, archers and people sitting and talking [**g**].

The west aisle
At the far end of the right-hand (**west**) aisle, a woman [**o**] reclines on a golden couch beneath an awning, with a male attendant and a woman seated on the ground nearby; at the head of the couch is a **bearded man** who pops up in many of the murals and who, archeologists have surmised, might have been in charge of the bathhouse. Above the figures are two peacocks and a Greek inscription referring to victory. Below is what looks like a walled city, and below that, a decorative geometric pattern runs at eye level around the room. Near the corner – and difficult to make out – are **six kings** [**p**], all conquered by Walid: the Byzantine emperor, the last Visigothic king of Spain, the Persian emperor, the king of Abyssinia and two others, now obscured (the king of India, the emperor of China or the Turkish khan). Next to them is a strikingly clear **nude female bather** [**q**], surrounded by onlookers, one of whom is the bearded man; he's also watching male gymnastics [**r**]. Above, wild asses, their ears pricked, are being driven into nets. Round near the entrance are some grapes and fragments showing curled toes [**s**].

The throne room
If the suite at the back – sometimes called the **throne room** – has not been closed off, you can see the leopards [**j**] and fruit trees [**k**] decorating the side walls. On either side of where the throne might have stood are male and female figures – one, very pregnant, representing fertility [**l**]. Dominating the back wall is a **seated king** [**h**], possibly Walid; two attendants with fans or fly-whisks keep him happy and there's a frieze of partridges around his head. On either side are what were presumably royal **withdrawing rooms**, with mosaic floors [**m**] and murals of fat grapes, giant pomegranates, acanthus leaves and peaches or heart-shaped fruit [**n**].

The east aisle
Back in the main hall the **east aisle** has, near the entrance, a large leaf design [**t**] beside hunters killing and butchering asses inside huge nets [**u**]. The whole of the east wall is devoted to a hunting scene of Saluki hounds chasing and capturing asses [**v**]. At the far end are the muses of History and Philosophy [**w**], alongside Poetry [**x**]. Dominating this aisle, though, are everyday scenes **overhead**, depicting metalworkers, carpenters, blacksmiths, hod-carriers and jolly working camels.

The baths
The door in the east wall leads into the **baths**, which show a more intimate style of decoration, probably the work of a different artist. The first room is thought to have been a changing room (*apodyterium*) or a cool room (*frigidarium*), originally floored in marble with benches on two sides. Above the door is a reclining woman, gazed on by a stubbled admirer and a cupid [**A**]. The south wall has a sequence of little figures in a diamond pattern, including a monkey [**B**] applauding a bear playing the lute [**C**]. Opposite the door is a woman with a 1960s hairdo [**D**]; next to her are a flautist [**E**] and a female dancer [**F**]. On the ceiling overhead, blackened by smoke, is a fine sequence showing the **three ages of man**, with the penetrating gaze of the same man in his 20s, 40s and 60s. Next door is a *tepidarium*, with a plunge pool and a hypocaust system to allow warm air to circulate beneath the floor and up flues in the wall. Beside the door is a tableau of three nude women [**G**], one of them holding a child; if you follow the picture round to the right, you'll see a woman is pouring water [**H**] and about to bathe the child [**J**].

The last room, a domed **steam room**, or *caldarium*, is next to the furnace; the holes in the wall all around supported marble wall slabs, and there are a couple of plunge pools. Above is the earliest surviving representation of the **zodiac** on a spherical surface [K]. Dead ahead you can easily identify Sagittarius, the centaur, with the tail of Scorpio to the left. Ophiuchus the serpent-holder is above Scorpio and below an upside-down, club-wielding Hercules. From Scorpio, follow the red band left to Gemini, the twins, and Orion. The whole map is centred on the North Star; just to the left of it is the Great Bear. Above and at right angles is the Little Bear, and twisting between the two is Draco, the snake. Just to the right, Cepheus is shrugging his shoulders, next to Andromeda with outspread arms. Cygnus the swan is just by Andromeda's left hand.

ARRIVAL AND DEPARTURE
QUSAYR AMRA

By car Amra lies 15km northeast of Qasr Kharana. It's roughly 75km southeast of Amman via the anticlockwise loop (see page 185), and 25km southwest of Azraq via the clockwise loop (see page 185).

Qasr Tuba
Open access • Free

Way off any road in the depths of the desert, about 110km southeast of Amman, **QASR TUBA** is the most southerly of the "Desert Castles", and, though ruined, is the only one which still has its original atmosphere of a grand estate reached after a long and difficult journey. It lies isolated in the deep desert. Set aside a day for the experience.

Although remote today, Tuba was built to be a **caravanserai** (inn) on the route between Syria, Azraq and northern Arabia. It was begun around 743 AD, the same time as Mushatta, and in a similar style, with bricks built up on a stone foundation. Tuba's bricks, though, are of sun-baked mud, unique among the "Desert Castles". The complex is very large and was originally planned as two enclosures, each 70m square, linked by a corridor – but only the northern half was completed. As you approach, keep an eye out for the building's **barrel vaults**, visible from some way off on the south side of the Wadi al-Ghadaf. You can discern **towers** around the external wall, and around the entrance are corridors, courtyards, passageways and rooms. The arched **doorways** are particularly striking, even if all the beautifully carved stone lintels have been smashed or taken away.

ARRIVAL AND DEPARTURE
QASR TUBA

By 4x4 To get to Qasr Tuba you need a 4x4 and a reliable guide – either a local villager from, say, Qatraneh or Muwaqqar or an archeology specialist from Amman or Azraq. There are three possible access routes. The best known is the desert track heading due south 47km from Qasr Kharana. A more difficult alternative leads 30km west from an unmarked point on the Azraq–Jafr road. Otherwise, from the Amman–Ma'an Desert Highway, about 14km north of Qatraneh, a road branches east towards Tuba – but the asphalt runs out after 30km, leaving you to negotiate the last 40km or so across the stony desert.

Azraq and around

As Jordan's only oasis, **AZRAQ**, 100km east of Amman, has always been a crossroads for international traffic. In the past, its location at the head of the Wadi Sirhan, the main caravan route from Arabia to Syria (known as the Wadi al-Azraq before its settlement by the bedouin Sirhan tribe), meant that Azraq was both a vital trading post and a defensive strongpoint. The Romans built a fort here – **Qasr Azraq** – which was continuously renovated over the succeeding centuries and chosen, in 1917, as his headquarters by **Lawrence of Arabia**.

Today, **traffic** passes through Azraq from **five directions**: from Syria to the north, Iraq to the east, Saudi Arabia to the south, Amman and Zarqa to the west, and the Red Sea port of Aqaba to the southwest. Heavy lorries thunder through the little town 24 hours a day on their way somewhere else. On the approach roads, it's not uncommon to see road trains of ten or twenty trucks nose to tail, trundling slowly through the desert together. As a consequence, half of Azraq is given over to **roadside restaurants**, the other half to **mechanics' workshops**.

It takes imagination to enjoy a stay in Azraq, but despite the drawbacks of traffic and neglect, this is a unique place with simple charms. It also has virtually the only tourist

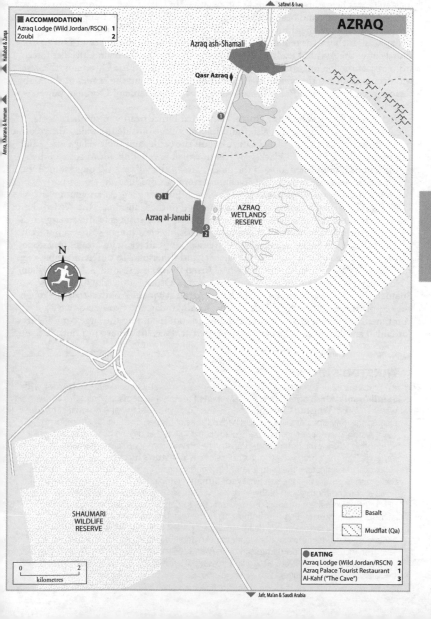

accommodation in the entire eastern desert region. Attractions include the unique oryx safaris on offer at the **Shaumari Wildlife Reserve**, a host of minor archeological sites and the rather extraordinary **holy tree of Biqyawiyya**.

Brief history

Large numbers of **Paleolithic** hand axes and flint tools have been discovered around Azraq oasis, indicating a substantial settlement up to 200,000 years ago: it seems that **malachite** was being brought from as far away as Ain Ghazal, near Amman, to be worked into delicate and beautiful earrings at Azraq. The Romans built a **fort** on the site of Qasr Azraq in the third century, also subsequently used by the Byzantines and Umayyads. The fort was rebuilt in 1237 by the Ayyubid governor Azz ad-Din Aybak, shortly after the Ayyubid leader Salah ad-Din had expelled the main Crusader force from east of the Jordan. Still in use under the Mamlukes and the Ottomans, the *qasr* was occupied during the winter of 1917–18 by Lawrence and the armies of the Arab Revolt; their final attack on Damascus, which saw the collapse of Ottoman power, was launched from here.

After World War I, wandering **Druze**, from Jabal Druze nearby in southern Syria, occupied the castle for a while, also founding the village outside the walls. The volcanic plains spreading south from Jabal Druze engulf the castle, and their village was – and still is – dominated by hard black-grey basalt, which is very difficult to cut and dress, giving a lumpy, unfinished look to the older parts of the village. Although some Druze became farmers, most earned their livelihood from salt production.

Barely a decade later, **Chechens** arrived at Azraq following a great emigration in 1898 from Russian persecution in their homeland in the Caucasus. They settled about 7km south of the Druze village, on flat ground near three springs feeding a large area of wetland marsh. The basalt runs out in a remarkably clear line of scarps about 4km south of the Druze village and the new settlement instead lay in an area of limestone. Most of the Chechen émigrés became farmers and fisherfolk. To differentiate between the two villages, the first became known as **Azraq Druze**, the second as **Azraq Shishan**.

Nowadays, with a more mixed population, Azraq Druze is officially **Azraq ash-Shamali** (North Azraq) and Azraq Shishan is **Azraq al-Janubi** (South Azraq) – though the old names survive in the minds of most locals. Today, the two Azraqs have a combined population of about twelve thousand, not including the large contingents of Jordanian and US air force personnel quartered at the giant **airbase** just outside town,

---

WINSTON'S HICCUP

Azraq is situated near the crook of the strange angle formed by Jordan's eastern **border with Saudi Arabia**, which zigzags here for no apparent reason. The demarcation of this border was the work of **Winston Churchill**, then British Colonial Secretary, who boasted of having created the new Emirate of Transjordan with a stroke of his pen one Sunday afternoon in 1921. A story grew up that, after a particularly liquid lunch that day, he had hiccupped while attempting to draw the border and – Winston being Winston – had refused to allow it to be redrawn. Thus the zigzag was written into history as **Winston's hiccup**.

On closer examination, the truth is rather less engaging: Churchill in fact carefully plotted the zigzag to ensure that the massive **Wadi Sirhan** – which stretches southeast of Azraq and holds a vital communications highway between Damascus and the Arabian interior – ended up excluded from the territory of the new emirate. Jordan's resulting "panhandle", a finger of desert territory extending east from Azraq to the Iraqi border, also had significance: with the French installed dangerously nearby in Syria, it meant that Britain was able to maintain a friendly air corridor between the Mediterranean and India at a time when aircraft were taking an increasingly important role in military and civilian communication. The fact that the new, ruler-straight borders cut arbitrarily across tribal lands in the desert appears not to have troubled the colonial planners.

DEATH OF AN OASIS

The reason why little Azraq attracts such attention is that it is – or was – the only permanent **oasis** in 30,000 square kilometres of desert. Fed by aquifers draining millions of cubic metres of filtered rainwater into a massive shallow basin, Azraq (which means "blue" in Arabic) was surrounded by freshwater pools and forests of palm and eucalyptus. Literally millions of migrating birds stopped off every year to recuperate in the highly improbable lushness on their long desert flights between Central Asia and Africa. Water buffalo and wild horses were common.

Azraq positively gushed with **water**, fed to the village from all points of the compass. Rain falling on Jabal Druze 80km to the north takes just a few years to filter through the basalt to Azraq's aquifers. Five **springs** (two in Azraq ash-Shamali and three in Azraq al-Janubi) poured 34 million litres of water every day into Azraq's pools. In addition, a total of ten river beds feed into Azraq's *qa* (depression), including the mighty Wadi Sirhan from the southeast and Wadi Rajil from the north, draining surface rainwater (separate from the underground aquifers) towards Azraq. In rainy years, the entire *qa* – 50 square kilometres in the midst of a parched and burning desert – was flooded to a depth of a metre or more with sweet water.

The abundance was too tempting to resist. In 1963, a small amount of **pumping** began from Azraq to Irbid; the oasis could replenish itself and no damage was done. But, following the 1967 war with Israel, the population of Amman in particular was swollen by hundreds of thousands of Palestinian refugees. Jordan's water infrastructure couldn't cope. In 1975, large-scale pumping to Amman began, Azraq alone supplying a quarter of the city's water. In addition, Syria dammed the Wadi Rajil, depriving the *qa* of a third of its run-off water. Jordan then tapped Azraq's aquifers deeper, this time fatally – yet still, in 1977, signed an international treaty protecting wetland habitats.

During the 1980s, Azraq gained a reputation as an attractive and fruitful place to farm: city folk began to move in and sink illegal private **wells** to irrigate their fields. Whereas in previous years such wells needed to be only 3m deep, by this time drilling ten times deeper produced no water. In 1992, after just seventeen years of abuse, the fragile wetlands dried up.

Almost three decades on, roughly 20 million cubic metres (mcm) of potable Azraq water is still being pumped annually to Amman – a city which, it's been claimed, loses 55 percent of its water through leaky pipes – while almost another 50mcm is drawn off by an estimated seven hundred wells for irrigation, far more than is replenished naturally. The natural balance in water pressure between the freshwater aquifers and neighbouring pockets of saltwater has been overturned. **Seepage of salt** is already occurring, and is irreversible: once brackish, an aquifer stays brackish forever. Ragged palms survive, but most migrating birds now head for Galilee instead. Recent work by the Royal Society for the Conservation of Nature (RSCN) to conserve and rejuvenate Azraq's **wetlands** has seen a good deal of success, but faces an uphill struggle.

Almost the only lifeline is the scheme piping drinking water to Amman from **Disi** (near Wadi Rum) and the proposed **Red–Dead Canal** (see page 115). The surplus they generate may mean that less water is pumped from Azraq. Time will tell whether the oasis can claw its way back from the brink.

and the recent influx of **Syrians** seeking refuge from the war. Over thirty thousand of them – roughly half under the age of 18 – bide their time in a vast, grim UN **refugee camp**, huddled on the scorching plains 25km west of Azraq.

Qasr Azraq

Azraq ash-Shamali • Daily 8am–6pm (Nov–Feb till 4pm) • Joint ticket for all "Desert Castles" JD3, free with JP

We hurried up the stony ridge in high excitement, talking of the wars and songs and passions of the early shepherd kings, with names like music, who had loved this place; and of the Roman legionaries who languished here as garrison in yet earlier times. Then the blue fort on its rock above the rustling palms, with the fresh meadows and shining springs of water, broke on our sight. T.E. Lawrence, Seven Pillars of Wisdom

Lawrence is turning in his grave at the fate of his "blue fort", **Qasr Azraq**. Leaving aside the 1927 earthquake, which shook some height from the walls and towers, apartment buildings now loom over the **castle**, the meadows have vanished and the "shining springs of water" have been diverted to keep Amman alive. Adding insult to injury, the main highway from Iraq thunders past the walls, slicing the castle away from the oasis that inspired it. Nonetheless, it remains a romantic and explorable place, with marvellous sunsets, and all the more poignant for its modest fame. A Druze family – currently in the third generation – have acted as guardians of the castle since the days of Lawrence.

As you enter the dogleg **gatehouse**, machicolation and an Arabic inscription commemorating the 1237 renovation of the castle are above your head. The massive basalt slab front door still swings on its hinges. Down at your feet, a double row of seven indentations in a threshold stone is for a gatekeeper's solitaire-type game using pebbles.

Within the **courtyard**, the rooms immediately to the left were patched up with palm fronds either by Lawrence's men or by later Druze occupiers. Further around, the west wall is dominated by a massive **tower**, at the base of which is a three-tonne basalt slab door, barely swingable to and fro: Lawrence described the whole west wall trembling as it was slammed shut. The supposed **prison** in the northwest corner features a locking hole in the doorframe rubbed smooth by centuries of curious fingers. To the north are the smoke-blackened **kitchens** and **dining hall**, and, beside them, the **stables**, supported by oddly shaped arches: a room here serves as a **museum**, displaying carved stone images of animals found nearby (which are probably Umayyad), and Roman milestones and inscribed blocks. A 7m **well** in the east wall was filled with water until the mid-1980s, but is now dry: the water table has dropped. Sitting skewed in the middle of the courtyard is a remarkably graceful little three-aisle **mosque**, probably built during the Ayyubid renovations.

The highlight, though, is the room above the gate you entered by. This was **Lawrence's room**, accessed by stairs and in a plum position to look out over the courtyard and the palms. In *Seven Pillars* he wrote:

In the evening when we had shut-to the gate, all guests would assemble… and coffee and stories would go round until the last meal, and after it, till sleep came. On stormy nights, we brought in brushwood and dung and lit a great fire in the middle of the floor. About it would be drawn the carpets and the saddle-sheepskins, and in its light we would tell over our own battles, or hear the visitors' traditions. The leaping flames chased our smoke-ruffled shadows strangely about the rough stone wall behind us, distorting them over the hollows and projections of its broken face.

Azraq Wetlands Reserve

Visitor Centre daily 8am–6pm (winter till 4pm) • Entrance fee JD8, waived if you book an activity or stay overnight; book everything at least a day in advance • ☎ 05 383 5225 or via the RSCN Wild Jordan centre in Amman on ☎ 06 461 6523, ⓦ wildjordan.com • A signpost opposite the petrol station in Azraq al-Janubi points down a side street to the reserve's Visitor Centre

Spreading east of Azraq al-Janubi village is the **Azraq Wetlands Reserve**, a sadly depleted shadow of its former self. Before the oasis dried up (see page 195), this whole area of marshes and lakes, in the midst of Azraq's *qa*, or depression, was the scene of vibrant life. Well over a hundred water buffalo roamed the area, along with wild horses and small livestock. In the winter of 1967, a staggering 240,000 ducks landed here, along with 180,000 teals, 100,000 pintails, 40,000 coots, 20,000 wigeons and 2000 mallards. Insects, molluscs and hundreds of thousands of frogs thrived; there's even a particular species of fish, the **killifish**, that is endemic to Azraq's pools. By 1992, though, after disastrous human intervention, there was very little left apart from some more or less deserted reed-beds and low muddy pools.

In 1998 the RSCN stepped in, and since then has launched a programme to protect the wetland area and focus efforts on conservation. The **Visitor Centre** has an **interpretation room** outlining Azraq's conservation issues – and a tank of tiny striped killifish.

WILD JORDAN RESERVE PRICES

Prices at Jordan's **RSCN-run nature reserves** are high. The RSCN make no apologies for this, saying that the reason they exist is to protect Jordan's natural environment, and that they have built lodges and developed tourism – under their **Wild Jordan** brand – as a tool for generating funds to help conservation and support rural communities. You may or may not agree with their pricing policy, but this kind of responsible tourism is virtually unknown in the Middle East, and the RSCN are pioneers. For now, until tourism schemes emerge that are truly community-owned, paying extra to visit the RSCN reserves is a good way to ensure that your money goes to benefit rural people and habitats.

From the Visitor Centre, the circular **Marsh Trail** (1.5km) heads off into the reed-beds. Brisk walkers could cover the circuit in ten minutes; dawdlers could find enough to keep them interested for hours, including ruins that are thought to be Umayyad or Roman. The water you can see gushing into the pools between the reeds has come from Amman: it's the minuscule amount that the government is pumping back into the wetlands as a gesture towards ecofriendliness. Overlooking a water hole near the end of the trail is a hide built of mud-brick, from where you can watch the **birdlife** – and, if you're lucky, the **water buffalo** which roam the reed-beds. Serious birders can arrange in advance with RSCN staff at the *Azraq Lodge* (see page 200) to be taken out to the hide at dawn. Ask, too, about following a longer route deeper into the reserve, known as the **Water Buffalo Trail** (guided; JD12).

Shaumari Wildlife Reserve

Open by appointment only • Book at least two days in advance – check details with RSCN staff at the *Azraq Lodge*, Azraq Wetlands Reserve or the Wild Jordan centre in Amman (see page 82) ☎ 06 461 6523, ⊛ wildjordan.com • Guided oryx safari: short (1hr; JD18pp) or long (2–3hr; JD22pp including tea and snack) • Guided oryx bike trail (2hr; JD14pp including bike and water) • Guided Wadi Shaumari trail (1–2hr; JD12pp) • Drive 7km south of Azraq al-Janubi and you'll see a sign for the reserve pointing right: the entrance lies 6km along this sometimes rough turn-off, though you must check in first at the Azraq reserve or lodge

Out in the baking desert south of Azraq, the highest point of land for miles around is the road, raised a metre or two above the dust. Here nestles the **Shaumari Wildlife Reserve**, 22 square kilometres of desert that is Jordan's leading centre for captive breeding of endangered **Arabian oryx**.

Shaumari accepts visitors for prebooked guided **oryx safari** tours, conducted in their own rugged 4x4 safari vehicles, in groups of up to seven people per car. These offer a close-at-hand experience of the desert habitat as it would be without the depredations of sheep and goats: the difference between the flora inside the fence and the over-grazed wilderness outside is striking. Notable species include shrubby giant fennel (*Ferula communis*) – *kalkh* in Arabic, known locally as *shaumar*, for which the area was named. Guides – all from Azraq village – explain more about local use of medicinal herbs during the tour, and point out the herds of roaming wild **onager** (the Syrian wild ass) as well as Shaumari's other inhabitants – gazelles, oryx, snakes, sand rats, lizards, the occasional caracal, jackal or wildcat, plus plenty of birdlife.

You can also book ahead to go cycling in the desert on the **Arabian Oryx Biking Trail** around the reserve, or to hike the short **Wadi Al Shaumari Hiking Trail** into the arid plains.

Asaykhim (Aseikhin/Useikhim)

As usual in this region, you can only get here with a 4x4 and a guide: it's a tough 30min drive east from the Safawi–Azraq road across stones and up steep gradients, although the hilltop ruins are clearly visible from some distance away; another option is to book Wild Jordan's bus tour (see page 181), organized through the *Azraq Lodge*: they'll drop you at the roadside, from where you begin an atmospheric guided hike between desert boulders to the ruins

About 15km north of Azraq ash-Shamali – or 39km south of Safawi, just past the experimental Tell Hassan renewable energy station (complete with wind pump and solar panels) – are the hilltop ruins of the Roman fort at **Asaykhim**, definitely worth the effort to reach for the extraordinary views and ravishing sunsets.

Simply wandering on foot in the natural Safaitic art gallery of the rugged basalt desert to the east of the hill can trump the scanty ruins. A surprising number of the boulders and rocks here feature some kind of **prehistoric inscription** or drawing, most of which are roughly 2000 years old: in this once-lush land, anonymous shepherds and farmers drew stylized people, camels and other animals, geometric patterns and random unknown markings on the only canvas they had available – **basalt**. The article "Safaitic art" by Jordanian artist Ammar Khammash, found under "Geology Tourism" at ⓦpellamuseum.org, explains more.

Asaykhim itself was one of a string of fortified stations built along the road between Azraq and Bosra, probably in the third century AD, to protect the empire's exposed eastern frontier. It occupies a commanding position. A scramble to the **summit** will reveal a series of small rooms built around a **courtyard**, the walls twelve courses high in places, with a **gatehouse** and some arched ceiling supports still standing. The arch in one room on the west wall has lost the ceiling it once supported, and stands alone facing the setting sun. It's the breathtaking 360° **panorama** that makes Asaykhim memorable, far more than the ruins. Locals say that you can see all the Badia from up here.

4 Biqyawiyya

Roughly 39km north of Azraq ash-Shamali and 15km south of Safawi – but without any signs or noticeable landmarks – a side-track branches off the highway on a lovely journey towards the **holy tree of Biqyawiyya** (also spelled **Bakieoah** and many other ways), well worth the tough, 35-minute ride by 4x4 across open country.

The approach

As soon as you leave the highway, the track deteriorates to reveal an old, 5m-wide cambered roadway, known to locals as the **"British Road"**, made of fieldstones packed together, with defined kerbstones and a central spine. This leads dead straight out across the undulating desert, visible for miles ahead without diversion; from satellite imagery it appears to follow the line of the Trans-Arabian Pipeline (or "Tapline"), built in 1947–50 to transport oil from the Saudi Gulf coast to Sidon in Lebanon, but disused in Jordan since 1990. Watch for kilometre markers all along the side of this route: the first, just off the highway, is 978; after 3km of a very bumpy ride you pass a modern brick hut marked "Km 975". Around 1500m further across the stony desert is a gentle rise, on the far side of which – in a memorable flourish of natural drama – stretches a vast area of fertile rolling **grassland**, often dotted with standing water, soft on the eye and echoing with the calls of swooping birds. A little after Km 970 is another small rise, which gives onto more gentle countryside in the area known as **Biqyawiyya**. Shortly after you'll be able to see the **holy tree** itself, located about 300m past Km 967.

Brief history

In his youth, the **Prophet Muhammad** is said to have travelled at the behest of a wealthy widow Khadija (who later became his wife) from his hometown of Mecca, north across the desert to Syria. Accompanying Muhammad on this trading mission was Khadija's slave, Maysarah. During the journey the caravan stopped for a break near the remote home of a Christian monk named **Bahira**. While Muhammad rested under a wild pistachio tree, Bahira came up to Maysarah and asked, "Who is that man?" – to which Maysarah replied, "That is one of the tribe of Quraysh, who guard the Kaaba in Mecca." In a reply which has passed into folklore, Bahira then said, "No one but a Prophet is sitting beneath that tree." Islamic tradition holds that the particular tree beneath which Muhammad rested still lives. There are competing claims, but the prime candidate is this one, far out in the desert northeast of Azraq. The fact that dendrochronologists have estimated the tree's age at only around 500 years detracts from the power of the legend not one jot.

The holy tree

The **holy tree of Biqyawiyya** stands in a beautiful setting on the edge of a flowing stream feeding a modern reservoir. It's the only tree within view – indeed, just about the only tree visible on the entire journey from Azraq – in a peaceful and pleasant spot, from where vast panoramas stretch out across the open desert. Bear in mind, however, that this is a holy place, and that the local bedouin as well as pilgrims from around Jordan and beyond make the long journey here specifically in order to pray and spend time alone or with their families in the presence of the Prophet. Frivolity, or stripping off to go bathing in the temptingly cool water, would be most disrespectful, as would tampering in any way either with the tree itself or with the strips of cloth which pilgrims leave tied to the lower branches as a mark of respect.

ARRIVAL AND DEPARTURE   **AZRAQ**

BY CAR

From Amman and Zarqa The quickest way from Amman to Azraq (roughly 100km) is the anticlockwise loop (see page 185) via Qasr Kharana and Amra. About 8km after the road merges with the road from Zarqa and Hallabat, all traffic is funnelled towards a T-junction with traffic lights, from where the restaurants of Azraq al-Janubi are visible to the right, extending for about 1km southwards. To the left, some 7km along the road, lie Qasr Azraq and the village of Azraq ash-Shamali.

North Safawi (see page 202) lies 54km north of Qasr Azraq, on the road signposted for Iraq.

South At a point roughly 23km south of Azraq, the road divides: a highway branches southeast to the Saudi border at Umari while the main road stays inside Jordan, heading south into the desert to Jafr, after 185km, and Ma'an, 58km further (see page 336). It is long on silent desert landscapes, short on anything else, and is used chiefly by trucks plying between Iraq and Aqaba port. Make sure you fill your tank, check your oil and tyres and buy plenty of drinking water before you head south.

BY BUS

The buses from Zarqa wander through Azraq al-Janubi first, then turn round and head for Azraq ash-Shamali, dropping off here and there. If you tell the driver where you want to be dropped beforehand, he'll take you to the door. The first buses to Zarqa depart around 6am, the last around 5pm – they start from Shamali, then pick up in both villages. Flag one down at any point. These buses also serve Hallabat. Destinations Hallabat (1hr); Zarqa (1hr 20min).

BY TAXI

No public transport serves Qusayr Amra (25km west of Azraq) or Qasr Kharana (15km further). Hiring a taxi in Azraq to see these two and bring you back would cost roughly JD50 – but you'd do better to fix something up in Amman beforehand (see page 185). An alternative is to take a Zarqa-bound bus (see above) 8km west to where the main roads split, then hitch along the Amman road to both sites and onwards to Amman (100km west of Azraq) – but fair payment for each ride wouldn't be less than a taxi anyway.

TOURS

The **RSCN** – through their **Wild Jordan** presence at Azraq Wetlands Reserve and *Azraq Lodge* – offer interesting ways to see the local area, on tours which include visits to village families and guided activities. Book everything at least a day in advance through the Wild Jordan office in Amman (☎ 06 461 6523, ✆ wildjordan.com; see page 82).

By bike RSCN staff can lead groups (min three, max nineteen) on guided cycling trails, including the Mudflat Trail (2–3hr; JD14/person) and Azraq Village Trail (4–5hr; JD25/person). Rates include bike rental and entrance to the

reserve; the Village Trail also includes brunch with a local Druze family and admission to Qasr Azraq.

By bus/on foot The RSCN offers combination bus and hiking tours around the area (min three, max seven). A half-day tour (JD23/person) covers Azraq itself and some outlying areas; the full-day tour (JD27/person) goes out as far as Asaykhim (see page 197). Both include a brunch with a local Druze family and admission to Qasr Azraq.

Jordan Eastern Badia Trail (JEBT) Due to launch just after this book went to press, this new concept from Wild

4

AZRAQ SALT

Strangely for a freshwater oasis, Azraq has separate, extensive underground pockets of extremely salty water, which for many years allowed the village to supply much of the **table salt** used in Jordan and Iraq. However, the growth of the Dead Sea salt works at Safi (which is a far bigger and more efficient operation) now means that there is no longer any profit in producing salt in Azraq. The failure of the salt business, which was once a major source of income and employment, has serious **ecological implications**. Azraq's brine, now untapped, is seeping into the freshwater aquifers beneath the desert and turning them brackish. Even worse, Safi's vast evaporation ponds are a major contributor to the shrinkage of the Dead Sea, operating at full capacity despite the lake's greatly reduced inflow. It makes ecological – if not economic – sense to share Jordan's salt production between Safi and Azraq, to limit environmental damage at both sites and distribute potential profits evenly. Yet there is no sign of that happening.

Jordan centres on guided 4x4 off-road driving routes starting (and ending) at the Azraq Lodge. The Black & White Trail (160km; 10hr) is a full-day trip south to the eroded chalk ridges of Wadi Dahik. The Bedouins Trail (220km; 2 days) extends this, including wild camping and the tree at Biqyawiyya. The Burqu Trail (528km; 2 days) takes you from the sites around Azraq for a night at Burqu, before returning on a looping route through deep desert. The Badia Stories Trail (476km; 3 days) covers all these and more. All include guiding and full support. Prices hadn't been fixed at the time of writing.

GETTING AROUND

By bus Although there are some local minibuses between the two halves of Azraq, most people just flag down any vehicle; a simple "*Shamali?*" or "*Janubi?*" to the driver suffices. A decent offer would be JD3.

By bike For independent exploration, rent a bike (half day JD7; full day JD15) at the Azraq Wetlands Reserve. Ideally book at least a day in advance through the Wild Jordan office in Amman (ⓦ wildjordan.com; see page 82) – or ask at the *Azraq Lodge* on the off chance.

ACCOMMODATION

Azraq – specifically Azraq al-Janubi – holds almost the only tourist accommodation in the entire eastern desert region.

★ **Azraq Lodge (Wild Jordan/RSCN)** Azraq al-Janubi ☏ 05 383 5017 or book via the RSCN Wild Jordan centre in Amman (see page 82) ☏ 06 461 6523, ⓦ wildjordan.com; map p.193. This atmospheric old British army field hospital, built in the 1940s on a small rise overlooking the oasis, served for a time as a hunting lodge. After extensive renovation by the Royal Society for the Conservation of Nature – which included restoration of period features as well as some new construction – it is now an excellent hotel. The atmosphere is friendly and informal, the sixteen rooms (which are all en suite, with a/c and heating) are simple but well designed, and service is faultless. Staff – all of whom are Azraq locals – can advise on activities and excursions, and arrange meals with advance notice. Within the lodge is an area of handicraft workshops (open to visitors by arrangement), where local women are employed in silk-screening, painting ostrich eggs and sewing textiles for sale at RSCN Nature Shops around Jordan. The hotel is located off the main highway about 600m west of Azraq's T-junction, signposted up a side road to the south. JD82

Zoubi Azraq al-Janubi ☏ 05 383 5012; map p.193. Small family-run hotel behind the *Refa'i* restaurant at the southern end of Azraq that gets most of its business from passing Saudi families. Rooms are decent enough and keenly priced. JD20

EATING

Azraq al-Janubi's main drag is lined with basic **restaurants**, alongside the no-nonsense butchers which service them: the juxtaposition of hanging carcasses and roadside cooking may not appeal to everyone. Plainer places cater for long-distance truckers, offering meat stew and spit-roasted chicken. Posher joints try to tempt in Saudi families with fancier decor, meze-style salads and kebabs. Take your pick.

★ **Azraq Lodge (Wild Jordan/RSCN)** Azraq al-Janubi ☏ 05 383 5017 or book via the RSCN Wild Jordan centre in Amman (see page 82) ☏ 06 461 6523, ⓦ wildjordan. com; map p.193. The lodge restaurant is run by a local Chechen family, and the meals they serve are outstanding – carefully presented Arabic dishes of kebabs and chicken and rice, salads and fresh fruit alongside delicately flavoured Chechen specialities, including cheese soup, *mantaish* (a hearty dish of mutton and onions), *gelnesh* (rather like chicken and veal wontons) and more. Meals cost JD14–21 a head. Booking at least two days ahead is essential –

preferably a week. To find it, head along the main road about 600m west of Azraq's T-junction, where you'll see a sign pointing south up a side road. Open for prebooking only.

Azraq Palace Tourist Restaurant Azraq al-Janubi ☎ 079 503 0356; map p.193. Almost every tour bus that stops in Azraq disgorges its passengers here, about 2.5km north of Azraq's T-junction, for lunch (roughly JD10–12). It's

basic, but adequate. Daily 11am–10pm.

Al-Kahf ("The Cave") Azraq al-Janubi ☎ 05 383 5444; map p.193. This is one of the better local restaurants on the main drag – a friendly place, with acceptably good food (around JD10 a head). There's no English sign, but it's the one that looks like a sunken den made of basalt stones, with a row of neon spiders and a giant *dalleh* coffeepot outside.

The Northern Badia

Jordan tends to be defined as a desert land, but most people – locals as well as visitors – don't ever get to know the desert, spending virtually all their time in the fertile, relatively well-watered strip of hilly territory running down the western part of the country. Yet more than eighty percent of Jordanian territory comprises the **Badia** (pronounced *bad-ya*; from the same root as "bedouin"). This hard-to-define term may be translated as "desert", but you should banish ideas of classic rolling dune-scapes. Gravelly *badia* desert, though arid and wild, is richer in both flora and fauna than the sandy *sahra* deserts of Arabia and North Africa.

Jordan's Badia divides into three sectors. The areas around Wadi Rum (see page 320) in the Southern Badia are now widely known, but outsiders understand much less about the vast stony deserts which stretch east of Amman and Mafraq, and south to Qatraneh. Beyond the Central Badia around Azraq, the **Northern Badia**, hemmed into Jordan's long panhandle, remains *terra incognita* for most visitors (and Jordanians). It lacks the drama of Rum's soaring cliffs and red sand dunes, yet holds some of the most striking scenery in the country, from the black, boulder-strewn, volcanic *harra* desert near the Syrian border out to the undulating limestone plateau of the *hamad* desert in the farthest corners of the country near Iraq.

This is also one of Jordan's most rewarding areas for **birdwatching**. Recent **animal** sightings have included the sand cat, the Levantine viper and Tilbury's Spring-Footed Lizard, all of them rarities, and ongoing investigations have turned up 49 plant species new to science. In addition, there's a handful of relatively minor archeological sites that serve as a useful hook on which to hang a visit. Everything centres on the small, dusty town of **Safawi**; north lie the ruins of **Jawa**, a long-abandoned city, while east, barely 50km from the Iraqi border, is the astonishing, mirage-like apparition of the glittering lake and ruined black castle of **Burqu**.

4

GETTING AROUND   THE NORTHERN BADIA

Transport in this most remote area of Jordan is difficult, and requires considerable forward planning. Relying on **public transport** won't get you far; the way to go is in a **4x4** with a guide.

BY BUS
There are buses from Mafraq to Safawi (1hr), with fewer heading on to Ruwayshid (2hr) and beyond, but none goes anywhere near sites of interest. Even if you reach Ruwayshid, your chances of being able to get out to Qasr Burqu independently are virtually nil.

BY 4X4
Your vehicle should be well equipped with spares, communications equipment, food and plenty of drinking water, plus a local guide who knows the area. A handful of

local and foreign tour operators (see page 48) organize tours focused on birdwatching or archeology and will take you out to sites such as Qasr Burqu.

RSCN/Wild Jordan Your best bet is the RSCN, who have the expertise to put a special itinerary together for you, with Azraq as the base from which to explore the area. Contact their "Wild Jordan" tourism unit in Amman well in advance (see page 82) to discuss what's possible. You might be able to fix something up on the spot with staff at the *Azraq Lodge* (see page 200), but don't rely on it.

BRP You could also seek advice – again, well in advance – from the Badia Research Programme, based in Amman (☎ 06 534 0401, ⊕ ncrd.gov.jo). They have a field office in Safawi (☎ 02 629 0111) where, with sufficient notice, you might be able to arrange a rudimentary overnight stay and desert guiding.

Safawi

Buses run west to Mafraq (1hr) and east to Ruwayshid (2hr)

The major town of the Northern Badia is **SAFAWI**, 75km east of Mafraq and 53km north of Azraq. It's an oil-stained, engine-roaring kind of place that's unlikely to inspire: there are no hotels and just a handful of restaurants. You may spot road signs to Safawi that include "H5" in brackets; this refers to a pumping station along the route of an **oil pipeline** constructed in the 1930s, which prompted the later construction of the highway alongside. Only operational for fifteen years up until the declaration of the State of Israel in 1948, the pipeline originated in Kirkuk, Iraq, with one branch running through Syria to Tripoli on the Lebanese coast, and the other through Jordan to Haifa, now in Israel. All the pumping stations along the Haifa branch were numbered with the prefix "H": H4 is just before Ruwayshid, while Safawi developed around the H5 pumping station, whose buildings are now part-occupied by a field office of the **Badia Research Programme** (see opposite).

Dayr al-Kahf, Dayr al-Qinn and Jawa

Sandwiched between Safawi and the Syrian border are the hilly expanses of the **Hawran**, a black desert of igneous rocks spewed out in antiquity by the now-extinct volcano of Jabal Druze, just over the border. Within this strip, east of Umm al-Jimal (see page 182), lie a string of rural communities and a handful of ancient sites, including the Roman forts at **Dayr al-Kahf** and **Dayr al-Qinn**, and the bleak and mysterious Bronze Age site of **Jawa**. However, with the war continuing nearby in Syria, we **do not recommend exploration** out here; for this edition of the Guide, we have removed our coverage, with the hope that it can be reinstated next time round.

East of Safawi: towards Iraq

On the western edge of Safawi town is the junction of the roads to Mafraq (signed for Syria) and Azraq (signed for Saudi Arabia). Towards Mafraq, after about 20km you'll spot the twin hills of **Aritayn** ("Two Lungs") to the side of the road, just before the road swings northwest around the aptly named **Jabal al-Asfar** ("Yellow Mountain"; 424m) towards the jutting scarp of Tell ar-Remah.

In the other direction, a short way **east of Safawi**, the highway crosses the **Wadi Rajil**, which feeds water falling on Jabal Druze in Syria south to Azraq. Soon after, you pass alongside the prominent **Jibal Ashqaf** mountains, looming on both sides above the rolling slopes of black rocks (overlaying yellowish sand) which fill the immensely long sightlines in all directions. The Ashqaf area marks a watershed, since the large **Wadi Ghsayn**, which runs alongside the road further east, drains water into the flat Qa Abul Ghsayn and then to Burqu and north into Syria. As you head on east, you cross the dividing line between the black stony *harra* desert and flatter limestone *hamad*, which stretches east to the Iraqi border and is much more soothing on the eye.

Some 90km east of Safawi, **Muqat** is the starting point for a journey north along the Wadi Muqat into the roadless desert towards Burqu.

Burqu

Guide essential: arrange through Wild Jordan (🌐 wildjordan.com), with at least a week's notice via their Amman office (see page 82), coordinated with guiding staff at *Azraq Lodge* (see page 200) • Burqu Ecolodge (run by Wild Jordan), offering meals and accommodation in an environmentally friendly new building near the castle, was not yet open at the time of writing; check for details before you visit

At the focal point of desert tracks roughly 18km north of Muqat and 25km northwest of Ruwayshid is the *qasr* of **BURQU** (pronounced "beurkaa" with a throaty gargle at the end: "berkoo" is wrong). The castle is all but impossible to locate without the help of a **guide** with intimate local knowledge; moreover, due to its

DEVELOPING THE BADIA

Jordan's arid areas, known as the **Badia**, cover approximately 85 percent of the country, yet are home to only five percent of the population. Although its annual rainfall is less than 200mm, the Badia provides Jordan with over half its groundwater needs and almost a quarter of national GDP – today, these arid regions are seen as the country's agricultural and industrial resource base. With Jordan's ongoing **population explosion**, urban areas are unable to cope, and in recent years growing numbers of people have abandoned the cities and moved out to make a life here.

Traditionally, the Badia was home to the nomadic **bedouin**, but the growing power of urban communities in the twentieth century increasingly affected bedouin social life as well as the physical environment. Key **resources** were exploited mainly for the urban population's benefit, and services and products generated by the urban community became integrated into the lifestyle of the bedouin, undercutting a sense of responsibility for the environment – countless discarded plastic bags, for example, now blow around the desert. Vegetation was destroyed, erosion increased, groundwater was tapped and scarce resources were squandered. The bedouin became more alienated from the central authorities.

Then, in 1990–91, **refugees** fleeing the Gulf War in Iraq brought an estimated 1.8 million sheep and goats into northeastern Jordan. The overgrazing that followed caused severe environmental damage, eliminating the production capability for pasture and forage, destroying wildlife habitats and wreaking havoc with existing patterns of agriculture.

Sheep have remained a constant problem; traditionally a small-scale livelihood for the bedouin, the industry now severely threatens land resources through overgrazing by hugely expanded flocks. In one sector of the Northern Badia, roughly eighteen thousand people live in an area of 11,000 square kilometres, yet they may, at certain times of year, share the land with 1.5 million sheep. Perversely, the local sheep industry is almost nonexistent: Jordan imports most of its mutton from Australia, and wool is a nonstarter, with most farmers shearing with hand-clippers for domestic use only. Another significant problem is education: a third of the Badia's children aren't enrolled in school at all. Graduates – especially women – have great difficulty finding jobs in the Badia, so the best local teachers tend to move to Amman. Badia schools give students little grounding in either the arts or vocational sciences such as agriculture or engineering; almost half the Badia's population over the age of 19 is illiterate, and just three percent are university graduates.

However, notions of the Badia and bedouin life are key to the Jordanian national character. In 1992, Jordan's Higher Council for Science and Technology, with the backing of Britain's Royal Geographical Society and Durham University, established the **Badia Research Programme** (BRP), to investigate the Badia's human and natural resources and the possibilities for sustainable development. They identified vast potential in the Badia, ranging from minerals to ecotourism, traditional crafts and renewable energy, and are having some success in turning around the priorities of local farmers. A royally backed investment plan followed (W badiafund. gov.jo) and then in 2005 the UN awarded Jordan US$162 million in compensation for the environmental damage caused by the 1990–91 refugee inflow. On the back of the award, in 2009 the government launched the **Badia Restoration Program** (W badiarp.gov.jo), a twenty-year plan focusing on wide-ranging environmental and socioeconomic rehabilitation. There's now an **Arid Lands Academy** in Zarqa, as a focus for research and development efforts, and implementation of **sustainable tourism** programmes – including the RSCN's **Jordan Eastern Badia Trail** – and a tourism lodge at **Beir Mathkour**, in the Southern Badia region of Wadi Araba (see page 339). Ideas to introduce sustainable development in the Badia are finally gaining traction.

4

proximity to both the Syrian and Iraqi borders, you should not attempt to venture out here independently.

This small Roman fort, occupied and expanded during the Islamic period, can be grouped – archeologically speaking – with the "Desert Castles" of Hallabat, Azraq and others. However, the ruins take a poor second place to Burqu's extraordinary **natural environment**, both on the off-road journey to reach the site and once you arrive. The

USEFUL ARABIC PLACE NAMES

Azraq al-Janubi	الأزرق الجنوبي	–Bedouin station	مجمع البدو
Azraq Lodge	نزل الأزرق	–Fellahin station	مجمع الفلاحين
Azraq ash-Shomali	الأزرق الشمالي	Muqat	مقاط
Dulayl	الضليل	Muwaqqar	الموقّر
Hallabat al-Gharbiyyeh	الحلابات الغربية	Sahab	سحاب
Hallabat ash-Sharqiyyeh	الحلابات الشرقية	Zarqa	الزرقاء
Khaw	خو	– New station	المجمع الجديد
Mafraq	المفرق	– Old station	المجمع القديم

qasr stands on the shores of **Ghadir Burqu**, a substantial lake some 2km long which is fabulous enough in itself, hidden in the depths of the desert, but which also serves as the lifeline and congregation point for an array of animals and local and migrating birds. Proposed to become a protected nature reserve, Burqu is a wild and dramatic place, well worth the long and difficult journey.

Burqu dam and castle

Burqu **dam**, 2km north of the *qasr* (which led to the lake's formation), and the jagged, broken-off tower which still rises above the ruined walls of the **castle**, are thought to have been constructed in the third century, possibly to guard the water source for caravans travelling between Syria and Arabia. Inhabited throughout the Byzantine period – possibly as a monastery – Burqu was expanded by Emir Walid in the year 700 AD; an inscription dated 1409 might indicate occupation up to that date. The entrance into the *qasr* is on the north wall, which gives access to two **inscriptions** – one naming Walid – above the lintel of the room in the far left-hand corner of the rubble-strewn **courtyard**, next to a room with a pointed arch. In the opposite corner is a small, freestanding circular room with a cross carved into its lintel; next to it is the original **tower**, still standing to around 8m, with a tiny, easily defended door (now blocked) in one wall.

Burqu lake

It's Burqu's **lake** and its flora and fauna which most impress. The drive from Muqat crosses a large, flat *qa* (depression), from which subterranean water rises to form the lake, full almost year-round and bordered in spring by poppies, irises and other wild flowers. Gently lapping wavelets fringe the most incongruous beach you're ever likely to stroll on.

The projected **nature reserve** is to be centred on this mirage-like apparition, which stands between two very different habitats. To the east is a vast expanse of *hamad*, or stony desert pavement, covered with bushes and grasses in winter. To the west sweeps the black *Harrat ash-Sham*, a moonscape of basalt rocks ranging in size from a few centimetres to a metre or more across. The rocks make the *harra* impassable even for 4x4 jeeps: hunters cannot penetrate the area, turning it into a perfect **wildlife** refuge. Gazelles roam here, in addition to hyenas, wolves, sand foxes, sand cats, caracals and hares. **Birders**, too, will be delighted: as well as regular sightings of sandpipers, larks, wheatears and finches, Burqu boasts herons, pelicans, storks and cranes, along with buzzards, owls, vultures and even the rare imperial eagle, pallid harrier and saker falcon. Rumours, as yet unsubstantiated, persist among the locals about the presence of cheetahs.

Ruwayshid

About 10km east of Muqat and 100km east of Safawi stands the last town in Jordan, **RUWAYSHID**, another shabby but bustling place with a couple of truckers' motels and a few diners. A dual-lane highway makes short work of the 79km to the border (not accessible for tourists), which is better known by the name of the Iraqi border-post **Turaybil** than by the Jordanian post of **Karama**. Baghdad is about 550km further east.

4

The King's Highway

DANA

The King's Highway

The King's Highway – the grandiose translation of an old Hebrew term which probably only meant "main road" – is a long, meandering squiggle of a road running through some of Jordan's loveliest countryside. It has been the route of north–south trade and the scene of battles since prehistoric times – but today is a simple byway, often rutted and narrow, which follows the contours of the rolling hills above the Dead Sea rift. Major stops include the historic town of Madaba, Crusader castles at Karak and Shobak, and the spectacular Dana Nature Reserve, set in an isolated valley with good facilities for camping and hiking. But the King's Highway also runs through fields and small towns, linking a series of springs and following the line of maximum hilltop rainfall: travelling on it can give a glimpse of the reality of rural life for many Jordanians.

The **King's Highway** is mentioned in the Old Testament: **Moses** was refused permission to travel on it by the king of Edom. Later, the **Nabateans**, from their power base in Petra, used it to trade luxury goods between Arabia and Syria. When the **Romans** annexed the Nabatean kingdom, Emperor Trajan renovated the ancient road to facilitate travel and communications between his regional capital at Bosra, in modern Syria, and Aqaba on the Red Sea coast. Early Christian pilgrims visited a number of sites on and off the road around Madaba, whose beautiful Byzantine mosaics still merit a pilgrimage today. The **Crusaders** used the highway as the linchpin of their Kingdom of Oultrejourdain, fortifying positions along the road at Karak and Shobak – where extensive remains of castles survive – and also at Petra and Aqaba.

However, with the development by the **Ottomans** of the faster and more direct Darb al-Hajj (Pilgrimage Route), from Damascus to Medina and Mecca through the desert further east – and the subsequent construction of both the Hejaz Railway and the modern Desert Highway along the same route – the King's Highway faded in importance. It was only asphalted along its entire length in the 1950s and 1960s.

GETTING AROUND   THE KING'S HIGHWAY

Amman to Petra via the King's Highway is around 280km – but there's a lot of ups and downs. You can make the whole distance in a day, but if you're taking it slow the best places to **break your trip** are at Madaba, where there's a choice of mid-range family-run hotels, and Dana, which has guesthouses and nature camping. Karak, the most obvious midway stop, is a disappointment, with poor accommodation and the plainest of restaurants.

By car Whether you have a day or a week, the best way to travel is by rental car (see page 33), since there's no public transport running the length of the road. Going more or less nonstop, allow 6–7hr for the drive.

By bus All public buses from Amman to towns along the highway start out on the faster but duller Desert Highway

and only cut west on feeder roads at the last moment. Thus, Amman–Karak buses bypass Madaba, Amman–Tafileh buses bypass Karak, Amman–Shobak buses bypass Tafileh, and buses to Petra or Aqaba bypass them all. Public transport along the King's Highway is limited to a series of point-to-point local bus routes: to make any sort of distance you either have to switch buses several times in small villages or resort to hitching.

By taxi or private bus Budget hotels in Amman are keen to service the market for day-trips in private buses or taxis along the King's Highway to Petra, but it's worth being aware of the scams that are common on this route (see page 91). You'd do better to talk to the *Mariam* hotel in Madaba (see page 219), which operates reliable, good-value private transport along the highway.

Madaba

Much as it did in antiquity, the initial portion of the King's Highway south of Amman runs through small farming villages interspersed among wide plains of wheat. The edge

MADABA

Highlights

❶ Madaba Amiable small town full of fine mosaics, among them a unique map of the Holy Land – for history, accessibility, outlook and fine mid-range hotels, this makes a great alternative base to Amman. See page 208

❷ Mount Nebo Awe-inspiring views stretch out from the mountain named in the Bible as the spot where Moses died. See page 220

❸ Wadi Mujib "Jordan's Grand Canyon", a vast fold in the landscape now protected as a nature reserve. See page 229

❹ Karak castle Crusader stronghold, still within its original walls, perched on a crag above a busy market town. See page 231

❺ Dana The country's finest nature reserve, with village atmosphere, walks, climbs and views to recharge the emptiest of batteries and stunning natural scenery. See page 238

❻ Shobak castle Often overlooked on routes approaching Petra, this majestically crumbling hilltop ruin offers an enticing sense of isolation, aided by some cheerfully low-key places to stay. See page 246

HIGHLIGHTS ARE MARKED ON THE MAP ON PAGE 210

Jerash

AMMAN

Wadi Seer
Iraq al Amir
Jericho
Shuneh
al-Janubiyyeh
Marj al
Hamam
Na'ur
ISRAEL
Baptism
Site
Hesban
Sweimeh
La Storia
Complex
Mt Nebo
Mukhayyat
Madaba
Jiza
Dead Sea
Hotels
Dead Sea
Panorama
Ma'in
Ma'in
Nitil
Amman
Beach
Ma'in hot
springs
Libb
Wadi Wala
DEAD SEA
Wadi Zarqa Ma'in
Mukawir
Wadi Hidan
Dhiban
Umm ar-Rasas
Mujib
Bridge
MUJIB
BIOSPHERE
RESERVE
Wadi Mujib
Ariha
Faqua
Wadi ibn Hammad
Qasr
Mazrafi
Wadi Karak
Rabba
Potash City
Bab adh-
Dhraa
Karak
al-
Iraq
Wadi Numeira
Muta
Safi
Mazar
Lot's
Sanctuary
Hammamat
Burbita
Khirbet Tannur
Wadi Hasa
Ayna
Fifa
Afra hot springs
(Hammamat Afra)

N

Tafileh (Tafila)

Sela
Ain al-Baydha
Busayra
Rashdiyyeh
Jurf ad-Darawish
DANA
BIOSPHERE
RESERVE
Dana
Qadisiyyeh
Feynan

Shobak

Petra
Wadi Musa

0   10
kilometres

HIGHLIGHTS
1. Madaba
2. Mount Nebo
3. Wadi Mujib
4. Karak castle
5. Dana
6. Shobak castle

of the plateau is never far from the road, and countless tracks lead off westwards into the hills teetering over the Dead Sea rift.

The easy-going market town of **MADABA**, 30km southwest of Amman, is best known for the fine Byzantine **mosaics** preserved in its churches and museums. An impressive sixth-century mosaic **map of the Holy Land** takes top billing in package tours, but the town's narrow streets, dotted with fine old Ottoman stone houses, lead to plenty more examples, notably the splendidly intricate mosaic at the **Church of the Apostles**. Excursions to the mosaics at **Mount Nebo** – the peak where Moses looked over the Promised Land – as well as natural and historical attractions galore (see page 224), make Madaba an ideal base for two or three days of exploration. A clutch of pleasant family-run hotels helps. Add easy access to Amman, the Dead Sea (see page 112) and the Baptism Site of Jesus (see page 122), and a location just 18km from Queen Alia International Airport, and Madaba becomes a viable, good-value alternative to basing yourself in the capital.

Brief history

Madaba is first mentioned in the Old Testament as having been conquered – along with the rest of the land of **Moab** – by the **Israelites**. The city was won back for Moab in the middle of the ninth century BC by **King Mesha**, as proclaimed in the Mesha stele (see page 231), at which point the Israelite prophet Isaiah stepped in, prophesying doom: "Moab shall howl over Nebo and over Medeba: on all their heads shall be baldness and every beard cut off … everyone shall howl, weeping abundantly." After some further turmoil during the Hellenistic period, when the city passed from Greek hands to Jewish to Nabatean, the **Roman** *Provincia Arabia* brought order.

Christianity spread rapidly and, by 451, Madaba had its own bishop. Mosaicists had been at work in and around the town since before the 390s, but **mosaic art** began to flourish in Madaba during the reign of the Emperor Justinian (527–65). Towards the end of that century, Bishop Sergius oversaw a golden age of artistic accomplishment: surviving mosaics from the Cathedral (576), the Church of the Apostles (578),

5

> ## MAKING THE MOST OF MADABA
>
> Although most visitors rush into Madaba to view the mosaic map and rush out again, the town is crammed with other **mosaics**, many of them more complete, and most more aesthetically pleasing. Within the central maze of streets is a large area of excavated mosaics dubbed the **Archeological Park**, while a small **museum** and the grand mosaic floor of the **Church of the Apostles** both lie a short stroll to the south.
>
> As well as mosaics, Madaba is known for its **carpets**. If you're in the market for such items, you'll find that prices are more reasonable, and quality often better, than in Amman. Many places in the town still weave carpets on traditional upright handlooms (although these days all the actual weaving is done by Egyptian employees). For other local crafts, **Haret Jdoudna**, a complex of small shops with a restaurant set round an attractive courtyard off Talal Street, merits a wander.

the Church of Bishop Sergius at Umm ar-Rasas (587), Madaba's Crypt of St Elianos and Church of the Virgin (both 595) and the Moses Memorial Church on Mount Nebo (597) – as well as, conceivably, the famed mosaic map of the Holy Land – all date from his period in office. When the **Persian** armies came through in 614, closely followed by the **Muslims**, Madaba surrendered without a fight and so retained its Christian identity and population; churches were still being built and mosaics laid for another hundred years or more. A mosaic discovered at Umm ar-Rasas mentions a bishop of Madaba as late as 785.

The modern era

Madaba was abandoned during the **Mamluke** period, and its ruins – by then strewn over a huge artificial mound, or *tell* – lay untouched for centuries. In 1879, conflict between Christian and Muslim tribes in Karak led to ninety Catholic and Orthodox families going into voluntary exile; they arrived at Madaba's uninhabited *tell* shortly after, laid claim to the surrounding land and began to farm. It was in 1884, during clearance work for a new church, that Madaba's remarkable **mosaic map of the Holy Land** was uncovered, closely followed by many more mosaics which lay in churches and houses all over the town. Scholars arrived from around the world, and their investigations still regularly uncover more mosaics and remnants of the past beneath the streets of the modern town centre.

These days Madaba's social and religious balance is changing, in a process of urbanization that has seen tens of thousands of **Muslim** families moving from nearby villages into suburbs and outskirts. Although **Christians** – Greek Orthodox, Roman Catholic and other denominations – still comprise the overwhelming majority of inhabitants in the city centre (estimates put the proportion at over 95 percent), Madaba's total Christian population today is around 14,000 in a greater municipality that has ballooned above 120,000.

St George's Church (Church of the Map)

Talal St • Sun 10.30am–6pm, Mon–Thurs & Sat 8am–6pm, Fri 9.30am–6pm; winter till 5pm • JD1

Madaba's prime attraction is a remarkable Byzantine **mosaic map** of the Holy Land, housed in the nineteenth-century **St George's Church**. Although heavily hyped – and thus suffering from over a thousand visitors a day in the high season – the map is well worth seeing, notwithstanding the cramped space inside the church. To one side of the church entrance is an interpretation room, where you could eavesdrop on tour guides briefing their groups on the history and layout of the map.

Although there is no evidence of a date of composition, or the identity of the artist, the map was laid at some time between 542 and 570 AD (a recent stylistic study suggests 557), in a Byzantine church that stood on the same site as the modern one

5

(8km) & Mount Nebo

Mount Nebo

(300m)

MADABA

Amman via Hesban

1 (50m)

2

3

4

AISHA UMM AL-MU'MENEEN ST

AL-QUDS STREET

YARMOUK STREET

5

6

TALAL STREET

MUHAFADHA
CIRCLE

Bus & serveece
to Mount Nebo ★

Municipality

**Tourist
Police**

TALAL STREET

7

KING HUSSEIN STREET

2

8

**St George's Church
(Map Church)**

9

HUSSEIN BIN ALI ST

10

TALAL STREET

AL-JAMEA' STREET

**Haret
Jdoudna** 3

**Martyrs'
Church**

**Burnt
Palace**

ABU BAKR AS-SADDEEQ ST

FIRAS AL-AJLOUNI STREET

P

Archeological Park

Roman Road

**Madaba Institute
for Mosaic Art**

KING ABDULLAH STREET

**Hussein bin
Talal Mosque**

Dar al-Saraya

HASHMI STREET

**Church of the Beheading
of St John the Baptist
(Catholic Church)**

**TELL
MADABA**

Bus & serveece
to Ma'in ★

PRINCE HASSAN STREET

5

AL-BALQA STREET

**Old Bus
Station**

AL-NUZHA ST

AL-BALQA ST

**Madaba
Museum**

KING'S HIGHWAY

Ma'in & Dead Sea Panorama

Mahabbah Circle (Dowaar Al-Mahabbah) & Amman via Airport Road

New bus station

0   100
metres

**Church of
the Apostles**

Dhiban & Karak   Nitil

N

THE MIRACLE OF THE BLUE HAND

St George's Church is the focus of Madaba's **Greek Orthodox** community, and services are held here every week, with carpets laid over the precious mosaic to protect it. One Sunday morning in 1976, worshippers passed in front of one of the church's many icons as normal, praying and touching it. Later in the service, someone chanced to look at the icon again – a picture of the Virgin and Child, which had been in full public view for years – and noticed that it had suddenly "grown" a third, **blue hand**, unseen by the full congregation an hour or so before. No one had an explanation, and it was declared to be a miracle, the Virgin showing Madaba a helping hand. Head down to the crypt to see the celebrated icon, still with its blue hand, now on public display behind glass.

but was possibly much larger; two of the original columns survive outside in the churchyard. The **map** is oriented to the east, its front edge being the Mediterranean coast, with north lying to the left.

Its **size** and **style** both mark it out as special. What survives today are fragments of the original, which comprised over two million pieces, measured an enormous 15.6m long by 6m wide and depicted virtually the entire Levant, from Lebanon in the north to the Nile Delta in the south, and from the Mediterranean coast to the open desert. Stylistically the map is unique in depicting the larger towns and cities with an **oblique perspective**, as if from a high vantage point: what you see of Jerusalem, Karak, Gaza and Nablus is the outside of the western city wall and the inside of the eastern one, with buildings inside shown accurately in 3D-style.

Indeed, the whole, novel purpose of laying a map on the floor of the church may have been – in addition to glorifying God's works in the lands of the Bible – to help **pilgrims** reach sites of significance. Although there are some inaccuracies, the mapmaker has reproduced settlements and geographical features very precisely: even by today's standards, the work is mostly cartographically correct.

The mosaic map: Jerusalem

What you come to first, as you walk up the aisle of the church, is **Jerusalem**, the "centre of the world" and the map's largest city, oval-shaped and labelled in red Η ΑΓΙΑ ΠΟΛΙC ΙΕΡΟΥCΑ[ΛΗΜ] ("The Holy City Jerusalem"). The six Byzantine gates of the city are shown in their exact locations and all survive to this day, including – at the northern edge of the city, marked by a tall column – the **Damascus Gate** (in Arabic, *Bab al-Amud*, or Gate of the Column). The long, colonnaded *cardo maximus* runs from here due south to the **Zion Gate**. In the western wall of the city, the only breach is for the **Jaffa Gate**, from which the *decumanus* (today's David Street) runs east to join the *cardo*, with a dogleg hooking south behind the Citadel. Of Jerusalem's many churches, the biggest is the Church of the Holy Sepulchre, a centrally located complex of buildings topped with a red roof and the Dome of the Resurrection. At the southern end of the *cardo* is the New Church of the Mother of God, with a double yellow doorway; this was consecrated on November 20, 542, which helps in dating the Madaba map. Outside the walls to the southeast, a large patch of damage obscures everything up to the Dead Sea, but the four letters ΓΗΘC ("GETHS") indicate the garden of **Gethsemane**.

The mosaic map: around Palestine

North of Jerusalem, a badly charred section conceals **Nablus**, identified as ΝΕΑΠΟΛΙC (Neapolis). From here, if you look between the pews against the left-hand wall of the church, you'll find an isolated fragment of mosaic showing a patch of modern-day Lebanon, giving an idea of the full extent of the original map. To the east of Nablus lies **Jericho** (ΙΕΡΙΧW), shown face on, surrounded by palm trees. Nearby, a small watchtower guards a crossing for rope-drawn ferries across the River Jordan – one

5

fish swims downriver to a salty death in the Dead Sea, while another tries frantically to swim against the current. On the east bank, a gazelle flees from a lion (obliterated in antiquity). Just below is an enclosed spring marked "Ainon, where now is Sapsafas" (AINWN ENΘA NYN O CAΠCAΦAC), the location of the **Baptism Site** of Jesus.

West of Jerusalem are crowded more place names and biblical references, including, outside the southwestern corner of the city, the "field of blood" (AKEΛ ΔAMA), bought with Judas Iscariot's thirty pieces of silver (Matthew 27). The nearest major town is the unwalled Lod (ΛWΔ); just below, in large red letters, is marked the allocation of land to the tribe of Dan ([KΛH]POC ΔAN). Below, and to the left of the patch of damage, is a tiny red-domed building, with the Mediterranean Sea beyond; this was one of the possible locations for **Jonah**'s being thrown up onto dry land out of the belly of the whale – TO TY AΓIY IWNA ("The [sanctuary] of St Jonah").

To the south of Jerusalem, on the edge of the surviving mosaic, lies **Bethlehem** (BHΘΛEEM), shown surprisingly small compared to less important towns. Due south is the land of Judah (IOYΔA). Hard up against the pillar of the church is the sacred tree of Abraham (Genesis 18), identified as H ΔPYC MAM[BPH] (the oak of Mambre) near **Hebron**.

The mosaic map: the Dead Sea, Transjordan and the Nile

Central to the map is the long, sausage-shaped **Dead Sea**, with shipping indicating trade links in antiquity. Of the two boats, the left one is being rowed with a cargo of what seems to be salt. The right one has an open sail and a yellowish cargo, which might be wheat. The detail of both crews, though, has been obliterated by iconoclasts. On the northeastern shore of the sea are the hot springs of Callirhoë (ΘEPMA KAΛΛIPOHC) at the outflow of the Wadi Zarqa Ma'in, showing pools and flowing water. To the east, all that remains of Transjordan is a stretch of mountainous land reaching out as far as **Karak** ([XAP]AXMWB[A] or Kharakh-Moba, the fortress of Moab), fortified and isolated on its hilltop. On the southeastern tip of the sea, near Zoora (ZOOPA), is **Lot's Sanctuary** (TO TY AΓIY Λ[WT]), a church commemorating the site where Lot was drunkenly seduced by his two daughters. The four letters EPHM are the beginning of the Greek word for "desert".

The final section of the map is the most difficult to relate to reality. Against the right-hand wall of the church curl the arms of the **Nile** delta; however, instead of flowing from south to north, the Nile is depicted as flowing from east to west. In order to squeeze the river onto his strictly rectangular map, and also to keep faith with the notion of all the Rivers of Paradise – the Nile being one of them – flowing from the east (Genesis 2), the mosaicist used artistic licence to twist things around. The major city of the region is **Gaza** ([Γ]AZA), on the westernmost edge of the surviving map, intricately depicted with walls, towers, streets and buildings.

Hussein bin Ali Street

A short stroll round the back of St George's Church brings you to **Hussein bin Ali Street**, in the heart of Madaba's old town. It's undeniably focused on tourists, with many carpet shops and souvenir outlets, but retains a good deal of charm.

Burnt Palace

Hussein bin Ali St · Sun–Thurs 8am–5.30pm, winter till 3.30pm · Free

Down a side street off Hussein bin Ali Street, a gateway between shops leads to the ruins of the **Burnt Palace**, a sixth-century patrician mansion destroyed by fire early in the seventh century. Its large floor mosaics include an image of the Roman city-goddess Tyche and several hunting scenes. Also within this area is a stretch of second-century **Roman road** and the ruined **Martyrs' Church**, which has fine floor mosaics.

5

Archeological Park

Hussein bin Ali St • Daily 8am–6pm; winter till 4pm • Joint ticket with Madaba Museum and Church of the Apostles JD3, free with JP

Hussein bin Ali Street doglegs to reach the impressive **Archeological Park**, housing some of Jordan's striking mosaics. Left of the ticket office hangs a Hellenistic-period mosaic, the oldest discovered in Jordan, taken from Herod's palace at Mukawir, as well as many more examples hung in a small colonnaded courtyard, some from nearby Ma'in. There are depictions of Hesban and Gadaron (Salt), but the most interesting piece is beside the entrance door, where a mosaic picture of an ox has been artfully obliterated with a tree (all that remains are hooves and a tail), following an eighth-century religious injunction against depicting living beings (see opposite). Similar care was taken in disfiguring many of the mosaic images in and around Madaba, implying that much iconoclasm was effected by local artists working under orders, rather than by religious zealots destroying whatever they saw.

Walking out to an open plaza, you can follow a catwalk over a stretch of the diagonally paved Roman road (some 2m below the present road surface) to reach the well-worn mosaic floor of the ruined **Church of the Prophet Elias**, dated to 607/8, and, below it, the tiny Crypt of Elianos, from 595/6.

Hippolytus Hall

Back across the Roman road stands the fine **Hippolytus Hall** mosaic, housed beneath a protective hangar. Dating from the early sixth century, probably from the reign of Justinian, the mosaic lay in what must have been a breathtakingly lavish private house. Less than a century later, though, the house was demolished and the mosaics buried to make way for the construction of the adjacent Church of the Virgin.

Closest to the doorway is a diamond grid showing birds and plants. Next to this, and damaged by the foundations of an ancient wall, is a panel depicting the myth of **Phaedra and Hippolytus**; an almond-eyed Phaedra, sick with love for her stepson Hippolytus, is supported by two handmaidens and awaits news of him with a falconer in attendance (the image of Hippolytus himself has been lost). Above is a riotous scene. To the right, a bare-breasted **Aphrodite**, sitting on a throne next to **Adonis**, is spanking a winged **cupid** with a sandal; all around, the **Three Graces** and a servant girl have their hands full dealing with several more mischievous cupids, one of which is upsetting a basket of petals.

Outside the acanthus-leaf border of the main mosaic – itself decorated with hunting scenes of leopards, lions and bears – are three women, personifications of (from the left) **Rome**, **Gregoria** and **Madaba**, seated next to a couple of hideous sea monsters.

Church of the Virgin

Adjoining the Hippolytus Hall, a stepped catwalk leads you on to overlook the circular nave of the **Church of the Virgin**. Just discernible around the edge of the main mosaic are images of flowers dating from the construction of the church, in the late sixth century. Most of what is now visible dates from a geometric redesign completed in 767, during the Muslim Abbasid period. Swirls, knots and endlessly twisting patterns encircle a central medallion, with an inscription urging the congregation to "purify mind, flesh and works" before looking on Mary.

Tell Madaba (old quarter)

Overlooking central Madaba from the south is the **tell**, site of settlement in antiquity – and resettlement in the nineteenth century. It's an atmospheric quarter, still residential, its narrow, crooked streets packed with Ottoman-era stonework and arched windows.

Take time to stroll. You'll spot the fine **Dar al-Saraya** of 1896, with its semicircular steps, built as the Ottoman administrative office and used as a police station right through to 2008. It's now beautifully restored, though plans for it to house either a museum or, perhaps, a restaurant seem to have stalled. To the west, a section of the *tell* – with Iron Age fortifications underlying Roman/Byzantine remains – is still currently off-limits following excavation as the **Tell Madaba Archeological Project** (Ⓦsites.utoronto.ca/tmap).

Church of the Beheading of St John the Baptist
King Talal St • Generally daylight hours • Free • Call ahead to confirm opening ☎05 324 4065 or ☎077 730 8159

The Latin (that is, Roman Catholic) **Church of the Beheading of St John the Baptist**, also dubbed Madaba's **cathedral**, was built in the 1910s over a demolished Ottoman fortress at the highest point of the town: as you drive in from Amman, this is the steeple you can see on the horizon from far away. The guardian will no doubt welcome you in to visit the church itself and the excellent adjacent **museum**, displaying images

---

THE MOSAICS OF JORDAN

Hundreds of floor-laid **mosaics** in stone have survived in Jordan, from a first-century-BC example at Herod's palace at Mukawir (now on display in Madaba) through to pieces from the eighth century AD, when Christian mosaicists were still at work under the Muslim caliphate. During the reign of the Byzantine Emperor Justinian, a retro taste for Classical motifs was popular: many secular buildings were decorated with scenes taken from **Greek and Roman mythology**. Churches couldn't be decorated with the same pagan designs, but instead featured **Christian symbols** such as the lamb and the fish, and **Classical-style personifications** of the sea, the earth and the seasons. These church mosaics served to dazzle and awe visitors to the house of God and to teach the events of the Bible pictorially; the many representations of buildings and great cities may also have served as a rudimentary atlas.

Mosaic artists worked from **pattern-books** compiled in regional cultural centres, above all Constantinople. **Pastoral** scenes predominate – in provincial backwaters such as Transjordan, they also represented the daily reality for many people. Vignettes of ducks, boats and fish were rooted in a Classical taste for representations of life on the **Nile**, and **hunting** scenes with lions or leopards grew out of the Roman practice of capturing animals for amphitheatre sports. In addition, Transjordanian mosaicists portrayed an encyclopedia of **flora and fauna** drawn from local experience, the tales of travellers (elephants, crocodiles and octopus), and the realms of imagination (sea monsters and phoenixes).

However, controversy concerning the **depiction of people** which raged across Byzantium and Transjordan – then already in the control of the Muslim armies – in the eighth and ninth centuries led to many mosaics being disfigured. For centuries, Christians in the East had been venerating religious images in paint, stone and mosaic in a way that more ascetic elements in the Byzantine hierarchy considered too close to paganism. In 726, Emperor **Leo III** banned the use of icons in worship. In Umayyad-controlled Transjordan, a parallel **iconoclastic** movement within Islam had similar impact. The Prophet Muhammad is reported to have taught that God is the only creator; interpreting this to imply that human "creation" of images of living creatures was blasphemous; the Umayyad caliph **Yazid II** (719–24) issued a directive to destroy all such depictions throughout the Muslim empire. Transjordan's mosaicists had no choice but to obliterate faces in existing mosaics with blank stones. Sometimes they did this with care, but it seems they were often in a panic: many of Jordan's mosaics now feature surreal clouds of haze hanging over what were once portraits. Some mosaics survived unscathed by having been buried in earlier years; others, laid after the order was given, avoided the issue by remaining studiously abstract. After 120 years of bitter controversy, the Christian ban was rescinded, but the Muslim injunction still applies today.

Madaba is keeping its mosaic tradition alive: alongside the Archeological Park in the town centre stands the **Madaba Institute for Mosaic Art and Restoration**, or MIMAR (☎05 324 0723, Ⓦmimarjordan.org), where students learn how to restore ancient mosaics as well as create their own designs. Call ahead – or try dropping in – for a tour of their workshops.

5

of old Madaba and some antiquities – as well as explore the cellars and ancient well beneath and the fine Twal house facade alongside. Climb the bell tower for spectacular views over the whole town and beyond.

Madaba Museum

Off Al-Nuzha St • Daily 8am–6pm; winter till 4pm • Joint ticket with Archeological Park and Church of the Apostles JD3, free with JP

Southwest of the old quarter, the small **Madaba Museum** is worth a quick look, though its future remains uncertain and you may find part of its collection has been dispersed to other sites around town. Nestled in a residential courtyard, the museum buildings were formerly houses themselves and feature mosaics uncovered during modern renovation work. Down some steps is a partly damaged mosaic featuring a naked satyr prancing in a Bacchic procession (although Bacchus himself is missing). Through an arch and to the right is the al-Masri house, with a mosaic showing a man's head and pairs of animals between fruit trees. Outside, steps lead down to the museum rooms, displaying pottery and coins, but the most appealing exhibit is at the very back – the tiny chapel of the Twal house, laid with an exquisite mosaic floor featuring a lamb nibbling at a tree. Climb the steps back up to a quiet courtyard at the top, where there's a mosaic pavement from Hesban and open views across the roofs and fields. An adjacent building houses folklore artefacts and traditional costumes.

Church of the Apostles

Corner of Al-Nuzha St and King's Highway • Daily 8am–6pm; winter till 4pm • Joint ticket with Archeological Park and Madaba Museum JD3, free with JP

Housed beneath a large and graceful modern arched building, the **Church of the Apostles** was a huge 24m by 15m basilica with a couple of side-chapels, built in 568, the high point of the Madaba school of mosaic art. The centrepiece of the floor mosaic is a personification of the sea, a spectacular portrait of a composed, regal woman emerging from the waves, surrounded by jumping fish, sharks, sea monsters and even an octopus. She holds a rudder up beside her face and is making a curious, undefinable hand gesture. The main body of the mosaic features pairs of long-tailed parrots; the acanthus-leaf border is filled with animals (a crouching cat, a wolf, a hen with her chicks) and boys at play. In the corners are distinctive, chubby human faces.

ARRIVAL AND DEPARTURE

MADABA

BY PLANE

Madaba is closer to Amman's Queen Alia International Airport than Amman, lying only 18km west (roughly 20min drive) – and is therefore a good option for your first or last night in Jordan. Book an airport pick-up or drop-off (about JD14–18) through any Madaba hotel.

BY BUS

Madaba's bus station is about 2km east of the town centre; a taxi to/from the centre is JD2. However, there's no need to head out that far: all buses drop off and pick up at various points around town.

Amman and Zarqa Buses to/from Amman (Tabarboor, Mahatta and Wihdat; 30min) and Zarqa (45min; for connections to Azraq) stop at Mahabbah Circle (Duwaar Al-Mahabbah), the big roundabout by the Al-Mahabbah Hospital on the north side of town, on the King's Highway

about 1.3km north of where it meets Hashmi St. Another bus route to Amman (Muhajireen; 35min) picks up at Muhafadha Circle (Municipality Circle/Duwaar Al-Muhafadha) on Al-Yarmuk St and follows a slightly longer route via Hesban (10min) and Na'ur.

Mt Nebo and the Dead Sea Muhafadha Circle is also the pick-up/drop-off point for buses to Mt Nebo (15min) and Shuneh al-Janubiyyeh (1hr) in the Jordan Valley; to reach the Dead Sea, ask a Shuneh driver if he'll go a bit further and drop you off at "Amman Beach", or just take a connecting bus to Amman Beach from Shuneh.

South of Madaba South of Madaba along the King's Highway, all regular buses – flag them down on the main street – terminate in Dhiban (40min), the last town before the dramatic gorge of Wadi Mujib. Aside from a single 6am bus, which only operates in university term-time, there are no buses to/from Karak.

BY TAXI
To Petra along the King's Highway Given the lack of buses to Karak or Petra, your best option is to charter a taxi through your hotel – best via the *Mariam* or *Black Iris*, which cater specifically for independent travellers. Drivers and prices are scrupulously honest: no commission is added. Some other hotels in Madaba offer a similar service, but generally in coordination with the *Mariam*, which is the booking hub. As long as at least three people have reserved in advance, the fare is JD20/person; otherwise you can charter a taxi for JD70. Check w facebook.com/mariamhotel to hook up with other travellers. Departure is from Madaba at 10am, stopping briefly at Wadi Mujib, then for an hour at Karak, then dropping off passengers at Dana on request,

arriving in Wadi Musa/Petra around 4 or 5pm. Note that it only runs from north to south; there is no return option.
Other routes The *Mariam* and *Black Iris* can also offer commission-free bargain rates on a number of other routes by taxi from Madaba – for example, to/from Amman (JD14); to Mt Nebo, the Dead Sea and the Baptism Site including an hour at each site (JD36); to those three plus the Ma'in hot springs and Dead Sea Panorama (JD52); to Jerash and Ajloun (JD46); to the "Desert Castles" (JD55); to Wadi Mujib Reserve, including a 4hr wait (JD52); to the airport (JD14); to Feynan Ecolodge (JD72); and direct to Wadi Rum (JD75). All these are for a full car of four people; check with the hotels to carpool.

INFORMATION
Tourist information There is a small, poorly equipped tourist office (daily 8am–5pm; ☎ 05 325 3563) in the Visitor Centre, reached from Abu Bakr as-Saddeeq St or the car park just below it.

ACCOMMODATION
Madaba is one of Jordan's most characterful towns, and has a pack of decent, good-value mid-range **hotels** – many of them family-run and most offering a genial, easy-going ambience that's hard to find in Amman. Note that a few hotels encourage guests heading to Petra to book ahead with the *Valentine Inn*, a hostel which this book explicitly does not recommend.

★ **Black Iris** Off Yarmouk St ☎ 05 324 1959, w black irishotel.com; map p.212. Clean, spacious and friendly family-run hotel, renowned for a warm welcome and excellent service. It's quiet and well run, with en-suite twins and doubles, decent breakfasts and competitive prices for taxi transport and airport pick-ups. **JD35**

Grand Hotel Madaba Aisha Umm al-Mumeneen St ☎ 05 324 0403, w grandhotelmadaba.com; map p.212. The highest-rated hotel in town, at four stars, located alongside the *Mariam* a short walk north of the centre. It's a classy choice, locally owned and run, with a pool, room service, swanky fittings and all, and 81 rooms done up in a neat, contemporary style. **JD51**

Madaba 1880 Talal St ☎ 05 325 3250, w madaba1880. com; map p.212. This large hotel building in the centre of town reopened in 2017 after a top-to-toe refit, and it's now a decent three-star option. Rooms are clean, beds are comfortable, service is unusually switched-on, there's free parking and you're just a stroll from al the sights. **JD45**

Madaba Hotel Al Jame'a St ☎ 05 324 0643; map p.212. Decent little place in a useful central location, just behind St George's Church (with the mosaic map), with a handful of rooms. Everything is pleasant and well kept, though pretty basic. Shared-bath **JD22**, en suite **JD26**

★ **Mariam** Aisha Umm al-Mumeneen St ☎ 05 325 1529, w mariamhotel.com; map p.212. The best hotel in Madaba (and one of the best in Jordan), family-run and located on a residential street 10min walk north of the centre. It is rated as two stars, though easily deserves three. The 57 rooms – spacious and bright, with en-suite bathrooms – are spotless and comfortable, while breakfast and other meals on request are served in the rooftop restaurant or on the poolside terrace. The welcoming and knowledgeable owner, Charl al-Twal, is a mine of information on the history of Madaba (which features his own family prominently) and on travelling around Jordan: he is director of the local tourism business consortium and has no commercial axes to grind other than promoting his city and country. Ask about commission-free bargain rates for local and long-distance taxis. Book well in advance, especially in high season. **JD36**

Moab Land Talal St ☎ 05 325 1318, w moablandhotel. com; map p.212. Reasonable choice directly opposite the "Church of the Map", run by a friendly, helpful family. Roomy en-suite twins and doubles include some with balconies overlooking the street, and there's a great roof terrace for breakfasts with a view over the whole town. It can be a touch noisy, though. **JD33**

★ **Mosaic City** Off Yarmouk St ☎ 05 325 1313, w mosaiccityhotel.com; map p.212. Another fine choice in a good location just north of the town centre – a new building, with a range of high-quality rooms that represent excellent value. It's family-run, with a warm welcome and good facilities, including bike rental (JD13/half day). **JD39**

★ **Pilgrim's House** St George's Church, Talal St ☎ 05 325 3701; map p.212. The Greek Orthodox "Church of the Map" has a side annexe with accommodation for pilgrims (but open to all). The spick-and-span rooms – all of them en suite – are ranged around an upper-level gallery of a brilliant white internal courtyard more reminiscent of Morocco than Jordan, with a warm welcome and a quiet night guaranteed.

5

Profits fund the church school alongside. JD35

Rumman Aisha Umm al-Mumeneen St ☎05 325 2555, Ⓦrummanhotel.com; map p.212. Fresh and friendly budget hotel a few steps from the *Mariam* and *Salome* – if one is full, the others invariably oblige. It's another family-run affair, with 22 modern, simply furnished rooms and

switched-on service. JD36

★ **Salome** Aisha Umm al-Mumeneen St ☎05 324 8606, Ⓦsalomehotel.com; map p.212. Excellent 45-room hotel that stands directly beside the *Mariam* (and so often serves as overflow). The rooms are airy and spacious, though they don't have quite the character of its neighbour. JD36

EATING

As an increasingly tourist-focused town, Madaba has a decent range of **restaurants** and **cafés**. Some cater specifically for groups, laying out lunch buffets to feed the hungry bus-loads; if you're travelling independently there are more congenial places for sustenance dotted around town, including a string of cheap diners along Nuzha St near the museum and along lively Yarmouk St, an atmospheric strip of local emporia that is worth exploring, especially after dark. All the hotels can rustle up simple JD10 meals of kebabs or roast chicken – the *Mariam*'s rooftop restaurant is one of the nicer venues. It's also worth driving the 5km out of town to dine at *Hekayet Nebo* (see page 223).

★ **Adonis** Beside Church of the Beheading of St John the Baptist (Catholic Church) ☎05 325 1771; map p.212. Top-quality restaurant occupying Beit Shweikat, a fine stone building hidden away in the old quarter – originally a family residence, built in 1920. Duck through to the cavernous interior: there are tables in the main hall as well as secreted into cave-like nooks to either side. The food is splendid, with a wide range of meze dishes and especially good *kofte*, washed down with top-quality Lebanese and Jordanian arak: expect to pay around JD15 a head. Book for weekend evenings in particular, when there's often live music. Daily roughly noon–midnight.

Ayola Café Talal St ☎05 325 1843; map p.212. One of the better options among the cluster of easy-going coffee shops ranged along the tourist streets, this cheery place has been revamped in an upmarket contemporary style, but still offers budget-priced sandwiches, snacks, light meals and drinks (roughly JD2–8). Daily 8am–11pm or so.

★ **Haret Jdoudna** Talal St ☎05 324 8650, Ⓦharet jdoudna.com; map p.212. One of the best restaurants in Jordan, located about 100m south of the Church of the Map. The restaurant (whose name means "Courtyard of our Forefathers") comprises two old houses beside each other, one with an elegant cross-vaulted interior dating from 1905, the other with its original colourful floor-tiles imported from Haifa in 1923. Perhaps the most pleasant place to eat is in the quiet courtyard between the two. A mere JD15–17 will buy you a meal of superb Arabic food in a tasteful, atmospheric setting; cold meze highlights are the *jibneh bil zaatar* (goat's cheese in thyme), the vegetarian *warag aynab* (stuffed vine leaves) and excellent *muhammara* (hot pepper dip), while the hot meze include stuffed mushrooms and *sambousek* (pastry filled with meat or cheese). As well as kebabs, there's a choice of chicken- or hummus-based *fatteh*. Although it does attract some tour groups, this remains a popular choice for locals (and gourmet Ammanis): bookings essential on Thurs and Fri. Daily 11.30am–midnight.

Mrah Salameh 20 Hashim Abdelmalik St ☎05 324 0400, Ⓦfacebook.com/mrahsalameh; map p.212. An extraordinary restaurant, opened in 2018, that is constructed over a 65-million-year-old cave in the bedrock: the floors are glass, so you have the eerie experience of floating above the exposed geology, and the owner, a geophysicist, can explain the whole thing. The food – standard meze and grill offerings – is excellent, too, with keen service. Expect a full meal to come in around JD15–20 a head. Daily roughly noon–11pm or so.

Mount Nebo

About 9km northwest of Madaba, a series of peaks referred to collectively as **MOUNT NEBO** (in Arabic, *Siyagha*) comprise one of the holiest sites in Jordan, with a unique resonance for Jews, Christians and Muslims. Having led the Israelites for forty years through the wilderness, **Moses** finally saw, from this dizzy vantage point, the Promised Land that God had forbidden him to enter. After he died on the mountain, his successor Joshua went on to lead the Israelites across the river into Canaan. In Christian and Jewish tradition, Moses was buried somewhere on or in Mount Nebo, but Muslims (who regard Moses as a prophet) hold that his body was carried across the river and placed in a tomb now lying off the modern Jericho–Jerusalem highway. The lack of earthly remains on Nebo, though, doesn't temper the drama accompanying a visit to the isolated mountain, and the ancient church on its summit. Besides, the marvellous **mosaics** on display in the church would be reason enough in themselves to visit.

5

ADVENTURE EXCURSIONS AROUND MADABA

Thanks to the folded landscape of canyons, gorges, valleys and hills around Madaba, Mukawir and the Ma'in hot springs, there are some great opportunities for **adventure trips** and excursions. Although many of the Jordanian specialist tour operators (see page 48) will be able to help, check first with **Terhaal** (☎06 581 3061, ⓦterhaal.com) and **Tropical Desert** (☎079 543 8708, ⓦtropicaldesert.me), excellent, professional adventure activity firms with intimate knowledge of Madaba's mountains and countryside. As an added enticement, some of Terhaal's day-trips include a meal hosted by a local family – a unique opportunity to sample rural village life and authentic home cooking.

WALKING AND CANYONING

Among the wide range of trips are relatively short, easy **gorge-walking** excursions down **Wadi Wala**, **Wadi Al Hidan** or **Wadi Karak**, as well as long, difficult **canyoning** adventures in **Wadi Manshala**, **Wadi Mukheiris** and others. One popular route leads down **Wadi Zarqa Ma'in**, from the spa hotel (see page 226) to the Dead Sea shore at ancient Callirhoë, while you may be lucky and find a guide for the hard-to-access routes into the stunning rainbow canyon of **Wadi Qseib**.

Most of these are full-day trips, involving anything from six to twelve hours of walking, canyoning, swimming through deep pools and, sometimes, abseiling down waterfalls. Expect to pay JD40–90 per person for the more straightforward trips; much more for the tougher adventures. Bear in mind that the terrain is often difficult: within the sweltering, breezeless gorges temperatures can soar and **dehydration** can strike even the most experienced of walkers. You need to be at least moderately fit and carry lots of water.

The *Ma'in Hot Springs* hotel may also lead shorter hikes, up onto the cliffs around the hot springs valley; contact them for details. Another option is to talk to the Wild Jordan team at the Royal Society for the Conservation of Nature (see page 49) about routes in the neighbouring **Mujib Biosphere Reserve** (see page 230) for a day of sightseeing, hiking, swimming and birdwatching.

These walks and others are described in more detail in *Jordan: Walks, Treks, Caves, Climbs & Canyons* by Tony Howard (see page 390).

CYCLING AND MOUNTAIN-BIKING

The hills around Madaba are also perfect for **cycling** and **mountain-biking**. Terhaal offers several trips – both on- and off-road – including routes from Madaba to Mount Nebo or Mukawir, as well as easy rides down to the Dead Sea and a half-day exploring dolmen fields. These run as scheduled trips (check website for dates; JD30–60/person) and also on request.

ULTRALIGHTING

From its base by the Dead Sea, the **Royal Aero Sports Club of Jordan** (☎079 730 0299, ⓦrascj.com) operates sightseeing flights over Mount Nebo by **ultralight** – a two-seater plane, where you sit behind the pilot (JD50/20min; JD75/30min; JD90/45min). Book well in advance.

Moses Memorial Church

Mt Nebo • Daily 8am–6pm; winter till 4pm • JD2 • ☎05 325 2938, ⓦmontenebo.org

The focus of a visit to Mount Nebo is the **Moses Memorial Church**. The first structure on this site may have dated from Classical times, but by 394 AD it had been converted into a triapsidal church floored with mosaics. The church was expanded during the sixth century and later, until it became the focus for a large and flourishing monastic community; the monastery is known to have been still thriving in 1217, but by 1564 it had been abandoned. In 1933, the ruined site was purchased by Franciscans, who began excavating and restoring the church and the surrounding area. Today, Siyagha (originally Aramaic for "monastery") remains both a monastic refuge and the headquarters of the energetic Franciscan Archeological Institute (ⓦcustodia.org).

Mount Nebo mosaics

Laid in the church's **Old Baptistry** is the most entertaining of all the **mosaics** in and around Madaba. Completed in August 531, it was discovered in 1976, when the

5

mosaic which had been laid over it in 597 (now displayed nearby) was removed for cleaning. The huge central panel features four beautiful and intricately designed tableaux. At the top, a tethered zebu is protected by a shepherd fighting off a huge lion, and a soldier lancing a lioness. Two mounted hunters with dogs are spearing a bear and a wild boar. Below, a shepherd sits under a tree watching his goat and fat-tailed sheep nibble at the leaves. A dark-skinned Persian has an ostrich on a leash, while a boy next to him is looking after a zebra and an extraordinary creature that is either a spotted camel or a creatively imagined giraffe.

Other mosaic panels include some from the **Church of St George** at Mukhayyat, near Mount Nebo, showing peacocks, a lion and other animals. One, featuring doves and a deer around a date palm, dates from 536 and has, on one side, the name *Saola* in Greek and, on the other, either the same name in old Aramaic script, or – some historians claim – the word *bislameh* ("with peace") in Arabic; were the latter to be correct, this would be the earliest example of Arabic script found in Jordan, predating Islam by a full century. However, due to the similar formation of letters in the two languages, it's impossible to be certain.

In another part of the church, what was formerly a funerary chapel became the **New Baptistry** in 597, also hosting several mosaics, while the apse of the **Theotokos (Virgin Mary) Chapel**, which was added to the main building in the seventh century, features a stylized representation of the Temple of Jerusalem and a perfect and endearingly bright-eyed gazelle, complete with a little bell around its neck.

Mount Nebo viewpoint

Make your way around the side of the church to Mount Nebo's most famous feature – a stunning **viewpoint terrace**. From here, a panoramic view of the Land of Milk and Honey takes in the northern shore of the Dead Sea, the dark stripe of the River Jordan in its valley, Jericho on the opposite bank and, haze permitting, the towers on the Mount of Olives in Jerusalem amid the hills opposite. It's truly biblical, both in scale and significance. To one side looms a giant **stylized cross** in the form of a serpent, a modern sculpture inspired by Jesus' words in John 3: "As Moses lifted up the serpent in the wilderness, so must the Son of Man be lifted up."

Mukhayyat

Roughly 6km northwest of Madaba on the road towards Mount Nebo stands the village of Faysaliyyeh, where there's a marked turn to **MUKHAYYAT**, site of the biblical town of Nebo and home to five ruined churches and yet another outstanding mosaic.

Church of Saints Lot and Procopius

Turn off the Mt Nebo road at the Mukhayyat sign, then take the older road (left) at the first fork – after about 2km you'll reach a small car park at the foot of a hill, 1min walk from the church

The **Church of Saints Lot and Procopius** sits on the summit of a small but steep hill. A modern building protects the large, well preserved floor mosaic, featuring bunches of grapes, tableaux of vine-harvesting and musically accompanied grape-treading, along with rabbit-chasing and lion-hunting. The most entertaining pieces are between the column stumps: nearest the door are a fisherman and a man rowing a boat either side of a church, and two peculiar fish-tailed monsters, while opposite lie vignettes of geese and ducks in a pond full of fish and lily pads.

Church of St George

Visible on the hilltop beyond Saints Lot and Procopius, the ruined sixth-century **Church of St George** occupies the highest peak on the mountain. Its mosaics are on display at Mount Nebo, but the view remains breathtaking. There are three more churches dotted around the valley nearby (the guardian can tell you where), but none has mosaics *in situ*.

La Storia complex

Beside the Madaba–Mt Nebo road, about 1km from the Moses Memorial Church • Daily 9am–5pm • Free

La Storia complex makes an entertaining diversion off the Madaba–Mount Nebo road. The focus is a kitschy but well-designed **folklore museum** of mannequins in scenes from the past. After a series of biblical tableaux geared towards teaching local schoolchildren stories from the Old and New Testaments – the parting of the Red Sea is quite an eye-opener – the trail leads into a genuinely fascinating section devoted to Madaba's history: after a tent of motorized bedouin figures busily making yoghurt and playing traditional instruments, you stroll past "streets" of traditional shops – a grocer, a weaver, even a hammam – all kitted out perfectly authentically, many with original artefacts. The same complex holds a **handicrafts centre**, with mosaicists working on site, and a large gift shop, as well as the excellent *Hekayet Nebo* restaurant (see below).

Ayoun Musa

Signed off the Madaba–Mt Nebo road, about 1km from the Moses Memorial Church; a clutch of restaurants marks a road leading steeply down to the spring

AYOUN MUSA, the Springs of Moses, is one of the reputed locations for Moses striking the rock and water gushing forth (the Ain Musa spring above Petra is another). The spring itself, marred by a modern pumping station, is overlooked by lush foliage and is set in beautiful countryside – the vineyards nearby produce some of Jordan's best wine – but aside from a couple of tiny ruined churches about ten minutes' walk beyond the spring, you'll find little of specific interest. All the mosaics discovered in the churches down here were long ago removed to Mount Nebo. Plans to build a cable car linking Ayoun Musa to Mount Nebo seem to have come to nothing, as has talk of opening an ecolodge of some kind down here.

ARRIVAL AND DEPARTURE   MOUNT NEBO

By car Mt Nebo is an easy 9km drive out of central Madaba. There's only one road – it's signposted initially, but then just keep going straight. Once out of town, past a roundabout with a fighter jet on it, you pass roadside souvenir shops, Faysaliyyeh village, a couple of restaurants and a large mosque before reaching a car park on the left, opposite the church gates. Park here: access to the church is on foot only. Beyond Mt Nebo the road continues ahead, plunging off the back of the mountain in a series of switchbacks down to the Amman–Dead Sea road, 1200m below – a spectacular drive at any time of day, truly epic in the couple of hours before sunset. The Dead Sea beaches (see page 115) and the Baptism Site (see page 122) are both nearby.

By bus or serveece Departures from central Madaba (15min) are frequent from beside Muhafadha Circle (Duwaar Al-Muhafadha), a roundabout on Al-Yarmuk St overlooked by the municipality building. They generally go only as far as Faysaliyyeh village, 2km short of Mt Nebo.

To get to the church, you'll either have to walk the last bit, offer the bus driver a tip to drive onwards, or wait instead at Madaba bus station for one of the less frequent buses to Shuneh al Janubiyyeh in the Jordan Valley, which run directly past the gates of Mt Nebo. Mukhayyat and Ayoun Musa have no public transport.

By taxi Getting a taxi to take you from Madaba to Mt Nebo, wait, and bring you back shouldn't cost more than JD12–14, a little more if you include other sites. For JD30, your hotel in Madaba can book you taxi transport to Mt Nebo and the Dead Sea, including an hour's waiting time at each and the return to Madaba.

By bike Book ahead with Terhaal (see page 221) for its afternoon guided bike ride from Madaba up to Mt Nebo, then back to Madaba via the Wadi Jdeid dolmen fields (25km; 2hr). From about JD30/person including bike and light refreshments.

EATING

★**Hekayet Nebo** La Storia complex, 1km from Mt Nebo ☎079 621 6063, ⓦfacebook.com/hekayetnebo restaurant; map p.212. Excellent Arabic restaurant, 5km from Madaba and in the same complex as the La Storia folklore museum, featuring spectacular views over biblical hillsides from the rear terrace. The welcome couldn't be warmer, and

the food is top-quality traditional Lebanese fare, prepared to order – there are no lukewarm tour-group buffets here. Meze cost around JD3 and mains roughly JD7–9; don't miss the fresh lemon juice with mint (JD3.50), or sip an arak or a (Jordanian-brewed) Carakale beer as the sun sinks behind the hills. Daily noon–4pm or so; May–Sept till 11pm or later.

5

Around Madaba

Even aside from Mount Nebo, the countryside around Madaba is packed with natural and historical attractions, including the World Heritage Site of **Umm ar-Rasas** and the biblical ruins of **Hesban** to the spa resort at **Ma'in hot springs**, ranged around a series of thermal waterfalls tumbling within an isolated canyon. Near the hot springs stands the excellent museum and restaurant at the remote **Dead Sea Panorama** complex (see page 117), while on a King's Highway journey southwards you might take the time to head into the hills to explore King Herod's ruined mountaintop palace at **Mukawir**.

GETTING AROUND   AROUND MADABA

By car Public transport in this area is thin or nonexistent, so driving is the best option. As well as roads to each individual sight, a cross-mountain road links the Ma'in hot springs with Mukawir, making it possible to follow a long, scenic and often steep circuit – south along the King's Highway, up to Mukawir, down to the hot springs, up again (to the Dead Sea Panorama, for example) and back to Madaba.

By taxi Taxis can be arranged through various hotels in Madaba (see page 219).

Hesban

Beside the modern village of **HESBAN**, 9km north of Madaba and about 22km southwest of Amman, rises a huge *tell* – rarely visited, despite interesting ruins and good signage. Remains testify to occupation from the Paleolithic Age onwards. In the thirteenth century BC, with the name Heshbon, this was "the city of Sihon, king of the Amorites" (Numbers 21). As the Israelites approached, they "sent messengers unto Sihon" seeking permission to pass through his territory "by the king's highway, until we be past thy borders". Sihon refused, and was defeated in battle by the Israelites, who then took up residence in Heshbon. After they departed to Canaan, the city was fortified by the Ammonites, abandoned, and then refortified in the second-century-BC Hellenistic period. The Roman historian Josephus named Hesbus, or Esbus, as one of the cities strengthened by Herod the Great; by the second century AD it was flourishing, due to its position at the junction of the Via Nova Traiana and a transverse Roman road connecting to Jericho and Jerusalem. From the fourth century, the city was an important Christian ecclesiastical centre, and remained a bishopric until after the Umayyad takeover. During the Abbasid period, after the eighth century, it became

---

DOLMENS

Hidden away in the hills near Madaba are hundreds of **dolmens** (prehistoric burial chambers) and **menhirs** (standing stones). Many are hard to access or of limited interest, but a couple of sites stand out.

On the road from Madaba towards Ma'in, if you fork left at an avenue of trees about 1km before Ma'in village, after about 5km you'll come to **Magheirat** (or Magheighat). Lines of Neolithic standing stones crisscross the road here; up on the hilltop to the right is a largely unexcavated **stone circle** in a double ring.

Back at Ma'in village, if you turn left and head south through orchards into open country – increasingly covered with white dust from a nearby quarry – you'll see, on the left in an unguarded field, a Neolithic **standing stone** known as *Hajar al-Mansub*, carved (in antiquity) on its reverse side as an enormous phallus. Theories abound as to its purpose and context.

For the full low-down, make contact with dolmen enthusiast Charl Al-Twal, owner of Madaba's *Mariam Hotel* (see page 219). He'll happily explain more about the dolmen fields in the area, including the one by Al-Faiha village at remote **Wadi Jadid/Jdeid**, 10km southwest of Madaba – and he'll be able to fix you up with taxi transport as well (roughly JD20 return). Alternatively, Terhaal (see page 221) runs an afternoon **cycling** tour from Madaba to Mount Nebo which passes by Wadi Jdeid (from JD30/person), meeting at the *Mariam* first. Book ahead.

a pilgrims' rest stop, and regained some significance as a regional capital under the Mamlukes in the fourteenth century. Hesban was repopulated in the 1870s by the local Ajarmeh bedouin, and remains a quiet agricultural village. The site guardian is happy to show visitors around.

Archeologists (see ⓦmadabaplains.org) have uncovered a network of Iron Age **caves** which riddle the *tell*, leading to speculation concerning their possible connection to Moses and the Israelites; one particularly significant find was an unbroken pottery cup dating from 1200 BC – precisely the right period. On the summit are the fallen columns of a Byzantine **church** (its mosaic floor is now in the Madaba museum), as well as a Mamluke **mosque**, and **baths** with furnace and plunge pools. Panoramic views extend west to Jericho and Jerusalem, north into Gilead, east to the desert highlands, and south to Dhiban and even Karak, bringing home the strategic value of the site.

ARRIVAL AND DEPARTURE   **HESBAN**

By car Coming from Amman, Hesban is signposted from Na'ur, off the Dead Sea highway. From Madaba, follow signs to Na'ur north for 9km.

By bus Buses run from Madaba (10min) and from Amman's Muhajireen station via Na'ur (25min). Before you get on, specify you want Hesban, since most Madaba–Amman buses follow a different road.

Ma'in

The road southwest from Madaba towards Ma'in hot springs passes first through fields and the small farming community of **MA'IN**; the village, perched on its *tell*, is mentioned in the Bible, and excavations in its Byzantine- and Umayyad-period churches revealed many mosaics, now on display in the Madaba Archeological Park. There is a **dolmen** field near here at **Magheirat** (see opposite).

Beyond Ma'in, the terrain dries out, and the road begins to heave and twist around the contours of land above the Dead Sea. Thin tracks off to the left give options for picnic spots on slopes perched high above cultivated sections of the Wadi Zarqa Ma'in; to the right, the **views** over the desert hills down to the fairy-tale Dead Sea, luminous blue in a valley of brown, are incredible. The road keeps coiling and recoiling in steep switchbacks until you come to a well-marked **T-junction**.

Turning **right** here will bring you to the **Dead Sea Panorama** museum and restaurant (see page 117). Past the Panorama the same road descends in a series of hairpin turns down to the Dead Sea shoreline road. Turning **left** at the T-junction leads steeply down over the cliff edge of the Wadi Zarqa Ma'in gorge via a series of switchbacks to the **Hammamat Ma'in hot springs** (see below), which make for a great side-trip off the King's Highway.

Ma'in hot springs (Hammamat Ma'in)

Daily 9am–8pm; closes earlier in winter • JD15 admission, waived if you're staying at the hotel

About 30km southwest of Madaba, at the end of one of Jordan's steepest, squiggliest roads, lies **MA'IN HOT SPRINGS** (Hammamat Ma'in in Arabic). Continuously dousing the precipitous desert cliffs of the Wadi Zarqa Ma'in with steaming water varying between a cosy 40°C and a scalding 60°C, the springs (and the whole valley, which lies more than 250m below sea level) have long been popular with weekend day-trippers. The waters have been channelled to form hot waterfalls, and there are hot spa pools with natural saunas, plus spa facilities at the adjacent hotel. Fridays, especially in spring and autumn, see the valley packed with day-trippers from Amman and Madaba. If you're seeking serenity, come another day, when it's not too hard find a quiet, steamy niche in the rock all to yourself. If you're feeling energetic, hiking past the springs down the deep gorge to the Dead Sea is an exhilarating counterpoint to lying around in hot water all day.

5

After the **main gate** into the valley, where you pay admission, the road continues down for 500m or so, past gardens and car parks. The **hot waterfalls** tumble down off the cliffs to one side of the valley, steam rising from a series of pools below, where you can sit and enjoy a shoulder-pounding from the water. There are waterfalls nearest the hotel are public and pools open to all, as are nearby pools, seating areas and sporadically open snack barsthe public, though repairs from winter flood-damage in 2017-18 were ongoing beneath the main waterfall at the time of writing. You may find that some zones are reserved for "families" (which means solo men do not have access). Men are fine in swimming gear; women should opt for a loose T-shirt and long shorts. Further down, other pools and waterfalls – as well as spa facilities and restaurants – are exclusively for the use of guests at the hotel.

ARRIVAL, DEPARTURE AND ACTIVITES

By car The road into the valley is signposted 30km south-west from Madaba, passing through Ma'in village. There is also road access over the hills from Mukawir.

By taxi Expect to pay JD22–26 return by taxi from Madaba, including waiting time at the hot springs.

Hiking and outdoor activities The classic route hereabouts is the hike (see page 221) through the hot water of the Wadi Zarqa Ma'in down to the Dead Sea. In and around the valley, the *Hot Springs* hotel may be able to offer a guide for walks above the waterfalls to the sources of the springs; check with them for details.

MA'IN HOT SPRINGS

Cascade Spa Part of the *Ma'in Hot Springs* hotel, this sympathetically designed retreat of pools and treatment zones stands alongside the hotel, in a secluded location directly beneath a mineral-rich hot waterfall. Admission (whether or not you're a hotel guest) costs JD40 for a day, and gets you access to the spa's sauna, hammam, natural hot-water pools, steam cave and relaxation facilities, with towels and herbal teas. If you book a treatment – say, an olive-oil massage (1hr; JD83), a body wrap of Dead Sea mud (1hr; JD90) or any of an array of exotic options to rebalance, rejuvenate and revivify – the admission fee is waived.

ACCOMMODATION

Ma'in Hot Springs ☎ 05 324 5500, ◉ mainhotsprings. jo. Tucked away in this isolated valley of springs and hot waterfalls 264m below sea level, this formerly-luxury hotel resort has reverted to local management; standards in service and presentation have dropped, but it remains a classy place to stay, though very expensive. The main

building itself is no beauty, but rooms inside are still spacious and well designed, with stone floors and dark wood. Every room has a balcony. Hotel restaurants include poolside dining and the off-site *Dead Sea Panorama* restaurant (see page 117), a short drive away. **JD137**

Mukawir (Machaerus)

Daily 8am–6pm (Nov–Feb till 4pm) • JD2, free with JP

The King's Highway heads south from Madaba through quiet, picturesque farmland for 13km to **Libb**, where a well-signed road branches right for a long, slow 20km across the windblown hilltops to the small village of **MUKAWIR** (pronounced "m-KAA-whirr"), views yawning away in all directions. The main reason for visiting is to make the short hike up to the isolated conical hill beyond the village, which is topped with the ruins of the **palace of Machaerus**, known gloomily to the locals as Qal'at al-Meshneqeh ("Citadel of the Gallows") – where Salome danced for King Herod, and where John the Baptist was beheaded.

During the first century BC, the hill was a stronghold of the Jewish Hasmonean revolt against the Seleucids, and was fortified to be a buffer against Nabatean power further south. In the last decades of that century, **Herod the Great**, king of Judea, constructed a walled citadel at Machaerus and developed road access to the site from the Dead Sea port at Callirhoë, 8km west, although trade on the King's Highway, just 22km east, remained under the control of the Nabateans. According to the Roman historian Josephus, it was at Machaerus that **Salome** danced her famously seductive dance for the head of **John the Baptist** (see opposite).

SALOME'S DANCE

In an act forbidden under Jewish law, **Herod Antipas**, son of Herod the Great, married his brother's wife, **Herodias**. When local holy man **John the Baptist** publicly accused the king of adultery, Herod had the troublemaker arrested and imprisoned at Machaerus. Some time later, at a birthday celebration in the Machaerus palace, Herod was so impressed by the dancing of **Salome**, Herodias' daughter, that he promised her anything she wanted. Salome, prompted by her mother (who wanted rid of the holy man), requested John's head on a platter – and Herod obliged.

Christian tradition holds that John was buried where he died, in a well-signposted **cave** near the hill, but Islam, according to which John (or **Yahya** in Arabic) is a prophet, keeps two shrines holy, one for his body (the same cave) and another in Damascus for his severed head, which was supposedly taken to that city and buried where the Great Mosque now stands.

In 66 AD, during a Jewish revolt against **Roman** rule, the rebels seized Machaerus and held it for seven years, eventually surrendering when faced by Roman forces preparing to assault the fortress (in an almost identical situation at Masada, west of the Dead Sea, a Jewish resistance force committed mass suicide rather than submit). The Romans immediately moved into Machaerus, razed the buildings, massacred the local civilian population and departed. The hill has remained quiet since.

Today, a visit entices for the truly awe-inspiring views and the beautiful, rolling countryside, carpeted with wild flowers in spring. Kestrels wheel against the Dead Sea haze above a handful of gleaming modern columns which sprout from the part-excavated hilltop. Of the palace ruins, a few rooms are discernible, as are the remains of the Roman **assault ramp** on the far slopes of the hill and the line of an **aqueduct** across the saddle. A **mosaic** – the oldest discovered in Jordan – once lay in the baths complex, but has been removed to Madaba for display.

Bani Hamida weaving centre

Mukawir village • Unreliable hours; at most Sun–Thurs 8am–2pm • Contact via Jordan River Foundation office in Amman ☎ 06 593 3211, ⓦ jordanriver.jo

The Mukawir area is the homeland of the **Bani Hamida** tribe, now well known in Jordan following the success of a highly publicized project to revive traditional weaving skills among the women of the tribe, providing them and their families with an additional source of income and vocational training possibilities. At the **Bani Hamida weaving centre**, sister outlet to the shop in Amman (see page 106), you can buy beautiful rugs, wall-hangings and other knick-knacks. As you'd expect for high-quality handmade goods, nothing is cheap – but there's no pressure to buy and the selection is outstanding. If you fancy splashing out, you can be certain that this is the genuine article.

ARRIVAL AND DEPARTURE   MUKAWIR

By car Mukawir lies roughly 35km southwest of Madaba, signed off the main road at Libb village, 13km south of Madaba itself. Drive 2km through the village to reach the car park opposite the hill, from where a steep but easy 15min climb across the saddle and up some steps brings you to the hilltop ruins. A road also comes into Mukawir village over the hilltops from Hammamat Ma'in, making it possible to follow a loop.

By bus Occasional buses run from Madaba to Mukawir village (1hr). You may be able to persuade the driver to take you the extra 2km to the car park by the hill; if not, it's

a pleasant walk.

By taxi A return taxi from Madaba, organized through one of the hotels, costs JD17–20, including an hour's waiting time, or about JD30 with Umm ar-Rasas as well.

By bike Although there are wilderness hiking routes aplenty, one of the best ways to experience Mukawir is by bike. Terhaal (see page 221) offers an afternoon cycling tour from Madaba to Mukawir, which includes a visit to the ruins and dinner with a local family (56km; 4hr; about JD62/ person). Book ahead.

5

Umm ar-Rasas

Daily 8am–6pm (Nov–Feb till 4pm) • JD3, free with JP

A small farming village on a backroad midway between the King's Highway and the Desert Highway, **UMM AR-RASAS** was the site of the Roman garrison town of Kastron Mefaa, which developed during the Byzantine and Umayyad periods into a relatively important city: large **mosaic** floors from some of its many churches survive and are on display. Nearby is a striking Stylite **tower**. It's a remote, windblown spot – worth a detour if you have your own transport.

Church of St Stephen

From the Visitor Centre, which stands alongside the (fenced) ruins, follow trails through the ancient city past buildings and arches to a modern shelter protecting the **mosaics**. Well-designed catwalks lead you over the intricate mosaic floor of the **Church of St Stephen**, dated to 785, over 150 years after Muslim rule was established in Jordan. The apse has a dazzling, kaleidoscopic diamond pattern swirling out from behind the altar, and the broad nave is framed by mosaic panels showing cities of the day: closest to the door is Jerusalem, with seven Palestinian cities below, including Nablus, Asqalan and, at the bottom, Gaza. On the far side are seven Transjordanian cities, headed by Kastron Mefaa itself, with Philadelphia (Amman), Madaba, Hesban, Ma'in, Rabba and Karak below. The central section is filled with scenes of fishermen, seashells, jellyfish and all kinds of intricate detail of animals, fruit and trees, although in antiquity iconoclasts blocked out virtually all representations of people. Alongside is an older mosaic belonging to the Church of Bishop Sergius, dated to 587. Its main feature is a rectangular panel in front of the altar featuring pomegranate trees and very wise-looking rams; on the other side of the catwalk, hard up against the exterior wall, a beautifully executed personification of one of the seasons survived the iconoclasts by having had a pulpit built over it at some point.

The tower

Attractive though they are, Umm ar-Rasas's mosaics are only half the story; don't leave without standing awhile at the foot of the village's peculiar square **tower**, 1km away from the ruins and represented on the church floor by Kastron Mefaa's own mosaicists as an identifying feature of their city. Windblown and mysterious, the 15m tower (known in Arabic as *Burj Sam'an*) is solid, without internal stairs, yet at the top is a room with windows in four directions. Rough crosses are carved on the three sides facing away from the city, but details of intricate carving survive on the topmost corbels. This would seem to have been the Stylite tower of a Christian holy man; the fifth-century ascetic **Simon Stylites** spent 38 years atop a pillar near Aleppo, and a cult of pilgrimage grew up around him and later imitators who isolated themselves from worldly distractions in order to concentrate on their prayers. At the foot of the tower once stood a church; nearby are cisterns and a building which may have been a hostel for pilgrims. Today, almost wrenched apart by earthquakes, the tower is home only to pigeons and kestrels. It is perhaps Jordan's single most evocative ancient building.

ARRIVAL AND DEPARTURE   **UMM AR-RASAS**

By car Though Umm ar-Rasas is accessible on 32km of poorly signed country backroads from Madaba via Nitil (signposted left at the Church of the Apostles in Madaba city centre), you'd be better advised to stick on the main King's Highway heading south from Madaba until Dhiban, where a signed turning to the east leads straight to Umm ar-Rasas in 16km – and, after another 14km, to a marked junction on

the Desert Highway south of the Amman airport turn-off.
By bus Buses run a few times daily from Madaba via Nitil to Umm ar-Rasas (50min).
By taxi A taxi from Madaba, organized through one of the hotels, costs JD20 return, including visits to both the main site and the tower, with an hour's waiting time, or about JD30 with Mukawir as well.

Crossing Wadi Mujib

South of Madaba, the King's Highway meanders up and down across several valleys draining rainwater off the hills, including the dramatic canyon of **Wadi Mujib**. One of Jordan's most spectacular natural features, lying midway between Madaba and Karak, the immense valley has been dubbed, with a canny eye on the tourist dollar, "Jordan's Grand Canyon". The name, however, is well earned, as the King's Highway delivers you to stunning viewpoints on either rim over a vast gash in the barren landscape, cutting through 1200m of altitude from the desert plateau in the east down to the Dead Sea in the west. It is every bit as awe-inspiring as its Arizonan cousin and has the added selling point of the memorable road journey winding down to the valley floor and up the other side. A large chunk of the surrounding territory now forms part of the protected **Mujib Biosphere Reserve**, offering the chance for wilderness hiking and canyoning as good as any you'll find in the Middle East.

GETTING AROUND   WADI MUJIB

By car This is a lovely drive south from Madaba through the rural heartland of Jordan, punctuated by farming villages crowding the ridgetops either side of deep valley canyons. You could reach Karak in a couple of hours without stopping – or pack a picnic and linger.

By bus Aside from a single early-morning bus, which only operates in university term-time, there is no public transport through Wadi Mujib – effectively all southbound buses from Madaba terminate at Dhiban. Although Dhibanis are aware of foreigners' desire to travel through the canyon, it may take a while of hanging around at the shops on Dhiban's central roundabout before you find someone willing to do the trip for you. The going rate for a full car to Ariha, the first village on the southern rim, is around JD15. From Ariha, local buses continue south along the King's Highway to Karak.

By taxi Private tours along the King's Highway can be arranged from Amman (see page 91) and Madaba (see page 219).

Wadi Wala and Wadi Hidan

About 15km south of Madaba, a little beyond Libb, the first of a series of large east–west valleys is the lush **Wadi Wala** – pleasantly dotted with vineyards and shaded by groves of pine and eucalyptus. From the valley floor, you can drive west on a riverside road for some 15km into the quiet and beautiful **Wadi Hidan**. This road terminates in a dead end, where you'll find a beautifully designed **visitor centre** with panoramic outlook: this is the meeting-point for **canyoning** hikes along the valley floor, offered by many local adventure outfits (ask around at hotels in Madaba for more details, and see page 219). The visitor centre is only open for pre-booked trips. Hidan itself goes on to meet the Mujib River just before the Dead Sea; with a guide, it's possible to follow the river on foot for about 6km between basaltic cliffs up to the edge of a 60m waterfall (which marks the start of an area off-limits to walkers), although you must then climb up the cliffside and make your way back to the road.

Dhiban

Back on the main King's Highway, when you reach the top of the southern slope of Wadi Wala, a stretch of the Roman Via Nova Traiana is visible on the valley floor behind. Some 10km further (33km south of Madaba), **DHIBAN** is the last town before the Mujib canyon – an ordinary, working place with few frills. A signposted turn here heads east for 16km to Umm ar-Rasas (see opposite), continuing for another 14km to reach the Desert Highway.

Wadi Mujib

Some 2km south of Dhiban, the vast canyon of **Wadi Mujib** opens up spectacularly in front, over 500m deep and 4km broad at the top. Just over the lip of the gorge is

5

MUJIB BIOSPHERE RESERVE: ACCESS FROM THE KING'S HIGHWAY

Much of the area between the King's Highway and the Dead Sea shore as far north as Ma'in, and including the lower 18km of the Mujib River, forms the **MUJIB BIOSPHERE RESERVE** (w wildjordan.com). This expanse of diverse terrain extends from the hills alongside the King's Highway, at 900m above sea level, all the way down to the Dead Sea shore at 400m below sea level, and includes seven permanently flowing wadis within its 212 square kilometres. The biodiversity of this apparently barren area is startling: during ecological surveys of the reserve, four plant species never before recorded in Jordan were discovered, along with the rare Syrian wolf, Egyptian mongoose, Blanford's fox, caracal, striped hyena, two species of viper, the venomous desert cobra and large numbers of raptors. Nubian ibex roam the mountains on Mujib's southern plateau. This is one of the most dramatic areas of natural beauty in Jordan – well worth the time and effort to experience.

Access to the reserve is generally from its lower entrance, by the Dead Sea road, which we cover in Chapter 2 (see page 118). The reserve's only base at the King's Highway end of the valley is a small office in **FAQUA** village, northwest of Qasr, but this is usually unstaffed and is not geared up for enquiries. In any case, everything must be **booked in advance** through the RSCN's Wild Jordan tourism unit in Amman (see page 82).

Most of the reserve's **hiking trails** begin from the Dead Sea side, going into canyons against the water flow, then turning round to exit. However, you could email Wild Jordan in advance to ask about the difficult full-day guided route from Faqua all the way down to the Dead Sea (April–Oct only), following the Mujib River with deviations at obstacles and passing through wild and varied scenery. This links up with the Malaqi Trail at the confluence of the Wadi Hidan for the final stretch down through the stunning Mujib Siq.

There are similar routes **outside the reserve**, around Wadi Zarqa Ma'in and Mukawir (see page 226) – and more further south around Karak, including the beautiful Wadi ibn Hammad (see page 235).

a small rest stop and viewing platform. The dramatic canyon is an obvious natural focal point, and in biblical times, Arnon, as it was named, was the heartland of Moab, although with shifts in regional power it frequently marked a border between tribal jurisdictions; today, it divides the governorates of Madaba and Karak. The sheer scale of the place takes your breath away, with vultures, eagles and kestrels wheeling silently on rising thermals all around, and the valley floor to the right losing itself in the mistiness of the Dead Sea. The broad, flat plain of the wadi bed, now dammed, is noticeably hotter and creaks with frog calls.

Ariha, Qasr and Rabba

After snaking up Mujib's southern slope, the King's Highway emerges onto the flat Moabite plateau, fields of wheat stretching off in all directions. The first village on the southern rim, about 3km from the gorge, is **ARIHA**; from here the highway ploughs a straight furrow south through small farming communities to two towns nurturing minor remnants of a more glorious past. **QASR**, 12km south of Ariha, boasts a Nabatean temple east of the town, while **RABBA**, 5km on – once an important Roman and Byzantine settlement – hosts the remains of a Roman temple west of the road behind the modern town. Midway between Qasr and Rabba, a side-turning gives access to hikes along the spectacular Wadi ibn Hammad (see page 235). The outskirts of Karak begin roughly 12km south of Rabba.

Karak

The southern stretches of the King's Highway pass through an increasingly arid landscape dotted with lushly watered settlements. **KARAK**, unofficial capital of southern

Jordan, still lies largely within its hilltop Crusader-era walls and boasts one of the best-preserved **Crusader castles** in the Middle East. Roughly 125km south of Amman, midway between the capital and Petra, it's also a natural place to break a journey. Unfortunately, Karak is not well geared up for overnight stays, with poor access and below-par hotels. Drop in to visit the castle, then press onwards to more enticing destinations – Madaba to the north, Dana or Petra to the south.

Everything you need in Karak is within a few minutes' stroll of the castle, at the highest point of town. Just in front of the castle is the **Castle Plaza** area, a tasteful complex of restored Ottoman buildings around a paved plaza beneath the castle walls, including the old Al-Hamidi mosque and a Visitor Centre. In sharp contrast is Karak's **town centre**. Venturing down any of the narrow streets that lead north from the castle – most of them lined with grand but grimy Ottoman-era balconied stone buildings – will bring you nose-to-nose with Karak's bustling everyday shops and markets. The focus of town is an equestrian statue of Salah ad-Din, occupying a traffic junction about 400m north of the castle, around which spreads Karak's ramshackle **souk** – tailors, butchers, cobblers and all.

Karak castle
Castle Plaza • Sun–Thurs & Sat 8am–5pm, Fri 10am–4pm • JD2, free with JP

Occupying a rocky spur on the southern edge of the town centre, **Karak castle** is first, and most impressively, visible on the approach from the east, its restored walls and glacis looming above the ravine below. Access is from behind the Castle Plaza complex, across a wooden footbridge spanning the moat. The castle has **seven levels**, some buried deep inside the hill, and the best way to explore is to take a **torch** and simply let your inquisitiveness run free: it's quite possible to spend two or three atmospheric hours poking into dark rooms and gloomy vaulted passageways.

Brief history
The hill on which Karak stands – with sheer cliffs on three sides and clear command over the Wadi Karak leading down to the Dead Sea – features both in the Old

---

THE MESHA STELE

These days a largely unregarded village, in the past **Dhiban** was an important city, capital of Moab and mentioned many times in the Old Testament. In around 850 BC, a man named **Mesha**, described as a "shepherd king", liberated Moab from Israelite aggression, built a palace in Dhiban and set about refortifying the King's Highway against future attack.

Almost three thousand years later, in 1868, a German missionary travelling in the wild country between Salt and Karak was shown by Dhibani bedouin a large **basalt stone** inscribed with strange characters. Unaware of its significance, he informed the German consul of his discovery, who then made quiet arrangements to obtain the stele on behalf of the Berlin Museum. However, a French diplomat in Jerusalem who heard of the discovery was less subtle; he travelled to Dhiban, took an imprint of the stele's text and there and then offered the locals a large sum of money. Suddenly finding themselves at the centre of an international furore over a seemingly very desirable lump of rock, the bedouin refused his offer and sent him packing; they then did the obvious thing and devised a way to make more money. By heating the stone over a fire, then pouring cold water on it, they successfully managed to shatter it, and thus sell off each valuable fragment to the covetous foreigners one by one. Meanwhile, scholars in Europe were studying and translating the imprint of the text, which turned out to be Mesha's own record of his achievements, significant as the longest inscription in the Moabite language and one of the longest and most detailed original inscriptions from the biblical period yet discovered. The mostly reconstructed stele now sits in the Louvre in Paris; having become something of a symbol of national pride, copies of it are displayed in museums all over Jordan.

5

Testament and on Madaba's Byzantine mosaic map as a natural defensive stronghold. The **Crusaders** began building a fortress on a rocky spur atop the hill in 1142.

The Crusaders

The castle's construction was initiated by the knights of the successful First Crusade, but its eventual downfall is inextricably linked with **Reynald of Chatillon**, a ruthless warrior who arrived in the Holy Land in 1147 on the Second Crusade. Reynald was both vicious and unscrupulous, and it was specifically to avenge his treachery that the Muslim commander, **Salah ad-Din**, launched a campaign to expel the foreign invaders. In 1177, Reynald married Lady Stephanie, widow of the Lord of Oultrejourdain. Safely ensconced in Karak, he began a reign characterized by wanton cruelty: not only did he throw prisoners from the castle walls, he encased their heads in boxes first, in the hope that this would stop them losing consciousness before they hit the rocks below. In 1180, he robbed a Mecca-bound caravan on the King's Highway in violation of a truce; Salah ad-Din was forced to swallow his anger until a suitable time for revenge could be found.

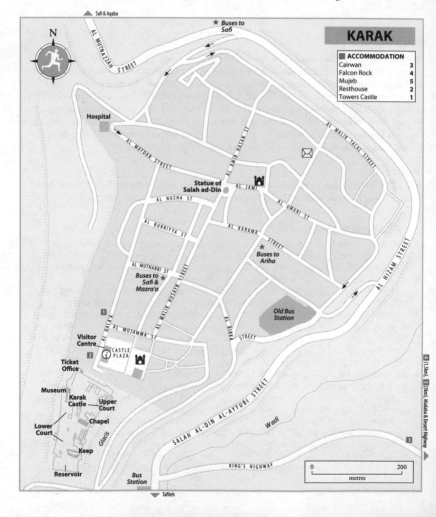

5

THE CRUSADERS IN TRANSJORDAN

Following an appeal from the Byzantine emperor for foreign military assistance to defeat the Seljuk Turks, it took only a few years from the pope's first call to arms of 1095 for invading Christian European armies to seize **Jerusalem**. European-run statelets were set up in quick succession. One of the Christian lords, **Baldwin**, was crowned King of Jerusalem on Christmas Day 1100, and it was under his rule that the Crusaders began to realize the benefit of controlling the Transjordanian land route from Syria into Egypt and Arabia, in order to divide the Muslim power bases in Damascus and Cairo and to be able to harass Mecca bound pilgrims.

In 1115, Baldwin set out to incorporate Transjordan into the Crusader realms, and began construction of a large castle at modern **Shobak** (see page 245), which he named *Le Krak de Montreal* ("Fortress of the Royal Mountain"). A string of Crusader fortresses soon followed, at Aila (Aqaba), Wu'ayra and Habees at Petra, and Tafileh. However, the Lordship of Oultrejourdain, as it came to be known, was far from impregnable, and infiltration across the River Jordan by a Muslim raiding party in 1139 seems to have persuaded Paganus the Butler, by then the effective ruler, to move his power base northwards from Shobak. Construction of the massive fortress at **Karak** began in 1142, and twenty years later, with the addition of another citadel at Ahamant (possibly Amman), Crusader-controlled territory in Transjordan extended from the River Zarqa to the Red Sea, and from the Jordan Valley to the desert.

Such power was short-lived, however. After 1169, the Karak headquarters underwent four sieges. By 1174 Salah ad-Din had united the Muslim forces and began methodically to oust the Crusaders from Transjordan. Karak withstood two more sieges during 1183, but the Latin armies were depleted, and their young king, Baldwin IV, was dying of leprosy. In 1187, at **Hattin** near Tiberias, they were roundly defeated by Salah ad-Din, who soon after took Jerusalem. Karak capitulated in late 1188, and Shobak – the last Transjordanian possession – fell in the spring of 1189. A century later, the entire Holy Land was once again under Arab rule.

In 1183, the wedding of Reynald's heir was celebrated within the walls of Karak castle at the very moment that Salah ad-Din and his army, having already invaded the town, were poised just beyond the north moat ready to attack. Lady Stephanie sent plates of food to the Muslim army beyond the walls. In response, while his men were trying to bridge the moat and catapulting rocks against the walls, Salah ad-Din enquired which tower the newlyweds were occupying – and then ordered his army to direct their fire elsewhere.

Karak withstood that siege, but at the **Battle of Hattin** in 1187, the Crusaders, stymied by the strategic ineptitude of Reynald and others, were defeated. The victorious Salah ad-Din characteristically spared the king and the Crusader lords – all apart from Reynald, whom he personally decapitated. The besieged Crusader garrison at Karak held out for months; they sold their wives and children in exchange for food, and resorted to eating horses and dogs, but surrender was inevitable. Karak capitulated in November 1188.

After the Crusaders

With the Europeans gone, **Ayyubid** and **Mamluke** occupiers of the castle rebuilt and strengthened its defences. Under the **Ottomans**, anarchy was the rule rather than the exception. During a rebellion in 1879, Karaki Christians abandoned their town, moving north to settle among the ruins of ancient Madaba. Soldiers only reimposed order in 1894, but Karak's ruling families – among them, the **Majali** clan – remained restless. In 1908 they rallied a local force and stormed Karak's government buildings, forcing the Ottoman garrison to seek refuge in the castle. After eight days, troops arrived from Damascus, publicly executed the rebel leaders and declared the Majalis outlaws. Even today Karak retains a reputation for political activism, yet – a little ironically, considering the family history – the Majalis are now at the heart of the Jordanian establishment, boasting government officials and even a prime minister or two among their number.

5

Exploring Karak castle

A good place to start is by heading up the slope once you enter, then doubling back on yourself into a long, vaulted passageway along the inside of the huge north wall built by the Crusaders. Down here, close to the original entrance of the castle in the northeastern corner, are a **barracks** and, on the right, the **kitchens**, complete with olive press and, further within, a huge oven. You emerge along the **east wall**, close to the ruined **chapel**. Over the battlements the restored glacis heralds a dizzy drop, and facing you is the partly complete Mamluke **keep**, the best-protected part of the castle. It's not difficult to climb to the highest point, from where there are scarily vertiginous views in all directions.

In a sunken area between the chapel and the keep lie the remains of a Mamluke **palace**, while at the bottom of some steps just behind the chapel's apse is a beautifully carved stone panel. Of the two rooms opposite the panel, the one on the right features some reused Nabatean blocks set into the wall; next door, Reynald's extensive and suitably dank **dungeons** lead off into the hill. Back at the carved panel, a passageway to the left eventually brings you out, after passing another barracks, near the entrance.

If you head down from here to the lower western side of the castle, you'll come across the **museum**, offering fascinating background to the history of the castle and the local area. Equally interesting is a restored Mamluke **gallery** nearby, running virtually the length of the west wall at the lowest level of the castle.

ARRIVAL AND DEPARTURE KARAK

BY CAR

The King's Highway makes a poorly signposted zigzag around Karak; it's easy to get confused. At a T-junction 12km south of Rabba, just by the *Mujeb* hotel, turning left leads 34km west to Qatraneh on the Desert Highway (see page 335), while turning right brings you 4km through hilly suburbs to another T-junction at the foot of Karak castle. From here, turn left for the King's Highway to Tafileh or right to spiral up the hill into Karak. As you drive up, the only road through the walls into Karak town centre is a poorly marked turning on the left at the crest of the hill, just before an archway. If you miss it and start going down the back of the hill, make a U-turn: this road continues for 26km all the way down to Mazra'a on the Dead Sea (see page 119) via the majestic Wadi Karak – one of Jordan's great scenic drives, especially in the afternoon, when low sunlight makes the walls of the steep canyon glow.

BY BUS AND TAXI

Karak's bus station is at the foot of the hill, by the King's Highway junction outside town. The only viable way to get to the castle from here is by taxi. If you're heading onwards, note that buses only depart Karak in the mornings (roughly 7am–noon); you might be lucky and find a bus after that time, but don't rely on it.

Amman and Aqaba Buses from Amman's Wihdat station via the Desert Highway (2hr), Aqaba via the Wadi Araba (3hr) and elsewhere arrive at the bus station.

Madaba via the King's Highway Buses for Ariha on the south rim of Wadi Mujeb leave from a side street in the middle of Karak. To get to Madaba from Ariha, you'll have to hitch (or take a local taxi) through the canyon to Dhiban and catch another bus there northwards.

Dana via the King's Highway To get to Dana, take a bus from the bus station to Tafileh via the King's Highway (1hr) and another from there to Qadisiyyeh, or opt for a taxi (about JD30).

Feynan A ride to Feynan, organized through the *Feynan Ecolodge* (see page 342), costs JD70.

Petra via the Desert Highway One bus may leave Karak in the afternoon for Wadi Musa/Petra (2hr; JD5), but only via the Desert Highway; the more reliable alternative is to catch a bus to Ma'an (2hr) and change there for a bus or *serveece* to Wadi Musa. A taxi is about JD30–35.

Petra via the King's Highway The slow way to reach Petra involves a bus to Tafileh (1hr), another to Qadisiyyeh, hitching to Shobak and a minibus or *serveece* to Wadi Musa/ Petra: it's likely to take all day. Otherwise, the quicker option by taxi (2hr 30min) costs JD60–70 for a full car (about double what it would be via the Desert Highway): ask your hotel or staff at the castle visitor centre to hunt down a driver, or just stop one on the street and ask.

Mazra'a and Safi Buses to Mazra'a (30min) and Safi (40min) on the Dead Sea leave from Karak town centre and go past Bab adh-Dhraa; those for Safi also go past the turn-off for Lot's Cave.

INFORMATION

Tourist information Karak's welcoming but modestly equipped visitor centre (April–Oct daily except Fri 8am– 4pm) is located in the plaza below the castle walls.

WALKS AROUND KARAK

As well as trails around Madaba (see page 221) and others within the Mujib reserve (see page 230), there are several attractive **canyons** near Karak that are worth exploring. Many of Jordan's specialist guides (see page 48) know some routes.

CANYON HIKES

The full-day gorge-walk down the stunning **Wadi ibn Hammad**, 34km north of Karak, starts from a pool fed by a hot spring, accessed down a tortuous side road midway between Qasr and Rabba. The canyon – briefly subterranean at first – extends for 12km down to the Dead Sea, 500m below, passing through beautiful mixed terrain, rich with palms, ferns and, in springtime, a breathtaking array of wild flowers. The only obstacle is a 5m waterfall, about 2km east of the Dead Sea road; the path around it leads right, up the cliffs, before descending to follow the lower river bed out to the Dead Sea road, where you can pick up buses between Mazra'a and Karak.

    Wadi Numeira, south of the village of Al-Iraq, 34km south of Karak, is equally enjoyable. If you start from the end of the tarmac road in Al-Iraq, it's a hike of 18km (8hr), but you can cover the first 5km of dirt track by 4x4, leaving 13km to do on foot (6hr). The route, which passes through a green canyon between barren mountains, climaxes in a narrow 100m gorge, bringing you out onto the Dead Sea road between Mazra'a and Safi. You may need a rope for a 5m drop at one point.

    These walks and others in the area are described in more detail in *Jordan: Walks, Treks, Caves, Climbs & Canyons* by Tony Howard (see page 390).

WALKING THE JORDAN TRAIL TO KARAK

It's not hard to adapt part of stage 4.4 of the national **Jordan Trail** (ⓦjordantrail.org; see page 50) into a roughly 15km walk – rated easy – from Rabba village to Karak. The stage officially starts further north in Majdalein village, west of Qasr, but you could join around the 7.5km mark beside the main road in Rabba (which is accessible by bus). Soon afterwards the route branches off into a valley, with views up to Karak castle, then crosses another wadi and climbs to end in Karak town. The Jordan Trail website has full information, maps, GPS points and detailed walking notes.

ACCOMMODATION

Karak stands halfway between Amman and Petra, and appears to make sense as an overnight stop, but in truth you'd do much better to press on to Dana: Karak's **hotels** are mostly a disappointment. In summer, a/c may cost extra; in winter, expect rooms to be very chilly (and for the heating to be on the blink).

Cairwan Facing the town across a valley ☎079 525 0216; map p.232. A cleanish guesthouse converted from a family home: interiors are cosy, with armchairs, sofas, polished brass and an old gramophone, while guest rooms (all en suite) are decent and comfortable. They also have a spacious apartment, holding two double rooms, two bathrooms (with a Jacuzzi), a lounge and a kitchenette (JD40–50, depending on the season). It's plain – but adequate. JD30

Falcon Rock Panorama Street, Al-Marj ☎079 764 4470, ⓦfacebook.com/falconrockhotel; map p.232. A modern 72-room hotel in the suburb of Al-Marj in a wonderful location, on a high plateau facing west directly to the castle walls. It rates itself as four stars, which is a touch ambitious – service can be slow – but the rooms are certainly the best in town: comfortable and clean, with those magnificent views. There's also a small rooftop pool. JD40

Mujeb 4km east of Karak ☎03 238 6090; map p.232. This long-standing tourist hotel continues to make its living mainly from serving lunches to passing tour groups, but it's not a bad overnight option. The welcome is matched by clean, airy rooms sporting laminate flooring and modern bathrooms with proper showers. However, it's located well outside town, at the junction of the King's Highway from Rabba and the link road from Qatraneh on the Desert Highway – and there's no public transport up to the castle (taxi JD4 or so). JD40

Resthouse About 50m north of the castle ☎03 235 1148; map p.232. Aged tourist hotel and restaurant beside the castle that is well past its best. The rooms (all en suite) are old and overpriced because of the location, though all have memorable views over the valley below. JD48

Towers Castle About 100m north of the castle ☎03 235 4289; map p.232. This budget hotel near the castle offers reasonable rooms that are fairly clean. Choose one on a higher floor for great valley views. Staff can advise on transport and hiking routes in the area. JD28

5

EATING AND DRINKING

Karak's **restaurants** are pretty uninspiring. Avoid all the restaurants near the castle – *Kings, Fida, Resthouse, Kir Heres, Kings Castle* and the rest: none is worth recommending. Instead, either walk down into the town centre – which is packed with ordinary local shawarma places – or take a taxi 3km east to the lively, student-oriented suburb Al-Marj, where you'll find a clutch of good hummus and falafel restaurants, terrace cafés for smoking *argileh* and the beautifully located Falcon Rock Hotel (see above), whose restaurant serves simple salads, wings, club sandwiches and plates of pasta (JD3–8).

South of Karak

South of Karak, the deep canyon of **Wadi Hasa**, overlooked by an extinct volcano, runs a close second to Wadi Mujib for natural drama. From **Tafileh** a little beyond, the King's Highway rises into the Shara mountains, well over 1500m above sea level (and considerably more above the deep Dead Sea rift to the west); up here are both the magnificent **Dana Nature Reserve** and another Crusader castle at **Shobak**. A little way south, the dry, jagged mountains conceal ancient Petra.

GETTING AROUND   SOUTH OF KARAK

For most visitors, it's a straight nonstop **drive** from Karak to Dana (or beyond); this is fairly sparse country, and though there are **buses** going from village to village – Tafileh is the regional hub – there's not much to stop for.

Muta and Mazar

The King's Highway floats along the wheat-sown plateau south of Karak for 10km to **MUTA**, best known today as the home of one of Jordan's leading universities, but also the scene, in 629 AD, of the first major battle between the Byzantine Empire and the nascent Muslim army on its first surge out of Arabia. On this occasion, the Muslims were routed, and its generals, including the Prophet Muhammad's adopted son Zaid bin Haritha and his deputy Jaafar bin Abi Talib, were killed. Some 3km south of Muta on the King's Highway, in the town of **MAZAR**, a large, royally funded mosque (with Islamic museum) has been constructed over the shrines of Zaid and Jaafar.

Wadi Hasa

South of Mazar, the landscape becomes increasingly wild. A little way out of Mazar, two roads, old and new, descend past the cultivated fields of Ayna village into the vast **Wadi Hasa** canyon, a natural boundary which marked the transition from Moab into the land of Edom. Dominating the wadi is a huge and elementally scary **black mountain** – actually an extinct volcano – which clashes so startlingly with the white limestone all around that it seems to be under a permanent, ominous cloud. The Nabateans clearly felt something similar, since they built a large temple complex on the conical hill of Jabal Tannur directly opposite, ruined today but still visitable.

Khirbet Tannur

As you rise out of the bed of Wadi Hasa, a broken concrete sign on the right side of the highway, 24km from Mazar, marks the track leading to **Khirbet Tannur**. This is passable for a little way by car, but eventually you'll have to get out and make the tough climb across a saddle and up the steep slope to the atmospheric ruins. The temple area dates from the second century AD. Unfortunately, excavations in the 1930s carted off virtually everything of any interest, and all the carving and statuary that used to adorn the site now gathers dust in museums in Amman and Cincinnati. Yet, however hard it is to imagine the complete structures which once stood here, the windswept isolation of this rugged summit resurrects the presence of the Nabatean gods more potently even than Petra's quietest cranny.

You arrive on the summit more or less where the Nabatean worshippers would have arrived: in front is a humped threshold, originally part of the entrance **gateway** to a paved courtyard. It's easy to make out the wall foundations of three **rooms** to the right, and although only random chunks of decorative carving survive, many of the courtyard's **flagstones** are still in place. Ahead is a raised platform on which stood the small **temple**, its entrance originally crowned with a large carved image of the goddess Atargatis bedecked with vines and fruit (now on display in Amman). Within the holy of holies stood images both of Atargatis and the god Zeus-Hadad.

Afra hot springs (Hammamat Afra)
Daylight hours • JD7

Barely 2km from the Khirbet Tannur turning, the King's Highway is carried over Wadi Laban, a tributary of Wadi Hasa, on a small bridge; no buses follow the small turning off to the right side, but private transport can take you further along this winding side road deep into the valley to reach a set of **hot springs**. It's a popular excursion for local families – empty during the week, packed on Fridays and Saturdays.

Once you've left the King's Highway and headed along the side road, you'll see a turn-off after 7km. This leads down to **Hammamat Burbita** (also spelled Barbeita and in other ways), in a broad and sunny part of the valley, with the river fringed by reed-beds and some cultivation. You could divert to the thermal springs here (admission costs JD5), but you'd do better to continue ahead. After another 5km of narrow switchbacks, high above the valley floor, you reach a gate across the road giving access to **HAMMAMAT AFRA**. There are some leisure facilities here, but nowhere to escape the crowds if you visit when it's packed. The hot pools (four outdoor ones for men, one indoors for women) are set down in a gorge between high, narrow cliffs that cut out most of the direct sunshine, and are well maintained. The water is a striking rust-red colour from the high iron content, and genuinely hot: the last pool on the left – popularly known as the *megla*, or frying pan – is a broiling 52°C. The walls all along the narrow valley drip water, with mineral reds and mossy greens daubing the white limestone. Splashing barefoot up or down the warm river here is as much pleasure as flopping around in the pools with everybody else (dress conservatively: men in long shorts; women with body and legs covered and only in the women's bathing section). A couple of kiosks sell snacks and cold drinks, but most people set up barbecues on the various terraces around the site.

Tafileh (Tafila)
South of Wadi Hasa, the King's Highway begins to climb into the Shara mountains, eventually reaching a small plateau where a road branches east (left) to the Desert Highway (if you're heading north along the King's Highway, the signposting at this junction is confusing and it's easy to lose the way; if necessary ask passers-by which road is which). It was near here that, in January 1918, the only fully fledged battle of the Arab Revolt took place, Feisal and Lawrence's armies sweeping away an Ottoman force only to be halted in their tracks by heavy snow.

Some 25km south of the turn-off for Hammamat Afra, the picturesque town of **TAFILEH** (also spelled **TAFILA**) comes into view, spread along gently curving terraces, with orchards of fruit and olives blanketing the hillside below. Although a governorate capital and a sizeable town, Tafileh has no specific attractions to make for (the signposted "castle" in the middle of town comprises a single, inaccessible tower, most likely Mamluke), and you'll probably find yourself stopping only to switch buses.

About 4km south of Tafileh is a turn-off westwards, signed for Aqaba and Fifa. It offers truly spectacular views out over the desert as it coils down to Fifa (see page 340), just south of the Dead Sea. This is the route to follow if you're driving between Dana and Feynan.

5

By bus Buses drop off in the town centre, but they stop running by about midday: if you arrive in the afternoon you'll find no buses to Dana, Petra or Amman – your only options will be hitching or negotiating with the local taxi drivers. Destinations Aqaba (2hr 30min); Karak (1hr); Ma'an (1hr); Qadisiyyeh (40min); Wihdat station (2hr 30min).

Sela

The village of Ain al-Baydha, about 10km south of Tafileh, marks a turn-off heading steeply down the cliffside to the hamlet of As-Sil, opposite Sela – As-Sil is just about accessible by ordinary car, but to go on you'll have to resort to 4x4 or on foot, and a guide is essential, since this is barren and inhospitable terrain; either start out early in the day, and ask around for help in Ain al-Baydha village, or consult the RSCN staff at Dana (see page 241) in advance

In the rugged hills south of Tafileh looms the remote mountain fastness of **SELA**, which offers a taxing but memorable hike up to a summit with magnificent views. The giant sandstone mountain looms on the other side of a deep ravine from the picturesque hamlet of **As-Sil**, where old stone cottages cluster higgledy-piggledy on an outcrop.

A biblical account in II Kings narrates the story of the seventh-century-BC King Amaziah of Judah, who attacked Edom, defeated a ten-thousand-strong army and seized "Selah", while II Chronicles says that, during the same campaign, Amaziah threw ten thousand captive Edomites off the "rock". Some archeologists have related present-day Sela with these events (the Hebrew word for "rock" is *sela*), but others have suggested that these events took place at the similarly remote, inaccessible mountain Umm al-Biyara at Petra – partly since the Greek word *petra* also means "rock". Neither case has been conclusively proved, and even the discovery of a worn **inscription** in Babylonian cuneiform, carved in a smoothed rectangle in the cliff face on the side of the mountain of Sela (and just about visible to the naked eye from As-Sil), hasn't provided any further insight.

The one-hour **hike** up to the summit from As-Sil heads down into the valley, then up via a Nabatean-style rock-cut stairway; once at the top, aside from exploring the various cisterns and chambers, you're rewarded with outstanding **views** over the rocky domes and towers of this folded landscape.

At the end of the road leading down through **Ain al-Baydha** into As-Sil is an open car park on a terrace viewpoint, beside a restored complex of stone cottages converted into a café and restaurant. Locals drive out here especially on a Thursday and Friday to play music, smoke *argileh* and generally hang out around sunset. Join them if you fancy.

Dana

In **Qadisiyyeh**, a small town located 27km south of Tafileh and 24km north of Shobak, a steep, cliffside road winds down off the King's Highway to **DANA**. This hamlet lies at the eastern edge of Jordan's flagship **Dana Biosphere Reserve**, which encompasses 320 square kilometres of terrain around the breathtaking Wadi Dana, stretching as far as Wadi Araba in the west. The village has been the scene of an extraordinary – and successful – social experiment to rejuvenate a dying community by protecting the natural environment. Clinging to the edge of the cliff below the King's Highway, Dana is the starting point for a series of walks and hikes through one of Jordan's loveliest protected areas. Or, of course, you could just hole up and enjoy the peace. Whether you stay for an hour or a week, you won't want to leave.

Dana village

ⓦ danacooperative.wordpress.com

A picturesque cluster of stone cottages huddled together on a cliffside outcrop, **Dana village** has rightly become celebrated as one of Jordan's loveliest hideaways. Long settled as a farming community, it was abandoned in the middle of last century, only to become the focus for sustained projects of renovation and redevelopment (see page 240). And the story continues: with funding from the US government's USAID programme, Dana is being reinvented as the hub for **ecotourism development** in southern Jordan, with new infrastructure laid for water, electricity and sewage bio-treatment, streets and cottages rebuilt, and new parks and play areas popping up. The focus is very much on retaining the village's Jordanian character, both to draw local tourism and create a base for sustainable, environmentally sound international tourism too.

It's worth taking a stroll around, to soak up the atmosphere and rural character. Drop into the Royal Society for the Conservation of Nature (RSCN) offices, by the *Guesthouse* on the left side of the village as you face the valley. They can fill you in on the latest developments and can advise on **walks**. An easy one to start with is the **Village Tour** (2km; 1hr 30min), a stroll around Dana – and up to the springs and gardens on the slopes above – to enjoy the views and visit the workshops where local women make silver jewellery and prepare dried fruit. In the same building as the nature shop (see page 245) is a small **museum**, where informative displays give a sense of Dana's natural context.

Dana Biosphere Reserve

Entrance fee JD8, waived if you book a walk or stay overnight in RSCN accommodation • Book everything at least a day in advance, on ☎ 03 227 0497 or via the RSCN Wild Jordan centre in Amman (see page 82) ☎ 06 461 6523, Ⓦ wildjordan.com

Dana village overlooks the **Dana Biosphere Reserve**, an immense tract of wilderness centred on the V-shaped Wadi Dana. It's a spectacular place to go walking. The reserve's terrain drops from 1500m above sea level at Dana to below sea level west of Feynan. Its **geology** switches from limestone to sandstone to granite, ecosystems varying from lush, well-watered mountain slopes and open oak and juniper woodlands to scrubland and arid sandy desert. The list of **flora** and resident **fauna** is dizzying: a brief roundup includes various kinds of eagles, falcons, kestrels and vultures, cuckoos, owls, the Sinai rosefinch and Tristram's serin; wildcats, caracals, hyenas, jackals, badgers, foxes, wolves, hares, bats, hedgehogs, porcupine and ibex; snakes, chameleons and lizards

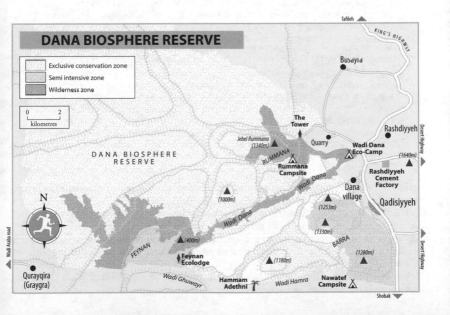

5

THE STORY OF DANA

Dana is unique, not only in Jordan but in the whole Middle East – the setting for a positive, visionary programme combining scientific research, social reconstruction and **sustainable tourism**. For most of the twentieth century Dana was a simple farming community thriving on a temperate climate, three abundant springs and good grazing; indeed, some inhabitants had previously left Tafileh specifically for a better life in the village. But as Jordan developed new technologies and the general standard of living rose, a growing number of villagers felt isolated in their mountain hamlet of Ottoman stone cottages. Some moved out in the late 1960s to establish a new village, **Qadisiyyeh**, on the main Tafileh–Shobak road, and the attractions of electricity and plumbing rapidly emptied primitive Dana. The construction of the huge Rashdiyyeh cement factory close by in the early 1980s was the last straw: with well-paid jobs for the taking, most locals saw the daily trek up from Dana to the factory as pointless, and almost everyone moved to Qadisiyyeh.

Dana lay semi-abandoned for a decade or more, its handful of impoverished farmers forced to compete in the local markets with bigger farms using more advanced methods of production. This was what a group of twelve women from Amman discovered in the early 1990s as they travelled across the country to catalogue the remnants of traditional culture. Realizing the deprivation faced by some of the poorest people in Jordan, these "**Friends of Dana**" embarked on a project to renovate and revitalize the fabric of the village under the auspices of the **Royal Society for the Conservation of Nature (RSCN)**. Electricity, telephones and a water supply were extended to the village and 65 cottages renovated. People started to drift back to Dana. The RSCN quickly realized the potential of the secluded Wadi Dana for scientific research. In a project funded partly by the World Bank and the UN, they turned the area into a protected **nature reserve**, built a small research station next to the village and, in 1994, launched a detailed ecological survey.

Continued grazing by thousands of domesticated goats, sheep and camels couldn't be reconciled with the need for environmental protection and so – not without controversy – was banned. Studies were undertaken into creating sustainable opportunities for villagers to gain a **livelihood** from the reserve. The ingenious solution came in redirecting the village's traditional crops to a new market. Dana's farmers produced their olives, figs, grapes, other fruits and nuts as before, but instead they sold everything to the RSCN, who employed the villagers to process these crops into **novelty products** such as organically produced jams and olive-oil soap for direct sale to relatively wealthy, environmentally aware consumers, both Jordanian and foreign. **Medicinal herbs** were introduced as a cash crop to aid the economic recovery, and the last Dana resident familiar with traditional **pottery-making** was encouraged to teach her craft to a younger generation.

Dana soon hit the headlines, and in 1996 the RSCN launched **low-impact tourism** to the reserve, with the traditional-style *Guesthouse* going up next to the research buildings. Local villagers – some of whom were already employed as research scientists – were taken on as managers and guides. "Green tourism" awards followed, and, with Dana becoming better known as a tourist destination, locals opened small, budget hotels within the village. A campsite was established in the hills at Rummana, and in 2005 the RSCN opened a "wilderness ecolodge" at the lower, western end of the reserve at Feynan – both of them built and staffed by local people. Dana sees 80–100,000 visitors a year, around a quarter of whom stay overnight, bringing money to the village economy and focusing attention on how sustainable tourism can benefit rural people.

In only one generation, moribund Dana has been given a new lease of life.

galore; freshwater crabs; and, so far, three plants new to science out of more than seven hundred plant species recorded.

The RSCN-run **Dana Guesthouse** is worth stopping at – whether you're staying there or not – both for the views from their terrace (binoculars are available if you'd like to do a spot of birdwatching) and to get some firsthand **information** about the reserve's walks and wildlife from the experts. Bear in mind you have to **book** everything with the RSCN well in advance.

You can also access the reserve from **Feynan**, at the far western end of Wadi Dana, which we cover in detail in Chapter 7 (see page 340).

Rummana Campsite

Early March to late Oct

A few kilometres northwest of Dana village, on the opposite flank of Wadi Dana, **Rummana Campsite** (see page 245) is another place to stay – and is also an alternative entry point to the reserve, with several good trails (see below). Near the campsite is a **bird hide** overlooking a small pool – ideal for early morning observation of birds and ibex – and should you fancy stretching your legs instead of sitting on the shuttle bus, the walk back up from the campsite to the "Tower" (the public access point for Rummana) takes about an hour.

ARRIVAL AND DEPARTURE   DANA

BY CAR
To/from Amman via the Desert Highway By the most direct driving route, Dana lies 202km south of Amman's 7th Circle junction. Head due south on the Desert Highway for 172km to Husseiniyya, then turn west (27km) to the large Rashdiyyeh cement factory, from where Qadisiyyeh is 3km

---

WALKS IN DANA BIOSPHERE RESERVE

WALKS FROM DANA VILLAGE

For all routes from Dana village other than the Wadi Dana Trail, **guides are compulsory**.

The most obvious walking route in the reserve is the magnificent **Wadi Dana Trail** (14km; 5–7hr) from the village along the downward-sloping floor of the wadi, a moderate walk passing from the lush green gardens of Dana through increasingly wild and desolate terrain to end at Feynan (see page 340). This can be done alone or with a guide (JD20pp).

The **White Dome Trail** (8km; 3–4hr; March–Oct only; JD15pp) is a beautiful one-way walk that follows a contour around the head of the valley, passing first through the spring-fed terraced gardens of Dana and then beneath the massive escarpment to Rummana.

Another highly explorable area is **Al-Barra**, a fifteen-minute drive south of the village, where lush woodlands give way to networks of canyons and gorges cutting into the mountainous landscape. This is the starting point for the superb **Shaq al-Reesh Trail** (3km; 4–5hr; JD15pp) to a Nabatean mountain retreat ("Canyon of the Feathers" in Arabic). The walk begins in flower-filled meadows and quiet terraces, but involves a bit of scrambling and climbing through a narrow gorge to reach the spectacular summit, dotted with cisterns and water channels. Al-Barra is also the start and finish for the **Nawatef Trail** (2km; 2hr; JD15pp), heading out to the springs and ruins at Nawatef and back on a different route.

The beautiful but difficult **Wadi Dathneh Trail** (19km; 8–10hr; March–Oct only; JD20pp) also starts from Al-Barra, passing between the red cliffs of Wadi Hamra before reaching the verdant oasis of Hammam Adethni and following flowing water all the way down to end at Feynan. One of the most celebrated long routes is the neighbouring **Wadi Ghweir Trail** (18km; 7–8hr; March–Oct only; JD20pp), starting from Mansoura near Shobak and leading through a magnificent high-walled canyon through a flowing stream down to Feynan.

WALKS FROM RUMMANA CAMPSITE

All these trails are open from early March to late October only.

The **White Dome Trail** (8km; 3–4hr; JD15pp) to Dana – the route is described in reverse above – is highly recommended, or you could try the alternative **Dana Village Trail** (5km; 4hr; JD12pp), following a rougher track. A **guide is compulsory** for both these trails.

All other trails can be walked **without a guide**. The easy **Rummana Campsite Trail** (1.5km; 1hr) leads on a circular route around the Rummana area, offering stunning views and birdwatching lookouts. The moderate **Rummana Mountain Trail** (2.5km; 2hr) follows a trail through the juniper trees up to the summit of Jabal Rummana ("Pomegranate Mountain") for the views down into Wadi Araba: it's also easy to spot raptors up here, and if you head up at dawn you may see ibex. Across from the campsite is the **Caves Trail** (1.5km; 1hr 30min), a short, rough walk leading to a set of caves above Shaq al-Kalb ("Dog Canyon"), residence of hyenas, wildcats and wolves.

5

THE DANA–PETRA TREK

One of the Middle East's most impressive long-distance treks – dubbed "Jordan's Inca Trail" – links Dana village and Feynan with **Petra** (45km; 3–5 days; guide compulsory). The route heads far off any beaten tracks, from Dana to Feynan, across open country towards Shobak, and then to "Little Petra" in order to arrive at Petra via a back route over the mountains. It's a challenging, but extraordinarily rewarding, walk.

However, it is not waymarked – and, in fact, there is no single accepted path. Many of Jordan's specialist independent **guides** can lead you from Dana to Petra, but they won't necessarily all go the same way – some paths are more beautiful than others. Some propose two nights camping out between Feynan and Little Petra; others say three.

A handful of **tour operators** in the UK and elsewhere offer the route as part of a Jordan package, but if you'd like to tackle it independently, talk well in advance to RSCN staff at the *Dana Guesthouse* or at the Wild Jordan centre in Amman for an idea of the logistics – and then compare with some of the independent specialists (see page 48). One key point is to determine what facilities are on offer at each overnight stop: some guides will carry everything with them, others will bring in trail support so that tea and meals are ready when you arrive.

The walk itself is epic, covering highland forests, wild, rolling hills and scorching deserts, dropping down to the floor of the Wadi Araba, then climbing again into the sandstone mountains. A version of it for independent walkers is outlined on the national Jordan Trail website (⊕jordantrail.org; see page 50), with maps, GPS points and detailed walking notes.

to the left (south). The turn-off down the cliffside into Dana is marked at the top end of Qadisiyyeh village. On the way down into Dana, a viewpoint gives a tremendous panorama of Wadi Dana. Further down, as you clatter down the steep cobbled street into the village centre, you come to a fork beside the *Dana Moon Hotel*: go straight on into the village or turn left to reach the RSCN *Dana Guesthouse*.

To/from Tafileh via the King's Highway Qadisiyyeh lies 27km south of Tafileh. As you get close you'll pass signs to the Dana Nature Reserve pointing off into the countryside: though they don't say so, these are indicating an access route into the northern fringe of the reserve around the *Rummana Campsite*. If you want Dana village, stay on the road until you reach the cement factory, then go 3km further to the turn-off in Qadisiyyeh.

To/from Petra Dana is 53km north of Petra. From Wadi Musa follow the main road through Shobak town, then pick up signs to Tafileh: ignore roads to the right signed Amman (they join the Desert Highway at Unayza). Keep going straight to reach Qadisiyyeh (24km north of Shobak), then drive all the way up Qadisiyyeh's long main street to find the turn-off (left) to Dana at the top of the village.

GETTING AROUND

At this upper end of the valley, there are two access points to the reserve: Dana village and *Rummana Campsite*. Getting between the two isn't difficult.

On foot The walk between Dana and Rummana is a straightforward 2–3hr around the head of the valley: ask someone to point you onto the path.

By shuttle bus You can request a free transfer between

BY BUS AND SERVEECE

The only bus into Dana shuttles to and from Qadisiyyeh on the King's Highway above the village (5min).

To/from Amman and north Qadisiyyeh has fairly regular bus links from Tafileh (40min), plus two or three buses a day to/from Amman's Wihdat station (2hr 40min). There may be one or two *serveeces* heading to/from Amman Wihdat as well.

To/from Shobak and south South of Dana, the section of the King's Highway between Qadisiyyeh and Shobak has little or no public transport; there may be one student bus in the early mornings to Shobak or Ma'an, but ask around the day before. Otherwise hitching is an option.

BY TAXI

A full car to Dana from Shobak or Tafileh should cost about JD15, or from Wadi Musa/Petra about JD35–40. Bargain hard. Hotels in Madaba may be able to organize a drop-off at Dana on a chartered taxi run to Petra (see page 219). A ride to/from Feynan, organized through the *Feynan Ecolodge* (see page 342), costs JD52.

Dana and Rummana at the *Dana Guesthouse*.

By car From Dana village, head up the access road to Qadisiyyeh. At the top, where you meet the main Qadisiyyeh–Tafileh road, turn left (up the hill) and follow this for about 5km. Just beyond where the road cuts straight through the middle of a small wood, turn left at a brown sign for the RSCN *Rummana Campsite*. (Coming the other

5

WILD JORDAN RESERVE PRICES

Prices at Jordan's **RSCN-run nature reserves** are high. The RSCN make no apologies for this, saying that the reason they exist is to protect Jordan's natural environment, and that they have built lodges and developed tourism – under their **Wild Jordan** brand – as a tool for generating funds to help conservation and support rural communities. You may or may not agree with their pricing policy, but this kind of responsible tourism is virtually unknown in the Middle East, and the RSCN are pioneers. For now, until tourism schemes emerge that are truly community-owned, paying extra to visit the RSCN reserves is a good way to ensure that your money goes to benefit rural people and habitats.

way, this turn lies 22km south of Tafileh.) The turn-off brings you down below the level of the main road onto a wide, gravel road; carry on, past a huge quarry on the left, and then down a signposted left turn. About 1km further you'll come to "The Tower" – a small building with an office and terrace – where you must park. This marks the entrance to the reserve. Check in at the Tower, and staff will radio ahead to summon the shuttle bus, which will take you down the hill to the *Rummana Campsite*. The shuttle to and from the Tower (and, on request, to the *Dana Guesthouse*) is free.

INFORMATION

RSCN/Wild Jordan Drop into the Royal Society for the Conservation of Nature (RSCN) offices beside the *Dana Guesthouse* to pick up leaflets detailing a number of walks and activities. Trained nature guides are available for any of the walks at a fixed rate: short walks cost JD12/person for 1–2hr or JD15/person for 3–4hr, both with a minimum of four people (so quadruple these prices if you're on your own), longer walks cost JD20/person for 5–8hr with a minimum of ten people. Many of the walks require you to take a guide – which you have to book well in advance, either direct (☎ 03 227 0497) or via the RSCN's Wild Jordan centre in Amman (see page 82): you can't just turn up and book one on the spot. However, there's a handful of self-guided trails on which you can strike out alone

(✆ wildjordan.com lists them all) and if you ask around in Dana village you may be passed to a non-RSCN guide who can take you onto trails outside the reserve boundary.

Dana Cooperative As part of Dana's ongoing renovations, a general (non-RSCN) Visitor Centre is planned for the village. It's unclear at the time of writing what form it will take. In the meantime check out ✆ facebook.com/ danacooperative.

Books All the walks outlined in this section, and others in the area, are described in *Jordan: Walks, Treks, Caves, Climbs & Canyons* by Tony Howard (see page 390). If you're keen to be able to identify plants, animals and birds while out walking, another good purchase – as book or smartphone app – is the *Field Guide to Jordan* (see page 390).

ACCOMMODATION AND EATING

Dana's **accommodation** is excellent, whether you choose the isolated country campsites, the budget hotels in the village or the pricier serenity and charm of the RSCN's *Guesthouse*. Either way, expect silence and an epic atmosphere of wide-open nature all around. Note that it gets cold here in winter (Nov–March), and heating is often rudimentary. The lack of **grocery shops** or **restaurants** means that you must either eat at your hotel or campsite, or bring in picnic supplies; a mix of the two is probably the best solution. The **Feynan Ecolodge** is at the far western end of the reserve (see page 342).

DANA VILLAGE

★ **Dana Guesthouse (RSCN)** South side of village ☎ 03 227 0497 or book via the RSCN's Wild Jordan centre in Amman (see page 82) on ☎ 06 461 6523, ✆ wildjordan.com. A night in this clifftop lodge – which combines isolated tranquillity with cosy comforts – is likely to be one of your most memorable in Jordan. Stay a few days and let the atmosphere seep into your bones. The original

building holds nine "economy" rooms, while an extension holds fifteen "deluxe" rooms. All rooms, and the main terrace, overlook the full length of the still Wadi Dana: at night, lights twinkling on the Dead Sea and the call of nightjars echoing eerily up the valley make for an unforgettable experience. The building and its furniture were designed by architect Ammar Khammash (✆ khammash.com) in a skilful and attractive blend of traditional Jordanian styles and a chic minimalism in stone and iron. Everything is kept spotlessly clean by the cheerful staff. All rooms have a private balcony. Of the "economy" rooms, one is en suite while the others share bathrooms. All the newer "deluxe" rooms are en suite. Rates include a good breakfast. With advance notice, staff can prepare lunches and dinners (JD14–21/person), as well as hikers' lunchboxes (around JD6.50/person): if you're staying the night, make sure to specify you want dinner at the time of booking. Reserve well in advance. Economy JD76, Deluxe JD100

★ **Dana Hotel** Village centre ☎ 03 227 0537 or ☎ 077 238 7787, ✆ facebook.com/danahoteljordan. Small village hotel run by the local Dana Cooperative: profits go to support local families (notably putting students through university). It's a great, atmospheric little place. The original building occupies one of the old stone cottages, sympathetically renovated, with simple rooms ranged around its quiet stone-flagged courtyard – or you could stay in one of the "villas" across the square nearby. There's also the option of sleeping in the tent on the roof. Breakfast is included; other meals cost JD5. Room JD20 Villa JD25

★ **Dana Moon Hotel** Village centre ☎03 227 0413 or ☎079 753 3581, ✉dana.moonhotel@hotmail.com. Tiny little place in a prominent location at the entrance to the village. Its five rooms are small and basic, with shared bathrooms, but they are comfortable enough – and the warmth of the welcome stands out. Rates include dinner and breakfast. JD20

Dana Tower Hotel West side of village ☎079 568 8853, ⓦfacebook.com/danatower1. Occupying four of the old cottages at the very back of the village, this less sympathetic restoration – its ugly breezeblock shack on the roof dominating sightlines – comes with backpacker graffiti on the walls, flags of the world, the aroma of joss sticks and trinkets dotted about. The owners have dissociated themselves from the RSCN and the village cooperative, so despite its hippyish appearance, this is a profit-making business. Rooms are clean, and include dinner and breakfast (other meals are about JD5). Transport to or from Qadisiyyeh and Petra is discounted. JD20

Wadi Dana Eco-Camp Above the village ☎077 224 7775, ⓦfacebook.com/wadidana. As you drive down into Dana, fork to the right, then park – a 20min walk leads to this beautiful, well-presented little site, set amid the orchards 1km above the village with stunning views down the length of the valley. They have four stone-built two-person chalets (en suite) and nine striped bedouin-style tents for one or two people, all with solid beds and bedding – basic but neat, clean and attractive. Breakfast is included and lunch/dinner can be requested (JD10/person), but there is no electricity – lighting after dark is by candles; bring a torch. Showers use water heated by the

sun: warm in summer, chilly at other times. The camp is run as a partnership between local farmers and the Dana village cooperative, who can provide trail guides (from JD35), and also take you out for a day with a local shepherd or to watch local women baking bread. Tents JD35, chalets JD45

IN THE RESERVE

★ **Rummana Campsite (RSCN)** Rummana ☎03 227 0497 or book via the RSCN's Wild Jordan centre in Amman (see page 82) on ☎06 461 6523, ⓦwildjordan.com. The great Dana outdoors is best experienced by camping, but to control numbers within the reserve you're not allowed to pitch your own tent. Instead, aim for the RSCN's *Rummana Campsite*, located in an idyllic spot at the foot of Jabal Rummana in the hills to the north of Wadi Dana. It has twenty solid, roomy tents, some sleeping two, others four. The sense of isolation, and the beauty of the environment, make this a fabulous place to spend the night. Book well in advance. Rates include all bedding plus access to a proper, clean toilet block with cold showers, as well as a hearty breakfast. With advance notice, staff can prepare lunches and dinners (around JD12/person), as well as hikers' lunchboxes (around JD6.50/person). Closed Nov to early March. JD64

NEARBY

★ **Nawatef Campsite** Nawatef ☎077 554 7048, ⓦbit.ly/nawatef. Another exceptional place to stay, this rock-bottom basic campsite is located in the next-door valley to Dana – drive a few kilometres south of Qadisiyyeh and the camp lies 1.7km along the signed turn-off. Perched up on a high spur, the site offers stupendous views over the rocky domes and silent cliffsides. Facilities are basic, comprising a few tented chalets and a shower block – or you can pitch your own tent (JD5) – but the setting, and the open-hearted welcome, more than make up for any inadequacies. Expect to be plied with tea, tasty food and loads of ideas for walks and excursions in the hills around. Staff will pick you up in Qadisiyyeh on request. Rates include dinner and breakfast. JD20

SHOPPING

RSCN/Wild Jordan Nature Shop Beside the RSCN Guesthouse. This is where you can buy local products such as herbs, fruit and jewellery, as well as textiles, gifts

and other handmade items from RSCN projects around the country. Sun–Thurs 8am–4pm.

Shobak

Perched dramatically like a ship on the crest of a hill, the castle at **SHOBAK** was the first to be built by the Crusaders (see page 233) in Transjordan. In a more ruinous state than Karak castle, and much rebuilt by Mamlukes and Ottomans, it's nonetheless well worth an exploratory detour on a route between Dana and Petra. In addition, the RSCN is exploring possibilities for a new **nature reserve** here: a fine canyon trail

5

already leads along **Wadi Ghwayr** between Mansoura village, about 10km north of Shobak, and Feynan (see page 340).

Shobak castle

3km from Shobak town • Sun–Thurs & Sat 8am–5pm, Fri 10am–4pm • JD1, free with JP • No buses run up to the castle, so without your own transport you'll need to persuade a taxi driver to take you or face a stiff climb

Shobak castle's walls and towers are Mamluke, and all the towers which stand have beautifully carved external **calligraphic inscriptions** dating from rebuilding work in the 1290s. As you enter, down and to the left is a small **chapel**, at the back of which are pools and channels of unknown usage. Below the chapel runs a long, dank and pitch-dark **secret passage**, which brings you out in the middle of the castle if you head right, and outside the walls if you head left.

Back alongside the chapel is the original **gatehouse**, to the left side of which are two round wells which presage an even scarier **secret passage** – a dark and foul opening with, according to legend, 375 broken and slippery steps leading down into the heart of the hill, followed by a tunnel 205m long. This was the castle's main water supply: somehow the Crusaders knew that by digging down so far they'd eventually hit water. It might be navigable when you visit, eventually emerging at the foot of the castle by a road – but take proper advice before venturing down: people who have gone unprepared (including a potholing expert who tried it in 2008) have ended up with serious injuries, telling of how the stairs crumbled away under their feet. You need a **guide** who's done it before, a torch and a disdain for claustrophobia.

The gatehouse gives onto a street, at the end of which is a building with three **arched entrances**, one topped by a calligraphic panel; up until the 1950s the castle was still inhabited, and this building was the old village school. If you head through to the back and turn right, a long vaulted corridor leads you out to the north side of the castle, and a maze of abandoned **Ottoman cottages**, beneath which is an exposed **Ayyubid palace** complex, with a large reception hall and baths. Further round towards the entrance stand the beautiful arches of a **church**, beneath which is a small room filled with catapult balls and chunks of carved masonry.

You might be lucky and stumble upon a **re-enactment of battles** between Crusaders and Muslim armies under Salah Ed-Din at Shobak, employing local army veterans in a choreographed show staged for tour groups. The Jordan Heritage Revival Company (⊕ jhrc.jo) has details.

ARRIVAL AND DEPARTURE   SHOBAK

By car The castle lies 3km west of Shobak town, which is 24km south of Qadisiyyeh and 27km north of Wadi Musa. From two points on the King's Highway the castle is clearly signposted: the turn-offs lead through Al-Muthallath, a modern suburb, to the old village of Al-Jaya, at the foot of the castle hill. A Visitor Centre stands on the adjacent hilltop, facing the castle, but there's little point heading there: just go up to the castle and park by the walls.

By bus Buses and some *serveeces* run to Shobak town direct from Amman's Wihdat station, in the mornings only, and all day from Wadi Musa and Ma'an, but there is virtually no public transport from Qadisiyyeh. If you're planning a bus journey out of Shobak, ask around the day before to check times and pick-up points.

Destinations Amman Wihdat (2hr 45min); Ma'an (30min); Wadi Musa (30min).

ACCOMMODATION

As well as the two places mentioned here, you'll find one or two small cave-style "**hotels**" in old Al-Jaya village at the foot of the castle hill. Ask Yassin, who runs the souvenir stall outside the castle gateway, for details.

Jaya Tourist Camp Near the Montreal Hotel ☎ 079 595 8958. Splendid little independent campsite just down from the *Montreal Hotel* run by the charming, happy-go-lucky

Saleh Rawashdeh. Everything is very basic, comprising tents and communal sleeping areas, with food rustled up in the camp kitchen – or you could contact Saleh to set up wilderness camping in the desert nearby, or homestays with local bedouin families. He also has guides for hikes in the area (JD70/day), including to Petra or down to Feynan via the epic Wadi Ghuweir. Rates cover standard double

5

USEFUL ARABIC PLACE NAMES

Ain al-Baydha	العين البيضاء	Mahabbah Circle	دوار المحبة
Busayra	بصيرا	Mansoura	المنصورة
Dana Guesthouse	بيت الضيافة – ضانا	Muhafadha Circle	دوار المحافظة
Dead Sea	البحر الميت	Mujib Reserve	محمية الموجب
Dead Sea Panorama	مجمع بانوراما البحر الميت	Nawatef Campsite	مخيم النواطف
Desert Highway	الطريق الصحراوي	Nitil	نتل
Faqua	فقوع	Qadisiyyeh	القادسية
Faysaliyyeh	الفيصلية	Qurayqira (Graygra)	القريقرة
Feynan	فينان	Rashdiyyeh	الرشادية
Hammamat Burbita	حمامات البربيطة	Rummana Campsite	مخيم الرمانة
al-Iraq	العراق (بجانب مؤتة)	Wadi Ghwayr	وادي الغوير
Jaya Campsite	مخيم الجاية السياحي	Wadi ibn Hammad	وادي ابن حماد
Libb	لب	Wadi Numeira	وادي النميرة

occupancy including dinner and breakfast. JD25
Montreal Hotel Opposite the castle ☎03 216 5440, ⓦmontrealhotel.jo. Occupying a former school, this modern, twenty-room tourist hotel enjoys a prime location, directly facing the castle across the valley-floor ruins of old Al-Jaya village. It's operated by the heritage revival firm JHRC, who also run the Crusader re-enactments at the castle; there's a strong social/community element to staying here (check ⓦfacebook.com/jhrcjor for more). Interiors are freshly done up in light pine, with carpets and good mid-range facilities, though the bathrooms are a touch basic. The welcome, as usual, is genial and accommodating but unless there's a group in – which is rare, this close to Petra – the hotel can feel a bit grandiose and empty. The hotel is signposted from the main road. JD50

EATING

Set in acres of lush orchards, Shobak is Jordan's leading producer of **apples**, but this quiet farming village has also been trying for years to reap some benefit from the tourists heading south to Petra. There are some decent local **restaurants** on the main drag as well as numerous **grocery** shops, which beat those in Wadi Musa on both price and quality; if you intend to picnic in Petra, you'd do well to stock up here in advance.

Petra

PETRA LANDSCAPE

Petra

Petra astounds. Tucked away in a remote valley basin in the heart of southern Jordan's Shara mountains and shielded from the outside world behind an impenetrable barrier of rock, this ancient city remains wreathed in mystery. Since a Western adventurer stumbled on the site in 1812, it has fired imaginations, its grandeur and dramatic setting pushing it – like the Pyramids or the Taj Mahal – into the realms of legend. Today, it's almost as if time has literally drawn a veil over the once-great city, which grew wealthy enough on the caravan trade to challenge the might of Rome: two millennia of wind and rain have blurred the sharp edges of its ornate Classical facades and rubbed away at its soft sandstone to expose vivid bands of colour beneath, putting the whole scene into soft focus.

The highlights of the ancient city do not disappoint. The epic walk in, through the tall, echoing **Siq** canyon, precedes a jaw-dropping encounter with the **Treasury**, Petra's iconic facade, its columns and exquisite detailing carved directly from the cliff face. Further on, past the huge **Theatre**, you reach the giant **Royal Tombs**, gazing out over the hidden valley that shelters Petra's city centre. Walk along the **Colonnaded Street**, then tackle the stepped climb to Petra's largest monument, the **Monastery**, carved from a mountain summit. Budget some downtime to take in the extraordinary late-afternoon views from the **Qasr al-Bint** temple up the Colonnaded Street towards the fiery East Cliff. Visiting these core sites, walking on stony (or, sometimes, sandy) footpaths the whole way, would fill a fairly exhausting entire day. Many people take longer over it than that.

Stay longer – most package tours allow a couple of days in Petra at least – and possibilities abound for wider exploration. The **High Place of Sacrifice** offers spectacular views from a mountaintop altar, easily reached by a stepped path. Walking in an outlying wadi – **Wadi Turkmaniyyeh** is a prime example – takes you out of the tourist hubbub into still landscapes of barren peaks and wild canyons, while **Little Petra**, a few kilometres to the north, hides a mini-Siq and carved facades of its own, far from the main site.

Where Petra sits, in a valley basin between two lines of jagged peaks, there's only one route in and out, and that passes through the **modern town** of **Wadi Musa** on the eastern side of the mountains. In the last few decades Wadi Musa has grown to serve the lucrative tourist trade to Petra; it has all the services, including **hotels** (see page 294) and **restaurants** (see page 297): there's nowhere to stay within the ancient city itself, and virtually nowhere to eat either. The single entrance gate into Petra is in Wadi Musa, but once you've crossed that barrier you're immediately thrown into the rocky landscape of the desert. Within Petra there is no urban development of any kind, and the local culture is all rural.

Spending a few days here is a constant to-and-fro – down-at-heel Wadi Musa providing all the necessities of life, majestic Petra all the historical and natural drama.

Brief history

The **history** of Petra – a Greek word meaning "rock" – encompasses more than a hundred centuries of human settlement. In prehistory, the Petra region saw some of the first experiments in farming. The hunter-gatherers of the **Paleolithic Age** gave way, over nine thousand years ago, to settled communities living in walled farming villages such as at **Beidha**, just north of Petra. Nomadic tribes passed through the Petra basin in

PETRA BY NIGHT

Highlights

❶ Petra By Night Magical late-night guided walks into Petra for traditional music and storytelling by candlelight. See page 261

❷ The Siq Dramatic entrance to the ancient city, walking through a high, narrow gorge flanked by towering cliffs. See page 263

❸ The Treasury Jordan's most recognizable monument, a towering Classical facade dominating the entrance to the city. See page 264

❹ East Cliff A line of impressive royal tombs gaze over Petra's ancient city centre from this immense cliffside, glowing fiery-red in the late afternoon sun. See page 268

❺ The Monastery Tackle the strenuous walk up eight hundred steps to be rewarded with a close-up viewing of Petra's largest and most imposing facade. See page 276

❻ High Place of Sacrifice A tough climb to this windblown summit reveals a mountaintop altar offering stunning views. See page 278

❼ Jabal Haroun Far off the beaten track stands one of Jordan's holiest sites – a shrine to Aaron, brother of Moses, perched on Petra's highest summit. See page 284

❽ Petra Kitchen Instead of another restaurant dinner, learn how to prepare a full three-course Jordanian feast – then consume your handiwork. See page 298

HIGHLIGHTS ARE MARKED ON THE MAP ON PAGE 252

the millennia following, but the spur to its development came with attempts at contact between the two great ancient powers of **Mesopotamia** and **Egypt**. The desert plateaux of Mesopotamia, to the east of the King's Highway, were sealed off by high mountains from the routes both across the Naqab (Negev) to Gaza and across the Sinai to Egypt; somehow a caravan route across the barrier had to be found if contact was to be made. Petra, where abundant springs tumble down into the Wadi Araba through a natural fault in the mountains, was prime choice, marking the spot on the north–south King's Highway where an east–west passage could connect the two empires.

The biblical era

The first significant mention of Petra is in the Old Testament, as the **Israelites** approached **Edom** after their forty years in the desert. Local legend – running against the geographical evidence – maintains that it was in the hills just above Petra that God ordered Moses to produce water for the Israelites by speaking to a rock. Moses instead struck the rock, and the spring that gushed is today named **Ain Musa** (Spring of Moses), its outflow housed beneath a small domed building at the eastern entrance to the town of Wadi Musa. **King Reqem** of Edom (Reqem was the Semitic name for Petra, and he was probably just a local chieftain) refused permission to the Israelites to

PETRA & WADI MUSA

0 2 kilometres

HIGHLIGHTS
1. Petra By Night
2. The Siq
3. The Treasury
4. East Cliff
5. The Monastery
6. High Place of Sacrifice
7. Jabal Haroun
8. Petra Kitchen

pass through his territory, but before they departed Moses' brother Aaron (Haroun in Arabic) died, and was buried supposedly on top of **Jabal Haroun** overlooking Petra. A white shrine atop the mountain is still a site of pilgrimage.

Just after 1000 BC, the Israelite **King David** moved to take control of Petra and the whole of Edom – by now rich on the proceeds of copper production as well as trade. His son **Solomon** consolidated the Israelite grip on trade and technology, and for fifty years diverted Petra's profits into his own coffers. However, after his death, the Israelite kingdom collapsed and feuding erupted. Some Edomites withdrew to a settlement on top of the impregnable **Umm al-Biyara** mountain overlooking central Petra and to a village at **Tawilan** above Ain Musa. Fluctuations in regional power soon after led to Petra passing from Edomite hands to **Assyrian** to **Babylonian** to **Persian**: such instability left the way open for a new people to stamp their authority on the land and stake a claim to its future.

The Nabateans

The first mention of the **Nabateans** was in 647 BC, when they were listed as one of the enemies of Ashurbanipal, last king of Assyria; at that stage, they were still a tribe of bedouin nomads inhabiting northern and northwestern Arabia. When the Babylonians depopulated much of Palestine during the sixth century BC, many Edomites came down from Petra to claim the empty land to the west. In turn, the Nabateans migrated out of the arid Arabian desert to the lusher and more temperate mountains of Edom, and, specifically, to the well-watered and easily defended prize of Petra. Whereas the Edomites had occupied the hills above Petra, the Nabateans quickly saw the potential for developing the central bowl of the valley floor. The migrants arrived slowly, though, and for several centuries it seems that most stuck to their bedouin lifestyle, building little other than a temple and refuge atop **Umm al-Biyara**. However, displaying the adaptability that was to become their trademark, the Nabateans soon gave up the traditional occupation of raiding the plentiful caravans that passed to and fro in favour of charging the merchants for safe passage and a place to do business. It was probably around this time that the first organized, permanent trading emporium was established at Petra, and Edom became known as **Arabia Petrea**.

The Roman author Diodorus Siculus reports that the Greek **Seleucid** ruler of Syria, **Antigonus**, attacked the Nabateans in 312 BC – though whether at Petra itself or another well-defended rocky hideout nearby is unknown; Sela (see page 238) is a candidate. Either way, his troops sneaked in under cover of darkness, and found that all the Nabatean men were away. The Greeks slaughtered a few women and children and made off with as much booty as they could carry – silver, myrrh and frankincense. However, someone managed to raise the alarm, since within an hour, the Nabateans were in pursuit. They rapidly caught up with the complacent army, massacred all but fifty, recovered the valuables and returned home. In true merchant style, though, the Nabateans instinctively recognized that war would do no good to their flourishing business, and so sent a mollifying letter of explanation to Antigonus. The general let some time pass before attacking again – only to be easily repelled. Comfortably ensconced in their unassailable headquarters, the Nabateans this time acted the wealthy tycoon: they bought peace from the humiliated Greeks.

Growth of Nabatean power

Over the following two centuries, the battling between Seleucid Syria and Ptolemaic Egypt for control of Alexander's empire enabled the Nabateans to fill the power vacuum in Transjordan and extend their kingdom far beyond Petra. By 80 BC they controlled Damascus. Petra grew ever more wealthy on its profits from **trade**, standing at the pivots between Egypt, Arabia and Syria, and between East Asia and the Mediterranean. Traditional commodities such as **copper, iron** and Dead Sea **bitumen**, used for embalming in Egypt, were losing ground to **spices** from the southern Arabian coast – myrrh, balsam and frankincense, the last of which was central to religious ritual all over the Hellenistic world. Pepper, ginger, sugar and cotton arrived from **India** for onward distribution. **Chinese** documents even talk of imports of silk, glass, gold, silver, henna and frankincense from a place known as Li-Kan, taken to be a corruption of "Reqem". Nabatean power seemed limitless. When **Pompey** sent troops against Petra in 62 BC, the Nabateans were even able to buy peace from the Roman Empire. Petran prosperity grew and grew.

Petra's golden age

The first centuries BC and AD saw Petra at its zenith, with a settled population of perhaps as many as thirty thousand. The Roman author **Strabo** describes it as a wealthy, cosmopolitan city, full of fine buildings and villas, gardens and watercourses, with Romans and other foreigners thronging the streets, and a democratic king. "The Nabateans", reported Strabo, "are so acquisitive that they give honours to those who increase their possessions, and publicly fine those who lose them."

However, the writing was on the wall. The discovery of the monsoon winds had begun to cause a shift in trade patterns: overland routes from Arabia were being abandoned in favour of transport by **sea**. In addition, Rome was diverting inland trade away from the upstart Petra, instead directing it into Egypt and Syria, presaging the rise of **Palmyra**. The pressure on Nabatea was inexorable. The last Nabatean king, **Rabbel II**, tried moving his capital from Petra north to Bosra, but eventually had to strike a deal with Rome. On his death in 106 AD the entire Nabatean kingdom passed peacefully into Roman hands.

The Romans and after

After the **Roman** annexation, Petra became a principal centre of the new Provincia Arabia, and seems to have undergone something of a cultural renaissance, with the theatre and Colonnaded Street both being renovated. The city was important enough to be visited by Emperor **Hadrian** in 130 AD, and possibly also by Emperor Severus in 199. However, the tide of history was turning, and by 300 Petra was in serious decline, with houses and temples falling derelict through lack of maintenance. Palmyra, an oasis entrepôt in the eastern Syrian desert, was on the ascendant, and sea trade into Egypt was well established; Petra was stuck between the two, and there was no reason to keep it alive. Roman patronage began to drift away from the city, and money followed.

Petra's decline was drawn out. **Christianity** was adopted as the official religion of the empire in 324, but for many decades afterwards the proud Nabateans mingled elements of the new faith with remnants of their own pagan heritage. An earthquake in 363, according to the contemporary bishop of Jerusalem, levelled half of Petra, although the city limped on for another couple of centuries. In 447, the **Urn Tomb** was converted into a huge church, and both the lavishly decorated **Petra Church** and plainer **Ridge Church** were built within the following century or so. Nonetheless, by the time of the seventh-century Islamic invasion, Petra was more or less deserted, and the earthquake of 749 probably forced the final stragglers to depart the crumbling city.

The Crusader era

On their push through Transjordan in the early twelfth century, the **Crusaders** built small forts within Petra at **Al-Habees** and **Wu'ayra**, though these were tiny outposts of their headquarters at nearby Shobak and were abandoned less than a century later. In 1276, the **Mamluke** sultan Baybars – on his way from Cairo to suppress a revolt in Karak – entered Petra from the southwest and proceeded through the deserted city "amidst most marvellous caves, the facades sculptured into the very rock face". He emerged from the Siq on June 6, 1276, and, as far as records show, was the last person, other than the local bedouin, to see Petra for over five hundred years.

"SHEIKH IBRAHIM" BURCKHARDT

Jean Louis Burckhardt was born in Lausanne, Switzerland, in 1784. He travelled to London when he was 22 and shortly after came under the wing of the Association for Promoting the Discovery of the Interior Parts of Africa, which offered him the mission of locating the source of the River Niger. Burckhardt accepted. Then, as now, Egypt was the gateway into Africa, and so he devised a plan to familiarize himself with Islam and Arab culture in preparation for the expedition. Journeys into the Middle East at this time were extremely dangerous: the territory was virtually unknown and local people (few of whom had ever seen Europeans) were engaged in continuous tribal skirmishing and were highly suspicious of outsiders. While still in England, Burckhardt embarked on crash courses in Arabic, astronomy and medicine, and took to sleeping on the ground and eating nothing but vegetables to toughen himself up.

On his arrival in Aleppo in 1809, locals immediately questioned him about his strange accent. Burckhardt told his cover story: that he was a Muslim trader from India and his mother tongue wasn't Arabic but Hindustani. Suspicion persisted, and he was pressed to say something in Hindustani, whereupon he let loose a volley of fluent Swiss-German – which seemed to satisfy the doubters. Burckhardt spent over two years in Aleppo, adopting local customs, taking the name **Sheikh Ibrahim ibn Abdallah**, perfecting his Arabic and becoming an expert in Quranic law.

In 1812, Burckhardt set off for Cairo, recording everything that he saw in a **secret journal**: had he been found out, no doubt he would have been killed as a spy. Around Karak, he heard the locals talking of an ancient city locked away in the heart of an impenetrable mountain. His curiosity was aroused, but there was no way he could openly declare an interest without bringing suspicion onto himself: a genuine devotee of Islam would know that such ruins were the work of infidels and of no concern. Burckhardt made up a story that he had vowed to sacrifice a goat at the shrine of the Prophet Aaron atop Jabal Haroun near the ruins: an unimpeachably honourable motive for pressing on.

As he and his guide approached Wadi Musa (then known by its old name of **Elji**), they were stopped by the Liyathneh tribe, camped near Ain Musa, who tried to persuade them to sacrifice their goat there and then, with the white shrine in plain view on the distant summit. But Sheikh Ibrahim insisted on going on, much to the irritation of his guide. They went down the steep hill, on into the Siq, and arrived at the Treasury. Burckhardt somehow managed to make detailed notes and a sketch of the facade, and they continued throughout the city in this way, Burckhardt writing and sketching in secret, his guide becoming ever more suspicious. They reached the foot of Jabal Haroun as dusk was falling, and Burckhardt finally submitted to his guide's insistence that they make the sacrifice and turn back.

Burckhardt's adventures continued: he arrived in Cairo to prepare for his great African expedition, but quickly got tangled in bureaucracy. In the meantime he travelled deep into Nubia, crossed the Red Sea to Jeddah (and was probably the first Christian ever to enter Mecca, where his Quranic learning deeply impressed the city's religious judge), and explored Sinai, but back in Egypt in 1817, he contracted dysentery and died in eleven days, with his journey to the Niger not even begun. All Burckhardt's journals were published after his death, *Travels in Nubia* and *Travels in Arabia* overshadowed by the news of his rediscovery of Petra, published in 1822 in ***Travels in Syria and the Holy Land***. His **grave**, bearing his pseudonym Sheikh Ibrahim, is visitable in a Muslim cemetery in Cairo. Its existence shows that, far from being simply a game or ploy, Burckhardt's alter ego took on a genuine life of its own.

Petra in the nineteenth century

On August 22, 1812, a Swiss explorer, Jean Louis **Burckhardt** (see above), entered the Siq in heavy Arab disguise in the company of a local guide. His short visit, and the notes and sketches he managed to make, brought the fable of Petra to the attention of the world once again. In 1818, two commanders of the British Royal Navy, Charles Irby and James Mangles, spent some days sightseeing in the ancient city, but it was the visits of **Léon de Laborde** in 1826 and the British artist **David Roberts** in 1839 that first brought plentiful images of Petra to the West. Laborde's engravings were often fanciful and over-romanticized, but Roberts's drawings were relatively accurate. As well as helping to shape the legend of Petra in Western minds – **Burgon**'s oft-quoted line about the "rose-red city" (see page 271) appeared within a few years – they also launched **tourism** to the place. The second half of the nineteenth century saw a steady trickle of earnest visitors, even though Petra could still be reached only with extreme hardship by horse or camel from Jerusalem. Serious archeological investigation began at the turn of the century, with specialists cataloguing all Petra's monuments in 1898 and producing the first accurate maps in 1925. The adjacent village – long known as **Elji**, then **Wadi Musa** (Moses Valley) – got its first telephone line in 1926.

The modern era

In 1931 the Thomas Cook travel company set up a camp in Petra for European tourists, offering the choice of tent or cave accommodation. It was followed in the 1950s by the first tourist hotel, the government-run *Rest House*. Nonetheless, until a regular bus service from Amman began in 1980, facilities around the site remained minimal. Wadi Musa town was a backwater, despite the designation of Petra as a national park. In the early 1980s the government ordered the **Bdul** tribe (see page 277), who had been resident in Petra's caves for as long as anyone could remember, to move out to **Umm Sayhoun**, a purpose-built settlement of small breezeblock houses 4km away. The prospect of electricity, running water, health care and better education for the kids proved irresistible, and, in dribs and drabs, the Bdul departed. Development of the site and archeological exploration then took off: Petra was named a **UNESCO World Heritage Site** in 1985, and four years later a group of concerned local establishment figures set up the **Petra National Trust** (PNT; ⓦ petranationaltrust.org), a not-for-profit NGO campaigning on issues of the environment, antiquities and the region's cultural heritage.

Today a buffer zone of over 750 square kilometres of land, from Shobak to well south of Rajif, is formally protected, while a core 264 square kilometres around the site itself is defined as the strictly regulated **Petra Archeological Park**. Recent years have seen a host of new projects, ranging from ongoing digs at several locations to major engineering works repaving the Siq, installing upgraded tourist facilities around the site and beautifying Wadi Musa town.

The ancient city

After you've finished dealing with the practicalities of transport and lodging in Wadi Musa (see page 289), **PETRA** comes as an assault on the senses. As you leave the entrance gate behind, the sense of exposure to the elements is thrilling; the natural drama of the location, the sensuous colouring of the sandstone, the stillness, heat and clarity of light – along with a lingering, under-the-skin quality of supernatural power that seems to seep out of the rock – make it an unforgettable adventure.

Whether you're in a group or alone, you'd do well to branch off the main routes every now and again. When tourism is buoyant, Petra can see three thousand visitors a day in peak season. The place is physically large enough to absorb that many (although archeologists and environmentalists lobby for controls on numbers), but the **central path** that runs past the major sights can get busy between about 10am and 4pm. Taking a ten- or fifteen-minute **detour** to explore either side of the path or wander along a side-valley is a good idea, since not only does it get you out of the hubbub, but it's also liable to yield previously unseen views and fascinating little carved niches or facades. All over Petra, the Nabateans carved for themselves paths and signposts, shrines and houses in what seem to us remote and desolate crags.

> ## PETRA: KEY DISTANCES
>
> **Petra** is approximately:
> - 250km south of **Amman** (3hr)
> - 125km north of **Aqaba** (1hr 45min)
> - 100km north of **Wadi Rum** (1hr 30min)
> - 50km south of **Dana** (1hr)

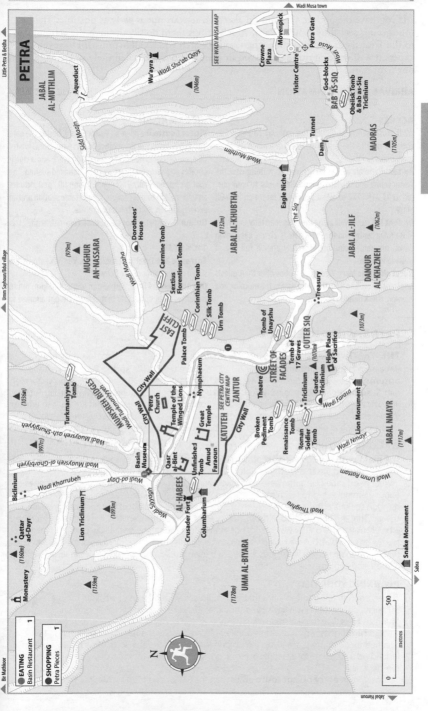

PETRA

6

EATING
Basin Restaurant 1

SHOPPING
Petra Pieces 1

6

If you have the option, you should also plan to start out as **early** as possible. The first tour groups set off by 8.30 or 9am, which brings them noisily through the echoing Siq to the Treasury as the sun strikes the facade (which you shouldn't miss). However, the experience of walking through the Siq in silence and alone is definitely worth at least one 6am start.

ARRIVAL AND INFORMATION   THE ANCIENT CITY

ACCESS

Wadi Musa (see page 289) is the gateway to Petra. The entrance gate to the Petra site lies 2km from Wadi Musa town centre.

By taxi There are always plenty of taxis waiting near the Visitor Centre and sharking around the streets; to book one, call ☎ 03 215 6777 or ask at your hotel reception in Wadi Musa.

On foot The steep walk along the main road between Wadi Musa town centre and the Petra gate is 2km – easy going down, miserable going up, especially after a full day of walking in Petra.

Hotel shuttles Many Wadi Musa hotels offer their guests free transport to and from the Petra gate in the morning and evening; check details in advance.

INFORMATION

Visitor Centre The open-air Visitor Centre, beside the gate into Petra, holds the ticket office (daily: 6am–5pm; winter till 4pm; ☎ 03 215 6044), the tour guide office and a clutch of cafés and souvenir shops, as well as shaded seating. The cool, a/c interior (daily: 7am–8pm; winter till 7pm) includes an information counter, toilets, comfortable seating and an excellent museum/interpretation centre.

Online ⓦ visitpetra.jo or ⓦ facebook.com/petravisit.

TICKETS

Entrance The ticket gate beside the Visitor Centre is the single public entrance into Petra.

Opening hours Daily: 6am–5pm; winter till 4pm; return permitted until dusk. Note that visitors are not allowed to

---

PETRA: WHAT TO EXPECT

THE WEATHER

Petra is up in the **mountains**, at around 1100m above sea level. In **spring** (March–May) and **autumn** (Sept–Oct) it is pleasantly warm, with highs around 25–30°C and virtually no chance of rain. In **summer** (late May to early Sept) it can be blisteringly hot during the day, perhaps above 40°C. However, with the altitude and the desert conditions, nights year-round are cool. In **winter** (Nov–Feb), Petra can be cold, often not getting above 10–15°C during the day and dropping below freezing at night: wind and rain are to be expected, and snow is not uncommon.

WALKING INTO PETRA

The **main path** through Petra's central valley starts at the ticket gate, leads through the Siq, past the Treasury and the Theatre to the Colonnaded Street, ending at the Qasr al-Bint.

Wear good shoes. From the gate, if you walk at a reasonable pace without stopping, it takes about 25 minutes just to reach the Treasury, downhill on stony ground all the way. From the gate through to Petra's city centre is more than 3km, the gentle gradient of five percent concealing the fact that the drop in altitude (from 1027m to 861m) is equivalent to a forty-storey skyscraper – barely noticeable on the way down, but murder for tired thighs on the way back up. Walking on stones isn't too bad, but walking on sand can be exhausting – and struggling across the stretches of worn, uneven Roman flagstones in the Siq is even worse. You can – in the Siq at least – resort to a horse-and-carriage (see page 260).

PLANNING YOUR TIME

There's enough to explore in Petra that you could easily spend days or weeks in the place. Shelling out for a one-day ticket will have you running around like crazy to get value for money; paying for four days buys time to pace yourself.

Major **highlights**, which count as unmissable, are the Siq, the Treasury, the High Place of Sacrifice, the Monastery, a walk up the Colonnaded Street, and the Royal Tombs. With a break for lunch, and a little time for personal exploration, seeing all this would occupy a pretty exhausting ten-hour day.

Choosing an **entry or exit route** other than the Siq for one trip – via Madras, Wadi Muthlim/

stay in Petra after sunset, and you may be asked to start on the long walk out well in advance. In any case it's potentially dangerous to do some of the longer descents (such as from the Monastery or the High Place) in low light.

Tickets Entry costs a frankly outrageous JD50 for one day, JD55 for two days, or JD60 for three or four days. This refers to blocks of consecutive days, with no chopping and changing allowed. The longer you stay, the better value you receive on each day's admission. If you flew to Jordan with Turkish Airlines, show your boarding pass to receive a 15 percent discount. Children under 15 go free, as do holders of the Jordan Pass (see page 55). If you come to Petra directly from the border or airport on your first day in Jordan, you may be charged the extortionate day-tripper rate (JD90) – if so, go back to the ticket office next morning to get JD40 back

(or JD35 back, if you want to re-enter for a second day).

How to pay Tickets are sold only from the Visitor Centre. Payment is in Jordanian dinars (no other currencies are accepted) or by credit card. Expect queues for tickets in the morning peak period (8–10am).

Ticket checks Tickets are dated, personalized and non-transferable, with ID checks in place; you may find a proposed system of e-ticketing has been brought in, further clamping down on the possibility of fare-dodging. Tickets are checked at varying points within Petra; even if you hike several kilometres out of the way to avoid the gate, there's no guarantee a police officer won't pop up on some remote crag and ask to see your ticket. Note that Little Petra, Beidha and Wu'ayra currently fall outside the (undefined) ticketed area, and so have free entry.

GETTING AROUND

Other than clambering aboard one of the camels or threadbare donkeys, whose handlers roam the main paths touting for customers (prices are very negotiable), the only way to get around Petra is on foot – and you can **walk** unguided to and from almost all of the main sights while comfortably staying this side of foolhardiness.

Nonetheless, there are some more remote spots where taking a guide would be prudent. We've mentioned this in our accounts where relevant. Aside from the dangers of twisted ankles (or worse) scrambling around rocky cliffs, once you leave the main routes it's easy to lose the path.

Mataha or Wadi Turkmaniyyeh – can give you a feel for outlying landscapes. Depending on your taste for archeology or nature, you could then devote more time to exploring the city-centre slopes and the East Cliff, or choose one or two of the many hikes and climbs.

With **Little Petra** (Siq al-Barid) being free-entry, plan a visit for the morning after your Petra ticket has expired.

It's also worth timing your trip to coincide with a Monday, Wednesday or Thursday – these are the days when **Petra By Night** operates.

There are **benches** at strategic points all the way down the main path, and **toilets** at various points throughout the site. Around the Theatre are clustered several little **tent cafés**, offering tea, coffee, cold drinks and light snacks; the only **restaurants** are down by the Qasr al-Bint (see page 275). Full details of **hotels** and **transport** come later in this chapter (see page 294).

MUSEUM AND INTERPRETATION CENTRE

By the time you read this, a major new JD5 million **museum** will be open alongside the Visitor Centre. If the standard of the **interpretation centre** it replaces was anything to go by, the museum will be excellent, and worth an hour or two of your time. With well-written information boards examining every detail of Petra's history and Nabatean society, and a carefully chosen illustrative selection of artefacts and statuary, it will deepen and broaden your experience of the ruins. The best advice is to visit before you enter the site – and since the Visitor Centre stays open until 8pm (winter 7pm), you could drop by the evening before you head into Petra for the first time.

FUTURE PLANS

Plans were in train, at the time of writing, to consolidate and surface the stony Wadi Turkmaniyyeh "**backroad**", leading from behind the *Basin Restaurant* out to the Bdul village of Umm Sayhoun. This means that when you've finished your day in Petra, instead of having to walk back up through the whole site to exit through the Siq, you could opt to board a free **shuttle bus** at the restaurant and be driven back direct to Wadi Musa. The scheme may already be running when you visit – ask around for details.

6

GUIDES

In the Visitor Centre is a tour guide office (daily: 6am–4pm; winter 7am–3pm), where you can hire a professional, accredited guide on a rota system at fixed prices. For JD50 on top of your entrance ticket, a guide will take you on a basic 90min tour of the major sights. JD100 buys a guide for the main sights plus either the High Place of Sacrifice or the Monastery. To be guided to other outlying sites, such as Jabal Haroun or Sabra, costs even more: check current prices when you visit.

HORSES

Horses and handlers Petra is famous for its horses, which are stabled alongside the gate. These 350-odd animals generate an income for more than 1200 families in Wadi Musa. As you walk past you'll be targeted by the handlers, proposing a horse-ride from the gate down to the dam at the entrance to the Siq – a walk of about 800m. Bizarrely, you've already paid for this: it's unavoidably wrapped into the cost of your entrance ticket. However, the horse owners (who get the financial benefit) are almost without exception not the people holding the reins. The only income gained by the handlers is in tips. If you agree to a ride, expect to hear a sob story on the way down, and then a firm (and not always friendly) request for extra money before you're allowed to dismount.

Carriages It's forbidden to ride horses through the Siq, but a horse-and-carriage seating two can be taken all the way through the Siq to the Treasury, for JD20 return. For the return leg, there are always plenty of carriages at the Treasury waiting for business from tired sightseers as the afternoon draws on, but if you arrange with a particular carriage-driver to be at the Treasury at a set time for your return ride, he will turn up: his fee depends on it. Resist the temptation to copy the many weary visitors who just get into the first carriage they see; this a breach of honour, and also leads to underhand competition between carriage-drivers to muscle in on each other's business. Ugly arguments over cash between two stalled carriages in the Siq are a feature of Petra afternoons. You can also take a carriage right through from the gate to the *Basin Restaurant* (JD40 return): this must be booked in advance at the Visitor Centre.

Mistreatment If you see a horse or donkey being mistreated, refer the matter either to the Visitor Centre or direct to the Petra Development and Tourism Region Authority (W pdtra.gov.jo); complaints are taken seriously. The PDTRA heads the international "Care for Petra" campaign on responsible tourism – one of its three core issues is the welfare of working animals. More than twenty years of work in Petra by the Brooke (W thebrooke.org), an English-run horse charity, has improved standards, bringing benefits such as professional farriery, provided by the Jordanian Horse Owners Association, and subsidized veterinary treatment.

EATING

There are only limited facilities for **eating** inside Petra – and prices are high (understandably, considering everything has to be trucked in). Along the path near the theatre are stalls offering tea and snacks, while around the Qasr al-Bint you'll find **tent café-restaurants** offering adequate – sometimes pretty good – buffet lunches for about JD10–14. The only formal restaurant in Petra itself is the *Basin Restaurant*. Your best option is to **carry supplies** with you for the day. All Wadi Musa hotels (see page 294) can provide a **lunchbox** on request – at a budget hotel, reckon on JD5–8 for bread, cheese, fruit, yoghurt and a drink. Groceries and minimarkets in the centre of Wadi Musa can provide simple **picnic fare**, and the town-centre Sanabel bakery, just below the Shaheed Roundabout, is open from before dawn. Bear in mind that in the summer you'll need to be drinking four or five litres of **water** a day, possibly more; unless you can carry it all, you should budget on shelling out JD2 at the tent cafés for a 1.5-litre bottle of water or a soft drink to keep yourself hydrated along the way.

Basin Restaurant Opposite the Qasr al-Bint ✆ 03 215 6266; map p.257. Situated beneath shady tree cover, the *Basin Restaurant* is run by the *Crowne Plaza* hotel, with whom it's a good idea to book in advance on the number above: busy times can see tour groups occupying every table. Buffet lunch, including a full range of salad dishes, falafel, barbecue/kebabs and dessert, costs JD18 – but it's barely worth it. Unless you're a dedicated carnivore, go for the salads-only option, at roughly half the price. They have cold beer in cans and on draught (JD6–8). Daily 11.30am–4pm, depending on weather conditions.

SHOPPING

Petra Pieces On the right of the path as you walk down from the theatre W marriedtoabedouin.com; map p.257. Unique silver jewellery, designed and handmade by local women and sold only at this stall inside Petra run by local author Marguerite van Geldermalsen, known as Umm Raami (see page 267).

Bab as-Siq

From the Petra entrance gate, a modern gravel path – one side for horses, the other for pedestrians – leads down through a lunar landscape of white rocky domes and looming

PETRA BY NIGHT

In times gone by, a visit to Petra wasn't complete without spending a night in the ruins, wandering the rocky paths by moonlight and sleeping in a tomb cave. This is now banned – which led an informal group of Wadi Musa tour operators to come up with a new approach to Petra that aims to recapture some of that romantic spirit of adventure (and largely succeeds). **Petra By Night** is an after-dark guided excursion into the ancient city that adds an entirely new dimension to your experience of the place; the **candlelit walk**, leaving the lights of Wadi Musa behind to enter the pitch-dark valley in silence (talking and mobile phones are banned), is magical. Nothing can match the atmosphere of walking through the Siq at night, with only the light of candles placed every few metres to guide the way. The climax comes as you reach the Treasury plaza, where candles throw flickering shadows onto the great facade as a **bedouin musician** plays on a pipe. The magic lingers while tea is served and you listen to a **story** told by a local guide.

PRACTICALITIES

Petra By Night runs every Monday, Wednesday and Thursday, departing at **8.30pm** from the Visitor Centre (arrive 15min early), and delivers you back to the Visitor Centre around 10.30pm. Tickets cost a pretty hefty JD17, in addition to your Petra admission ticket. You must **book in advance** – even just a couple of hours ahead is fine – either through your hotel or directly with a local tour company, such as Petra Moon (see page 295).

The walk has become so popular that it's not uncommon to have 150 or 200 people setting out together. The best advice in these circumstances is to linger at the very back of the crowd: that way, you avoid most of the chatter on the way down and will be walking through the Siq more or less alone in the moonlight. The bedouin piper keeps playing until everyone has arrived at the Treasury, so you won't miss anything. Then there's nothing to stop you heading back early, before the crowd, for another lonesome walk in silence through the Siq, beneath moon and stars. But, either way, and notwithstanding the guide's urgent pleas for silence, be prepared to have to put up with other people's noise, laughter, chit-chat and – of course – camera flashes. It's rarely reverential.

cliffs known as the **Bab as-Siq** ("Gate of the Siq"). The bed of the Wadi Musa, carrying water during the winter and early spring, curves alongside. In all but the bleached-out midday hours, the light is soft enough to pick up earth tones of browns and beiges in the rock, but it's only with the last rays of the sunset that there's any hint of the pink that Petra is famous for.

Almost immediately, you can see evidence of Nabatean endeavour: three huge **god-blocks**, 6 to 8m high, loom next to the path just round the first corner, carved probably to serve as both representations of and repositories for the gods to stand sentinel over the city's vital water supply. Twenty-five such god-blocks exist in Petra, deemed by the locals to have been the work of *jinn*, or genies, and so also termed **jinn-blocks**; another name is **sahrij**, or water tanks (which has been loosely interpreted to mean tanks holding divine energy next to flowing water). The middle one has shaft graves cut into it, implying that it may also have served as some kind of funerary monument. Opposite the god-blocks are **caves**, one of which has an obelisk carved in relief, representing the soul of a dead person. Such carved shrines abound in every corner of Petra's mountains – for those with time to explore, the small side-valleys off this section of the Bab as-Siq, filled with tombs, water channels, niches and shrines, are worth seeking out. Behind the blocks, the area of domes known as **Ramleh** is cut through by parallel wadis, one of which is Wadi Muthlim (see page 263), and is equally explorable.

Obelisk Tomb and Bab as-Siq Triclinium

ⓦ auac.ch/iap

The first major Nabatean monuments are a few metres further on from the first god-blocks, and – being on an exposed corner – badly eroded. Although apparently the upper and lower halves of a single monument, the **Obelisk Tomb** and **Bab as-Siq**

6

NABATEAN RELIGION

As much as they created a blend of Arab culture with Mediterranean, the **Nabateans** also blended inherited elements of the ancient **religions** of Egypt, Syria, Canaan, Assyria and Babylon with elements of the Greek and Roman pantheons, to create specifically Petran forms of worship.

Central to their religion was **rock**. Jehovah, the god of the Israelites, was said to inhabit a blank rock called **Bet-El** ("House of God") – and this insistence on nonfigurative representation was shared by many Levantine and Arabian peoples. It was passed on to the Nabateans, in contrast to the Egyptians' and Assyrians' lavish portrayals of gods and goddesses. Concepts such as "the Lord is my rock" also appear many times in the Old Testament, implying an extension of the "House of God" idea so that the rock actually represents the deity itself. Nabatean deities were thus often represented simply by squared-off rocks, termed "**god-blocks**". In addition, a later development gave the rock a third aspect: that of the altar, the contact point between the divine and the material.

At the head of the Nabatean pantheon was **Dushara**, "He of the Shara" (the mountains around Petra), later identified with the Greek god Zeus and the Syrian Hadad. The fact that his name is so closely tied to the locality indicates that he may originally have been an Edomite, rather than a Nabatean, god. To the Nabateans, Dushara was the sun, the Creator, and he was often represented by an obelisk – the visual materialization of a beam of light striking the earth. With the mingling of Semitic and Mediterranean ideas, Dushara also came to be associated with Dionysus, god of wine, and so began to assume human form, bedecked with vines and grapes (as at the Nabatean temple on Jabal Tannur).

At Dushara's side were **Atargatis**, the goddess of fertility, of grain, fruit and fish; **Allat** (which means simply "The Goddess"), who represented the moon; **Manat**, the goddess of luck and fate, suggested to have been the patron deity of Petra and possibly the goddess worshipped at the Treasury; and **al-Uzza** ("The Mighty One"), assimilated with the Egyptian goddess Isis and the Roman goddesses Diana, deity of water and fertility, and Venus, embodied by the evening star and representing spiritual and erotic love. Allat, al-Uzza and Manat are all mentioned by name in the Quran, implying that their cult was still active and popular in Mecca as late as the seventh century, the time of the Prophet Muhammad.

The Nabateans also had many smaller gods, including **al-Kutbay**, god of writing; **She'a-al-Qawm**, the patron deity of caravans; **Qos**, originally an Edomite god; and **Baal-Shamin**, a Phoenician god especially popular in northern Nabatea, who had a temple somewhere near the modern mosque in the centre of Wadi Musa town.

Triclinium may be separate entities, carved at different times. Above, four pyramidal obelisks guard the entrance to a cave in the rock; such freestanding obelisks may have been like the god-blocks, representing a god and storing divine energy in a material form. Between the four is an eroded figure in a niche; the cave behind holds graves. Below, the *triclinium*, or dining room, is a single chamber with stone benches on three walls, for holding banquets in honour of the dead. On the opposite side of the path, 5m off the ground, a bilingual **inscription** in Nabatean and Greek records that one Abdmank chose this spot to build a tomb for himself and his children, although it's not certain that this refers to the monuments opposite.

Madras

Just past the Obelisk Tomb is a path leading to the hidden Petran suburb of **Madras**, tucked into the hills to the left (south), from where it's possible to cross the hilltops over the Jabal al-Jilf plateau, avoiding the Siq, to the top of the high, narrow Danqur al-Khazneh Valley leading down to the Treasury. The views are stunning, and the sense of isolation is worth the scramble if you've already seen the Siq. However, the route is far from clear, relying on worn Nabatean rock-cut stairs, and you'll need a guide.

The dam and tunnel

The curving northern bank of the wadi is liberally pockmarked with caves and niches, round to the point where the path is taken over the wadi bed by a bridge and the Wadi

Musa itself is blocked by a modern **dam**. This is almost exactly the same configuration as was built by the Nabateans in about 50 AD, and for the same reasons: to divert the floodwaters of the Wadi Musa away from the Siq so that the principal entry into the city could remain clear year round. On the opposite bank of the wadi are four obelisks, one mentioning a man who lived in Reqem (Petra) but died in Jerash.

It's here, at the mouth of the Siq, that all horse riders must dismount. Entrance tickets are sometimes checked. To the right, the Nabatean-carved, 8m-high **tunnel** – guarded by another, solitary god-block – enabled the floodwaters to feed into the Wadi Muthlim leading north around the gigantic Jabal al-Khubtha. Today, this is an alternative way into Petra (see below).

6

The Siq

From the crowded, horse-smelly bridge, the path drops sharply down over the lip of the dam into Petra's most dramatic and awe-inspiring natural feature – the **Siq** (meaning "gorge"), principal entrance into the city, yet invisible until you're almost upon it.

The Siq was formed when **tectonic forces** split the mountain in two. The waters of the Wadi Musa subsequently found their way into the fault, laying a bed of gravel and eroding the sharp corners into curves as smooth as eggshell, helped by the cool winds that blow in your face all the way down. At the entrance to the gorge, the path was originally framed overhead by an ornamental **arch**, which collapsed in 1896 although its abutments survive, decorated by the smoothed-out remnants of niches flanked by pilasters.

Walking the Siq

The path along the wadi bed twists and turns between high, bizarrely eroded sandstone cliffs for 1.2km, sometimes widening to form broad, sunlit open spaces in the echoing heart of the mountain, dotted with a tree or two and cut through by the cries of birds;

THE WADI MUTHLIM ROUTE

Although you should definitely follow the Siq into Petra at least once (and probably more than once, at different times of day), if you've allocated several days to a visit, the beautiful **Wadi Muthlim** is a good alternative entry route through stunning scenery, but taking no less than two hours to deliver you to the Nymphaeum in the city centre. Due to the very real danger of flash floods, you shouldn't attempt it at all during the rainy season – roughly November to March – and even as late as May, there may be difficult-to-avoid standing pools of water harbouring water snakes: wading would be a mistake.

Before beginning the walk, you can take a small detour from the dam at the Siq entrance up to the **Eagle Niche**, set in the rocks 400m to the northwest. Cross the wadi over the roof of the tunnel and head left up the second side-valley; it's a short scramble over the smooth, hot rock up to a set of small niches carved in the right-hand wall, one of which features a strikingly carved eagle with wings outspread.

Back at the tunnel, Wadi Muthlim – full of oleanders, but with high walls cutting out all sound bar the occasional birdsong – is easily passable up to the remains of another Nabatean dam; beyond here, the path gets steadily narrower until you reach a point where a massive boulder all but blocks the way. It's possible to squeeze past, and the path continues to narrow until, with the wadi floor no wider than your foot, you reach a T-junction; arrows on the solid walls all around will point you left. This cross-wadi is the **Sidd Maajn**, equally narrow, but beautifully eroded by flowing water. As you proceed, seemingly moving through the heart of the mountain, you'll notice the Nabateans were here before you: there are dozens of carved niches, some featuring pediments, other curving horns. It's around here that the way might be blocked by rockpools.

Eventually, you'll emerge into the open **Wadi Mataha** (see page 287), about 600m northeast of Dorotheos' House, and the best part of 2km northeast of the Nymphaeum.

6

in other places, the looming 150m-high walls close in to little more than a couple of metres apart, blocking out sound, warmth and even daylight.

All the way along the left-hand wall is a Nabatean rock-cut **water channel**, and on the right-hand wall you'll see the remains of terracotta pipes for water, both probably dating from the same time as the reorganization of the city water supply that prompted the building of the dam. At various points, you'll be walking over worn patches of the **Roman/Nabatean road** which originally paved the Siq along its entire length, in between stretches of newly consolidated pathway. High, narrow wadis feed into the Siq from either side, most of them blocked by modern dams (often set back to show the remains of the original Nabatean dams) to limit both flood danger and unauthorized exploration: once you're in the Siq, the only way is onward or backward.

Dotted along the walls at many points are small **votive niches**, some Greek-style with pediments, others with mini god-blocks. After about 350m, a small **shrine** has been carved on the downhill side of a freestanding outcrop of rock, with two god-blocks, the larger of which is carved with eyes and a nose. A little further on, on the left-hand wall at a sharp right-hand bend, is a merchant in Egyptian-style dress leading two large **camels**; the water channel originally ran behind all five sets of legs, and it's just possible to trace the worn outline of the camels' humps in the rock wall.

When you think the gorge can't possibly go on any longer, there comes a dark, narrow defile, framing at its end a strip of elegant Classical architecture. With your eye softened to the natural flows of eroded rock in the Siq, the clean lines of columns and pediments come as a revelation. As you step out into the daylight, there is no more dramatic or breathtaking vision in the whole of Jordan than the facade of the Treasury.

The Treasury

Perfectly positioned opposite the main route into Petra, the **Treasury** (*al-Khazneh* in Arabic) was designed to impress, and, two thousand years on, the effect is undiminished. What strikes you first is how well preserved it is; carved deep into the rock face and concealed in a high-walled ellipse of a valley (known as Wadi al-Jarra, "Urn Valley"), it has been protected from wind and rain from day one. The detailing of the capitals and pediments on the 40m by 30m facade is still crisp. It is normally dated to the first century BC, possibly to the reign of King Aretas III Philhellene ("the Greek-lover"), who brought architects to Petra from the centres of Hellenistic culture throughout the Mediterranean.

The best times to view the Treasury are when the sun strikes it directly, between about 9 and 11am, and late in the afternoon, around 5 or 6pm, when the whole facade is suffused with a reflected reddish-pink glow from the walls all around.

To the left of the facade, a set of stairs comes down into the valley from the Danqur al-Khazneh area. Off to the right, a wall blocks the narrow north end of the Wadi al-Jarra; if you climb over the wall, then double back to scramble up the rocks, you'll reach a small, jutting **plateau**, with a perfect view from above of the Treasury and the whole bustling plaza in front of it.

The Treasury facade

The **carvings** on the **Treasury facade**, though much damaged by iconoclasts, are still discernible and show to what extent Nabatean culture was an amalgam of elements from the Hellenistic and Middle Eastern worlds.

Atop the broken pediments, framing the upper storey, are two large **eagles**, symbols of the Nabateans' chief male deity, **Dushara**. In a central position on the rounded *tholos* below the urn is what's been identified as a representation of **Isis**, an Egyptian goddess equated with the Nabatean goddess al-Uzza. In the recesses behind are two **Winged Victories**, although the remaining four figures, all of whom seem to

6

be holding axes aloft, haven't been identified. Two **lions**, also symbolizing al-Uzza, adorn the entablature between the two storeys. At ground level, the mounted riders are **Castor and Pollux**, sons of Zeus. The parallel marks up the side of the facade, which occur in a couple of other places in Petra, may well have been footholds for the sculptors and masons.

One column is obviously new, a brick-and-plaster replacement for the original, which fell in antiquity. This neatly demonstrates one of the most extraordinary features of **Nabatean architecture**. A normal building that lost a main support like this would have come crashing down soon after; these Nabatean columns, though, support nothing. Like most of Petra's surviving monuments, the entire Treasury "building" was sculpted *in situ*, gouged out of the unshaped rock in a kind of reverse architecture.

At the base of the facade, **excavations** into the 4m of gravel that overlie the original Nabatean road surface revealed that the Treasury was carved above a line of older facades, also probably **tombs**, which are now viewable through a grille set into the ground.

The Treasury interior

Inside the Treasury doorway – unlike the scene in *Indiana Jones and the Last Crusade*, when Indy finds stone lions and Crusader seals set into the floor – there's only a blank **square chamber**, with smaller rooms opening off it, the entrance portico flanked by rooms featuring unusual round windows above their doors. Access to the interior is barred, but you may be able to poke your nose in. The function of the Treasury is unknown, but a significant clue is the recessed **basin** on its threshold with a channel leading outside, clearly for libations or ritual washing. None of Petra's tomb-monuments has this feature, but the High Place of Sacrifice does, suggesting that the Treasury may have been a place of worship, possibly a tomb-temple.

The Outer Siq

Beyond the Treasury, the path – known here as the **Outer Siq** – broadens and is lined with tombs in varying states of erosion. Steps lead up to a large cavern on the right, lined with benches inside. Opposite is a line of tombs at different heights, showing how the wadi floor rose during Nabatean occupation of Petra; most are badly eroded. One has the crow-step ornamental design that originated in Assyria and was adapted by the Nabateans to reappear in dozens of Petra's facades: a band of rising and falling zigzags running horizontally across the top of the facade. As the path broadens, in the corner of the right-hand cliff – pointed to by the terracotta pipe that has emerged from the Siq – is the restored **Tomb of 17 Graves**. If you look up and to the left of it, you'll spot one of the clearest examples of Nabatean facade-building; the **Tomb of Unayshu** (see page 268) presents a sharp profile of a clean Classical facade facing left, carved from a rough outcrop of rock behind that looks barely capable of supporting it.

Street of Facades

As the Outer Siq opens up, the path curves left to expose the **Street of Facades**, an agglomeration of dozens of facades carved side by side out of the rock on at least four different levels. Most are simple, cornice-free designs, probably some of the earliest carving in Petra.

It's around here that you'll come across the first of Petra's many **cafés**, offering water, shade and soft drinks. You'll also spot steps signposted to the left which begin the short but steep climb to the High Place of Sacrifice (see page 278), a spectacular addition to a standard walking tour.

6

Theatre

Just past the Street of Facades sits Petra's massive **Theatre**. Obviously Classical in design and inspiration, it's nonetheless been dated to the first century AD, before the Romans annexed Nabatea but at a time when links between the two powers must have been strong. Though the Romans refurbished the building after they took over in 106, the basic design is **Hellenistic**, with seats coming right down to the orchestra's floor level. As many as 8500 people could be accommodated, more even than in the vast theatre at Amman. Aside from the stage backdrop and the ends of the banks of seating, the entire edifice was carved out of the mountainside; one whole row of tombs was wiped out to form the back wall of the auditorium, leaving some of their interiors behind as incongruous gaps. Recent renovation work has built up the stage area, with its niches in front and elaborate *scaenae frons* behind (tumbled in the earthquake of 363), the high back wall of which would have sealed off the theatre from the street outside.

The path continues past cafés and stalls on both sides down to a point at which the Wadi Musa turns sharp left (west) into the city centre (see page 289). Straight ahead the valley opens up towards Beidha, with the Wadi Mataha (see page 287) coming

---

MARRIED TO A BEDOUIN

When New Zealander **Marguerite van Geldermalsen** came to Petra on holiday in 1978, she fell in love with a local souvenir-seller – and then stayed with him to get married, settle down and raise a family. In 2006 she published *Married To A Bedouin* (W marriedtoabedouin. com; see page 389), a wonderfully evocative account of their life together. Here, Marguerite reflects on the changes she has witnessed.

"I started writing Married To A Bedouin *when I realised how much our way of life had changed.*

When Mohammad and I were married in Petra in 1978, about seventy families lived in the ancient site; some in tents of woven goat-hair and others, like us, in 2000-year-old caves. They herded goats, planted winter crops and sold trinkets and old coins to the tourists. I learned to live like them – carting water from the spring, baking bread on an open fire and using kerosene for our lamps.

In 1985 we were moved to the overlooking hillside of Umm Sayhoon, partly to protect the archeological site but also to improve our quality of life with running water and electricity. Our children attended the village school and we became commuters – going into Petra to tend our souvenir and coffee shops, then riding home on camels and donkeys to turn on our televisions, put laundry into our washing machines and, eventually, hook up to the internet.

Mohammad and I had been married 24 years when he died. Soon after, I left Jordan. I felt my reason for living there had gone.

Now I understand that I left to write my story; I needed the distance to see clearly. Although Mohammad is no longer in Petra, through him I have become woven into the fabric of the place. In 2007 I returned – and settled straight back in."

Today Marguerite – known as Umm Raami – still lives and works in Petra. You'll spot her **stall** (see page 260) on the right of the path as you walk down from the theatre, near the bathrooms: Marguerite is there every day, selling her book (which she will sign for you) as well as unique silver jewellery designed and made by local women. It's a perfect opportunity to inject a little cash into the local economy.

6

in from the northeast, while way up to the right, some of Petra's grandest monuments have been etched into the East Cliff.

East Cliff

About 250m beyond the theatre, just before the Wadi Musa makes its sharp left turn, modern steps lead to the **East Cliff**, looming up to the right. This whole elbow of Jabal al-Khubtha is ranged with some of Petra's most impressive facades, collectively known as the **Royal Tombs**. If you have anything more than half a day in Petra, you should fit them in; the climb is easy and the views are marvellous. From down below, in the direct, reddish light of late afternoon, the entire cliff seems to glow with an inner translucence, and is one of the most striking sights of Petra. However, it's probably best to aim to be up here in the morning shadows, with the sun lighting up the valley and the mountains opposite.

From **right to left**, the first tomb on the cliff – separate from the big ones, and missable if you're short of time – is the **Tomb of Unayshu**, viewed in profile from the Outer Siq and easiest to get to by scrambling up the rocks opposite the High Place staircase. This is part of a complete Nabatean tomb complex, and features a once-porticoed courtyard in front, with a *triclinium* to one side.

Urn Tomb

Heading north from the Tomb of Unayshu, past another well-preserved tomb facade, you join the modern steps leading up to the soaring facade of the **Urn Tomb**, with its large colonnaded forecourt partially supported on several storeys of arched vaults. The Bdul know the tomb as Al-Mahkamah, "**the Court**", dubbing the vaults As-Sijin, "**the Jail**". Whether or not it was later used in this way, the whole structure would seem originally to have been the tomb of somebody extremely important, quite probably one of the Nabatean kings – but who exactly isn't known. Set into the facade high above the forecourt between the engaged columns are spaces for three bodies; this is a unique configuration in Petra, since such *loculi* are normally inside the monument, and they seem to have been placed here as an indication of the importance of their occupants. The central one – possibly that of the king himself – is still partially sealed by a stone which formerly depicted the bust of a man wearing a toga. The urn which gave the tomb its name is at the very top.

Due, no doubt, to its dominating position in the city's landscape, the Urn Tomb was later converted into a major **church**, possibly Petra's cathedral; the large interior room features, near the left-hand corner of the back wall, a Greek inscription in red paint recording the dedication of the church by Bishop Jason in 447 AD. Probably at the same time, two central recesses of the original four were combined to make a kind of apse, and myriad holes were drilled in the floor to support all the relevant ecclesiastical furniture: chancel screens, a pulpit, maybe a table, and so on.

The **view** from the forecourt, which takes in the full sweep of the valley (and even the urn atop the Monastery), is one of Petra's best.

Silk Tomb

Working your way around the cliff from the Urn Tomb, you'll come to the **Silk Tomb**, unremarkable but for its brilliant colouring. It was named for its streaks of vibrant colour, from pinks and blues to yellows and ochres, which appeared to archeologists and historians similar to the rippled sheen of moire (watered or "shot" silk).

Corinthian Tomb

Next to the Silk Tomb, the facade of the **Corinthian Tomb** (named by a nineteenth-century visitor, though it's Nabatean, not Corinthian) is something like a squat, hybrid Treasury. It has the Treasury's style on the upper level – a *tholos* flanked by a broken pediment – but below, it's a mess, the symmetry thrown out by extra doors on the left. It has also suffered badly at the hands of the wind. However, such an exposed position on the corner of the cliff – directly in line with the Colonnaded Street – points to the fact that, like the Urn Tomb, this may well have been the tomb of another Nabatean king, visible from everywhere in the city.

Palace Tomb

Adjacent to the Corinthian Tomb is an even more ramshackle jumble, the very broad **Palace Tomb**, boasting one of Petra's largest facades. It has at least five different storeys, the top portions of which were built of masonry because the cliff turned out to be too low, and so subsequently collapsed. The unevenly spaced line of engaged columns on the second row clashes nastily with the orthodox lower level. Protected by the cliff, the extreme right-hand edge of the facade still has some sharply carved detail surviving.

Sextius Florentinus Tomb

From the Palace Tomb, tracks lead west towards the city centre. Continue hugging the cliff northeast to find the peaceful **Sextius Florentinus Tomb**, positioned facing north where a finger of the cliff reaches the ground. Sextius Florentinus was a Roman governor of the Province of Arabia who died about 130 AD, and must have chosen to be buried in Petra rather than in the provincial capital of Bosra. The facade of his tomb, with a graceful semicircular pediment, is one of the most charming in the city.

Carmine Tomb

A few metres north of Sextius Florentinus, behind a tree, stands the spectacular **Carmine Tomb**, girt with breathtaking bands of colour, but, by virtue of its position, hardly ever noticed. Wadi Zarnug al-Khubtha, which divides the two, holds a path which gives reasonably easy, if steep, access to little-visited High Places and a few scattered ruins perched atop the massive **Jabal al-Khubtha**, the main barrier standing between Petra and Wadi Musa town. The views from on top are tremendous – especially of the theatre – but you'd have to be keen (and sure-footed) to try it.

We cover the continuation of this path, northeast along the Wadi Mataha, later in the chapter (see page 287).

Petra city centre

As you round the corner of the path leading from the theatre, **Petra city centre**, focused along the Cardo Maximus, or **Colonnaded Street**, stretches out ahead, framed by the barrier range of mountains – and the flat-topped giant Umm al-Biyara – behind. Although there are excavations continuing on the flat, rounded hills to either side, the overall impression is of rocky desolation; nonetheless, in Petra's prime, the landscape in all directions was covered with buildings – houses big and small, temples, market-places – all of them long since collapsed. Many archeologists theorize that most of Petra is in fact still hidden beneath the dusty soil, and that all the facades and what few buildings have so far been exposed are the tip of the iceberg.

Until you reach the Temenos at the far end of the Colonnaded Street, the only monument actually on the street is the Nymphaeum, although both the northern (right-hand) and southern (left-hand) slopes hold plenty of interest.

Nymphaeum

One of the few trees in the city centre – a huge, lush pistachio – stands proudly over the ruined **Nymphaeum**, originally a Roman public fountain, these days more popular as a shady hangout for the bedouin police than anything else. Virtually nothing remains of the ancient superstructure, and even the retaining wall is modern. However, its location is key, at the confluence of the **Wadi Musa**, flowing from east to west, and the Wadi Mataha, bringing the water diverted by the dam at the Siq entrance into the city from the northeast. It may also have been the terminus for the terracotta pipes and channels bringing water through the Siq itself. The sight and sound of water tumbling from such a monument must have been wonderful in such a parched city centre.

The Nymphaeum is where you'll end up if you've walked the Wadi Muthlim route from the dam (see page 263); it's equally possible to walk the route in reverse, although the initial stretch will be down in the wadi bed, and less appealing than following the East Cliff around to join Wadi Mataha further north (see page 287).

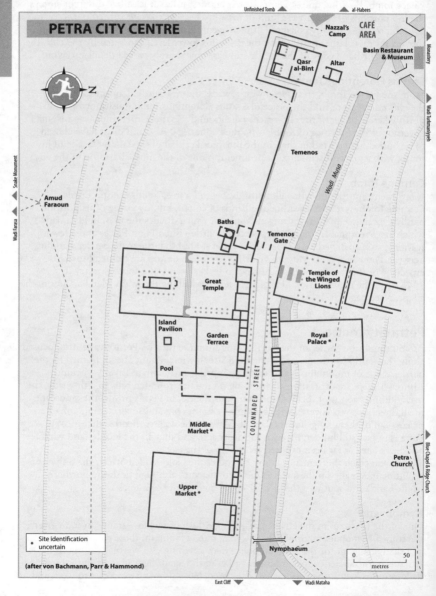

PETRA CITY CENTRE

Unfinished Tomb
al-Habees
Nazzal's Camp
CAFÉ AREA
Basin Restaurant & Museum
Monastery
Qasr al-Bint
Altar
Wadi Turkmaniyeh
Temenos
Wadi Musa
Snake Monument
Amud Faraoun
Wadi Farasa
Baths
Temenos Gate
Great Temple
Temple of the Winged Lions
Island Pavilion
Garden Terrace
Royal Palace *
Pool
COLONNADED STREET
Middle Market *
Petra Church
Blue Chapel & Ridge Church
Upper Market *
Nymphaeum

* Site identification uncertain

(after von Bachmann, Parr & Hammond)

0   50
metres

East Cliff   Wadi Mataha

PETRA COLOURS

One of the most breathtaking aspects of Petra – for many people surpassing even the architecture – is its **colourful sandstone**, famously celebrated in a particular tourist's memoirs almost 150 years ago. As the artist **Edward Lear** strolled up the Colonnaded Street on a visit in 1858, coolly noting "the tint of the stone … brilliant and gay beyond my anticipation", his manservant and cook, Giorgio Kokali, burst out in delight, "Oh master, we have come into a world of chocolate, ham, curry powder and salmon!"

Agatha Christie, who visited in the 1930s, preferred to see the rocks as "blood-red". A character in her *Appointment with Death*, set in Petra, comes out with a line describing the place as "very much the colour of raw beef".

Unfortunately for posterity, however, the most famous lines on Petra's colours are less engaging. In 1845, **John William Burgon**, later to become Dean of Chichester, wrote in his poem *Petra*:

It seems no work of Man's creative hand,
By labour wrought as wavering fancy planned;
But from the rock as if by magic grown,
Eternal, silent, beautiful, alone!
Not virgin-white like that old Doric shrine,
Where erst Athena held her rites divine;
Not saintly-grey, like many a minister fane,
That crowns the hill and consecrates the plain;
But rose-red as if the blush of dawn
That first beheld them were not yet withdrawn;
The hues of youth upon a brow of woe,
Which Man deemed old two thousand years ago,
Match me such a marvel save in Eastern clime,
A rose-red city half as old as Time.

No advertising copywriter could have dreamt up a better final line, and Burgon's words have hung over Petra ever since: you'll be sick of reading "**rose-red city**" on every map, poster and booklet by the time you leave. Tellingly, Burgon had never been to Petra when he wrote it; he finally went sixteen years later, and at least then had the humility to write, if only in a letter to his sister, "there is nothing rosy about Petra".

Over the centuries, wind has rubbed away at the soft sandstone of Petra's cliffs to reveal an extraordinary array of colours streaking through the stone. The most colourful facades are the **Silk Tomb** and the **Carmine Tomb**, both on the East Cliff and bedecked in bands of rainbow colours, while the cafés on the path below are set in caves no less breathtaking. Elsewhere, the lower walls of the **Wadi Farasa** are streaked with colour, and the **Siq cliffs** are striped with everything from scarlet to yellow to purple to brown, to complement the green foliage on the trees, the pink of the oleander flowers and the deep-blue sky. The one place in Petra that's truly "rose-red" is the **Treasury**, lit in the afternoons by low reflected sunlight off the pinkish walls.

You should allow around three hours from the Nymphaeum to circumambulate Jabal al-Khubtha and get back to the gate.

Colonnaded Street

From the Nymphaeum all the way along the paved **Colonnaded Street** westwards, columns on your left (south) stand in front of what have been dubbed Petra's **markets**. Ranged along street level, to either side of grand staircases, were small shops, which may have been refitted in the Byzantine period; some have been renovated, but work to excavate the floors and outbuildings remains ongoing.

To your right (north), slopes – formally dubbed **Jabal Qabr Jumayan** – host the Petra Church (see below), with its superb mosaics, and a clutch of smaller Byzantine sites on the hills above, as well as one of the city's longest-running excavations, the Temple of the Winged Lions (see page 273).

6

If you walk dead ahead down the Colonnaded Street, without diverting to either side, you reach a ruined gateway giving into Petra's sacred temple precinct, the Temenos (see page 275).

Petra Church

Above and behind the Nymphaeum stands a modern shelter protecting the Byzantine **Petra Church**, as it's been called. This is a large tripartite basilica, roughly 26m by 15m, with three apses to the east and three entrances to the west, accessed from a stone-paved atrium. It was built in the late fifth century, and remodelled about fifty years later. Around 600 it was burned, and remained derelict until earthquakes shook it down shortly afterwards. Surviving in both aisles of the church, though, are superbly detailed **floor mosaics** depicting the bounty of creation, dated stylistically to the early sixth century. The presence of such a large church so richly decorated – and the discovery of the Petra scrolls (see opposite) – merely highlights how little is known about Byzantine Petra, and how much awaits discovery. Much of the stone used to build the church was pilfered from the ruined Nabatean and Roman monuments all around, and now lies tumbled down the slopes in front.

From beside the Petra Church, fine **views** extend over the valley. To the left is the East Cliff; ahead is the Great Temple; and to the right you can clearly see the unusual **Unfinished Tomb** (see page 281), carved into the base of Al-Habees.

The interior

The spectacular **south-aisle mosaics** are in three rows, the central line of personifications of the seasons flanked by rows of animals, birds and fish. From door to altar, the middle line features fishermen and hunters interspersed with Ocean (with one foot on a fish), a delightfully clear-faced Spring, and Summer with her breast bared and holding a fish. The **north-aisle mosaics** depict people and indigenous and exotic animals and birds, including a camel-like giraffe, a hyena, boar, bear and leopard. Archeologists also found thousands of gilded glass tesserae, indicating that lavish **wall mosaics** once adorned the church, and they managed to reconstruct – from more than a hundred pieces – a huge marble tub with panthers for handles (which is now in the Basin Museum).

At the rear (west) of the atrium is a superbly well-preserved fifth-century **Baptistry**, with a cruciform font surrounded by four limestone columns.

Blue Chapel

On a ridge just above the Petra Church is the partially reconstructed fifth-century **Blue Chapel**, so named for its bluish Egyptian granite columns, which were moved here

---

IMAGES OF NABATEAN PETRA

It is often very difficult to grasp what Petra must have looked like in its Nabatean "**golden age**", when it was an extravagantly wealthy city, home to tens of thousands of people. What today are rubbly excavation sites were once grand temples and public buildings, soaring to their full height. Watercourses flowed to irrigate lush gardens in what looks now like dusty waste ground. Natural earth tones in the landscape were tempered with brightly coloured plasterwork adorning many of the buildings.

Many architects and artists have tried to depict Petra's ancient reality, with varying degrees of accuracy. One in particular – **Chrysanthos Kanellopoulos**, an archeologist in his own right – has worked over many years with a number of teams in Petra and around Jordan. Search his name online to find his vivid, full-colour renderings of what Petra would have looked like two thousand years ago. As an impression of original Nabatean architecture, they are remarkable – though bear in mind that since archeological work is ongoing, some details may now have been superseded by new discoveries.

THE PETRA SCROLLS

A hugely significant archeological find was made by accident in a storage room at the northeast corner of the Petra Church on December 4, 1993: archeologists stumbled on a cache of 152 **papyrus scrolls**, tumbled higgledy-piggledy from the shelves that presumably once carried them, which had lain buried beneath 4m of rubble. Analysis of the scrolls is still incomplete, but they have given tantalizing glimpses of life in Byzantine Petra, a period that is rarely accounted for.

The whole archive seems to have belonged to one **Theodore**, born in 514, who at the age of 24 married a young woman from a family already connected with his own by marriage in a previous generation. Theodore became archdeacon of the "Most Holy Church of NN in the metropolis" – presumably the Petra Church. Most of the documents date from a sixty-year period, roughly 528 to 588, and comprise property contracts, out-of-court settlements and tax receipts, providing a wealth of detail about everyday life. Transfers from one family to another of vineyards, arable land, orchards, living quarters and stables within a 50km radius of Petra were all dutifully recorded. One man's will specifies that after his mother's death, all her assets were to be donated to the "House of Aron", the Byzantine monastery atop Jabal Haroun. Farmers, tailors, doctors, slaves and soldiers are all mentioned by name, including one Abu Karib ibn Jabala, known to have been a military commander of the Arab tribes.

Petra was decisively Christian at this time, and **monks and priests** feature prominently, not least a Bishop Theodore, who may have been the same Theodore who took part in a synod at Jerusalem in 536. Another reference is to a priest "of her, our All-Holy, Praised Lady, the Glorious God-Bearing and Eternally Virgin Mary", indicating that there may be a **church to Mary** yet to be uncovered in Petra. Only once the content of the scrolls has been fully published can investigation proceed any further, but this is yet another sign that archeologists have only just begun to scratch Petra's surface.

Separately, Jane Taylor's fine book **Petra and the Lost Kingdom of the Nabataeans** (see page 389) includes a fascinating chapter on an earlier Nabatean archive, left in a cave above the Dead Sea by Babatha, a Jewish woman living in the second century AD. Worth a read.

presumably from a destroyed nearby monument or building. It's tiny, and seems to have had access only via a small staircase from above, leading archeologists to theorize that this may have been the private chapel of a resident bishop, rather than a public building.

Ridge Church

A short climb to the top of the hill that peaks behind the Petra Church brings you to the austere **Ridge Church**, another small building (some 18m by 13m) perched on a ridge at the northwestern edge of Byzantine-era Petra, overlooking the Wadi Turkmaniyyeh behind, and the whole of the city centre in front. Its position suggests it may originally have been a military lookout post, which was converted in the late fourth century into a church. Much of the interior paving survives, but there's no decoration. What's most interesting about the place is that archeologists found almost no remnants of the building's superstructure nearby, although they did find a hoard of water-washed stones in the church courtyard brought up from the wadi below. From this confusing evidence, they came up with an elaborate theory for the church's destruction. At a time of increasing political instability, they postulate, the Petrans deliberately dismantled the church – which lay hard up against the city wall – in order to use its stones as missiles against invaders approaching from below. When the church had been razed, they collected more stones from the wadi to hoard against future attacks, but these were forgotten as, possibly, the city was overrun from a different direction. Any truth in this tale has yet to be confirmed.

Temple of the Winged Lions

Overlooking the Temenos Gate west of the Petra Church is the **Temple of the Winged Lions**, the principal building of the northern slope. It was named for

6

unusual column capitals featuring winged lions (one of which is in the Basin Museum), but would – so the excavator suggests – have been more appropriately named the Temple of **al-Uzza**, for it seems to have been dedicated to her. Dated approximately to the early first century AD, the building was approached via a bridge across the Wadi Musa, parts of which you can still see on the banks. Worshippers would have proceeded across ascending terraces, an open colonnaded courtyard and a portico into the temple itself, featuring close-packed columns and an altar platform. The floors were paved in contrasting black, brown and white marble, and the walls decorated with painted plaster. Archeologists uncovered both a **painter's workshop** – with paints and pigments still in their ceramic pots – and a **marble-cutter's workshop** adjoining the temple.

One of the most spectacular discoveries, also now on display in the Basin Museum, was a small rectangular **stone idol**, complete with a stylized face and a hole between the eyes (possibly for a set of horns, the symbol of the goddess Isis, to be inserted); the inscription along the base reads "Goddess of Hayyan son of Nybat". Adjacent to the temple to the east is a large unexcavated area of rubble deemed to have been a **royal palace**, also with a bridge over the wadi, but no work has as yet been done on it.

Garden and Pool Complex

Ⓦ petragardenexcavation.wordpress.com

On the southern side of the Colonnaded Street, on the slopes above street level, once stood an expanse of ornamental gardens, now dubbed the **Garden and Pool Complex**. This was laid out in Petra's "golden age" – the late first century BC – as a place of refuge in the city centre, tucked in among the grand public buildings and busy shops all around. In front, nearest the street, was a flat area that comprised the gardens themselves. Behind, occupying the whole southern part of the **terrace**, was a large **pool**, 43m long by 23m wide (and about 2.5m deep), surrounded by a colonnade. Occupying an **island** in the centre of the pool was a small, rectangular pavilion. The beauty of such a site can only be imagined.

Great Temple

Ⓦ brown.edu/Departments/Joukowsky_Institute/Petra

Alongside the Garden Complex at the western end of the street, and accessed by a set of steps leading up from the street, is a late first-century-BC building that has been dubbed the **Great Temple**, though not even the deity who was worshipped here is known. Ongoing excavation work by a US team suggests that this extremely grand affair, one of the largest complexes in the city at 7000 square metres, might not have been a temple at all. Originally designed perhaps as some kind of gathering place or trade centre, then later adapted into a council chamber or even quasi-religious performance space, it seems as though the building – whatever it was – went through several incarnations, from one function to another, over centuries.

In its final, grandest phase access was via a staircase from street level through a monumental gateway onto a hexagonally paved **lower courtyard**, featuring triple colonnades to east and west culminating in semicircular benched alcoves.

Steps climbed again to the **temple** itself – if that's what it was – some 25m above street level, fronted by four enormous columns which were originally stuccoed in red and white. Within stands a renovated Nabatean **theatre**, about 7m in diameter, which would have seated up to six hundred people, perhaps for performances, perhaps as a debating hall of sorts. The whole building is extremely complex, set on different levels, with internal and external corridors flanking it on east and west. Columns and chunks of architectural elements (many of them beautifully carved) all point to the fact that this was one of Petra's most important monuments. You can even spot capitals here carved with the heads of **Indian elephants** – a symbol, perhaps, of just how cosmopolitan and well connected the Nabatean traders were in their heyday.

Scramble to the highest point of the walls for **views** west to the arches of the Crusader fort atop Al-Habees, north across the wadi to the Temple of the Winged Lions, behind which lie the valley tombs of Wadi Muaysreh ash-Shargiyyeh, and northeast to the Petra Church, with Umm Sayhoun behind it and Mughur an-Nassara to one side.

Temenos

In most Roman cities, the main east–west and north–south streets ploughed straight furrows from city gate to city gate. However, as at Bosra, the heterodox Nabateans blocked off Petra's main street at one end and turned the area beyond – hard up against the mountain cliffs – into a **Temenos**, or sacred temple precinct.

Framing the western end of the Colonnaded Street stand the partially reconstructed remains of the **Temenos Gate**, marking the end of the commercial sector of Petra and the entrance to the main area of worship. Sockets in the threshold indicate that great doors once closed off all three entrances of the gate; the floral frieze which survives on the easternmost facade of the gate was originally framed by freestanding columns which stood just in front and to either side.

Temenos courtyard

As you pass through the Temenos Gate, the impression remains of having left the city behind; the **Temenos courtyard** – occupied at the far end by, on one side, camels and, on the other, the bulk of a temple – is huge, paved and open, and at times of religious celebration would have been thronged with people. Low walls enclosed the Temenos on both sides, although the northern one has been eroded away by the waters of the Wadi Musa. Just inside the Temenos Gate to the south are three domed rooms tentatively identified as **baths**, only partially excavated. All along the south wall is a double row of stone benches, some 73m in length, leading almost up to the main feature of the Temenos, the Qasr al-Bint, the only freestanding monument as yet uncovered in the whole of Petra. Just visible from the Temenos, over the hill to the south, is the tip of the Amud Faraoun (see page 281).

Qasr al-Bint

The **Qasr al-Bint al-Faraoun** ("Palace of Pharaoh's Daughter") is nothing of the sort. Its name derives from a far-fetched bedouin tale of the pharaoh, who, it's said, after stashing his riches in the Treasury, and still desperate to let nothing slow him down in his pursuit of the Israelites, built this place to stash his daughter away for safekeeping. Interestingly enough though, an inscription naming Suudat, daughter of the Nabatean king Malchus II (40–70 AD), and probably from the base of a statue, was found on the steps; according to historian Iain Browning, this indicates that some link between the *qasr* and the daughter of a powerful man may not be so fanciful after all.

The building is a huge, square Nabatean temple, dating from the late first century BC, oriented to the north and facing a huge, freestanding altar, some 13m by 12m and at least 3m high. The **altar**, clad in marble, showed a blank wall to the north, and was originally approached by steps from in front of the temple. From here looking back, the four gigantic columns of the temple portico, standing at the head of a broad staircase wider than the building and topped by an architrave and pediment, would have made a deeply impressive sight. The huge arch that survives today was probably only a relieving arch for a lower, horizontal lintel of the doorway into the *cella*, which spanned the width of the building and was lit by windows high up in each wall. Behind, the holy of holies was divided into three separate chambers, or *adyta*. The central one is slightly raised, and has engaged columns along the walls and another relieving arch overhead; this is where the god-block or cult statue would have stood. The temple's dedication is unknown, but Dushara is the most obvious candidate.

Tent cafés and camel-drivers crowd the courtyard in front of the Qasr al-Bint, and this is the main rest area for gathering strength before you continue to explore or start the long walk back to the gate (which takes a full hour uphill by the most direct route through the Siq). In front of the *qasr*, a bridge crosses the Wadi Musa to the *Basin Restaurant* (see page 260) and adjacent Basin Museum; from the other bank, the **Wadi Turkmaniyyeh** dirt road (see page 287) wends its way out of the city to the Bdul village Umm Sayhoun.

Nazzal's Camp

The modern building next to the Qasr al-Bint is known as **Nazzal's Camp**. It was formerly Petra's sole hotel (of eleven rooms), built by the Nazzal family in 1943 on the site of the Thomas Cook campsite established a few years before. (Early Cook's tourists were also offered the option of sleeping in one of the caves cut into Al-Habees looming overhead.) The Nazzal's Camp building is now used by the Department of Antiquities as a base for archeological teams working in Petra.

Basin Museum

Closed at time of writing; formerly daily 8am–3.30pm • Free

Shaded by a prominent grove of trees opposite the Qasr al-Bint, beside the *Basin Restaurant* (see page 260), the **Basin Museum** was closed at the time of writing, pending the opening of the new Petra Museum in Wadi Musa town beside the Visitor Centre. It's likely that some (or, perhaps, all) of the archeological pieces that used to be on display here will have been transferred to the new museum – and, for now, the future of this building remains unclear.

The Monastery route

Petra's most awe-inspiring monument is also one of the most taxing to reach. The **Monastery** (*Ad-Dayr* or *Ad-Deir* in Arabic) boasts a massive facade almost 50m square, carved from a chunk of mountain nearly an hour's climb northwest of the city centre, 220m above the elevation of the Qasr al-Bint. Daunting though this sounds, there's a well-trodden route the whole way – involving roughly **eight hundred steps** – as well as plenty of places to rest; a tranquil holy spring two-thirds of the way up is almost worth the climb by itself. Even if you've had your fill of facades, the stupendous views from the mountaintop over the entire Petra basin and the Wadi Araba make the trip essential.

Whether you want to **ride a donkey** to the summit or not (prices are *very* negotiable), you'll most likely have to beat off the hordes of kids riding alongside offering them as "Air-condition taxi, mister?" Bear in mind that the archeological authorities would prefer that you walked: all those hooves are seriously degrading the Nabatean-carved sandstone steps on the route up. The best time to attempt the climb is in the **afternoon**; not only is the way up mostly in shadow by then, but the sun has moved around enough to hit the facade full-on.

Walking up to the Monastery

The walking route passes in front of the *Basin Restaurant* and museum, and leads dead ahead into the soft sandy bed of the Wadi ad-Dayr. The steps begin after a short distance, and soon after there's a diversion pointed left to the **Lion Triclinium**, a small Classical shrine in a peaceful, bushy wadi, named for the worn lions that flank its entrance. A small, round window above the door and the doorway itself have been eroded together to form a strange keyhole shape. The frieze above has Medusas at either end; to the left of the facade is a small god-block set into a niche.

The processional way up is broken after another patch of steps by a sharp left turn where the Wadi Kharrubeh joins from in front; a little way along this wadi – off the

THE BEDOUIN NAMED FOR CHANGING

From time immemorial, the caves and dens of Petra have been occupied by one of Jordan's poorest and most downtrodden tribes, the **Bdul**. Surrounded by tribes living traditional tent-based lifestyles (the **Saidiyeen** to the south and west, the **Ammareen** to the north and the **Liyathneh** to the east), the Bdul remain a community apart, looked down upon for their poverty, small numbers (only about three hundred families) and cave-centred lifestyle.

Most bedouin tribes can trace their **lineage** back to a single founding father (whether real or fictitious), but mystery surrounds the origin of the Bdul. Some Bdul, naturally enough, claim descent from the Nabateans, but this may just be wishful thinking. Most claim that the name Bdul derives from the Arabic word *badal*, meaning to swap or change, and was given to the tribe after the survivors of a massacre at the hands of Moses and the Israelites had agreed to convert to Judaism; at some point in the centuries following, the tribe converted again, this time to Islam. Much more plausible is the possibility that the Bdul earned their name from being a nomadic tribe that decided to settle in the ruins of Petra, changing their habits to suit a more stable existence.

The Bdul were slow to benefit from the growth in tourism in Petra, largely because of cut-throat competition with the more cosmopolitan and better-educated Liyathneh of Wadi Musa. When the *Resthouse* hotel opened in the 1950s, Liyathneh were hired as construction workers, hotel staff, book- and postcard-sellers and even to provide horses for rides into Petra; their near-monopoly on tourist facilities in Wadi Musa has persisted to this day. Adding insult to injury, a USAID report dating from the establishment of Petra as a National Park in 1968 acknowledged that the Bdul held traditional rights over park lands, but nonetheless recommended that they be **resettled** elsewhere. This sparked a twenty-year battle to oust the Bdul from Petra, which saw the tribe's traditional lifestyle of agriculture and goat herding decimated; instead, income dribbled in from the refreshment cafés within Petra and the few individuals offering crafts and antiquities – real and fake – to tourists. In the mid-1980s, tempted by material comforts in the new, purpose-built village of Umm Sayhoun, many Bdul families finally left the caves of Petra for the breezeblock houses on the ridge. Some still herd a few goats, others cultivate small plots, but most Bdul make their living providing services to tourists. You'll meet Bdul adults and children in all corners of Petra, running the tent cafés or offering tea and trinkets in the hills, and often happy to chat (in perhaps surprisingly fluent English). The "bedouin named for changing", as archeologist Kenneth Russell dubbed them, are embracing change yet again.

MORE INFORMATION

The best modern account of Bdul life in Petra is *Married to a Bedouin* by Marguerite van Geldermalsen, which we outline earlier in this chapter (see page 267) and review in the "Books" section (see page 389). There's some excellent background on the Bdul by researcher Rami Sajdi at ⓦacacialand.com.

main path – you'll find on the right-hand side a small **biclinium**, a ceremonial dining room with two stepped benches facing each other. Back on the path, after a step-free patch, the climb recommences. Some twenty or thirty minutes from the *Basin*, where the steps turn sharply left, you can branch right off the main path into a narrow wadi; double-back to the left, follow a track up and then right onto a broad, cool, protected ledge overlooking a deep ravine below. This is the **Qattar ad-Dayr**, once an enchanted mossy grotto enclosed by high walls, completely silent but for the cries of wheeling birds and the continual dripping of water; now, however, it's almost always dry, and choked with litter. Here, the one place in Petra where water used to flow year-round, the Nabateans built a *triclinium* and cisterns, and made dozens of carvings, including a two-armed cross.

As the steps drag on, the views begin to open up, and you get a sense of the vastness of the mountains and valleys all around. With tired legs, it's about another twenty minutes to a small sign pointing right to the **Hermitage**, a sheer-sided pinnacle of rock featuring a less-than-gripping set of caves carved with crosses. Another ten minutes, after a squeeze between two boulders and a short descent, and you emerge onto a wide, flat plateau, where you should turn right for the Monastery.

The Monastery

The **Monastery** facade is so big that it seems like an optical illusion – the doorway alone is taller than a house. A local entrepreneur has thoughtfully set up a café in a cave opposite: sink down at one of the shaded tables in front to take in the full vastness of the view. At first glance, the facade looks much like the Treasury's, but it's much less ornate; indeed, there's virtually no decoration at all. The name "Monastery" is again a misnomer, probably suggested by some crosses scratched inside; this was almost certainly a **temple**, possibly dedicated to the Nabatean king **Obodas I**, who reigned in the first century BC and was posthumously deified. Inside is a single chamber, with the same configuration of double staircases leading up to a cultic niche as in the Qasr al-Bint and the Temple of the Winged Lions. The flat plaza in front of the monument isn't natural: it was levelled deliberately, probably to contain the huge crowds that gathered here for religious ceremonies. You can pick out traces of a wall and colonnade in the ground to the south of the plaza, near where you entered. The opposite side (the left flank of the monument as you face it) has a scramble-path leading up to the **urn** on the top of the facade, which is no less than 10m high. Leaping around on the urn is a test of mettle for the local goat-footed kids, and some even shimmy to the very top; follow them with your life in your hands.

Around the Monastery

There are dozens more monuments and carvings to explore **around the Monastery**, not least of which is a cave and stone circle directly behind the refreshments cave. At any point, once you climb off ground level, the views are breathtaking. The cliff to the north (left) of the facade is punctuated for well over 100m with Nabatean caves, tombs and cisterns; some 200m or so north of the Monastery, you'll find a dramatically isolated **High Place**, with godlike **views** over the peaks down to the far-distant Wadi Araba, over 1000m below.

The only route back into Petra from the Monastery is the way you came up. Like all these descents, it's too rocky and isolated even to think about attempting it after sunset.

The High Place of Sacrifice route

Near the theatre and Street of Facades, a signposted set of steps leads south up a rocky slope to the **High Place of Sacrifice**, a diversion off the main path, but an unmissable part of a visit. Even if you have only one day in Petra, this is still worth the climb, about thirty or forty minutes with safe steps at all tricky points – there's no scrambling or mountaineering involved. You can return the same way, but steps also lead down off the back of the mountain into **Wadi Farasa**, forming a long but interesting loop that delivers you (after about two and a half hours) to the Qasr al-Bint. The breathtaking **views** and some of Petra's most extraordinary **rock-colouring** make the hike worthwhile, quite apart from the wealth of Nabatean architecture at every turn and the dramatic High Place itself. The path is well travelled, and you're unlikely to find yourself alone for more than a few minutes at a time.

Walking up to the High Place of Sacrifice

The **steps** up are clearly marked beside a souvenir stall and toilet block. They are guarded by several god-blocks, and wind their way into the deep ravine of the beautiful **Wadi al-Mahfur**. At several points, the Nabatean engineers took their chisels to what were otherwise impassable outcrops and sliced deep-cut corridors through the rock to house the stairs. It's a dramatic walk.

The sign that you're reaching the top, apart from one or two rickety café-stalls, is the appearance on your left of two very prominent **obelisks**, both over 6m high. As in the

Bab as-Siq and elsewhere, these probably represent the chief male and female Nabatean deities, Dushara and al-Uzza, although far more extraordinary is to realize that they are solid: instead of being placed there, this entire side of the mountaintop was instead levelled to leave them sticking up. The ridge on which they stand is still marked on modern maps with the bedouin name of Zibb Attuf, the Phallus of Mercy (often adapted to Amud Attuf, the Column of Mercy), implying that the notion of these obelisks representing beneficial fertility was somehow passed down unchanged from the Nabateans to the modern age. Opposite stand very ruined walls, the last remnants of what could have been a **Crusader fort** or a Nabatean structure. Broken steps lead beside it up to the summit.

The High Place of Sacrifice

As you emerge onto the hand-levelled platform atop the ridge, the sense of exposure after the climb is suddenly liberating. The **High Place of Sacrifice** (*al-Madhbah* in Arabic) is one of the highest easily accessible points in Petra, perched on cliffs that drop an almost sheer 170m to the Wadi Musa below. It's just one of dozens of High Places perched on ridges and mountaintops around Petra, all of which are of similar design and function. A platform about 15m long and 6m wide served as the venue for religious ceremonies, oriented towards an altar, set up on four steps, with a basin to one side and a socket into which may have slotted a stone representation of the god. Within the courtyard is a small dais, on which probably stood a table of (bloodless) offerings.

What exactly took place up here – probably in honour of Dushara – can only be guessed at, but there were almost certainly libations, smoking of frankincense and animal sacrifice. What is less sure is whether **human sacrifice** took place, although boys and girls were known to have been sacrificed to al-Uzza elsewhere: the second-century philosopher Porphyrius reports that a boy's throat was cut annually at the Nabatean town of Dunat, 300km from Petra. At Hegra, a Nabatean city in the Arabian interior, an inscription states explicitly: "Abd-Wadd, priest of Wadd, and his son Salim … have consecrated the young man Salim to be immolated to Dhu Gabat. Their double happiness!" If such sacrifices took place in Petra, the High Place would surely have seen at least some of them.

It's also been suggested that Nabatean religion incorporated **ritual exposure of the dead**, as practised among the Zoroastrians of Persia; if so, the High Place would also have been an obvious choice as an exposure platform. You can survey the vastness of Petra's mountain terrain from here, and the tomb of Aaron atop **Jabal Haroun** is in clear sight in the distance.

The ridge extends a short distance north of the High Place, nosing out directly above the theatre, with the tombs of the Outer Siq minuscule below. From here, it's easy to see that the city of Petra lay in a broad valley, about a kilometre wide and hemmed in to east and west by mountain barriers. North, the valley extends to Beidha, south to Sabra. It looks tempting to scramble down the front of the ridge, but there is no easily manageable path this way; it would be dangerous to try it.

Walking down from the High Place via Wadi Farasa

ⓦ auac.ch/iwfp

It's easy to go back down from the High Place the same way you came up, but the route down the western cliff of the Attuf ridge via **Wadi Farasa** is preferable. The route leads directly straight ahead (south) as you scramble down past the ruined Crusader walls. After 50m you'll come to stairs winding downward to your right along the valley wall; the way is often narrow and steep but always clear. Note that it's also possible to descend via **Wadi Nmayr**, parallel to Wadi Farasa, but this is a very difficult, concealed path and should only be attempted with a knowledgeable guide.

Lion Monument

Part of the way down into the Wadi Farasa, you'll come to the **Lion Monument** carved into a wall. This may have been a drinking fountain, since a pipe seems to have fed water to emerge from the lion's mouth. The creature itself, as on the Treasury facade, represented al-Uzza, and the monument was probably intended both to refresh devotees on their way up and prepare them for the ceremonies about to be held at the High Place.

Garden Triclinium

The precipitous stairs beyond the Lion Monument, which give views of the facades below, bring you down to the **Garden Triclinium**, a simple cave overlooked by a huge tree in a beautiful, hidden setting, which got its name from the carpet of green that sprouts in springtime in front of the portico. Two freestanding columns are framed by two engaged ones; within is a small square shrine. Stairs to the right of the facade lead to a huge cistern on the roof, serving the Roman Soldier Tomb below.

Roman Soldier Tomb

A beautiful set of rock-cut stairs to the left of the Garden Triclinium brings you down to the complex of the **Roman Soldier Tomb**. Although not immediately apparent, the two facades facing each other here across the wadi formed part of a unified area, with an elaborate colonnaded courtyard and garden between them, long vanished. The tomb is on your left, a Classical facade with three framed niches holding figures probably representing those buried within; the interior chamber has a number of recesses for the dead. Its name is based on the middle of the three figures, a headless man wearing a cuirass – but it's misleading: the tomb is Nabatean, not Roman.

Opposite the tomb, with an eroded but undecorated facade, is a startlingly colourful **triclinium**, unique in Petra for having a carved interior. The walls have been decorated with fluted columns and bays, all worn to show streaks of mauves, blues, pinks, crimsons and silver. Why this *triclinium* was decorated so carefully, and who was buried in the tomb opposite, is not known.

Renaissance Tomb and Broken Pediment Tomb

Stairs lead down over the lip of a retaining wall to the wadi floor, and it is around here that the colouring in the rock is at its most gorgeous. Plenty of tombs crowd the lower reaches of the wadi; one of the most interesting is the **Renaissance Tomb**, topped by an urn and with an unusual arch above its doorway also carrying three urns. Nearby is the **Broken Pediment Tomb**, above the level of the path, displaying an early forerunner of the kind of broken pediment found on Petra's grandest monuments, the Treasury and the Monastery.

Zantur

Ⓦ auac.ch/iezp

As you emerge from Wadi Farasa into the open, you should bear in mind that you're still the best part of half an hour from reaching the main routes again. From here onwards, though, there's not a scrap of shade and you're quite often walking in stifling, breezeless dips between hills. In addition, the path isn't immediately clear. You should bear a little right, initially keeping out of the wadi bed, and aim for the left flank of the smooth rounded hill dead ahead. This hill is **Zantur**, where a Swiss team have excavated the residential mansion of a wealthy first-century-AD Nabatean merchant – a lavish two-storey affair which would have towered above the city, offering sweeping views. More houses have been uncovered on the Zantur slopes, which crunch underfoot with fragments of pottery: as well as coarse, crudely decorated modern shards, there are countless chips of beautiful original Nabatean ware – very thin, smooth pottery that's been skilfully painted. As long as you don't start digging, you can take whatever you like.

Amud Faraoun

The path from Wadi Farasa eventually curls around to the western flank of the Zantur hill, and **Amud Faraoun** ("Pharaoh's Column"), also called Zibb Faraoun ("Pharaoh's Phallus"). This standing column, which must have formed part of the portico of a building – part-visible buried in the rubbly hill behind – now serves as a useful landmark and resting spot. Paths converge here from all sides; to the **southwest** is the main route into Wadi Thughra towards Umm al-Biyara, Jabal Haroun and Sabra; to the **west** is a path accessing a route up al-Habees; to the **northwest** are the Qasr al-Bint and the tent cafés; and to the **northeast** a path runs behind the markets area of the city centre, parallel to the Colonnaded Street.

Al-Habees

The caves of **Al-Habees**, looming beside the Qasr al-Bint, are used now as storage areas and offices for the police, but you can follow a path up and around the mountain on the initial stretches of a processional way to the summit. A little way around is an open area overlooking the beautiful Wadi Siyyagh, with plenty of rock-cut caves – whether they're tombs or houses isn't certain – as well as a small **High Place**, in perfect isolation above a prominent crow-step facade and sunken courtyard in the so-called **Convent Group** of monuments. Beyond, though, the Nabatean stairway is worn and dangerous, and the best way up to the summit is now via a staircase on the southern flank of the mountain, for which you must return to Nazzal's Camp.

The Unfinished Tomb and Columbarium

Overlooking the rubbly hill directly behind Nazzal's Camp is one of Petra's most interesting monuments, the **Unfinished Tomb**. This is a part-complete facade, and shows how Nabatean craftsmen worked from the top down, scooping out the interior as they went. Beside it is the **Columbarium**, a strange monument covered inside and out with hundreds of tiny square niches of unknown function: the name literally means "dovecote", implying that each niche held a bird, but no dove could roost here and the niches seem too small to hold funerary urns, as has also been suggested.

Crusader fort

To reach the **Crusader fort** on the top of Al-Habees, you should continue south up the rubbly hill from the Columbarium, and follow a sign pointing right, even though it appears to point at the blank rubbly cliffside. As you get nearer, you'll spot the modern stairs which take you up to the summit; it's an easy fifteen-minute climb, although there is one wooden footbridge without railings on the way. A gate with a rock-cut bench marks the approach to the fort, after which you'll have to scramble over loose stones up to a gatehouse. From here, you must find your own way the last little bit to the top; steps rise at one point over the barrel vault of a small room. The layout of the ruined fort itself – only occupied for a few decades in the twelfth century – is jumbled and confusing, but the 360° views are exceptional.

Wadi Siyyagh

Just to the north of Al-Habees, **Wadi Siyyagh** – which takes the waters of the Wadi Musa down to Wadi Araba – was formerly one of the most gorgeous and quiet short walks you could make in Petra. This was once an exclusive residential neighbourhood of the city, enclosed between high walls, and there are plenty of houses and tombs, a Nabatean quarry and a well to explore. However, the wadi is now a short-cut for local people driving their pick-ups, and there's a depressing amount of litter.

Persevere with the walk – which is accessible on the flat, beside the *Basin Restaurant* – and after half an hour or so you'll reach the well-tended "**Roman Gardens**" (not Roman at all), now maintained by local people. Beyond, you'll find modest pools and waterfalls en route to Bir Mathkoor (see page 339) in the desert of Wadi Araba, 16km from Petra, but route-finding is not always obvious in this harsh terrain and some scrambling on steep cliffs is necessary; you should be fully confident in your skills, or hire a guide for the journey.

Umm al-Biyara

W auac.ch/iubp

Petra's hardest climb (other than off-route scrambling) is up **Umm al-Biyara**, the flat-topped mountain overlooking the whole of Petra. It's likely to take three or four hours from the Qasr al-Bint to the summit and back, and requires something of a head for heights: a couple of exposed scrambles might give you the flutters. You definitely need a guide, and should only make the **thousand-step climb** in the afternoon when the east face of the mountain is in shadow.

The processional way

As you head southwest from the Amud Faraoun, dropping down to follow the main Wadi Thughra along the base of the cliffs, Wadi Umm Rattam comes in from the left after 350m; keep straight and, a little beyond, branch right (west) on a path directly towards a gully on the western edge of the massif, itself dotted all the way along with facades at different levels. The initial stages of the Nabatean **processional way** have collapsed, but a little to the south you'll find some modern steps, which lead you round to join the Nabatean path again higher up, part original, part restored. A little further is a sweeping hairpin ramp, deeply gouged out of the rock face to form a high corridor. Beyond here, the way is often eroded and, though there are some cairns to mark it, the drops are precipitous.

The summit plateau

You emerge at the south edge of the **summit plateau**, a scrubby slope that rises another 30m to the highest point on the northwest. A seventh-century-BC **Edomite settlement** is dead ahead, with many high dry-stone walls and corridors excavated; from the evidence of lamps, jars and looms, it seems that this community was a quiet, peaceful one, but it must have been important enough to receive a letter from Qaush-Gabr, king of Edom around 670 BC: his seal was discovered in the ruins. *Biyara* means "cisterns", and there are plenty up here, probably Nabatean. All along the eastern rim are part-excavated ruins of Nabatean buildings commanding spectacular bird's-eye views over the Petra basin, 275 sheer metres below; the mountain vistas to the west, from the highest point of the plateau, are no less stunning. There are only two ways down: the fast way, and the way you came up.

Snake Monument

The 2km path to the **Snake Monument** – a single block carved as a huge snake – is the same as for Umm al-Biyara in the initial stretches, except instead of branching off the Wadi Thughra you should keep going ahead through the undulating countryside. This was (and is) the main road into Petra from the south. After around thirty minutes you'll see a very prominent, top-heavy **god-block** atop an area of caves and tombs which has been dubbed the "Southern Graves"; these caves are still inhabited by Bdul families, so you shouldn't be exploring too inquisitively without being invited in. Poised above and to the left of the god-block, not immediately apparent, is the monument itself, a worn block carved with a large, coiled serpent overlooking the tombs and houses below.

If you head another five minutes or so along the valley, you'll come to a flat area with trees that's been fenced around and cultivated; it's here that paths divide – south to Sabra, southeast towards the foot of Jabal Haroun.

PETRA UNPACKAGED

Of all Jordan's tourist destinations, Petra is the most celebrated – and the most packaged. A modern gateway marks entry to the site; you follow a path neatly laid with gravel and defined with kerbstones; you pass standardized souvenir kiosks; you explore on predefined trails. Yet 25 years ago you could roam at will – there were no trails and no kiosks – and 25 years before that you could spend the night in the ancient city. Tourism has forced the pace of change, but there are still many unusual perspectives to explore.

PETRA BY NIGHT

One of the most powerful – and, oddly, easiest – ways of capturing some of the old magic of exploring Petra is to book for the locally run **Petra By Night** walking excursion. We give a full account of the practicalities, timings and prices earlier in this chapter (see page 261).

INTO THE PAST

Although Petra is **visually stunning** even if you know nothing of the site's history, a little knowledge of who built these monuments (and why) can add hugely to your experience of the site – and allows your imagination to re-create some of what Petra must have felt like in its heyday. What today appear to us to be heaps of dusty ruins at one time formed a graceful, elegant city. Grand temples and busy shops lined the main streets. Fountains played alongside lush gardens. A cosmopolitan mix of merchants and townspeople relaxed in cool, shady spots out of the sun. Learning about **Petra's past** – for instance at the excellent new museum beside the Visitor Centre (see page 290) – enriches any stroll through its present. We give ideas for specialist history tours in Basics (see page 26) and recommendations for further reading in Contexts (see page 388).

LOCAL LIFE

Ideas of the value of **community-based tourism** – dodging the big group model in favour of one-to-one interactions and personal experiences – are starting to take hold in Jordan, and there are now ways you can get a flavour of **local life** in Petra, beyond the ancient history and the whirlwind of commercial tourism. We list some contacts later in this chapter (see page 294).

POETIC INSPIRATION

The tiny nonprofit US firm Tavern Books (⩊ tavernbooks.org) publishes **Petra: the Concealed Rose**, the English translation of an extended **poem** by celebrated Jordanian writer Amjad Nasser (born 1955). It's devastatingly beautiful, evoking the oddly diffident splendour of "this endless rose" and discussing meanings behind Petra's nineteenth-century rediscovery and contemporary ambience. Bring it with you while you explore.

THROUGH THE BACK DOOR

Almost everybody who visits Petra stays in a hotel in the adjacent town of **Wadi Musa**, walks in and out through the main gateway, follows the main path for most of the day and sees Petra's major monuments – the Treasury, the Theatre, the Monastery, and so on – in the same order. This works fine if you have limited time, but if you have more than one day there is much to be said for tackling some new approaches.

There's no need to stay in Wadi Musa: you may find small, locally run guesthouses opening soon in the neighbouring Bdul village of Umm Sayhoun, or you could opt to stay with the **Ammarin** tribe, who operate an excellent camp (see page 296) near Little Petra. Staying with the Ammarin takes you completely out of Petra's usual run of packaged experiences, and also gains you access to Ammarin guides, who are able to lead you on their own paths through the hills and into the ancient city **the back way** – so that you walk through the site against the tide. The epic **Dana–Petra trek** (see page 242) often includes this route, too.

In future years, look out for a new **nature reserve** that may be set up by Jordan's Royal Society for the Conservation of Nature around **Shobak**, north of Petra. As well as new walking trails and lodge-style accommodation, this may offer more unusual approaches – riding into Petra on horseback or camel, perhaps.

6

6

Jabal Haroun (Mount Aaron)

Jabal Haroun (**Mount Aaron**) is the holiest site in Petra and one of the holiest in Jordan, venerated by Muslims as the resting place of Prophet Haroun, as well as by Christians and Jews (Haroun is Aaron, brother of Moses). Some local resistance to tourists casually climbing the mountain simply for the views, or to gawk, still persists: you should bear in mind that this is a place of pilgrimage. The trip there and back takes at least **six hours** from Petra city centre, involving a strenuous climb of almost 500m (a donkey can take you for all but the last twenty minutes), and you shouldn't attempt it without a guide, six to eight litres of water, some food, respectable clothing and a sense of humility. Don't bother if you're expecting an impressive shrine (it's small and unremarkable) or outstanding views (they're equally good from the Monastery and Umm al-Biyara). If you choose to visit, you should consider bringing a sum of money with you to leave as a donation.

Rosalyn Maqsood, in her excellent book on Petra, explained the power of Jabal Haroun well:

Believers in the "numinous universe" accept that certain localities can be impregnated with the life-giving force of some saint or hero – transforming the sites into powerhouses of spiritual blessing. Traces of their essential virtue would cling to their mortal leavings even though their spirits had passed to another and better world. Holiness was seen as a kind of invisible substance, which clung to whatever it touched. So the virtues (the Latin word virtu means "power") of saints would remain and be continually renewed and built up by the constant stream of prayer and devotion emanating from the pilgrims who found their way there. These places are visited to gain healing, or fertility, or protection against dangers psychic and physical, or to gain whatever is the desire of the heart. Jabal Haroun is such a place … There is nothing there, really, and no one to watch you – so why should you remove your shoes, or leave an offering? Only you can answer this.

From the cultivated area near the Snake Monument, a path leads down into the Wadi Magtal ad-Dikh. A little beyond a cemetery on the right-hand side, and past a rock ledge called **Settuh Haroun** (Aaron's Terrace) at the foot of the mountain, where pilgrims unable to climb make an offering (Burckhardt slaughtered his goat here in 1812), there is a reasonably clear path up the mountain. Check in the tent at the bottom of the mountain whether the guardian will be around to open the shrine at the top; if not, you should collect the keys from him before heading up. Read a detailed account of the route at ⊕walkingjordan.com.

The summit

A plateau just below the **summit** was the location of a **Byzantine monastery** dedicated to Aaron; excavations here are ongoing. The small domed **shrine of Haroun** (shrine of Aaron) on the peak – visible from all over Petra and Wadi Musa – was renovated by the Mamluke sultan Qalawun in 1459, replacing earlier buildings which had stood on the same site. Up until then, the caretakers had been Greek Christians, and it was in the late sixth century that the Prophet Muhammad, on a journey from Mecca to Damascus, passed through Petra and climbed Jabal Haroun with his uncle. The Christian guardian of the shrine, a monk named Bahira, prophesied that the boy – then aged 10 – would change the world. Today, pilgrims bedeck the shrine with rags, twined threads and shells, the Muslim equivalent of lighting a candle to the saint.

Sabra

At the zenith of its economic power, Petra must have been processing goods from dozens, possibly hundreds, of caravans at a time, and it was obviously not desirable to have hordes of foreign merchants – not to mention camels, random travellers

6

A TWO-DAY HIKE TO JABAL HAROUN AND SABRA

A fascinating **walking route** from Petra involves a technically not-too-challenging **seven-hour trek** (20km) over **Jabal Haroun** to the solitude of the Roman theatre in **Wadi Sabra**, beyond which is a palm-fringed spring, followed on the second day by a direct route back to Petra (9km).

Though the Sabra Valley is obvious when looking south from the summit of Jabal Haroun, the best way into it is not. After you've returned down the zigzag path from the summit, note the small paths which lead southeast across the upper edge of the valley to a ridge on its far side. Follow this ridge down to reach Wadi Sabra, and continue down to find the theatre partially concealed by oleanders. The "**Waters of Sabra**" spring lies just beyond. There are rough spots for wilderness camping nearby. On the second day, the route back to Petra takes a direct line northeast up Wadi Sabra, following the main (right) fork of the watercourse where the valley splits. Finding your route only becomes tricky after emerging from the valley, 4km before Wadi Musa: your objective is clear but the way to it is not, and you're faced either with a scramble up the long hillside to the Scenic Road hotels, or devious route-finding along the lower slopes to arrive near the Petra gate. This is not a trek for the inexperienced, but anyone familiar with mountain terrain should be able to hike it with confidence.

The national **Jordan Trail** (🌐 jordantrail.org; see page 50) passes Sabra as part of the long and difficult stage 7.1 (22.1km; 8hr). Check the website for maps, GPS points and walking notes.

and all the hangers-on associated with the caravan trade – pouring into the city centre. Archeologists theorize that the Nabateans therefore built for themselves "suburbs" on all the main routes into the city, where business could be done, camels fed and watered, and goods stored well away from the sensitive corridors of power. **Bir Mathkoor** (see page 339) in Wadi Araba was the western suburb dealing with trade to and from Gaza; **Siq al-Barid** (see page 288), the northern, for trade with Palestine and Syria; **al-Khan** (the area near the modern ticket gate) may have been the eastern, receiving goods from the Arabian interior; and the southern suburb – with goods arriving from the Red Sea and Hejaz – was **Sabra**. Little has been excavated here, and the walk from Petra (9km) could take two and a half hours or more, much more appealing as a day-long round-trip hike in open country than a ruin hunt.

Routes to Sabra

There are two **routes to Sabra**, both on the flat but unsigned. The first, and more open, goes from the cultivated area near the Snake Monument, around the humped Ras Slayman hill and through the Ragbat al-Btahi pass between peaks before dropping to the sandy wadi floor; shortly after, **Wadi Sabra** joins from the left. As an alternative, you could head southwest from Amud Faraoun, then after 350m turn left (southeast) along Wadi Umm Rattam, which crosses to hug the eastern side of the valley below Jabal Nmayr; after a little less than an hour, aim right (southwest) to follow Wadi Sabra, which is eventually joined by the first path.

The ruins

A little ahead are the **ruins** of Sabra, set in beautifully green, rolling countryside well watered by a spring, **Ain Sabra**. On the left is a large rock-cut **theatre** topped by a large cistern that was used to flood the place so that the Nabateans could apparently indulge in mock sea battles. Ruinous evidence of the size of Nabatean Sabra is all around – houses, monumental buildings, niches and several temples.

Continuing south from Sabra through the **canyons** of lower Sabra and Tibn is a more serious prospect and takes a further day or two to reach Taybeh or Rajif. It's wild and magnificent country, described in detail in Tony Howard's book on trekking in Jordan (see page 390).

Wadi Turkmaniyyeh

Joining the Wadi Musa between the Qasr al-Bint and the *Basin Restaurant*, **Wadi Turkmaniyyeh** – also often called **Wadi Abu Ullaygeh** – is a very pleasant walking route to follow out of Petra to the north, a small sandy valley with the 100m-high jagged cliffs on your left contorted into weird shapes. Along the bank runs the only driveable track into and out of Petra, currently forbidden to non-locals without written permission from the Wadi Musa tourist police (though plans are afoot to consolidate the road and open it to shuttle buses: you may find the work has altered access when you visit).

Along the way there are two groups of tombs: if you enter the Wadi Muaysreh ash-Shargiyyeh, which joins Wadi Turkmaniyyeh on the left barely five minutes from the restaurant, after about 350m you'll come to a dense gathering of facades. Back in Wadi Turkmaniyyeh, after five minutes' walk further northeast you'll see, ranged up on the Muaysreh Ridges to your left, plenty more **rock-cut facades**, with niches, double-height courtyards and a tiny High Place dotted among them. Either of these areas would repay scrambled exploration, well away from the crowds. Both Wadi Muaysreh ash-Shargiyyeh and its neighbour Wadi Muaysreh al-Gharbiyyeh provide walks (7km; 2hr 30min) linking Petra with Little Petra, emerging from Petra's valley onto a cultivated plateau 4km southwest of Little Petra (which is concealed behind a small hill).

Turkmaniyyeh Tomb

About 1km along Wadi Turkmaniyyeh from the *Basin* restaurant you'll see the facade of the **Turkmaniyyeh Tomb** on the left, with the entire bottom half broken away. Between the two pilasters is the longest inscription in Petra in Nabatean, a dialect of Aramaic, dedicating the tomb and the surrounding property to Dushara. All the gardens, cisterns and walls mentioned in the inscription must have been swept away by the floodwaters of the wadi, as, indeed, the facade almost has been.

From here, the road begins 1500m of tight switchbacks as it climbs the ridge to the police post on the outskirts of the modern Bdul village of **Umm Sayhoun**. Buses shuttle regularly from Umm Sayhoun's main street into Wadi Musa town, about 4km away, curling around the head of the valley.

Wadi Mataha and beyond

From the Sextius Florentinus Tomb (see page 269), a path hugs the **Jabal al-Khubtha** cliffs northeast along the broad Wadi Mataha. After 300m or so, you'll spot a complex of rock-cut dwellings known as **Dorotheos' House** set into the cliff on your right, so called because the name "Dorotheos" occurs twice in Greek inscriptions within a large *triclinium* here. Opposite, on the western side of the wadi, are **Mughur an-Nassara** (the "Caves of the Christians") a still-populated rocky crag dotted with dozens of tombs and rock-cut houses, many of which are carved with crosses (thus the name). The whole outcrop is worth exploring and commands an excellent view of Petra from the north. About 600m northeast from Dorotheos' House is the point at which the narrow Sidd Maajn canyon joins the larger Wadi Mataha from the east.

Walking out of Petra via Wadi Sha'ab Qays

There are **two routes** back to civilization from the Wadi Mataha–Sidd Maajn junction, neither of them particularly easy, and both susceptible to flash-flooding in the winter and spring. First – and less complicated – is to follow the Wadi Muthlim route (see page 263) in reverse; this brings you to the dam at the mouth of the Siq. The other route takes you into the heart of the craggy domes west of Wu'ayra, where it's easy to get lost; from the Wadi Mataha, you should be certain you have at least two hours of good daylight left, or you may find dusk falling with you stranded in a 100m-high blind gorge and nobody in earshot. From the Sidd Maajn junction, continue north only another 100m or so along Wadi Mataha, and scale the dark rusty rocks to your right. This ridge gives you a view down into the Sidd Maajn from above, and along the parallel wadis leading south away from you into the mountain. As you walk left (east), you'll spot – like an enchanted bridge – a Nabatean aqueduct, gracefully spanning a wadi below. You need to aim for the wadi which leads south-southeast into the domes from a point directly at the foot of the aqueduct; make a wrong move at this point, and you'll have trouble later on extricating yourself. This is **Wadi Sha'ab Qays** and, like all of the wadis hereabouts, is long, straight and perfectly still; tracks and fresh goat droppings are good signs that you're going roughly in the right direction. You'll have to scrape past woody oleanders rooted in the sandy bed, but the going is easy enough until you reach a gigantic boulder (featuring an endearing little niche) all but blocking the way. There's just enough room to squeeze through on the right. Much further along, you'll come across a Nabatean water channel, which you can follow all the way out of the domes and towards the *Crowne Plaza* hotel.

Wu'ayra

On the edge of the mass of rocky domes east of Jabal al-Khubtha stands the Crusader fort of **Wu'ayra**. The ruins themselves are only of passing interest, but the location of the place is fairy-tale stuff, balanced on a razor-edge pinnacle of rock with sheer ravines on all sides and a single bridge giving access.

After **King Baldwin** led the Crusaders into Transjordan in 1115, founding their headquarters at Shobak, his forces rapidly set about consolidating their defences; Wu'ayra (called by them Li Vaux Moise, or "Moses' Valley") was one outpost constructed the following year, al-Habees another, with forts also going up at Aqaba and Tafileh. Wu'ayra was only briefly in Frankish hands, though: after some tussling over possession, Salah ad-Din seized control for good only seventy years later.

The fort is only accessible off the road towards Umm Sayhoun about 1km north of the *Mövenpick* hotel, the spot handily marked out by a gaping rectangular tomb to the left of the road. Aim for a gap in the rocks about 10m left of the tomb, and you'll find the straightforward path down to where the **bridge** spans the chasm. The **gatehouse** on the other side, with benches and a graffitied niche, gives into the castle **interior**, rough, rocky and ruined.

Little Petra (Siq al-Barid)

Daylight hours • Free • Taxi from Wadi Musa, including waiting time and return, about JD15–20

Petra's northern suburb of **Siq al-Barid**, 9km north of Wadi Musa town, is often touted to tourists as **Little Petra** – which, with its short, high gorge and familiar carved facades, isn't far wrong. However, although it sees its share of tour buses, the place retains an atmosphere and a stillness that have largely disappeared from the central areas of Petra. Adding in its location in gorgeous countryside and its proximity to **Beidha** (a rather less inspiring Neolithic village), it's well worth half a day of your time.

The **route** to Little Petra follows the road north from the *Mövenpick* hotel. A short way along, where the road curves left, you can park on the shoulder for one of Petra's best **views**, a breathtaking sweep over the central valley of the ancient city, with many of the monuments in view, dwarfed by the mountains.

Further on, past the Bdul village Umm Sayhoun, the road heads on across rolling, cultivated uplands that are breathtakingly beautiful after Petra's barren rockscapes. About 8km from the *Mövenpick*, at a T-junction, head left for 800m to the end of the road. You are now beyond Bdul territory in the lands of the Ammareen tribe; a signpost points off the road to the Ammarin Camp (see page 296). In the small car park you'll likely be approached by Ammareen kids hawking trinkets and guides offering their services.

The site

This whole area was a thriving community in Nabatean times, and there's evidence in almost every cranny of Nabatean occupation. Just before you reach the Siq entrance, there's a particularly striking **facade** on the right, with a strange, narrow passage for an interior.

As you enter, you'll realize why this was dubbed Siq al-Barid (the "Cold Siq"): almost no sun can reach inside to warm the place. It's only about 350m long, with alternating narrow and open sections, and differs from most areas of Petra, firstly in the density of carved houses, temples and *triclinia* – there are very few blank areas – and secondly in the endearingly quaint rock-cut stairs which lead off on all sides, turning it into a multistorey alleyway that must once have hummed with life. Feel free to explore. In the first open area is what was probably a temple, fronted by a portico, below which is a little rock-cut house. The second open area has four large *triclinia*, which could have been used to wine and dine merchants and traders on their stopover in Petra. A little further on the left, stairs climb up to the Painted House, a *biclinium* featuring one of the very few Nabatean painted interiors to have survived the centuries: on the ceiling at the back is a winged cupid with a bow and arrow; just above is a bird, to the left of which is a Pan figure playing a flute. The third open area culminates in rock-cut stairs which lead through a narrow gap out onto a wide flat ledge; the path drops down into the wadi (Petra is to the left), but you can scramble up to the right for some excellent views.

6

Beidha

From the Little Petra car park, if you head left on a track that hugs the cliff all the way round, after fifteen minutes or so you'll come to the Neolithic ruins of **Beidha**, which date from around nine thousand years ago, when the first experiments in settled agriculture were happening. There are two main levels of occupation: the first, from about 7000 BC, involved building a wall around what was formerly a temporary camping ground. The round stone houses inside were partly sunk into the ground and supported on a framework of vertical wooden posts (now rotted away). The occupants seemed to have farmed goats and possibly other animals, as well as cultivating a wide variety of cereals and nuts: querns, tools and stones for grinding and flints are dotted all over the site. After a fire sometime around 6650 BC, the village was rebuilt with "corridor houses", characterized by long, straight walls and large communal areas in addition to smaller rooms. Sometime around 6500 BC, and for a reason as yet unknown, Beidha was abandoned. Although the Nabateans later farmed the site, no one lived here permanently again.

Wadi Musa town

As the main tourist gateway to Petra, **WADI MUSA** is an anomaly, a modern southern Jordanian town given an unfamiliar twist with lots of signs in English, a huge number of hotels and a noticeable diminution in the usual hospitality towards foreigners. In sharp contrast to the rest of Jordan, where decency and respect are the unswerving norm, Wadi Musa shows a distressing tendency towards rip-offs, wheedling and outright hassle – the last of these directed particularly at women. Businesses and individuals all too often overcharge and under-deliver. It's a seedy little place, run with just one aim in mind: to milk its world-famous cash cow dry.

There's precious little to do. But then again, after a day of hard walking most visitors aren't looking for rip-roaring entertainment anyway: shopping (see page 298), eating (see page 297) – especially the hands-on Petra Kitchen experience – or sitting around in a Turkish bath (see page 297) is about most people's limit. Plans have long been touted to create an artisans' district in Wadi Musa's historic quarter of **Elgee** (or Elji) – a cluster of restored stone cottages behind the main mosque in the town centre – but have so far come to nothing.

Petra Museum

Beside the Visitor Centre • Hours not fixed at time of writing: probably daily 7am–8pm (winter till 7pm) • Admission not fixed at time of writing: probably free • ⓦ visitpetra.jo

By the time you read this, the new, JD5 million **Petra Museum** (funded by the Japanese government) will be open alongside the Visitor Centre. It will have eight themed galleries, with displays on religion, Nabatean life, ancient water technologies and so

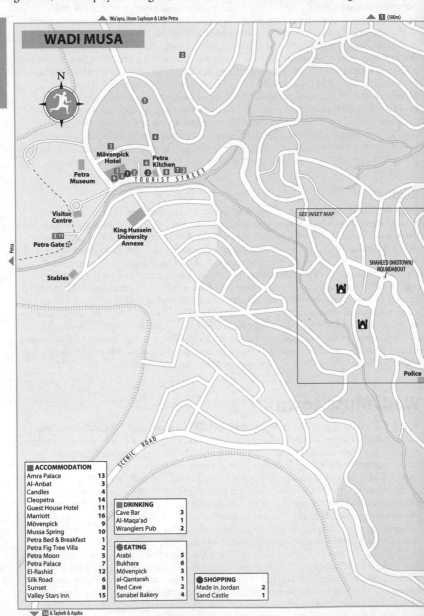

6

▲ Wu'ayra, Umm Sayhoun & Little Petra   ▲ 🏚 (500m)

WADI MUSA

N

Mövenpick Hotel

Petra Kitchen

Petra Museum

TOURIST STREET

Visitor Centre

Petra Gate 🏚

Petra ◄

Stables

King Hussein University Annexe

SEE INSET MAP

SHAHEED (MIDTOWN) ROUNDABOUT

Police

SCENIC ROAD

▼ 🏚 & Taybeh & Aqaba

▮ ACCOMMODATION	
Amra Palace	13
Al-Anbat	3
Candles	4
Cleopetra	14
Guest House Hotel	11
Marriott	16
Mövenpick	9
Mussa Spring	10
Petra Bed & Breakfast	1
Petra Fig Tree Villa	2
Petra Moon	5
Petra Palace	7
El-Rashid	12
Silk Road	6
Sunset	8
Valley Stars Inn	15

▮ DRINKING	
Cave Bar	3
Al-Maqa'ad	1
Wranglers Pub	2

● EATING	
Arabi	5
Bukhara	6
Mövenpick	3
al-Qantarah	1
Red Cave	2
Sanabel Bakery	4

● SHOPPING	
Made In Jordan	2
Sand Castle	1

on, enhanced by well-written information boards examining every detail of Petra's history and Nabatean society, and a carefully chosen illustrative selection of artefacts and statuary. Whatever form it takes, it will deepen and broaden your experience of the ruins. The best advice is to visit before you enter the site – and if, as seems likely, it stays open late, you could drop by on the evening before you head into Petra for the first time.

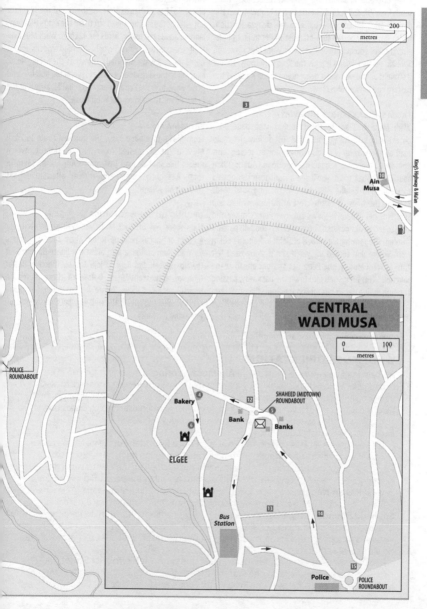

6

ARRIVAL AND DEPARTURE

BY CAR

FROM AMMAN (DESERT HIGHWAY)

From Amman, the most direct route to Petra is 235km, safely driveable in around 2hr 45min without stops. Head south from 7th or 8th Circle on the Desert Highway past the airport: after 180km you'll come to the Unayza junction, which has a signposted turn-off west to Petra. From here, a road takes you quickly and easily to Wadi Musa through Shobak; partway along it joins the King's Highway. Follow it straight all the way and it delivers you to Ain Musa, at the eastern end of Wadi Musa town.

FROM SHOBAK (KING'S HIGHWAY)

Wadi Musa is 27km south of Shobak (see page 245) on the King's Highway. You could just follow the main road all the way, or – if you fancy a slower, more scenic approach – opt for a beautiful backroad. About 13km south of Shobak town, you'll see a right turn signposted to Hesha and Beidha. This narrow, twisting road leads through the trees up to the crest of a ridge, where you suddenly get expansive views out over Petra's valley and the jagged peaks beyond. Carry on down the hill, passing through the ramshackle village of Beidha. Roughly 10km from where you turned off you'll see a signposted left turn to Wadi Musa (Little Petra lies straight ahead at the junction). This brings you into town the back way, passing through rolling desert terrain and the Bdul village at Umm Sayhoun before ending up, 8km on, at the *Crowne Plaza* and *Mövenpick* hotels.

FROM WADI RUM OR AQABA

Wadi Musa is 105km from Wadi Rum (see page 320) and 126km from Aqaba (see page 302). From either, head north on the main highway towards Amman, to the point where the road climbs off the desert floor to crest the plateau of Ras an-Naqab. Here, at the top of the hill, turn left – this is the southernmost stretch of the King's Highway, leading across the rolling fields for 42km to Wadi Musa via Rajif, then Taybeh. After Taybeh the road widens into a multilane highway unofficially known as the Scenic Road, clinging to the cliffside as it passes several big hotels – and great views over the Petra mountains – until it arrives at the Police Roundabout in central Wadi Musa.

FROM MA'AN

From Ma'an (see page 336), the quickest route to Wadi Musa is the signposted road through Udhruh, which meets the Shobak road just above Ain Musa: 33km in total. A slightly longer and trickier alternative goes through Ail village.

DRIVING OUT OF WADI MUSA

Main roads out of Wadi Musa are well signposted. For Amman or Shobak head up to Ain Musa and keep going; for Wadi Rum or Aqaba turn off at the Police Roundabout towards Taybeh and Rajif to join the southbound Desert Highway at Ras an-Naqab. Details of these routes (in reverse) are given above. Before you get going, fill up and check your oil and tyres at the well-equipped service station just above Ain Musa.

WADI MUSA ORIENTATION

All main roads to Petra meet just above **Ain Musa**, a **spring** in the hills at the top (eastern) end of Wadi Musa which is marked by a small triple-domed building sheltering a rock – traditionally, the rock struck in anger by Moses – from beneath which water emerges. From here, the whole of the town is strung out for 4km along a **main road** which heads downhill all the way, offering spectacular views out over the craggy mountains and eventually terminating at the ticket gate into Petra.

Partway down is an intersection known as the **Police Roundabout** (Wadi Musa's police station is alongside it), from where a turn-off heads left through residential districts and eventually out of town, passing big hotels such as the *Marriott* on the way towards the neighbouring villages of **Taybeh** and **Rajif**, eventually joining the Desert Highway 42km away at **Ras an-Naqab** (see page 338) on the route towards Rum and Aqaba.

The centre of Wadi Musa, just below the police intersection, is marked by the small **Shaheed Roundabout**, although there are no signs naming it (it's often dubbed the Central or Midtown Roundabout instead). Clustered near the junction – which, thanks to the one-way system, is no longer a roundabout – are most of Wadi Musa's shops, banks, mosques, cafés and hotels, as well as the bus station.

Past the town centre, the road coils down to a strip known as the **Tourist Street**, with hotels, cafés and restaurants on one side and the valley bed on the other. It ends at the landmark *Mövenpick* hotel, with the Petra Visitor Centre and ticket gate just beyond.

BY BUS AND SERVEECE

Bus station Wadi Musa's bus station is in the centre of town, down the hill behind the main mosque about 300m south of the Shaheed Roundabout. Instead of being dropped here, you could ask the bus driver to let you out at the hotel of your choice along the way. All routes have fewer buses running on Fridays.

Hassles and scams Regrettably, buses from Amman, Aqaba and Wadi Rum are often met at the bus station by touts, who try to bamboozle new arrivals into staying at particular hotels; needless to say, it's only the nastier places which engage in this kind of thing. In a *serveece* you may find that the driver "recommends" a particular hotel by taking you to the hotel: he does this to earn a commission from the hotel, who will correspondingly charge you more for your room. Hotels which encourage this kind of deception are unlikely to be the best in town. We cover similar scams employed by some Wadi Musa *serveece*-drivers in Chapter 1 (see page 91).

Reservations The few bus routes out of Wadi Musa are all very popular: you should always book seats in advance and be prepared to pay inflated fares of JD5–8 (including bags). Ask your hotel manager the day before to reserve you a place on a bus for the next morning. All buses start from the bus station, but if you've reserved a seat the bus should come to your hotel's door; if you're not ready when it arrives, it won't wait. If you know you'll be departing on a Friday – when there are far fewer buses – check schedules in advance with your hotel.

AMMAN (VIA DESERT HIGHWAY)

Minibuses and serveeces From Amman's Wihdat station, six or seven minibuses – and a few *serveeces* – head for Wadi Musa in the early morning and mid-afternoon, though on Fridays there may be nothing after midday. We cover these in more detail in Chapter 1 (see page 91). On the return journey, six or seven minibuses and a few *serveeces* depart Wadi Musa for Amman Wihdat between about 6am and noon/1pm. All run via the Desert Highway (3hr).

JETT buses A more comfortable coach from Amman, run by JETT, departs its Abdali office at 224 King Hussein St (☎06 566 4146, ⊕jett.com.jo) daily at 6.30am, dropping off at the Petra Visitor Centre by the gate, not the bus station. The JETT bus is the last public transport to leave Wadi Musa for Amman, departing from the Visitor Centre daily around 4.30 or 5pm (winter 4pm)

and terminating at JETT's Abdali office; buy tickets (JD11) from stalls near the Visitor Centre. It runs via the Desert Highway (3hr).

MADABA (VIA KING'S HIGHWAY)

A private bus (or, sometimes, taxi) runs daily from Madaba to Wadi Musa along the King's Highway (6–7hr). We cover this in detail in Chapter 5 (see page 219). It will drop you off wherever you ask. It only operates in the Madaba–Petra direction.

AQABA

From Aqaba (1hr 45min), four or five buses arrive in two clusters: morning and early afternoon. The same four or five buses depart Wadi Musa in two clusters: 6–8am, then 10am–noon. There might be one departure at around 3–4pm.

WADI RUM

One bus a day (1hr 30min) departs Wadi Musa for Rum at about 6.30am, and then leaves Rum around 8am for the journey to Wadi Musa.

KARAK

If it's running, one bus heads to Karak (2hr) via the Desert Highway about noon, returning to Wadi Musa in mid-afternoon.

MA'AN AND SHOBAK

Buses arrive and depart throughout the day (until mid-afternoon) to and from Ma'an (40min) and Shobak (30min). Bear in mind that if you want to get to Petra from Amman, Aqaba or just about any other town in southern Jordan, and there are no direct buses, take a bus to Ma'an instead: frequent connections leave Ma'an for Wadi Musa, or it's easy to find a taxi for around JD10–12. Shobak has no connections to anywhere, but is a good place to start a hitch up the King's Highway to Qadisiyyeh and beyond.

BY TAXI

Chartering a taxi (seating up to four passengers) between Wadi Musa and Dana costs about JD30, Wadi Rum JD40–45, Aqaba JD45, Karak JD50–55, Amman on the Desert Highway JD70–80, or Amman along the King's Highway JD100 or more. A ride to Feynan, organized through the *Feynan Ecolodge* (see page 342), costs JD52.

GETTING AROUND

By bus Local minibuses shuttle from Wadi Musa north to the Bdul village of Umm Sayhoun (10min) and Beidha/Little Petra (20min), and south to Taybeh (20min).

By taxi The only means of transport within Wadi Musa is taxi. The tourist rate for a ride through town – from the Petra ticket gate to Ain Musa or anywhere in between – is JD2–3, but you'll probably have to bargain each time.

6

LOCAL TOUR OPTIONS

The ruins take top billing, but it's easy to tap into local knowledge for ways to enhance your stay in Petra. **Excursions** include a sunset horse ride in the hills, a half- or full day's hiking in the countryside nearby, wilderness mountain biking, a two-day camel trek, and so on.

FULL-SERVICE TOUR COMPANIES

Tour agency offices on the Tourist Street near the Petra ticket gate, where you could pop in for a face-to-face chat, include: **Petra Moon** (☎ 03 215 6665, ⓦ petramoon.com), **Zaman Tours** (☎ 03 215 7723, ⓦ zamantours.com), **La Beduina** (☎ 03 215 7099, ⓦ labeduinatours.com) and **Jordan Tours & Travel** (☎ 03 215 4666, ⓦ jordantours-travel.com).

SMALLER TOUR COMPANIES

There are many smaller operations, run by recommended individual guides and focused mainly on **hiking** and low-key **wilderness exploration. They** include **Jordan Beauty Tours** (☎ 03 215 4999, ⓦ jordanbeauty.com) and **Jordan Inspiration Tours** (☎ 03 215 7317, ⓦ jitours.com). Petra-born guide **Mahmoud Twaissi** (☎ 077 725 4658, ⓦ mahmoudtwaissi. wordpress.com) is one of the best guides in the country, highly experienced and with a focus on hiking and nature tourism.

COMMUNITY-BASED TOURISM

To get well off the beaten track, contact the **Ammareen tribe** through their campsite at Little Petra (ⓦ ammarinbedouincamp.com; see page 296): their website includes outlines of guided treks on foot and by camel through areas of southern Jordan little known to outsiders.

    A Piece of Jordan (☎ 079 990 2916, ⓦ apieceofjordan.com), run by the wonderful Stephanie Altwassi – who has roots in both Wadi Musa and Birmingham (UK) – is a fantastic community tourism project. As well as supporting crafts projects, it offers "eco experiences" (JD25–55/person), where you join local families to harvest olives, spend a day on a farm, practise baking bread, dine in local homes and so on. Check online for details.

    Patricia, at **Petra Bed and Breakfast** (see page 296), and Jolanda, at **Petra Fig Tree Villa** (see page 296), can advise on horseriding and yoga retreats – and both are also connected with **In2Jordan** (☎ 079 110 2629, ⓦ in2jordan.com), an innovative UK/European/Jordanian firm based in Wadi Musa that specializes in yoga/relaxation weekends and horseriding retreats in the nearby mountains, as well as dinners hosted by local families. In2Jordan can also assemble tailor-made itineraries around the country.

ACCOMMODATION

Wadi Musa has dozens of **hotels**, but many are drab mid-range places without much style or comfort; our recommendations pick out the best. Hotel **prices** here are more open to bargaining than anywhere else in Jordan. Another feature of Wadi Musa is that all hotels have rates for "room only", "bed and breakfast" and "half board" (breakfast and dinner): make sure you confirm what you want when you check in. All rates we quote in this section are for **bed and breakfast**. In a budget hotel the main thing to look out for is **heating**: summer nights are pleasantly cool (several places offer cut-price rates for sleeping on a mattress on the roof), but all during winter and even as late as April, mornings and evenings can be chilly. **Location** is also an issue: you have to weigh up whether you'd rather pay more to be closer to the Petra gate, or would prefer to be up in the town centre near local life. Most mid-range hotels rely on tour-group business – and so may have **price flexibility** when demand is low. At the top end, for such

a famous location you might expect world-class design, service and amenities, but nowhere truly matches up.

NEAR THE GATE

Candles On the road leading north off Tourist St ☎ 077 777 7379, ⓦ candlespetra.com; map p.290. A tired and uninspired place, which scrapes a recommendation here for its location, a short walk from the Petra gate, and for its upper-floor rooms, particularly the corner room 101 and the junior suite 311, both of which offer space and views that might make up for the small and disappointing bathrooms. Some rooms have enclosed balconies; others can be connected for families. **JD33**

Guest House Hotel Beside Petra gate ☎ 03 215 6266, ⓦ guesthouse-petra.com; map p.290. Neither a guesthouse nor a "rest house" (its previous name) but a 72-room hotel, which forms part of the adjacent (closed) *Crowne Plaza* resort. It isn't up to much by itself:

the welcome is warm enough but the rooms – in generic chain-hotel style – could do with a revamp. What sells it is the location, right beside the gate into Petra and with the *Cave Bar*, (a pub in a 2000-year-old tomb, see page 298), directly beside the hotel entrance. JD85

Mövenpick Tourist St ☎03 215 7111, ⓦmovenpick. com; map p.290. Petra's top choice, superbly designed in traditional Damascene style right down to the last exquisite detail. The stunning four-storey courtyard atrium, with its mosaic-tiled fountain and palm trees, vies for gasps with the adjacent bar, where hand-carved wooden screens and embroidered fabrics are backed by hand-painted walls inlaid with turquoise and gold leaf. The 183 guest rooms are immaculate, service is calm and efficient, and the location – metres from the Petra gate – ideal. Don't miss the roof garden at sunset. Its sister property, the similarly grand *Mövenpick Nabatean Castle*, located 6.5km out on the Scenic Rd, is often used only for tour groups and sometimes has restricted opening: check with the main hotel. JD130

Petra Moon Just north of Tourist St ☎03 215 6220, ⓦpetramoonhotel.com; map p.290. This locally owned and run four-star property is easily the sassiest hotel in town, the tone set by the lobby's striking blend of Damascene-style traditional design with a nightclub-chic colour scheme in black and gold – deep sofas, venetian blinds, sparkly mosaic tiles and all. The 52 rooms are of an excellent standard, with quality fabrics and textures set off by tasteful contemporary design, as well as soundproofing and double-glazing. Considering the quality of service and amenities, and the location – a short walk from the Petra gate – this is a bargain. JD85

Petra Palace Tourist St ☎03 215 6723, ⓦpetrapalace. com; map p.290. A fine local upper-three-star hotel near the Petra gate with a long history – opened in 1989, extended first in 2007 and then in stages thereafter, now offering 190 rooms in total. The soundproofed rooms are spacious and well appointed – marble-floored in one wing, carpeted in the other, all of them overlooking one of the two swimming pools. Service is tip-top: the tour operators from around the world who book groups here year after year expect nothing less. As an individual, bargain to bring the quoted rate down a tad. JD75

Silk Road Just north of Tourist St ☎03 215 7222, ⓦpetrasilkroad.com; map p.290. Pleasant upper-three-star property down by the Petra gate, frequently used by tour groups and – because of the location – representing decent value for money. Rooms are comfortable, though some of the infrastructure is a bit make-do. Rooms overlooking the street can be a bit noisy. Nonetheless this is a reliable hotel with a reputation to uphold. JD55

Sunset Tourist St ☎03 215 6579, ⓦpetrasunset.com; map p.290. The only remotely budget-like hotel located on the Tourist St, close to the gate – an adequate option

if you lower your expectations. Service isn't up to much at all. Rooms are all en suite, in two distinct classes: the standard rooms (without a/c) can be a bit too poky for comfort, but the roomier deluxe a/c ones are overpriced (JD55) and characterless. Bargain hard: rates may well move. JD35

TOWN CENTRE

Amra Palace 250m south of Midtown Roundabout ☎03 215 7070, ⓦamrapalace.com; map p.290. Reasonable upper-three-star hotel on a quiet backstreet in the town centre – big, too, with 72 rooms. It has attractive pine decor, a nice little palm-shaded garden and a covered swimming pool with Turkish bath. Rooms are a little ho-hum in terms of decor, but the hotel gets a lot of tour-group business, which is a vote of confidence in itself. Briskly efficient service can sometimes lack the personal touch. Bargain to bring the quoted rate down. JD50

★ **Cleopatra** 250m south of Midtown Roundabout ☎077 636 6243; map p.290. Wadi Musa's best budget hotel by a country mile, with clean, comfortable rooms, decent food and super-friendly staff willing to go the extra mile for you – ask for details of onward transport around the country. It's located in a quiet spot above the town centre, with easy access and free parking. This is a cheerful, well-equipped, genuinely welcoming place. JD34

El-Rashid Beside Midtown Roundabout ☎03 215 6800; map p.290. Decent option overlooking Wadi Musa's central roundabout, with 25 rooms that are clean and moderately well kitted out, though perhaps a little tired round the edges. Service, though, is excellent and the place has a good reputation among travellers. Worth a look. JD40

Valley Stars Inn Off Police Roundabout ☎03 215 5733; map p.290. This two-star is the closest Petra gets to a boutique hotel, located slightly above the town centre: just eight rooms, spacious, clean and quiet, with stone-tiled floors and mildly stylish interiors. A great choice for individual travellers seeking to escape Petra's mass-market tourism. JD50

FURTHER OUT

★ **Al-Anbat** Just below Ain Musa ☎03 215 6265, ⓦalanbat.com; map p.290. Great-value, low-priced mid-range option, with friendly service and a long-standing reputation (it opened in 1979). Its 91 rooms are among the largest in Wadi Musa: airy and spacious, with

6

high ceilings, decent furniture and balconies offering exceptional sunset views from this elevated location high above Wadi Musa town. Tile floors and (on the uppermost level) double-glazing as well as free transport to and from the gate, a place to pitch a tent (or park a caravan) and a shaded swimming pool with Turkish bath add to the appeal. There are cheaper rooms at the *Al-Anbat II* annexe down in the town centre. Rates include half board. JD40

Marriott Scenic Rd ☎03 215 6407, ⓦmarriott.com/mpqmc; map p.290. An excellent five-star choice, located 4.5km out of town high up on the Scenic Rd, with spectacular views over the mountains. Public areas are comfortable but not excessively grand, and there's a good swimming pool with a panoramic view across the valley. It has 99 rooms, all good, with big windows, well-appointed bathrooms and large beds. Service is outstanding – perhaps the best in Wadi Musa. JD85

Mussa Spring Beside Ain Musa ☎03 215 6310; map p.290. Long-standing backpackers' favourite, situated right up at the top of the town beside Ain Musa, with mostly friendly staff and a sociable atmosphere. Rooms are basic but clean: there are singles, doubles and dorms, both en suite and with shared bathrooms. Dorms JD7, doubles JD16

★ **Petra Bed & Breakfast** 1.5km northwest of town centre ☎077 722 0825, ⓦpetrabedandbreakfast.com; map p.290. Lovely little family-run B&B. Four guest rooms occupy the upper floor in the home of Belgian-Jordanian couple Patricia Enkels and Eid Al Hasanat (who live on the ground floor). Rooms – two doubles, a twin and a quad – are big, airy and comfortable, with carpets or bedouin rugs underfoot and well-equipped en-suite bathrooms. There's a pleasant guest lounge, as well as a shaded balcony gazing out over the town; everything has that personal touch. The

house stands in a peaceful location on the stony hillsides of the (unsigned) Zeitun district on the north side of Wadi Musa: call ahead for directions or a pick-up. Patricia is a charming host, keeping the place spotless, serving a generous breakfast inside or alfresco – and both she and Eid are experienced horse riders, offering excursions out into the hills from JD20/hr. JD65

★ **Petra Fig Tree Villa** A few hundred metres north of Tourist St ☎077 909 2675, ⓦpetrafigtreevilla.com; map p.290. Beautifully presented B&B in the cat-friendly home of Jolanda Koopman, who moved here in 2015. Accommodation is spread across four rooms – a four-poster single, a twin and two doubles, one with a private terrace looking over Petra's mountains. Everything is spotless and charmingly decorated, with taste and simplicity, but none of the rooms is en suite: guests share a bathroom. It's in a great location, on a hillside behind the Tourist St, walkable down into Petra (though you'd want a taxi back up). However, the main draw is the warmth of the welcome and the home-cooked food. Jolanda is a qualified masseur, and also hosts yoga retreats. JD60

CAMPSITES

Camping is forbidden within Petra itself. Other than pitching a tent at the *Al-Anbat* hotel (see page 295) or the *Ammarin Camp* (see below), there aren't many options nearby. As you drive north of Wadi Musa towards Beidha/Little Petra, you'll see some locally run camps signposted off to the side of the road – but the "luxury" ones aren't luxurious and the "bedouin" ones aren't bedouin. Have a look on ⓦcouchsurfing.com for the unusual option of spending a night in a cave in one of Petra's far-flung corners.

★ **Ammarin Camp** Little Petra ☎079 975 5551, ⓦammarinbedouincamp.com. Petra's best camping

---

WADI MUSA ACCOMMODATION SCAMS

If you're travelling on a budget, be aware that in Wadi Musa – as in Wadi Rum – there are people involved in the lower echelons of the tourism industry who **target backpackers** for money or sex. If you keep your ear to the ground, and monitor online forums, you'll come across stories of pushy staff at particular hotels, rip-off taxi drivers, restaurant owners playing the gigolo, and worse. If we haven't reviewed a particular hotel, there's probably a good reason why you should avoid it.

Common petty deceptions include paying **taxi drivers** to bring tourists to the door (and then charging the tourists higher rates to make it up) and/or setting a **loss-leading room rate** before extracting profit on meals, transport, internet, beers and so on. One particularly lucrative line is selling **cheap desert tours** of Wadi Rum; check out our warning in Chapter 7 (see page 320).

There's also **sexual harassment**: a favoured ploy of local slimeballs is to offer to show you some amazing remote viewpoint, or invite you to an evening meal at a special campsite. Women travellers in Wadi Musa should never accept such an offer. Even if things start OK, stories abound of alcohol-emboldened hosts starting after-dinner games teaching you the Arabic words for parts of the body. Situations can rapidly escalate.

6

TURKISH BATHS

After a day of walking in the heat, steaming the dust out of your pores in a **Turkish bath** (or hammam) has become a popular evening pastime in Wadi Musa (usually 5–10pm). Many of the mid-range and luxury hotels have their own on-site Turkish baths, some with separate sections for men and women, others mixed – though you'll only ever be among tourists; the only local men in these places are the attendants. An hour's steaming, soaking, scrubbing and rudimentary massaging starts from around JD25 per person. In town, aim for the **Al-Anbat**, **Amra Palace** or **Petra Palace** hotels – or the stand-alone **Salome Turkish Bath** (☎03 215 7342), which offers free transport to and from your hotel. For a more sophisticated, up-market experience, plump for the *Marriott* hotel out of town.

option, a permanent encampment run by the Ammareen bedouin tribe, and located in a beautiful, quiet spot out near Little Petra: from the Little Petra access road, you turn off at the camp's signpost and drive for 1km on a marked dirt track to reach the campsite, which is tucked away out of site behind a crag. A taxi from Wadi Musa is about JD8–10. The site has a series of long, low bedouin goat-hair tents divided up into sections and given concrete floors: you sleep on reasonably comfortable beds with mattresses, and there's a block with flushing toilets and hot and cold running water. The big plus is that you're completely away from the hustle and bustle of Wadi Musa, nestling in among the mountains under a starry sky – and that your money is going straight to the Ammareen community cooperative. It's a wonderful experience. You can also pitch your own tent here (JD15/ person). See online for full price list; this rate is for two people including dinner and breakfast. **JD56**

EATING

For **eating** in Wadi Musa, most travellers either stick with whatever's on offer from their hotel buffet or end up chewing pizza at one of the distinctly ordinary restaurants on the Tourist St down by the Petra gate. There are some better options up in town – though, as usual, the most visible places clustered around the central roundabout tend to be the worst. Note that – even for locals – food in Wadi Musa is **expensive**, with fruit and veg costing up to double the price in Amman. Most staples are also prone to significant **price hikes** for foreigners: a falafel sandwich, for which a local would pay less than JD0.50, might cost you more than JD1. There's little to be done about this, and not much point arguing, just so long as you don't end up paying silly money. Your best bet is to check prices in advance, tiresome though that is. Within Petra itself, eating options are pretty limited (see page 260).

★ **Arabi** By Midtown Roundabout ☎03 215 7661; map p.290. One of Wadi Musa's best local restaurants, located just up from the main roundabout. It's always busy, and does a wide range of basic dishes – falafel, hummus, *fuul*, salads, kebabs and more, served with fresh flatbread. The place is clean, staff are friendly and prices are acceptable: a meal shouldn't cost more than JD6–9. Daily 6am–10pm.

Bukhara Town centre ☎03 215 4225; map p.290. A sociable restaurant in the centre of town, with streetside tables offering views of the mountains. The speciality is grilled meat: mouthwateringly aromatic smoke from the barbecuing kebabs regularly wafts over the street. A locals' favourite. Expect to pay JD8–10 a head. Daily noon–10pm.

Mövenpick Tourist St ☎03 215 7111, ⊛movenpick. com; map p.290. The hotel's *Al-Saraya* restaurant has a lavish dinner buffet (daily 6.30–11pm), from fresh vegetables wok-fried as you watch, through gourmet breads, kebabs, fresh fish and an array of salads to proper Black Forest gateau. It's not cheap (about JD25), but the quality and variety are consistently excellent. They also do a la carte. Alongside, but several notches up the scale, *Al-Iwan* restaurant (daily 7–11.30pm) offers seriously sophisticated a la carte dining off a Mediterranean-inspired menu for JD50 and up, in a romantic candlelit setting. For lighter bites, after a day in Petra you could cool off in the *Mövenpick's* splendid Syrian-style atrium lounge with a Swiss ice cream sundae – or head up to the roof garden (summer daily 4pm–midnight) for tea and/or an *argileh* as the sun sets behind the mountains. In addition, the Caravan Stop shop (daily 9am–midnight) sells delicious croissants, ice creams, espresso and fresh-baked loaves.

★ **al-Qantarah** North of Tourist St ☎03 215 5535, ⊛al-qantarah.com; map p.290. Excellent choice for traditional Arabic cuisine, in an impressive setting of a purpose-built townhouse on the northern edge of the centre. Although relying on tour-group business (it can seat 450, with seventy more on the terrace), this place unusually also draws local families for its range of Jordanian specialities, including less common dishes such as *gidreh* (or *qidreh*), a local variety of tagine, where

6

lamb or chicken is baked with rice and chickpeas in an earthenware pot. Expect a buffet at lunchtime and a la carte at dinner. A meal is around JD15. Daily 11.30am–4.30pm & 6.30–10pm.

Red Cave Tourist St ☎03 215 7799; map p.290. The interior of the *Red Cave* – a good choice near the gate – is large and cool, and the food is excellent, including, among many staple dishes, a bedouin *gallaya* (rice with lamb or chicken in a spicy tomato/onion sauce). Meze are JD2–3,

most mains JD6–10. Daily 10am–10pm.

Sanabel Bakery Town centre ☎03 215 7925; map p.290. Busy local bakery in the centre of town, open from before dawn, churning out bread as well as tasty cheese pastries, *manaqish*, baklava, biscuits and other sweet nibbles: assemble picnic fare for under JD5. Mostly for takeaway, though there's a small seating area. Daily 5am–10pm.

DRINKING

The only places for **drinking alcohol** are in the big hotels or a couple of specifically designated bars.

Cave Bar By the Petra gate ☎03 215 6266; map p.290. Essentially a rather cheesy pub which has been crowbarred into an evocative 2000-year-old Nabatean tomb, elegantly carved in sandstone. Wadi Musa town has grown up around it, and the tomb/bar now stands directly outside, and is catered by, the *Guest House Hotel* (see page 294). It's dim and dark, with plenty of quiet corners in which to hole up with a beer (JD5–8). They also have a long food menu. Daily noon–midnight.

Al-Maqa'ad Mövenpick hotel, Tourist St ☎03 215 7111;

map p.290. The *Mövenpick*'s bar is a stunning place to kick back with a sundowner (from JD5). It's designed in a beautifully ornate Arabian style, with hand-carved wooden screens, embroidered fabrics and cushions and a gilded wood ceiling. Daily 4pm–midnight.

Wranglers Pub Petra Palace hotel, Tourist St ☎03 215 6723; map p.290. The third of the hotel bars on the Tourist St is the *Wranglers Pub*, a cosy little den inside this big hotel that's a pleasantly sociable spot for a beer or two (JD4–7), though everything is in cans or bottles – no draught. Daily 2pm–midnight.

SHOPPING

For shopping, head down to the Tourist St near the gate, where you'll find a string of **craft and souvenir shops** – all open long hours, roughly 9am to 11pm – selling postcards and trinkets as well as rugs and antiques. Several are the retail outlets for local women's cooperatives, selling handmade crafts.

Made In Jordan Tourist St ☎03 215 5700; map p.290. A gallery and gift shop where the crafts come from charitable suppliers such as the Royal Society for the Conservation of Nature, the Jordan River Foundation, the Noor al-Hussein Foundation and the Royal Marine Conservation Society

(JREDS) – all of which employ chiefly rural women (in JREDS' case, the wives and daughters of Aqaba fishermen) to produce traditional crafts and handmade items of the highest quality. Also on show are pieces made by individual artisans from Wadi Musa and around Jordan.

Sand Castle Tourist St ☎03 215 7326, ⊕petra sandcastle.com; map p.290. This shop is notable for its high-quality antiques, including pieces in copper, brass, silver and wood from Syria, Yemen and elsewhere, as well as hand-woven carpets.

PETRA KITCHEN

Located on the Tourist Street near the gate into Petra, the **Petra Kitchen** is a fine local initiative. This is not a true restaurant; rather, it is a way for a small number of visitors to get hands-on experience of Jordanian culture by working with a team of locals (both men and women) to prepare ingredients, cook an evening meal and then eat together.

After a menu briefing, you're let loose to chop, mix and assemble under guidance a range of salads, soup, hot and cold meze (starters), a main course such as *mansaf* or *maqlouba*, and bedouin coffee and tea – the idea being that you learn new culinary techniques, handle possibly unfamiliar products and break the social ice at the same time. The ingredients are all locally sourced; the tableware comes from the women's ceramics workshop at Iraq al-Amir, near Amman; and the aprons, tablecloths and napkins are all hand-embroidered by women working with the Jordan River Foundation.

The evening starts at 7.30pm (winter 6.30pm), running for three hours, and takes place when demand is sufficient – generally every night in high season. It costs JD35 per person, excluding wine. To take part you must **book in advance** (☎03 215 5900, ⊕petrakitchen. com). They can also extend the concept to run as a five-day **culinary course**.

USEFUL ARABIC PLACE NAMES

Ain Musa	عين موسى	Ras an-Naqab	رأس النقب
Ammareen camp	مخيم العمارين	Taybeh	الطيبة
Bdul village	إسكان البدول	Udhruh	أذرح
Bir Mathkoor	بئر مذكور	Umm Sayhoun	أم صيحون
Rajif	الراجف	Visitor Centre	مركز الزوار

DIRECTORY

6

Hospital Queen Rania Hospital (☎ 03 215 0628) – with 24hr emergency room – is about 5km out of town on the Scenic Rd towards Taybeh.

Pharmacies Pharmacies in Wadi Musa town centre have qualified English-speaking staff.

Police In an emergency, dial ☎ 911. English-speaking Tourist Police patrol most parts of the Petra ruins in daylight hours, and are available 24hr at their office (☎ 03 215 6487) by the Visitor Centre. Police headquarters (☎ 03 215 6551) is beside the Police Roundabout.

Aqaba and the southern desert

WADI RUM

Aqaba and the southern desert

The huge eastern deserts of Jordan are mostly stony plains of limestone or basalt, but much of the southern desert is sand, presaging the dunes and vast emptinesses of the Arabian interior. In the far south, squeezed onto Jordan's only stretch of coastline, Aqaba forms a pleasant urban counterpoint to the breathtaking marine flora and fauna which thrive in the warm Red Sea waters just offshore. The real highlights, though, lie inland. You shouldn't leave Jordan without spending time in the extraordinary desert moonscape of Wadi Rum, haunt of Lawrence of Arabia and starting point for camel treks into the red sands, while the award-winning ecolodge at Feynan makes a fabulous hideaway for walks, cultural encounters and off-the-beaten-track exploration in the little-visited Wadi Araba desert.

Two of the three north–south highways connecting Amman with Aqaba are desert roads, only really of interest as access routes to and from southern Jordan, so we've included them in this chapter. The easternmost of the three, the so-called **Desert Highway**, follows the line of the old Hejaz Railway and serves as a demarcation boundary between well-watered hills to the west and the open desert. The westernmost of the three is the **Wadi Araba** road, which hugs the line of the Israeli border south of the Dead Sea. The middle route of the three – the King's Highway – is covered in detail in Chapter 5.

GETTING AROUND	AQABA AND THE SOUTHERN DESERT

Plenty of **buses** serve the south's biggest cities – Aqaba and Ma'an – and you can get connections from both of them to other destinations in the region. Aqaba is also a major entry point to Jordan, with an international **airport**, a **ferry** port serving **Egypt** and land crossings with **Israel** and **Saudi Arabia**. Destinations in the south are often at least as appealing as the epic journeys to get to them: the freedom

renting a car (see page 33) gives really comes into its own when you're travelling in the desert here. Being able to pull over and walk even 100m away from the highway, to get a firsthand experience of the wide open vistas rather than seeing them skim past a dirty window, is worth paying for.

Aqaba

Jordan's beach resort of **AQABA** (say it "acka-buh") glories in an idyllic, sunny setting on the shores of the Red Sea, at the country's southernmost tip. From a rather dowdy backwater, in the last fifteen years or so Aqaba has transformed itself into a pleasant, if still under-resourced, **leisure destination**. Hotels at all grades are springing up in the town as well as at luxury waterfront developments up and down the coast; investment is coming in to improve the city's infrastructure and facilities; and flights direct into Aqaba's under-used international airport are enabling holiday-makers to bypass Amman and the north of the country altogether. Some of the best **diving and snorkelling** in the world is centred on the unspoiled coral reefs that hug the coast just south of the town – an engaging contrast with the nearby desert attractions of Petra and Wadi Rum.

The city centre forms a dense network of streets and alleys clustered just behind the beach road (called the "**Corniche**"). Aside from shopping and promenading after dark, sights are limited to a **Mamluke fort** and some scanty archeological remains. You're likely to have more fun in the **water** – hotel pool, Red Sea or both.

FEYNAN ECOLODGE

Highlights

❶ **Aqaba** Red Sea diving, snorkelling and year-round sunbathing at Jordan's only beach resort, ranged alongside spectacular coral reefs. See page 302

❷ **Wadi Rum** One of the world's most alluring desert destinations, rugged, majestic and endlessly memorable. Think immense vistas, towering cliffs, red dunes and sleeping under the stars. Book ahead with a bedouin guide for an experience to savour. See page 320

❸ **Desert driving** Three long desert drives capture the spirit and look of southern Jordan's epic landscapes: the Desert Highway from

Amman, the Wadi Araba road, and, least travelled of all, the Ma'an–Azraq road through Jafr. See page 335

❹ **Ras an-Naqab** Take in stupendous panoramic views out over the sandy Hisma desert from this roadside stop at the edge of Jordan's highland plateau. See page 338

❺ **Feynan Ecolodge** This remote desert hotel offers a unique experience of environmentally friendly low-impact nature tourism amid traditional bedouin cultures. A stylish, evocative retreat for canyon trekkers and desert dreamers alike. See page 341

HIGHLIGHTS ARE MARKED ON THE MAP ON PAGE 304

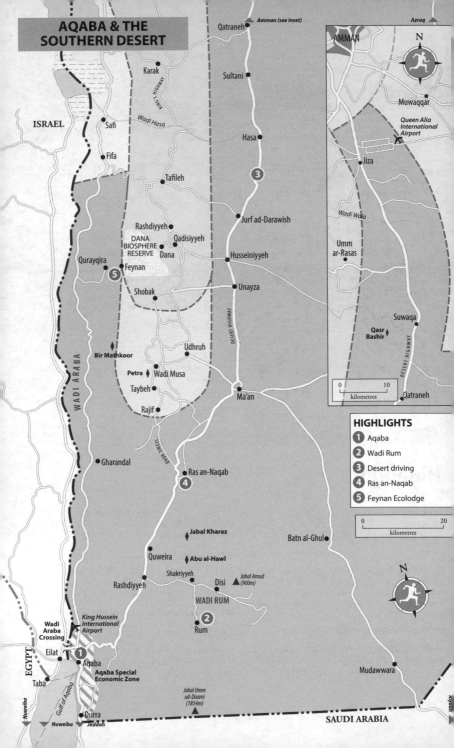

AQABA & THE SOUTHERN DESERT

ISRAEL

Qatraneh

Azraq

AMMAN

Amman (see inset)

Karak

Sultani

Muwaqqar

Safi

Wadi Hasa

Hasa

Queen Alia
International
Airport

Fifa

③

Jiza

Tafileh

Wadi Wala

Rashdiyyeh

Jurf ad-Darawish

Qadisiyyeh

DANA
BIOSPHERE
RESERVE   Dana

Husseiniyyeh

Umm
ar-Rasas

Qurayqira

Feynan

⑤

Suwaqa

Shobak

Unayza

Qasr
Bashir

0   10
kilometres

Bir Mathkoor

Udhruh

Petra ♦ Wadi Musa

Taybeh

Qatraneh

Rajif

Ma'an

HIGHLIGHTS

① Aqaba

② Wadi Rum

③ Desert driving

④ Ras an-Naqab

⑤ Feynan Ecolodge

Gharandal

Ras an-Naqab

④

0   20
kilometres

Jabal Kharaz

Batn al-Ghul

Quweira

♦ Abu al-Hawl

Shakriyyeh   Disi

Jabal Amud
(900m)

Rashdiyyeh

WADI RUM

King Hussein
International
Airport

②
Rum

N

Wadi
Araba
Crossing

Eilat

①

Taba

Aqaba

Aqaba Special
Economic Zone

Mudawwara

EGYPT

Gulf of Aqaba

Jabal Umm
ad-Daami
(1854m)

Durra

SAUDI ARABIA

Nuweiba

Nuweiba   Jeddah

WADI ARABA

KING'S HIGHWAY

DESERT HIGHWAY

SCENIC ROAD

DESERT HIGHWAY

What to expect

Despite package tourists (many from Scandinavia and Eastern Europe) flip-flopping through the streets in shorts or bikinis, Aqaba's proximity to – and cultural links with – Saudi Arabia make this actually one of the more socially **conservative** urban centres in Jordan. Historically neither a trading port nor a commercial hub, Aqaba was only ever significant as a stopping-off point for pilgrims travelling to and from Mecca: if you've come expecting a pacy, cosmopolitan mini-Dubai, you'll be disappointed. The contradictions between deep-set tradition, big business and mass tourism are giving Aqaba plenty to think about.

There's now a year-round **high season**. Jordan's standard peaks (March–May & Sept–Nov) are supplemented by European tourists seeking Aqaba's winter sun (Dec–Feb). Summer (June–Aug) is the main Saudi and Gulf holiday season, and also when Europeans come to sizzle on the beaches. The hajj pilgrimage – currently in July and August – is an added complication, with thousands of Egyptian and North African pilgrims stopping off in Aqaba on their way home. And holiday weekends can see Aqaba booked solid with domestic tourists, as Ammanis and others head for a short break by the seaside.

Another factor to reckon with is the extreme **heat and humidity**. During the four mild months around Christmas, a few days in Aqaba can pleasantly warm the chill of Amman from your bones (not for nothing does King Abdullah keep a winter residence here), but for the rest of the year, daytime temperatures damply soar. The four months of summer can be stifling, with July and August's 50° days and 30° nights too much to bear.

Brief history

The presence of freshwater springs rising just below Aqaba's beaches has ensured almost continuous habitation of this bit of shore for thousands of years, though names have changed many times – from Biblical **Elot** to Aela, Ailana or Aila during the Roman and Islamic periods. The Arabic word *aqaba* means "alley", and is a shortening of "**Aqabat Aila**", referring to the narrow Wadi Yitm pass that was formerly the only route into the town through the mountains to the north.

The biblical era

One of the earliest references to a settlement here comes in the Old Testament (I Kings). **King Solomon** built a large port at Ezion Geber "beside Elot on the shore of the Red Sea" both for trade and also to house his new navy. During the 1930s, excavations at Tell al-Khaleifeh, a little west of Aqaba, seemed to indicate occupation around the time of Solomon, but archeologists – hampered by construction of the modern Jordanian–Israeli border fence – later pinpointed occupation to have begun during the eighth century BC, much later than Solomon. Ongoing investigation is suspended while the *tell* lies in a militarily restricted zone, but nonetheless the real Ezion Geber must have been close by.

The **Nabateans** controlled a series of ports from Aqaba all down the eastern Gulf coast. Aqaba's fresh water also ensured that the town became a caravan stop for merchants arriving from Arabia, with routes leading north to Petra and Syria, northwest to the Mediterranean coast at Gaza and west across the Sinai desert into Egypt. A highway constructed by the Roman Emperor Trajan in 111–14 AD led to Aqaba from his provincial capital at Bosra (Syria). Recent excavations beneath the beach revealed the world's oldest purpose-built church, dated to around 300 AD.

The Crusaders and after

During the **Byzantine** period, Aqaba was the seat of a bishopric, and the town was the first prize to fall to the **Muslims** on their military advance northwards out of Arabia in 630. It flourished throughout the early Islamic period, hosting a theological seminary. By the tenth century, Aqaba was an important stop on the pilgrimage route to Mecca.

On their push into Transjordan after 1115, the **Crusaders** – led by Baldwin of Jerusalem – seized the town and built a castle, although no trace of it survives. In response, the Muslim resistance fortified a small offshore island, known to the Crusaders as the Île de Graye (today dubbed **Pharaoh's Island**), and within a century Salah ad-Din had retaken Aqaba on a campaign which eventually led to Jerusalem.

A small **Mamluke fort** on the shore was rebuilt in the early sixteenth century, just before the Ottoman seizure of power. For three hundred years, Aqaba again became an important **caravan stop**, but the opening of the **Suez Canal** in 1869 dealt a death blow. For the first time, seaborne trade around the region, and between Europe and Asia, became an economically viable alternative to the camel caravans. Equally, making the pilgrimage to the Holy Places by sea through Suez was infinitely preferable to the arduous journey through the desert via Aqaba. The town's fortunes rapidly declined, and during the 1917 Arab Revolt, the forces of **Faisal and Lawrence** were able to surprise the small Ottoman garrison by approaching through the desert from the north. With all defensive artillery directed towards the sea, Aqaba fell with barely a skirmish.

Ironically, when David Lean arrived in 1962 to stage the same incident for *Lawrence of Arabia*, he thought Aqaba looked wrong – and so departed to film the sequence in southern Spain instead.

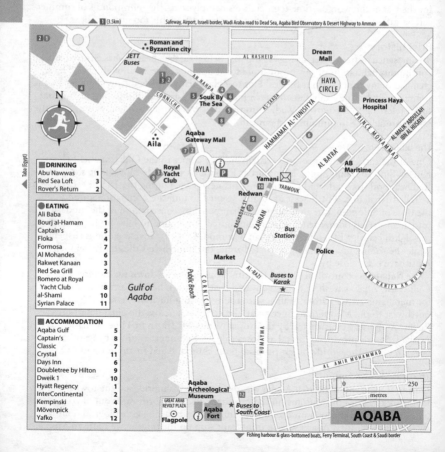

DEVELOPING AQABA

With tax breaks stimulating international investment into Aqaba, the range of **development projects** in and around the city is dizzying. In recent years, the entire city centre has been revamped, with new street furniture, public art and extensive replanting of palm trees (after the natural palm groves that used to line Aqaba's shore had all sadly been uprooted by previous, less visionary city authorities). New **shopping malls** have gone up, large numbers of **hotels** have opened or are due to open and extensive **residential suburbs** are being built to cater for the city's ballooning population.

Tala Bay (🌐 talabay.net), a wedge of luxury apartments, hotels and restaurants around a marina and sandy beach 15km south of Aqaba city centre, was the first. Work continues on the **Saraya** development (🌐 sarayaaqaba.com), comprising villas, apartments, hotels, water parks and beach facilities, and the adjacent **Ayla** (🌐 ayla.com.jo), featuring a leisure complex around a large inland lagoon and a Greg Norman-designed eighteen-hole golf course. Luxury hotels – invariably the first arrivals – are now open at both.

Work also continues on **Marsa Zayed** (🌐 marsazayed.org), a $12 billion Abu Dhabi-funded ten-year scheme to rebuild an entire chunk of the city centre by demolishing Aqaba's sea-port and building a new one 20km south beside the Saudi border (a process nearing completion in 2019), then filling the liberated 2km of prime urban waterfront with skyscrapers and marinas.

Another headline-grabbing scheme is the **Red Sea Astrarium** (🌐 rubiconholding.com), a $1.5 billion entertainment resort in the mountains above Aqaba, offering luxury hotels, shows, shopping and dining alongside an immersive space-flight experience in a Star Trek-themed zone. King Abdullah is known to be a Trekkie, and in 1995 appeared as an extra in the *Star Trek: Voyager* TV show (searchable on YouTube). All very bold, but at the time of writing, plans for the resort had been put on hold for a second time.

7

Into the 21st century

The sleepy fishing village was only dragged into modernity following a 1965 readjustment of the international border: Saudi Arabia got a patch of interior desert in exchange for Jordan's gaining an extra few kilometres of coastline and coral reef south of Aqaba. This made room for construction of full-size **port** facilities, and since then Aqaba has seen a resurgence in overland trade, although the camel caravans of antiquity have been replaced by a continuous stream of juggernauts: Aqaba port is the sole outlet for Jordan's principal export, phosphates, as well as a transit point for goods trucked to and from Iraq.

For years Aqaba was overshadowed by its huge Israeli neighbour **Eilat**, established in 1949 and clearly visible sprawling around the opposite shore of the Gulf of Aqaba. With the recent shift in priorities away from industry towards **beach tourism**, the endearingly run-down Aqaba of old is being unceremoniously shouldered aside – and its long-standing **fishing** industry has been reduced to just a hundred individuals. In tourism terms, what levelled the playing field was the establishment in 2000 of the **Aqaba Special Economic Zone** (ASEZ; 🌐 aqabazone.com), which covers the city and its surrounds. Set up with tax breaks for business and lowered customs duties, it has had a good deal of success, driving growth and spurring innovation. After 2008, Aqaba was the home of the Steven Spielberg-backed (but regrettably now defunct) **Red Sea Institute of Cinematic Arts**, training students from across the region in acting, cinematography and direction – and the city remains the home of several of Jordan's multibillion-dollar megaprojects. Aqaba is on the up.

Aqaba flagpole

Great Arab Revolt Plaza • Open access • Free

Aqaba's most identifiable landmark soars above the waterfront, visible not just from around town, but also from the Israeli, Egyptian and Saudi coasts at this end of the gulf. The giant **Aqaba flagpole**, at 132m, is one of the tallest freestanding flagpoles in

FREE WITH JORDAN PASS

Throughout this Guide, "free with JP" means that the attraction grants free admission to holders of the **Jordan Pass** (see page 55).

the world, more than 2.5m thick at the base. Despite a popular misconception, it doesn't fly the Jordanian flag. The huge black-green-white standard (30m by 60m) which flaps in the prevailing northerlies is the **flag of the Great Arab Revolt**, also adopted for a time by the short-lived Kingdom of the Hejaz (which fell to Saudi forces in 1925). It commemorates the successful attack on Aqaba in 1917 by Arab armies under Faisal and Lawrence, which ousted an Ottoman garrison and opened the way for the capture of Damascus the following year. The waterfront square in which the flagpole stands is named **Great Arab Revolt Plaza**; it's an unromantically bare concrete space, flanked by a couple of ordinary cafés, which acts as a focus for the evening *passeggiata*.

Aqaba fort

Beside Aqaba flagpole • Closed for renovation at the time of writing; formerly daily 8am–6pm (winter till 4pm) • Joint ticket with archeological museum JD3, free with JP

The flagpole looms above the atmospheric **Aqaba fort**, just back from the beach. Semicircular towers flanking the Mamluke fort's impressive entrance each bear a calligraphic invocation to Allah; the arch that currently spans the gap between them is much narrower than the original, the line of which can still be traced. Overhead is a panel bearing the Hashemite coat of arms, installed following the victory in 1917.

The fort itself was built in 1320; inside the gloomy cross-vaulted entranceway, a long inscription runs around the walls, celebrating renovations by the penultimate Mamluke sultan **Qansawh al-Ghawni** ("slayer of the unbelievers and the polytheists, reviver of justice in the universe") in either 1504–05 or 1514–15. A roundel commemorates further rebuilding work in 996 AH (1587 AD), by which time the Ottomans were in power.

Through a dark passageway lies a domed area, beyond which opens the large **courtyard**, dominated by a huge eucalyptus. This fort was the main focus of Aqaba's caravan trade for centuries, right through into the modern era. Rooms all around the walls – some of which have been restored – testify to its function as caravanserai for much of its later life. The ruined section to the right as you enter the courtyard was destroyed mostly by shells fired from British gunboats during the Arab Revolt. Opposite the entrance is a concrete-and-plaster mosque; steps to the left of it can bring you up onto the highest point of the walls for a dreamy view through the palm trees and over the blue gulf waters.

Aqaba Archeological Museum

Beside Aqaba fort • Closed for renovation at the time of writing; formerly daily 8am–6pm (winter till 4pm) • Joint ticket with fort JD3, free with JP

The rather dusty collection in the little **Aqaba Archeological Museum** includes coins and pottery from Egypt (including a fine lustreware bowl from tenth-century Fatimid Cairo), Iraq and Ethiopia, as well as some exquisite tenth- and eleventh-century Chinese ceramics. Among Islamic-era frescoes and three exquisite Nabatean bronze figurines, found at Wadi Rum, you'll spot the first milestone of the Roman Via Nova Traiana, inscribed "from the borders of Syria to the Red Sea" and discovered on the beach. The museum occupies part of the **House of Sheikh Hussein bin Ali**. Hussein – the current king's great-great-grandfather – spent six months here during 1924, in an attempt to overturn the 1923 Anglo-Jordanian Treaty, which had separated Transjordan from the Hejaz and Palestine (and had excluded him from power). A room contains mementoes of the visit: huge *mansaf* platters, coffee grinders, camel saddles and copperware.

Across from the fort is a small shop selling an excellent range of crafts, textiles, ceramics and jewellery from charitable projects all over Jordan.

The public beach

The only stretch of free-entry **public beach** in town comprises the few hundred metres north of the flagpole square, known variously as Palm Beach or Al-Ghandour Beach. It's a great place to soak up some local atmosphere, especially on a Friday when the whole area is packed with weekending families. Steps lead down from the Corniche road, past patches of cultivated garden beneath the palm trees, to the beachfront **promenade**, where families stroll and kids sell chewing gum and knick-knacks. The cafés that formerly spread across the sand have now been cleared – but there are still impromptu refreshment stalls galore, with radios blaring, children splashing and women sitting in the shallows fully clothed. It's a great spot to catch a flavour of what Aqaba used to be like, before the developers moved in. Needless to say, this is not the place either for sunbathing or for women to take a dip wearing anything less than an overcoat.

7

Aqaba Gateway Mall

Ayla Square (the main traffic circle on the Corniche, at the northern end of the public beach)

The odd little **Aqaba Gateway** Mall, fronted with a *McDonalds*, was conceived by Hollywood director Irvin "Shorty" Yeaworth, famous for 1958's *The Blob*. He planned a mini-theme park, hosting costumed characters parading amid a traditional-style souk of spices and jewellery. It was only part-completed when, in 2004, Yeaworth was killed in a traffic accident near Tafileh. Subsequently, the building works were rushed through and the retail units filled as quickly as possible – with the sad result that it has become just another mall of fast food and dismal shops, albeit with a replica Arab *dhow* moored on a lagoon in the middle.

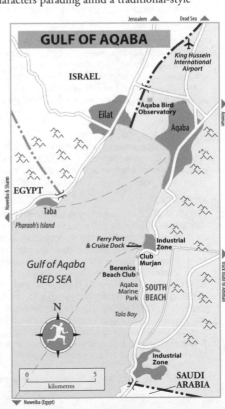

Souk By The Sea

An Nahda St beside *Captain's Hotel* • Oct–May Fri 5–11pm • Free • ⊕ soukbythesea.com (also Facebook)

The cheerful **Souk By The Sea** outdoor crafts market and bazaar was begun in 2011 as a community development scheme to keep tourist money in local hands, rather than having large national – or multinational – tourism businesses siphon off every penny. It's a lively affair, running in the middle of town every Friday evening (except in summer), and hosting dozens of stalls from Aqabawi artisans as well as crafts projects all across southern Jordan: expect the ubiquitous soaps, sand bottles and trinkets, but also a range of unique, handmade items from carpets to jewellery. There's also a small stage, with music and performances livening up proceedings during the evening.

Aila

Corniche, opposite *Aqaba Gulf* hotel • Daylight hours • Free

---

DIVING AND SNORKELLING AT AQABA

Some of the world's best **diving and snorkelling** is packed along the 20km or so of coastline between Aqaba and the Saudi border. If you've never been snorkelling before Aqaba is an easier, and more instantly attractive, place to start than nearby Eilat (Israel) or Sharm el-Sheikh (Egypt), with the reef shelving gently directly from the beach, cutting out the need for boat entries. Diving beginners can go down accompanied by an instructor at any of more than a dozen dive sites.

The major advantages of diving here are the condition of the **coral**, especially below the 6m line, and the excellent **biodiversity**. Aqaba was a relatively slow and careful starter in dive tourism, and so has managed to avoid severe deterioration of the reefs. It's also quiet: compared to the Sinai's two million annual dives, and Eilat's 750,000, Aqaba sees fewer than twenty thousand dives a year. Work by local environmental NGOs – principally the Royal Marine Conservation Society (ⓦfacebook.com/thejreds) – is raising awareness of conservation issues. Almost 9km of Aqaba's south coast is protected as the Aqaba Marine Park, which extends 350m offshore and 50m inland.

With the demolition of the town-centre port (completed in 2019), and ongoing construction of a new industrial port complex beside the Saudi border, **expect major changes** from the information we give here: dive sites and access could well be different when you visit.

WHAT TO EXPECT

Wherever you choose to dive or snorkel, wide fields of near-perfect soft **corals** stretch off into the startlingly clear blue water, huge heads of stony corals growing literally as big as a house. **Fish** life is also thrillingly diverse, with endless species of small and large multicoloured swimmers goggling back at you from all sides. Butterflyfish, angelfish, parrotfish and groupers are all common, as are shoals of damselfish, jewelfish and even moray eels. Experienced divers should not miss the chance to go down at **night**. All the dive centres listed below offer one-off dives, boat dives, PADI courses and more. Small groups could book ahead for a trip in a fancier craft, such as the submarine boat *Neptune* (ⓦfacebook.com/neptuneboat) or the wooden Phoenician-style vessel *Alissar* (ⓦc-guard.net).

It can be dangerous to **fly**, or climb to altitude, soon after diving. If you're driving from Aqaba (at sea level) up to Wadi Rum (at 950m), Petra (1100m) or Amman (800m), allow **eight hours** on land in Aqaba after diving to let your body adjust. The sea-level drive to the Dead Sea is fine. If you're flying out of Aqaba, give yourself at least **eighteen hours** on land before departure.

DIVE SITES

Aqaba's south coast hosts more than a dozen **dive sites**, although, confusingly, different dive centres use different names, and sometimes divide one site into two or more areas (Dive Aqaba, for instance, lists more than thirty sites, including several technical dives in deep water). Always consult a dive centre in advance about the latest conditions; the account below – which runs from north to south – is not meant to be exhaustive.

Just south of the Marine Science Station's fenced-off area is **First Bay**, with the popular **Cazar Reef** directly offshore from Club Murjan beach beside the gently sloping **Eel Garden**. South is the **King Abdullah Reef**, which extends for several hundred metres offshore and is good for snorkelling as well as diving; close by is the steeply sloping **Black Rock**, with a wide variety of massive hard corals and the added attraction of occasional turtle sightings.

About 13km south of town and barely 50m from the shore lies the **wreck of the Cedar Pride**, a Lebanese cargo ship sunk here in 1986 as an artificial reef. Lying in 30m of water, it's now covered in soft corals. Very close by is the gently undulating **Japanese Gardens**, colourful and good for snorkellers.

A little further south are the unmissable **Gorgonion I** and **II**, the reef gently inclining down to

The shadeless ruins of the Islamic-period town of **Aila** lie in an unromantic location sandwiched between buildings off the Corniche. You enter through a gateway which is roughly where the original **Syrian Gate** would have met the road from the northeast. To the right, the foundations of towers projecting out of the city wall can be followed down to the **Egyptian Gate**, the history of which reflects the history of the whole city. In the early Islamic period, the gate was about 3m wide, flanked by the two

30m or so with spectacular fish life and perfectly preserved coral growth of all kinds stretching off to all sides. The **Canyon** has a shallow slope leading off for several hundred metres to a drop-off plunging over 45m, the whole slope split from the shallows outwards by a steep-sided ravine; its neighbour, the **New Canyon**, hosts an old field tank, sunk here to create a barrier to encourage reef growth. **Blue Coral**, named for a bluish lacework coral found here, is a little south, while nearby, 17m down, lies a huge C-130 Hercules military aircraft, cleaned and scuttled here in 2017 – great for snorkellers as well as divers from novice to expert.

Just north of a fenced-off nature reserve, **Moon Valley** offers an undulating reef framed by sandy beds, and is also the entry point for the **Long Swim**, taking divers or experienced snorkellers 700m south beyond the reserve fence, past patches of dense coral interspersed with sandy valleys.

CORAL CONSERVATION

Coral reefs are formed of millions of individual creatures called **polyps**, which come together to create a single, compound organism. The various species of polyp produce hard external skeletons, which remain intact after the polyp dies; sand and other detritus fills up holes and cracks, and the reef is built up little by little, with new corals growing on the surface of the stony mass. Some coral colonies are several centuries old. To avoid damaging the reefs:

• **Never stand on the coral** – any kind of pressure can damage or kill the outermost polyps. If you opt for a boat dive, make certain that the captain ties up to one of the mooring buoys already in place all round Aqaba, and doesn't just drop anchor onto the reef. If he claims that his selected site has no buoy, then insist that you be taken instead to a site that does have one.
• **Don't enter the sea from the beach** – the reef begins directly from the shallows. Instead, use jetties or boat entries.
• **Never break the coral** – snapping off a particularly colourful bit of coral not only kills that section of the reef, it's also pointless: after a few days out of water, all coral turns grey.
• **Avoid kicking up sand** – clouds of grit settling on the reef can smother the outermost polyps.
• **Don't litter, feed the fish or buy marine souvenirs**, such as corals, shells or starfish.

INDEPENDENT DIVE CENTRES

Aqaba has at least a dozen **dive centres** – more, if you include the dive operations attached to the big hotels. The tourist office can supply a full list and contact information; this is a selection of the better-known ones.

Aqaba Adventure Divers 12km south of town ☎ 079 907 8450, ⓦ aqaba-diving.com. Small, flexible team with a great reputation, also with its own beachside accommodation.

Arab Divers 12km south of town ☎ 079 507 8565, ⓦ arabdivers.jo. Excellent, top-rated outfit with long experience in Aqaba.

Dive Aqaba Town centre, Al-Saada St opposite Captain's restaurant ☎ 079 669 9008, ⓦ diveaqaba. com. Leading centre that is known for its outstanding service and expertise from a knowledgeable Jordanian-British team.

Red Sea Dive Center 12km south of town ☎ 079 742 2331, ⓦ aqabascubadiving.com. Well-regarded family-run operation on South Beach, with on-site hotel to boot.

Sea Guard Operating out of Royal Yacht Club ☎ 079 502 7853, ⓦ c-guard.net. Welcoming, accomplished and well-regarded operation with a personal touch.

SeaStar Club Murjan, 10km south of town ☎ 03 201 8335, ⓦ aqabadivingseastar.com. Long-established dive centre with a great reputation, working closely with local tour company Above And Below.

Sinai Divers At Movenpick Resort Tala Bay ☎ 077 677 2772, ⓦ sinaidiversaqaba.com. Local branch of this Egypt-based operation, with high standards and a professional outlook.

Sindbad Dive Club 1 At Berenice Beach Club, 11km south of town ☎ 079 610 1629, ⓦ berenice.com. jo. Friendly, well-respected operation, at a fine private beach.

7

semicircular towers still apparent and featuring a round arch overhead. A stump in front is the remnant of a central column, built in the eighth century to narrow the arch. A century or two followed during which Aila was at its zenith; however, debris dumped outside the walls caused the ground level to rise, when the towers were converted to storerooms. Rebuilding work resulted in the current smaller, pointed arch over the gate, but Aila's days were numbered, and eventually the gate was sealed, serving only as a drain.

From the Egyptian Gate you can walk along a street – well below current beach level – past remains of shops and houses. Some 50m along, the **Pavilion Building** was, in the ninth or tenth century, a two-storey residence, with rooms set around a courtyard. The road would have continued straight across to the **Hejaz Gate**, now in the grounds of the yacht club opposite. A cross street led from the Pavilion Building right to the **Sea Gate** and left to the Syrian Gate. Towards the Corniche lies what was a large **mosque**, with *mihrab* and double row of columns. In 2018, an underwater archeological survey discovered traces of Aila's port just outside the Sea Gate, dating back around a thousand years: more work is planned to interpret the findings and continue the search.

The Roman and Byzantine city

Some 200m northwest of the Aila ruins, in an open area behind the JETT bus station, excavations have uncovered the earlier **Roman and Byzantine city**, including rooms, a city wall and remains of a **church**, dated to 290 or 300 AD. Though older buildings, in Syria and elsewhere, are known to have been converted into churches in the 260s, this is the oldest-known structure in the world to have been designed and built as a church. It was abandoned after an earthquake in 363 and sand has preserved the mud-brick walls to a height of almost 5m.

Aqaba Bird Observatory

About 8km north of town • Daily except Fri 8am–4pm, last entry 3pm • JD10; contact observatory manager Feras Rahahleh (☎ 079 799 0450, ✉ feras.rahahleh@rscn.org.jo) in advance to confirm your visit • ☎ 03 205 8825, ⓦ facebook.com/aqababirds • Drive north, turning left before the airport at the sign for Eilat – you must surrender your passport at the first checkpoint, continue on and you'll find the observatory on the left, a little before the Wadi Araba border post • Return taxi (including waiting time) roughly JD20 • Contact ⓦ aboveandbelow.info for all-inclusive package, including transport and admission (about JD40pp, min two people)

As a key stopping-off point for migratory birds, Aqaba has long attracted intrepid **birdwatchers** – particularly to the artificial pools and vegetation around a wastewater treatment plant north of town beside the Israeli border. The Royal Society for the Conservation of Nature manages the modest **Aqaba Bird Observatory** beside the pools here. Follow 1.5km of trails around a long, narrow lake, or hole up in a hide: more than two hundred bird species stop here, almost half of Jordan's total species count. It's prized as the country's best place to spot waders, and the area also hosts the world's largest concentration of white-eyed gulls.

ARRIVAL AND DEPARTURE
AQABA

BY PLANE
Airport Aqaba's King Hussein International Airport (code AQJ; ☎ 03 203 4010, ⓦ aac.jo) is 9km north of the city, off the Wadi Araba road. If you're arriving on a charter flight, you'll have ground transfers laid on. Taxis gather to meet the few scheduled flights, charging around JD15 into the city centre.

Domestic flights Royal Jordanian (☎ 06 510 0000, ⓦ rj. com) has two or three flights a day between Aqaba and Amman Queen Alia airport. At around JD50 one-way, this isn't prohibitively expensive, and means you can travel from city centre to city centre in around 1hr 30min (including check-in and ground transfers), compared with more than 4hr overland. In addition, the airborne views over the

BEACHES, WATERSPORTS AND EXCURSIONS FROM AQABA

If you're staying at a hotel in Aqaba that does not have its own **beach**, ask at reception whether any deals are in place to allow guests beach access. Otherwise, all the five-star beach hotels will admit non-guests – though for a hefty **fee** (anything from JD20 to JD50) and at busy times they may turn you away.

SOUTH BEACH AREA

Other than at big hotels, the best and cleanest non-hotel beaches are at the South Beach zone, beginning around 8km south of town – **Berenice Beach Club** (ⓦberenice.com.jo) a great, family-friendly mini-resort complex of pools, café-restaurants and beach access and nearby tourist-focused beach resort **Club Murjan** (ⓦaqabadivingseastar.com). Both these recommendable places run deals with hotels around town, discounting walk-in admission prices and often including free transport and/or snorkelling gear; ask on the day. There is also a broad stretch of **public beach** here – but facilities are few and women may be the focus of unwanted attention.

WATERSPORTS

All the big hotels, beach clubs and dive centres (see page 310) offer a range of **watersports**. Prices and options vary, but expect speedboat trips, waterskiing, banana/inner-tube rides, jetskiing, canoeing, windsurfing, parasailing and more. Many of the hotels work with the local **Sindbad Group** (ⓣ078 022 2935, ⓦfacebook.com/sindbadgrp), so you could check prices and offers with them directly.

CRUISES

A number of operators (including Sindbad) feature **cruises** – many run only for groups, but there are also regular scheduled trips each week that are bookable by individuals. Prices are around JD30–35 per person for a four-hour lunchtime cruise, including a meal on the yacht plus snorkelling, or JD15–20 per person for an hour-and-a-half sunset cruise. Many firms also rent out sailing yachts and motor yachts for private excursions or fishing trips. Check online or with the tourist office for full details.

GLASS-BOTTOMED BOATS

A popular budget option is a quick trip in a **glass-bottomed boat**, which has a viewing window to see below the surface. Dozens of simple craft gather near the big flagpole. A trip in one of these should cost around JD35–40 per hour for a full boat. (Note that some disreputable boat captains will dive down and snap off bits of coral to hand to their oohing-and-aahing clients. This is not only illegal but also kills the reef. If it happens, refuse to pay for the trip and report the incident to the tourist office.) A more up-market alternative – and a better way to actually get to see some marine life – is to go with a glass-bottomed boat trip through a big hotel (or Sindbad; see above). A comfortable four-hour trip, including snorkelling kit and refreshments on board, costs about JD30/JD35 per person – or you could splash out on a submarine adventure on the *Neptune* (ⓦfacebook.com/neptuneboat), which operates out of Tala Bay.

PHARAOH'S ISLAND

Perhaps the best day-voyage is to **Pharaoh's Island**, a rocky islet in Egyptian waters about 17km southwest of Aqaba (and 250m off the Egyptian coast). In the twelfth century, to counter a castle at Aqaba built by the Crusaders (now lost), Salah ad-Din's Muslim resistance fortified this barren islet, dubbed by the Crusaders the Île de Graye. The castle's towers and passageways have been restored, but the main reason for coming is to **dive or snorkel** in the maze of reefs off the northeastern tip of the island.

The only way to reach Pharaoh's Island is on one of the organized tours that run whenever there's sufficient demand (and whenever the security situation allows). Just about any hotel or dive centre can take a booking; expect to pay JD45–50 per person, which includes everything, including lunch on board. Departure is around 8.30am, and you're back in Aqaba by 4.30pm. You must book at least one day ahead, and leave your passport: the operator has to organize a temporary Egyptian visa. It's not possible to cross from the island to the Egyptian mainland.

desert, Dead Sea and Petra mountains are exceptional; sit on the left-hand side heading north.

BY CAR

Driving into Aqaba Coming from Amman, Petra or Wadi Rum, the main Desert Highway enters Aqaba from the north, coiling along the line of the Wadi Yitm, still (as in antiquity) the only negotiable route through the mountains that seal Aqaba off. Signed bypass routes to the port ensure that heavy trucks are diverted away from the city. Beyond the cursory customs check, if you go straight at every junction and roundabout, you eventually reach the main Ayla Circle, where the Corniche coast road hugs the shore right (west) to a hotel zone, and left (east) past the city centre to the south coast, location of more hotels and beaches, plus the port and ferry terminal.

Routes out of Aqaba For the drive north out of Aqaba, take your pick between the Desert Highway towards Amman (see page 335) – from which turn-offs lead to Wadi Rum and Petra – and the Dead Sea road (see page 330).

Customs check Because Aqaba is a low-tax zone (see page 54), there are customs checkpoints on all roads into and out of the city. In theory you should declare high-value goods. In practice, checks rarely amount to more than a flick through your passport: you're likely simply to be waved on.

BY BUS AND SERVEECE

Bus station Aqaba's bus station stands opposite the police station in the city centre, though a couple of routes terminate in the streets nearby. All routes are restricted – or nonexistent – on Fridays.

To Amman Minibuses (5hr; about JD6–7) and some quicker serveeces (4hr; about JD7–8) run regularly to Amman. In addition, JETT (☎ 03 201 5222, ⊚ jett.com.jo), runs large a/c coaches roughly 6–8 times daily from its office on the Corniche near the *Mövenpick* hotel to each of four Amman locations (first bus 7–8am, last 6–7pm; 4hr 30min; JD9): Tabarboor station, 224 King Hussein St in Abdali, Wihdat station and 7th Circle. There are also more comfortable "VIP" departures to Abdali and 7th Circle (1–3 daily; JD11–19), and one overnight departure to Abdali (daily 1am; JD9). Call ahead to confirm schedules and book a seat.

To Petra/Wadi Musa Four or five buses a day (1hr 45min; about JD5–7) run to Wadi Musa at around 7–8am and 11am–1pm, although timings depend on demand. Others run via Rajif to Taybeh village, a short bus ride from Wadi Musa. More regular buses serve Ma'an (1hr 20min; JD2), from where you can catch another bus (or taxi) to Wadi Musa.

To Wadi Rum Buses to Wadi Rum (1hr; about JD4–6) depart at around 1pm and sometimes also 3pm, with an additional bus sometimes around 11am. As an alternative, take just about any bus heading north out of Aqaba (to Amman, Ma'an, Wadi Musa or Quweira, for example) and ask to be let out at the Rashdiyyeh junction on the highway,

---

> ## AQABA: KEY DISTANCES
> Aqaba is approximately:
> - 330km south of **Amman** (3hr 45min)
> - 280km south of **Dead Sea hotels** (3hr 30min)
> - 120km south of **Petra** (1hr 30min)
> - 60km south of **Wadi Rum** (1hr)

7

from where hitching into Rum is easy (be prepared to pay about JD2–3/person for the hitch).

To Karak (via Safi) Buses (3hr; JD3.50–4) depart from a street 100m south of the bus station.

To Irbid JETT runs two to three buses a day (6hr; JD11); book in advance.

BY TAXI

A taxi one-way from Aqaba to Wadi Rum costs about JD30–40; to Petra JD50–70; or to the Dead Sea JD80–95. A ride to Feynan for up to four people, organized through the *Feynan Ecolodge* (see page 342), costs JD75.

TO/FROM ISRAEL

Arrivals Routes from Eilat to Aqaba are covered in Basics (see page 30).

Aqaba to Eilat Aqaba's land crossing into Israel (Sun–Thurs 6.30am–8pm, Fri & Sat 8am–8pm; ☎ 03 201 9784) – the Wadi Araba border, also known as the "Southern Crossing", or in Israel as the Yitzhak Rabin or Arava crossing – is 5km north of Aqaba, signposted off the airport road. Entering Jordan, taxis do the run into Aqaba for a hefty JD20 or more. If you're leaving Jordan this way, you'll have to pay a JD10 departure tax and most nationalities are issued with free Israeli visas on arrival. Once you're through, a taxi into Eilat is about NIS80 – or walk from the border about 500m to the Kibbutz Elot bus stop on the main road, from where you can flag down any bus for the last couple of kilometres into Eilat. Note that during the Jewish *shabbat* – effectively from Friday 2pm until Saturday dusk – all Israeli public transport and many services shut down. Egged buses (⊚ egged.co.il) depart Eilat frequently for Tel Aviv or Jerusalem (both 5hr; NIS70).

TO/FROM EGYPT

Travel advice At the time of writing, the British Foreign Office (⊚ fco.gov.uk) advised against all but essential travel to many of the places we mention in this section, including Dahab, Nuweiba and Taba. Check the security situation carefully before you travel.

Visa for Egypt The easiest method for many nationalities is to apply and pay for a printable e-Visa at the government website ⊚ visa2egypt.gov.eg.

Egyptian Consulate 46 9th-of-Shaaban St, in the 3rd District, an outlying suburb also known as Zahra (☎ 03

WADI RUM TOURS FROM AQABA

Tours to **Wadi Rum** are advertised at one-man-band tour "companies" and budget hotels all over Aqaba – if you express interest, they'll dig out a photo album of their adventures, plus glowing testimonials from happy customers, to try to convince you to book. If all you want is to be driven out to a campsite somewhere in the desert near Rum, have dinner and be brought back to Aqaba in the morning – often in the company of "guides" who may not be Jordanian and/or speak little or no English – then these jaunts are great value, at JD30–40 per person. But in truth they're nothing like the real McCoy. And horror stories abound; one favourite ploy (apart from money upfront and tips, of course) is to demand more cash once you're at the campsite. Refuse, and your "guide" may threaten to abandon you in the desert unless you cough up.

On the whole, you're better off talking to a proper tour company (see page 48). In Aqaba, reliable firms include **Above and Below** (☎ 03 201 3735, ⓦ aboveandbelow.info), located on As-Saada Street, and **Captains** (☎ 03 206 0710, ⓦ captains.jo), at the *Captain's Hotel*.

7

201 6171). It's difficult to find by yourself; the best advice is to ask the tourist office to fix up a taxi for you (around JD5–8 including waiting time). Visa applications are taken Sun–Thurs 9am–noon. One photo is needed (or they might photocopy your passport photo instead). Collection is on the spot, after a short wait. A three-month full Egyptian tourist visa costs JD17. "Sinai-only" visas, valid only for travel along the east Sinai coast as far as Sharm el-Sheikh (including St Catherine's), are issued free.

TO EGYPT BY SEA

Arrivals Routes from Egypt to Aqaba are covered in Basics (see page 31).

Ferry company AB Maritime (☎ 03 209 2000, ⓦ abmaritime. com.jo) operates both routes outlined below. Book in person at their city-centre office on Al-Batra St (Sun–Thurs 8am–4pm).
Aqaba to Nuweiba by slow/fast ferry Service to Egypt from Aqaba's ferry terminal, located 5km south of town (taxi about JD8), is chaotic. To Nuweiba, 70km southwest of Aqaba, there is a fast ferry (catamaran; 1hr) – though this was suspended at the time of writing – and a slow ferry (daily 11pm; US$90; 3hr). The timetable is notoriously unreliable and can change from month to month. Expect lengthy delays. There's a departure tax of JD10. Although it's possible to get an Egyptian visa on the boat, getting one in advance will save considerable time and confusion. At Nuweiba port, taxi drivers do the run into town (8km) for about LE50. Beside the port is Nuweiba's bus station, with buses to Cairo (8hr), Dahab (1hr) and Sharm (3hr), plus *serveeces*. There may be extra boats laid on in peak season – summer, at the end of Ramadan, and around the hajj and Eid al-Adha.

Aqaba to Taba by tourist catamaran A smaller tourist ferry operates from Taba, 70km north of Nuweiba, to Aqaba, but it is intended for hotel guests in Egypt who want to visit Jordan for a day or two: you can't buy a one-way ticket, and if you try to board with bags or suitcases, you may be stopped from travelling. A return ticket, valid up to eight days, costs US$106.

TO EGYPT OVERLAND VIA ISRAEL

It's cheaper and often easier to go overland to Egypt through Israel (total journey time about 2–3hr) – but note that the passport stamps you pick up will disqualify you from subsequently entering many Middle Eastern countries. Avoid crossing during the Jewish *shabbat* (between about 2pm Fri and sunset Sat), when it's difficult to find transport in Israel.
Aqaba to Eilat Start by crossing from Aqaba into Israel (see page 30).
Eilat to Taba City bus #15 runs from Eilat bus station to the Egyptian border (*hagvul hamitzri* in Hebrew), 10km south of Eilat, but it's easier to take a taxi directly from the Jordanian entry-point (around NIS80–100). The Israel–Egypt border is open 24hr; there's an Israeli departure tax of NIS101 and an Egyptian entry tax of about US$8. From Taba's bus station, buses run to destinations including Sharm (4hr) and Cairo (7hr), but loitering *serveece*-taxi drivers will nab you first; bargain hard.
Egyptian visas If you enter Egypt by land from Israel, the only visa obtainable on the border is a Sinai-only pass (free), valid solely for the coast between Taba and Sharm el-Sheikh. If you intend to travel on to Cairo, you must hold a full Egyptian visa in advance before you cross, obtainable online, in your home country or in Amman or Aqaba.

GETTING AROUND

On foot The simplest way to get around town is on foot: walking the length of the Corniche (from the *InterContinental* hotel to the fort) takes around 30min. If it's too hot to walk, you need only lift a finger for a taxi to screech to a stop for you.
By taxi Metered taxis prowl constantly. You'll pay no more than JD2–4 for any ride within the city centre, or roughly JD10–12 to reach the South Beach/Tala Bay area.

By bus Aqaba's city buses mostly serve only the residential suburbs. Public buses run between the city centre (on the Corniche by the fort) and the South Beach/Saudi border area (daily about 8am–7pm every 30min; JD0.50), stopping anywhere on request. Several of the Tala Bay hotels and South Beach dive centres operate private shuttles for guests; ask for details.

INFORMATION

Tourist office Aqaba's tourist office (daily 9am–6pm, Nov–March till 5pm, shorter hours on Fri; ☎03 203 5360, ⓦaqaba.jo) is in a shaded hut on Hammamat Al Tunisiyyeh St, diagonally opposite the Aqaba Gateway Mall, a short walk from most of the hotels. Staff are friendly and knowledgeable, offering free maps and information about goings-on around town.

Car rental All the big global firms are represented in Aqaba – walk from one to the other on and around An-Nahda St to compare prices, or opt for local agencies: the Above and Below tour company (☎03 201 3735, ⓦaboveandbelow. info) can offer competitive rates with Save Rent-a-Car.

ACCOMMODATION

Aqaba has a broad range of **hotel** options, with more luxury properties on the way as the new beachfront leisure developments open up. At budget/mid-range level, also bear in mind that several of the South Beach dive centres (see page 310) have their own simple accommodation onsite, though they're all far from town; factor in taxi costs if you're not keen on holing up in one place. Many places around town (and in Tala Bay) offer **furnished apartments** for rent – check with the tourist office for details. When **choosing a room**, factor in the stifling heat: the romance of a sea view – along with a beautiful panorama westwards across the bay towards Eilat – brings with it exposure to the scorching force of the sun all afternoon. For the sake of a cool night's sleep, you might do better to choose a room facing east to the mountains or north over the city. Either way, keep windows and curtains closed during the day.

IN TOWN

Aqaba Gulf Corniche ☎03 201 6636, ⓦaqabagulf.com; map p.306. Aged landmark city-centre hotel which was the best in town a few decades back – the public areas today are not so much retro as unrenovated. However, the two hundred rooms are functional and adequate, even if maintenance can be poor. A drawback is that it has no private beach of its own, though guests are offered a shuttle bus to the *Berenice* resort facility on the South Beach. **JD75**
★ **Captain's** Al-Nahda St ☎03 206 0710, ⓦcaptains. jo; map p.306. Excellent locally owned upper-three-star hotel (nearer four-star) in the centre of town, with sleek well-kept rooms offering a touch of designer style – gadgets, good fabrics, tile floors, chic bathrooms with bowl basins and multijet showers, and so on. Rooms are a touch on the compact side, but still very comfortable. Service is quick and professional. **JD77**
Classic Prince Mohammed St ☎03 205 0070; map p.306. Surprisingly good, modest-looking boutique-style hotel on a busy traffic corner slightly away from the tourist strip, just off the roundabout opposite the Princess Haya Hospital. It has 45 rooms spread over four floors – generally spacious and well kept, with bargain rates. **JD38**
Crystal Al-Razi St ☎03 202 2001, ⓦcrystal-international.com; map p.306. Adequate budget hotel in the centre, overlooking shopping streets and near the souk. A grandiose lobby preludes 63 big but shabby rooms that could do with some TLC. It's not fancy, but staff are friendly and at slow times have been known to offer bargain rates to walk-up customers. Go, if you can, for the huge corner rooms (108, 208, 308 or 408) – the higher the better, to avoid street noise. **JD35**
Days Inn Al-Saada St ☎03 203 1901, ⓦdaysinn.com; map p.306. Occupying an odd building (begun as a shopping mall, then converted partway up into a hotel), this is a handsome, competitively priced holiday hotel with a rooftop mini-pool that sizzles in summer. All but a handful of the 110 rooms have balconies, and those that don't are huge corner rooms. Also has several connected family suites. **JD55**
★ **Doubletree by Hilton** Al-Nahda St ☎03 209 3209, ⓦdoubletree.com; map p.306. This world-class upper-four-star hotel in the centre of town gives a kick in the pants to some of its more complacent neighbours, with classy contemporary styling, spacious rooms (some with sea view, some not), a long list of amenities and a shaded infinity pool. **JD78**
Dweik 1 Behind Raghadan St ☎03 201 2984; map p.306. A basic little hotel in the alleyways behind the town-centre souk streets, shabby and down-at-heel but mostly acceptable – and welcoming enough at these prices. No breakfast. **JD22**
Hyatt Regency Marina Village, Ayla ☎03 204 1234, ⓦhyatt.com; map p.306. This super-sleek behemoth opened in late 2018 as the first hotel in the new Ayla resort complex, just west of the city centre. Resplendent beside its own marina, with watery views in every direction (though no beach), this place offers huge, airy rooms with private balconies and marble bathrooms, and a sense of exclusivity that's hard to find in Aqaba's other big hotels. **JD118**

7

★ **InterContinental** Corniche ☎03 209 2222, ⓦintercontinental.com; map p.306. Outstanding five-star hotel on its own slice of beach, gazing south over the water. Rooms are large and very well appointed, and the hotel's facilities range from top-notch restaurants to a spa and fitness centre. Super-stylish. <u>JD120</u>

Kempinski Corniche ☎03 209 0888, ⓦkempinski-aqaba.com; map p.306. Another top-class holiday hotel on its own sandy beach, offering chic, state-of-the-art interiors. Every one of the 201 rooms and suites has a sea view, thanks to the building's curved design. <u>JD120</u>

★ **Mövenpick** Corniche ☎03 203 4020, ⓦmovenpick. com; map p.306. Lavish five-star complex, variously dubbed by the locals "the fairy palace" for its twinkling lights and "the prison" for the curiously designed set of bars that slides across every window. Inside, it's airy, spacious and beautifully designed, with the pool placed up on a bridge over the road that connects the hotel proper (on the north side of the road) with the condominium section on the beach to the south. Rooms are very well appointed, with everything you'd expect. <u>JD100</u>

Yafko Corniche ☎03 204 2222, ⓦyafko.com; map p.306. Great little mid-range hotel on the Corniche opposite the fort, with a sense of style and very competitive prices. It's not grand, but it ticks all the right boxes, even if service is a bit vague. Go for one of the sea-view rooms. <u>JD38</u>

OUT OF TOWN

★ **Bedouin Garden Village** 12km south of town ☎079 560 2521. This is about as bedouin as a bikini, but nonetheless qualifies as a decent, attractive option for budget beachside accommodation, with an easy-going, hippyish atmosphere. There's a mix of a/c "chalets" plus clean toilets and showers and a pleasant, shaded tent area for lounging. They do inexpensive meals (fish barbecues are an evening favourite), and snorkelling excursions. Located 100m from the beach, above the road. <u>JD38</u>

★ **Darna Village** 12km south of town ☎079 671 2831, ⓦdarnavillage.com. Of the little cluster of good-quality mid-range "village" accommodation just behind the public beach hereabouts – which include the *Bedouin Garden Village*, as well as *Bedouin Moon Village, Aqaba Adventure Divers, Red Sea Dive Center, International Arab Divers Village* and more – this is probably top choice, a genuinely welcoming, laid-back little family-run resort around a lovely swimming pool. The a/c chalet-style rooms are spotless, with a touch of domestic pride – and the welcome stands out. Grilled fish, salads, kebabs and more are keenly priced, and there's snorkelling and diving on request. <u>JD37</u>

Mövenpick Tala Bay Tala Bay, 15km south of town ☎03 209 0300, ⓦmovenpick.com. Self-contained five-star luxury beachfront resort complex offering 306 large, tastefully designed rooms ranged around a network of swimming pools and leisure facilities, from a mini-shopping mall to the world-class Zara spa complex. There's diving and other watersports on offer, too, as well as a private stretch of sandy beach. <u>JD110</u>

EATING

Aqaba shakes a leg when the sun goes down, and many **restaurants and cafés** have terrace tables (or balconies) for alfresco dining. The compact area around An-Nahda and As-Saada streets, extending onto the main Hammamet al-Tunisiyyeh St (with illuminated fountains along its central strip), is a great place to stroll after dark – here you'll find lots of lounge-style **cafés** and **espresso bars**, families and friends walking together and people hanging out.

What to eat The obvious thing to plump for when you're by the sea is fish – but be aware that the big hotel restaurants generally import their fish and seafood frozen (mostly from Dubai, or Mediterranean sources such as Cyprus). Only a few bottom-end restaurants serve fish from Aqaba's local market – which doesn't help much, since that's almost always imported too. The famous dish around town is *sayyadieh* – fish (most often spiced red mullet) on buttery rice with pine nuts, originally Lebanese but done in multiple Aqabawi varieties. You'll also spot lots of familiar Western-style fast-food outlets around town, from burgers to pizza to fried chicken.

COMMUNITY TOURISM IN AQABA

Aqaba focuses on mass-market tourism and big-ticket investment projects: you can tell, as you wander around, that the city lives another, less glitzy life, but options for accessing it, or even just for getting under the skin of the place a little, are rare. The Souk By The Sea (see page 309) offers one window, while local tour company Above And Below (☎03 201 3735, ⓦaboveandbelow.info) has another couple of possibilities. Through them, you could join local artisans at a **handicraft class** run by social enterprise Green Creations (ⓦgreencreations. org), designing jewellery or making new products from recycled materials (from JD35pp). Alternatively, try a **cooking class** with a local family where you're taught how to make Jordanian specialities – such as the Aqabawi fish dish *sayyadieh* – in their kitchen before dining together on your creation (from JD32pp). Both have a minimum of three participants. Book at least one day ahead.

What to drink Traditional coffee houses all over town come into their own in the evening, laying out chairs and setting up a TV for locals to while away the twilight hours with a hubbly-bubbly. Around Zahran and Al-Razi streets, juice bars offer anything from plain orange juice to sensational mango-guava-strawberry-banana concoctions, interspersed with parlours doing a roaring trade in cups of supersweet, strangely elastic local ice cream. All the big hotels serve alcohol; most other places around town do not.

Picnic food If you're heading to Rum or Petra for a few days, stock up on supplies beforehand, since even basic food in both places is priced at a premium. Check out Aqaba's early-morning fruit and veg market, the good local Humam supermarket on Al-Batra St, or the big Safeway supermarket north of the centre.

CAFÉS AND RESTAURANTS

Ali Baba Raghadan St ☎03 201 3901; map p.306. Landmark restaurant on the central roundabout, with a full complement of meze and Arabic main courses, as well as a good fish selection. Once the best restaurant in town; it's not that any more, but it's OK – though you rarely see locals eating here. Expect around JD10–15 a head. Alcohol served. Daily 9am–3am.

★ **Bourj al-Hamam** InterContinental hotel, Corniche ☎03 209 2222; map p.306. Aqaba's best upmarket Lebanese restaurant by miles, serving exquisite speciality dishes on the open sea-view terrace. Everything, from the fresh-baked flatbread to the salads, grills and hot and cold meze, is top quality, service is warm and the setting lovely. An expensive treat, upwards of JD20 a head. Daily 7–11pm.

★ **Captain's** An-Nahda St ☎03 206 0710, ⓦ captains.jo; map p.306. Large, busy maritime-themed tourist restaurant on the main drag with a well-deserved reputation for quality – and thus often full. The fish is good, and you can also get dishes like pasta and all the normal Arabic staples for around JD15. Daily noon–11pm.

Floka An-Nahda St ☎03 203 0860; map p.306. A rather good fish restaurant in the heart of the hotel district. Their *sayyadich* is excellent, and a range of other, more familiar European dishes are well prepared and courteously served. Expect a bill somewhere around JD15. Alcohol served. Daily noon–midnight.

★ **Formosa** Aqaba Gateway Mall, Corniche ☎03 206 0098, ⓦ facebook.com/formosachineserestaurantaqaba; map p.306. The warmest welcome in Aqaba. This cosy little family-run Chinese restaurant inside the Aqaba Gateway Mall has an impeccable local reputation for quality, both in food and service. The menu takes in a range of familiar favourites – including many fish and seafood dishes – priced keenly

(mains around JD7–11), and the tastefully artistic setting is perfect. Daily noon–1pm.

★ **Al Mohandes** Tabari St ☎03 201 3454; map p.306. For decades, this perpetually busy diner ("The Engineer" in Arabic) has been churning out the best staple Arabic food in town – plates of hummus, falafel, *fuul* and simple salads, scooped up with fresh flat bread and washed down with super-sweet tea. It's not fancy, but wow is it good. Stuff yourself for under JD5 a head. Daily 6am–11pm.

Rakwet Kanaan Al-Saada St ☎077 757 7700, ⓦ facebook.com/rakwetkanaanrestaurantcafe; map p.306. Cheery, stylish little café-restaurant in the middle of the town-centre action. Lounge on comfortable seating with a coffee or a hubbly-bubbly, or order from the menu of traditional Jordanian dishes – meze, mixed grills and the like. Mains around JD8. Daily 10am–1am.

Red Sea Grill Mövenpick hotel, Corniche ☎03 203 4020; map p.306. Of the hotel's range of fine-dining restaurants, this is the stand-out choice – a romantic, open-air spot down on the beach, serving up excellent fish and seafood in a pleasant, candlelit ambience right by the water. Not cheap, obviously (from JD20 a head). Daily 7pm–midnight.

Romero at Royal Yacht Club Off the Corniche ☎03 202 2404, ⓦ romerogroup.jo; map p.306. Calm, classy restaurant at the yacht club – but open to all – run by the highly recommended *Romero* of Amman (see page 104) and with efficient, friendly service. A top-quality Italian menu is padded out a little incongruously with Lebanese meze and Japanese sushi, but ignore all that and concentrate on the main attractions: pasta, authentic pizza and fish mains, with an excellent wine list to accompany. Also has a terrace overlooking the marina. Expect over JD20 a head. There's also a spectacular rooftop bar. Daily noon–11pm.

★ **al-Shami** Raghadan St ☎03 201 6107; map p.306. The narrow Raghadan St behind the main market area is shoulder-to-shoulder Arabic restaurants, serving simple fare at inexpensive prices. Despite its touristy appearance, this is one of the best, with good food and an upstairs terrace (with a/c). It's invariably packed with local families scarfing down fish, kebabs and salads, which says it all. Eat well for JD6–10. Daily 8am–11pm.

Syrian Palace Raghadan St ☎03 201 4788; map p.306. Beside *al-Shami*, this is another great choice for low-budget local dishes – particularly strong on the fried fish, but with a full range of Arabic dishes. As with most places on this street, the decor is a bit shabby but service is generally very good. Expect to pay a few dinars. Daily 8am–11pm.

DRINKING

As a rather conservative, Islamically observant town, Aqaba doesn't have much local demand for **bars**: independent

places tend to come and go, while those that survive on the tourist trade can be rather bereft of atmosphere. A better bet is to aim for one of the big hotels, all of which have decent pubs.

Abu Nawwas Mövenpick hotel, Corniche ☏03 203 4020, ⊛movenpick.com; map p.306. Cosy little bar in this five-star hotel that serves as a comfortable bolthole, and can sometimes drum up a whisper of atmosphere too. Beers from about JD6. Daily 8pm–2am.

Red Sea Loft Royal Yacht Club, off the Corniche ☏03 202 2404, ⊛facebook.com/TheRedSeaLoftRYC; map p.306. This classy lounge bar on the roof terrace of the Royal Yacht Club is a great spot for cocktails (around JD7),

beers (from JD6/pint) or a glass of wine (from JD6/glass) after sunset, and also serves food catered by the excellent *Romero* restaurant downstairs. Daily 6pm–late.

Rover's Return Aqaba Gateway Mall ☏03 203 2030, ⊛roversreturnjordan.com; map p.306. Hidden up some stairs within the mall, in a fake lighthouse, this pub-restaurant can get rather cramped – but if beer (from around JD5), football on big-screen TVs and familiar food (fish-and-chips JD10, lamb chops JD17) are your thing, it's perfect. Daily noon–midnight.

DIRECTORY

Bookshops The Yamani (☏03 201 2221) and Redwan (☏03 201 3704) bookshops, beside each other on Zahran St (both daily roughly 9am–1pm & 5–9pm), have excellent ranges of English-language books and international newspapers.

Hospital Princess Haya hospital (☏03 201 4111) has a 24hr emergency room and recompression chamber, as well as staff trained to deal with diving accidents.

Police In emergency, dial ☏911. The tourist police are headquartered at the Wadi Araba border (☏03 201 9717), also with officers working out of the town-centre police station by the bus station (☏03 203 4118). The main police directorate (☏03 201 2411) is in the outskirts.

Post office Yarmouk St (Sun–Thurs & Sat 7.30am–7pm, Fri 7.30am–1pm).

Wadi Rum

One of the most spectacular natural environments in the Middle East, the desert scenery of **WADI RUM** (rhymes with "dumb", not "doom") is a major highlight of a visit to Jordan. The wadi itself is one of a sequence of parallel faults forming valleys in the sandy desert south of the Shara mountains. They are oriented almost perfectly north–south, shaped and characterized by giant granite, basalt and sandstone mountains rising up to 800m sheer from the desert floor. The rocky landscape has been weathered over the millennia into bulbous domes and weird ridges and textures that look like nothing so much as molten candle-wax, but it's the sheer bulk of these mountains that awes – some with vertical, smooth flanks, others scarred and distorted, seemingly dripping and melting under the burning sun. The intervening level corridors of soft red sand only add to the image of the mountains as monumental islands in a dry sea. Split through by networks of canyons and ravines, spanned by naturally formed rock bridges and watered by hidden springs, the mountains offer opportunities galore for scrambling and rock climbing, where you could walk for hours or days without seeing another soul.

Although an arid, open desert, the Rum area is far from depopulated. Aside from the tents of seminomadic bedouin scattered in the desert, there's a handful of modern villages in the area, including **Rum** itself in the heart of its eponymous wadi, and **Disi**, a few kilometres away.

However you choose to do it – and the best way is to **book in advance** for a one- or two-day tour with a local guide (see page 330) – you should clear at least one night in your schedule to **sleep in the desert**. The sunsets are extraordinary; evening coolness after the heat of the day is blissful; the clarity of the desert air helps produce a starry sky of stunning beauty; and the tranquillity of the pitch-dark desert night is simply magical. It's an unforgettable experience.

Brief history

Wadi Rum has extensive evidence of past cultures, with plenty of **rock-carved drawings** and ancient **Thamudic inscriptions** still visible (the Thamud were a tribe, cousins of the

Nabateans, who lived as nomads in the deserts of northern Arabia between about the eighth century BC and roughly the seventh century AD), as well as a single, semi-ruined **Nabatean temple**.

T.E. Lawrence ("of Arabia") waxed lyrical about the Rum area, describing it as "vast, echoing and godlike" when he passed through in the years either side of the 1916–18 Great Arab Revolt. Appropriately enough, much of the epic *Lawrence of Arabia* was filmed here in the early 1960s, prompting tourists to visit in dribs and drabs during the years after. But until the late 1980s, Rum village was still comprised mostly of bedouin

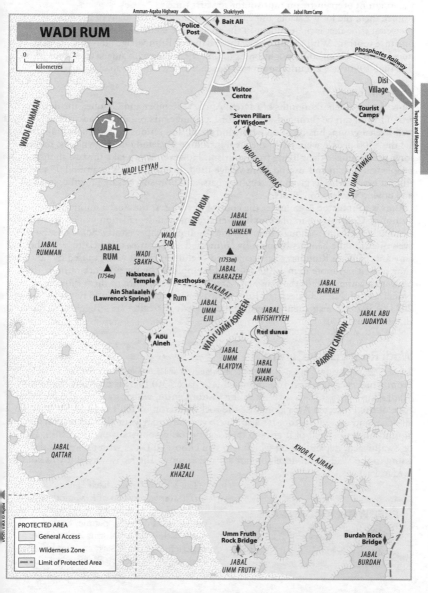

WADI RUM

0   2
kilometres

N

Amman-Aqaba Highway   Shakriyyeh   Jabal Rum Camp
Police Post   Bait Ali
Phosphates Railway
Disi Village
WADI RUMMAN
Visitor Centre
"Seven Pillars of Wisdom"
Tourist Camps
Twaybeh and Mensheer
WADI LEYYAH
WADI SIQ MAKHRAS
SIQ UMM TAWAGI
WADI RUM
JABAL UMM ASHREEN
JABAL RUMMAN
JABAL RUM
(1754m)
WADI SID
WADI SBAKH
Nabatean Temple
Ain Shalaaleh (Lawrence's Spring)
Resthouse
Rum
RAKABAT
(1753m)
JABAL KHARAZEH
JABAL BARRAH
JABAL UMM EJIL
WADI UMM ASHREEN
JABAL ANFISHIYYEH
Red dunes
BARRAH CANYON
JABAL ABU JUDAYDA
ABU Aineh
JABAL UMM ALAYDYA
JABAL UMM KHARG
JABAL QATTAR
KHOR AL AJRAM
JABAL KHAZALI

PROTECTED AREA
General Access
Wilderness Zone
Limit of Protected Area

Umm Fruth Rock Bridge
Burdah Rock Bridge
JABAL BURDAH
JABAL UMM FRUTH

DESERT TRACK TO AQABA

7

tents at the end of a rough track, with a single radiophone serving the lone Desert Patrol fort.

The growth of tourism

In 1984, a British climbing team led by **Tony Howard** and **Di Taylor** requested permission from the Ministry of Tourism to explore the possibilities for serious **mountaineering** in and around Wadi Rum. With assistance from the bedouin and the backing of the ministry, a pioneering **guidebook** resulted, which brought the area into the forefront of mainstream tourism for the first time.

Since then, the local Zalabia and Zuwaydeh bedouin – sub-clans of the great Howeitat tribe that is pre-eminent in the area – have established **cooperatives** to organize tourism. With the proceeds, the Zalabia of Rum village built breezeblock houses and a school, and bought buses to link the village with Aqaba and Wadi Musa. The mid-1990s saw a **tourist boom** that has shown few signs of abating.

Wadi Rum today

Now, during the peak months of March, April, September and October, the deserts around Rum can be thronged with visitors, a strange mix of budget backpackers, well-heeled groups bussed in on whirlwind tours, and serious professional climbers. Of the 5500 people who live in the area, including Disi and outlying villages, roughly forty percent make their living from tourism. However, if you take the two thousand people who live in and around Rum village itself, that figure rises to around 95 percent. Almost everybody has given up keeping goats, and now survives by providing **guide and driving services** to visitors.

Rum is a **Protected Area** under the control of ASEZA, the Aqaba municipal authority. Controls are in place to limit environmental degradation while supporting sustainable tourism – though bureaucratic disputes hamper efforts. Some observers even question the benefits brought by "protected area" status, amid claims that the core area of Wadi Rum has seen accelerated decline in recent years, caused by (at the time of writing) more than 1200 4x4s and exemplified by the presence of more than 65 tourist camps within the Protected Area alone, over a third of them unlicensed. Nonetheless UNESCO declared Rum a mixed natural/cultural **World Heritage Site** in 2011. ASEZA management teams installed shortly thereafter are struggling to turn things around.

Wadi Rum Visitor Centre

Daily 7am–7pm; shops and restaurant 8am–4pm • Free • Admission to desert areas JD5; free with JP • ☏ 03 209 0600

From whichever direction you approach (see page 330) there is only one road into Wadi Rum – and it leads directly to the **Visitor Centre**, which stands at the northern edge of the Protected Area alongside the rocky outcrop of Tell Hassan. This is where all buses and cars must stop. It's also where you must pay your JD5 **admission fee**; around fifteen percent of it goes to the local bedouin cooperative (either Rum, Disi or Swalhiyeen, depending on which trip you choose to take), with the remainder going to the Wadi Rum development administration. The fee is waived if you hold a Jordan Pass.

> **FREE WITH JORDAN PASS**
>
> Throughout this Guide, "free with JP" means that the attraction grants free admission to holders of the **Jordan Pass** (see page 55).

The Visitor Centre itself is not unattractive, a sweep of low, modern buildings set around a large gravel courtyard. For many people, bussed in on whistle-stop tours, this is their sole experience of the desert, and it has been designed with their needs in mind. Aside from the **guides office**, which handles

> **THE SEVEN PILLARS?**
>
> Although the free handout map, and almost all tourist literature, names the soaring pinnacles of rock directly opposite the Visitor Centre as the **"Seven Pillars of Wisdom"**, this is a fabrication, made up in the last few years by marketing executives to cash in on the legend of Lawrence. (Five of the pinnacles are in plain view; the other two are round the side.) Lawrence never mentioned this mountain, and took the title of his most famous work from the Book of Proverbs (9:1): "Wisdom has built a house; she has hewn out her seven pillars". The local bedouin referred to this mountain as **Jabal al-Mazmar** (roughly, "The Fluted Mountain") long before outsiders had ever heard of Rum. It seems tragic that even they are now calling it the "Seven Pillars".

payments and allocates drivers for visitors who turn up without a booking (see page 333), there are a few small **shops** selling locally produced crafts and jewellery items, and a pleasant **restaurant**, which serves simple salads and a few daily specials to lunching tour groups. Their rear terrace – open to all – gives spectacular **views** across the desert landscape. You can also climb the Visitor Centre's two little towers, for more eagle-eye views.

7

However, hanging around the Visitor Centre amid the hubbub makes it obvious very quickly that the best course of action is to escape into the desert as soon as possible.

Exploring the desert

Although most drivers and guides follow a set pattern of routes – the highlights of which we cover in this section – you shouldn't feel restricted: if you have a couple of hours to spare, there's nothing to stop you walking out across the sands in whichever direction you fancy.

Walking to the east side of Wadi Rum from the Visitor Centre – towards the misnamed **"Seven Pillars of Wisdom"** (see above) – transfers you from tour-group hubbub into stillness and solitude. Following the cliffs of the massif south for a few minutes will give you a more intimate flavour of the desert environment than a bouncing 4x4 ride ever could.

Another way to lose the bustle, if you have a rental car, is to drive back out towards **Disi** and onwards – on asphalt road – to the unvisited villages of **Twayseh** and **Mensheer**. The desert out here is just as explorable, and the views just as awesome, as in and around Wadi Rum itself.

Nabatean temple

From the Visitor Centre, the road continues south along the west side of Wadi Rum for 7km to Rum village. **Jabal Rum** rises to the right, **Jabal Umm Ashreen** to the left. Plans to turn the village's former police post into a small archeology museum have so far come to nothing. From the *Resthouse*, which is the first building you come to (on the right-hand side), walk alongside the telephone poles that lead away behind towards the daunting cliffs of Jabal Rum, and within five minutes you'll come to a small, ruined **Nabatean temple** dating from the first or second centuries AD, with Nabatean inscriptions on the walls and columns overlaid by later Thamudic graffiti.

Most tours include the temple as standard; alternatively, once you've paid your admission at the Visitor Centre, you could walk or cadge a lift down the road into Rum village to explore for yourself.

Ain Shalaaleh (Lawrence's Spring)

From the Nabatean temple, a modern cylindrical water tank is in plain view a little way south; follow a path from the tank up the hillside and around the cliffs above the mouth of a little valley, past springs lush with mint. On the south side of the little valley, at the head of a Nabatean rock-cut aqueduct, you'll reach **Ain Shalaaleh**, a beautiful, tranquil spot cool with water and shaded by ferns and trees, evocatively described by Lawrence in Chapter 63 of *Seven Pillars of Wisdom*. Nabatean (and modern) inscriptions are all around and there are stunning views out across Wadi Rum. Taking your time, you could devote a gentle half-day to visiting just the temple and the spring.

Most camel and car drivers, though, can't be bothered with climbing the slope to reach the spring, and instead lead visitors who have requested "**Lawrence's Spring**" south along the valley floor to the rather mundane spring at **Abu Aineh**, which is marked by a square concrete pumping block near a scree slope. Both this and Ain Shalaaleh are valid destinations, but the confusion has now become written into history, with the official map marking Abu Aineh as "Lawrence's Spring". Insist on Ain Shalaaleh, if that's where you want to go.

From Ain Shalaaleh, it's not hard to work your way east around an outcrop and south over a pass onto a path above the desert floor. About 500m further on, another pass to the right will deliver you to the bedouin tent and spring at Abu Aineh – also easily reachable on a simple one-hour valley-floor walk, 3km south from Rum village.

Around Jabal Rum

For a long and serious walk, you can **circumnavigate Jabal Rum** – from Rum village to just beyond Abu Aineh, then north, passing to the east of Jabal Rumman and across a saddle into Wadi Leyyah. This could take nine hours or more and is only for the fit. A much easier prospect is walking northwest from the *Resthouse* along the small, well-

---

WADI RUM: WHAT TO EXPECT

THE WEATHER
Wadi Rum is elevated at around 950m above sea level. Bear in mind the **extremes of temperature**. Although it may be killingly hot during the day, nights even in summer can be chilly and, in winter, a dusting of frost isn't uncommon.

TRIBAL TERRITORIES
Although the landscapes in and around Rum look similar, three clearly defined **tribal areas** intersect here. The Protected Area of Wadi Rum itself, in and around Rum village, is the territory of the **Zalabia**. The area around Disi village, east and northeast of Wadi Rum (including the easternmost part of the Protected Area) is **Zuwaydeh** land. North and west of Wadi Rum, around the village of Shakriyyeh, live the **Swalhiyeen** tribe.

As you approach the Visitor Centre, the jeeps parked outside the walls belong to the Zuwaydeh: they are permitted to follow routes only in the outlying zone dubbed "Operator 2". Beyond the Visitor Centre, through the gateway, are cars belonging to the Zalabia; they stick to routes in the central heartland of Wadi Rum, dubbed "Operator 1". The Bait Ali complex (see page 329) is in Swalhiyeen territory, and has guides for camel, horse and 4x4 trips in this less-explored area.

There's much jockeying for position, with the Protected Area administrators bending over backwards to upset nobody (and thereby pleasing nobody either). Although Wadi Rum itself falls within Zalabia territory, there is nothing to stop you exploring further afield.

PLANNING YOUR TIME
Visiting the desert is at least as much about the people as it is about the sand. The best way to see Wadi Rum is to **prebook with a named guide** (see page 330). The scenery is stunning but it can be hard to make sense of it – or see the best of it – on your own. The bedouin of Rum and Disi are, on the whole, skilled, business-minded professionals who know how to deliver an experience to remember. Book ahead and you'll be met at the Visitor Centre at a prearranged time to be whisked off for your agreed tour. If you choose to stay overnight, all meals and accommodation will be included as part of

watered **Wadi Sbakh**, between the cliffs of Jabal Rum and the outcrop of **Jabal Mayeen**; you'll eventually have to make a short scramble over a saddle into the tiny, narrow **Wadi Sid**, often dotted with pools, from where a scramble leads down to the road a little north of Rum village, making a pleasant three-hour round trip.

Canyons of Umm Ashreen

The west face of **Jabal Umm Ashreen** (also spelled **Um Ishrin**) – the "Mother of Twenty", named (depending on whom you talk to) for twenty bedouin killed on the mountain, or twenty hikers swept away in a flash flood, or a crafty woman who killed nineteen suitors before marrying the twentieth – is pierced by a number of explorable ravines and canyons.

Northeast of Rum village, between the highest peak of the Umm Ashreen massif and Jabal Kharazeh, is **Makhman Canyon**, explorable for about a kilometre along its length.

Directly east of the *Resthouse* is an enormous ravine splitting Jabal Kharazeh from Jabal Umm Ejil. Just beside it, a complex maze of canyons is negotiable all the way through the mountain. Once up and over a concealed gully alongside the ravine – the only way into the mountain – you emerge on a hidden plateau dotted with wind-eroded towers and framed by looming molten cliffs. Diagonally left is **Kharazeh Canyon**, and you can work your way along it for some distance before the cliffs close in. The main route follows **Rakabat Canyon** southeast from the plateau, but path-finding is complex in this closed-in, rocky gorge, requiring plenty of scrambling up and down through interlinking ravines. You eventually emerge beneath the magnificent orange dunes of **Wadi Umm Ashreen** on the east side of the mountain, from where you could walk south around the massif back to Rum village. To do the full trip (10km; at least

7

the deal. If you arrive at the Visitor Centre **without a booking**, all is not lost (see page 333).

Either way, there's a collection of specific sites to visit in the deep desert, which we've outlined in this account along with a few pointers for walkers to get off the beaten track. There are literally dozens of possible **itineraries**. Any of the routes can be strung together to form a two-, three- or four-day adventure, with intervening nights spent camping in the desert. There are also plenty of opportunities for journeys further afield, including the **desert track to Aqaba** (50–70km), covered in a day by 4x4, two or three by camel. It's possible to reach Mudawwara by camel in about four days, Petra or Ma'an in five or six.

A NIGHT IN THE DESERT

There are no **hotels** in or near Wadi Rum: the only places to sleep are the numerous bedouin-run **camps** dotted around the desert. At most places, washing facilities are somewhat rudimentary and beds (and bedding) rather make-do, though some are rather fancier, with real beds and proper bathrooms. Camps within the Protected Area tend to be small, placed in isolation from one another far out in the desert, accessible only by 4x4 and sleep ten or fifteen people maximum in bedouin-style goat-hair tents. Most camps at Disi are larger, sometimes cheek-by-jowl with one another; they are often accessible by tour buses driving on dirt tracks, frequently set around circular performance areas with amplified music and electric floodlights, and sleep anywhere from fifty to two hundred and fifty people, often in army-style canvas tents pitched in rows.

WALKING ALONE: A WARNING

A final note. It barely needs saying, but here goes: it would be **suicidally reckless** to tackle any of the mountain routes in and around Wadi Rum without a local guide. Walking on the desert floor is fine – if you're fit enough to cope with hours on soft sand – but even then, if you choose to do a long-distance walk alone, you should register your intended route at the Visitor Centre and let staff know when you are planning to return. For multiday walks, and all types of scrambling or climbing, it is essential to have a **knowledgeable local guide**: this is exceptionally harsh terrain and even apparently safe rock can be treacherous.

WILDLIFE IN RUM

Wadi Rum is the setting for an ongoing experiment in wildlife reintroduction. The **Arabian oryx** (*Oryx leucoryx*) – a white antelope with long, straight horns that formerly roamed the deserts of the Middle East – has been extinct in the wild in Jordan for many decades. A captive breeding programme in the 1970s and 80s at Shaumari (see page 197) was successful, but after the first Gulf War 1.7 million sheep and goats, brought into Jordan by refugees from Iraq, decimated the rangelands through overgrazing, rendering the planned oryx release impossible. Oryx have remained **in captivity** at Shaumari ever since. Other regional projects have fared little better: Oman's oryx reintroduction failed due to excessive poaching, and schemes in Dubai, Abu Dhabi, Syria and elsewhere have had varying degrees of success – always (bar one release area in Saudi Arabia) with the oryx remaining behind fences.

In 2009, after meticulous planning, twenty oryx were brought to Wadi Rum from Abu Dhabi for acclimatization in a large, fenced zone behind Jabal Rum, away from tourist routes, before release into the open desert. Twenty more followed in 2012, boosting the herd's viability – by 2014 there were 73 oryx. A hundred **gazelle** also live alongside, and in 2015 sixty **ibex** (a kind of wild mountain goat) were released into the wild, ten with satellite tracking devices. The UAE is funding solar-powered surveillance cameras in the area to deter illegal poaching. By all accounts, the local bedouin are thrilled to see the animals back in the area: oryx have a uniquely poetic resonance in bedouin culture. They have vowed to protect them, not least because they also recognize that **oryx-spotting safaris** could become a major money-spinner. For up-to-date information, ask at the Visitor Centre.

half a day), you need confidence on easy rock, a good head for heights and experience of route-finding; if in any doubt, take a local guide.

Wadi Siq Makhras

Heading east from the Visitor Centre takes you across the valley into **Wadi Siq Makhras**, which narrows as it cuts southeast through the Umm Ashreen massif, eventually delivering incredible views over the vast and silent **Wadi Umm Ashreen**. The walk from here south around the massif to Rum village (12km) can be shortened by navigating Rakabat Canyon from east to west. Other routes of 10–12km from the eastern opening of Wadi Siq Makhras involve heading northeast through Siq Umm Tawagi to get picked up in Disi village, or southeast to camp overnight in Barrah Canyon. If you don't fancy such long hikes, you can arrange in advance to be picked up at any identifiable intermediate spot by camels or 4x4 for the return journey.

Jabal Qattar

About 8km south of Rum, on the desert track to Aqaba, rises **Jabal Qattar** ("Mountain of Dripping"), origin of several freshwater springs. A short walk up the hillside brings you to the largest spring, **Ain Qattar**, which was converted by the Nabateans into a well. Stone steps in an area of lush greenery descend into a hidden, underground pool of cold, sweet water, drinkable if a little mossy. South and west of Qattar, just off the Aqaba track in the beautiful hiking area around **al-Maghrar**, are a handful of **"sunset sites"**, popular spots for late-afternoon 4x4 excursions (though the exact places that give the best sunset views change according to the seasons).

Khazali canyon

The titanic chunk of mountain opposite Qattar is **Jabal Khazali** – a highlight of any tour in Rum and included on even the shortest excursions. It's supposedly named for a criminal, Khazal, who was pursued up to the summit and, with nowhere to run, leapt off, whereupon he miraculously floated to earth and landed unharmed. The mountain's north face is split by a mammoth **canyon**, entered by a ledge on the right, the inner walls of which are covered at different heights with stylized **Thamudic rock drawings** of people, horses and pairs of feet. It's possible to scramble your way up through the cool, narrowing ravine, dodging the pools of stagnant water, for about 200m until you meet unscaleable rock.

Umm Fruth rock bridge

The area east and south of Khazali is full of small domes and outcrops, with a cat's cradle of wadis and hidden valleys running through and between the peaks. To the south, a small, easily climbed **rock bridge** rises from the desert floor at **Jabal Umm Fruth**, another very popular stopping-off point which features in many photos of Rum.

Red dunes and Jabal Anfishiyyeh

East of Wadi Umm Ashreen is an area of soft sand, with some scrambleable **red dunes** rising to 20m or more against the north face of Jabal Umm Alaydya. Very close by, some of the best **Thamudic inscriptions** can be seen on **Jabal Anfishiyyeh**, including a herd of camels – some ridden by hunters, others suckling their calves – and some strange circle-and-line symbols. A little southeast, **Jabal Umm Kharg** has on its eastern side a small Ottoman structure, named – wrongly – "**Lawrence's House**", which commands spectacular panoramic views out over the desert.

7

THE WADI RUM BEDOUIN: AN INSIDER'S VIEW

Ruth Caswell has been visiting Wadi Rum for many years. In this piece, written almost two decades ago, she sheds some light on the background of a generation of bedouin who now make their living as tourist guides.

Two cousins I know, Muhammad and Mahmoud [names have been changed], who are guides at Rum, are both from the Zilabia tribe, a branch of the great Aneizat tribal confederation. Both of them were born in the mid-1970s, in the desert, in the family tent. When they were children they attended the army school in Wadi Rum, usually walking up to 10km in the mornings and then returning to the family camps in the afternoon (school finishes at about 2pm). Sometimes they rode a donkey, sharing it with their friends. After school and during school holidays they looked after their family's animals, often moving tens of kilometres across the desert in search of grazing. They learned to hunt for meat in the mountains, and to gather the medicinal herbs they found there. Both families had a number of goats, but they were (and still are) too valuable to be killed for meat except for special occasions.

The usual transport was by camel. Muhammad's father bought one of the first jeeps to be seen in Wadi Rum when Muhammad was 12 years old; they quickly realized that the jeep was more expensive to run than the camel was, so its use was strictly rationed. It certainly wasn't to be used for things like taking the children to school. Muhammad's family used to spend the winters sheltered in the Barra canyon; during the spring they made their way slowly across the desert, spending the high summers on a plateau across the border in Saudi Arabia. Then back again during the autumn. Mahmoud's father preferred to travel from east to west, from the Mudawwara mudflats to the Abu Aina spring in Wadi Rum.

It is not surprising that these men and their families know the desert and the mountains intimately, nor that they are good walkers.

Another trait that they nearly all share is complete independence whenever possible. Because they were not brought up to be able to call a doctor, a vet or a mechanic, they all know a fair bit about treating an injury or an illness, caring for a sick or injured animal or repairing a car. They are confident in their own abilities in almost any situation. Most of the bedouin guides in Wadi Rum have the same or similar backgrounds. The few exceptions are from the families that preferred to remain near to the fort in Wadi Rum that was built by the Desert Patrol and a sure source of water, rather than moving with the seasons. These people might know the deep desert less well than the others, but nonetheless all the Rum guides are still bedouin to the core.

Barrah Canyon

East of Anfishiyyeh lie Jabal Barrah and Jabal Abu Judayda, divided by the sandy, easily negotiable and very atmospheric **Barrah Canyon**, which winds between the cliffs for some 5km; this is an often-used overnight camping stop, the journey best done with camels.

Siq Umm Tawagi ("Siq Lawrence")

North of Barrah, between a group of three peaks, the beautiful hidden valley of **Siq Umm Tawagi** is another classic destination, featuring plenty of Thamudic rock drawings as well as carvings of faces done in the 1980s – with the date "1917" – which tour guides describe as an original depiction of Lawrence and Emir Abdullah. Tragically, in the spirit of the theme park that Wadi Rum threatens to become, this canyon is now being dubbed "**Siq Lawrence**" as a result. Umm Tawagi is a good second-day route from Barrah to a pick-up point in Disi village, about 15km north. From Barrah, it's also possible to round the Umm Ashreen massif and return to Rum.

7

LAWRENCE OF ARABIA

Very few of the events concerning **T.E. Lawrence** and the Arab Revolt can be pinned down with any accuracy. The Arab protagonists left no record of their actions and motivations, and the single account of the Revolt is Lawrence's own, his famous **Seven Pillars of Wisdom**, written after the war, lost, rewritten from memory and published in 1926. By then, though, the image of Lawrence as a true British hero was firmly in place; he was almost universally seen as a soldier of integrity and a brilliant strategist, honest and courageous, who acted with genuine altruism in leading the Arabs to victory and was betrayed by his own officers. The image is a beguiling one, and stood the test of dozens of biographies. Even one of his closest friends describing him as "an infernal liar" didn't crack the facade.

But with the gradual declassifying of British war secrets – and dozens more biographies – elements of a different truth have slowly been taking hold. Lawrence was undoubtedly close to **British Intelligence**. Indeed, even in his early 20s, Lawrence's work on an archeological dig in northern Syria may have been a front, enabling him to photograph engineering work on the nearby Berlin–Baghdad railway. His supposed altruism during the **Arab Revolt** seems to have been firmly rooted in a loyalty to his own country and a hatred of the French. During the Revolt, Lawrence was well aware of the Sykes-Picot Agreement that was to carve up the Levant, and seems to have wanted to establish Arab self-rule mostly to stop the French gaining any control. Although his own conscious betrayal of the Arabs racked him with guilt, he justified himself on the grounds that it was more important to defeat Germany and the Ottomans. Details have also emerged of Lawrence's dishonesty and self-glorification: biographers who have compared Seven Pillars to documentary evidence have regularly come up against inconsistencies and outright lies perpetrated by Lawrence, often for his own self-aggrandizement.

Lawrence is much less highly regarded in Jordan, where he is often seen as an **imperialist** who sought to play up his role in what was essentially an Arab military victory, achieved and led by Faisal. Although he pretended to have Arab interests at heart, in fact – as was shown by the events after the Revolt – his loyalty to British interests never wavered.

Nonetheless, as the years pass and the biographies pile up, the **myth** persists of Lawrence the square-jawed, blue-eyed buccaneering English bedouin as portrayed by Peter O'Toole in David Lean's 1962 film epic Lawrence of Arabia. But in 1919, Lawrence's friend Colonel Richard Meinertzhagen recorded a conversation that they'd had about the text of Seven Pillars: "He confesses that he has overdone it, and is now terrified lest he is found out and deflated. He told me that ever since childhood he had wanted to be a hero. And now he is terrified at his brazen imagination. He hates himself and is having a great struggle with his conscience." This seems as appropriate an epitaph as any to a life still shrouded in mystery.

Burdah rock bridge

For intrepid types, one of the highlights of Rum is the impressive **Burdah rock bridge** perched way off the desert floor on the north ridge of Jabal Burdah. Best photographed from the east, the bridge is best scaled from the west; it's an easy but serious climb, especially if you're not that good with heights, and should only be attempted in the company of a guide – preferably one who has a rope to protect the last few metres of climbing, which is a bit exposed. The sense of achievement at reaching the bridge, though, is marvellous, and the views are stupendous.

Jabal Umm ad-Daami

A guided ascent of Jabal Rum requires climbing competence, but an ascent of Jordan's highest mountain, **Jabal Umm ad-Daami** (1854m), identified as such by climbing guide Difallah Atieq (who died in 2011) and located some 40km south of Rum on the Saudi border, can be achieved by anyone. In truth, it's often harder to find a driver who knows the way than it is to reach the summit. Once you've driven there, the scramble up the north ridge is straightforward, and the summit provides superb views over both countries. You can overnight in the desert, perhaps at a bedouin camp among the beautiful **Domes of Abu Khsheibah**, midway back to Rum.

7

North of Disi and Shakriyyeh

The wild landscape **north of Disi and Shakriyyeh** is just as impressive as the core areas further south – but a fraction as well known. Three easily accessible sites stand out to give a taste of the area. In the foothills just east of Disi, at the base of **Jabal Amud** amid dozens of Thamudic inscriptions, is a large slab of rock covered in lines and interconnected circles which, it has been theorized, is an ancient map – although what it refers to isn't known. About 6km north of Shakriyyeh are some amazing Thamudic drawings at **Abu al-Hawl**; the name means "the Terrifying One" and suits well the extraordinary experience of coming across stark 2m-high figures with stubby outstretched limbs carved into a remote desert cliff. About the same distance again north is a breathtaking rock arch at **Jabal Kharaz**.

You could either take a half-day drive out to these two spots, or treat them as stop-offs on a long desert journey northwest to Petra or northeast to Ma'an. Also in this area is "The Palace", a castle-like compound which some guides claim featured in *Lawrence of Arabia*. It was in fact built in 2001 for the French TV game show *The Desert Forges*.

Bait Ali

Shakriyyeh • ☎ 079 925 7222, ⓦ facebook.com/baitaliwadirum • Signposted off the main road into Wadi Rum, 15km east of the Amman–Aqaba highway junction and about 2km west of the police post marking the fork to Disi; the signpost leads you north across the railway line and onto a short desert track – passable in an ordinary car – to the site itself

The comfortable, upmarket, fully serviced desert compound of **Bait Ali**, located just outside Rum, is a great place to hole up and do nothing all day in comfort (surprisingly difficult at most camps, which often stand empty between 9am and 5pm). Hidden behind a rocky outcrop, the site has open views across the desert plains. Owned and run by genial Tahseen and Susie Shinaco, the place – and its team of local staff – is the height of hospitality. Public lounge areas, decorated in traditional style, are sheltered and cool, and include a dining and entertainment zone. Their **accommodation** is excellent (see page 334) and they have Wadi Rum's only **swimming pool**, fed by water from aquifers beneath the desert.

Bait Ali lies within the territory of the **Swalhiyeen** tribe, who are quite separate from the Zalabia of Rum and the Zuwaydeh of Disi, and so are able to offer unique trips by camel, horse or 4x4, at their own rates, into landscapes that most visitors don't get to experience. Owner Susie Shinaco is herself an accomplished horse rider. Added draws include **adventure activities** such as dune-buggies (JD45/person/hr), as well as hot-air ballooning and ultralighting.

7

ARRIVAL AND DEPARTURE
WADI RUM

BY CAR
There's only one road into Wadi Rum, signposted east off the Desert Highway at the village of Rashdiyyeh, which lies 41km south of Ras an-Naqab and 42km north of Aqaba. This road, shadowed by a freight-only railway track, skirts the mountains and a couple of hamlets for some 17km to a fork in the road marked by a police post and railway station: the village of Disi (also spelled Diseh, Ad-Disa and so on) and other hamlets lie to the left, while the road ahead bends right into the long avenue of Wadi Rum itself, reaching the Visitor Centre after 4km. Some 7km beyond the Visitor Centre lies Rum village (also spelled Rhum, Ram and so on), where the road ends.

BY BUS
With most visitors booked on all-inclusive bus tours, there's very little public transport in or out of Wadi Rum. It's impossible to make a day-trip without your own transport. Check details of buses the day before with guides or staff at the Visitor Centre (which is where buses pick up and drop off). Bus services on Fridays are curtailed or nonexistent.

To Aqaba One bus (1hr; JD6) departs around 7am or 7.30am, with perhaps another at around 8.30am (see page 315).

To Petra (Wadi Musa) There's only one bus to Wadi Musa/Petra (1hr 30min; JD7), departing around 8am or 8.30am (see page 293).

Buses from Rashdiyyeh If you miss the buses listed above, or if you want to reach any other point, it's fairly easy to hitch a ride out to the highway junction at Rashdiyyeh (be prepared to pay JD2–3/person for the hitch), from where buses pass fairly frequently, south (left) to Aqaba and north (right) to Ma'an and Amman.

BY TAXI
Chartering a taxi is a viable way of getting to Rum. Split between three or four passengers, fares are reasonable value: one-way to/from Aqaba about JD25–35, Wadi Musa about JD50–60, Amman about JD80–100.

INFORMATION
Visitor Centre You can pick up a sketch map and a pamphlet or two at the Visitor Centre (see page 322).

Books If you intend to stay in Rum for more than a day or two, or if you're at all serious about trekking (guided or independent) or climbing, get hold of the excellent books by Tony Howard and Di Taylor (see page 390): *Treks and Climbs in Wadi Rum, Jordan* has detailed, technical route descriptions, *Walks & Scrambles in Wadi Rum* is a booklet of short, easy-to-accomplish excursions, and some of the routes from both also feature in *Jordan: Walks, Treks, Caves, Climbs and Canyons*. Links to all at ⓦ nomadstravel.co.uk. They can't be recommended highly enough.

Money There is no bank or ATM in or near Wadi Rum – the nearest are in Aqaba, Ma'an or Wadi Musa. The Visitor Centre booking office accepts credit cards, but nobody else does. Bring cash with you.

Warning If you're travelling on a budget, be aware that some people in the lower echelons of the tourism industry in Wadi Rum – as in Wadi Musa – target backpackers for money or sex. If you keep your ear to the ground, and monitor online forums, you'll come across reports of harassment and sexual assault. A favoured strategy is to offer to show you some amazing remote viewpoint, or invite you to an evening meal at a special campsite. Women travellers in Wadi Rum should never accept such an offer. Even if things start OK, stories abound of alcohol-emboldened hosts proposing after-dinner games teaching you the Arabic words for parts of the body. Situations can rapidly escalate.

PREBOOKED TOURS
The most rewarding, cost-effective and – in short – best way to see Wadi Rum independently is to **choose a guide in advance** and **book directly** with them. Itineraries can be arranged for anything from a couple of hours to an overnight stay or longer, hosted at the guide's own campsite out in the desert. They always include transport, accommodation, food and sightseeing. You're the boss. If you'd prefer to see the desert from the back of a **camel** – or even a **horse** – rather than in a 4x4, say so: most guides can oblige, or will pass you on to a specialist. And if you want to be **alone**, say so: the easy-to-overlook downside of 4x4 excursions, and, to a lesser extent, camel treks is that neither allows you to soak up the silence and isolation of the desert at your own walking pace. It's perfectly possible to hire a guide to drive your gear out to a campsite in the desert while you take your time and walk there, or you could arrange for a **one-way ride** by 4x4 or camel out to a particular spot from where you then walk back.

What to expect Every guide has his own camp in the deep desert, usually sleeping no more than about a dozen people at a time in traditional long, low tents made from black

WADI RUM: KEY DISTANCES
Wadi Rum is approximately:
- 300km south of **Amman** (3hr 30min)
- 100km south of **Petra** (1hr 30min)
- 60km north of **Aqaba** (1hr)

goat hair; there might be communal tents for sleeping, or individual cabins – or you can choose to sleep out under the stars. Either way, all bedding is provided. Some camps have full shower blocks, with flushing toilets, hot showers and basins for washing, others have simpler make-do facilities. There's rarely any mobile phone coverage or electricity; a head-torch would be useful.

WADI RUM DIVERSIONS

HORSERIDING

Horseriding through the desert sands is perennially popular, and a handful of guides offer anything from short excursions (roughly JD30/hr) to a full week or more, exploring far and wide, camping each night. These are not for novices, though; you should have some experience of handling horses. On the drive into Rum you'll pass signs for the stables of **Atallah Sweilhin** (☎079 580 2108, ⓦwadirumhorses.com), acknowledged as the leading specialist, contactable through Bait Ali (see page 329).

ROCK CLIMBING

If you're intending to do technical **rock climbing**, you should contact one of Rum's handful of UK-trained **mountain guides**, all of whom have full equipment and plenty of experience. Talk first to the guys at ⓦshababsahra.com. A few other locals also guide rock climbs; like many Rum bedouin they are naturally competent climbers, and have learnt rope techniques by climbing with experienced visitors. However, Jordan has no system of qualification for mountain guides: staff at the Visitor Centre can put you in touch with someone suitable, but you should establish his experience before agreeing terms. There is an informative leaflet on environmental and safety guidelines, *Climbing and Trekking in Wadi Rum Protected Area*, available free at the Visitor Centre. For more information and contacts, see ⓦnomadstravel.co.uk, ⓦwadirum.net and ⓦwadiram.userhome.ch.

HOT-AIR BALLOONING AND MICROLIGHTING

Hot-air ballooning offers an incomparably romantic way to experience the grandeur of Wadi Rum. You take off – usually at dawn – from near Bait Ali for a serene float over the mountains: an hour's flight costs JD130 per person (minimum three people). Alternatively you could buzz the sands in a **microlight**, an open-air powered glider operated in tandem with a qualified pilot (JD55/20min; JD80/30min; JD150/1hr). Book with the **Royal Aero Sports Club of Jordan** (☎079 730 0299, ⓦrascj.com) well in advance.

CAMEL RACES

The locals (and visiting sheikhs) regularly **race camels**, but often at short notice with no outside promotion; ask around when you visit. Most events take place in spring and autumn, notably the star-studded two-day **Sheikh Zayed Camel Racing Festival** at a racetrack in Disi in late October: if you're nearby at the time, don't miss it.

YOGA AND MEDITATION

New-agey ideas are now part of Rum's tourism profile, with a few guides now hosting desert **yoga or meditation retreats**. Check with resident yoga teachers Sandra Jelly or Alena Bartoli on a variety of websites, including ⓦpinkspiritjordan.com, ⓦjordanmeditation.com and ⓦin2jordan.com.

A FOUR-DAY WALK TO THE SEA

The national **Jordan Trail** (ⓦjordantrail.org; see page 50) passes through Rum. With suitable preparation, you could turn the final section into an epic **four-day walk to the sea**. Outdoor skills, camping gear and prearranged support are essential (there are no food or water supplies along the route, and guides are needed for at least part of the way). Begin with the 17.9km trail south from Rum village past Jabal Qattar to Al-Qider, then a mazy flattish 15.4km route between domes to the isolated hamlet of Titen. Day 3 plots an 18.6km route through desert valleys to a campsite at the foot of a final barrier of peaks. The last day is a tough 12km, up and over the mountains: you're rewarded with views of the Red Sea on the gentle descent past industrial works, ending at the public beach south of Aqaba – perfect for a dip. The Jordan Trail website has full information, maps, GPS points and detailed walking notes.

7

CUT-PRICE TOURS OF WADI RUM: A WARNING

Numerous scammers – notably at cheap hotels in Wadi Musa and, to a lesser extent, in Aqaba, Amman and Dana – offer **cut-price tours** of Wadi Rum that may leave you disappointed. Here's why.

- **Wadi Rum or Disi?** Unlicensed operators are not permitted to bring tourists into the Wadi Rum Protected Area, which is patrolled by rangers. This means that anyone offering cut-price tours of Wadi Rum – such as a budget hotel in Aqaba or Petra – will not be taking you into Wadi Rum*: they will, instead, drive you around the deserts of Disi nearby, and host you at one of the Disi tourist camps. There's nothing wrong with Disi – it's beautiful – but it's not what you're paying for. Yet these scammers will swear blind that you're being taken to the real Wadi Rum – even to the extent of lying to you about which camp you're in (we've had reports of tourists being dumped at one of the Disi camps by a driver who told them it was Bait Ali). Rum camps are invariably smaller, cosier, quieter and less commercialized than those in Disi.
- **Commission?** If you pay, say, JD30 to a hotel in Petra for a tour of Wadi Rum, it's likely that around JD15 of that will go straight into the pocket of the hotelier. That leaves JD15 for the man who's actually going to drive you around – which means you'll get a very short tour. For comparison, the going rate for a decent tour of Wadi Rum booked directly with a reputable guide, including overnight camping, all transport, meals and facilities, is roughly JD50–60 per person. Pay significantly less than that, and you can be sure you'll be short-changed.
- **Guide or driver?** At cut-price rates you are unlikely to be hosted by a guide – that is, someone who lives in Wadi Rum, speaks English and can explain the area and its sights to you. Instead you're likely to get someone who can drive the car, but little else – probably friendly enough, but possibly not even Jordanian.

Being taken around the desert in a 4x4 is never cheap – why should it be? – and that's even more true for somewhere as extraordinary (and fragile) as Wadi Rum. Out here, you really do get what you pay for.

The Cleopatra hotel in Wadi Musa is an exception – to our knowledge, this is the only Petra hotel offering tours that genuinely do enter Wadi Rum.

Food and drink If you're staying late or overnight, dinner will be cooked for you – perhaps roast chicken, or lamb cooked in a *zarb* (a traditional sand oven, where the meat slow-cooks for hours in a hole in the ground), along with veg, salads and bread. Breakfast is usually bread, salads, cheese, olives and eggs. Tea and coffee flow on request.

VIP options You can, of course, choose to spurn all this, and ask to be set up with a private tent of your own, far out in some remote spot, with or without meals provided. Anything is possible, if the price is right.

CHOOSING A GUIDE

It pays to do a bit of advance planning. Work out your arrival and departure dates, how much time you have available in between, and roughly what you'd like to see or do. Then compare our listings with the guide recommendations at trustworthy websites such as ⓦ nomadstravel.co.uk. It also makes sense to read the online travel forums to get a sense of other people's experiences – though bear in mind that reviewers can get confused about which camp they're talking about, or who their guide was (there are lots of Sabbahs, Salems, Salims and Suleimans in Wadi Rum, and

one common Arabic name may be transliterated multiple ways as "*Attayak*", "*Atayek*", "*Atieq*" or "*Ateeg*").

Getting a quote Once you've selected a handful of guides that seem suitable, contact them by email or online messaging to get a quote for what they can offer at what price. Some guides have their email answered by helpful European or American friends outside Jordan; others tackle their own office admin – don't take fluency in English (or lack of it) as indicative of the service you'll receive on the ground.

Confirming the tour Be aware that there are strict rules in place surrounding guide services. Once you've chosen a guide, give a firm written confirmation by email as far in advance as possible – at the very least two days before your arrival. Make sure you receive an acknowledgement back. Your guide is then permitted to meet you at the Visitor Centre (or elsewhere; some will meet you at the Rashdiyyeh highway junction on request), and escort you into the desert for your agreed programme. Guides are not permitted to pick up tourists at the Visitor Centre without a booking.

Booking through a tour operator An alternative option is to book through a Jordanian tour operator (see page 27), who can sort everything out for you – though you will pay extra for their services. Many are excellent: some work with particular guides; others maintain their own campsite within the Protected Area. Beware the horde of unlicensed operators – including budget hotels in Petra and elsewhere – who will try to convince you that their "special" cut-price tour is a great way to see Wadi Rum on the cheap: it rarely is (see opposite).

SOME RECOMMENDED GUIDES

This is a small selection of recommended guides; there are many more, and we couldn't possibly list them all – don't take a particular guide's omission from this list as necessarily implying we're withholding a recommendation. Regrettably, no impartial list of all guides and camps exists, so until ASEZA or some other entity produces one, travellers are flying blind. Many guides are also on Facebook.

Ahmad Zalabia (Rum Stars) ☏ 079 512 7025, ⓦ rum stars.com. A team of cheery young guides with good desert knowledge.

Aodeh Abdullah (Bedouin Whispers) ☏ 079 561 7902, ⓦ bedouinwhispers.com. Budget tours by jeep and camel, plus overnight desert camping.

Attayak Ali (Bedouin Roads) ☏ 079 589 9723, ⓦ bedouinroads.com. Highly respected guide, offering top-quality jeep tours as well as excellent hiking and trekking programmes. Often booked solid.

Khaled Sabbah (Khaled's Camp) ☏ 079 560 9691, ⓦ facebook.com/wadirumcamping. Great little team with a flexible approach, impeccable credentials and access to an excellent camp.

Mater & Anne Zalabia (Milky Way Ecolodge) ☏ 077 734 9574, ⓦ tevamilkyway.com. Soft adventure excursions by jeep or on foot, based at one of Rum's best lodge-style camps. Great for families.

Mehedi Saleh (Bedouin Directions) ☏ 077 688 6481, ⓦ wadirumjeeptours.com. Wide-ranging tours and a very isolated, far-flung campsite.

Mohammed Hammad ☏ 077 266 0319, ⓦ wadirum bedouincamp.com. Dedicated mountain specialist, managing scrambling and rock climbing trips of all kinds.

Mohammed Mutlak/Salem & Suleiman Mutlak ☏ 077 742 4837, ⓦ wadirum.org. A good choice of well-managed tours, reaching some unusual spots in the deep desert, plus excellent overnight camping. They also run yoga retreats and cooking classes.

Mzied Atieq ☏ 077 730 4501, ⓦ mzied.com. A wonderful host, charming and knowledgeable, with many years of experience. Offers a wide range of options for hiking, trekking, camel treks and jeep trips, as well as overnight stays at his excellent campsite in the deep desert.

Obeid Naser (Bedouin Life) ☏ 079 584 0672, ⓦ facebook.com/bedouinlifecamp. Genial jeep tours and camping, with a hospitable welcome from Obeid or his family and a deep knowledge of the desert.

Sabah Atayek, with his sons Musalam & Suleiman Sabah (Fox Camp) ☏ 079 590 2127, ⓦ bedouins ofwadirum.com. Highly accomplished mountain guides, also offering a wide range of camel and jeep tours.

Sabbah Eid (Golden Sand Camp) ☏ 077 789 1243, ⓦ facebook.com/sabbaheid. Very experienced specialist in hiking, trekking, desert tours and rock climbing. Knowledgeable and good company.

Salem & Saleem Lafi (Jordan Tracks) ☏ 079 648 2801, ⓦ jordantracks.com. Brothers who run the only fully accredited travel agency in Rum, authorized to make hotel bookings and tourist arrangements all round Jordan. Offers a range of jeep and hiking trips within Rum, including some climbing and scrambling, plus horseriding.

Shabab Sahra ☏ 077 697 6356, ⓦ shababsahra.com. Wadi Rum's first proper climbing club (the "Desert Youth" in Arabic), established in 2015 with government accreditation, and staffed by local specialists who know the mountains intimately and can guide professionally and safely on even the toughest routes. They also offer shorter excursions and tailor-made cultural trips.

Zedane al-Zalabia (Bedouin Meditation Camp) ☏ 079 550 6417, ⓦ wadirumbedouinmeditationcamp. com. Last but not least – recommended budget-priced jeep trips and overnight desert camping.

ON-THE-SPOT TOURS

If you turn up in Wadi Rum **without a booking**, check the noticeboards by the Visitor Centre ticket office which describe a dozen desert itineraries by 4x4 (and some others by camel), with prices for each. If you want to stay overnight, you'll have to fix up accommodation yourself – we give some options later in this section (see page 334).

How to book Simply choose which route you'd like to do, pay the fee (credit cards are accepted) and you're then assigned the next driver (or camel boy) in line. This can be a perfectly satisfactory way to see the desert: most drivers (there are dozens) are friendly and professional.

However, be aware that these guys are not guides: they may not speak English, may only know a few sites of interest and may not be driving the most comfortable 4x4 in the world.

Routes Turn-up-and-go excursions booked at the Visitor Centre are divided into areas: "Operator 1" routes cover ground within the heartland of Wadi Rum; "Operator 2" routes are in more outlying (but not necessarily any less beautiful) areas to the north and east around Disi. Both are possible by 4x4 or by camel.

Costs by 4x4 At the time of writing, a basic 2hr tour by

4x4 taking in the Nabatean temple at Rum village, Abu Aina spring and the Khazali inscriptions (Operator 1) – or, alternatively, the scenic drive through Siq Lawrence/Umm Tawagi (Operator 2) – costs JD35 for a full car, seating between four and six people. Several different tours, on various routes, last 3–5hr, up to an 8hr tour covering all major sites as far south as the rock bridges at Umm Fruth and Burdah, plus a sunset viewpoint, for JD80 for the car.

Costs by camel A short camel ride of 1–2hr costs JD10–15/person, rising to JD30/person for a full day.

SELF-DRIVE

You can drive your own 4x4 into Wadi Rum for a fee (JD20/day) or rent a 4x4 at the Visitor Centre (JD35/day).

A warning Driving yourself around the desert is not a great idea. Unless you've been to Rum before (and even then), it's very easy to get confused and lost in the open desert, to say nothing of ending up bogged in soft sand. Punctures and axle damage are common. There are also regulations in place to try and limit environmental degradation within the Protected Area by restricting drivers to certain tracks – unless you know where those tracks run, you'll basically be carving up a UNESCO World Heritage Site at random. Not big, not clever. Leave the driving to the locals.

ACCOMMODATION AND EATING

If you've **prebooked a tour** with a specific guide, all your sleeping arrangements and meals will be taken care of as part of the agreed package (see page 330).

ON-THE-SPOT ACCOMMODATION

Facilities for independent arrivals are not great: the whole system of tourism at Rum is geared up best for large tour groups and individuals who have prebooked. Since no public transport leaves Rum during the afternoon, it's impossible to arrive by bus, do a tour in the desert and then leave (unless you shell out for a taxi to your next destination). And options for fixing up decent accommodation on the fly are limited.

Disi tourist camps It's possible to turn up on spec at one of the big tourist camps outside the Protected Area – which all focus on tour-group business – and negotiate a bed for the night. Most are ranged side-by-side around the base of Jabal Umm Bdoun just outside Disi village; it's fairly easy to hitch a ride out there. None has guides or transport available, but if you ask you'll be shunted along to someone who can help. However, many of these places are owned by tourism businesses in Aqaba or Amman, meaning that little money stays within the community.

Other options A few owners of camps within the Protected Area publish rates for overnight stays without touring – ⓦ tevamilkyway.com is one – or you could ask the Visitor Centre to phone around on your behalf. Otherwise, your best bet is Bait Ali.

DISI

Captain's Desert Camp ⊙ 079 520 2038, ⓦ captains. jo. A popular choice, sleeping a total of 140 people in comfortable little half-tented suites with proper beds and bed linen. Groups often get bussed in and out for dinner or a quick glass of tea under the (imported) palm trees, but it remains fairly congenial. JD45

Hillawi Camp ⊙ 079 553 3244. Vast campground, sleeping up to five hundred people in army-style tents

pitched in rows – when a big group is in this can feel almost like a small town in the desert, with electric lights strung across the mountainsides, cauldrons of food cooking and dancers entertaining the crowds. Its neighbours – *Moon Valley (Wadi Qamar), Oasis Desert, Desert Palm, Caravan* and more – are in the same mould. About JD40

Jabal Rum Camp ⊙ 079 557 3144. Another huge camp, located near the road on the plains behind Shakriyyeh, sleeping 260 people in army-style tents, with music and dancing nightly. Great, if you like that kind of thing. About JD40

Zawaideh Camp ⊙ 079 584 0664, ⓦ zawaideh desertcamp.com. Small, simple but well-equipped (and locally run) desert campsite near Disi, with goat-hair tents and a peaceful location, away from the Disi hubbub. This one is run by Hasan Zawaideh; not far away you'll also find the *Zawaideh Insights Camp, Salman Zwaidh Camp, Rahayeb Camp* and *Um Al Bdoun Eco Camp* in roughly similar vein. About JD35

RUM VILLAGE

Resthouse ⊙ 03 201 8867. The first building you come to in Rum village. For twenty-odd years this place served the function of being Rum's information centre, meeting point, restaurant, café, campsite and social centre. These days, with most tourists remaining back at the Visitor Centre, it's quieter than it was, but is still an OK place for a meal (JD12–15) or a beer. Across the road are a couple of local cafés.

BAIT ALI

Bait Ali ⊙ 079 925 7222, ⓦ facebook.com/baitali wadirum. This desert compound outside Rum (see page 329) is a great option – comfortable, upmarket and warmly welcoming. Accommodation is in three grades of adobe chalets, all nicely done in vaguely ethnic style, with stone floors, rugs, fancy mirrors, bamboo ceilings, tiled bathrooms and proper beds – everything spotlessly clean and comfortable. All are en suite, and all bar the "small" chalets have a/c. They also have thirty army-style tents, basic but with electric sockets. Bear in mind that Fri nights in particular can be busy, perhaps with DJs entertaining large groups from Amman or, sometimes, weddings or business get-togethers. Check in advance. Rates quoted here are for double occupancy including dinner and breakfast. Tent JD70, chalet from JD84

Amman to Aqaba: the Desert Highway

The fastest but least romantic of the three routes linking Amman and the south of Jordan, the **Desert Highway** can whisk you from the capital to Petra and beyond in a fraction of the time the same journey would take on the slow King's Highway – but with a fraction of the interest. For the most part, the journey south is framed by bleached-out desert hills rolling off into the distance, the monotony broken only by feeder roads branching west at regular intervals to towns on the King's Highway – in north-to-south order, Dhiban, Karak, Tafileh, Dana and Shobak (all described in Chapter 5) and Wadi Musa/Petra (Chapter 6).

The Desert Highway is the route followed by tankers and heavy lorries running between Aqaba's port and the industrial zones around Amman and Zarqa; it is a dual-lane highway but **traffic** can still be dense in parts. This is also the principal road into and out of **Saudi Arabia**, and all summer long features a tide of big, well-suspensioned minivans packed with holidaying Saudi or Gulf families heading north to cooler climes. Most people prefer doing these huge cross-desert drives in the cool of the night, so you'll find services on the highway open until the small hours but often shut in the heat of the afternoon.

This route is older than it appears, as the road was built mostly along the line of the **Hejaz Railway** (see page 88), which itself shadowed earlier Ottoman **pilgrimage** routes through the desert from Damascus to Mecca. During the sixteenth century, the Ottoman authorities built forts roughly a day's journey (about 30km) apart all down the length of the route, to guard local water sources and to serve as accommodation for the pilgrims; some of these "**hajj forts**" survive today, but almost all are ruined and/or inaccessible, the preserve of kestrels and archeologists.

Jiza and Suwaqa

From Amman's 7th and 8th Circles, the Desert Highway (doubling up in its initial stretches as the Airport Road) heads more or less due south. After exits for the Dead Sea, then Madaba and then the airport itself – at which point the glitzy billboard ads lining the highway abruptly halt – traffic swishes on south past the busy town of **JIZA** (with its Mamluke fort, now a bedouin police station) and the infamous desert prison at **SUWAQA**. Just before Suwaqa, some 74km south of 7th Circle, is a small blue sign for Qasr Tuba pointing east into the desert; the ruins repay the effort needed to reach them (see page 192), but you need a 4x4 and a knowledgeable guide for the journey 54km into the desert.

Qasr Bshir

Roughly 10km west of Suwaqa, on the other side of the highway, lies the superbly well-preserved late-Roman fortress **Qasr Bshir** (or Bashir), built in the early fourth century AD for an auxiliary cavalry unit on what was the far-flung southeastern border of the Roman Empire. Its walls still stand 3 or 4m high in parts, with thick corner towers flanking an internal courtyard lined with stables. It's an evocative sight, rising out of the desert on the short off-road journey to reach it (passable only in a 4x4). You'll need a guide who knows the way.

7

Qatraneh and Sultani

At **QATRANEH**, 90km south of Amman, a small, well-preserved two-storey hajj **fort** (signed as Qatraneh Castle), built under the sixteenth-century Ottoman sultan Suleiman the Magnificent, is signposted by a wadi 300m west of the highway. A wander round the empty, restored interior makes for an atmospheric interlude. Just beyond the fort is the highway exit heading west to Karak.

Antiquities aside, dusty Qatraneh has made a living out of providing roadside refreshment: a handful of generally decrepit and overpriced snack bars line the highway in the town centre, exploiting nod-and-wink understandings with bus operators to fleece hungry passengers. If you have your own transport, a better option is the *Baalbaki Tourist Complex*, 9km north – but if you're in a group (or on the JETT bus to Petra), you might well be taken instead to the *Midway Castle*, 23km south of Qatraneh at **SULTANI**.

Beyond there, the highway ploughs ahead. Around **Hasa**, 50km south of Qatraneh, are some phosphate mines. Other major signposted turn-offs include at **Jurf ad-Darawish** (69km south of Qatraneh) west to Tafileh; at **Husseiniyyeh** (83km south of Qatraneh) west to Dana and east to Jafr; and at **Unayza** (92km south of Qatraneh) west to Shobak and Petra.

ACCOMMODATION AND EATING   **QATRANEH AND SULTANI**

Baalbaki Tourist Complex Ad-Damkhi, 9km north of Qatraneh ☎079 553 6910. Curiously subtitled "The Legend", this well-equipped refreshment area – run by the Baalbaki catering conglomerate – is kept very clean: it boasts spotless public toilets (ask for the "Western toilets", which are usually kept locked), a basic canteen-style restaurant, a small minimarket, authentic crafts from Bani Hamida and other charitable foundations (priced no higher than in Amman) and a bookshop of sorts. Out back, alongside a simple garden shaded by olive trees, are a few plain but comfortable motel rooms, all en suite. JD30

Midway Castle As-Sultani, 23km south of Qatraneh ☎079 556 1245. This lone roadside rest area – so popular with drivers of tour buses on their way to Petra, it makes you wonder if some hidden inducement to stop might not be at play – includes a fancy souvenir shop (with sky-high prices), a simple restaurant and – the main attraction – well-kept toilets.

Ma'an

MA'AN, 214km south of Amman, is the capital of the southern desert, a bedouin town at the meeting point of highways from Amman, Iraq, Aqaba and Saudi Arabia. A frontier staging post from its earliest days, Ma'an only began to assert itself after the **Hejaz Railway** came through in 1904, transforming a desert encampment into a thriving settlement. Even after the establishment of Transjordan, Ma'an lay in a poorly demarcated frontier zone, with closer links to the Arabian Hejaz than to Amman. These days farmers come to do business in the markets, and the Hussein bin Talal University brings a little student colour to the streets, but for the most part Ma'an is a tough, hard-working city with a reputation for Islamic conservatism. It is bypassed by the Desert Highway, and there's little reason to visit other than to change buses.

The bus station lies on the edge of the **old quarter**, where Hejazi-style mud-brick houses cluster around palm-laden wadis, and shady gardens – sealed off from the outside world behind crumbling walls – make for a pleasantly cool retreat in such a hot, dry city. A short stroll from the bus station is the signposted **Ma'an Castle** – not a castle, but a sixteenth-century hajj fort, used as a prison right through to the 1980s. It is currently occupied by government offices, but if the doors are open you're free to wander around the courtyard and peek into the old rooms. Behind, on the banks of a wadi, is the **King Abdullah Gardens**, featuring shady spots under the palms, a children's playground and small café.

King Abdullah I Palace

Closed at the time of writing • No public transport; head 2km east of town on the road towards Mudawwara and Azraq, then follow the signed turn-off right for 1km

Ma'an's sole touristic draw is the **King Abdullah I Palace**, a grandiose title for a modest, late-Ottoman stone building beside the old railway station, which was where Abdullah stopped in 1920 on his intended push northwards from the Hejaz to Damascus. After he left in February 1921, it was used briefly as a hotel before lapsing into disuse, prior to renovation as a small heritage museum (displays included the first-ever Jordanian flag, flown in 1918, before the country existed). However, royally directed plans for restoration as a site of national historic importance ground to a halt in 2010 over contractual disputes, and the building remains closed. Check at the "castle" in town for the latest news. The **railway** – just beyond the palace – is now used solely for transporting phosphates from desert mines to Aqaba port.

ARRIVAL AND DEPARTURE   MA'AN

By bus Ma'an is the hub of public transport in the south, and if you can't find a bus running directly from one southern town to another you can almost always find a connection from Ma'an instead. The bus station is 500m southeast of the city centre. There are reasonably regular services to Amman, Aqaba, Wadi Musa and other southern towns, although things slow down noticeably after about 2pm. Less regular services run to the desert outposts of Disi near Rum, Mudawwara and Jafr.

Destinations Amman (2hr 30min); Aqaba (1hr 30min); Disi (1hr 20min); Jafr (50min); Karak (2hr); Mudawwara (1hr 30min); Shobak (1hr); Tafileh (1hr 30min); Wadi Musa (40min).

Ma'an to Aqaba

The principal route from Ma'an to Petra (33km) runs from the centre of town across the Desert Highway and through **Udhruh**. Continuing south from Ma'an on the Desert Highway itself you'll pass another couple of exits marked for Petra (both of which meet the road from Udhruh just above Ain Musa), and then the *Al-Anbat Tourist Complex*, another rest stop. Just past here is the final turn-off for Petra, some 33km southwest of Ma'an; this is the start of the so-called "**Scenic Road**" which runs into Wadi Musa through Rajif and Taybeh (see page 292).

A few hundred metres further, the Desert Highway reaches the edge of the highland plateau at **RAS AN-NAQAB**, from where the most stupendous panoramic views over the sandy deserts of the **Hisma** region suddenly open up in front of you. Pull off, if you can, to savour them.

The highway comes down off Ras an-Naqab before scooting away across the sandy floor of the desert, with the sheer mountains of Rum clearly visible off to the left of the road for much of the way. To the right lie the ruins of **Humayma**, a Nabatean village that was fortified by the Romans and later used by the Abbasid family to launch their overthrow of the Umayyads; it's a significant historical site but the ruins are scanty and hard to interpret.

Some 41km from Ras an-Naqab and a little beyond the village of **QUWEIRA**, a marked left turn at Rashdiyyeh points the way to **Wadi Rum** (see page 320). From here it's a clear run onwards as the highway threads a twisting path between the mountains, following the Wadi Yitm down towards **Aqaba** (see page 302).

Jafr

A junction 7km east of Ma'an town centre marks the start of two long, desolate roads through the desert. One route heads **northeast to Azraq** (see page 199) and onwards towards Iraq, but the only buses along here terminate at **JAFR**, an amiable but rather dilapidated village 58km out of Ma'an. Few vehicles pass this way, and getting stuck out here without a ride in the endless Plains of Flint under a scorching sun wouldn't be much fun. Jafr is set on the edge of a huge salt flat, smooth and hard as a tabletop, where in 1997 a British team clocked up an impressive 869km/h in the world's fastest car, *ThrustSSC*, before going on to the Nevada desert to set a new world land speed record of 1228km/h.

From Jafr, a road heads west past a large air force base to reach Husseiniyyeh on the Desert Highway, but if you continue north towards Azraq the only thing breaking the long desert drive is a speed bump located outside a police post 71km north of Jafr. From then on, there's only the regular *tha-dum* of the concrete road under your wheels until you reach Azraq, 209km north of Jafr. With a 4x4, you can follow the rough desert track 15km east of the police post to the remote settlement of **BAYIR**, site of an ancient Nabatean fort and well, still used by the bedouin today.

Mudawwara

The other road from the junction 7km east of Ma'an leads southeast to the Saudi border post of **MUDAWWARA**, though there are few reasons to venture onto this long, quiet road if you're not actually intending to cross the border. Some 80km beyond Ma'an is a well-preserved station of the Hejaz Railway at **Batn al-Ghul**, while at Mudawwara itself, 113km southeast of Ma'an – also with a well-preserved station, now occupied by a friendly extended family – an old **railway carriage** blown up in 1917 by Lawrence and the Arab armies still rests near the disused tracks. If you have a 4x4, you could try searching out a guide to help you navigate the three-hour, hard-to-follow route across the desert west from Mudawwara to Rum. The Saudi border lies 15km beyond Mudawwara.

7

Aqaba to the Dead Sea (Wadi Araba)

The road running due north from Aqaba along the floor of the vast **Wadi Araba** desert is the fastest way to the **Dead Sea** – and a scenic alternative route back to Amman, much preferable to the tedious Desert Highway (see page 335). However, it's a lonely drive – 280km to reach the Dead Sea hotels, passing through only a few villages, with lots of speed traps.

In the southern parts, expect sandy desert, acacia trees and rolling dunes, backed by giant mountains. Local bedouin allow their camels to graze freely beside the road. At some points, the border fence with Israel runs beside the road: traffic on the mirror-image Israeli highway is clearly visible, as are the irrigated fields cultivated by a string of desert kibbutzes.

Past the mudflats at **QATAR**, proposed as a new nature reserve, the Chinese company that built this road in the 1980s left a pagoda as a memento at **GHARANDAL**, 70km north of Aqaba.

Bir Mathkoor

Some 110km north of Aqaba, there's the welcome sight of the *Beir Mathkoor Café* (☎03 206 3650), a **refreshment stop** and petrol station open all hours. Shortly after, a sign points to **BIR MATHKOOR** (also spelled Beir Madhkur, Beer Mathkur, etc), which was the westernmost caravan suburb of Petra, tucked away in the mountains to the east of the road; you can spot the white shrine atop Jabal Haroun from here (see page 284). The village's Nabatean ruins, however, are likely to inspire only the most enthusiastic of archeologists. You'll also spot signs from the highway for the **Beir Mathkour Tourism Lodge**, an isolated spot out in the wilderness.

ACCOMMODATION   **BIR MATHKOOR**

Beir Madhkour Tourism Lodge Bir Mathkoor ☎077 212 3520, 🌐 facebook.com/beirmathkoor. This lodge comprises a cluster of 23 small houses – originally gifted to local bedouin by King Hussein in 1970 – isolated on the

7

> ### FEYNAN'S CASHLESS SOCIETY
> Feynan runs a near-**all-inclusive** pricing model. Your room rate (see page 344) – eye-wateringly high at first glance – includes an impressive pile of extras, from three meals a day (CNN named Feynan in a review of the world's eleven best vegetarian destinations) to teas, coffees, unlimited mineral water and "free" access to a wide range of activities, including guided walks, cooking classes, learning encounters with local bedouin families, and more. We cover all options in our account. The idea is to limit the exchange of cash as much as possible – and it works. Removing money from the experience is beguiling; Feynan is the softest sell in Jordan.

scorching desert plains 10km from Bir Mathkoor village. The bedouin preferred not to use the buildings, and they have now been renovated by a royally backed development NGO (⌨ badiafund.gov.jo; see page 203) to serve as visitor accommodation. Small and simple, each house has its own courtyard and bathroom. Access is by 4x4 only. As well as a rustic desert overnight experience, you could ask about guided hikes (from JD35/2hr) – including a challenging full-day walk to Jabal Haroun. Book ahead: if you turn up without a reservation you're likely to find the place empty and unstaffed. Price includes dinner and breakfast. <u>JD50</u>

Fifa

About 130km north of Aqaba, a turn-off is signposted east to **Feynan** (see below), after which a gently rising 35km of highway brings you to the edge of a scarp with the whole of the Dead Sea plain stretching in front. The small agricultural settlement of **FIFA** is at the bottom of the slope, with a signed turn-off climbing east into the mountains to Tafileh (see page 237). Our account of the stretch from Fifa northwards past Safi to the Dead Sea is in Chapter 2 (see page 121).

Feynan

As Jordan develops into a niche ecotourism destination of world renown, so one small project has gained a reputation as the country's – if not the Middle East's – leading example of how sustainable development can run hand-in-hand with low-impact nature tourism. **FEYNAN** (also spelled **Faynan**, **Feinan**, etc), an isolated rural community in Wadi Araba at the lower western end of the Dana Biosphere Reserve (see page 239), now hosts the **Feynan Ecolodge**, a Jordanian-owned, Jordanian-run 26-room desert hotel which has won global acclaim for both the quality of its environmentally friendly tourism product and the way in which it has established a sustainable socioeconomic partnership with local people.

Situated well away from any road, the ecolodge is not somewhere you stumble across. Book to stay here, though, and you gain access to a world that is effectively otherwise closed to outsiders: ordinary life for **rural bedouin** across Jordan, largely unchanged (for now) by tourism – older generations maintaining their traditional tent-based lifestyle, younger generations making new lives in the village.

Don't come expecting Dubai-style desert luxury – it's a long, bumpy drive to get here, across stony slopes that remain furnace-hot from May to September, and the lodge itself is charming but simple. Do come, though, expecting an **atmosphere of calm**, a stunning **natural landscape** opened up with **walks** and **mountain-biking**, an exceptionally long history evoked at remote **archeological sites**, and the rarest kind of genial, unfussy service from staff who have lived in the area all their lives. Austere but richly rewarding, Feynan shouldn't be missed.

Brief history

Marking a topographical meeting point between the mountains and the desert, where valleys coming down from the east bring constantly flowing water to an open alluvial plain fanning westwards, Feynan has seen human settlement for millennia. **Neolithic** villages on the slopes suggest people cultivated figs, pistachios and wild barley, hunted gazelle and perhaps herded goats and cattle here as early as 12,000 years ago. The 2011 discovery of an amphitheatre-like structure has led archeologists to theorize that the earliest human buildings were not houses, as previously thought, but community centres for processing foodstuffs. The economic shift which caused hunter-gatherers to domesticate crops and animals is well understood; what Feynan suggests is that a **social shift** may have occurred before that, from nomadic independence to shared labour.

Feynan is also extremely rich in minerals, particularly **copper**. As early as 6500 years ago, simple wind-fired kilns were being used to extract copper for ornaments and tools. Mining and smelting techniques progressed through the Bronze and Iron Ages, reaching a peak under the **Romans**, when Feynan – by then effectively a giant penal colony – hosted the largest copper **mines** in the Roman Empire. The third and fourth centuries AD saw numberless prisoners – many of them Christians – sent to Feynan to be literally worked to death, bound in chains and forced to labour night and day. The prisoners were overseen by imperial administrators based in a town overlooking the confluence of Wadi Dana and Wadi Ghwayr, now ruined and known as **Khirbet Feynan** (*khirbet* means ruins). Wealth-generation continued into the Byzantine era, when Feynan was the seat of a bishopric.

FEYNAN ECOLODGE ACTIVITIES

As well as hiking, Feynan offers several appealing **activities**, all run in conjunction with local communities.

MOUNTAIN BIKING

Feynan is developing **mountain-bike** trails, both on- and off-road around the lodge, nearby archeological ruins and the neighbouring villages. They supply bikes (JD20/day) and all the gear, and can also arrange a guide if needed (JD86/half-day, JD118/day).

STAR-GAZING

Out here in the desert, where there is no light pollution, stars fill the sky every night. After dinner each evening, staff set up Feynan's seriously high-powered telescope on the roof for a spot of **star-gazing** – amateur for sure, but guides have been trained by astronomers and are able to point out constellations and astronomical features with considerable knowledge. Join in if you like (it's free), or just lie back on a mattress to take in the galactic splendour.

COMMUNITY EXPERIENCES

Feynan offers a programme of **community experiences** with local **bedouin families**, where you'll be welcomed into a family tent to be served coffee around the fire, with a Feynan guide on hand to explain the intricacies and significance of the traditional coffee ceremony, and the deep cultural significance of coffee itself to the bedouin (see page 46). There's also the chance to participate in making *arbood*, a doughy, crusty bread baked in the embers of the fire, *shugga* weaving with goat hair to produce tent panels, or *kohl*, a form of natural eyeliner. These each cost JD3 per person, with all the money going to the host family. Another idea is spending a day with a shepherd, shadowing one of the local kids as they move up the mountainsides with their flocks searching for grazing (JD5/person), or joining the lodge chefs for a cooking class to learn how to make popular Jordanian dishes (free).

Feynan Ecolodge

Feynan • ☎ 06 464 5580, ⦿ ecohotels.me/feynan

British archeologists have been digging at several sites in Feynan since the 1990s. In 2005 the **Royal Society for the Conservation of Nature** (RSCN) brought in Jordanian architect Ammar Khammash (⦿ khammash.com) to design a tourist lodge to replace the archeologists' campsite. His style marries local materials with traditional arid-zone building techniques – thick walls, recessed windows, ribs to cast shadow on exterior walls, shaded interior courtyard, and so on – in the **Feynan Ecolodge**, a unique building that is functional, sympathetic and attractive.

The lodge is still owned by the RSCN but since 2009 it has been run by Amman-based firm EcoHotels, whose director, **Nabil Tarazi**, takes a refreshingly hands-on approach: you'll often find him at Feynan, listening to the local community's concerns and ideas, negotiating between tribal elders, refining how the lodge operates. Staying overnight here is a delight (see page 345). Staff at the lodge, and the associated income-generating crafts projects making candles and goat leather, are drawn from the **Azazmeh** bedouin tribe, who live in the area around Feynan. The drivers who shuttle guests to the lodge from a Reception Centre in the nearby village, where the asphalt road ends, are all from the neighbouring **Rashaydeh** bedouin – and every penny of the transport fee goes to them. Benefits are being spread around. The lodge is creating extra income for around eighty local families – perhaps five hundred people or more.

The lodge's **green** credentials are impeccable. It is not connected to the grid, and generates all its own electricity through **solar panels** – but only the reception office, bathrooms and kitchen have power; the rest of the building is lit by **candles** (which are made locally by hand). Water comes from local springs, and is heated by the sun for showers and kitchen use. Over the few chilly weeks of winter, the lodge's fireplaces burn not wood but **jift**, a by-product of olive-oil production made from compacted olive stones and dry residue. The lodge **composts** and **recycles**, serving only **vegetarian food** made from locally sourced products: bread is baked fresh each day by a woman from the local bedouin community.

And the place has **atmosphere**. Sit out on the terrace, lounge on the sofas, try a spot of star-gazing on the roof, walk in the hills – it's bewitchingly calm and contemplative. Set down below stony crags under a scorching sun, the lodge feels remote, but crucially not cut off from its surroundings. This is no luxury tourist hidey-hole planted down amid rural poverty. Quite the opposite: thanks, above all, to the endlessly cheerful and accommodating **local staff**, staying here you feel a part of things – protected in a stark natural wilderness yet also with privileged access to the culture of people for whom it is home. Feynan has been named one of the world's best ecolodges for a reason.

Short walks from the lodge

The choice of **walks** from Feynan is dizzying. If you want a private guide, rates start at JD86 for up to four hours, but the lodge's guides – all local bedouin – also lead two **guided group hikes** each day, open to all, at no extra charge on top of your room rate. Routes are scheduled ahead – publicized in advance on the website – and could include a challenging sunrise hike to a local summit (2hr); the informative Copper Mines trail (3–4hr), explaining the significance of Feynan for ancient copper-smelting, and visiting Roman mineshafts and slag heaps; sampler trails into Wadi Ghwayr, past Roman ruins into a perpetually flowing stream bed (3–4hr); Wadi Dana, for birdwatching and spectacular views (3–4hr); or the Feynan Plants Hike (2hr 30min), pointing out medicinal herbs. There's also a self-guided option for a walk to nearby archeological sites (2–4hr), including a Roman aqueduct, Byzantine church and Neolithic village.

> ## FROM COPPER TO LEATHER
>
> Feynan's economy, founded on copper, long ago shifted to farming – specifically **goatherding**. To the local Azazmeh bedouin, goats provide milk, cheese, yoghurt, *jameed* (a type of preserved dried yoghurt), hair for tent-weaving, rarely meat and above all cash from selling the male kids. Today the Azazmeh are participating in an RSCN scheme that is altering the rural economy to place greater emphasis on environmental protection. For years, goats have been overgrazing the land and decimating local flora, but rather than banning them within the Dana reserve area – which would merely foment ill will and shift the problem elsewhere – the RSCN are investing in them, fattening the goats in large pens outside the reserve and training local women to produce craft items out of **goat leather**. Both projects mean that the goats sell for higher prices at market and that their owners can additionally raise the value of each animal by selling the hide. You can ask to visit the leather workshops at Feynan to see more. Crafts made from Feynan goat leather are used in the lodge and sold at RSCN nature shops around Jordan.

7

Every day, a guided **sunset walk** (2hr) leads from the lodge on a short stroll up to a nearby ridgetop, for freshly brewed bedouin tea and stunning views westwards as the sun sets over the vast Wadi Araba deserts.

Long walks from the lodge

Longer guided day-hikes venture deeper into the mountains. One varied trail combines the lower reaches of both Wadi Dana and Wadi Ghwayr (closed for a month in autumn for the ibex breeding season). There's a challenging circular route to **Um Alamad**, to visit Roman ruins and abandoned mineshafts – but the two best routes are both one-way treks, requiring either vehicle transfers back to Feynan or onward travel.

The walk all the way up **Wadi Dana** (14km), rising from 325m at Feynan to 1200m at Dana village, passes from stony desert to Mediterranean scrub forest, taking in a multitude of flora and – occasionally – fauna. You can take the steep walk up and then either stay in Dana (see page 238) or book ahead for a transfer back to Feynan (3hr; JD52/car). Alternatively, do it the easy way: be driven up and then do the full-day walk back down to Feynan. Either way, you can take a guide or go it alone.

Perhaps even better is the full day adventure in **Wadi Ghwayr** (16km; closed in winter), negotiating a path through a gorge narrowing into a slot canyon, past palms and giant boulders. The hard way is uphill from Feynan, ending on the plateau at the highland village of Mansoura for the vehicle transfer back (2hr; JD52/car), though there are accommodation options near Mansoura at Shobak (see page 245) – or you can go in reverse, being driven to Mansoura for the hike down to Feynan. In either direction, this route requires a guide.

Faynan Archeological Museum

Faynan • Hours not fixed at time of writing; check at Ecolodge • ⓦ cbrl.ac.uk

In 2018 the small **Faynan Archeological Museum** opened near the Ecolodge as a joint project between Jordan's Department of Antiquities and the Council for British Research in the Levant (CBRL). Its purpose is to collate and display results from thirty years of archeological work done here by UK teams. Displays include a timeline of informational panels and a large horizontal relief model of the landscape around Feynan, with more ambitious exhibits planned for the future. For more details, see the project website ⓦ faynanheritage.com.

USEFUL ARABIC PLACE NAMES

Batn al-Ghul	بطن الغول	Jurf ad-Darawish	جرف الدراويش
Bayir	باير	Nuweiba	نويبع
Bir Mathkoor	بير مذكور	Qurayqira	قريقرة
Disi	الديسة	Quweira	القويرة
Durra	الدرة	Ras an-Naqab	رأس النقب
Eilat	إيلات	Rashdiyyeh	الراشدية
Gharandal	غرندل	Rum	رم
Graygra	قريقرة	Udhruh	أذرح
Humayma	الحميمة	Unayza	عنيزة
Husseiniyyeh	الحسينية	Wadi Araba	وادي عربة

ARRIVAL AND DEPARTURE

Feynan Ecolodge's website ⓦ ecohotels.me/feynan gives comprehensive detail on how to reach Feynan from points all over Jordan.

BY CAR

There is no access to the lodge by paved road: all guests must park at the Reception Centre (ⓞ 078 777 7260) located outside the village of Qurayqira (pronounced "Graygra") and be driven the last 8km off-road to the lodge by 4x4. If you're in your own 4x4, still check in at the Reception Centre, where staff will give you directions. Call the Reception Centre if you get lost.

From Aqaba or Dead Sea/Amman To reach the Reception Centre, turn off the Aqaba–Dead Sea highway at a turn (signposted Feynan) located about 135km north of Aqaba and 134km south of Amman Beach on the Dead Sea. Follow this road for 15km, then turn right; after 1.3km bear left; after another 1km turn left, and after 3.7km you'll see the Reception Centre on your left.

From Petra There's a beautiful back route to Feynan following the scenic Wadi Namla road. From the Petra *Mövenpick*, drive north 8.4km to the T-junction at Little Petra. Turn right, then immediately left (signed Wadi Araba) and follow this road all the way down a series of switchbacks to the desert floor (it's badly potholed in parts, but usually passable in an ordinary car: ask locally in Petra before you set out). At a T-junction 44km from Petra turn right; after 5.9km turn right again. After 1.3km bear left; after another 1km turn left, and after 3.7km you'll see the Reception Centre on your left.

At the Reception Centre There is sheltered parking (free) at the Reception Centre, which is staffed 24hr. From here, a bedouin driver with 4x4 will drive you to the lodge.

FEYNAN ECOLODGE

It costs JD14.50 for up to four people with luggage, but you don't need to give the driver anything; he'll receive the full amount later, and the charge will be added to your final bill at the lodge.

BY BUS

Minibuses for Graygra leave from Amman's Wihdat station around noon–1.30pm (4hr; JD3.50) and from Aqaba around noon (2hr; JD3). Ask the bus driver to drop you at the Feynan Reception Centre (and call ahead to let them know you're coming). Return buses leave Graygra around 6am – ask ecolodge staff the day before to request the bus picks you up at the Reception Centre. No buses run on Fridays.

BY TAXI

Although you could get a taxi to Feynan from anywhere, the lodge can arrange transport with a local bedouin driver at broadly competitive prices – the difference being, all proceeds stay within the Feynan community. A pick-up carrying up to four people costs JD52 from Dana or Petra, JD70 from the Dead Sea or Karak, JD75 from Aqaba, or JD81 from Amman, Madaba or Wadi Rum.

ON FOOT

The most straightforward approach to Feynan is from Dana village (see page 238), along the bed of the great Wadi Dana (6hr; guided or self-guided). An adventurous alternative is to hike from Mansoura village near Shobak (see page 245) down the Wadi Ghwayr canyon (8hr; guide essential). Call ahead to Feynan and they can arrange for your bags to be transported to the ecolodge from Dana or Mansoura (JD52).

INFORMATION

Money There is no bank or ATM anywhere near Feynan, and though the lodge does accept credit cards, the machines at reception often can't connect wirelessly to process payments. Bring cash for any activities that aren't covered under your prepaid room rate.

ACCOMMODATION AND EATING

★ **Feynan Ecolodge** ☎ 06 464 5580, ⓦ ecohotels.me/ feynan. Designed in simple style, with quirks and details retrofitted, no two of the ecolodge's 26 rooms are the same. Choose from Economy twin rooms, Standard twins or doubles, or Deluxe twins or doubles with private balcony, each larger than the last, and all with an en-suite bathroom with shower. Quads are also available. All feature rough adobe-style render on thick walls, mosquito nets draping every bed, colourful cushions and pillows in *saya* (a striped silky fabric from Syria) and candles tucked into mirrored niches around the walls casting flickering shadows. To avoid relying on plastic bottles, each room has a clay jar (made by a women's cooperative in Taybeh near Petra) filled with local spring water. Bear in mind the lack of electricity: there are sockets to charge phones and cameras in reception, but the building has no a/c. It's designed well enough for this to be no serious problem until high summer, when staff will set up beds for guests to sleep on the roof. The lodge dining room (with terrace) serves only vegetarian food: the kitchens have only enough solar electricity to power two small fridges, and storing meat simply isn't viable. But that shouldn't put you off: meals are sumptuous, featuring hearty soups and stews, salads, dips, fresh juices, jams, teas – everything made on the spot from sustainably and/ or organically farmed ingredients. An online booking form lets you advise of all guide/meal requirements: everything must be booked in advance. Each adult pays an additional conservation fee of JD4/stay. Quoted here is the lowest rate in high season (March–May & mid-Sept to Nov) covering full board and activities for two people; prices drop at other times. **JD132**

7

MADABA

Contexts

History

The history of Jordan is a history of occupation. Never the seat of an empire, the country has been tramped by foreign armies and merchants since the pharaohs. Until independence in the mid-twentieth century, the indigenous people, chiefly bedouin tribes, tended to live under the nominal – and often ineffectual – rule of governors sent from more powerful neighbours.

The area of the modern kingdom became a distinct entity only when borders were drawn for the first time by British colonial planners. In naming their new creation, they used the geographical term "**Transjordan**" (ie the land across the Jordan river), later shortened to "Jordan". But for most of recorded history there was no such place: after the fall of early fiefdoms, the centre and north tended to be identified as part of **Syria**, along with Palestine and other areas, while the south was seen more as part of **Arabia**. The term "Transjordan", though it reveals a foreign perspective, remains a useful shorthand to refer to an area that was only ever a bit of somewhere else.

In addition, only relatively small parts of the country – the well-watered northern highlands and Jordan Valley – have ever been able to support large populations. Since prehistoric times, huge tracts of land to the south and east have received very little rainfall and have no rivers; only tiny populations of nomadic or seminomadic bedouin have been able to live there. Thus the history of Jordan revolves largely around events in the fertile north and west. The **history of the desert** survives only in the culture and oral traditions of the bedouin themselves.

The Stone Age: up to 3200 BC

During the **Paleolithic** period (c.500,000–17,000 BC), Jordan's climate was a good deal wetter than it is today, and what is now desert was then semi-fertile savanna. The local population of hunter-gatherer hominids, as well as foraging for wild plants, preyed upon the area's native big game, which included lions, elephants, bears and gazelle. Flint and stone handaxes from this time have been found all over the country, most significantly in enormous quantities at the **Azraq oasis** in the eastern desert.

Some time around 17,000 BC, at the beginning of the **Epipaleolithic** period, major changes took place in Transjordan. The previously nomadic hunter-gatherers began to make seasonal camps, broadened their diet to include small mammals and – most importantly – learnt how to domesticate goats and cultivate some wild grains. These new proto-farmers, who used complex tools such as sickles and pestles and mortars, have left evidence of their building work all over Jordan: small, circular enclosures and huts solidly built with subterranean foundations.

The Neolithic and Chalcolithic periods

From about 8500 BC onwards, during the **Neolithic** period, three profound shifts altered the pattern of life. First, responding to the introduction of new food sources from agriculture and animal husbandry, people began to opt for the certainties of community

17,000 BC	8500 BC	6500 BC	4000 BC
Hunter-gatherers begin to domesticate animals	People begin settling permanently, establishing villages and farms	Complex societies develop at settlements such as Ain Ghazal, near Amman	Copper-smelting develops in Wadi Araba and the Jordan Valley

life, establishing permanent villages such as at **Baydha**, near Petra. The large Neolithic settlement at **Ain Ghazal**, northeast of Amman, was made up of many rectangular, multiroomed houses, some with plastered floors. From the discovery here and across the region of skulls covered with plaster, their eye sockets stuffed with bitumen, it seems that one aspect of village life was veneration – or even worship – of the dead. The oldest statues in the world, dating from around 6000 BC, were uncovered at Ain Ghazal: 1m-high androgynous figures with huge, painted eyes, now on display in Amman.

A second shift resulted from changing weather patterns: as temperatures rose, the eastern savanna dried out and became virtually uninhabitable. Desertification marked a clear distinction between Transjordan's arid east and fertile west, forcing most people to congregate in the western areas that, today, still hold the greater population.

But the most important innovation of Neolithic times was the discovery of how to make **pottery**. Around 5000 BC, potters arrived in Transjordan from the more advanced civilizations of Mesopotamia (in modern Iraq). By 4000 BC or so, during the **Chalcolithic** period, copper had been smelted for the first time for use in fashioning hooks, axes and arrowheads, and the new metal began to be used in conjunction with pottery and flint-working to considerably improve the quality of life. People slowly began to turn away from subsistence hunting towards planned cultivation: olives, lentils, dates, barley and wheat were all common, as was sheep and goat breeding. The area's principal copper deposits were at **Feynan** in Wadi Araba, but the largest Chalcolithic village discovered in Jordan is at **Teleilat Ghassul** in the Jordan Valley, where mud-brick houses with roofs of wood, mud and reeds were constructed around large courtyards. Here, pots were decorated and of good quality, and woven baskets were sturdy. From the evidence of the village's mysterious murals of masked figures, stars and geometric motifs, it seems that Ghassulian women decorated themselves with necklaces of shells and stones, while men took pride in tattoos.

The Bronze Age: 3200–1200 BC

Towns from the **Early Bronze Age** (c.3200–1950 BC), although still relying on copper ("Bronze Age" is a misnomer from the early days of archeology), often included strong defensive fortifications, probably to keep the marauding nomadic tribes of the open countryside away. The new technology of water management led to collection and some storage of supply against drier times. New customs of burial also developed, sometimes involving the digging of deep shaft tombs: at **Bab adh-Dhraa** on the Dead Sea, archeologists have uncovered over twenty thousand such shafts, perhaps containing up to a quarter of a million corpses in total. Other burial customs – possibly brought from Syria or Anatolia – involved the construction of **dolmens** (two or more stone slabs standing side by side, capped by another slab), which can be found throughout the Jordanian countryside.

Elsewhere in the region at this time, the extraordinary innovation of **writing** was leading to the development of highly sophisticated civilizations. To the south, Egypt was unified into one kingdom, while to the north and east, Anatolia and Mesopotamia saw the rise of equally complex urbanized cultures. Occupying the area midway between the three, the simpler people of the Levant, who wouldn't start to use writing for another millennium or so, fell into the role of merchant middlemen. The first significant commerce began to flow between the great powers.

3000 BC	2000 BC	1550 BC
Cultural interaction with Syria, Egypt and Anatolia develops, bringing new ideas to Jordan	Discovery of bronze, and invasion by neighbouring peoples, spur the development of fortified towns	Strong trade links develop with Pharaonic Egypt and Mycenean Greece

Around 2300 BC, many of the fortified towns in Transjordan were destroyed, although there is some controversy as to whether this was due to conquest by a new people, the Amorites, or simply an earthquake. A decrease in rainfall levels coupled with a general rise in temperature almost certainly played its part, too.

The Middle and Late Bronze Age

The **Middle Bronze Age** (c.1950–1550 BC) saw trade between Egypt, Arabia and the city-states of Syria and Palestine continuing to flow through Transjordan, generating wealth and facilitating the spread of ideas and culture. It was during this period that artisans mixed copper with tin for the first time; the resulting metal, **bronze**, allowed much harder and more durable tools and weapons to be made than before. Transjordanian towns such as Amman, Irbid and Pella (as well as Jericho, on the western bank of the river) built massive, banked earth ramparts, implying a need for security – as borne out by the eighteenth-century-BC conquests of the Hyksos who overran much of the Levant. Probably nomadic herders from Central Asia, the Hyksos interrupted the steady indigenous cultural growth of Transjordan, replacing it with new, foreign elements. As well as importing a more graceful and technically accomplished style of pottery, they also introduced both horses and chariots to the Middle East.

Following the expulsion of the Hyksos around 1550 BC by the Egyptian Seventeenth Dynasty, Transjordan – and the rest of the Levant – saw an expansion of Egyptian influence during the **Late Bronze Age** (c.1550–1200 BC), especially under Pharaoh Tuthmosis III. Despite conflict further north, occupied Transjordan remained relatively peaceful and prosperous, and the presence of pottery from Mycenaean Greece and Cyprus indicates strong trade links.

By 1200 BC, however, the peace and prosperity of the eastern Mediterranean had been shattered, probably by the arrival of unknown invaders collectively termed "**Peoples of the Sea**", one group of whom, the Philistines, settled around Gaza (giving rise to the name Palestine). The principal cities of Greece and Cyprus fell to these foreigners, the Hittite Empire in Anatolia collapsed, wealthy city-states in Syria were razed and the Egyptian occupiers of Transjordan retreated to face the onslaught at home. In addition, events surrounding a group of tribes known as the **Israelites** – about which ample, if contradictory, records survive (see page 350) – began to alter the power balance in Transjordan and Palestine.

The Iron Age: 1200–332 BC

On the east side of the Jordan, the years after 1200 BC saw a consolidation and development of the Transjordanian kingdoms of **Ammon**, **Moab** and **Edom**, all three of which lay on the lucrative Arabian–Syrian trade route for gold, spices and other precious goods.

By about 1000 BC the Israelites were strong enough to declare a united Kingdom of Israel; under **King David**, they seized control of virtually the entire Levant and won several victories in Transjordan. Edom managed to regain some independence following David's death in 960 BC, but it wasn't until David's son **Solomon** died some thirty years later that the Israelite empire fell. The last vestiges of Israelite control in Transjordan were erased during the mid-ninth century BC, partly by the efforts of Mesha, apparently king of Moab, who recorded his victories on the "**Mesha stele**", a

c.1230 BC	c.1200 BC	c.1200 BC
The Exodus – Israelites expelled from Egypt arrive in Jordan, travelling along the King's Highway	Moses dies on Mount Nebo, near Madaba	Joshua leads Israelites across River Jordan to Jericho

BIBLICAL ACCOUNTS OF THE BRONZE AGE

Genesis records that **Abram**, a native of the city of Ur – most likely in modern Iraq – travelled at some time probably well before 2000 BC with his wife and extended family to Canaan (Palestine). After some years, the land – already home to existing tribes of Canaanites and others – was unable to support so many people, and bickering ensued between Abram's tribe and that of his nephew **Lot**. Abram offered a separation: Lot would be given the choice of taking his tribe and flocks either east or west of the River Jordan, and whichever direction he chose, Abram and his tribe would go the other way. Lot chose to go east and pitched his tents at the southeastern corner of the Dead Sea. Abram went west and eventually settled near Hebron, meanwhile having a vision of God granting him in perpetuity the land that Lot had spurned.

SODOM AND GOMORRAH

After the adaptation of Abram's name to **Abraham** following another vision, Lot's home city of Sodom – and others nearby – were destroyed. The only survivors were Lot and his two daughters, who lived for a time in a cave in the desert. Fearful that their tribe would die out since no man had escaped with them other than their father, the elder of Lot's two daughters hatched a plan to get their father so drunk he wouldn't be able to tell who they were, whereupon they would seduce him and thus preserve the family. Everything worked to plan and both daughters gave birth to sons; the elder named her child **Moab**, and the younger **Ben-Ammi**, or "father of Ammon".

THE SONS OF ABRAHAM

Meanwhile Abraham had had two sons, the first – **Ishmael** – by his Egyptian mistress Hagar, and the second – **Isaac** – by his wife Sarah. On Sarah's insistence, Hagar and Ishmael were banished to the desert, and the biblical record concentrates on Isaac's two sons, Esau and Jacob. (The Qu'ran, though, concentrates on Ishmael, who had twelve children and died at the age of 137; Muslims and especially Arabs view him as their forebear. The hajj pilgrimage centres on commemoration of Hagar and Ishmael's banishment.) Jacob persuaded Esau to sell his inheritance and, by dint of trickery, also gained the blessing of his father to rule over his brother. The two then separated, Jacob fleeing to an

basalt stone set up in the Moabite capital, Dhiban. To the north, Ammon, centred on modern Amman, prospered, while to the south, Edom had developed skill in mining and smelting copper and had major settlements near Busayrah, Petra and Aqaba, although much of the Edomite population may have been nomadic or seminomadic.

By the mid-eighth century BC **Assyrian** forces had captured Damascus and parts of Israel. It was only by paying tribute that Ammon, Moab and Edom managed to retain their independence and continue to exploit the north–south flow of trade.

Barely a century later, in 612 BC, the Assyrians were themselves defeated by an alliance of Medes (from modern Iran) and **Babylonians** (from Iraq); the latter then took control in the Levant, limiting the independence of the Transjordanian kingdoms and, in 587 BC, destroying Jerusalem and deporting thousands of Jews. Chaotic Babylonian rule was then overrun by the **Persian Empire**, the largest yet seen in the region. The Persians released the Jews from captivity in Babylon and permitted them to rebuild their temple at Jerusalem. The indignant Ammonites and Moabites took this to be a declaration of sovereignty and attacked, only to be repulsed by the direct intervention of the Persian leadership.

Two centuries of relatively stable Persian rule were brought to a swift end by the military adventures of the Greek general known as **Alexander the Great**. In 333 BC, at

c.850 BC	c.750 BC	587 BC
"King Mesha" frees Moab from Israelite control	Invasion of Assyrian forces	Babylonians under Nebuchadnezzar destroy Jerusalem

uncle's house and after a series of visions changing his name to **Israel** (which means "he who wrestled with God"). Esau married into Ishmael's family and settled in the southern part of Transjordan, known as **Edom**. Its southern neighbour **Midian** (modern Hejaz), and its northern neighbours **Moab** and **Ammon**, as well as Edom itself, were all established kingdoms by soon after 2000 BC.

THE EXODUS

The Bible makes no further mention of Transjordan until the **Exodus**, which occurred several centuries after Esau. The most accepted chronology places it during the reign of Pharaoh Merneptah (c.1236–1217 BC), but it may have been over two centuries earlier. The Book of Numbers records that, after expulsion from Egypt and several generations of wandering in the Sinai, the Israelites, an extended group of twelve related tribes descended from Abraham's grandson, Israel, arrived in the southern Palestinian desert near Aqaba, on a journey towards the lands west of the Jordan that had been granted by God to the tribal patriarch Abraham. The Israelite sheikh Moses and his brother Aaron had a vision from God instructing them to speak to a rock to produce water for their tribes; Moses, though, struck the rock, and for this transgression both he and his brother were denied future entry to the Promised Land.

After Aaron's death on **Mount Hor** (possibly Jabal Haroun near Petra), the Israelites apparently followed the route of the present Desert Highway northwards. A little way north of modern Qatraneh, the Israelites defeated the **Amorites** in battle and destroyed their cities, including Hesban, Dhiban and Madaba. They proceeded north to Dera'a (just over the modern Syrian border), defeated King Og and returned to make camp in "the plain of Moab" opposite Jericho, probably near modern Shuneh al-Janubiyyeh. Alarmed at the presence of such powerful newcomers on his borders, the king of Moab made a military pact with the kings of Midian, but after a seer prophesied only victory for the Israelites, the combined Moabite-Midianite forces lost heart, and were attacked and routed. Three Israelite tribes occupied Transjordan from Dhiban as far north as Gilead (the hills around modern Jerash) and the Golan Heights. Moses then had several visions and, sometime probably around 1200 BC, at the age of 120, died on **Mount Nebo** near Madaba. Soon afterwards, his successor Joshua led the Israelite tribes across the Jordan into the Promised Land.

the age of 21, he defeated the Persian army in southeastern Turkey and proceeded to conquer the entire Levant and Egypt before heading east. At his death in Babylon in 323 BC, Alexander controlled an empire stretching from Greece to India.

The Greeks and the Nabateans: 332–64 BC

Alexander's conquest of the Persian capital Persepolis in 332 BC confirmed **Hellenistic** control over the formerly Persian lands of the Levant, and ushered in a period of dominance over Transjordan by Alexander's successors that lasted for three centuries. On Alexander's death, his generals **Seleucus** and **Ptolemy** divided the eastern part of his empire between them: Palestine, Transjordan and southern Syria went to Ptolemy, while Seleucus took northern Syria and Mesopotamia. Bitter struggles for the upper hand ensued, with much of Transjordan caught in the crossfire. After more than a century of fighting, the Seleucids finally wrested Transjordan away from the Ptolemies in 198 BC. Meanwhile, many new and rebuilt Transjordanian cities had been flourishing, including Philadelphia (Amman), Gerasa (Jerash), Pella and Gadara (Umm Qais) – though virtually the only Hellenistic monument to survive today is a lone palace in the countryside west of Amman, **Qasr al-Abd**.

332 BC	150 BC	64 BC
Alexander the Great defeats the Persian army, secures control over the entire Middle East	Nabatean kingdom dominates Jordan alongside Seleucid rule	Roman general Pompey seizes Damascus and annexes Jordan

Long before these events, and possibly as early as the sixth century BC, a nomadic tribe of Arabs had wandered out of the deserts to the south and taken up residence in and around Edom. Slowly these **Nabateans** had abandoned their nomadic ways and founded a number of settlements in southern Transjordan, northern Arabia and the Naqab (Negev) desert of modern Israel, probably using their position to plunder the caravans heading out of Arabia loaded with luxury goods. The Roman historian Diodorus Siculus, writing much later, describes "Arabs who are called Nabatei" occupying Petra around 312 BC. The Nabateans – who had switched from plundering caravans to providing them with safe passage – managed to remain largely independent throughout the Seleucid-Ptolemaic power battles.

With the Seleucid victory of 198 BC, trade again prospered in Transjordan and the Nabateans expanded their realm, absorbing many Hellenistic influences which worked their way into the art and architecture of Petra. By 150 BC – coexisting alongside Seleucid rule in western Transjordan – the independent **Kingdom of Nabatea** extended along a strip of eastern Transjordan as far north as the Hawran, and south into the Hejaz. The Nabateans were accumulating vast profits from trade across the Middle East in everything from Indian silks and spices to Dead Sea bitumen and, most importantly, a monopoly over trade in frankincense and myrrh. Both were central in religious ceremonies throughout the West and both were produced only in southern Arabia; transport overland from the Arabian coast terminated at the sole taxation and international distribution centre at Petra.

Meanwhile, riots were breaking out in Judea against Hellenistic rule. In three successive years – 167 to 165 BC – Jewish rebels defeated the Greek army four times. The Jewish leader **Judas Maccabeus** then invaded northern Transjordan. Less than a century later, Judas's successor occupied the whole of Transjordan as far south as Wadi Hasa, with the Nabatean kingdom – by now extended to Damascus but still confined only to a slice of the country east of the King's Highway – remaining independent. With nothing appearing likely to put a stop to the growth of Nabatean wealth and influence, and faced by an increasingly unstable political situation, the generals of **Rome** decided that the time had come to impose some law and order.

Rome and the Nabateans: 64 BC–324 AD

In 64 BC, the Roman general **Pompey** took Damascus and ordered Nabatean forces to pull back from the city. After proceeding to annex most of the region, Pompey sent a force to Petra to subdue the Nabateans, but the Nabatean king was able easily to repulse the attack and dip into his treasury to pay the Romans off.

Pompey turned his attention elsewhere. The group of Hellenized northern Transjordanian cities that included Gerasa, Gadara, Philadelphia and Pella had been badly damaged under the Jewish occupation; Pompey restored their infrastructure and granted them some local autonomy. With shared cultural and economic ties, these cities – in a region of Transjordan known as the **Decapolis**, or "Ten Cities" – agreed to pay taxes to the Romans and so retained independence.

Herod the Great and Herod Antipas

In 44 BC, Julius Caesar was assassinated in Rome. The **Parthians** – based in Mesopotamia and Persia – took the chance to attack, and the Nabateans sided with them; following Rome's reassertion of its power, the Nabatean king was forced to dip into his treasury

c.29 AD	c.31 AD	106
Jesus visits Jordan and is baptized in the River Jordan	Beheading of John the Baptist at Mukawir	Romans establish control over Jordan as part of the Province of Arabia

again to placate the generals. The local Roman placeman, Herod the Great, twice attacked the Nabateans to ensure consistent payments. By the time of Herod's death in 4 BC, Rome was in control of the region, with Transjordan divided into three spheres of influence: to the north, the **Decapolis** remained independent; Palestinian Jewish puppet-kings ruled **central Transjordan** (although Philadelphia remained part of the Decapolis); and **the south** comprised the rump Kingdom of Nabatea, still nominally independent, though coming under increasing pressure to submit to Rome.

Herod the Great's successor, Herod Antipas, married a daughter of the Nabatean king Aretas IV, but soon afterwards divorced her, and married his brother's wife instead. Unable to ignore such an insult, Aretas sent an army against Herod and won, but showed magnanimity in withdrawing peacefully. A local holy man, John the Baptist, condemned Herod's incestuous marriage, was imprisoned at the royal palace at **Machaerus** and, at the behest of Herod's step-daughter Salome, beheaded.

Rebellion and decline

Jewish uprisings in Palestine during the mid-first century AD gave a chance for the Nabateans to weigh in militarily and so restore amicable relations with Rome. The Nabatean king was personally present at the Roman capture of Jerusalem in 70 AD. Many Palestinian Jewish rebels sought refuge at Machaerus, but the Roman army razed the palace in 72 AD and slaughtered everyone inside.

By this stage it was clear to the Nabateans that their days of independence were numbered. A new trading centre far to the north, **Palmyra** – positioned on Roman-sponsored routes that were growing in popularity – was chipping away at Petra's business, and the Nabatean king Rabbel II, seeing Roman dominance all around, almost certainly made a deal permitting the Romans to annex the Nabatean lands peacefully. In 106, on Rabbel's death, the whole of Transjordan – with the exception of the Decapolis – was incorporated into the new Roman **Province of Arabia**, under the Emperor **Trajan**, with a new capital at Bosra, in Syria.

From Trajan to Constantine: 106–324 AD

Roman city planners, engineers and construction workers moved into Transjordan. Large forts were built near Karak, Petra and in the north to house the massed legions; Petra itself, along with Philadelphia, Gerasa, Gadara and other cities, was renovated and Romanized; and, by 114 AD, a new fortified road – the **Via Nova Traiana** – was in place, running from Bosra right the way through Transjordan to the Red Sea at Aila (Aqaba). Trajan's successor, Hadrian, paid the province a visit in 130, staying in **Gerasa**, by this time one of the most splendid of Rome's provincial cities. During the second and third centuries, Transjordan gained new sophistication under the Romans, and prosperity rose to an unprecedented level. In 199, the Emperor Septimius Severus toured the province with his Syrian wife; although many overland trade routes from Arabia had been diverted to Palmyra and seaborne trade along the Red Sea was flourishing, Petra was still important enough to merit a visit. It was around this time that **Azraq**, at the head of a major route to and from the Arabian peninsula, was fortified for the first time.

Nonetheless, the desert fringes of the empire remained open to infiltration, and in 260, Persian **Sassanians** invaded from the north. Six years later, the Roman military commander, based in Palmyra, was murdered, precipitating a rebellion throughout

130	324	527
Emperor Hadrian visits Jordan, staying in Jerash	Christianity becomes the official religion of the eastern Roman Empire	Madaba becomes a centre for mosaic art, under Emperor Justinian

Syria led by a local queen, Zenobia. The situation was perilous enough to force the Emperor **Diocletian** (284–305) to take drastic measures. Retaining overall command from his base in Turkey, Diocletian split the empire into eastern and western administrations under separate emperors, and then proceeded to strengthen the infrastructure of the eastern fringes, building forts and new roads, among them the **Strata Diocletiana** linking Azraq with Damascus. Meanwhile, with Palmyra's predominance annulled through its association with rebellion, trade through Transjordan once again began to flourish, and the Red Sea port of Aila took on a new importance.

A new force was also beginning to make itself felt. The influence of **Christianity** went much deeper than the extent of its practice (by a mere fourteen percent or so of the empire's population) might show. The Emperor **Constantine** had already converted by 324 when he made Christianity the official religion of the eastern empire. Six years later, he confirmed the eclipse of Rome by founding a new Christian imperial capital – Constantinople (modern Istanbul).

The Byzantine period: 324–636

The **Byzantine** period – so named because Constantinople had been built over the ancient Greek colony of Byzantium – saw long-lived Roman institutions coexisting with the new Christian faith, which flourished within a broadly Greek culture. Transjordan experienced a steady growth of population coupled with energetic construction projects and important artistic development.

Constantine's mother, Helena, started a trend of **pilgrimage** by journeying to Jerusalem in 326. It was around this time that the first church on Mount Nebo was built to commemorate Moses' death, and the area around Nebo and Madaba became the focus for pilgrimage in Transjordan. Following the final divorce between Rome and Constantinople in 395, many churches were built, often on the foundations of Roman temples and often decorated with ornate **mosaics**. Madaba, in particular, was a flourishing centre for mosaicists, especially during the reign of **Justinian** (527–65). Church building and mosaic art in Transjordan entered a golden age.

Twin disasters were to bring both artistic development and, indirectly, the empire itself to an end. The first was **plague**, which struck Transjordan during Justinian's reign and wiped out much of the population. A far more sustained threat came from the Persian **Sassanians**, who, in the sixth century, launched a series of raids against the Euphrates frontier, breaking through to sack Antioch in 540. There followed over eighty years of titanic, but inconclusive, struggle in Syria between Byzantium and Persia – Transjordan remaining quiet throughout – which was only ended by the Emperor **Heraclius**' recapture of Syria in 628.

During the struggles (and unknown to either combatant), far to the south an Arab holy man named **Muhammad** had been gathering around himself a large band of followers following a series of divine visions. Initial sorties northwards had won over a few desert tribes but the **Muslims**, as they styled themselves, lost their first battle with Byzantium, near Karak in 629. Muhammad himself died in Mecca in 632, but his armies, led by Abu Bakr, the first **caliph** ("successor"), and fired by the zeal of a new religion, pushed northwards again, seizing Damascus from Heraclius in 635. On

636	661
Muslim armies victorious at Battle of Yarmouk, seizing control of the region	Umayyad caliphs rule from Damascus, later building the "Desert Castles" in Jordan

the banks of the River Yarmouk the following year, they defeated a Byzantine army exhausted from decades of war.

The early caliphs of Islam: 636–1250

After the Yarmouk victory, it took the Muslim armies barely ten years to dismantle Byzantine control over the Levant, although the Byzantine Empire itself limped on for another eight hundred years. By 656, the whole of Persia and the Middle East was ruled from the Muslim capital at Medina. That year, the third caliph, Othman, was murdered. When his successor, Ali, dismissed many of Othman's appointees – including Muawiya, governor of Syria – civil war broke out among the Muslims, brought to an end only by negotiations held probably at Udhruh near Petra in 659. Ali was subsequently assassinated, and Muawiya, a member of the **Umayyad** clan, was acclaimed caliph in 661. This marked a schism in Islam, which persists today, between the **Sunnis** – the orthodox majority who accept the Umayyad succession – and the minority **Shi'ites**, who believe the succession should have passed instead to Ali, a relative of Muhammad's, and his descendants.

The Umayyads: 661–750

Muawiya's first decision was to relocate the Muslim capital away from Arabia to the vibrant metropolis of Damascus. At one stroke, Transjordan was transformed: not only was it on the direct pilgrimage route between the imperial capital and the holy sites in Mecca and Medina, but it also suddenly lay at the heart of a rapidly expanding empire, which, at its fullest extent, reached from India virtually to the Pyrenees. The Umayyad caliphs began a vigorous campaign of monument-building throughout the Levant, which included both the Dome of the Rock in Jerusalem and the Great Mosque of Damascus. At heart, however, they were desert people, and their most enduring legacy to Transjordan is a series of buildings in the eastern desert, now known as the "Desert Castles": some, such as **Qasr Kharana**, were places where the caliphs could meet with the bedouin tribes of the area, while others – **Qusayr Amra**, **Qasr Mushatta** – were lavish country mansions or hunting lodges. Motivated less by adherence to Islamic orthodoxy than by older Arab notions of honour, loyalty and rule by negotiation, the Umayyads had a lively aesthetic sense, valuing intellectual curiosity, poetry and wine in roughly equal quantities. Christianity was widely tolerated, and churches were still being built in Transjordan up to the middle of the eighth century.

Abbasids and Fatimids: 750–1097

Followers of stricter interpretations of Islam eventually gained the upper hand, possibly aided by a devastating earthquake which struck the region in 749. A year later, Damascus fell to a new dynasty, the **Abbasids**, who shifted the Muslim capital eastwards to Baghdad, a symbolic move embodying a rejection of the liberal Umayyad spirit in preference for more strait-laced Mesopotamian methods. Transjordan – instantly reduced to a provincial backwater – fell into obscurity.

During the ninth century, internal dissent whittled away at the power of the Abbasid caliphate, and by 969 a rival, Shi'ite-derived caliphate had been proclaimed in Cairo by the Tunisian **Fatimid** dynasty, who took control of Palestine, Transjordan and southern Syria soon after, destroying many churches and harassing Christian pilgrims. In 1037,

749	1099
Major earthquake in Jordan destroys Petra, Amman and many other sites	Crusader armies seize Jerusalem, establish control across Jordan

Seljuk Turks took power in Baghdad and within fifty years had defeated both the Fatimids and the Byzantines to regain Transjordan for orthodox Islam.

These tides of Muslim conquest and reconquest sweeping the Holy Land, coupled with the anti-Christian feeling aroused by the Fatimids and a Byzantine request for military aid against the Seljuks, didn't go unnoticed in the West. In 1095 Pope Urban II, speaking in France, launched an appeal for a European force to intervene in the chaos in the Middle East, to restore Christian rule in Palestine and, above all, to liberate Jerusalem. This holy war was termed a **crusade**.

Crusaders and Ayyubids: 1097–1250

In 1097, a 100,000-strong Christian army – comprising seasoned troops and peasant rabble alike – arrived at Constantinople. Two years later, they seized Jerusalem, slaughtering every man, woman and child in the city. Within forty years, there was a strip of Crusader-held territory running from southern Turkey to the Red Sea, part of it incorporating the Lordship of Oultrejourdain (Transjordan) with its two castle strongholds at **Karak** and **Shobak**. In 1144, local Muslim forces started to eat into Crusader realms in northern Syria, inspiring a wave of strong Muslim resistance to the invaders, led after 1176 by a Kurdish officer named **Salah ad-Din al-Ayyubi** (or Saladin). Having already disposed of the Fatimids in Cairo (and by doing so uniting the Muslim world), Salah ad-Din routed the Crusaders on the battlefield in 1187 and retook Jerusalem, coastal Palestine and Transjordan. After his death in 1193, his dynasty, the **Ayyubids**, ruled the Muslim forces from their power base in Cairo. Waves of Crusaders nonetheless continued to arrive from Europe over the next decades, and rule of Levantine coastal areas shifted to and fro.

Mamlukes and Ottomans: 1250–1915

The Ayyubids came to rely for their military strength upon a band of highly disciplined and trained slave-troops, known as "the owned ones". Most of these **Mamlukes** were Turks or Caucasians from southern Russia who had been bought at market. Once trained, they were given property, goods and women; their lack of local tribal allegiance guaranteed loyalty to their master. In 1250, however, the worm turned: with the Ayyubid sultan on his deathbed, the Mamlukes seized power for themselves.

They soon faced a challenge. In 1258, a **Mongol** army under Genghis Khan's grandson Hulagu destroyed Baghdad and swept westward through Transjordan to Galilee, where they were halted by a Mamluke army. The victorious general, **Baybars**, claimed the title of sultan and proceeded to eject the last remaining Crusaders from the Levant.

During the fourteenth century, the Mamluke unification of Syria and Egypt provided some peace for the embattled Transjordanian population, who continued to facilitate north–south commerce and provide shelter to Muslim pilgrims. Another Mongol invasion in 1400 under Tamerlane overran much of Syria; Mamluke finances – which relied on the Red Sea shipping trade – were further undermined by the Portuguese discovery of a new sea route around Africa to India.

Ottoman rule after 1453

Meanwhile, in northwestern Turkey a new dynasty had been gathering power, and, in 1453, these **Ottomans** seized Constantinople, erasing what was left of the Byzantine Empire. The

1176	1453	1812
Salah ad-Din leads Muslim resistance to Crusaders, eventually expelling them	Ottoman Turks occupy Jordan	Swiss adventurer Jean Louis Burckhardt rediscovers the "lost city" of Petra

Ottoman leader **Selim the Grim** occupied Damascus, Transjordan and Jerusalem in quick succession, eventually suspending the last Mamluke sultan from the gallows in Cairo.

Ottoman expansion continued apace (halted only at the gates of Vienna in 1683) but although imperial architects lavished care and attention on Damascus and Jerusalem, Transjordan, apart from inns built along the pilgrimage route between Damascus and Mecca, was allowed to fall into decline, its people left largely to themselves. European merchants based in ports and cities all around the region quietly siphoned wealth away from the imperial coffers, and the Ottoman Empire crumbled.

In 1798, **Napoleon Bonaparte** invaded Egypt, but lost power less than a decade later. In the 1830s, the new Egyptian ruler Ibrahim Pasha embarked on a military adventure through Transjordan and the Levant which looked poised to overthrow Ottoman rule altogether but for the intervention of the British, who preferred the presence of a feeble and ineffective sultan to that of an enthusiastic and powerful young general. Trade on the Red Sea was revivified by the opening of the Suez Canal in 1869, but the canal itself, which represented the fastest sea route from Europe to India, remained under sole control of the British, who were by now firmly installed in Egypt and nurturing imperialist designs on Palestine.

In the 1870s, Russian persecution of Muslims in the Caucasus region east of the Black Sea led to waves of refugees arriving in Turkey. The Ottoman authorities dumped them onto ships bound for Levantine ports. These **Circassian** and **Chechen** farmers settled throughout the region, working their way inland to Transjordan and colonizing the long-abandoned ruins at Amman, Jerash and elsewhere. In a separate but contemporary development, Russian persecution of **Jews** in modern Poland and Lithuania also created refugees who settled in the Levant, this time in Palestine. Jewish activists soon codified a philosophy of organized Jewish settlement of Palestine – **Zionism**.

The end of the Ottoman Empire: 1900–15

By the turn of the century, there was a spate of railway building around the Levant. The French were establishing a network in Syria; the German Berlin–Baghdad railway had reached Aleppo; and in Palestine, the British had long been operating a line from Jaffa to Jerusalem. To counter this European influence, and in a bid to bolster his religious authority, the sultan announced the construction of an Ottoman-sponsored **Hejaz Railway**, to run from Damascus south through Transjordan, terminating at the holy city of Mecca. As well as transporting Muslim pilgrims, the sultan also had an eye on facilitating the rapid mobilization of Ottoman troops should the Arab nationalism that was beginning to stir in the Hejaz come to a head. Transjordanian labour was vital in the construction of the line – as were the thick forests around Ajloun and Shobak, felled indiscriminately for fuel. By 1908, the track had reached Medina, 400km short of Mecca. A coup in Constantinople the following year led to seizure of power by secular Turkish nationalists, and the railway got no further.

On the outbreak of **World War I**, the puppet sultan sided with the Germans, bringing the Ottoman Empire into conflict with both Britain – eagerly eyeing the newly discovered oilfields in Iraq and Persia – and France. Turkification was proceeding apace, with a ban on the use of Arabic in schools and offices, arrests of Arab nationalist leaders in Damascus and Beirut, and, in 1915, the first of the twentieth century's genocides, when over a million Armenians were killed. Observing from Cairo, the British conspired on the best way to foment ill will towards Turkish authority into full-scale rebellion. Negotiations

1870s	1915	1916
Circassian and Chechen refugees from Russia are resettled in Jordan	Britain promises to support Arab independence if the Arabs overthrow Ottoman rule	Britain secretly agrees with France to carve up the Middle East between them

with opposition leaders in Cairo and Damascus to involve Arab forces in a revolt against the Turks broke down, but contact with **Sharif Hussein**, the ruler of Mecca and self-styled "King of the Arabs", was more fruitful. Its consequences, and the events surrounding the end of World War I, have directly caused more than a century of war in the Middle East.

British promises and the Arab Revolt: 1915–18

When the Ottoman Empire entered World War I, the sultan had declared a *jihad* (an Islamically sanctioned struggle) against the Western powers. Alarmed at the possible repercussions of this in Muslim areas under their control, the British were keen to enlist for their side the support of Sharif Hussein, an authoritative religious dignitary and direct descendant of the Prophet Muhammad. In 1915, ten letters, known as the **McMahon Correspondence**, passed between Sir Henry McMahon, British High Commissioner in Egypt, and Hussein, in which Britain pledged to support Arab claims for independence if Hussein sparked a revolt against Turkish authority. Hussein's initial claims were for an independent Arab state stretching from Aleppo to the Yemeni coast, but McMahon countered this by stating that Arab claims were excluded from three areas: the districts of Basra and Baghdad in Iraq (which the British wanted for themselves), the Turkish Hatay region around modern Antakya, and – most significantly – "portions of Syria lying to the west of the districts of Damascus, Homs, Hama and Aleppo". Sharif Hussein took this clause to refer to Lebanon, and accepted the terms. Confident of British backing, he proclaimed Arab independence on June 16, 1916, and declared war on the Turks.

Meanwhile, the British had other ideas. Following negotiation with France and Russia, the secret **Sykes-Picot Agreement** of May 1916 carved up the Middle East into areas of colonial dominance, riding roughshod over the promises made to Sharif Hussein about Arab independence. Under the agreement, France was handed power in southeastern Turkey, Lebanon, Syria and northern Iraq, Britain in a belt of land stretching from Haifa to Baghdad and the Gulf, with most of Palestine to be administered by an international body. The colonial powers told nobody of their plans (Sharif Hussein only learnt of them more than a year later).

Also in 1917, in a letter addressed to a leader of Britain's Jewish community, which came to be known as the **Balfour Declaration**, the British Foreign Secretary Arthur Balfour wrote that "His Majesty's Government view with favour the establishment in Palestine of a national home for the Jewish people." Hussein had agreed to Arab claims being excluded from the "portion of Syria lying to the west of Damascus", and, in an attempt to cover their backs, British ministers later claimed – extraordinarily – that this clause referred to Palestine. The Balfour Declaration thus completed an astonishing triangle of mutually incompatible promises and agreements made by the British government between 1915 and 1917. Their consequences are still being suffered today.

The Great Arab Revolt: 1917–18

Meanwhile, still assuming wholehearted British support, Sharif Hussein – aided by two of his sons, **Abdullah** and **Faisal** – had launched the **Great Arab Revolt**. A ragtag army of thirty thousand tribesmen quickly seized Mecca and Jeddah from Ottoman forces, and, in January 1917, local notables, as well as Britain, France and Italy, recognized Sharif Hussein as "King of the Hejaz", leader of the first independent Arab state. In its initial stages, the British lent

1917	1918
Britain backs the creation of a Jewish homeland in Palestine	The Great Arab Revolt, led by Faisal and Lawrence ("of Arabia"), ejects the Ottoman Turks from Damascus

JORDAN'S FLAG

Jordan's **flag** is adapted from the banner of the Great Arab Revolt of 1916–17, when Arab armies under the Hashemite dynasty overthrew the rule of the Ottoman Empire in the Middle East.

The flag's three bands represent medieval caliphates: **black**, for the Abbasids who ruled from Baghdad; **white**, for the Umayyads who ruled from Damascus; and **green**, for the Fatimids who ruled from Cairo. On the side is a **red triangle** representing the Great Arab Revolt, with a seven-pointed **white star** which symbolizes the seven verses of the opening *sura* (verse) of the Quran.

their support to the Arab Revolt principally in the form of Second Lieutenant **T.E. Lawrence**, later mythologized as "Lawrence of Arabia". Leaving Abdullah to pin down a forlorn Turkish garrison in Medina, Faisal – with Lawrence – led an army northwards to the port of Aqaba, a strategic prize through which the Arabs would be able to receive weaponry and material support from the British Army in Egypt. Ottoman defences in the town, protected on two sides by arid mountains, focused all their attention on attack from the sea. Holed up to the south, Lawrence instead planned a looping overland route through the desert, and with a small force emerged from the mountains to launch a surprise attack on the town from the north. The plan worked, and Aqaba fell on July 6, 1917.

Faisal's Arab forces then came under the command of the British general **Allenby**, who was leading several divisions from Egypt towards Jerusalem. The Arabs and the British worked their way northwards, the Arabs using the old castle at Azraq as a base during the winter of 1917–18. After Jerusalem fell to the British, the Arab armies skirmished up the Hejaz Railway line, taking Ma'an, Karak and Amman. The final assault was launched from Azraq, and on October 1, 1918, Faisal and Lawrence entered Damascus, ending Ottoman rule in the Levant.

The establishment of the emirate: 1918–23

By now, the French (working to the Sykes-Picot Agreement) had designs on Syria and Lebanon, while the British and the Zionist Jews (working to the Balfour Declaration) had designs on Palestine. When, in 1920, elected Arab delegates to the government in Damascus declared the Levant independent under King Faisal, and Iraq independent under King Abdullah (who was still in the Hejaz), both Britain and France came out in sharp denunciation. Within six weeks, administrative control – termed a "**mandate**" – over the Middle East was awarded by an international conference to the colonial powers, forming borders within the Levant for the first time and splitting Palestine and Iraq (awarded to Britain) away from Syria and Lebanon (handed to France). The French forcibly ejected Faisal from Damascus and the British suppressed open rebellion in Iraq. In Mecca, the stunned Sharif Hussein realized the extent of the betrayal. "I listened to the faithless Englishmen," he muttered to a group of confidants. "I let myself be tempted and won over by them."

The arrival of Abdullah

The position of Transjordan remained unclear for some time. Britain informed a meeting of sheikhs at Salt that it favoured self-government for Transjordan, but then

1920	1923	1928
Abdullah Bin Al-Hussein arrives in Ma'an	Abdullah I installed as Emir of Transjordan	Jordan's first constitution drawn up

did little to foster it. Arab discontent was growing at British and French duplicity: Abdullah raised an army in Mecca, intending to liberate Damascus from the French. He arrived in Ma'an on November 21, 1920, to a rousing reception of Transjordanian sheikhs and Arab nationalists.

From Ma'an, Abdullah's path lay through British-held Transjordan, still neither part of the Palestine Mandate nor fully autonomous. He proceeded north without hindrance, arriving in the village of Amman on March 2, 1921, to cheering crowds of mounted tribesmen. Confronted by a fait accompli, but obligated to prevent attack on the French from British territory, the new British Colonial Secretary **Winston Churchill** (accompanied by his special adviser T.E. Lawrence) proposed a separate British mandate to be established in Transjordan; in exchange for Abdullah's abdication of the throne of Iraq in favour of Faisal, Britain would offer Abdullah the temporary title of Emir (Prince) of Transjordan, until "some accommodation" could be made with the French in Damascus. With the knowledge that he was being brought to heel, Abdullah attempted to secure the unification of Palestine with Transjordan, but was told that Britain had other plans for Palestine which took account of Jewish national aspirations. Well aware that Transjordan was the best he and the Arabs were likely to get for the moment, Abdullah accepted.

The Emirate of Transjordan

The territory that Abdullah took control of in April 1921 was undeveloped and anarchic. The borders drawn by Churchill were more or less arbitrary, frequently cutting across tribal areas and grazing grounds. The three existing Transjordanian governments – centred in Irbid, Salt and Karak – had virtually no authority and were overlaid by a patchwork of unstable local sheikhdoms. The population numbered about 230,000, of which over 200,000 were Muslim Arabs, the remainder Christian Arabs and Muslim Circassians. Over half were **fellaheen**, or landowning tribal village-dwellers (there were only four towns holding more than ten thousand people); a quarter were seminomadic bedouin concentrated in the north and west, and the rest were fully nomadic, relying on their livestock and on raiding the *fellaheen*, pilgrimage caravans and each other for survival. Amman held around 2400 people. Political loyalties were rooted in tribalism, and although the population at large tended towards common aims – desire for an Arab ruler, hatred of the French for their destruction of the Kingdom of Syria, distrust of the British for their double-dealing – they lacked a collective voice. When Abdullah arrived, apart from a brief challenge in Salt, he was accepted without question as a unifying leader.

For their part, the British wrote Transjordan out of the Palestine Mandate. On May 15, 1923, under an **Anglo-Jordanian Treaty**, the British formally recognized Abdullah as head of the new **Emirate of Transjordan**, describing it as a national state being prepared for full independence under the supervision of the British High Commissioner in Jerusalem.

Consolidation of the emirate: 1923–28

In Mecca, Abdullah's father Sharif Hussein was furious at being supplanted. In January 1924, he departed for Aqaba, where he ignored his son's, and British, authority and started to rule in his own right. It rapidly became apparent, though, that his dream of becoming "king of the Arabs" was in tatters – much as was the Arab heartland itself. Syria was controlled by the French, who had carved Lebanon from it; Iraq was ruled by one son,

1946	**1948**
Jordan gains independence from Britain	Establishment of the State of Israel; Jordan secures control of East Jerusalem and the West Bank

Faisal, Transjordan by another, Abdullah; Palestine was under the thumb of the British; and late in 1924 the Hejaz was invaded by a fundamentalist central Arabian tribe led by **Abd al-Aziz al-Saud**, who shortly afterwards established the Kingdom of Saudi Arabia. As a crowning ignominy, the British exiled Hussein to Cyprus, where he spent his last days.

Meanwhile, Abdullah set about consolidating power in his newly chosen capital of **Amman** (favoured over the fractious Salt). The 1920s and 1930s saw the forging of a cohesive political unity from among the disparate tribes, with one of Abdullah's earliest acts being the creation of a centralized security force, named the **Arab Legion**.

Throughout this period, the British guaranteed funding for central government, in exchange for British advisers maintaining close contact with Abdullah. A pragmatist, as visionary as he was realistic, Abdullah knew that the British still called the shots, and that without Britain – specifically, without military assistance and money – the emirate could never survive. By compromising where necessary, Abdullah maintained progress towards his ultimate goal of independence, though his concessions to the British tarnished his reputation among Arab nationalists. To assuage growing discontent, Abdullah promulgated the **first Transjordanian constitution** in 1928. A year later, representative elections to a legislative council placed Transjordanians in real power for the first time.

With his domestic affairs stable, Abdullah was able to turn his attention further afield – specifically to the increasingly fraught situation in Palestine.

Abdullah I and Palestine: 1920–39

Palestine had always had a small native Jewish community, resident for the most part in the towns, Arabic-speaking and culturally Palestinian. Since the 1880s, however, Jews from central and eastern Europe had been arriving, many of them tough-minded nationalistic **Zionists**, for whom the area was not simply a holy land to be shared among religious communities but the rightful national homeland of the Jews of the world. As it became obvious that the Balfour Declaration was to become official mandate policy in Palestine, a **militant Arab reaction** to Zionism developed, denouncing Britain's perceived right to hand the country over to the Jews. In Amman, Abdullah quickly grasped the political reality – principally that Britain was in a position to dictate its will and that at least some degree of Jewish immigration to Palestine was inevitable. He put forward the proposal that if the Jews were prepared to accept the extension of his own rule over Palestine, they would be left free to govern themselves with all civil rights guaranteed; this would not only secure the Jewish position in Palestine with minimum cost to the existing local population, but it would also enable Jews to settle in Transjordan, where they could contribute much-needed money and skills to the country's development.

Amid the increasingly hot-headed politics of the time, such a vision was doomed to failure. The Jews wanted more in Palestine than mere political autonomy under a Muslim king, and rejected his proposals. Mainstream Arab opinion viewed Abdullah's plan as overly concessionary, and from this time on, doubts were laid in Palestinian minds as to Abdullah's motives. Reservations were fuelled by the leader of the Palestinians, **Hajj Amin al-Husseini**, Mufti of Jerusalem. A strict hardliner who refused to compromise an inch with the Jews, Hajj Amin led calls for a complete ban on Jewish immigration and land purchase, ahead of a declaration of Palestinian independence; he was aided by a silent alliance with the British, who had no desire to see Abdullah

1951	1952	1957
King Abdullah I assassinated in Jerusalem	King Hussein accedes to the throne	The last British troops leave Jordan

extending influence over a land he wasn't supposed to be ruling. Amman became the focus for the Palestinian opposition to Hajj Amin, which believed that the only way of saving Palestine for the Arabs was to cultivate British goodwill and offer limited concessions to the already entrenched Zionist settlers.

Anti-Zionist feeling among Palestinian Arabs exploded into violence in the 1920s and 1930s, put down with increasing harshness by the British. With the coming to power of the Nazis in Germany in 1933, Jewish immigration to Palestine increased dramatically, as did Arab attacks on both Jewish and British targets. From 1933 onwards, Abdullah began to appoint Palestinians to positions of power in Amman, but in such a charged atmosphere, his pragmatism in backing both Arab dialogue with the Jews and Arab concessions to the British merely fanned Palestinian distrust of his motives. In 1937, a **Royal Commission** arrived from London to assess the political situation. The Palestinian leadership boycotted the commission's proceedings; under threat of arrest, Hajj Amin fled to Lebanon.

The build-up to World War II: 1937–39

With war in Europe looking increasingly likely, Britain attempted to secure its position in the Middle East, an area commanding vital land and water routes and, most important, harbouring oil. The Royal Commission report of 1937 recommended **partitioning** Palestine between Arabs and Jews, but this was rejected by the all-or-nothing Palestinian leadership. In May 1939, with war imminent, the British suddenly offered a dramatic U-turn. On the table was **full independence** for Palestine after ten years, with severe limitations in the meantime on land transfers to Jews and with Jewish immigration permitted only subject to Arab approval. The Jews immediately rejected the proposal. In Amman, Abdullah hailed it as the best the Palestinian Arabs could ever hope to get, but Hajj Amin denounced the deal as a British ploy. The rejectionists won the day.

Seeing reason dissipating before him, Abdullah wrote: "The pillars of Zionism in Palestine are three: the Balfour promise; the European nations that have decided to expel the Jews from their lands; and the extremists among the Arabs who do not accept any solution. So behold Palestine, breathing its last."

Independence and the loss of Palestine: 1939–52

World War II had little impact in Transjordan, other than to delay advances towards independence. However, Abdullah's Arab Legion served loyally alongside the British elsewhere in the Middle East, helping to retake Baghdad from the Axis powers in 1941 (which paved the way for the British victory at El-Alamein the following year), and helping to eject the Vichy French from Syria and Lebanon. Abdullah deserved reward. What he hoped for – as he had done for decades – was the throne of a new Greater Syria. However, neither the Syrians nor the Lebanese would accept anything less than independence now the French had been removed from power; and the king of Saudi Arabia, already faced by a strong monarchy in Iraq, had no desire to see another in Transjordan (Britain and the United States were both aware by now of the vast oil reserves in Saudi Arabia, and were willing to bend over backwards to avoid upsetting King Saud). Syria and Lebanon were granted independence, but Transjordan remained under British mandate until the 1946 **Treaty of London**, which granted the emirate independence. In May, the Transjordanian cabinet

1958	1960	1964
Jordan and Iraq merge in a short-lived Arab Federation	Jordanian prime minister Hazza al-Majali assassinated	Palestine Liberation Organization founded in Jerusalem

GLUBB PASHA

The name of **General Sir John Bagot Glubb** is generally better known in Jordan than T.E. Lawrence: there are still old-timers in Amman who remember him with some affection as an upstanding soldier and asset to the young emirate – though many other Jordanians associate his name with the colonialist treachery of the British.

Glubb was instrumental in establishing the Arab Legion, as the British-officered Transjordanian army was known. From 1918, he served first in British-controlled Iraq, famously halting incursions of bedouin fighters from the desert by establishing a loyal bedouin force. In 1930 he was posted to Transjordan, which was suffering from similar tribal raids. Glubb set up the bedouin **"Desert Patrol"**, which, after subduing the raids, went on to evolve into an elite army unit, serving in World War II and the 1948 war with Israel. In 1939, Glubb took over supreme command of the Arab Legion and became known as **"Pasha"**, an honorific title awarded to senior Jordanian officers. However, with the rise of Arab nationalism and the accession to the throne of the young King Hussein in 1953, Glubb began to appear increasingly outdated, and, worse, a tool of British imperialism. Dismissed in 1956, he went on to write dozens of well-respected books on Jordan and Arab history, including his autobiography *A Soldier with the Arabs*. He died in England in 1986.

switched Abdullah's title from emir to king, and officially changed the name of the country to the **Hashemite Kingdom of Jordan**; we explain the term "Hashemite" later in this section.

Palestine 1947–49

Meanwhile, the situation in Palestine had been worsening, with a flood of post-Holocaust Jewish immigration and a simultaneous campaign of terror by underground Jewish groups aimed at the British. In 1947, Britain announced that it would unilaterally pull out of its Palestine mandate. That November, the UN approved a plan to partition Palestine into a Jewish and an Arab state, with Jerusalem administered internationally. The Jews were unhappy, having been denied Jerusalem, and mainstream Arab opinion was outraged at the whole idea of conceding any kind of Jewish state in Palestine. On May 15, 1948, the last British troops departed from Haifa. Jewish forces immediately declared an independent **State of Israel**. Disorganized Arab armies, led by Jordan's Arab Legion, simultaneously entered the region intent on taking the land allotted to the Jews by the UN. By the time fighting ended in July, Jordan had occupied a swathe of the interior of Palestine, as well as the eastern districts – and Holy Places – of Jerusalem. The entire Galilee region and the valuable fertile coastal strip, including the towns of Haifa, Jaffa, Lydda and Ramle, had been lost to Israel. Hundreds of thousands of Palestinians fled, or were forcibly ejected, from towns and villages throughout the country, most seeking refuge in the Jordanian-held sector, known as the **West Bank**. In four years, the kingdom's population jumped from 435,000 to 1.5 million, of whom two-thirds were Palestinian (including more than half a million refugees living in temporary camps).

Aftermath and assassination: 1950–52

After the hostilities, Abdullah convened a meeting in Jericho of Palestinian notables to proclaim the absorption of the Jordanian-occupied West Bank into Jordan proper. In April 1950, Jordan formally annexed the West Bank under the guise of "**uniting the two banks**".

1967	**1970**
Jordan defeated by Israel in the Six-Day War, loses control of East Jerusalem and the West Bank	"Black September": Palestinian fighters in Jordan spark civil war

Meanwhile the newly formed **Arab League** ruled that Arab countries should not grant citizenship to Palestinian refugees, lest the disowned and displaced should then lose their claim to their homeland. To this day, Palestinians who sought refuge in Lebanon, Syria and Egypt remain stateless and without rights. Jordan was the only Arab country to go against this policy; it formally resettled its Palestinian refugees, granting them full Jordanian citizenship and civil rights. Abdullah's policy enabled Palestinians in Jordan to rebuild their lives, but it ran entirely against mainstream Arab thinking that refused to accept the fact of Israel's existence. Citizenship notwithstanding, most Palestinians – in Jordan and elsewhere – felt betrayed by Abdullah's policies from as far back as the 1920s, and particularly by his perceived eagerness to absorb Arab Palestine under the Hashemite banner. On July 20, 1951, as Abdullah was entering the al-Aqsa mosque in Jerusalem for Friday prayers, a young Palestinian stepped up and shot him dead. A bullet intended for Abdullah's 15-year-old grandson, Hussein, ricocheted off a medal on the boy's chest.

On Abdullah's assassination, the throne passed to Abdullah's 40-year-old son **Talal**, who was in Switzerland receiving medical treatment. Talal returned to Amman, but his increasingly erratic behaviour made it clear that he was unfit to rule. In 1952, he abdicated in favour of his eldest son, Hussein.

King Hussein's early years: 1952–67

Born in 1935, **King Hussein** was educated in Britain, at Harrow School and Sandhurst military academy. He succeeded to the throne before his seventeenth birthday, and was crowned king in May 1953. The Cold War was well established, and the new king found himself caught between a powerful Egyptian-Syrian-Saudi bloc on the one hand, closely allied with the Soviets, and on the other, the controlling British presence at the heart of his government pushing him towards the pro-Western Baghdad Pact (a British-designed defensive treaty against Soviet aggression, subscribed to by Iraq, Turkey, Iran and Pakistan). In addition, the 1948 war had utterly changed the character of Jordan, and had thrown a cosmopolitan, well-educated and urbanized Palestinian population into the midst of an outnumbered Transjordanian population with an entirely different, rural and bedouin-based culture. Most of the Palestinians yearned to return to their lost homeland, and were unwilling to follow the conciliatory and pro-Western Hashemite line; many favoured instead the **pan-Arabism** espoused by the charismatic Egyptian leader, **Nasser**.

Suez and beyond

Crisis loomed for Hussein in 1955 and 1956. In nine months, five prime ministers came and went. Jordan's declaration of Cold War neutrality angered the British, which in turn led to violent street protests in Amman. Hussein dismissed the British commander-in-chief of the Jordanian army, **Glubb Pasha**, and replaced him with a Jordanian, but anti-Western feeling continued to run high, especially after the British-French-Israeli invasion of Egypt during the **Suez Crisis** of 1956. Jordan's pro-Soviet prime minister **Suleiman Nabulsi** ended the 1948 Anglo-Jordanian treaty, replacing the British subsidy to Jordan with contributions from Saudi Arabia, Syria and Egypt (the last two soon defaulted). British troops left Jordan for good in July 1957.

To make up the financial shortfall, Hussein requested aid from the US and soon afterwards took control of army appointments and suppressed political parties and trade unions. The

1971	1973
Jordanian prime minister Wasfi Al-Tal assassinated	Israel defeats Egypt and Syria in the "October War" or "Yom Kippur War"

US declared its determination to preserve Jordan's independence, and when Syria allied itself with the USSR in September 1957, US forces sent a large airlift of arms to Amman.

Hussein and Nasser
Throughout the 1950s Egypt and Syria, both then revolutionary republics, kept up a bombardment of anti-Hashemite propaganda, with Nasser's **Radio Cairo** particularly vocal in denigrating both the Jordanian government and King Hussein. On February 1, 1958, Egypt and Syria announced – to wild celebrations on the streets of Jordan as everywhere in the Arab world – their merger in a **United Arab Republic** (UAR); as a counter-move, two weeks later, the Hashemite monarchies of Jordan and Iraq announced their own merger in an **Arab Federation**. The latter body survived barely five months, with the entire Iraqi royal family being slaughtered in a military coup in July. Meanwhile there was open Muslim insurrection in Lebanon, supported by the new UAR against the Christian-led and staunchly pro-American Lebanese government. Anti-Western feeling in the Middle East was at a peak, and the only obstacles most observers saw standing in the way of pan-Arab unity were the Lebanese Christians and Jordan's Hashemite monarchy. Few gave the latter much chance of survival.

The American response to the crisis was to bomb Lebanon. Meanwhile, the US administration had received a request for help from Jordan, which had run out of oil. However, with the revolutionary forces in Syria and Iraq sealing off their borders, and the Saudi king in thrall to Nasser's popularity, the only remaining direction by which the US could deliver oil to Jordan was over **Israeli airspace**. Amazingly, Hussein applied to Israel for permission, which was granted, and the airlift commenced, to a barrage of scorn from all Arab sides. Soon after, Britain flew troops into Amman to bolster the regime; they too arrived over Israel and the insults rang out again. Nonetheless, in Jordan, democracy had been sacrificed for stability, and Hussein's **security services** kept a tight lid on the simmering discontent. Palestinian bombs exploded in Amman, and, in 1960, the prime minister was assassinated, but repeated attempts on the king's life were foiled.

Economic development
Opposition to Hussein died down, not least because US aid – and substantial remittances from Jordanians working in the Gulf – were fostering tangible **economic development**: Jordan's potash and phosphate industries were taking off, modern highways were being built, unemployment was down as construction teams expanded East and West Bank cities, and tourism to Jordanian Jerusalem, Bethlehem, Hebron and the West Bank, as well as East Bank sites, was bringing in much-needed hard currency. Ties with the Saudi Arabian monarchy were also strengthening in the face of communism and Arab nationalism. Perhaps most important of all, Hussein reluctantly approved the creation of a political body to represent the Palestinians, the **Palestine Liberation Organization (PLO)**, founded in 1964. Its charter, in a specific rebuff to Jordanian claims on the West Bank, stated that it was to be the "only legitimate spokesman" for the Palestinian people.

The Six-Day War and beyond: 1967–70
During 1966, relations with Syria deteriorated and Jordan suspended support for the PLO, accusing its secretary of pro-Communist activity. Syria and the PLO both

1974

Jordan surrenders its claim to represent the Palestinian people

1978

Egypt signs peace treaty with Israel

appealed to the Jordanian people to revolt against King Hussein. Clashes followed and PLO-laid bombs exploded in Amman. At the same time, skirmishes with Israeli troops led Jordan to introduce conscription. The prospect of war with Israel seemed inevitable. In May 1967 Hussein flew to Cairo to throw in his lot with Egypt and Syria.

On June 5, Israel launched a pre-emptive strike against its Arab neighbours. By the end of the **Six-Day War**, Jordanian losses were devastating: Israel was occupying East Jerusalem and the entire West Bank. Israel had seized the Jawlan (Golan Heights) from Syria and the Gaza Strip and Sinai Peninsula from Egypt. In the eyes of the entire Arab world, this was a catastrophe: Egypt and Syria had lost relatively small areas of strategic importance, but Jordan had lost fully half its inhabited territory, a third of its population, its prime agricultural land and – most ignominious – control over the Muslim and Christian holy sites in Jerusalem. Up to a quarter of a million refugees crossed to the East Bank, putting the government, economy and social services under intolerable pressures.

The crushing defeat gave Palestinians in Jordan cause to believe that King Hussein and the other Arab leaders were unable or unwilling (or both) to liberate their homeland. King Hussein rapidly included equal representation from the East and West Banks in the National Assembly, but this was never going to satisfy Palestinian demands. The rift grew between the government and the Palestinian guerrilla organizations in Jordan – principally Fatah, led by **Yasser Arafat**, chairman of the umbrella PLO. After 1967, these groupings – funded by the Gulf states and receiving arms and training from Syria – took control in Jordan's refugee camps, backed also by widespread grassroots support from Jordan's majority Palestinian population. A **fedayeen** ("martyrs") movement developed within the camps, which took on the appearance of a state-within-a-state, intent on liberating Palestine by their own independent efforts. The *fedayeen* took for granted their ability to overrule King Hussein in his own country, and launched military operations against Israel. The ensuing reprisals, however, caused extensive damage to the border areas – now Jordan's only remaining agricultural land – and seriously undermined any possibilities for a peace settlement with Israel, on which the country's long-term future depended.

Black September and its aftermath: 1970–74

Fedayeen opposition to the Hashemite monarchy, rooted in revolutionary socialism, remained implacable. Street battles flared in 1968, and in June 1970, the Jordanian army mobilized in Amman to assert authority over the guerrilla movements. There was an attempt on the king's life. In September, *fedayeen* **hijacked** three international aircraft to an airfield near Mafraq, ostensibly demanding the release of imprisoned comrades, but equally intent on embarrassing King Hussein in the eyes of the world and forcing the issue of the Palestinian revolution in Jordan. Once emptied of passengers and crew, all three aircraft were spectacularly blown up; the *fedayeen* then took over Irbid proclaiming a "people's government", and the country exploded into violence. By the end of "**Black September**", full civil war was raging, with thousands dead and injured. Conflict continued for months but by April 1971, the Jordanian army had pushed the *fedayeen* out of Amman. Three months later, after a violent offensive on Palestinian positions around Jerash and Ajloun, forces loyal to the king were back in control. The *fedayeen* fled to Lebanon to continue their fight (within four

1984

Elections in Jordan introduce limited democracy for the first time

1987

The first Palestinian *intifada* breaks out against Israeli occupation

> **THE HASHEMITES**
>
> The aristocratic Hashemite dynasty, headed by Jordan's King Abdullah II, traces its genealogy back to the Prophet Muhammad – and beyond. An Arab chieftain **Quraysh**, claimed to be a descendant of Ishmael (and thus of Abraham), is said to have first arrived in Mecca in the second century AD. By 480, his family ruled the city. One of his descendants, **Hashem**, was the great-grandfather of the Prophet Muhammad, who was born into the tribe of Quraysh in Mecca in around 571. Muhammad's daughter had two sons, and the direct descendants of the elder son have been known as "**Sharifs**" (nobles) since that time. Different Sharifian families ruled the Hejaz from 967 onwards, with King Abdullah's own branch ruling Mecca itself from 1201 right through to 1925, when the Saudis seized control from Sharif Hussein.
>
> Jordan's King Abdullah II is the 43rd-generation direct descendant of the Prophet Muhammad. You can find a full account of Hashemite history, including family trees going back 54 generations to Quraysh, at Ⓦ **kingabdullah.jo**.

years, civil war had broken out in Lebanon as well). Palestinian commandos made three unsuccessful attempts to hijack Jordanian aircraft, and, in September 1971, members of the Black September faction of Fatah assassinated another Jordanian prime minister.

In March 1972 King Hussein made an attempt to regain Palestinian political credibility by announcing plans for a **federation** of Jordan and Palestine, but criticism of the plan was almost universal, from Israel, from the exiled Palestinian organizations and from Egypt. A military coup was only just averted. Jordan's isolation in the Arab world was almost complete. Nonetheless, Hussein attended a **reconciliation summit** with presidents Sadat of Egypt and Assad of Syria, which resulted in a general amnesty for all political prisoners in Jordan, including Fatah activists. Jordanian security services and intelligence organizations were beefed up to deter dissident activity; political parties remained banned and the country had no elected parliament. Jordan stayed out of the 1973 Egyptian-Syrian **October War** (or Yom Kippur War) against Israel, but garnered little kudos for doing so.

The Rabat summit and Camp David: 1974–80

Throughout 1974, King Hussein attempted to preserve his claim over the West Bank, flying in the face of the increasing power and prestige of the PLO (Yasser Arafat had that year been invited to address the UN General Assembly). In October 1974, at the **Arab Summit Conference** in Rabat, Morocco, twenty Arab heads of state passed a resolution recognizing the PLO as the "sole legitimate representative of the Palestinian people". King Hussein reluctantly agreed to this, effectively ceding Jordan's claims both to represent the Palestinians and to reincorporate the West Bank into the Hashemite realm.

In 1974, Egypt and Syria signed disengagement agreements with Israel; in 1975 and 1976, King Hussein held secret talks with Israel over the West Bank, which later collapsed due to Israel's proposal to retain control over thirty percent of the territory. The new realities were thrown into turmoil by Egyptian President Sadat's peace initiative in visiting Jerusalem in 1977; Hussein tried to stand as an arbiter between Egypt and the rejectionist Arab states (led by Syria), while still demanding Israel's complete withdrawal from East Jerusalem, the West Bank and Gaza. Jordan joined the

1988	1989
Jordan severs all legal and administrative ties with the West Bank, handing control to the PLO	Antigovernment riots break out in Karak and Ma'an

rest of the Arab world in scorning the US-sponsored Egypt-Israel **Camp David accords** of 1978, and, as a reward, was promised $1.25 billion annually by wealthy **Iraq**. Throughout the 1970s, economic relations with Iraq had been improving, with Iraq funding the expansion of Aqaba port and construction of major highways. When Iraq invaded Iran in September 1980, launching the bloody **Iran–Iraq War**, Jordan benefited greatly from the passage of goods through Aqaba bound for Iraq.

The Palestinians and the first intifada: 1980–89

Since Black September, the PLO's bid for authority over Palestinians on the East Bank had – bizarrely – reinforced the stand of both Transjordanian and Israeli hardliners. The former had never viewed the Palestinians as true Jordanians anyway. The latter saw the Hashemite monarchy as the sole obstacle to annexation of the West Bank by Israel; under the slogan "**Jordan is Palestine**", they pressed for a Palestinian revolution east of the Jordan, offering to help it along by expelling Palestinians from the West Bank. Needless to say, this rapidly dampened Palestinian opposition to King Hussein in Jordan.

In 1982, the PLO was ejected from its Beirut headquarters by the **Israeli invasion of Lebanon**, and sent into further exile in Tunis; humiliated, Arafat looked to King Hussein for some way to challenge Israeli hegemony. Hussein reconvened Jordan's National Assembly, comprising representatives from both banks of the Jordan, for the first time since 1967, as a forum for discussion of moderate Palestinian opinion away from the extremist intransigence of the Syrian position. Israel even permitted West Bank deputies to travel to Amman. In March 1984, the first **elections** in Jordan for seventeen years (and the first in which women could vote) took place, although political parties were still banned and the eight seats up for grabs were East Bank only.

"Land for Peace"

Less than a year later, in opposition to a widely denounced peace plan put forward by US President Reagan (who refused to talk to the PLO), Hussein and Arafat agreed to allow Jordan to start direct negotiations with Israel under UN auspices, on the basis of Hussein's formula of "**land for peace**" – that is, the return of lands occupied by Israel in 1967 in exchange for a comprehensive Arab-Israeli peace. Hardline Syria, though, forced Hussein to drop the initiative, partly by assassinating Jordanian diplomats and partly by uniting the Abu Nidal Palestinian guerrilla organization with Arafat's main PLO rival, George Habash, to attack the accord. At the end of 1985, Hussein and Syria's President Assad issued a joint statement rejecting any direct peace negotiations with Israel; Hussein's motivation for this was also to put pressure on Arafat to accept **UN Resolution 242**, without which the PLO could gain no international credibility. "242" had been a thorn in the side of the Arabs since 1967, since it called ambiguously for Israel to withdraw from "occupied territories" (which could be taken to mean whatever anyone wanted) and referred to the Palestinians as "refugees", thus implying a denial of the existence of a Palestinian nation and the right of Palestinians to self-determination, and accepting the right of Israel to exist. Hamstrung by extremist attitudes embedded within the PLO, Arafat couldn't stop the PLO Executive Committee reiterating its opposition to 242 in December 1985.

Although rumours of secret talks between Hussein and the Israeli Prime Minister Shimon Peres persisted through the mid-1980s, publicly Jordan continued to reject

1990	1991
Iraq invades Kuwait, prompting UN sanctions which cause economic crisis in Jordan	First Gulf War ends with Kuwait expelling 300,000 Jordanians and Palestinians to Jordan

Israeli proposals for peace talks which excluded PLO participation. In November 1987, King Hussein managed to convene in Amman the first full meeting of the Arab League for eight years and, acting in the interests of Arab unity, was able to draw Egypt back into the fold after its expulsion for making peace with Israel.

The first intifada and Jordan's West Bank pull-out: 1987–89

In December 1987, an incident in the Gaza Strip sparked a widespread violent Palestinian uprising against Israeli occupation of the West Bank and Gaza, termed the **intifada**, or "shaking-off". Israel was unable to suppress the uprising, and, alarmed at the possibility of demonstrations turning violent, the Jordanian security services enforced their own clampdown on any shows of solidarity. The intensity of the revolt, as well as the Israeli response to it and the news that emerged of horrendous living conditions among Palestinians under Israeli occupation, alerted world opinion to the necessity of a comprehensive settlement in the Middle East. The US Secretary of State, George Shultz, came up with a plan, but since it refused participation by the PLO and also neglected to address the Palestinian right to self-determination, it was rejected by every Arab state.

In a momentous decision on July 31, 1988, with the *intifada* in full swing, King Hussein announced the **severing** of all legal and administrative links between Jordan and the West Bank. By doing so, he effectively ended Hashemite claims to Arab Palestine which had been playing beneath the surface of political machinations in the region since 1917. The 850,000 Palestinians on the West Bank welcomed the clean break. Israel, however, immediately began restricting the activities of West Bank Palestinian institutions. Anti-Hashemite opinion cynically suggested that Hussein wanted to demonstrate the inability of the PLO to run public services and conduct international diplomacy without the backing of Jordan.

Shortly afterwards, on November 15, the PLO unilaterally proclaimed an independent **State of Palestine**, endorsing UN Resolution 242 and thus implicitly recognizing the right of Israel to exist (within its pre-1967 frontiers). Jordan and sixty other countries recognized the new state. The following month, Yasser Arafat renounced violence on behalf of the PLO in front of the UN General Assembly.

Democracy and the first Gulf War: 1989–91

In Jordan, the pull-out from the West Bank caused the value of the dinar to fall dramatically, and the austerity measures that followed resulted in **price rises** of up to fifty percent on basic goods and services. In April 1989, anti-government **riots** broke out in depressed southern towns such as Karak and Ma'an. The prime minister and the entire cabinet resigned, forcing a **general election** that gave a surprising boost to the Islamist and leftist opposition. 1990 was a year of desperate crisis for Jordan. The dinar had lost two-thirds of its value in two years and unemployment was running at twenty percent. Fraud and embezzlement had been uncovered at the country's second-largest bank, and the scandal had spread to the national airline and some 37 other companies. In addition, a huge influx of Jews into Israel from the former Soviet Union was resulting in ever more settlements going up on the West Bank and a consequent flood of Palestinians crossing the river into Jordan. With the West Bank Palestinians under almost continuous curfew, the *intifada* seemed to have fizzled out.

1993	1994	1996
Jordan's first one-person-one-vote multiparty elections	Jordan signs peace treaty with Israel	The ending of grain subsidies precipitates rioting in southern Jordanian towns

The first Gulf War: 1990–91

As the 1980–88 Iran-Iraq war juddered to a halt, it became clear that Iraq was in no position to repay its loans from the Gulf states. President Saddam Hussein campaigned to have the loans cancelled, but **Kuwait** stood out by refusing to accede. This quarrel was complicated by a long-standing border dispute between the two countries – and by the fact that the disputed area was rich in oil. King Hussein of Jordan pressed for a resolution to the crisis by Arab mediation, but before steps could be taken, Iraq suddenly **invaded** Kuwait on August 2, 1990. Saddam Hussein quickly proclaimed the annexation of Kuwait to Iraq.

The UN Security Council imposed **economic sanctions** on Iraq four days later, precipitating a further crisis in Jordan. Thousands of Jordanian refugees returned destitute from Iraq and Kuwait, ending substantial foreign remittances to the kingdom and placing a huge burden on the country's social services. Petroleum prices rose sharply, as Jordan's supply of free Iraqi oil (in return for loans) dried up; fully a quarter of Jordan's export trade had been to Iraq, and this was terminated; and business at Aqaba port was cut overnight, as the road to Iraq was closed to trade.

It was clear that Saddam Hussein's actions flouted international law. King Hussein attempted to get the Arab League to mediate in the crisis, but he was countered by Saudi Arabia, Egypt and Syria leading calls for international action. In August, King Hussein started a round of peacemaking, giving a televised address to the US Congress urging withdrawal of the multinational force in Saudi Arabia. In November, he warned the World Climate Conference of the potentially disastrous environmental effects of war – borne out by Iraq's later ignition of Kuwaiti oil installations. The following month, he proposed a peace plan linking the Iraq-Kuwait dispute with the Arab-Israeli conflict, and advocating dialogue among Arab leaders.

His efforts proved fruitless: on January 16, 1991, the **Gulf War** began, sparking widespread anti-Western and anti-Israel demonstrations throughout Jordan. Petrol rationing was introduced in Jordan, which only bolstered pro-Iraqi sentiment. Popular opinion held that the US-led coalition was pursuing double standards, condemning Iraqi aggression against Kuwait yet condoning Israeli aggression in the occupied territories; that the Gulf States were greedy, unwilling to share their new-found oil wealth with other Arabs; and that the West, by weighing in against Iraq, was supporting the oil-rich states against the poorer Arab states. In the region, King Hussein was highly regarded for being the only leader to articulate this opinion fully, although he was lambasted for it in the West.

After hostilities ceased in March, the US Congress cancelled an aid programme to Jordan in punishment for the king's stance. Kuwait regarded its sizeable Jordanian and Palestinian community as collaborators with the Iraqis, and expelled them all – about 300,000 people – to Jordan, a further burden on the country's social infrastructure.

Peace and crises: 1991–99

In 1991, a new **National Charter** improved openness within government, eased bureaucracy and lifted the ban on political parties, which had been in effect since 1963. Martial law, which had been in force since 1967, was repealed. Jordan's first one-person one-vote, multiparty **elections** of November 1993 saw a 68 percent turnout, with the majority of candidates being independent centrists loyally backing the king, although the Islamic Action Front (the political arm of the Muslim Brotherhood) gained strong support.

1997	1999	1999
Israel botches an assassination attempt on Hamas leader Khaled Meshaal in Amman	King Hussein dies	King Abdullah II accedes to the throne

New moves in the Middle East **peace process** were initiated by the US in Madrid in October 1991, Jordan participating in a joint delegation with the Palestinians. The peace talks soon hit deadlock, but, unknown even to King Hussein, Israel's new left-wing government and the PLO were engaged in secret talks in Oslo. In September 1993, they emerged with a **Declaration of Principles** on Palestinian self-rule in the occupied territories. Soon after, Jordan and the PLO signed agreements on economic and security cooperation, closely bonding the ongoing Israeli-Palestinian and Israeli-Jordanian peace talks together into a single framework.

On July 25, 1994, in Washington, King Hussein and Israeli Prime Minister Yitzhak Rabin formally ended the state of war that had existed between their two countries since 1948. A full **peace treaty** followed in October, opposed both by Syria and by Islamists within Jordan. A clause in the treaty acknowledging King Hussein as the custodian of the Holy Places in Jerusalem initially brought complaints from the PLO that it undermined Palestinian claims to the city, later mollified.

In August 1996, under intense pressure from the International Monetary Fund to institute austerity measures, the government ended **subsidies** on grain which were producing a ballooning economic deficit. The result was an immediate doubling of bread prices, and discontent, especially strong in the poorer towns of the south, flared into open **rioting**. King Hussein suspended parliament and sent troops and tanks into Karak and elsewhere to suppress the disturbances, but the austerities remained. The election in 1996 of an extreme right-wing government in Israel, headed by **Binyamin Netanyahu**, brought the ongoing Middle East peace process to a grinding halt.

Shattered confidence

For many Jordanians, 1997 was a year of shattered confidence, as the country was exposed to a series of domestic and regional crises. Early in the year, a Jordanian soldier opened fire on Israeli schoolgirls visiting Baqoura in northern Jordan, killing seven. King Hussein attempted to mend ties with Israel by personally visiting the bereaved families, a gesture which inspired much admiration in Israel and much contempt in the Arab world (no bereaved Arab families have ever been consoled by an Israeli leader, the argument ran). Anti-Israel feeling surged in Jordan. In July, nine major political parties announced their intention to boycott the November parliamentary election, as a sign of their opposition to normalizing relations with Israel. Diplomatic relations with Israel were almost terminated in September, after a botched assassination attempt in Amman by Mossad, the Israeli intelligence service, on an official at the Jordanian bureau of the Palestinian Islamist group Hamas. Days before the Jordanian elections in November, Human Rights Watch issued a damning report on the state of human rights in Jordan. The elections themselves were held to be a whitewash, with extremely low voter turnout and 62 out of 80 seats won by pro-government or independent centrist candidates. Only 19 out of 524 candidates were women, none of whom was elected (the king later appointed three women to the Senate). A report from Jordan University showed unemployment in the country standing at a crippling 22–27 percent, double the official estimate.

The death of King Hussein

Throughout the 1990s, concern had been bubbling under Jordanian politics about the **health** of King Hussein. In August 1992, one of his kidneys was removed during

2000	2003	2005
The second Palestinian *intifada* breaks out against Israeli occupation	The Second Gulf War leads to hundreds of thousands of Iraqi refugees entering Jordan	Al Qaeda suicide bomb attacks in Amman kill sixty people

an operation for cancer; spring 1996 saw an operation for an enlarged prostate, and during 1998 he underwent chemotherapy for lymph cancer. All these procedures were done in the US, his youngest brother, **Prince Hassan**, being sworn in as regent on each occasion. In October 1998, Hussein witnessed the **Wye River Accords**, guaranteeing Israeli withdrawal from more West Bank land in return for security safeguards from the Palestinians. (Two months later Israel suspended the agreement in the face of deepening domestic tension, and the Netanyahu government collapsed.) The king's appearance at Wye River, to free the negotiations from deadlock despite obvious physical frailty, inspired respect but also doubts about his ability to continue his public duties.

In January 1999, after six months of treatment in the US, Hussein flew back to Jordan. It was clear his health was failing. In a controversially abrupt letter, he publicly removed Hassan from the **succession** after 34 years as Crown Prince, and placed in his stead his own eldest son, Abdullah. Within hours, Hussein had suffered a relapse. After unsuccessful treatment in the US, he returned again to Amman where he died three days later, on February 7, 1999, at the age of 63, having been in power for 46 years – one of the longest-serving executive heads of state in the world. His funeral drew worldwide media attention, with more than **fifty heads of state** in attendance. Even at a time of tragedy, such a turnout, demonstrating the international community's high regard for Jordan and its king, was a significant fillip to national confidence.

Jordan under Abdullah II

On the death of Hussein, a swearing-in ceremony confirmed the succession to **King Abdullah II**, who was crowned in July 1999. Abdullah was born in 1962 to Hussein's second wife, an Englishwoman, formerly Toni Gardiner, who took the name Princess Muna al-Hussein when she converted to Islam. Abdullah was educated at Oxford and Sandhurst; when he acceded, it was said at first that he spoke better English than Arabic. His prominent role in the Jordanian military ensured wholehearted support among East Bankers, while the fact that his wife, **Queen Rania**, is a scion of a notable Palestinian family from Tulkarem on the West Bank safeguarded his reputation among Jordanians of Palestinian origin.

Faced with continuing turmoil in Israel and Palestine, Abdullah has played only a minor role in suing for regional peace. In September 2000, the notorious right-wing Israeli general **Ariel Sharon** sparked outrage by touring Jerusalem's Haram ash-Sharif, the third-holiest site in Islam. Within weeks Sharon had won the Israeli elections, his bullish presence as prime minister effectively halting progress in international peace negotiations. The **second intifada** which followed, incomparably bloodier than its forebear of the late 1980s, continued past the death in November 2004 of Yasser Arafat, fizzling out soon before the January 2006 stroke which incapacitated Ariel Sharon. Throughout, it was widely supported by the Jordanian people, aided by such vocal bodies as Jordan's **Anti-Normalization Committee**, an informal grouping which agitates against any contacts – political, social or cultural – with Israel or Israelis. The **Gaza War** of December 2008 to January 2009, which saw heavy Israeli bombardment of civilian areas within the Gaza Strip, shocked many in Jordan.

When a coalition of forces led by the US invaded Iraq in March 2003, launching the **Second Gulf War**, Jordan limited its involvement, refusing to open its airspace to

2007	2011
Elections solidify support for conservative tribal leaders	Antigovernment protests break out in Amman and other cities. Syrian government forces attack peaceful protesters, sparking civil war

coalition aircraft and staying out of the ground war. One poll stated that just nine percent of Jordanians supported military action. One consequence of the war is that Jordan has absorbed hundreds of thousands of **Iraqi refugees**. Such vast numbers have put considerable strain on the country's health care, housing and education systems. Coordinated **suicide bomb attacks** on three hotels in Amman in 2005 that killed sixty people – for which Abu Musab al-Zarqawi, the Jordanian leader of "Al-Qaeda in Iraq", claimed responsibility – had the unintended effect of turning many ordinary Jordanians against Al-Qaeda. US forces killed Zarqawi in an airstrike inside Iraq in 2006, reportedly on a tip-off from Jordanian intelligence.

Economic reform
Economic reform is where Abdullah has made most impact. Jordan became the first country (other than Israel) to negotiate a **free trade agreement** with the US, and now has several Qualifying Industrial Zones (QIZs), where goods are manufactured or processed jointly by Jordan and Israel for distribution to the US duty- and quota-free. In 2001, the low-tax Aqaba Special Economic Zone (ASEZ) was launched to attract investment to Jordan's Red Sea coast, significant foreign investment flowing soon thereafter. **Privatization** of state concerns, such as Jordan Telecom and the airline Royal Jordanian, have proceeded apace. Jordan joined the World Trade Organization and has hosted several full meetings of the World Economic Forum.

After 9/11
For many people living in the Middle East, the "9/11" attacks on New York and Washington in September 2001 reinforced the urgency of establishing peace and prosperity in their region, and the general need for **dialogue** between the West and the Muslim world. In Jordan, as in virtually all Arab states, there is a discrepancy between the motivations and preoccupations of government and those of the general population. The vast majority of Jordanians have no problem with their government's policy of maintaining warm relations with the West, as long as this is based on mutual respect and a fair crack at social and economic development. However, many people instead face unemployment and poverty, and feel that their beliefs and concerns are being slighted while injustice persists both at home and across the region. This alienates them not only from decision-makers in their own country but also from the source, as many see it, of wider cultural and political oppression – the West and, specifically, the US. Radicalization can follow.

The Arab uprisings and beyond
During the **revolutionary unrest** which swept across the Arab world after 2011, Jordan remained mostly quiet, with protesters directing their anger at corrupt politicians rather than demanding revolutionary overthrow. Protests in major cities generally passed off without violence, although they exposed fault lines running across Jordanian society: calls for **reform** of the monarchy and an end to political **corruption** came most tellingly from deeply conservative leaders of East Bank tribes formerly mutely loyal to the throne.

2014	2015
Jordan takes part in air strikes on IS positions in Syria	IS murder of Jordanian pilot Muath Kasasbeh evokes outrage and sympathy

Israel's destructive bombing of **Gaza** in 2014 was met with almost universal outrage in Jordan, deepening public opposition to Jordanian political and commercial contacts with the Israeli state.

When Syrian dictator Bashar Al Assad responded to peaceful protests in his country with lethal violence, sparking a catastrophic **war**, most Jordanians looked on in horror. Since 2011, their neighbour has been eviscerated, with devastating consequences. By 2018 Jordan had absorbed an estimated 1.3 million **Syrian refugees** fleeing the conflict, only around 670,000 of whom are registered with the UN. Some 80 percent are living dispersed among towns and cities, mostly in the north of Jordan; the remainder eke out their existence in vast camps that have been set up in the desert, such as **Zaatari** and **Azraq**. Utterly reliant on the international community for funding support, Jordan has struggled to absorb such numbers: resources are under intense strain and the economy is buckling.

Jordan has also become a vital bulwark in the fight against **IS** or **Daesh** (the transliteration of an Arabic acronym meaning "the Islamic State in Iraq and the Levant"), hosting sizeable contingents of military and special forces from the US, UK and other countries.

But for most people, the main concerns are economic – simply surviving day to day. **Mass protests** against the imposition of austerity measures in 2018 forced the prime minister, Hani Al Mulki, to resign. His replacement, economist Omar Razzaz, has pledged reform, though few Jordanians expect much in the way of progress. The principal challenge for King Abdullah, as for many Arab leaders, is to foster the rise of a practical, responsive **body politic** that is able, in Jordan's case, to incorporate strands of liberal democracy, home-grown tribalism and Islam, and give each an outlet for expression. Of equal importance is the development of a tolerant, participatory **civil society** to limit polarization and extremism. On both fronts, Jordan has some way to go – though it is generally held to be leaps and bounds ahead of most states in the region.

Nonetheless, life remains hard for many Jordanians, with the domestic economy squeezed by corruption, the lack of progress on a comprehensive resolution of the Israeli-Palestinian conflict and uncertainty fostered by the war in Syria as well as the sabotaged revolution – and dictatorial retrenchment – in Egypt. Economic reforms have raised living standards but also deepened class divisions. Many Jordanians are increasingly anxious about the future.

2016	2017	2018
Parliamentary elections under reformed system of proportional representation	With defeat of IS, Jordan's border with Iraq reopens to civilian traffic	Street protests against austerity bring down the government; the king appoints Omar Razzaz as new prime minister

Flora and fauna

Jordan has a great variety of wildlife, not least because it lies at the crossroads of the Mediterranean, Arabia and Africa. The deserts contain a rich flora and fauna especially adapted to the harsh environment, and there's even life in the Dead Sea – you just need a microscope to see the species of bacteria which are known to occur.

Mosaics, rock art and frescoes paint a picture of Jordan's wildlife at a time when its significance was as a source of food (and, later, sport). Ancient rock art in the eastern deserts depicts gazelles, ibex and ostriches, and stone corrals remain as evidence of systematic trapping by previous generations of bedouin. Eighth-century frescoes at Qusayr Amra suggest that hunting game, such as the onager (a wild ass from Persia), was a great attraction for visitors from Damascus. These images also afford a glimpse of some larger animals which have subsequently become extinct due to excessive hunting and habitat destruction. It's hard to imagine today that leopards, Asiatic lions, cheetah, Syrian bears and crocodiles once roamed Jordan's deserts, forests and rivers. It's also hard to appreciate how quickly the thousands of gazelles present until the mid-1940s were reduced to near-extinction following the arrival of automatic weapons and motor vehicles; ostrich, Houbara bustard, oryx and onagers all went the same way.

For many years, Jordan's Royal Society for the Conservation of Nature (**RSCN**) has pursued a plan to **re-establish populations** of some of the country's extinct mammals in the wild. Projects involving oryx, Nubian ibex and roe deer have all been marked by success, even though most of these animals' former ranges have been overgrazed by goats and sheep.

Major habitats

Jordan's varied topography, climate and geology interact to produce a patchwork of often tightly packed **habitats**: you can travel from pine forest to desert in an hour's drive. Broadly speaking, the country can be divided into four major regions: the rift valley, rift margins, highlands and interior deserts. Each of these contains a range of habitats which vary from north to south, west to east and from low to high altitudes. In addition, there are habitats specific to the desert oases, rivers and coast.

The **rift valley** comprises – from north to south – the Jordan Valley, the Dead Sea, Southern Ghor, Wadi Araba and the Gulf of Aqaba (before continuing on to the Red Sea and the East African Rift Valley). The whole valley is warm to hot, the only appreciable rain falling in the north, which is exposed to rainfall from Mediterranean weather systems and thus lushly vegetated.

The **highlands** constitute a spine of hills running north–south down the length of the country, dissected by major wadi systems flowing westwards. Terrain in the north, up to 1250m above sea level, comprises the country's richest agricultural land. Further south and east, a reduction in altitude and rainfall produces an undulating, steppe terrain (now mostly arable). The Shara mountains in the south, behind Petra, reach 1700m; their steppe habitat is unique in Jordan. Towards Aqaba, dissected granite mountains add further variation to this upland range.

Between the highlands and the rift valley, a deeply incised, west-facing escarpment contains some of the most dramatic of Jordan's scenery, including Petra and Dana. As you descend, habitats within this **rift margin** change with the drop in rainfall.

The interior **deserts**, covering eighty percent of Jordan's area, are typically flat, with geological variations controlling a complex pattern of fascinating habitats. Flint and limestone deserts predominate, with sand deserts rarer. Of considerable interest is the basalt desert, a vast expanse of boulders harbouring a unique fauna adapted to live in this harsh habitat. The Rum desert is far from flat, with Jordan's highest mountains (reaching above 1800m) among its towering peaks; the valleys between contain the country's finest sand dunes, largely stabilized with broom and other scrub. Much of the eastern desert's sporadic rainfall drains into mudflats or *qas* which, for brief, irregular periods, support huge quantities of life from invertebrates to the birds that feed on them.

Water is a valuable resource, and **rivers** are in short supply. Much of the flow of the Jordan River is now diverted for agriculture: a mere trickle remains. Many of its tributaries are now dammed, and as a result, the future for riverine wildlife in Jordan looks uncertain. Azraq was a textbook **oasis** until water extraction put an end to the natural flow of its springs. Other oases are small, such as those along the base of the rift margins and at Aqaba. Jordan's few kilometres of arid, sparsely vegetated **coastline** are fringed by coral reef, before the seabed plunges to depths of over 500m.

Mammals

A little detective work is needed to spot Jordan's mammalian wildlife, as many of the larger animals survive only in the remotest corners and the smaller animals are typically nocturnal. Discarded quills offer the only clue that nocturnal **porcupines** have been through; the **Palestinian mole rat** gives itself away by leaving telltale molehills. The pine forests around Dibeen are home to **Persian squirrels**, closely related to Europe's red squirrel; even if you don't see one, you can look for the chewed pine cones they leave behind.

Excepting a chance sighting of **Nubian ibex** at Dana or Mujib, or a **Dorcas gazelle** in Wadi Araba, the largest wild mammal you are likely to see in Jordan is a **red fox**, not to be confused with the ubiquitous feral dogs. Jordan's few **wolves**, **jackals** and **striped hyenas** keep well away from humans. Felines are represented by the wildcat and the **caracal**, both quite rare. Next largest is probably the **Cape hare**, which has evolved to become more rabbit-sized in the warm Arabian climate. But by far the most abundant are the varieties of **mice**, **gerbils**, **jerboas** and **jirds** – hamster-like rodents that make their home in desert burrows. A few **rock hyrax** – a burrowing rodent that's a close relative of the elephant, though just the size of a cat – remain in Dana and Rum. You may glimpse a **mongoose** scurrying along the banks of the River Zarqa.

The one-humped **dromedary**, the camel found in Arabia, has a history inextricably associated with that of the bedouin, and it has been a beast of burden as well as a source of milk and meat for many thousands of years. All Jordan's camels are domesticated, any vestiges of wild stock having vanished long ago.

Birds

Jordan has a lot to offer the birdwatcher: there are many resident bird species, some native to the Middle East, while others have European and even African affinities. Some species migrate vast distances to breed in Jordan, others winter here from points further north. Add to these the through-migration of literally millions of birds in spring and autumn – either dropping in for a rest or just flying over – and it is not difficult to imagine how well over four hundred species have been identified in a relatively small country, with additional species being added each year.

Although some locals do **hunt** under licence from the RSCN, it is a relief that Jordanian culture differs from that of much of the Mediterranean, where birds are slaughtered in their millions using nets, bird-lime and guns. Traditional Arab hunting with falcons (or even bringing falcons into the country) is also illegal, and it is regrettable that visiting hunters and falconers continue to have an impact by trapping migratory birds of prey in the eastern deserts.

To connect with local birders, consult ⓦjordanbirdwatch.com.

Native species

Jordan has eight endemic Near East species – **sooty falcon**, **sand partridge**, **Tristram's grackle**, **Hume's tawny owl**, **Arabian babbler**, **hooded wheatear**, **Arabian warbler** and **Syrian serin**; their breeding ranges include Jordan's southern rift valley, rift margins and Rum desert. Of these, the starling-like grackle, with its orange wing flash and evocative whistling call, is the most likely to be seen.

Jordan's **deserts** are home to many characteristic birds. These include the many larks and wheatears, each of which is superbly adapted to its chosen habitat, such as **Temminck's horned lark** in the flat, eastern deserts, **hoopoe lark** in sandier areas and **white-crowned black wheatear** in the rockiest mountains. Although Jordan's national bird, the **Sinai rosefinch**, is only the size of a small sparrow, the male's vivid pink plumage evokes Jordan's "rose-red city" of Petra and the red cliffs and desert sands of Wadi Rum. Sunbirds are the Old World equivalent of the hummingbird, and in Jordan the male **Palestine sunbirds** flash iridescent purple and blue as they hover – for example, by the borage flowers in the campsite at Dana. The basalt desert is also home to a unique population of **mourning wheatears**, whose virtually all-black colouring better matches its surroundings.

Migrant and breeding species

Jordan's position at the crossroads between Europe, Asia and Africa results in a cosmopolitan bird community. Species such as **black-eared wheatear**, **woodchat shrike**, **hoopoe** and **black-headed bunting** have affinities with southeastern Europe. Jordan is on the southern extreme of several species' ranges, such as **blue** and **great tits**. The **Cyprus warbler** and **Cyprus wheatear** also have restricted breeding ranges, and occur in Jordan on migration. The African influence is less obvious, though many migrant species retreat to Africa in winter. Isolated pairs of the **Verreaux's eagle**, more at home feeding on hyraxes in east and southern Africa, are also found in Jordan.

The country also hosts several species that are globally or regionally threatened, including **griffon vulture** and **lesser kestrel** (which breed in Jordan) and **imperial eagle**, **Levant sparrowhawk** and **corncrake** (which are found in Jordan on migration or in winter).

Spring migration sees millions of birds returning from wintering in Africa to their breeding grounds in eastern Europe and western Russia, via the rift valley. Migrant **warblers**, **pipits** and **wagtails**, for instance, use every available scrap of cover in which to shelter and refuel, whether on a traffic island in Aqaba, a sewage works, a clump of bushes in the open desert or in the meagre shade underneath a parked car. From late February through to May, vast numbers of **raptors**, including eagles, buzzards, kites, hawks and falcons, use traditional routes over Jordan's rift margins, typically seeking out a remote hillside to roost overnight before continuing. The head of the Gulf of Aqaba is a migration bottleneck, and north from here they peel off to get to their specific destinations. In contrast, the migration front is much broader in autumn, when birds are not averse to stopping off to eat or drink.

In wet winters, the inflow of the River Jordan into the Dead Sea gives rise to a layer of fresh water which persists for some time above the salt water before mixing; in these circumstances, it's possible to witness the rather incongruous sight of **ducks** swimming on the Dead Sea. **Herons** often gather at places like the Mujib delta to feed on the fish that die when they reach the saline water.

Insects

Insects are particularly obvious in the hotter seasons. **Butterflies** are colourful and easy to spot, though, as with birds, where you are will dictate whether you see European or Arabian species. Representatives of the swallowtails, blues, coppers, whites, marbled whites, fritillaries, painted ladies and tortoiseshells all occur, some migrating in spectacular fashion in their hundreds of millions. One of the rarest and most beautiful of the migrant butterflies is the large orange, black and white **plain tiger**, which is commoner in some springtimes than others.

It is easy to see all shapes and sizes of beetles in Jordan – around 1700 species have been identified in the country. The long-legged, black **pitted beetle** is one of the most obvious, as are **scarab beetles** and **dung beetles**. Large black **millipedes** are a feature of Jordan's ruins, such as Jerash.

Jordan has three species of **scorpion** (pale yellow and black in colour), all of which can inflict sufficiently painful stings to warrant a visit to hospital. Unless you are particularly lucky (or unlucky), you're unlikely even to see one, unless you make a habit of turning over stones. Solifugids, or **camel spiders**, are formidable hunters, but are not venomous despite having a strong bite.

Grasshoppers, moths, dragonflies, solitary wasps, cicadas, locusts and praying and ground mantises are other obvious insects, with the list practically endless. Bluebottle-like flies are a pest, especially in the hot Jordan Valley summer. Mosquitoes tend to be more of an irritation than a pest or health hazard.

Reptiles, amphibians and freshwater fish

No desert would be complete without **lizards**. Around fifty species have been identified in Jordan, the largest of which is the **desert monitor**, reaching 130cm in length. There are nocturnal **geckos** with their sticky toe-pads, hammer-headed **agamas**, smooth-skinned **skinks** and long-tongued **chameleons**. In Wadi Araba, you may glimpse the 65cm **spiny-tailed** (or **Dhab**) **lizard** – with its chunky, scaly tail – before it flees down its burrow. At Petra the dazzlingly turquoise male **Sinai agama** is one of the most eye-catching.

Snakes are much talked about and feared, but rarely seen. There are 24 species, including five that are venomous, particularly the **Palestine viper** and the **horned viper**.

Where there is water, **marsh frogs** occur in an extraordinary variety of colours and patterns, though it's easier to hear their croaking than it is to find them. There are a small number of freshwater **fish** in the River Jordan and its tributaries. On the mudflats of Azraq, millions of dormant eggs hatch when the area floods, giving rise to vast populations of the small **killifish**, which provide a valuable food source to migrating birds.

Red Sea life

The clear, warm waters of the **Gulf of Aqaba** host a fringing **coral reef**, the most northerly in the world, which is particularly rich in coral and fish species. The shallow reef flat lies closest to the shore, but this soon gives way at the reef crest to the steeply shelving reef slope. Elsewhere, in sandy bays and at the head of the gulf, sea-grass beds host colonies of **garden-eels**. Looking like blades of tall grass at first glance, these long sinuous creatures soon disappear into their burrows when approached.

Some one thousand species of fish occur off Aqaba, including the slimline **angel-** and **butterfly fishes**, coral-eating **parrot fishes**, predatory **groupers**, parasite-picking **cleaner wrasse**, shoals of red **jewelfish**, luminescent "**flashlight fish**", and the oddly shaped **box fishes**. Of the venomous fish, the **lionfish** is one of the most beautiful in the reef with its feather-like fins, whereas the **stonefish** is as ugly as they come, dull, bulky and covered in wart-like protrusions. Seeing a **turtle**, **shark** or **porpoise** off Aqaba requires a calm sea and a lot of luck; diving affords a better chance than watching from the shore or in a glass-bottomed boat.

Flora

For a country that is eighty percent semi-desert, Jordan's **plant** list is outstanding. Visit the higher ground in March or April, especially after a wet winter, and you will witness swathe after swathe of green, red and blue blanketing the hillsides.

On the downside, the desert landscape has changed dramatically following human introduction of sheep and goats, which has accelerated wind and rain erosion and desertification, putting tremendous pressure on the native wildlife. **Overgrazing** of the fragile semi-desert flora is ubiquitous, with the effects visible at Shaumari; compare the thick bushes inside the enclosures with the pitiful remnants outside. Many of Jordan's trees are grazed – the evergreen oaks, for example – and have responded by growing small, tough leaves at grazing height. Other trees are much hacked for firewood. Unusually heavy snow in the highlands can even snap mature trees under its weight.

Shrubs and herbaceous plants

Cyclamen are one of the earliest blooms, making their first appearance in late winter, followed by poppies, anemones and crocuses in March. Most of Jordan's 22 species of **orchid** flower in April in the highland forests of the northwest. April is also the optimum time to see the **black iris**, Jordan's national flower. One of at least four irises that are endemic to this region, it isn't actually jet-black, rather a very dark purple. The upland hillsides are often carpeted with low spiky bushes and aromatic herbs such as thyme and sagebrush (*Artemesia*). In summer, **thistles**, which grow in profusion and in great varieties, take on a new beauty as the six rainless months of fierce heat turn almost everything into a desiccated, buff-brown relic. However, some flowers do bloom at this time, for example the **sea-onion**, which carpets the flatter ground inside Petra and flowers in July; in autumn, **crocuses** add the only touch of colour when everything else is parched.

In early spring, if the ground warms up after winter rains, the **deserts** can become flushed with grasses and flowers, though this isn't on a dramatic scale and is often short-lived: if the sheep and goats don't eat the new arrivals, they soon succumb to the heat. White **broom** bushes line the wadis; a parasitic broomrape, the **cistanche**, is a spike of yellow in the semi-desert. **Desert melons**, found in the eastern desert, are poisonous and avoided by animals, and wild **capers** grow in the Jordan Valley.

Trees

Trees are largely restricted to the highlands, especially the Mediterranean regions of the northwest. Several species of evergreen and deciduous **oaks**, **Aleppo pines**, **carob** and **strawberry trees** can still be found in Jordan, along with fast-growing, introduced **eucalyptus**, **cypress** and **casuarinas**. **Almond** trees bloom early and **figs** grow wild near water sources in the hills. Ancient, gnarled **junipers** are characteristic of the Petra and Dana mountains. Natural **forest** remains only in parts of the northern highlands (mainly pines) and in the inaccessible mountain landscape around Dana and Petra (oak and juniper). Forests were undoubtedly more extensive in the past, and the operation of the Hejaz Railway is often cited as a major destroyer of woodlands, which were cut down to fuel the trains.

On lower ground, **acacias** give Wadi Araba a distinctly African look, while palms are found by freshwater springs such as Aqaba and Azraq. Wadi Butm, at Qusayr Amra, gets its name from the Arabic word for the ancient **Atlantic pistachio** trees that line the wadi. Although not nut-producing, they provide vital shelter for much resident and migrant wildlife. Similarly rare is the **funeral cypress**, of which a small number of reportedly native trees remain near Dana.

By Ian J. Andrews

Islam

It's almost impossible to make any sense out of the Middle East – or Jordan – without knowing something of Islam. Well over ninety percent of Jordanians are Muslim, and the practice and philosophy of Islam permeate most aspects of daily life. What follows is the briefest of backgrounds.

Islam was the third of the great monotheistic religions to originate in the Middle East, and places itself firmly in the tradition begun by Judaism and Christianity. Abraham is seen as the first Muslim, and Islam itself is defined as a reaffirmation, correction and consummation of the earlier faiths.

Islam was propagated in the seventh century AD by a merchant named **Muhammad** from the city of Mecca, in the Hejaz region of what is now Saudi Arabia. Muhammad is seen as the last of a series of prophets sent by God to earth; among earlier prophets were Abraham, Noah, Moses, Solomon, John the Baptist and Jesus, whose messages, for whatever reason, had been lost or corrupted over the centuries. Muhammad was sent to revive and refine the words of past prophets.

The basic principles of Islam are that there is one God (in Arabic, Allah), and he must be worshipped; and that Muhammad is his final prophet. The main sources of the religion are the Quran (or Koran) – the revelation Muhammad received during his lifetime – and Muhammad's own actions.

The Quran

Muslims regard the **Quran** (literally, "recitation") to be the word of God, as revealed by the angel Jibril (Gabriel) to Muhammad from about 610 AD, when Muhammad was about 40, until his death in 632. There is a noticeable difference in the style of the Quran between the early portions – which have the ring of soothsaying about them, arising from Muhammad's early role as mystic – and the later portions, which go into detail about the conduct of Muslim life, as befits Muhammad's status as the leader of a large group of followers.

The principal emphasis of the Quran is on the **indivisibility of God**. Human duty is to demonstrate gratitude to God by obedience and worship – *islam* itself means "submission" – for he will judge the world on the Day of Resurrection. Islamic concepts of heaven, as reward, and hell, as punishment, are close to Christian ideas, although the way they are described in the Quran is very physical, even earthy. God sent the prophets to humankind in order to provide the guidance necessary to attain eternal reward.

THE AMMAN MESSAGE

In 2004, King Abdullah published the **Amman Message**, a communiqué drawn up with Muslim authorities from around the world to declare – as its summary states – "what Islam is and what it is not, and what actions represent it and what actions do not. Its goal [is] to clarify to the modern world the true nature of Islam and the nature of true Islam." The message specifically rejects extremism as being a deviation from Islamic belief and the accompanying press release talks of Abdullah's "determination to ward off Muslim image-tarnishing, marginalization and isolation".

A subsequent **convention** of two hundred Muslim scholars from over fifty countries issued a three-point declaration confirming the Amman Message. This recognized diversity of opinion within Islam, prohibited the practice (common among extremists) of declaring other Muslims as apostates and clarified who (and who may not) issue religious edicts, or fatwas.

THE ISLAMIC CALENDAR

The **Islamic calendar** is dated from sunset on July 15, 622 AD, the start of the *hijra* (migration) of the Prophet Muhammad from Mecca to the city of Medina; the Western (Gregorian) year 2016 AD mostly coincides with the Islamic year 1437 (AH 1437). Whereas the Western calendar is solar, the Islamic one (like the Jewish) is lunar, and thus one Muslim year contains slightly over 354 days. The effect of this is that Muslim religious festivals move in a slow cycle backwards through the seasons, each one arriving about eleven days earlier, according to the western calendar, than it did the previous year. To convert from an Islamic year to a western one, consult an online calendar, such as the one at ⓦislamicfinder.org.

The names of the Islamic **months** are: Muharram, Safar, Rabia Awwal, Rabia Thaani, Jumada Awwal, Jumada Thaani, Rajab, Shaaban, Ramadan, Shawwal, Dhul Qida and Dhul Hijja. All have either 29 or 30 days, with the new month declared only when the crescent moon has been sighted.

The Quran is divided into 114 chapters, or *suras*. The first *sura*, known as Al-Fatiha, is a prayer which Muslims recite frequently. It begins *Bismillah il-rahman il-rahim* ("In the name of God, the Compassionate, the Merciful") and continues: "Praise be to God, Lord of the Worlds, the Compassionate, the Merciful, King of the Day of Judgement. We worship you and seek your aid. Guide us on the straight path, the path of those on whom you have bestowed your Grace, not the path of those who incur your anger nor of those who go astray." After this, the *suras* are in approximate order of length, starting with the longest and ending with the shortest; many are patched together from passages revealed to Muhammad at different periods of his life.

According to traditional Islamic belief, the Quran is the word of God which has existed forever. It is unique, and is the miracle which Muhammad presented to the world to prove his prophethood. However, not everything the Quran reveals is comprehensible; the book itself declares that it contains "clear" verses and "obscure" verses. On occasions, it appears to contradict itself. As a result, an elaborate literature of **interpretation** of the Quran developed. Early specialists put forward the idea that some revelations were made for a particular place or time and were cancelled out by later revelations.

The Hadith

The Quran provided a basic framework for the practices and beliefs necessary for Muslims, but it didn't go into much specific detail: of 6616 verses, only eighty concern issues of conduct. For precise guidance, Muslims also look to the example and habitual practice *sunna* of the Prophet Muhammad himself, as well as his words and actions. These were remembered by those who had known him, and transmitted in the form of reports, **hadith**, handed down within the Muslim community – *hadith* is generally translated into English as "**traditions**".

Although Muhammad himself didn't claim any infallibility outside revealing the Quran, Muslims around him seem to have collected these *hadith* from a very early time. Scholars soon began categorizing them by subject. It was obvious, though, that many of the reports of what the Prophet said or did weren't authentic; tales wove their way into his legend, and some of those who transmitted reports of his doings undoubtedly invented or exaggerated them. Scholars therefore developed a science of *hadith* criticism, requiring both specific content of what the Prophet is supposed to have said or done, and, more importantly, a traceable chain of transmission back to the Companion of the Prophet who had originally seen or heard it. Biographical dictionaries – to ascertain just how reliable a transmitter was – rapidly became a distinctive feature of Arabic literature. Two particularly refined collections of *hadith* from the late ninth century are generally held to have an authority second only to that of the Quran.

The pillars of Islam

Drawn both from the Quran and the *hadith*, there are five basic religious duties every Muslim must perform.

Statement of faith

Firstly, and most simply, is the **statement of faith** (*shahada*): "I testify that there is no god but God, and that Muhammad is the Messenger of God." If you say this with sincerity, you become a Muslim.

Prayer

A Sunni Muslim must perform formal **prayer** (*salat*) five times a day. Since the day begins at sunset, the five times are sunset (*maghrib*), evening (*isha*), dawn (*fajr*), midday (*duhr*) and afternoon (*asr*), the exact times set in advance by the religious authorities. Before performing the *salat*, a Sunni Muslim must be in a state of **ritual purity**, achieved by rinsing out the mouth, sniffing water into the nostrils, washing the face, head, ears, back of the neck, feet, and lastly the hands and forearms. All mosques, big or small, have ablutions fountains adjacent for worshippers to cleanse themselves.

The faithful are summoned to prayer by the **muezzin**; in previous centuries, he would climb the minaret of the mosque and call by shouting, but almost everywhere in Jordan this has now been overtaken either by a taped call to prayer or by amplification. Nonetheless, the sound of the *adhan* (call to prayer) has a captivating beauty all its own, especially down in the echoing valleys of Amman when dozens of mosques are calling simultaneously, repeating in long, melodious strings: "God is most great! (*Allahu akbar!*) I testify that there is no god but God. (*Ashhadu an la ilaha illallah.*) I testify that Muhammad is the Messenger of God. (*Ashhadu anna Muhammadan rasulullah.*) Come to prayer! (*Hayya alas-salah!*) Come to salvation! (*Hayya alal-falah!*) God is most great! (*Allahu akbar!*)" The dawn call has another phrase added: "Prayer is better than sleep."

Once worshippers have assembled in the mosque, another call to prayer is given. Prayers are led by an **imam**, and are performed in a **ritualized cycle** facing towards Mecca without shoes on: standing with hands slightly raised, bowing, prostrating, sitting on one's haunches, and prostrating again. During the cycle, worshippers recite verses of the Quran, particularly the opening *sura*. Repetition of the cycles is completed by everyone turning and wishing peace on each other.

One way in which Islam differs from Christianity and Judaism is that it has **no priests**. The *imam* who leads the prayers has no special qualification to do so, other than enough knowledge of the Quran to enable him to recite, or perhaps some standing in the local community. Anyone may lead prayers, and there is no claim to special religious knowledge or holiness marking out an *imam* from any other Muslim.

The midday prayer on Fridays is a special congregational prayer, and Muslims are expected to attend a large mosque of assembly, where a religious or political **sermon** is also given (and generally broadcast on loudspeakers). The sermon must include a mention of the legitimate ruler – in fact, this is one of the traditional ways for a population to bestow legitimacy on a ruler. If the mosque is controlled by the government, the sermon is often used to endorse government policy; if it is independent, the Friday sermon can be used as a means to incite rebellion among the faithful. This is part of the reason why many political demonstrations in the Muslim world begin from the mosque after the midday prayer on a Friday.

Although it's preferable for men to pray together in the mosque, it's not obligatory, and you'll see many men throughout Jordan instead laying down a small **prayer mat** in their shops, or by the side of the road, to mark out a space for them to pray alone. **Women** almost always pray at home. Non-Muslims are permitted to enter mosques in Jordan, but only at the discretion of the officials of that particular mosque; however, you must always be dressed suitably modestly. If you're not praying, you don't have to go through any ritual ablutions.

VISITING MOSQUES

There are no laws prohibiting non-Muslims from entering **mosques** in Jordan. If you want to go into one, avoid prayer times, and always ask permission from the mosque guardian, *imam* or local people first; if no one is about, don't just float in regardless. Take off your shoes at the door – there's generally a shin-high threshold to remind you – and, of course, wear clothing which covers your legs, upper arms and chest: no shorts, no vest-tops, no cleavage, and so on. Always ask before taking any photos.

That said, the vast majority of mosques around the country are simple working buildings, built plainly, without adornment, and with nothing much to see outside or in. Aside from the historic **Husseini Mosque** in Downtown Amman, the only conceivable exceptions are the capital's two showpiece mosques – the blue-domed **King Abdullah I Mosque** in Abdali and the large **King Hussein Bin Talal Mosque** in Dabouq. The former, built in the 1980s, is less of an architectural draw than the latter, inaugurated in 2006 amid expansive parkland on the western outskirts, clad in local limestone and designed around shaded halls and cloisters in serene white and brown stone.

A very common sight in Jordan is to see men holding strings of "worry beads", passing them rhythmically through their fingers in an almost unconscious action as they walk or sit quietly. The beads – *tasbih* or *subhah* – are **prayer beads**, and they always come in strings of 33 or 99, representing the 99 revealed names of God. As one passes through the fingers, the prayer is *subhanallah* ("Glory to God"); the next one is *al-hamdulillah* ("Thanks be to God"), the next *Allahu akbar* ("God is most great"), these three being repeated in a mantra until the cycle of 99 has been completed.

Alms

All Muslims who are able to do so should pay one-fortieth of their own wealth for purposes laid down in the Quran: for the poor, for those whose hearts need to be reconciled, for the freeing of slaves, those who are burdened with debts, for travellers, for the cause of God, and so on. This payment of **alms** is called *zakat*, literally "purification", and is primarily regarded as an act of worship: the recipients are less important than the giving, which is always done anonymously.

Fasting in the month of Ramadan

Ramadan is the ninth month of the Muslim year, and was the time at which Muhammad received his first revelation; it's a holy month, during which all Muslims must **fast** from dawn to sunset each day. All forms of consumption are forbidden during daylight hours, including eating, drinking and smoking, and any form of sexual contact. However, this is only the outward show of what is required: one *hadith* says, "There are many who fast all day and pray all night, but they gain nothing but hunger and sleeplessness." Ramadan is a time of spiritual cleansing.

As the Muslim calendar is lunar, Ramadan doesn't fall in a specific season each year: summer Ramadans in the Middle East, when the days are fourteen or fifteen hours long and the heat draining, can be particularly taxing, but Ramadan is an intense month at any time of year. Families get up together before dawn for a quick breakfast (many people then go back to bed for another few hours' sleep). During the day, shops, offices and public services all operate limited hours. As the afternoon draws on, people hurry home to be with their families for **iftar**, the fast-breaking meal eaten at sunset (often confusingly referred to as "breakfast"). After dark, a hectic round of socializing over large meals often brings distant relatives together for the only time in the year. The month ends with a three-day festival, **Eid al-Fitr**, also a time for family get-togethers.

Pilgrimage

Mecca was a sacred place long before the time of Muhammad, its central feature the **Kaaba**, a 15m-high stone cube inset with a smaller, holy black stone. Islam incorporated both the Kaaba and a set of rituals involved with pagan worship at Mecca into its own set of rituals around the hajj, or **pilgrimage**, which takes place in the twelfth month, Dhul Hijja. (A lesser pilgrimage, known as the *umrah*, can be undertaken at any time of year.) Every Muslim who has the means must make the pilgrimage to Mecca at least once in his lifetime. These days, over two million pilgrims arrive each year from all over the world, the whole operation coordinated by the Saudi Ministry of Hajj.

The Kaaba, now in the central precinct of the vast Grand Mosque at Mecca, is held to have been built by Abraham and his son Ishmael on the ruins of a shrine built by Adam, the first human. Male pilgrims wear only two lengths of plain, unsewn cotton cloth (symbolizing the equality of all before God); women veil their hair but must leave their faces uncovered, to express confidence and an atmosphere of purity. Everybody circumambulates the Kaaba seven times, emulating the angels who circle the throne of God, and kisses the black stone if they can. They go to the Well of Zamzam, discovered by Ishmael, and run between two small hills, commemorating the frantic running in search of water by Hagar – Abraham's concubine and Ishmael's mother – after Abraham had left them both in the desert. One day is spent on the arid Plain of Arafat, listening to sermons, praying and standing on the Mount of Mercy. All the pilgrims go to Mina, a suburb of Mecca, and hurl stones at three pillars, symbolically stoning the Devil. The hajj ends with the four-day festival of **Eid al-Adha**, celebrated throughout the Islamic world, when all who are able slaughter a sheep to commemorate Abraham's sacrifice – he was about to kill his son but God stopped him and provided a ram instead (Jews and Christians hold that the victim was to have been Isaac, but Muslims believe it was Ishmael).

There are often parties and celebrations to welcome home those who have returned from the hajj, and in Jordan you'll sometimes see murals painted by pilgrims on the outside walls of their houses, depicting the mosque at Mecca (with the Islamic symbol of the crescent often prominent), the Kaaba and other details of what they saw and experienced on their journey.

The bedouin today

This article, by Jordan-based scholar Dr Géraldine Chatelard, is an edited version of her introduction to Bédouins Aujourd'hui en Jordanie, *an outstanding book of photos by Nabil Boutros that was published by Amman's Institut Français (W ifjordan.com) in 2008. The English translation is by Isabelle Ruben.*

For centuries the **bedouin** have been in transition between a nomadic life in the arid margins and a settled, urban life. Transition and mobility are difficult notions for sedentary people to grasp, for they defy categorization. The sedentary outlook through which the world is normally perceived is so dominant that the bedouin themselves sometimes have doubts about what makes them distinctive: is it their nomadic lifestyle, their skill as herders in an arid environment, their tribal organization, or their values and morality? These questions are a reflection of the diversity of bedouin society, which is neither isolated nor separated but, rather, is dynamic and eager to harness the benefits of the modern world while preserving its values of solidarity, pride and honour.

Many of today's bedouin have transformed their spatial mobility into **social mobility**, a process which, in Jordan, began in the 1930s. First was recruitment into the armed forces and the government, then came widespread schooling. Bedouin families developed agriculture, mostly abandoning camel husbandry in favour of sheep and goats. They took advantage of modern technology – motor vehicles (particularly the water tankers that made them less dependent on natural constraints) and now mobile phones. The nomads who formerly moved seasonally across several hundred kilometres became transhumant herders living in tents for only part of the year, or sometimes not leaving their villages at all and entrusting their herds to shepherds. At the same time, a new generation has been settling in the towns, completing higher education and taking up professional careers while still maintaining strong links with their original villages and tribes – a process which has ensured the preservation of bedouin values and identity in an urban setting.

Use of space

The **bedouin tent** (known as *beit ash-sha'ar*, meaning "house of hair") is a mobile shelter with internal spaces that can be rearranged using movable partitions: transitions from exterior to interior, sunlight to shade, heat to cool are adjustable according to need. There is always a clear division between the public and private sides of the tent, usually in the form of a partition – decorated on the public side, backed by furniture (a chest, mattresses, bed coverings) on the private side.

Domestic tents are erected and maintained by the **women** of the family, or under their supervision. They make the tent from goat hair and sheep's wool, weaving strips on a horizontal loom which they then sew together. They also repair the tent regularly. In remote areas of Wadi Araba or the Hisma, single or widowed men who live alone will often choose a rock shelter or cave: a tent has little meaning without a female presence.

The symbolic function of the tent, over and above its practical aspect, is that of a space where guests can enjoy the **hospitality** and protection of the master of the house, expressed by the preparation and ritualized serving of Arabic coffee around the central hearth of the public side. This tradition is anchored in bedouin values: even when the tent has completely lost its domestic function and is erected alongside a house, it still represents the continuation of those values and thus of bedouin identity.

The domestic tent is adapted to the social norms that regulate relations between men and women and which allow **family honour** to be preserved. However, there are no areas that are reserved exclusively for either sex. Movement between the tent's public and private spaces depends on whether only close family, or outsiders, are present. The basic rule is that the women leave the reception area when guests are present who are not close family members. However, the matriarch of the family will always make it her duty to receive visitors in the reception area if her husband is absent. In any case, the women can listen to conversation from the private side of the tent and take a peek through the weave of the partition – a common practice when marriage negotiations are being discussed between men.

Associations with the tent remain strong, even in **houses** (which most bedouin own), where the reception area – clearly separated from family space – is large and has a fireplace to serve as a hearth as well as thick curtains recalling the tent's partitions. The house's interior is often extended outside, with a tent erected nearby.

Today, the poorest bedouin live on the outskirts of towns, or in the most arid and rocky zones overlooking the Dead Sea, the Jordan Valley and the Wadi Araba. These last real nomads can be recognized by their tents of sewn sack-cloth, which is cheaper than woven goat hair.

Figures of authority

Photographs of **figures of authority** are often on display in reception tents and salons, cars and offices. Their prominence is a way of demonstrating to whom the owner acknowledges authority – and, equally, from whom the owner's authority originates. Respect and authority are intimately linked values, above all with regard to the respect universally shown to Islam.

Respect for authority is one of the fundamentals of bedouin society, and of Arab society in general. The head of the family is required to make decisions concerning his wife and children, yet bedouin families are only moderately patriarchal: wives, particularly as they get older, take active part in family decisions. Bedouin men recognize the importance of **female responsibility** in a traditional lifestyle and many encourage their daughters in academic study and professional careers. Nevertheless, the father of the family always retains the right of absolute veto on personal choices. Grandfather's photo on display reminds everyone of the respect due to him, but also shows that his son – now the head of the family – is authorized to exercise domestic authority in his place.

At a higher social level, heads of families recognize the authority of a man to whom they are all related. This individual – generally given the title "**sheikh**" – has to represent his kinship group amongst other groups (for example, when there are conflicts to resolve) or to outside institutions. He is a mediator, and his authority does not replace that of the father of the family, who remains master of his own decisions. Adherence by family heads to collective action is not a foregone conclusion.

Codes of honour

A sense of **honour** is an essential masculine quality for the bedouin, to the extent that if a man loses his honour, he also loses his right to participate fully in bedouin society. This explains the efforts that every man makes to maintain and increase his honour, and that of his tribe. The welcome of guests has resisted changes in lifestyle: a man of honour must be **generous** – excessively so if he can afford it.

He must also be generous with his time – listening to the complaints of members of the tribe and others and helping them get a job or a place at university, assisting with administrative dealings, mediating between individuals or families in conflict. Every bedouin man must respond to a request for assistance even if he does not have the means to do so. This is why bedouin are sometimes more apt to "say" than to "do", which upsets only those who don't understand their code of honour.

The behaviour of **women** is also an essential part of family and tribal honour: virtue, high morals and respect for the rules of separation between men and women are obligatory. Following these rules does not imply meekness or lack of character. Many strong female personalities in bedouin society enjoy broad respect because they follow the code of honour unfailingly.

Transmissions

Visit a bedouin village and you might have the impression that **children** have free rein, with very few constraints placed on them. In fact, they are living an education in which they learn limits for themselves and make the direct experience of pain and danger – though within a framework: if the parents are absent, another member of the community is almost certainly nearby and can exercise authority. It is a tough education with no pampering, where from their earliest years children become accustomed to the realities that will be their adult lives, including familiarity with livestock and the responsibilities of pastoral and domestic work.

Children used to be educated by spending time with adults. Nowadays, traditional methods of transference of knowledge and behaviour compete with widespread **schooling**. Not many bedouin families choose a transhumant life for their children when they can send them to school instead. Even the poorest families time their seasonal movements to match the school calendar. It is not unusual to meet young women or men at university whose illiterate parents still live in a tent.

Yet schooling creates a distancing from **traditional knowledge**. Tribal history and the immensely rich oral literature of the bedouin that has been transmitted for generations have lost out to new media. Knowledge of animal husbandry, of herbal remedies for both humans and animals, of weaving techniques, of effective management of water resources are not being passed on. While people in wealthy, urbanized countries are rediscovering the importance of traditional knowledge, entire swathes of bedouin culture and tradition are disappearing largely unregarded. The staged bedouin encounters offered by tour operators in the theme park that Wadi Rum has become are a pale reflection of genuine bedouin culture.

There is no need to mourn the loss of a difficult way of life (which most of those still living it aspire to leave). But one can reflect, with the bedouin themselves, on ways of validating and preserving their knowledge and culture.

By Dr Géraldine Chatelard

Books

It can be difficult to find books focused on Jordan. Millions of words have been written about Palestine, Israel, Lebanon, Egypt and Syria, but Jordan is all too often relegated to mentions in passing. If you fancy going direct to specialist English-language publishers, start with Al-Saqi (ⓦsaqibooks.co.uk), Garnet/Ithaca (ⓦithacapress.co.uk), Interlink (ⓦinterlinkbooks.com), Stacey International (ⓦstacey-international.co.uk) and I.B. Tauris (ⓦibtauris.com). The selection below is a personal one, and necessarily omits much.

LITERATURE

★ **Maan Abu Taleb** *All The Battles*. A strikingly original novel set within the world of a run-down boxing club in Amman that explores ideas and issues of transformation and male identity within Arab culture.

Mahmoud Darwish *Memory for Forgetfulness: August, Beirut, 1982*. Startling prose poems, written as the Israeli army was laying siege to the city. Darwish (1942–2008) was the Arab world's best-loved modern poet; this is a good way into his extraordinarily visceral and moving style.

★ **Fadia Faqir** *Pillars of Salt*, *My Name is Salma* and *Willow Trees Don't Weep*. This Jordanian-British writer's 1996 lyrical novel *Pillars of Salt* is set in mandate-period Jordan. Two women, one from the city, the other from a bedouin tribe, resist domination by their male relatives. *My Name is Salma* (2007) focuses on a young asylum-seeker in England who is running from her vengeful family. It's a fine evocation of an outsider's view of British society. *Willow Trees Don't Weep* (2014) is a story of anger and forgiveness as a woman searches for her father, absent since she was 4. Fluid writing draws out themes of radicalization amid the contradictions of family love.

★ **Malu Halasa** *Mother of All Pigs*. Witty and amusing novel set in a small Jordanian border town centred on a matriarchal family and what happens when its unusual father-figure – the only pig butcher in the Middle East – comes face to face with his uncomfortable past.

Ghassan Kanafani *Men in the Sun*. Perhaps the best-known modern Arabic short story, about three men journeying across the desert from Amman to Kuwait. Kanafani was a Palestinian activist; his tender stories are superbly plotted.

T.E. Lawrence *Seven Pillars of Wisdom*. Doorstop classic, the only firsthand account of the Arab Revolt of 1917–18, which swept across Jordanian territory. It can be a bit of a slog, with Lawrence's day-by-day recounting of battles and intrigues wearing thin, despite the beauty of the language.

Ibtihal Mahmood & Alexander Haddad (eds) *Snow in Amman*. A slender anthology of eleven contemporary short stories by Jordanian writers, shining an unexpected light on issues of society and feminism in Jordan.

★ **Amjad Nasser** *Petra: the Concealed Rose*. An extended poem by this celebrated Jordanian writer, evoking the oddly diffident splendour of Petra, discussing meanings behind the ancient city's nineteenth-century rediscovery and contemporary ambience. Bring it with you when you visit.

Fadi Zaghmout *The Bride of Amman*. A controversial Arabic bestseller, now in English translation. Zaghmout weaves stories of love, sex, tradition and taboos into an engaging tale of intersecting lives in contemporary Amman.

HISTORY

★ **Raouf Sa'd Abujaber & Felicity Cobbing** *Beyond the River: Ottoman Transjordan in Original Photographs*. An absorbing collection of archive images, including the first-ever photos of Petra (dated 1852), interspersed with knowledgeable accounts of Victorian exploration.

★ **Amin Maalouf** *The Crusades through Arab Eyes*. Fascinating take on all the noble stories of valiant crusading normally touted in the West. Drawing on the extensive chronicles kept by Arab historians at the time, Maalouf paints a picture of a civilized Arab society suddenly having to face the violent onslaught of a bunch of European barbarians. Superbly readable.

Suleiman Mousa *T.E. Lawrence: An Arab View*. Unique, iconoclastic account by this leading Jordanian historian of the events surrounding Lawrence and the Great Arab Revolt, sourced from local records and interviews with survivors. Published 1960 in Arabic; English translation 1966.

James Nicholson *The Hejaz Railway*. Lavish tome devoted to the history of the famous Ottoman-built Damascus–Medina railway. Filled with fascinating photographs, detailed maps and blow-by-blow accounts of the railway's operation and eventual demise.

Avi Shlaim *Lion of Jordan: the Life of King Hussein in War and Peace*. Wide-ranging and broadly sympathetic biography by this eminent Oxford historian.

Adaia and Abraham Shumsky *A Bridge across the Jordan*. Engaging tale based on personal memoirs of the friendship that developed between a Jewish master

JORDANIAN FILM

Film is in its infancy in Jordan. After the gangster thriller-cum-tourist documentary *Struggle in Jerash* (1957), literally fifty years went past with virtually nothing being produced locally, though Jordan remained popular as an epic location for foreign crews shooting everything from *Lawrence of Arabia* (1962) and *Indiana Jones and the Last Crusade* (1989) to *The Hurt Locker* (2008) and *The Martian* (2015).

Captain Abu Raed (see below) broke the local drought in 2007. Its global success spurred new creativity. Jordan's film industry, championed by the **Royal Film Commission** (⊕film.jo), is starting to gain widespread recognition.

Nadine Toukan, an independent producer who is one of Jordan's most enthusiastic supporter of creativity in film, offers her (alphabetical) list of must-sees:

Captain Abu Raed (2007; 102min) by Amin Matalqa. A grey-haired janitor at Amman airport finds a captain's hat in the trash and gets pulled into the lives of children in his poor neighbourhood as he weaves imaginary stories to ease the harsh reality of their daily existence.
Caution! Comment Ahead (2006; 35min) by Dalia Al Kury. Deft short highlighting the social, psychological and moral complexities that combine to normalize the verbal harassment of women on the streets of Amman.
Recycle (2007; 78min) by Mahmoud Al Massad. An ordinary man living in Jordan's second city, Zarqa, struggles to support his family and define his identity amid political and social tension.
Theeb (2014; 100min) by Naji Abu Nowar. A brilliantly dramatic evocation of Wadi Rum anchors this intimate study of character: a young boy pursues an English army officer through the desert as the violence of World War I starts to impinge on traditional ways of life.
Torfa, Last of the Nomadic Bedouins (2007; 54min) by Majida Kabariti. Portrait of a seasoned seminomadic bedouin woman from the south of Jordan who chooses a life of freedom over the temptations of modern society.
When Monaliza Smiled (2012; 90min) by Fadi G. Haddad. Grumpy Jordanian Monaliza gets a job in a dusty government office, where she meets the jolly Egyptian tea guy, Hamdi. Their journey of transformation leads across Amman, among a quirky cast of characters and stereotypical attitudes.

carpenter from Jerusalem and Emir Abdullah of Transjordan, when the former was invited to Amman in 1937 to work at the Royal Palace.
★ **Jane Taylor** *Petra and the Lost Kingdom of the Nabataeans*. An infectiously enthusiastic evocation of the history of Petra and wider Nabatean society, liberally scattered throughout with the author's beautiful photographs. This is a work as appealing intellectually as visually, penetrating the myths surrounding the Nabateans with clarity and providing unparalleled perspective for a visit to their capital.

LOCAL INSIGHT

★ **Marguerite van Geldermalsen** *Married to a Bedouin*. Wonderful insight into bedouin life by this remarkable New Zealander, who visited Petra on holiday in 1978, fell in love with a local souvenir-seller, and stayed to marry him and raise a family. Her fascinating tales of learning how to adjust to bedouin society and how she built the life she wanted are told with humour and compassion.
Amal Ghandour *About This Man Called Ali: the purple life of an Arab artist*. Intimate biography of Ali Al Jabri, a prominent Syrian-Jordanian artist whose life ended in violent circumstances in 2002, evoking one man's struggle within changing attitudes towards society, sexuality and culture.
★ **Leon McCarron** *The Land Beyond*. Entertaining account of a thousand-mile walk across the Middle East from Jerusalem to Mount Sinai by this explorer/adventurer, including poignant accounts of extraordinary encounters in back-country Jordan.
Abd al-Rahman Munif *Story of a City: A Childhood in Amman*. Tales of life in Amman in the 1940s, recalling the city passing from a period of bucolic innocence through World War II and the tragic loss of Palestine, padded out with digressions and family stories.
HRH Princess Alia Al Hussein & Peter Upton *Royal Heritage: the Story of Jordan's Arab Horses*. A beautifully illustrated account of the role played by Arab horses in Jordan's modern history.
Jonathan Raban *Arabia*. Engaging tales of the Gulf States, Yemen, Egypt and Jordan in 1978 at the height of oil wealth, and before the Lebanese civil war and attempts at peace with Israel had had much impact. Much more than mere travelogue, the book is perceptive and sympathetic, still relevant today.
Isabelle Ruben & Jane Taylor *Beyond the Jordan*. This large-format book showcases the wealth of Christian history to be found in modern Jordan, with detailed accounts of biblical events – including the baptism of Jesus Christ – and outstanding photography.
Ann Hutchison Sawalha *Through the Palace Keyhole*. A

lively memoir that tells the story of the family built after Ann, from Detroit, met Sami Sawalha, from Jordan, in 1956. They married and moved to Jordan, where Ann still lives. She reflects on more than fifty years in the Sawalha family business: hotels.

★ **Rana F. Sweis** *Voices of Jordan*. An intimate portrait of the country, as this celebrated journalist talks in detail to ordinary Jordanians – a cartoonist, a refugee, a parliamentarian, a jihadi – with their everyday struggles bringing new insight to the reality of life at a time of upheaval.

★ **Jane Taylor** *Jordan: Images from the Air*. Beautiful, large-format book of aerial photographs of Jordan, taken in all seasons and at numerous destinations. The images are stunning, given added force by the authoritative accompanying text.

ISLAM

★ **Karen Armstrong** *The Battle for God*. Sympathetic investigation of fundamentalism in Judaism, Christianity and Islam, explaining motivations and mindsets. Armstrong's other works, all similarly brilliant, include *A History of God*, *A History of Jerusalem* and *Islam: A Short History*.

John L. Esposito *Islam: The Straight Path*. Intelligent handbook to what Islam means, where it came from and where it seems to be going.

★ **Barnaby Rogerson** *The Prophet Muhammad: A Biography*. Engrossing retelling of the life of the Prophet by this brilliant writer.

SPECIALIST GUIDES

Ian J. Andrews The *Birds of the Hashemite Kingdom of Jordan* (o/p). Ornithological field guide privately published by a longtime leader of birdwatching tours.

Chris Grant & Gregory Maassen *Hiking in Jordan*. Encyclopedic hiking guide, with massively detailed notes, maps and a website – ⓦ hiking-in-jordan.com – that includes GPS data, itinerary planners and day-trip ideas.

★ **Tony Howard** *Treks and Climbs in Wadi Rum, Jordan*. Written by a professional climber with years of experience in Rum, and containing detailed rock-face plans and precise descriptions of equipment-assisted ascents, this is an invaluable full-length guide for dedicated pros.

★ **Jarir Maani** *Field Guide to Jordan*. Superb full-colour pocket-sized field guide to Jordan's natural environment, with detailed notes – and outstanding photographs – of every flower, bird, animal and insect listed. Also with useful sections on history, geology and archeology. Available in Jordan and at ⓦ maani.us/jordan. Alternatively, download the smartphone app.

Isabelle Ruben *Field Guide to the Plants and Animals of Petra*. Full-colour field guide to the mammals, birds, reptiles and insects to be seen at Petra, with detailed notes on each and informative text on the medicinal uses of plants, herbs and flowers. Available at ⓦ petranationaltrust.org.

★ **Di Taylor and Tony Howard** *Jordan: Walks, Treks, Caves, Climbs and Canyons*. Published in the US as *Walking in Jordan*. Outstanding selection of more than a hundred walking routes across the country. Taylor and Howard have been climbing and trekking in Jordan since 1984: this is an invaluable companion if you're planning to explore independently. The same authors' *Walks, Treks, Climbs & Caves in Al Ayoun Jordan* is a lovely handbook to trails through the hilly green forests of the north, sensitively written and packed with insight.

★ **Jane Taylor** *Petra*. Beautiful work on the history and sites of Petra, with some engaging tales and magnificent photos. Jane Taylor is a longtime resident of Jordan and writes with grace and authority.

CUISINE

Anissa Helou *Feast: Food of the Islamic World*. Superb collection of recipes from the Middle East and beyond, described and contextualized with cultural insights by one of the world's leading authorities.

★ **Cecil Hourani** *Jordan – The Land and the Table*. Slim volume that is unique for examining the centrality of food to the different elements within Jordanian society, including (unusually) the Armenians, Chechens and Circassians. Fascinating recipes for rarely seen dishes are interspersed with insightful accounts of culture and agriculture. If you can't find it online, try in Amman at Al-Aydi craft shop.

Claudia Roden *A New Book of Middle Eastern Food*. Food as cultural history; invaluable for getting a handle on the importance of food in Arab and Middle Eastern societies.

Arabic

Many people in Jordan are fluent in English, and many more have a working knowledge. However, plain communication isn't necessarily the only consideration. Jordanian culture is deeply rooted in the verbal complexities of the Arabic language, and being able to exchange pleasantries in Arabic, or offer the appropriate response to an Arabic greeting, will endear you to people more than anything else. The most halting *"assalaamu alaykoom"* is likely to provoke beams of joy and cries of "You speak Arabic better than I do!"

Arabic is phenomenally hard for an English-speaker to learn. There are virtually no familiar points of contact between the two languages: the script is written in cursive from **right to left**; there's a host of often guttural sounds which take much vocal contortion to master; and the **grammar**, founded on utterly different principles from English, is proclaimed as one of the most pedantic in the world.

Briefly, the three forms of Arabic are:

Classical – the language of the Quran, with many words and forms which are now obsolete.
Modern Standard (*fuss-ha*) – the written language of books and newspapers, and the Arabic spoken in news broadcasts and on formal occasions. Identical throughout the Arab world and understandable from Morocco to Oman. Although most people can read *fuss-ha*, nobody uses it in everyday life and few ordinary people can speak it.
Colloquial (*aamayya*) – umbrella term for the many dialects of spoken Arabic. In Jordan, as in all other Arabic-speaking countries, the colloquial language has no proper written form. Pronunciation varies from district to district and, furthermore, the vocabulary and verb forms of Jordanian Arabic can be markedly different from the related Palestinian, Syrian and Iraqi dialects. Further afield, the Arabic spoken in Morocco is a foreign language to Jordanians, who find it more or less incomprehensible. Egyptian Arabic is a lingua franca, understandable throughout the Arab world because of the prevalence of movies and TV soap operas emanating from Cairo.

One of the few **phrasebooks** that covers Jordanian Arabic is *How to Speak Arabic in Jordan* by Eszter Papai – or you could plump for the excellent **teach-yourself course** *Colloquial Arabic (Levantine)* by Leslie McLoughlin. *Diwan Baladna* (ⓦdiwanbaladna. com) is a course in Arabic language and culture developed in Jordan, with books available online and in Amman. The clearest introduction to writing and **reading Arabic script** is *The Arabic Alphabet* by Nicholas Awde and Putros Samano, a slim volume that is invaluable for getting a handle on how the language works.

Pronunciation

Throughout this book, Arabic has been transliterated using a common-sense what-you-see-is-what-you-say system. However, Arabic vowel-sounds in particular often cannot be rendered accurately in English letters, and stress patterns are a minefield – the only way to pick them up is to mimic a native speaker. The following are four of the most difficult **common sounds**:

kh represents the throaty rasp at the end of the Scottish "loch".
gh is the same sound as *kh*, but voiced: it sounds like the gargled French "r".
q represents a very guttural *k* sound made far back in the throat; it approximates to the sound you might make when imitating the glugging of a wine bottle being emptied. In some Palestinian accents this becomes an unsounded glottal stop (*baqlawa* becomes *ba'lawa*), while in bedouin areas many people change it into a straightforward hard *g* sound (*baqlawa* becomes *baglawa*).

aa is especially tricky: constrict your throat muscles tightly like you're about to retch, open your mouth wide and make a strangulated "aaah" sound. Ridiculous as it feels, this is about as close as an English-speaker can get, and won't make Jordanians laugh. To keep things simple, the sound hasn't always been transliterated (it stands at the beginning of "Amman", for instance).

In this book, **ay** has been written where the Arabic rhymes roughly with "say", except where common usage dictates otherwise. Arabic **f** and **s** are always soft ("Muslim" not "Muzlim"; "Islam" not "Izlam"), and **r** is heavily trilled. Generally pronounce an **h** sound: *ahlan* (welcome) features a clear and definite exhalation of breath, as does *mneeh* (happy). Where **two consonants** fall together, pronounce them both: *hamam* means "pigeon" but *hammam* means "bathroom". The subtleties between the two different kinds of **s**, **t**, **d**, **h** and **th** are too rarefied to get into here.

USEFUL WORDS AND PHRASES

Where the form of a word or phrase differs depending on whether the speaker is male or female, we've shown this with (m) and (f): to say "I'm sorry", a man says "*mitaasef*", a woman "*mitaasfeh*". Where the form differs depending on who you're speaking to,

GREETINGS

Arabic takes **greetings** seriously. In the same way that English uses "How are you?" "I'm fine" as a verbal space-filler, meaningless in itself but allowing both parties a few seconds of thinking time, Arabic deploys volleys of greetings, often said in long strings, barely waiting for a response, while pumping your interlocutor's hand, and – if you're the same sex – looking him/her in the eyes. Old friends might also indulge in a complex ritual of double and triple kisses on both cheeks (and, in some bedouin areas, on the tip of the nose), but as a foreigner you won't be roped into this.

"PEACE BE UPON YOU"
• Greeting:
assalaamu alaykoom peace be upon you
• Response:
wa alaykoom assalaam and upon you be peace
This is the standard Muslim greeting, suitable in any situation, formal or informal. Say it as you enter a shop (to the shopkeeper and anyone else present), to a hotel receptionist, to a taxi driver as you get in, to a group of people in a café, and so on. If you're in a shop when someone else enters, or if you're one of the group to whom it is said, give the response. Note that Christians tend not to use it, preferring instead *marhaba* (hello); if you're in Madaba or another Christian area, try *marhaba* first.

GOOD MORNING/AFTERNOON/EVENING
• Greetings:
sabahl-khayr good morning (lit. morning of abundance)
masa il-khayr good afternoon/evening
tisbah (tisbahi to a woman) ala-khayr good night
• Responses:
sabahn-noor morning of light (response to *sabahl-khayr*)
masa an-noor afternoon/evening of light (response to *masa il-khayr*)
wa inta (inti to a woman) min ahlo the response to *tisbah/tisbahi ala-khayr*

HELLOS AND GOODBYES
• Greetings:
ahlan wa sahlan welcome and make yourself at home (see page 43)
ahlan welcome (generally formal)
itfuddal (itfuddalee to a woman) come in/go ahead etc (see page 43)
marhaba hello (generally said by one already settled to someone arriving from outside)
salaam hi
ma assalaameh goodbye

we've shown the two separated by a slash, with the form for addressing a man first, thus: "*allah yaafeek/yaafeeki* (to a woman)". Note also that all words and phrases ending *-ak* are for addressing a man; if you're addressing a woman, substitute *-ik*.

BASIC TERMS

yes naam
no leh
OK maashi
thank you shukran
you're welcome afwan
please minfadlak
excuse me (to attract afwan/lao samaht someone's attention) (samahti to a woman)
excuse me (if you bump afwaninto somebody, or tosqueeze past)
I'm sorry mitaasef (m)/mitaasfeh (f)
hopefully, God willing insha'allah

what's your name? aysh ismak?
my name is… ismi…
do you speak English? btihki ingleezee?
I'm British ana biritanee (add -yyeh if you're a woman)
I'm Irish ana irlandee (add -yyeh if you're a woman)
I'm American ana amerkanee (add -yyeh if you're a woman)
I'm Canadian ana canadee (add -yyeh if you're a woman)
I'm Australian ana ostraalee (add -yyeh if you're a woman)
I'm from New Zealand ana noozeelandee (add -yyeh if you're a woman)

• **Responses:**
ahlan feek or beek (ahlan feeki or beeki to a woman) it is you who are welcome (response to *ahlan*)
ahlayn two welcomes [back to you] (response to *ahlan*)
marhabtayn two hellos [back to you] (response to *marhaba*)
allah ysalmak God keep you safe (response to *ma assalaameh*)

HOW ARE YOU?
• **Greetings:**
keefak? how are you?
keef halak? (also keef il-hal?) how are you doing?
keef sahtak? how's your health?
keef shughulak? how's your work?
keef al-awlad? how are the kids?
keef hal ahlak? how's the family?
shoo akhbarak what's your news?
gawak? how are you? (literally "how's your strength?", only in rural dialects)
shlawnak? how are you? (literally "how's your colour?"; only in rural dialects)
al-afyeh hope you're keeping well (literally "good health")
• **Responses:**
al-hamdulillah thank God (all-purpose response to any of the above, covering a range of moods from "Fine, thanks" and "Really good!" to "Mustn't grumble" and even "Don't ask")
tayyib (m)/taybeh (f) I'm doing fine
mneeh (m)/mneeha (f) I'm well
maashi il-hal I'm OK
(kulshee) kwayyis (m)/kwayyseh (f) (everything's) good
(kulshee) tamam (everything's) perfect
allah yaafeek (yaafeeki to a woman) May God give you health
hala no translation; just an acknowledgement of having been greeted

THANK GOD
al-hamdulillah thank God
If you learn only one word of Arabic, make it this one. You can get away with deploying it in just about any situation – as a respectful response to any form of greeting, as "yes" if you want more of something, as "no" if you've had enough, as "leave me alone" if you want someone to stop pestering you, as "I'm so pleased to get to know you" if you're enjoying someone's company – and so on.

I don't speak/understand Arabic mabahki/mabafham arabee

I understand a little Arabic ana bafham shwayyet arabee

I don't understand ana mish fahem (m)/ fahmeh (f)

what's the meaning of that in English? shoo manato bil ingleezee?

could you write it for me, mumkin, tooktoobliyaha please? lao samaht?

never mind/forget it/it's OK/don't worry maalesh

no problem mafee mushkelah

as you like mittel ma biddak

I'm 25 years old ana khamseh wa-ashreen senneh

I'm (not) married ana (mish) mitjowez (m)/ mitjowzeh (f)

we're getting married next year rah nitjowez essenneh al-jay

congratulations! mabrook!

God bless you (the response allah ybarrak feek (feekito *mabrook*, but also used to a woman) widely to acknowledge someone's kindness to you)

I have no children maandi awlad

I have one/two/three children aandi walad/waladayn/ thalaath awlad

let's go yalla

it's none of your business ma dakhalak

get your hands off me! eem eedak!

leave me alone! utruknee le-halee!

go away rooh

I don't know mabaaraf

I can't (do that) mabagdar (aamalo)

slowly shwayy-shwayy

quickly bsooraa

immediately hela

enough/finished/stop it khalas

it's impossible mish mumkin

I'm tired ana taaban (m)/ taabaneh (f)

I'm unwell ana mareed (m)/ mareedeh (f)

get me to a doctor khuthni ala al-doktoor

DIRECTIONS AND TRAVEL

left/right/straight on shmal/ymeen/dooghri

near/far gareeb/baeed

here/there hawn/hunak

where is... wayn...

the Hotel Petra? funduq Petra?

the bus station? al-mujemma al-bussat?

the train station? al-mahattat al-sikkat al-hadeed?

the nearest serveece stop? agrab mawqaf lal-servees?

the post office? maktab al-bareed?

the police station? makhfar al-shurtah?

the bank? al-bank?

when does the first/last bus leave for Amman? imta bitrik awwal/akher bus la Amman?

does this bus go to Jerash? hadal-bus birooh ala Jerash?

BANKS, SHOPS AND HOTELS

money or cash masari

open/closed maftooh/msekker

when will it be open? imta rah yiftah?

I want to change... biddi asruf...

 dollars dollarat

 British pounds masari ingleeziyyeh

 travellers' cheques shikaat siyahiyyeh

how many JDs will I get? kam dinaar rah aakhoud?

is there a commission? fee comishon?

do you have the Jordan Times? andak Jordan Times?

I want... biddi...

 something else ishi thaani

 better than this ahsan min hada

 cheaper/like this arkhas/zay hada

 a big/small one kbir/zgheer

 a bigger/smaller one akbar/azghar

how much is it? gadaysh hada?

I don't want this mabiddi hada

it's too expensive ktir ghali

do you have a room free? andak ghurfeh fadiyyeh?

 for one person le-shakhs wahad

 for two people le-shakhsayn

 for three people le-thalaath ashkhas

can I see the room? bagdar ashouf al- ghurfeh?

is there... fee...

 a balcony? balconeh?

 a double bed? takht mizwej?

 hot water? my sukhneh?

 an en-suite bathroom? hammam bil-ghurfeh?

 a fan? marwaha?

it's not clean, show me another one hada mish nutheef, ferjeenee wahad thaani

is there a toilet here? fee hammam hawn?

how much for one night? gadaysh al-layleh?

NUMBERS

Note that, unlike words, numbers are written from left to right.

zero . sifr

one \ wahad

two ٢ ithnayn

three ٣ thalaatheh

four ٤ arbaa

five ٥ khamseh

six ٦ sitteh

seven ٧ sabaa

eight ٨ thamanyeh

nine ٩ tisaa

ten \ . ashra

eleven \ \ hidash

twelve \ ٢ ithnash

thirteen \ ٣ thalaatash

fourteen \ ٤ arbatash

fifteen ١٥ khamstash
sixteen ١٦ sittash
seventeen ١٧ sabatash
eighteen ١٨ thamantash
nineteen ١٩ tisatash
twenty ٢٠ ashreen
twenty-one ٢١ wahad wa-ashreen
thirty ٣٠ thalatheen
forty ٤٠ arbaeen
fifty ٥٠ khamseen
sixty ٦٠ sitteen
seventy ٧٠ sabaeen
eighty ٨٠ thamaneen
ninety ٩٠ tisaeen
a hundred ١٠٠ miyyeh
a hundred and one ١٠١ miyyeh wa-wahad
a hundred and twenty six ١٢٦ miyyeh wa-sitteh wa-ashreen
two hundred ٢٠٠ meetayn
three hundred ٣٠٠ thalaath miyyeh
one thousand ١٠٠٠ elf
two thousand ٢٠٠٠ elfayn
4594 ٤٥٩٤ arbaat alaaf wa-khame smiyyeh wa-arbaa wa-tisaeen
million milyon
one quarter rube
one half nuss

TELLING THE TIME

what time is it? gadaysh se'aa?
it's ten o'clock se'aa ashra
 10.05 ashra wa-khamseh
 10.10 ashra wa-ashra
 10.15 ashra wa-rube
 10.20 ashra wa-toolt
 10.25 ashra wa-nuss illa- khamseh
 10.30 ashra wa-nuss
 10.35 ashra wa-nuss wa- khamseh
 10.40 hidash illa-toolt
 10.45 hidash illa-rube
 10.50 hidash illa-ashra
 10.55 hidash illa-khamseh

DAYS AND MONTHS

day yom
night layl
week isbooa
month shahr
year senneh
yesterday imbaarih
today al-yom
tomorrow bukra
this morning essubbeh
this afternoon baad edduhr
this evening al-messa
tonight al-layleh
tomorrow night bukra bil-layl
Saturday essebt
Sunday al-ahad
Monday al-ithnayn
Tuesday al-thalaatha
Wednesday al-arbaa
Thursday al-khamees
Friday al-juma
January kanoon thaani
February shbaat
March athaar
April nisaan
May ayyar
June huzayran
July tamooz
August aab
September aylool
October tishreen awwal
November tishreen thaani
December kanoon awwal

FOOD AND DRINK GLOSSARY

BASIC STOMACH-FILLERS

khubez flat, round bread
falafel spiced chickpea mixture, deep-fried; stuffed into *khubez* with salad to make a *sandweesh* (sandwich)
shawarma shreds of lamb or chicken in *khubez*
fuul spiced fava beans, mashed with lemon juice, olive oil and chopped chillis; side dishes include raw onion (*basal*), fresh mint and/or pickled vegetables
fuul masri blander Egyptian-style *fuul*; without chilli but served with a dollop of *tahini* instead
hummus dip of chickpeas mashed with *tahini*, lemon juice, garlic and olive oil

manaqeesh zaatar small round of dough sprinkled with olive oil and *zaatar* (a mixture of dried thyme, marjoram, salt and sesame seeds), and baked until crispy
batatas potatoes; by extension, French fries
tahini sesame-seed paste
rooz rice

RESTAURANT APPETIZERS (MEZE)

shorba (taddas) (lentil) soup
s'laata salad; chopped tomato and cucumber
tabbouleh parsley and tomato salad with cracked wheat

fattoush Lebanese salad with chopped parsley and squares of crispy fried bread

baba ghanouj dip made from roasted mashed aubergine

moutabbel *baba ghanouj* with added *tahini*

labneh thick-set yoghurt, similar to sour cream

shanklish crumbly goat's cheese with tomato

warag aynab stuffed vine leaves

kibbeh ovals of spiced minced meat and cracked wheat

sujuk fried spicy mini-sausages

mahshi "stuffed"; by extension, a selection of stuffed vegetables such as peppers and aubergines

makdoos pickled aubergine

THE MAIN COURSE

mansaf boiled lamb or mutton on rice with a tangy yoghurt-based sauce, pine nuts and spices

musakhan chicken steamed with onions, sumac (a lemon- flavoured berry) and pine nuts, served on flatbread

magloobeh literally "upside-down": chicken on steamed rice with grilled vegetables

(nuss) farooj (half-)chicken; usually spit-roasted

kebab pieces of lamb or chicken chargrilled on a skewer with onions and tomatoes

kebab halaby spiced minced meat chargrilled

shish tawook chicken kebab

fatteh spiced meat or chicken baked with rice, hummus, pine nuts, yoghurt or bread

mulukhayyeh lamb or chicken stewed with spinach-like greens

fasooliyeh bean stew, often in meat broth

mujeddrah rice and lentils with onions

Daoud Pasha meatballs stewed with onions and tomatoes

lahmeh meat

djaj chicken

kharouf mutton or lamb

khanzir pork

kibdeh liver

kelaawy kidney

samak fish

khoodar vegetables

zayt oil

meleh salt

filfil pepper

ARABIC SWEETS (HALAWIYYAT)

k'naffy shredded-wheat squares filled with goat's cheese, smothered in hot honey syrup

baglawa layered flaky pastry with nuts

gatayyif pancakes filled with nuts and drenched in syrup

ftayer triangles of flaky pastry with different fillings

hareeseh syrupy almond and semolina cake

muhallabiyyeh rose-scented almond cream pudding

Umm Ali corn cake soaked in milk, sugar, raisins, coconut and cinnamon, served hot

maamoul rose-scented biscuits with dates or nuts

barazik thin sesame biscuits

awameh syrup-coated deep-fried balls of dough

asabya zaynab syrupy figs

mushabbak crunchy honey-coated pastries

karabeedj halaby sugar-coated curly fried dough

rooz b'laban rice pudding with yoghurt

halwa dense, flaky sweet made from sesame

DRINKS (MASHROOBAT)

my water

gahweh coffee

shy tea

naana/yansoon mint/fennel (tea)

zaatar/helbeh thyme/fenugreek (tea)

marrameeya sage (tea)

babbohnidj camomile (tea)

sahleb thick, sweet, milky winter drink

haleeb milk

tamarhindi tamarind drink

kharroub carob drink

soos liquorice-root drink

luz sweet almond-milk

aseer/koktayl juice/juice cocktail

FRUITS (FAWAKEH)

mooz banana

boordan orange

tfah apple

njas pear

grayfroot grapefruit

jezer carrot

manga mango

jowaffah guava

dourrag peach

limoon lemon (also drink)

aynab grapes

karaz cherries

rummaan pomegranate

mishmish apricot

teen fig

battikh watermelon

shimmam melon

balah crunchy unripe dates

tamar soft ripe dates

NUTS, SEEDS AND SIMPLE PROVISIONS

foustoug peanuts

foustoug halaby pistachios

boondoog hazelnuts
luz almonds
kashoo cashews
bizr dry-roasted seeds
zbeeb raisins
bayd eggs
zaytoon olives

jibneh cheese
laban yoghurt
zabadi high-fat yoghurt with cream
zibdeh butter
asal honey
marrabeh jam

Glossary

The first list below is a glossary of Arabic terms in common usage in Jordan. Common alternative spellings, as well as singulars and plurals, are given where appropriate in brackets. Afterwards is a list of English terms used in the guide to describe features of architecture.

ARABIC TERMS

abu Literally "Father of" – used as a familiar term of respect in conjunction with the name of the man's eldest son, as in "Abu Muhammad".

ain (ayn, ein) Spring.

argileh (arjileh, narjileh, nargileh) Floor-standing water pipe designed to let the smoke from the tobacco – which is kept smouldering by small coals – cool before being inhaled through a chamber of water. The sound of the smoke bubbling through the water gives the pipe its common name in Jordan of "hubbly-bubbly".

bab Gate or door.

badia Jordan's desert areas.

bahr Sea.

balad Nation or city.

baladi Countryfied, rural.

Balqa (Balka, Balga) The fertile hill country around Salt, west of Amman.

bani (beni) Tribe.

bayt (beit, bait; pl. byoot) House.

bedouin (also bedu) Generally refers to nomadic or seminomadic people who live in desert areas within a tribal social structure. Some Jordanian bedouin tribes, however, have long been settled in towns and cities and, although taking pride in their bedouin culture and ancestry, are indistinguishable in dress and lifestyle from urbanized Jordanians.

bir (beer) Well.

birkeh (birka, birket) Reservoir, pool, lake.

burj Tower.

daraj Flight of steps.

darb Path or way – "Darb al-Hajj" is the ancient pilgrimage route from Damascus to Mecca, following the present Desert Highway.

dayr (deir) Literally monastery or convent; by extension, a catch-all term for any ancient ruin of unknown usage.

diwan Formal architectural space, not necessarily within a house, intended for tribal discussions.

duwaar Circle (ie traffic intersection).

Druze A religious community, living chiefly in Lebanon and southern Syria, that follows a heterodox offshoot of Shia Islam.

fellaheen (fellahin; sing. fellah) Settled peasant farmers.

ghor "Sunken land", ie the Jordan Valley.

hajj (haj, hadj; f. hajjeh) The holy Muslim pilgrimage to Mecca and Medina; by extension, a title of respect, either for one who has literally made the pilgrimage, or – more commonly – simply for one who is of advancing years and thus deserving of honourable treatment.

hamad Stony desert pavement.

hammam (pl. hammamat) Turkish steam bath; bathroom or toilet; or a natural hot spring.

harra Rocky desert.

Hawran (Hauran) The basalt desert plains around Mafraq.

imam Prayer leader of a mosque, cleric.

iwan (liwan) Arched reception area at one end of a courtyard in traditional Arab architecture.

jabal (jebel; pl. jibal) Hill or mountain.

jamia "Place of assembly", ie a large, congregational mosque.

Jawlan Arabic equivalent for the Hebrew Golan.

jellabiyyeh Ankle-length outer robe worn by men.

jissr Bridge.

keffiyeh (quffiyeh, kafiya, etc) Patterned headscarf worn by men.

khirbet Ruin.

k'neeseh Church.

manara Minaret, the tower attached to a mosque, from which the call to prayer sounds.

masjid "Place of prostration", ie a small, everyday mosque.

maydan (midan) Public square, or traffic intersection.

mihrab Niche in the wall of a mosque indicating the direction of Mecca, and thus the direction of prayer.

minbar Pulpit in a mosque, from which the Friday sermon is given.

muezzin (mueththin) The one who gives the call to prayer.

mujemma "Assembly point", used to describe an open-air bus or service station.

nahr River.

qa Topographical depression, pan.

qal'a (kalaa) Fortress, citadel.

qasr (kasr; pl. qusoor) Palace, mansion; by extension, castle, fortress or a catch-all term for any ancient ruin of unknown usage.

qibla The direction in which Mecca lies, and therefore the direction in which Muslims pray.

qubba Dome; by extension any domed building.
Quran (Koran) The holy book of Islam.
qusayr (kuseir) Diminutive of qasr.
Ramadan Holy month in the Muslim calendar.
riwaq Colonnade.
sahra General term for desert; can also refer to sandy desert in particular.
sharia Street or way.
shari'a Set of laws based on Quranic precepts.
shebab Literally "youth", but used most commonly where English uses "guys", as a casual term of greeting to peers.
sheikh (shaykh) Tribal leader; consequently, mayor of a town or village.

souk (suq, souq) Market or bazaar.
tariq Way, path or road.
tell (tal, tall) Hill; by extension, an artificial mound concealing ancient remains, resulting from the continuous collapse and rebuilding of settlements, one on top of another.
umm (um, oum) "Mother of" – used as a term of respect in conjunction with the name of the woman's eldest son, as in "Umm Muhammad".
wadi Valley or watercourse (also refers to dry or seasonal riverbeds).
waha Oasis.

ARCHITECTURAL TERMS

apse Semicircular recess behind the altar of a church.
architrave Lintel resting on columns or piers, forming the lowest part of an entablature.
atrium Open inner courtyard of a Roman villa; also the court in front of a Byzantine church.
basilica Rectangular, apsed building; the earliest style of church.
biclinium Room with two benches, often a banqueting hall.
cardo Colonnaded main street of a Roman city; usually running north–south.
cella Inner sanctum of a Classical temple.
corbel Projection from the face of a wall supporting a horizontal beam.
Corinthian Order of Classical architecture, identifiable by acanthus-leaf decoration on column capitals.
cornice The upper part of an entablature; also a moulding running along the top of a wall.
decumanus Main street of a Roman city; usually running east–west.
engaged Column attached to or partly set into a wall.
entablature Element of Roman architecture positioned between the columns and the pediment; consists of architrave, frieze and cornice.
frieze Part of an entablature between the architrave and cornice, often decorated with figures.
glacis Steep slope below the walls of a castle, designed to be difficult to scale.
hypocaust Roman heating system allowing hot air to circulate beneath a floor raised on small pillars.

Ionic Order of Classical architecture, identifiable by fluted columns with scrolled capitals.
loculus Niche designed to hold a single body in a communal or family cave-tomb.
machicolation A projecting parapet of a castle or fort often above a doorway with holes below through which to pour boiling oil, etc.
narthex In a church, an area spanning the width of the building at the end furthest from the altar.
nave Central part of church, normally flanked by aisles.
nymphaeum A Roman public fountain dedicated to water nymphs and decorated with statues.
orchestra In a Classical theatre, the semicircular area in front of the stage.
pediment The shallow triangular gable over a door, window, etc.
propylaeum Monumental entrance gateway to a temple precinct.
scaenae frons The wall at the back of a stage in a Classical theatre.
squinch Small arch which spans the right angle formed by two walls, thus supporting a ceiling dome.
temenos Sacred enclosure of a temple.
tetrapylon Monumental four-sided structure supported on arches, usually at an important intersection of streets.
tholos Round section of building surrounded by columns.
triclinium Roman dining hall, most often with three benches.

Small print and index

A ROUGH GUIDE TO ROUGH GUIDES

Published in 1982, the first Rough Guide – to Greece – was a student scheme that became a publishing phenomenon. Mark Ellingham, a recent graduate in English from Bristol University, had been travelling in Greece the previous summer and couldn't find the right guidebook. With a small group of friends he wrote his own guide, combining a contemporary, journalistic style with a thoroughly practical approach to travellers' needs.

The immediate success of the book spawned a series that rapidly covered dozens of destinations. And, in addition to impecunious backpackers, Rough Guides soon acquired a much broader readership that relished the guides' wit and inquisitiveness as much as their enthusiastic, critical approach and value-for-money ethos. These days, Rough Guides include recommendations from budget to luxury and cover more than 120 destinations around the globe, from Amsterdam to Zanzibar, all regularly updated by our team of roaming writers.

Browse all our latest guides, read inspirational features and book your trip at **roughguides.com**.

Rough Guide credits

Editor(s): Zara Sekhavati
Cartography: Katie Bennett
Managing editor: Rachel Lawrence
Picture editor(s): Michelle Bhatia

Cover photo research: Tom Smyth
Senior DTP coordinator: Dan May
Head of DTP and Pre-Press: Rebeka Davies

Publishing information

Seventh edition 2019

Distribution

UK, Ireland and Europe
Apa Publications (UK) Ltd; sales@roughguides.com
United States and Canada
Ingram Publisher Services; ips@ingramcontent.com
Australia and New Zealand
Woodslane; info@woodslane.com.au
Southeast Asia
Apa Publications (SN) Pte; sales@roughguides.com
Worldwide
Apa Publications (UK) Ltd; sales@roughguides.com
Special Sales, Content Licensing and CoPublishing
Rough Guides can be purchased in bulk quantities
at discounted prices. We can create special editions,
personalised jackets and corporate imprints tailored to
your needs. sales@roughguides.com.

roughguides.com
Printed in China by CTPS
All rights reserved
© 2019 Apa Digital (CH) AG
License edition © Apa Publications Ltd UK
All rights reserved. No part of this publication may be
reproduced, stored in or introduced into a retrieval system,
or transmitted in any form, or by any means (electronic,
mechanical, photocopying, recording or otherwise) without
the prior written permission of the copyright owner.
A catalogue record for this book is available from the
British Library
The publishers and authors have done their best to
ensure the accuracy and currency of all the information in
The Rough Guide to Jordan, however, they can accept
no responsibility for any loss, injury, or inconvenience
sustained by any traveller as a result of information or
advice contained in the guide.

Help us update

We've gone to a lot of effort to ensure that this edition of
The Rough Guide to Jordan is accurate and up-to-date.
However, things change – places get "discovered", opening
hours are notoriously fickle, restaurants and rooms raise
prices or lower standards. If you feel we've got It wrong
or left something out, we'd like to know, and if you can
remember the address, the price, the hours, the phone
number, so much the better.

Please send your comments with the subject line
"**Rough Guide Jordan Update**" to mail@uk.roughguides.
com. We'll credit all contributions and send a copy of the
next edition (or any other Rough Guide if you prefer) for
the very best emails.

ABOUT THE AUTHOR

Matthew Teller first visited the Middle East in 1980, at the age of 11, when he kept nagging
to be taken back to Jerusalem's spice market to smell the smells. He has lived in Amman and
other cities in the region, travelled widely and is now an award-winning author, journalist and
BBC documentary-maker based in the UK. He has written for Rough Guides for more than
twenty years. Follow him on Twitter at @matthewteller and at Ⓦ matthewteller.com.

Photo credits
(Key: T-top; C-centre; B-bottom; L-left; R-right)

Index

Map symbols

The symbols below are used on maps throughout the book

––– – –	International boundary	◆	Point of interest	∴	Ruin	National park/wildlife reserve
–––––––– ·	Other boundary	✉	Post office	⊠	Gate	Mosque
––––––––	Major road	ⓘ	Tourist information	⊙	Flagpole	Shrine
-·-·-·-	Unpaved road	✚	Hospital	⤳	Mountain range	Monastery
⊓⊓⊓⊓	Steps	E	Embassy	▲	Mountain peak	Tomb
– – – –	Footpath	⊤	Fountain	⌂	Cave	Building
–– ––	Ferry route	✲	Viewpoint	‖‖‖	Cliff	Church
–––––	Wall	♟	Museum	⚠	Campsite	Stadium
✈	Airport	🏛	Monument	⋀⋀	Spring	Salt pan
★	Transport stop	♟	Fort	⋰	Swamp	Park
P	Parking	♜	Castle	🌴	Palm tree	Beach

Listings key

- Accommodation
- Eating
- Drinking & Nightlife
- Shopping

YOUR TAILOR-MADE TRIP
STARTS HERE

Tailor-made trips and unique adventures crafted by local experts

Rough Guides has been inspiring travellers with lively and thought-provoking guidebooks for more than 35 years. Now we're linking you up with selected local experts to craft your dream trip. They will put together your perfect itinerary and book it at local rates.

Don't follow the crowd – find your own path.

HOW ROUGHGUIDES.COM/TRIPS WORKS

STEP 1

Pick your dream destination, tell us what you want and submit an enquiry.

STEP 2

Fill in a short form to tell your local expert about your dream trip and preferences.

STEP 3

Our local expert will craft your tailor-made itinerary. You'll be able to tweak and refine it until you're completely satisfied.

STEP 4

Book online with ease, pack your bags and enjoy the trip! Our local expert will be on hand 24/7 while you're on the road.

BENEFITS OF PLANNING AND BOOKING AT ROUGHGUIDES.COM/TRIPS

PLAN YOUR ADVENTURE WITH LOCAL EXPERTS

Rough Guides' English-speaking local experts are hand-picked, based on their experience in the travel industry and their impeccable standards of customer service.

SAVE TIME AND GET ACCESS TO LOCAL KNOWLEDGE

When a local expert plans your trip, you save time and money when you book, even during high season. You won't be charged for using a credit card either.

MAKE TRAVEL A BREEZE: BOOK WITH PIECE OF MIND

Enjoy stress-free travel when you use Rough Guides' secure online booking platform. All bookings come with a money-back guarantee.

WHAT DO OTHER TRAVELLERS THINK ABOUT ROUGH GUIDES TRIPS?

Trip to Spain

This Spain tour company did a fantastic job to make our dream trip perfect. We gave them our travel budget, told them where we would like to go, and they did all of the planning. Our drivers and tour guides were always on time and very knowledgable. The hotel accommodations were better than we would have found on our own. Only one time did we end up in a location that we had not intended to be in. We called the 24 hour phone number, and they immediately fixed the situation.

Don A, USA

Trip to Morocco

Our trip was fantastic! Transportation, accommodations, guides - all were well chosen! The hotels were well situated, well appointed and had helpful, friendly staff. All of the guides we had were very knowledgeable, patient, and flexible with our varied interests in the different sites. We particularly enjoyed the side trip to Tangier! Well done! The itinerary you arranged for us allowed maximum coverage of the country with time in each city for seeing the important places.

Sharon, USA

PLAN AND BOOK YOUR TRIP AT ROUGHGUIDES.COM/TRIPS